H-11

W9-CDT-958

THE DICTIONARY OF FASHION HISTORY

THE
DICTIONARY

OF FASHION HISTORY

Valerie Cumming, C. W. Cunnington and P. E. Cunnington

Based on *A Dictionary of English Costume 900–1900*
by C. W. and P. E. Cunnington and Charles Beard,
now completely revised, updated and supplemented
to the present day by Valerie Cumming

Oxford • New York

This edition first published in 2010 by
Berg
Editorial offices:
First Floor, Angel Court, 81 St Clements Street, Oxford OX4 1AW, UK
175 Fifth Avenue, New York, NY 10010, USA

Berg is the imprint of Oxford International Publishers Ltd.

Library of Congress Cataloging-in-Publication Data

A catalogue record for this book is available from the Library of Congress.

British Library Cataloguing-in-Publication Data

A catalogue record for this book is available from the British Library.

ISBN   978 1 84788 534 0 (Cloth)
       978 1 84788 533 3 (Paper)

Typeset by JS Typesetting Ltd, Porthcawl, Mid Glamorgan
Printed in the UK by the MPG Books Group

www.bergpublishers.com

CONTENTS

We are ill informed even of the names of the articles we wear. People come to years of discretion scarce know the difference between a plain Hat and a Lunardi; and I have heard a lady, who I was told had a very good education, mistake a Parachute for a Fitzherbert.

1786. The Lounger no. 76

History is a gallery of pictures in which there are few originals and many copies.

The Old Regime and the Revolution, Alexis de Tocqueville, 1856

ACKNOWLEDGEMENTS

I would never have contemplated lexicography, even in an area with which I am familiar, without the encouragement of Kathryn Earle at Berg. She has left me to do the work of revision and addition without interference and has regularly provided useful texts for me to dip into or reject. The Cunningtons are totemic figures in fashion history and I am pleased and somewhat alarmed to have my name linked with theirs; and for that I offer my thanks to their daughter Susan Luckham and the literary estate who administer their considerable *oeuvre* for agreeing to this revised and updated version of the dictionary.

Over the past three years, my involvement with volume 8 of the *Berg Encyclopedia of World Dress and Fashion* provided useful evidence about how and why the words about costume, dress and fashion need careful thought because of the many different cultural and practical traditions from which they spring. Obviously, the bane of all lexicographers is that there are constant shifts in usage, new research within discrete areas, and the problem of what to include and what to leave out. Whenever I felt overwhelmed by the scale of the revision and update, I found the Cunningtons' original approach inordinately helpful. Colleagues within the Costume Society and CHODA, former students and email correspondents have patiently answered questions about arcane fabrics or unlikely usage; I am grateful for their ideas but any errors are mine.

Finding appropriate illustrations was not easy but again I found help among colleagues and friends with private collections. As always, John Cumming has been generous with his expertise and good humoured as the dictionary invaded every aspect of our lives. Last, but by no means least, I owe a huge debt of gratitude to the staff at Chertsey Museum, especially Grace Evans, Keeper of Costume, for her help with selecting strong and multi-applicable images from the outstanding Olive Matthews Collection curated and displayed at that museum.

Picture credits

I am indebted to the following individuals and organizations for the use of their images:

National Portrait Gallery
Olive Matthews Collection, Chertsey Museum
Private collections
Victoria & Albert Museum

INTRODUCTION

This revised and updated edition of what was once known as *A Dictionary of English Costume 900–1900* builds on a successful formula which encompassed four reprints and minor revisions between 1960 and 1976. C. Willett Cunnington (1879–1961) and his wife Phillis (1887–1974) separately, together and in partnership with other authors dominated the discipline of costume history in Great Britain for several decades from the 1930s. Key texts from their publishing history are listed in the Bibliography for this book.

Although they were familiar with the work of earlier dress historians, notably J. R. Planché (1796–1880) whose encyclopedic approach had inspired Charles Beard, their innate curiosity and collecting instincts ensured that they re-examined sources and redefined the role of costume history, as it was then known. Their dictionary was an important addition to their output, in terms of both the summation and the distillation of their long commitment to the discipline. Today we use different words to describe the study of human apparel – clothing, dress and fashion; "costume" is often perceived as being descriptive of theatrical disguise but terminology in this discipline is fluid and full of surprises.

The Cunningtons' dictionary covered the period starting from 900 and ending at 1900. However, they certainly went beyond 1900 in their research and information gathering, thereby leaving a legacy of information which has informed this revised dictionary, alongside much more recent work into many aspects of post-1900 clothing, fashionable or otherwise. A major difference between the pre-1900 period and the succeeding 110 years is that fashion becomes increasingly associated with fame; couturiers, their internationally known clients, film stars and that awkward group that we define as "celebrities" redefine the construction of personal appearance. This revised dictionary includes a limited number of these but only when strictly necessary; there are other sources through which they can be tracked and which are specifically devoted to them.

Since the 1980s, several dictionaries have been published in Europe and North America, complementing rather than challenging the dictionary of Cunnington and Beard. They include earlier information, such as on Greek and Roman dress; offer a wider and more inclusive world view of clothing terminology; consider post-1900 developments in dress and fashion; or describe themselves as dictionaries when they are companions or directories offering descriptions of processes, and biographies of designers, producers and purveyors of fashion. There are infinitely more sources of information about this subject than when the Cunningtons were writing books and students of this discipline will either own or be able to find these in libraries or, increasingly, online. Also, there are academic projects operating within the dictionary tradition, such as The Lexis of Cloth and Clothing Project c. 700–1450 led by Professor Gale Owen-Crocker, which is producing an 'analytical corpus of medieval dress and textiles terminology of the British Isles in the form of a searchable database innovatively illustrated'. This will be a rich resource for early period specialists when it is available.

The intention of this revised edition of the dictionary is to continue the best elements of the Cunnington–Beard volume, such as its cautious use of cross-referencing. Drainpipe trousers will appear under the appropriate alphabetical letter "D" and not under "T" for trousers. Also, where in English and American-English there are different meanings, these will be noted under the appropriate letter; for instance, the fact that trousers in American are called pants, whereas in English pants usually means an item of underwear. Ignoring these differences perpetuates the notion that one is correct and the other can be ignored; both are correct but in different parts of the world. It will be obvious to readers that American usage becomes increasingly important to fashion in the twentieth century, though possibly not as overarchingly influential as the many terms from European languages, especially French in earlier centuries.

The main dictionary in this edition contains both additions and amendments to existing entries. Some original entries were almost mini-essays; these have been kept but adjusted and updated when appropriate but there are relatively few *new* mini-essays. The practice of including dates at which terms emerge or change their meanings is retained, as is the occasional use of quotations to place the term in context. A useful organizational feature of the original dictionary is the categorization – the main dictionary deals with articles of clothing, mainly fashionable clothing, with appendices devoted to fabrics, lace and outdated names for colours. There are notable omissions – armour; classical and ecclesiastical dress; jewellery and embroidery are mentioned in passing and dressmakers and fashion designers barely rate a mention; to rectify this omission is impossible due to constraints of length but several gaps have been filled. The revised edition contains more information about people, practices and processes that support the production and wearing of clothing. Basic terms descriptive of the processes of dressmaking, tailoring and allied skills have been expanded and rationalized. The section originally called "Glossary of Materials" has been enlarged to include major twentieth-century fibres and fabrics but could be even longer. Trying to include each and every term in each and every language which has affected descriptions of fashionable clothing and fabrics in English would be impossible without several unwieldy volumes. Inevitably, any dictionary will always be a "work-in-progress" as more terms emerge and are added, and new evidence requires adjustments to early entries.

An obvious visual difference is the omission of the drawings which illustrated the earlier dictionary; instead, there are original images. These are fewer in number and have been chosen to prompt the reader to look at images online – a wonderful new resource that no book can emulate in range.

Valerie Cumming

PREFACE TO FIRST EDITION

The authorship of this dictionary requires a word of explanation. For a number of years the late Charles Beard had been collecting material for an encyclopaedic work on English Costume on the lines and dimensions of Planché's familiar volumes. As a mediaevalist Mr. Beard's chief interest lay in the early centuries with particular attention to armour and heraldry. At his death it appeared that the later centuries had not yet been adequately explored by him. We, on the other hand, unaware of his researches, had started to make a concise reference dictionary of English Costume; and now, invited to incorporate as much of Mr. Beard's material as might be relevant to our design, we have gladly accepted his mediaeval items as authoritative while reluctantly discarding much that lay outside our own plan.

At a rough computation about a sixth of the text of this volume may be attributed to him while for the rest we alone are responsible. In Part 1 the name of each garment is followed by the date when it came into use (in England) with, in many cases the date when, approximately it ceased to be fashionable; and the sex—M. or F.—which wore it.

Part 2 is a glossary of materials with the dates when they came into use.

C. Willlett Cunnington
Phillis Cunnington

GUIDE TO USING THE DICTIONARY

Using the Dictionary

This is simple. Cross-referencing is light-handed or entries would be impossible to read; the term "accessory" has been left with heavy cross-referencing to indicate the absurdity of this approach. Key words are cross-referenced; cloths, fabrics and materials including lace are found in the extra glossaries leaving the reader to decide whether to pursue that extra level of information.

Conversion Tables

Imperial to metric measurements:

1 inch = 2.54 cm.
1 foot = 0.3048 m.
1 yard = 0.9144 m.

£. s. d. to Decimal Currency

240 d. = 100 p. = £1

There are useful conversion tables online for readers who want fractional accuracy.

A photograph of one part of the exhibition, *Vanity Fair*, held at Chertsey Museum in 2008–9. This group displays clothing from ca. 1800–37, a range of female garments including a **spencer**, an evening **shawl** and other **accessories**, a **cap**, **boots** and **shoes** and a man's **frock coat**. Museum **collections** are a major source of information about historic and contemporary fashions. Copyright the Olive Matthews Collection, Chertsey Museum.

Abillements, habillements
See Billiments.

Accessory
(F & M)
Period: Medieval onwards.
An item which contributes to the overall effect but is of secondary importance is the dictionary definition of an accessory, but the term has only been applied in relation to personal appearance since the 19th century. As defined by dress historians, accessories usually complete an outfit and are chosen to complement it.

Accessories fall into two groups: those worn, such as **bonnets**, **caps** and **hats**, **boots** and **shoes**, **cravats** and **ties**, **gloves**, **mittens** and **muffs**, **jewellery**, **scarves** and **shawls**, **socks** and **stockings**, and those that are carried, such as **bags**, **canes**, **fans**, **parasols** and **umbrellas**, and **swords**.

If a detachable nature defines an accessory, there are many more, from **aigrets** to **shoe-roses**, thereby ensuring a limitless supply of such "secondary" items.

Accordion-pleating
(F)
Period: ca. 1889 onwards.
A form of close-pleating which enables the garment to expand its shape on movement, inspiring the fashion for "skirt-dancing" introduced by Loie Fuller, the American dancer (1862–1928). Also used for sleeves of some day dresses, the pleating ending at the elbow, with the fullness gathered into a close, long cuff.

Adelaide boots
(F)
Period: ca. 1830–1870s.
Side-laced, cloth top boots with patent toe-cap and flat, heel-less soles.

Adonis
(M)
Period: 18th century.

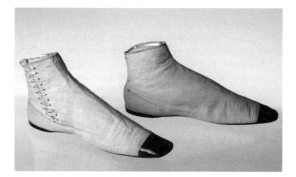

Woman's **ankle boots** called **Adelaide boots** of buff linen with black **patent** toes. Side-laced with a single silk **lace**. Inside a printed **label** "Wrigglesworth, 31 South Audley Street, London", ca. 1835–45. Copyright the Olive Matthews Collection, Chertsey Museum. Photograph by John Chase.

A long, bushy, white wig, "like the twigs of a gooseberry bush in a deep snow" (1734, *The London Magazine*). "A fine flowing Adonis or white periwig" (1773, R. Graves, *The Spiritual Quixote*).

Adonising
Period: 1807.
A fashionable expression for "dressing for dinner".

Adrienne, Andrienne
(F)
Period: 1703 to mid-18th century.
A style of **sac** gown; named after the character Andria played by the French actress Marie Dancourt who wore such a gown in a 1703 version of the eponymous play by Terence.

Aesthetic dress
(F)
Period: 1870s to early 20th century.
An attempt to revive in modified form the "artistic" dress of the 14th century. Encouraged and espoused by those associated with the Pre-Raphaelite circle of artists; a well-known enthusiast was the celebrated actress Ellen Terry (1847–1928). It took the form of high-waisted, flowing garments using natural dyes, with patterned materials in "indescribable tints", or variants of oriental styles, such as **kimonos**.
Satirized by W. S. Gilbert as the "Greenery-yallery, Grosvenor Gallery" costume and depicted by George du Maurier in his *Punch* cartoons. The Regent Street shop of **Liberty & Co.** provided fabrics and also produced a catalogue of dresses which captured the quasi-medieval, classical lines which suited those with such tastes.

(M)
Period: 1870s–1890s.
The best-known male exponent of aesthetic dress was the Irish critic and dramatist Oscar Wilde (1854–1900), who wore knee breeches, velvet jackets and shoulder-length hair and is associated with the poet Bunthorne in Gilbert and Sullivan's *Patience* of 1881, though Swinburne and Whistler had also prompted amusement with their aesthetic attitudes and appearance.
See Dress reform.

Afro
(F & M)
Period: From the 1960s onwards.
A hair style popular among African-Americans and widely copied in Europe and elsewhere. The hair is left to curl naturally, grown a few inches and styled to form a circle around the face.

Afternoon dress
(F)
Period: 19th to mid-20th century.
The rigid **etiquette** of carefully defined social occasions was matched by many differing styles and forms of clothing worn from early morning to late at night by elite women. Afternoon visits quickly acquired afternoon gowns or dresses.

Aggrafes, aggrapes
Period: 16th century onwards.
Hooks and eyes; also a clasp or buckle.

Period: 19th century.
An ornamental clasp or a hook, known as an "agrafe".

Aggravators
(M)
Period: ca. 1830–1870.
"His hair carefully twisted into the outer corner of each eye till it formed that description of semi-curls usually known as "aggravators" (1835–6, *Sketches by Boz*).

Aglets, aiglets, aigulets
(M, later F)
Period: 15th to mid-17th century.
Ornamental metal tags at each end of the ties called **points**, used to join **hose** to a **doublet** in the 15th century. Often of gold or silver or sometimes cut into the shape of little images; hence the term "aglet-baby" meant a diminutive person. From the 16th century aglets were used by both sexes as trimming, either as tags to short lengths of ribbon or sewn on in pairs or bunches.

Agnes Sorel bodice
(F)
Period: 1861.
A type of bodice for day wear, with the neckline cut square but not low at front and back, with full **bishop sleeves**.

Agnes Sorel corsage
(F)
Period: 1851.
A corsage of a **pelisse-robe** or **redingote** in the form of a day jacket with a plain or tabbed **basque**; either worn closed to the neck or open, showing a waistcoat-front.

Agnes Sorel style
(F)
Period: 1861 onwards.
French term for the English **princess** style of dress, the bodice and skirt cut in one without a seam at the waist. Agnes Sorel (1421–1450) was the mistress of the French king Charles VII and noted for her beauty.

Aigret, aigrette, egret
(F)
Period: 18th century onwards.
An upright plume of feathers or a jewelled ornament in the shape of feathers, worn on the head, fashionable in the last decades of the 18th century. "A bracelet or a well-fancied aigret" (1772, S. Foote, *The Nabob*).

Period: 1880s–1940s.
Aigrettes were worn on hats for day and also on or as an evening head-dress. The favourite feathers in the 19th century were osprey and heron. In the 1990s there was

a revival in the fashion for small feather head-dresses, now called **fascinators**.

Aile de pigeon
(M)

Period: ca. 1750–1770.

The "pigeon-wing" periwig; a **toupee** with one or two stiff, horizontal, roll curls projecting above the ears, with the foretop and sides smooth and plain.

À la marinière
(M)

Period: 1750–1800.

A small, round cuff crossed in front by a vertical flap, often scalloped, with three or four buttons matching those on the coat.

Albert boots
(M)

Period: 1840–ca. 1870.

Side-lacing boots with cloth tops and patent-leather toe-caps; often with "a close row of little mother-of-pearl buttons down the front; not for any purpose, for the real method of fastening being by the humble lace and tag at the side" (1847, Albert Smith, *The Natural History of the Gent*).

Albert collar
(M)

Period: ca. 1850 to early 20th century.

A separate **stand collar** of starched white linen, fastened at the back to a button attached to the shirt.

Albert driving cape, sac
(M)

Period: 1860 to early 20th century.

A very loose form of single or double-breasted **Chesterfield** overcoat, sometimes called simply a driving-cape or a **sac**. The back was usually made without a seam down the centre. "Sometimes these coats are cut without a seam under the arms in which case there must of course be a back-seam" (Minister's *Complete Guide to Practical Cutting*, 3rd edn).

Albert jacket
(M)

Period: ca. 1848.

A very short, skirted coat; single-breasted and slightly waisted, with or without a seam at the waist, and with or without side pleats. No breast pocket.

Albert overcoat
(M)

Period: 1877.

A loose overcoat with **fly-front fastening** and a half-circle cape cut to lie flat on the shoulders. Vertical slit pockets on each breast; flapped pocket on hips. Deep back vent closed by buttons under a fly. Length to mid-calf. Close-fitting sleeves with stitched cuffs.

Albert riding coat
(M)

Period: 1841.

A single-breasted coat, "the fronts slanted rather like the Newmarket style", with a broad collar and narrow lapels; buttoned high on the chest. Full skirts with rounded corners and pockets on the hips.

Albert slipper
(M)

Period: After 1840.

A slipper with an extended vamp in the form of a tongue covering the foot; named after Prince Albert of Saxe Coburg Gotha (1819–1861), consort of Queen Victoria. Many items of clothing were given his name after his marriage to Victoria in 1840.

Albert top frock
(M)

Period: ca. 1860–1900.

An overcoat in the form of a **frock coat** with a velvet collar three inches deep, a short waist, long skirts and flapped pockets on the hips. The collar, lapels and cuffs were broader than those on the ordinary **top frock** and the cloth was usually heavy. In 1893 it was made in a double-breasted version, very long and close-fitting.

Albert watch-chain
(M)

Period: ca. 1870 to mid-20th century.

A heavy chain worn across the front of the waistcoat from one pocket to the opposite, with the **watch** at one end and a "guard" (short rod of the metal) at the other; the chain passed through a buttonhole or, after ca. 1888, through a special "chain-hole" in the waistcoat.

Alexandra jacket
(F)

Period: 1863.

A day jacket without a centre back seam, the front with small revers and a collar, the sleeves with epaulettes and cuffs.

Presumably named after Princess Alexandra of Denmark (1844–1925) who married the Prince of Wales in 1863; various "Alexandra" and "princess" styles were named after this elegant woman.

Alexandra petticoat
(F)

Period: 1863.

A daytime undergarment of poplin with a broad plaid border above the hem.

Algerian burnouse
See Burnouse.

Alice band
(F)

Period: 1865 onwards.

The publication of Lewis Carroll's two novels, *Alice's Adventures in Wonderland* (1865) and *Through the Looking Glass* (1871), popularized a style of children's clothing including the narrow band of ribbon which held Alice's long hair away from her face in some, though not all, of Sir John Tenniel's illustrations. In the late 20th century, velvet Alice bands, the fabric covering a half circle of plastic or similar, were a feature of **Sloane Ranger** appearance in the UK.

A-line
(F)

Period: 1955.

One of three lines (H, A and Y) introduced by French designer Christian Dior (1905–1957) between 1954 and 1955. The A-line was a reworking of the 1954 H-line and coats, dresses and suits with this cut formed a triangle from shoulder to hem, with the cross-bar of the A below the bust or on the waist or the hips.

All-rounder
(M)

Period: 1854.

A rigid **stand collar** attached to the shirt and completely encircling the neck. "No military stock ever strangled an unfortunate soldier half so cruelly as these all-round collars" (1854, *Punch*).

Almain coat, Almain jacket
(M)

Period: ca. 1450 to 16th century.

A short, close-fitting coat or jacket with short, flared skirts and long, pendant sleeves open in the front seams; worn over the **doublet**. Almain meant "German" at that time.

Almain hose, German hose
(M)

Period: Late 16th century.

Very baggy, paned hose with voluminous puffs or pullings out.

See Pluderhose.

Alpine hat
(M)

Period: 1890s.

A soft felt hat with a low, round crown slightly depressed circularly.

Alpine jacket
(M)

Period: 1876.

An "improved" form of **Norfolk jacket**; double-breasted with a pleat down the centre of the back skirt; vertical pockets in the side seams, ornamented with side edges. Worn fastened to the neck, often without a waistcoat.

Alternative fashion
(F & M)

Period: ca. 1950 onwards.

Term encompassing all styles of youth, or non-mainstream, styles of clothing; also described as sub-cultural and discussed as **Goths**, **hippies**, **Mods**, **Rockers**, **Teddy boys**, etc.

Amadis sleeve
(F)

Period: 1830.

A style of sleeve with a tight cuff at the wrist. Fashionable

for day wear in the 1830s; revived in the 1850s when the tightness extended to the elbow and was closed by buttons. To be distinguished from the turned-back cuff end.

See Mousquetaire cuff.

Amazon corsage
(F)

Period: 1842.

A plain, high bodice tightly buttoned up to the throat, with a small cambric collar and cuffs; for day wear.

Amazon corset
(F)

Period: 1850s.

A riding **corset** with elastic lacings. "By pulling a concealed cord can be shortened 3" for riding."

Amazone
(F)

Period: Early 18th century.

A form of riding dress, probably named after the legendary Amazons, the Greek female warriors; "...a coat and waistcoat of blue camlet trimmed and embroidered with silver...this Amazonian hunting-habit for ladies, was, I take it, first imported from France..." (R. Steele, *Spectator,* Friday 29 June 1711, no. 104).

American coat
(M)

Period: 1829.

"A new kind of coat called an "American" has very broad collar, narrow lapels, skirt flaps, very long and wide, and is made S-B (single breasted). It may be in black cloth."

American neckcloth, Yankee neckcloth
(M)

Period: 1818–1830s.

A form of stock with vertical pleating on each side of the central portion in front, and with narrow ends brought forward and tied low down in a small knot called a "Gordian Knot".

American shoulders
(M)

Period: 1875.

The padding inserted in the shoulders of men's coats to produce the effect of "square", broad shoulders. "In New York they place the thickest part of the wadding about 2" in front of the shoulder seam" (*The Tailor & Cutter*).

See Padded shoulders.

American trousers
(M)

Period: 1857 onwards.

The cloth was gathered into a narrow waistband with a strap and buckle behind; worn without **braces**.

American vest
(M)

Period: 1860s onwards.

A single-breasted **waistcoat**, without collar or lapels

and buttoned high. Later, known also as the **French vest**.

Anademe
(F)

Period: Late 16th and early 17th centuries.

A **fillet** or garland of flowers or leaves for the head.

Andalouse cape
(F)

Period: 1846.

An outdoor cape of silk trimmed with broad streamers of fringed *crêpe lisse*; the front borders cut straight, the arms being free.

Andalusian casaque
(F)

Period: 1809.

A **tunic** worn with evening dress; fastened down the centre and sloping away to knee-level behind.

Androgynous styles
Period: Late 1960s onwards.

(M)

The appropriation of elements of female dress – feather boas, lurex, satin and sequins, and cosmetics – by pop and rock stars such as Marc Bolan, David Bowie and used as performance clothing and as a mark of sexual ambiguity.

(F)

Experimentation with forms of culottes, knickerbockers, trousers and jackets by designers of womenswear. The innovative French designer Yves Saint Laurent (1936–2008) developed a distinctive style for female day and evening wear using trousers and a jacket; the evening version was a variant of a dinner jacket, le smoking.

Angel overskirt
(F)

Period: 1894.

Day wear; a short upper skirt made with two deep points on each side.

Angel sleeve
(F)

Period: 1889.

Long, square panels reaching nearly to the ground, covering the arm-holes and attached to some **mantles**.

the Anglaise
(M)

Period: 1840 onwards.

Term describing "the collar and fold of the turnover" of a coat or waistcoat.

Angle-fronted coat, university coat
(M)

Period: 1870–1880.

A fashionable variant of the **morning coat**. Instead of the fronts sloping away in a curve from the second button, the fronts were cut so that the gap between them formed an angle, exposing much of the waistcoat.

The bottoms were cut into obtuse angles instead of being rounded. Usually single-breasted, occasionally double-breasted.

Anglesea hat
(M)

Period: ca. 1830.

A hat with a high, cylindrical crown and flat brim.

Anglo-Greek bodice
(F)

Period: 1820s.

A bodice made with **fichu-robings**, the lapels broad and wide apart, often edged with lace. For day or evening wear.

Angoulême bonnet
(F)

Period: 1814.

A bonnet made of straw with a high crown and broad front brim, tied on one side.

Ankle boots
(F & M)

Period: 14th century onwards.

General term for any boot that covers the foot and reaches up to just above the ankle.

See half boots.

Ankle bracelet
(F)

Period: Late 20th century onwards.

Although ankle bracelets or chains were worn by performers at earlier periods, it was only in the later 20th century that they became fashionable. Usually one bracelet was worn; often a thin chain in a precious metal; its position on one or other ankle supposedly signalled availability, or otherwise, to a potential partner.

Ankle-breeches
(M)

Period: ca. 1600–1650.

A nickname for **Spanish breeches**, generally called **Spanish hose**.

Ankle-jacks
(M)

Period: 1840s–1870s.

Short boots fitting round the ankles and laced up in front through eyelets, five on each side. "The laced-up shoes called ankle-jacks" (1874, T. Hardy, *Far from the Madding Crowd*).

Ankle-length
(F)

Period: Early 20th century onwards.

Term describing the length of a coat, dress or skirt; occasionally applied to trousers but rarely used for male styles.

Ankle socks
(F)

Period: 1930s onwards.

Short woollen or cotton socks, often with a turnover

cuff, worn for sports such as tennis; during the 1939–45 war they often replaced stockings, which were rationed, and patterns for hand-knitted ones were popular. From the late 1940s they were associated with schoolchildren until new yarns, colours and patterns made them fashionable again from the 1970s, and in 1983 Sock Shop was founded in the UK.

Ankle straps

(F)

Period: 1880s onwards.

Throughout the long history of footwear a ribbon, strap or tie attached to a shoe or slipper has often been passed around the ankle to decorate and/or secure the shoe. However, as skirts shortened this feature became apparent and a buttoned or tied strap became an element in shoe design.

Anorak

(F & M)

Period: 1920s onwards.

The term describes a traditional, hooded, waterproof garment, originally made of hide, birdskin or treated cloth, worn in Greenland and Canada. Adapted for use in other countries, the word now applies to a type of sturdy, hooded, waterproof jacket worn by men, women and children.

See Parka.

Anslet

See Hanslet.

Antigropolis

(M)

Period: 1850s.

A form of high gaiter "adapted to either walking or riding; generally of leather, similar in shape to the mud boot but fastens at the side by means of a spring. The back part is cut away at the ham and the front is raised to protect the thigh" (1855, *The Gentleman's Magazine of Fashion*).

Antique

Term found in complimentary and derogatory forms; the former suggestive of an admired detail, fabric or style from an earlier period, e.g. antique lace; the latter indicative of something old-fashioned, e.g. "a suit of rather antique appearance".

Antique bodice

(F)

Period: ca. 1830–1850.

An evening bodice with low **décolletage** and deeply pointed waist.

Antoinette fichu

(F)

Period: 1857.

Worn for summer morning wear, a "fichu Antoinette" of muslin trimmed with black lace and narrow velvet, covering the shoulders and crossing at the front but

An **apron** of ivory silk embroidered with floral motifs in silk and metal threads; the apron has a scalloped edge, ca. 1740. Copyright the Olive Matthews Collection, Chertsey Museum. Photograph by John Chase.

fastening behind with a bow, with the long ends floating at the back.

See Fichu.

Apollo corset

(F & M)

Period: 1810.

A form of whalebone corset worn by dandies; a rival of the **Brummell bodice** and the **Cumberland corset**. Also "worn by the ladies to make their waists look slender and genteel" (1813, *Spirit of the Public Journals*).

Apollo knot

(F)

Period: 1824–1838.

False hair plaited into a loop or loops and wired to stand above the head; for evening and some day hair styles.

Apparel

(F & M)

Period: Early 14th century onwards.

A term used to denote clothing, in particular a suit of clothes. In the late 14th century it also described the embroidered borders of ecclesiastical garments and the embellishment of a harness or armour.

Appliqué

French term to describe fabric cut into decorative shapes and applied to another fabric with plain or fancy stitching. In the 1950s the use of felt motifs on circular skirts was popular; from the 1970s motifs were applied to jackets and jeans to customize them.

Après-ski wear

(F & M)

Period: 1954 onwards.

Designed for the evening activities after a day of skiing. Ski-wear is streamlined but too bulky and warm for indoor wear, so the idea of "après-ski wear" was developed; the informality of these trousers, **sweaters** and loose jackets was often based on Scandinavian colours, patterns and styles.

Apron
Period: 13th century onwards.
Also "aporne" and **napron**, the latter term used in 14th and first half of the 15th century; subsequently "apron" was used.

(M)
Worn by artisans and workmen to protect the front of their clothing; tied at the waist and often cut in one to spread up over the chest. "Checkered apron men" were 16th century barbers who wore check-patterned aprons. "Blue-aproned men" often meant tradesmen from the 16th to the 18th century. "Green-aproned men" applied to London porters in the 18th century, and green baize aprons were worn by furniture removers, and in auction-rooms, in the 19th century.

(F)
Sometimes worn to protect the clothing but also used as a decorative feature. The fabric was gathered into a waistband and tied round the waist; some working aprons had an attached bib extending up from the waist to protect the bodice. Decorative aprons were of fine fabrics, usually without bibs, and often embroidered. They were fashionable from the late 16th century to ca. 1640, and especially fashionable throughout the 18th century and again in the 1870s. The latter were very small, of black silk sometimes embroidered in colours and popularly known as "fig-leaves". From the 20th century onwards aprons were practical rather than decorative, and came in washable cotton and wipeable PVC.

Apron skirt
(F)
Period: Late 19th century onwards.
Either an overskirt to a dress, simulating an apron, or a half-skirt worn when riding to conceal breeches.

Aquascutum
Period: 1850 onwards.
Along with **Burberry**, a name synonymous with rainwear since the 19th century. Originally an English tailoring firm funded in 1851 by John Emary and widely known after he introduced a waterproof garment in 1853; this London-based business became internationally celebrated during the 1914–18 war when they provided waterproof **trench coats** for British officers to wear. An innovative approach with new fabrics, processes and styles has ensured that the firm has retained its reputation for chic but practical outerwear while adding many other product ranges.
See Classic style.

Aquatic shirt
(M)
Period: ca. 1830 to late 19th century.

An early form of sports shirt worn for boating; also for country and seaside wear. Of cotton in coloured stripes or checks or in whole colours (red, blue, green). Decorated with sporting motifs and popular in the 1840s and 1850s.

Aragonese bonnet
(F)
Period: 1834.
A bonnet mainly of silk, with arched front brim, and pyramid-shaped crown.

Aran knitwear
(F & M)
Period: 9th century onwards.
A distinctive style of knitting found in the Aran Islands which used thick unbleached wool and incorporating raised motifs including bobbles, cables and twists. There were different traditions and patterns to the east and west coasts of Scotland and Ireland. One tradition produced horizontal patterns, another produced vertical patterns. Originally produced as **sweaters** for fishermen, from the mid-20th century the motifs have been used on other informal garments, such as cardigans, coats, etc., and copied in different countries.
See Guernsey.

Argyle knitwear
(F & M)
Period: ca. 1920 onwards.
A diamond-shaped motif knitted in coloured wools and used on sweaters and socks; often associated with golf and other outdoor activities. Possibly connected to the Dukes of Argyll (the modern spelling), though their **tartan** is that of the Clan Campbell.

Arisaid
(F)
Period: 16th to mid-/late-18th century.
An item of traditional clothing worn in the Highlands and Islands of Scotland. The name may derive from the Gaelic and is a term applied to a large rectangle of woollen fabric worn over the shoulders, draped across the body, reaching as low as the ankles, and held by a brooch or decorative pin. It was possibly a sign of wealth and/or status and worn as outerwear for special occasions. Surviving examples indicate that it usually had a white ground, woven with colours to produce a **tartan** or checkered pattern.

Armenian mantle
(F)
Period: 1847.
A loose **pelisse** without a cape, the front trimmed with **passementerie**.

Army surplus
(F & M)
Period: From 1920s onwards.
Clothing worn by British air-force, army and navy personnel that was surplus to requirement and was sold to

the public. This started after World War I but was more significant after World War II. **Duffle** coats, issued to the navy, were much sought after as warm winter coats and were joined by battle dress, bomber jackets, trousers, sweaters and boots. The quality was good and students found army surplus stores a vital source of clothing and mixed these **classic styles** with modern fashions and colours.

Arrow collars and shirts

(M)

Period: 1889 onwards.

Detachable and stiffened shirt collars were an American invention of the 1820s but Arrow collars and shirts (Arrow was a patented trademark) are symbolic of American masculine elegance. The combination of the crisp, rounded collar with a contrasting coloured or striped shirt became known through the advertisement drawings by J. C. Leyendecker which appeared from 1913. By the 1920s there were many colours, sizes and types of shirt and the company adapted to changing tastes by introducing integral collars and sleekly fitted shirts.

Art Deco

Period: ca. 1910–1939.

A fashionable artistic movement which supposedly took its name from the *Exposition Internationale des Arts Décoratifs et Industriels Moderne* which took place in Paris in 1925. In fact, the name first appears in the 1960s and was popularized by Bevis Hillier's book. However, the highly ornate and decorative styles, often influenced by 18th-century revivalism, are perceived to have started soon after the decline of **Art Nouveau** and to have reached their apogee in the 1920s, but continued into the 1930s as an aspect of the modernist aesthetic which was prevalent in clothing and textile design. The German fashion designer Karl Lagerfeld (b. 1938) adapted Art Deco motifs for his work in the early 1970s.

Artificial crinoline

See Crinoline.

Artificial flowers

Period: 19th century onwards.

Flowers, exotic, natural or wild, have been a source of inspiration to embroiderers, designers, printers and weavers from the earliest times. Real flowers were often held in portraits, woven into the hair, etc. Artificial flowers, often made of silk, were much used on millinery from the early 19th century onwards. Artificial flowers also decorate garments, individually or in groups, are regular substitutes for brooches, and are an integral feature on many **fascinators** – the hat substitute of the 1990s onwards.

Artistic dress

(F, occasionally M)

Period: 1848–ca. 1900.

The influence of the pre-Raphaelite brotherhood, a group of painters founded in 1848 by Holman Hunt, Millais and Dante Gabriel Rossetti, on clothing was reflected later by Walter Crane: "…the dress of women in our own time may be seen to have been transformed for a while, and, though the pendulum of fashion swings to and fro, it does not much affect, except in small details, a distinct type of dress which has become associated with artistic people…" (1894, *Aglaia*, p. 7).

The ideal pre-Raphaelite woman had thick, softly curling hair, a pale complexion, strong features and a taste for unstructured garments in natural colours. This alternative style, one of the first successful movements antithetical to fashion, continued and evolved, and was caricatured and satirized, but the ideas of comfort and timeless elegance influenced designers such as Paul Poiret and Mariano Fortuny in the 20th century.

See Aesthetic dress, Delphos dress, Liberty & Co.

Artist's smock

(F & M)

A loosely fitting cotton or sailcloth garment, usually between thigh- and knee-length, with long sleeves, not dissimilar to the female **smock** and worn to protect clothing. Portraits and self-portraits of artists are uninformative until the mid-to-late 19th century when photographs depict painters in smocks, often with a loose bow at the neck and a soft beret. Smocks are made in a range of colours.

Art Nouveau

Period: ca. 1890–1914.

A decorative art form using sinuous, curving lines and flower-and-leaf motifs, often exaggerated in scale. The name was attributed to the Paris shop *L'Art Nouveau* opened in 1895, but a celebrated British exponent was **Liberty** in London. Fabrics, embroidery and jewellery of this type were popular from the 1890s up to about 1910. Liberty revived interest in the textile designs in the 1960s.

Artois buckle

(M)

Period: ca. 1775–1790.

The very large, decorative and fashionable shoe buckle named after the Comte d"Artois (1757–1836), younger brother of Louis XVI of France and later Charles X of France.

Ascot jacket

(M)

Period: 1876.

A double-breasted jacket with its skirts rounded off at the front bottom edges, and a belt of the same cloth passing through loops at the sides, drawing in the fullness.

Ascot tie

(M)

Period: 1876 onwards.

The plain form of this tie was similar to the **Octagon tie**. The "Puffed Ascot" was puffed out in the centre. Both versions, usually of patterned silk, were often self-tied but some were ready made-up.

Asooch, aswash

(M)

Period: 17th century.

A term signifying sash-wise or scarf-wise; a garment worn "asooch" or "aswash" was draped diagonally across the body instead of hanging normally; a fashionable style for cloaks and sometimes for **shamews**.

Assasin, veney-a-moy

(F)

Period: Late 17th century.

"A certain Breast-knot, as much as to say, Come to me, Sir" (1690, J. Evelyn, *Fop-Dictionary*).

Attaché case

(F & M)

Period: Late 19th or early 20th century.

A rectangular, lockable case with two handles and of a size to take business papers. Often made of leather, but inexpensive versions in canvas or fibre were made. Also called a **briefcase**.

Attire

(F)

Period: 15th century onwards.

A head-dress of goldsmith's work and gemstones, worn on state occasions. Later shortened to "tire".

(F & M)

Clothing worn by men and women.

Aulmoniere, aumoniere, almoner, aumer

(M)

Period: Medieval.

A pouch or purse suspended from the **girdle** and worn by nobles. The first two terms are comparatively recent pseudo-archaic forms.

Aurum potabile

Period: 16th and 17th centuries.

A cosmetic; "a red dye for the tongue furred by too much indulgence"; "a blood-red, gummie or honey-like substance" (1678, Phillips).

Automobile coat

(F & M)

Period: Late 19th century onwards.

Literally a coat worn in early automobiles as a protection against the elements; made of leather or cloth with a thick lining, often of fur in winter and linen in summer. Later, a loose informal coat, often three-quarter length. Also called a motoring coat, a car coat, or a travelling coat.

See Dust coat.

B

Babet bonnet

(F)

Period: 1838.

A small bonnet of tulle covering the back of the head and descending over the ears; for evening wear.

Babet cap

(F)

Period: 1836–1840s.

A morning cap of muslin with a small, round **caul**, the sides descending over the cheeks; trimmed with ribbon.

Baby

Period: 16th century onwards.

Used as a suffix to describe items worn by small children, such as **babygro**, or items suggestive of infants' clothing or of its diminutive scale if intended for adults, such as **baby doll**.

Baby bodice

(F)

Period: 1878–ca. 1900.

A day bodice with a square neck, vertical pleats down the centre, and a large **basque** extending below

the waistband. In 1897 the neck was drawn in with threaded ribbons, and a wide sash with hanging ends replaced the belt.

Baby cap

(F)

Period: Late 16th and early 17th centuries.

Term used for a fashionable woman's **coif** of lawn or lace resembling a baby's bonnet.

Baby doll

(F)

Period: 1956 onwards.

The film *Baby Doll*, based on Nabokov's novel of the same name, inspired a range of childlike nightwear, including a type of short, loose top worn with short **panties** and a short nightdress, both similar to 19th-century children's garments.

Babygro

(F & M)

Period: 1959 onwards.

Term patented by the North American company Lisle Mills. This multi-purpose item of baby clothing was a

one-piece garment which allowed the baby movement when sleeping or awake. Now worn throughout
the world, this style of baby clothing is made in easily
laundered stretch fabrics, often in natural yarns such as
cotton and wool.

Bachlick
(F)
Period: 1868.
A **fichu** with a hood-like point behind having a tassel;
of cashmere edged with swansdown; worn over day
dress.

Back, bak
Period: 14th century.
Term used loosely for any outer garment; also, in the
plural, for clothing in general. "Oure bakkes…that moth-
etan be" (1377, Langland, *Piers Plowman*).

Drawstring **bag** of **Berlin wool-work**, lined with yellow
silk; a cord is threaded through brass rings to form two
drawstring handles. The bag has two **chenille** tassels;
ca. 1845–55. Copyright the Olive Matthews Collection,
Chertsey Museum.

Back breadth
(M)
Period: 19th century onwards.
Tailor's term for the combined width of the two back
pieces of a man's coat, at waist level.

Backpack
(F & M)
Period: Early 20th century onwards.
Originally a carrier for outdoor activities such as camp-
ing and hiking, the term later became associated with
rucksacks and other smaller, more fashionable bags
worn on the back, especially in the late 20th century,
allowing posture to benefit as a result of not carrying
heavy items suspended from one arm.

Back piece
(M)
Period: 19th century.
Tailor's term for the part of the back of a coat between
the midline seam and the side seam.

Back string
Period: 18th century.
A child's **leading strings** attached to the shoulders of
the dress. 'Misses at whose age their mother wore. The
back-string and the bib" (1785, Cowper, *The Task*).

Bag
(M)
Period: Late Medieval and 16th century.
Term for the girdle pouch.

Period: 16th century.
Term sometimes used for the padding of **doublets**.

Period: 18th century.
A wig.
See Bag-wig.

(F & M)
Period: 20th century onwards.
Term used for a **handbag** or similar.

A **bag** for the **queue** of a **wig**; these were a method of protecting the coat collar when hair was powdered. Essential
for formal occasions and when **court dress** was worn they
are found as attachments to the collars of court dress coats
until the twentieth century, ca. 1780–1800. Copyright the
Olive Matthews Collection, Chertsey Museum.

Bag bodice
(F)
Period: 1883.
A day-wear blouse bodice, the front of which sagged pouch-like over the waistband.

Bag bonnet
(F)
Period: Early 19th century.
An outdoor and daytime style of **capote** with a soft crown loosely covering the back of the head.

Bagging shoe
(M)
Period: 16th and 17th centuries.
A loose shoe roughly made for country wear; the term sometimes applied to **startups**.

Bag-irons, bag-rings
(M)
Period: 15th and early 16th centuries.
The cross-bar and swivel for suspension of a **pouch** and the pendant concentric semicircular rings which acted as stiffeners for the pouch-mouth and the covering flap. The bag-irons might also be of bronze, silver or latten (a mixed metal similar to brass) and were occasionally engraved with posies or mottoes.

Bagpipe sleeves, pokys
(F & M)
Period: 15th century.
Very wide sleeves, deeply pendant from a closed wrist and forming a huge hanging pouch, often used as a pocket. These sleeves were peculiar to **houppelandes**.

Bag plastron
(F)
Period: 1884.
A **plastron** or front panel of a day bodice, the plastron sagging in front and forming a "bag". Sometimes worn instead of a waistcoat-front.

Bags
(M)
Period: 19th century onwards.
Slang term for trousers; in the 1920s trousers with wide legs were called **Oxford bags**.
See Unmentionables.

Bag-waistcoat
(F)
Period: 1883.
A day waistcoat sagging in front to form a pouch.

Bag-wig, bag
(M)
Period: 18th century.
The **queue** of this **wig** was enclosed in a square, black, silk bag drawn in at the nape of the neck with a running string, concealed by a stiff, black bow. Worn with "dress" and "full dress" from the 1720s until the end of the century.

Period: 19th century.
A black silk bag in the form of a rosette attached to the back collar of a court suit even when wigs and their powder were no longer used.

Bahut
(F & M)
Period: 18th century.
A masquerade dress or **domino**.

Balaclava
(M)
Period: 1854 onwards.
A woollen cap which covered the head and neck leaving the face revealed; worn by military personnel and named after the Crimean village of Balaclava where a battle was fought in 1854.

Balandrana
Period: 12th and 13th centuries.
A wide cloak or **mantle** worn by travellers.

Balayeuse
(F)
Period: 1870s onwards.
A flounce or frill of stiff white muslin protecting the inner surface of the hem of a skirt and detachable for laundering.

Baldric, baldrick
(M)
Period: 13th century to 1700.
A belt worn diagonally across the chest, or sometimes across the abdomen, for suspending the sword, dagger, bugle, horn or pouch.

Period: 16th century.
The bugle baldrick was called the "corse".

Period: 17th century.
The term "shoulder-belt" was used; it suspended a rapier.

Ballerina skirt
(F)
Period: Early 20th century onwards.
A wide skirt, often of several layers of light fabric, of mid-calf length and inspired by classical ballets such as *Giselle*. Especially popular in the 1930s and 1950s.

Ballet-skirt
(F)
Period: 1883.
For evening dress, a skirt of tulle composed of three or four skirts diminishing from below upwards and mounted on a silk or satin foundation; the uppermost skirt spotted with stars, pearls or beetle-wings. Worn with a velvet, plush or satin bodice. 'A ballet skirt is three yards wide and required 20 yards of material" (C. W. Cunnington, *Englishwomen's Clothing in the Nineteenth Century*, 1937).

Ballets Russes
Period: Early 20th century.

The first of these Russian ballets, the idea of the impresario Serge Diaghilev, was seen in Paris in 1909 and in London in 1910. The exotic, innovative designs by Leon Bakst (1866–1924) had an impact on fashion and influenced designers such as Paul Poiret (1879–1944) and Mariano Fortuny (1871–1949). **Harem pants**, **hobble skirts** and **turbans**, all in brilliant colours can be traced to designs for the Ballets Russes. Bakst designed fashionable clothing for Madame Paquin (fl. 1891–1956) and Natalia Goncharova (1881–1962), a Cubist-inspired designer for Diaghilev, designed for Myrbor, a Paris textiles boutique in the 1920s.

Ball gown
(F)

Period: Early 19th century onwards.

Ball gowns or ball dresses are regularly illustrated and described in women's magazines from the 19th century, when minute distinctions between ball, dinner, evening and opera gowns became noticeable. Styles have changed, but the principal features are expensive silk fabrics, light or heavy, decorated with lace, embroidery or beading, with low-cut bodice, short or no sleeves, and a full skirt.

Balloon hat, Lunardi, parachute hat
(F)

Period: 1783–1785.

A hat with a large, balloon-shaped crown and wide brim made of gauze or sarcenet over a wire or chip foundation. Very fashionable in those years as a compliment to Vincenzo Lunardi (1759–1806) and his balloon ascents.

Balloon skirt
(F)

Period: 1950s onwards.

A full skirt curving out from a narrow waistband to resemble a balloon and narrowing towards the hem. Also called a "bubble skirt" or "tulip skirt".

Balloon sleeve
(F)

Period: 1890s.

Term sometimes used for a **gigot sleeve** or puffed sleeve, the very full upper sleeve for day and evening wear.

Ball-room neckcloth
(M)

Period: 1830s.

A white, starched **neckcloth**, the ends crossing in front in broad folds and secured to the braces. A brilliant brooch or pin in the centre held the neckcloth in place.

Balmacaan
(F & M)

Period: 19th century onwards.

Originally a single-breasted male **overcoat** of heavy tweed or wool, calf-length and loose-fitting, with a small collar and **raglan sleeves**. This style had been adapted for women by the end of the 19th century. The name is taken from a Scottish estate in Inverness-shire.

Balmoral bodice
(F)

Period: 1867.

The name then given to the postilion corsage with two short **basques**, similar to a postilion's coat-tails, falling over the upper part of the back of the day skirt.

Balmoral boot
(F)

Period: Late 1850s–1870s.

A short, black boot lacing up the front, often with coloured laces and generally worn with country or walking dress.

Balmoral cloak
(F)

Period: 1852.

A short, sleeveless cloak with a narrow hood. The name appeared in the year that Queen Victoria bought Balmoral Castle in Scotland.

Balmoral jacket
(F)

Period: 1867.

A jacket simulating a waistcoat, with pointed fronts and long pointed ends behind; buttoned up to the throat. For day wear.

Period: 1870.

A tailor-made version: "Resembles the Riding Habit but not made to fit so close; the back cut without a centre seam; side bodies added; D-B foreparts with lapels. The fronts rounded off; pocket flaps on the front of the skirts of the jacket. Sleeves with small gauntlet cuffs. Band or belt round the waist" (*The Tailor & Cutter*).

Balmoral mantle
(F)

Period: 1866.

A mantle made like an **Inverness** cape, of velvet, cashmere or cloth; for outdoor wear.

Band
(F & M)

Period: 16th and 17th centuries.

A white collar, the word being transferred from the shirt-band to a separate collar. A **falling band** or **fall** was a turned-down collar whether raised or flat. A standing-band was an upright collar without a turnover. Short bands were a pair of short, narrow pendants of white linen worn by ministers of religion, barristers and collegians. After ca. 1850 they were gradually discarded by High Church clergy and later by all Church of England clergy, but still used by evangelicals and nonconformist ministers into the 20th century.

Bandana, bandanna handkerchief
(M)

Period: 18th century onwards.

A handkerchief, originally of silk, later of cotton, having

a dark ground commonly of Turkey red or blue with small white or yellow spots. Imported from India and used, in the 18th century for **neckcloths**; later as snuff-handkerchiefs.

Band-box

Period: 16th and 17th centuries.

A box in which **collars** and **ruffs** were kept.

Bandeau

(F & M)

Period: ca. 1800 onwards.

A band of fabric worn around the head to contain the hair or for decorative effect; a style associated with women from the early 19th century, until elasticated bandeaux became popular amongst both sports men and women in the 1970s.

Bandelet

(F & M)

Period: 16th century.

"Any sort of scarf" (1598, Florio).

Bandore and peak

(F)

Period: 1700–ca. 1730.

A widow's head-dress, a black bonnet curving to a point over the forehead; worn with a black **veil** flowing behind.

See Mourning attire.

Band-strings

(F & M)

Period: 16th and 17th centuries.

Tasselled ties to fasten **bands** or **ruffs** in front; sometimes several pairs were used. In the 17th century, "snake-bone" band-strings were woven to resemble the backbone of a snake.

Bang

(F)

Period: 1880s onwards.

An American term for hair cut in a straight fringe across the forehead.

Banging chignon

(F)

Period: 1770s.

A wide, flat loop of hair dressed to hang from the top down to the nape of the neck; sometimes tied round with ribbon.

Bangle

(F)

Period: Late 18th century onwards.

A ring worn around the wrist or ankle as a decorative item of jewellery; unlike a bracelet it is slipped on or off and has no fastener. Many different styles were popular and ranged from simple bangles of precious metal to beads, plastic and plaited leather.

Banian, banyan, banjan, Indian nightgown

(M)

Period: ca. 1650 to early 19th century.

A loose-skirted coat, knee-length, with a short back vent and fastened by a clasp, or buttoned or hooked down the front; sleeves close and slit. Worn domestically and in 1780s often out of doors, when it was very fashionable and of expensive fabrics. In the early 19th century it had become a superior kind of **dressing-gown**, made without a back vent but with a **banyan pleat** and ankle-length. The name derives from the term for an Indian trader in the province of Gujarat.

Banyan pleat

(M)

Period: 19th century.

Tailor's term for a pleat at the back of a garment made with a **tackover** but without a back vent.

Barbe

(F)

Period: 14th to late 16th century.

The head-dress of widows and mourners. A length of vertically pleated linen encircling the chin and falling to the bosom; worn with a black hood and pendant veil behind. The barbe covered the chin of elite women; by all others it was worn with the chin exposed.

See Mourning attire.

Barbette

(F)

Period: ca. 1200–ca. 1350.

A French term for the **wimple** and also for the linen band worn under the chin and pinned on the top or sides of the head; usually worn with a white **fillet**.

Barbour

(F & M)

Period: 1894 onwards.

Originally a general drapery firm in South Shields, Tyneside, England; by 1908 it had a 12-page mail-order catalogue which included the waxed and waterproof garments for which it became famous. By the late 1950s it had its own factory and diversified in subsequent decades to produce a wide range of clothing and accessories. Its reputation was further enhanced by Helen Mirren wearing its traditional waxed jacket in the film *The Queen* (2006).

Barcelona handkerchief

(F & M)

Period: 18th and 19th centuries.

A handkerchief of soft, twilled silk from Barcelona, usually black; used as a **neckerchief**. "A Barcelona black and tight" pinned round the neck. (Peter Pindar).

Also used as a **handkerchief**; "Barcelona silk snuff-handkerchiefs" (1734, Essex Record Office, Inventory).

Barme cloth, barm cloth, barmhatre

(M, later F)

Period: Early Medieval.

An apron; a term used to the end of the 14th century and then gradually replaced by **apron**.

b

Barmfell, barmskin
(M)
Period: 14th–17th centuries.
A leather **apron**.

Barouche coat
(F)
Period: 1809.
A three-quarter-length, close-fitting outdoor coat, with shaped bodice and full sleeves; fastened down the front with **barrel-snaps** and a buckled girdle round the waist.

Barrel hose
(M)
Period: 1570–1620.
Breeches voluminous throughout; after 1610 heavily pleated or gathered from top to bottom. Certain Cambridge students were seen "waring greate Galligaskins and Barreld hooese stuffed with horse tayles, with Skabilonians and knitt nether-stockes too fine for schollers" (1570, MS in Corpus Christi College, Cambridge).

Barrel shape
(F)
Period: 20th century onwards.
A term describing a skirt which is, like a barrel, narrow at top and bottom but much fuller between, in this instance, the waist and hem. Descriptive of the **hobble skirts** of ca. 1908 and found also in the 1960s and occasionally later.

Barrel-snaps
Period: 1800–1830.
Tubular snap-fastenings of gilt metal; fashionable for cloaks and **pelisses**.

Barrette
(F)
Period: ca. 1850 onwards.
The instep of low-cut shoes was covered with several decorative bars known as barrettes.

Period: 20th century.
From the French term for a biretta or small cap, the term was used to describe a support for long hair early in the century, and then a decorative hair grip.

Barrow, barrow-coat
Period: 19th century.
A baby's flannel garment wrapped round the body and turned up over the feet. "The barrow-coats are best made of real Welsh flannel" (*Cassell's Magazine*, April 1884).

Baseball cap
(M, occasionally F)
Period: Mid-19th century onwards.
Specifically associated with the American game of baseball, these caps were originally soft and flexible but always with a brim to shield the eyes attached at the front. The segmented sections of the dome-shaped cap gradually acquired air-holes or vents and the brim

was offered in straight and curved forms. Many improvements took place in the second half of the 20th century using synthetic fabrics, **Velcro** fastenings, etc. A team, college or sponsor logo was often prominently displayed on the front of the cap and many colours and combinations of fabrics were devised. Since the 1980s these caps have become a general form of headwear and groups of young people often wear them with the brim to one side or at the back, shielding the neck.

Base coat
(M)
Period: 1490–1540.
A jacket or **jerkin** with deep skirts called **bases** hanging in tubular pleats to just above the knees; with a square neck and short sleeves. The half-base coat was a military garment.

Bases
(M)
Period: 1490–1540.
The tubular, pleated skirts of a jacket or jerkin; sometimes separate items, especially when worn with armour.

Base socks
(M)
Period: 16th century.
A sock worn beneath the outer one for added comfort.

Basket
(F)
Period: ca. 1550–1600.
A tall, wickerwork hat. "Their maried Women weare on their heades fine wickre Basquettes of a foot and a half long" (1555, *Fardle of Facions*).

Basket buttons
Period: 1700 onwards.
Buttons decorated with an interlacing pattern, in a basketwork pattern or a metal imitation thereof; especially fashionable on men's coats in the 18th century.

Basque
(F)
Period: 19th century onwards.
French term for an extension of the bodice below the waist.

Basque-habit
(F)
Period: 1860s–ca. 1900.
A bodice with square-cut **basques**.

Basque-waistband
(F)
Period: 1867–ca. 1900.
A waistband with five **vandyked** tabs; for afternoon-dress styles.

Basquin-body
(F)
Period: 1850s.
A day bodice with **basques** sometimes cut in one piece with the bodice.

Basquine, basquin

(F)

Period: 1857.

A coat with deep **basques**, fringed trimming, a **bertha** and **pagoda sleeves**.

Period: 1860s.

A new name for a fashionable outdoor jacket.

Bass Weejuns

(M)

Period: 1936 onwards.

A leather slip-on shoe first called "Norwegian moccasins" and made by G. H. Bass of Maine, USA. Sometimes called "penny loafers" because there is a slot in the band across the tongue into which a coin can be placed.

See Loafer.

An elite Englishwoman, in an engraving by the Bohemian artist Wenceslas Hollar of 1639. She is dressed in the styles worn at the English court; the back-laced **bodice** has deep **basques** and the front section mimics a **stomacher**. The wide collar and cuffs are edged with **lace**. The **petticoat** is probably worn over hip pads. A **sash** encircles the waist and ribbon rosettes and **pearl** jewellery complete the fashionable appearance. Private collection.

Bast hat

Period: 17th century.

A hat made of plaited bast or bass, the inner bark of the lime or linden. "Bast or Straw-Hats both knotted and plain" (1670–5, *Book of Rates*).

Bateau neckline

(F)

Period: 1920s onwards.

Shallow neckline, the same depth at front and back and running from one shoulder to the other; named after the curving upper line of a boat (*bateau* in French).

Bathing costume, bathing dress

(F & M)

Period: Medieval to late 16th century.

In rivers, in the sea, or at spas men usually bathed naked, but at Baden in Germany in 1416 and in the Bath spa waters in 1449 men wore **drawers** and women wore **smocks**, probably undergarments used for modesty.

Period: From 17th century onwards.

(M)

Voluminous flannel gowns, spoken of as "flannels", were worn at public baths in the 17th and up to the early 19th centuries. For seaside bathing nothing was worn by men until ca. 1870 when brief, triangular trunks, longer, woollen, all-in-one garments and, from the 20th century, various forms of swimming trunks using new fabrics were introduced, usually because they were required in swimming pools or by local regulations preventing nude bathing. From the late 20th century they became fashion items with seasonal changes in colour and cut.

(F)

Until 1865 a loose, ankle-length, flannel gown with sleeves was worn. In that year "the Zouave Marine Swimming Costume" with "body and trousers cut in one", of stout brown holland or dark-blue serge appeared. In 1868 an attached knee-length skirt was added; in 1878 the skirt was shorter and a separate item. By 1880 the garment became combinations, often of stockinette, and was knee-length, sleeveless, with a short, detachable skirt. "Ladies Navy Blue Stockingette Bathing Costumes, trimmed with white work; sale price 2s. 11 ½d. each", (1900, August 4, Daily Mail). In the 20th century shorter, simpler one-piece bathing costumes were introduced, and as early as the 1920s two-piece costumes were worn, well in advance of the **bikini** of 1946.

Bathing suit

(F & M)

Period: 1900 onwards.

Another description for **bathing costume**, but the term **swimsuit** was usual by the 1930s, suggestive of physical exercise rather than taking the waters.

Batswing tie

(M)

Period: 1896.

A **bow tie**, the ends shaped to resemble bats' wings; for day wear.

Battenburg jacket

(F)

Period: 1880s.

An outdoor short jacket with loose fronts, large buttons and a turned-down collar. Probably named after Princess Beatrice of Battenberg (the correct spelling but often ignored at the time), the youngest daughter of Queen Victoria who married Prince Henry of Battenberg in 1885.

Battledress jacket

(M)

Period: 1939 onwards.

A waist-length, khaki, wool jacket, buttoned and single-breasted with two buttoned chest pockets worn by conscripts and regular soldiers during the 1939–45 war and for several subsequent decades. Correctly termed a battledress blouse, it had a cross-over fastening band at the waist, not dissimilar to certain blouses. It was one of many garments which could be acquired from **army surplus** outlets and was popular with students.

Batts

(M, possibly F)

Period: 17th century.

Heavy, low shoes laced in front; for country wear.

Batwing sleeve

See Dolman sleeve.

Bavarette

Period: 17th century.

"A bib, mocet or mocheter to put before the bosom of a child" (1611, Cotgrave).

See Muckinder.

Bavarian pelisse-robe

(F)

Period: 1826.

A **pelisse-robe** with two lines of trimming descending from the shoulders to the bottom of the skirt *en tablier* (the French term which is an elegant way of describing an apron or a feature which copies the look of an apron).

Bavarian-style dress

(F)

Period: 1826.

A carriage dress with rows of decorative bands down the front in the Bavarian style.

Bavaroy, beveroy

(M)

Period: Early 18th century.

A coat, the exact nature of which is unknown but possibly from *bavarois* (Bavarian), a garment introduced during the War of the Spanish Succession, 1701–1713). "A sandy colour Beveroy broadcloth coat" (1711, *London Gazette*).

Bavolet

(F)

Period: 1830 onwards.

The curtain or pendant fabric at the back of a **bonnet** shading the neck.

Bayadere trimming

(F)

Period: 1850s.

Flat trimming of velvet woven in or sewn on to the dress fabric.

Beachwear

(F & M)

Period: 1920s onwards.

As seaside holidays increased in popularity a range of informal garments emerged, including beach gowns, beach pyjamas, beach robes, beach sandals, beach shirts and beach wraps. These were often brightly coloured and sometimes made of towelling.

Beanie

(F & M)

Period: 1920s onwards.

An American term originally describing a small, round, felt **cap** worn by schoolchildren. This developed into a female hat in the 1940s. In the late 20th and early 21st centuries it describes a knitted cap, with or without a turnover edge.

Beard

(M)

Period: ca. 1550–ca. 1650.

Although the beard was worn by men in earlier periods, it was from the mid-16th century that it acquired a peculiar social significance; in that hundred years there were over fifty named cuts of beard in fashion. The traveller returning from abroad would sport a style of beard indicating the country he had visited; his beard might reveal his social rank or occupation, or express "every man in his humour". The following are documented and important styles:-

Cadiz beard: sometimes called Cads beard, after the expedition to Cadiz in 1596. A large and disordered growth. "His face, Furr'd with Cads-beard" (1598, E. Guilpin, *Skialetheia*).

Goat beard: "How, Sir, will you be trimmed? Your moustachios sharp at the ends like a shoemaker's awls, or hanging down to your mouth like goat's flakes?" (1591, J. Lyly, *Midas*).

Peak: a common name for the beard, exclusive of the **moustache**. The beard cut to a point and often starched. "Some spruce yonker with a starcht beard and his whiskers turned up" (1623, J. Mabbe, *The Rogue*).

Pencil beard: a slight tuft of hair on the point of the chin. "Sir, you with the pencil on your chin" (1599, Ben Jonson, *Cynthia's Revels*).

Pick-a-devant, or Barbula: so called "when it ends in a point under the chin and on the higher lip, chin, and cheeks" (1688, R. Holme, *The Academy* of *Armory*).

Pisa beard: synonymous with "stiletto beard". "Play with your Pisa beard! Why, where's your brush, pupil?" (1618, Fletcher, *Queen of Corinth*).

Roman T beard, also called Hammer cut: a straight tuft under the lower lip, forming the "handle", the waxed moustache horizontal forms the cross-piece of the hammer or T 1618–1650.

Round beard, or Bush beard: "Some made round like a rubbing brush" (1587, Harrison's *England*).

Spade beard: a beard in the shape of a pioneer's spade (that of an ace of spades on a playing card), broad above with curved sides to a point below. Thought to give a martial appearance and favoured by soldiers. "... whether he will have his peake cut broade pendant like a spade, to be terrible like a warrior?" (1592, R. Greene, *Quip for an Upstart Courtier*). "His spade peake is as sharpe as if he had been a Pioneer" (1592, T. Nashe, *Piers Pennilesse*). Beards "some like a spade, some like a fork, some square" (1621, J. Taylor, *Superbiae Flagellum*).

Marquisetto, also Marquisotte: cut close to the chin, neatly trimmed 1570–ca. 1620.

Stiletto beard: "Some sharpe steletto fashion, dagger like" 1610–1640 (1621, J. Taylor, *Superbiae Flagellum*).

Swallow's tail beard: a version of the forked 1560–1600 beard but with the ends longer and more widely spread.

Period: Mid-19th century to ca. 1930.

In the 1830s, long side whiskers and moustaches began to be worn and developed into beards which were bushy and long, or trimmed to follow the contours of the face. "By the 1920"s (they) were confined to the elderly, literary, artistic and eccentric" (1973, A. Mansfield & P. Cunnington, *Handbook of English Costume in the 20th Century 1900–1950*).

Period: Late 20th century onwards.

Beards are worn but are often considered an impediment to a public career and tend to be associated with the young and experimental, alternative attitudes, or as in the earlier quote about the 1920s.

Beard-brush

(M)

Period: ca. 1600–1650.

A small brush for the beard; very popular and used in public.

Beard-comb

(M)

Period: ca. 1600–1650.

A small comb for the beard; uncommon.

Bearer

(M)

Period: 17th century.

Stiffening for **boot hose** tops; "...a paire of bearers for my toppes" (1656, Sir M. Stapleton's *Household Books*).

(F)

Period: ca. 1650 to early 18th century.

Padded rolls acting as **bustles**, worn "under the skirts of gowns at their setting on at the bodies, which raise up the skirt at that place to what breadth the wearer pleaseth and as the fashion is" (1688, R. Holme, *Armory*).

(M)

Period: 19th century.

A band buttoned across the inside of the top of breeches or trousers which were made with **falls**. The bearer, placed behind the falls flap, was deeper at the sides than in the centre where the two parts were buttoned together; rising a couple of inches above the top of the flap. A Bilston bearer meant that the bearer band of the breeches was extra-wide to give more abdominal support; a type used by labourers. A French bearer described the band cut very narrow.

Bearing cloth

Period: 16th–18th century.

The **mantle** or cloth used to cover an infant when carried to baptism; often embroidered and of the finest silks. "For 5 yeard of dameske to mak a bearing cloth £3:6:6" (1623, Lord William Howard of Naworth, *Household Books*).

Beatnik

(F & M)

Period: Late 1940s–1960s.

A movement found on the Left Bank in Paris and San Francisco in America. In France it was an intellectual, left-wing challenging of convention and included philosophers like Sartre and Simone de Beauvoir, writers and film-makers, and its most memorable fashion statements were made by the singer Juliette Gréco (b. 1927), whose sleek, dark hair, black **polo neck** sweater, black slacks or chic black evening dresses focused attention on her face, with its exaggerated eye make-up. This pared-down style was hugely influential, and black was also the preferred colour of the clothing worn by the San Francisco-based beat generation, whose unconventional behaviour led to the term beatnik (ca. 1955). The men wore black **berets**, black slacks, sandals and dark glasses, and the women adopted dancers' **leotards** worn with black skirts, black stockings, flat shoes and elaborate eye make-up to rival that of Gréco.

Beau

(M)

Period: ca. 1680 to mid-19th century.

A gentleman very particular as to his dress; not necessarily as effeminate as a **fop**. Used satirically in the 20th and 21st centuries to denote overly exquisite attention to all aspects of personal appearance.

Beaufort coat

(M)

Period: 1880.

A **lounge jacket** with four buttons, and closing high; seams raised or double-stitched; narrow, straight sleeves. Also known as a **jumper coat**.

Beaver, beaver hat

(F & M)

Period: 14th century onwards.

A hat originally made of beaver skin but from the 16th century of felted beaver-fur wool.

Period: 19th century.

"…the bodies of beaver hats are made of a firm felt wrought up of fine wool, rabbits' hair, etc.…over this is placed the nap prepared from the hair of the beaver" (1862, Mayhew, *London Labour and the London Poor*). Beaver coats were fashionable in the late 19th century but were practical, rather than sophisticated, fur coats.

Bébé bodice

(F)

Period: 1883.

A round-waisted bodice with a sash.

Bébé bonnet

(F)

Period: 1877.

A very small outdoor bonnet, the border turned up to show a cap; trimming of tulle, ribbons (narrow "bébé ribbon" in the 1880s) and flowers.

Beck

(F)

Period: Late 15th and early 16th centuries.

A beak-shaped accessory to a **mourning** hood.

Bedgown

(F & M)

Period: 18th century.

A loose-sleeved **dressing-gown**, worn only as négligée in the bedroom or for comfort. "Why must the wrapping bed-gown hide. Your snowy bosom's swelling pride?" (ca. 1744, Edward Moore).

Bed jacket

(F)

Period: 19th century onwards.

A short jacket worn in bed; of various fabrics and often, in the early to mid-20th century, home-made and/or hand-knitted.

Beehive hair style

(F)

Period: Late 1950s and 1960s.

A tall, dome-shaped hair style achieved by back-combing and hair spray.

Beehive hat, hive bonnet

(F)

Period: ca. 1770–1790.

A hat with a tall, rounded crown, beehive-shaped, and with a narrow brim.

Belcher, Belcher handkerchief

(M)

Period: ca. 1800–1870.

A blue **neckerchief** with large white spots, each with a dark-blue "eye"; as worn by the pugilist Jim Belcher (fl. 1800–1807).

Belette, bilett

(F & M)

Period: 1300 to mid-16th century.

A jewel or ornament.

Bell

(F & M)

Period: Late 13th–15th century.

A travelling cloak with a circular cut; some hooded, some buttoned at the neck, and sometimes made with side vents and back vent.

Bell bottoms

(F & M)

Period: 1960s onwards.

Sailors traditionally wore trousers which flared out from knee to ankle but, in terms of fashion, this style appeared in the 1960s with an exaggeratedly tight fit on the upper leg and a wide bottom flare.

Bell hoop, cupola coat

(F)

Period: 1710–1780.

An under-petticoat distended with whalebone hoops to the shape of a bell.

Bellied doublet

See Long-bellied doublet.

Bellows pocket

(M)

Period: Late 19th century.

A patch pocket with side folds capable of expanding or lying flat, like a bellows; a common feature of **Norfolk jackets** from 1890 on.

Bell skirt

(F)

Period: 1891.

A gored skirt, the front breadth shaped with darts; the foot of the skirt stiffened with muslin lining or, for walking, lined throughout; the skirt sometimes buttoned up on each side instead of having a placket hole behind. Commonly **tailor-made**.

Bell sleeve

(F)

Period: 1850 onwards.

A sleeve that is close-fitting to mid-forearm, then expanding into a bell-shaped opening.

Belly-chete

(F, possibly M)

Period: 16th century.

Slang term for an **apron**.

Belly-piece

(M)

Period: ca. 1620–1670.

A triangular stiffening of pasteboard, or whalebone and buckram, sewn into the lining of the **doublet** in front, on each side of the opening at waist-level, with the base of the triangle placed vertically along the front border, thus forming a corset-like ridge down the belly.

Below

See Furbelow.

Belt

(M)

Period: Early 15th century onwards.

Military belt of a **knightly girdle**.

Also a shoulder belt or **baldric**.

Also a waist belt, namely a strip of leather or fabric to confine or support clothes or weapons.

(F)

Period: 1800 onwards.

A single-layer strip of fabric or leather, or a firmly lined and sometimes wider strip, to accentuate the waist. In the 20th century belts became a major fashion accessory, often contrasting with the clothing with which they were worn.

Bend

(F & M)

Period: ca. 1000–1600.

Primarily a band of fabric worn in association with dress. It was used as a **fillet** or other circular ornament worn on the head, or as a hat-band. "My bende for an hat of black sylk and silver" (1463, Bury Wills).

Also a synonym for a stripe.

Bendel

(F & M)

Period: 15th and 16th centuries.

A small band, **scarf** or **fillet** of fabric. "She wyped it… with a bendel of sylk" (1483, Caxton, *Golden Legend*).

Bendigo

(M)

Period: 19th century.

A rough, fur cap worn by workers.

Benjamin

(M)

Period: 19th century.

A loose **overcoat**.

Benjy

(M)

Period: 19th century.

Slang term for a **waistcoat**.

Benoitan chains

(F)

Period: 1866.

Chains of metal or jet hanging at either side of the head, over the chignon or across the bosom; so named from Sardou's play, *La Famille Benoîton,* of that year.

Bents

(F)

Period: Late 16th and early 17th centuries.

Strips of whalebone or rushes used to distend **bum rolls** or **farthingales**. "Their bents of whalebone to beare out their bummes" (1588, W. Averell, *Combat Contrar…*).

Beret

(F)

Period: ca. 1820–1850.

A cap with a large, flat crown, similar to a halo; extensively trimmed. Usually of velvet and worn with evening dress.

(F & M)

Period: 20th century onwards.

A plain, circular style of enlarged cap, usually of wool and worn informally; the Basque beret was imported into the UK after 1918 by the founder of the firm Kangol, whose tradename became synonymous with this type of headwear in war and peace time. It became especially popular with young women after the film *Bonnie*

EVENING DRESS.

Engraved Expressly for THE LADIES MAGAZINE Improved Series

Evening dress for July 1830; the full sleeves are in the **beret** style. Copyright the Olive Matthews Collection, Chertsey Museum.

and Clyde (1967) and with young men emulating the actor Samuel L. Jackson in the 1990s.

Beret hat

(F)

Period: 1872.

An outdoor hat of white chip, shaped like a small **mob cap**, trimmed with roses and with pendant ribbons behind.

Beret sleeve

(F)

Period: 1829.

An evening-dress shoulder sleeve, short, circular and widely distended so as to resemble a beret head-dress. It was closed by a band round the arm, and the shape was sustained by a stiff lining of book muslin. Occasionally the beret was double, one above the other.

Berger

(F)

Period: 17th century.

A lock of hair. "A small lock (*à la* Shepherdess) turned up with a puff" (1690, J. Evelyn, *Mundus Muliebris*).

Bergère hat, milkmaid hat

(F)

Period: 1730–1800; also 1860s.

A large straw hat with a flexible brim and low crown.

Berlin gloves

(M)

Period: From 1830 onwards.

Washable gloves worn by servants and the less well-off. "Made of a kind of strong cotton which should be very-thin and neat."

Bermuda hat

(F)

Period: ca. 1700–1750.

A hat of straw for country wear. "Women's Hatts made of fine Bermuda Platt" (1727, *New England Weekly Journal*).

Bergère hat of plaited straw covered with cream silk, edged with narrow **lace** and decorated with **ribbons**. Worn by a bride as part of her **wedding** outfit, ca. 1780. Copyright the Olive Matthews Collection, Chertsey Museum. Photograph by John Chase.

Bermuda shorts

(F & M)

Period: 1930s onwards.

Knee-length shorts originally worn on the island of Bermuda, which when worn by women as "short" shorts were banned. Later, men also started wearing them; they can be vibrantly coloured and/or patterned.

Bernhardt mantle

(F)

Period: 1886.

A short outdoor cape, the back shaped, the front loose; with a turned-down collar and **sling sleeves**. The name reflects the international fame of the French actress Sarah Bernhardt (1844–1923).

Bertha

(F)

Period: 1839–1920s.

A deep fall of lace or silk encircling the neck and shoulders, or merely the shoulders, in a low **décolletage**; a Victorian revival of the mid-17th century fashion.

Bertha-pelerine

(F)

Period: 1840s.

A bertha carried down the centre front to the waist; worn with evening dress.

Bespoke

(M, later F)

Period: 19th century onwards.

In tailoring terms this means a garment is created to clothe an individual customer, who is measured by a tailor so that a pattern is cut to reflect his or her exact measurements; the customer also has choice in cloth, colour, style and the suit, for instance, is tailored to his or her wishes. It is a lengthy process, uses the finest pattern-cutting and tailoring skills, and is expensive.

See Made-to-measure, Ready-made clothes.

Beten

Period: Medieval.

Embroidered with fancy subjects.

Bettina blouse

(F)

Period: 1950s.

The designer Hubert de Givenchy (b. 1927) introduced this style of blouse which was cut like a shirt but had full sleeves of ruffled broderie anglaise. It was named after Bettina Graziani who modelled for Givenchy and was a celebrated **model** before the age of supermodels.

Bewdley cap

(M)

Period: 1570–ca. 1825.

A **Monmouth cap** made at Bewdley, Worcestershire, and used by country-folk.

Bias, byesse

Period: Medieval onwards.

A term used from the 15th century for fabric cut on the cross, a method used for the early kind of hose in order to obtain a close fit. "Hozen knitte at ye knees and lyned within with Lynnen cloth *byesse*as the hose is" (1434, John Hyll's *Traytese upon Worship in Armes*).

Bias-cut women's dresses were especially fashionable in the 1920s and 1930s and intermittently at later dates.

Bib

Period: 16th century onwards.

A small square of linen hung in front of a child's neck to protect the clothes from being soiled. Later versions were shaped, made of cotton or thin towelling, and held by ties around the neck.

See Muckinder.

Bib-apron

(F & M)

Period: 17th century onwards.

An **apron** with a bib extension above the waist.

Bib-cravat

(M)

Period: Late 17th century.

A broad bib like **cravat**, usually edged with lace; secured at the neck by a cravat-string or knot of ribbon, and usually coloured.

Bibi bonnet

(F)

Period: 1831–1836.

Also known as a **cottage bonnet**. A bonnet of which the sides projected forward with an upward tilt.

Bibi capote

(F)

Period: 1830s.

Name applied to any **capote** with a projecting brim in front, sloping down to a small crown at the back of the head, and shaped like a baby's bonnet.

Bicorne

(F & M)

A modern term to describe a hat worn in the late 18th and early 19th centuries with a brim turned up at front and back, with the front blocked into a slight peak and sometimes trimmed with a cockade or rosette.

Biggin, biggon

Period: 16th and 17th centuries.

A term for a child's cap shaped like a **coif**; used in Scotland in 1329.

(M)

Period: ca. 1550–1700.

A man's night-cap worn in bed.

(F)

Period: Early 19th century.

A large form of **mob cap** but without ties under the chin.

Bigote
Period: 17th century.
A rare term for a **moustache**.

Big shirt
(F)
Period: 1950s onwards.
Literally an oversized shirt worn by women, sometimes appropriating men's shirts. The term was coined in the 1980s when it became a recognized fashion garment.

Biker clothes
(M, sometimes F)
Period: 1950s onwards.
Clothing specially designed for wear by cyclists and motorcyclists for increased velocity and/or protection. Lycra tops, **shorts** and **leggings** were worn by cyclists, and leather, usually black, was worn by motorcyclists. Elements of both styles were adopted by non-bikers.

Bikini
(F)
Period: 1946 onwards.
A two-piece bathing costume supposedly named after the Bikini atholl in the Pacific Ocean. Although such bathing costumes had been worn earlier in the century (and by female Roman wrestlers much earlier), this version, designed by French engineer Louis Réard, was more abbreviated and set a trend for decreasing usage of fabric and maximum exposure of flesh.

Bilboquets
See Roulettes.

Billiment, billment, habillement, abillement
(F)
Period: 16th century.
The decorated border to a **French hood**. The upper billiment adorned the crown, the nether billiment the front of the bonnet. "Upper and nether habiliments of goldsmith's work for the French hood" (1541, Letters and Papers of Henry VIII).
Also, a head ornament popular with brides.

Billycock
(M)
Period: 19th century.
A colloquial term for a low-crowned, flexible, felt hat with wide, curving brim. There are two explanations of the name; that it derived from the "bully-cocked" hat of 18th century; or that it was "First used by Billy Coke [Mr William Coke] at the great shooting parties at Holkham" (Dr Cobham Brewer, 1894).
See Bully-cocked.

Bilston bearer
See Bearer.

Binding cloth
(F)
Period: 17th century.
A rare synonym for **forehead cloth**. "When shall I have my binding cloth for my forehead? Shall I have no forehead cloth?" (1605, Peter Erondelle, *The French Garden*).

Biretta
(M)
Period: 16th century onwards.
A square-cornered ecclesiastical cap worn by clergy in the Roman Catholic Church; it is black for priests, purple for bishops and red for cardinals. After World War II it was briefly imitated by milliners for female customers.

Birkenstock sandals
(F & M)
Period: 1967 onwards.
The name derives from a German firm of shoemakers who can trace their history back to the late 18th century. In the early 20th century a contoured arch was developed, the first to be placed into footwear. This was the origin of the Birkenstock sandal, known in Europe before being produced in the USA and marketed worldwide after 1967. In addition to sandals, there are shoes with the same distinctive arch-supports.

Birlet, burlet, bourrelet
(M)
Period: 15th century.
A circular, padded roll as worn with **chaperons**.

Birthday suit
(M)
Period: 18th century.
A court suit for wearing at a royal birthday celebration.
See Court dress.

Bishop sleeve
(F)
Period: 19th century onwards.
A day sleeve in light fabrics, very full from the shoulder to the wrist, where it was gathered into a closed cuff. Worn from ca. 1810 off and on until the end of the century. In the 1850s the "full bishop" was very large; in the 1890s the "small bishop" was preferred and popular for blouses. In the 20th century bishop sleeves were popular on blouses, coats and dresses.

Bivouac mantle
(F)
Period: 1814.
A large, loose **mantle** descending nearly to the feet and having a high collar; made of scarlet cloth wadded and lined with ermine.

Blacking
Period: 16th century onwards.
A composition containing lamp-black and oil, applied to the surface of shoes and boots. "Shoes that stink of blacking" (1611, Middleton, *The Roaring Girl*).

Blacks
(F & M)
Period: Medieval to late 18th century.
Mourning apparel for both sexes. In the Middle Ages only the cloak had to be black, the rest might be

coloured. From the end of the 15th century all outer garments were black.

See Mourning attire.

Black work

Period: ca. 1510–1630s.

Embroidery in black silk, generally on linen; often worked in an all-over pattern in continuous scrolling. Very popular for collars, wristbands, smocks and handkerchiefs.

Blanchet, blanch, blanc

Period: 12th–14th century.

Blanchet

Period: 17th century.

Blanch

Period: 18th century.

Blanc

Terms denoting white paint or powder used as a cosmetic for the skin.

Blazer

(F & M)

Period: 1890 onwards.

Originally a scarlet jacket worn by men as part of boating or cricketing clothing; later an unlined, flannel jacket in club or plain colours, worn for games and then as **leisure wear**. From the 1930s similar styles were worn by women and gradually the garment became a **classic style** and lost its association with sportswear.

Bliaut, bliaunt, blehant, blehand

(F & M)

Period: 12th to early 14th century.

A term denoting either a loose, ankle-length **super tunic**, usually having wide sleeves, or a costly fabric.

Blistered

Period: Late 16th and early 17th century.

A form of decoration synonymous with **slashing**.

Bloomers

(F)

Period: 1851.

Name given to young women who imitated the American Mrs Amelia Bloomer in wearing a modified form of trousers below a knee-length full skirt. "A young lady of a certain age – an ardent Bloomer" (1853, Surtees, *Mr Sponge's Sporting Tour*). The outfit, called Bloomer costume or Bloomer dress, was also implied.

Period: 1890 onwards.

Name given to the baggy **knickerbockers** worn by some women cyclists and also, to loose, knee-length underpants.

Blouse

(M)

Period: Early 19th century onwards.

A loose, smock-like garment, usually of cotton or linen, associated with the blue blouse of French workmen.

Also a term denoting the upper part of battledress worn by airmen and soldiers in the 20th century.

(F)

Period: ca. 1850 onwards.

A loose separate bodice of different fabric from the skirt, always worn with a belt, and with or without a jacket over it. An early form was the **Garibaldi shirt** of 1863. Usually for day wear, but in 1895 evening blouses were introduced. In the 20th century blouses came in various styles, loose or tight-fitting, long-sleeved or short-sleeved, with or without collars.

Blouse-bodice

(F)

Period: 1877.

A day bodice in blouse form, falling over the hips and worn with a belt.

Blouse dress

(M)

Period: 1870s.

A loose, sac-like blouse worn by boys outside the trousers and confined round the waist by a belt; a vertical pleat was down each side of the front.

Blouson

(F & M)

Period: 20th century onwards.

A short, casual jacket with the looseness of structure associated with early **blouses** but often with a drawstring inside the bottom hem to adjust the fit.

Bluchers

(M)

Period: ca. 1820–1850.

Half boots, close-fitting and laced up in front over a tongue, having six eyelet holes on each side.

Blue Billy

(M)

Period: ca. 1800–1820.

A blue **neckcloth** with white spots, as worn by the pugilist William Mace.

Blue coat

(M)

Period: Late 16th century to ca. 1700.

A coat of blue worn by apprentices and serving men, and therefore a colour avoided by gentlemen.

Boa

(F)

Period: 19th century onwards.

A long, round **tippet**, called by the French "Boa" (1829) but worn all through the 19th century; especially fashionable in the 1890s. Made of swansdown, feathers or fur.

Intermittently fashionable in later periods such as the 1930s and 1960s.

Boater

(F & M)

Period: 19th century onwards.

A stiff, straw hat with moderately shallow, flat-topped crown and straight, narrow brim with a hat-band of Petersham ribbon. The Henley boater of 1894 was a blue or drab felt hat of similar shape.

Women and schoolchildren wore boaters without any association with rowing.

Boating shoes

See Deck shoes.

Bob, bob-wig

(M)

Period: 18th century.

A wig without a **queue**. The long bob covered the back of the neck; the short bob ended above the neck. Always an "undress" wig.

Bobby socks

(F & M)

Period: 1940s onwards.

Short socks, often white, worn by American teenagers; similar in style to **ankle socks**.

Bodice

(F)

Period: 15th century onwards.

The inner section of a garment above the waist, of linen, with or without padding, and occasionally strengthened with boning. Usually a term for a female garment, but sometimes found describing a male item of clothing.

Period: 19th century.

The upper part of a woman's dress, often structured and boned, of which there were many named varieties such as:

Period: 1822.

En Blouse – the front gathered and pouched; the neck half high and round;

Period: 1820s.

En Cœur – heart-shaped front descending to a slight point and having a number of narrow pleats along the upper edge of a low neck;

Period: 1820s.

à l'Edith – a variation of the *Roxalane* and *Sévigné* (see below);

Period: 1820s.

à l'Enfant – the neck half-high and round, gathered by a draw-string;

Period: 1820s.

en Gerbe – the front folds pleated fan-wise from the shoulders;

Period: 1828.

à la Polonese – a cross-over front, the folds crossing high up;

Period: 1829.

à la Roxalane – similar to the *Sévigné*, the pleats across

the top, sloping down towards the central vertical bone of the bodice;

Period: 1820s.

à la Sévigné – the bodice with pleated folds crossing the bosom nearly horizontally, divided by a central bone in the lining, down to the waist.

Period: 20th century.

Term describing the close-fitting upper section of a child's or woman's dress.

Bodies, pair of bodies

(F & M)

Period: 16th and 17th centuries.

An under-bodice made in two sections and joined at the sides and stiffened with whalebone, wood or steel, and sometimes padded; corresponding to a pair of **stays**.

Spinner.

A spinner from the *The Book of English Trades*, 1823 edition. The illustration suggests a healthy outdoor activity but only the highly skilled could earn "one shilling in a day". The style of dress is late eighteenth century with a plain **cap**, a **smock** can be glimpsed beneath the low-cut **bodice** and a capacious **apron** covers the skirt. Private collection.

Bodkin

(F)

Period: 16th–19th century.

A long pin, plain or decorated, used for fastening women's hair.

Bodkin-beard

(M)

Period: 1520 to early 17th century.

A long, pointed **beard** decorating the centre of the chin only.

Body

(F)

Period: 15th–17th century.

A term denoting the **bodice**; the forebody was the front portion of the bodice.

Body coat

(M)

Period: 19th century onwards.

Tailoring term to distinguish the upper garment of a suit from the outdoor **overcoat** or **top coat**.

Body piercing

(F & M)

Period: Late 20th century onwards.

A perforation or hole is made in the flesh, usually the brow, ear, nose, nipple or belly to take an item of jewellery, often a stud or ring. **Ear-rings** were more usual than other piercing in Western society until the 1980s when there was more experimentation amongst young people. Zara Phillips (b. 1981), granddaughter of Queen Elizabeth II, had a stud in her tongue for a brief period.

Body stocking

(F)

Period: Mid-1960s onwards.

A complete body-covering in Lycra, often flesh-coloured and similar to a dancer's **leotard** but with leg coverings. Worn in place of all other underwear and often beneath transparent dresses.

Body warmer

(F & M)

Period: 1980s onwards.

Term for a sleeveless **jerkin** or **waistcoat**, often of quilted fabric with a soft interlining, which fastens from neck to waist, with a zip and/or buttons, and can be worn as an extra layer of warmth over other garments.

Boiler suit

(F & M)

Period: Early 20th century onwards.

Originally a protective outer garment, usually of sturdy cotton or denim, which combined **overalls** and shirt to provide a sleeved, buttoned layer over other clothing; often worn by manual workers. Women wore boiler suits in factories during World War II and the British Prime Minister Winston Churchill was photographed wearing one.

See Siren suit.

Boisson

(F)

Period: 1780s.

A short cloak with a hood. "Small boissongs, craped with a small handkerchief and hood, made very narrow round the shoulders" (1782, *The Lady's Magazine*); for half-dress.

Bolero

(F)

Period: 1853 onwards.

A loose-fitting jacket with **basques** cut in points and fringed. Inspired by Spanish styles of dress as a tribute to the Empress Eugénie of France (1826–1920) who was Spanish. Revived in the 1890s and then made very short without basques, the fronts curved away just above waist-level. Some had narrow revers peaked up over the shoulders and came with or without sleeves. A popular style intermittently throughout the 20th century, especially for young women, often worn unfastened and sometimes sleeveless.

Bolero bodice

(F)

Period: 1896.

A day bodice trimmed to simulate the wearing of a bolero; rounded in front.

Bolero coat, bolero jacket

(F)

Period: 1890s.

A short jacket in the style of a bolero, worn open over a blouse.

Bolero mantle

(F)

Period: 1899.

A short **mantle** with bolero-shaped fronts.

Bolero toque

(F)

Period: 1887.

A small **toque** of velvet, dress fabric, astrakhan or fur, with back trimming rising over the crown.

Bollinger

(M)

Period: 1858–1860s.

The **hemispherical hat** with bowl-shaped crown and narrow, circular brim; there was a button or knob on the centre of the crown. Originally worn by cab-drivers, then adopted by gentlemen for country wear.

Bolster

Period: 15th–17th century.

Term denoting a pad inserted into a garment to produce the required shape.

Bombast

(F & M)

Period: 16th and 17th centuries.

Padding used to distend garments, especially **trunk-hose** and sleeves; using horsehair, flock, wool, rags, flax, bran and cotton.

b

Bomber jacket

(F & M)

Period: 1940 onwards.

A jacket similar to that worn by USAF flight crew; usually of leather, zipped at the front and with close-fitting wrists and lower edge. Worn by young of both genders and acquired from **army surplus** outlets, this became a type of jacket occasionally hybridized and/or reinvented by designers later in the 20th century.

Bondage styles

(F & M)

Period: Late 1970s onwards.

A style of dress associated with **Punks**, and later with **Goths**, which used black leather and Lycra, chains, straps, studding and other physically uncomfortable features. The British fashion designer Vivienne Westwood (b. 1941) produced such styles of clothing early in her career.

See Body piercing.

Bongrace

(F)

Period: 16th and early 17th centuries.

As a separate article, a flat, stiffened, oblong head-covering which projected over the forehead in front and fell down over the back of the head to the shoulders. It could be worn alone or over a **coif**.

As part of the **French hood**, the pendant flap behind, which was turned up over the crown and fixed so as to project forward above the forehead. "(My face) was spoiled for want of a bongrace when I was young" (1612, Beaumont and Fletcher, *The Captain*).

Bonnet

(F & M)

Period: Medieval onwards.

Often used as a synonym for **cap**, but there were subtle differences. A bonnet usually was a soft, semi-structured form of head-covering with a crown and brim; a cap was unstructured, fitted the head closely, and had an optional brim or edge.

(F)

Period: 19th century.

Usually a form of hat of which the brim at the back was absent or greatly diminished; generally tied by ribbon-strings under the chin.

Period: 20th century onwards.

Bonnets were associated with the elderly or old-fashioned, with the exception of straw bonnets worn in the summer, but gradually the term was overtaken by hat.

Boot cuff

(M)

Period: 1727–ca. 1740.

A very deep, closed, turned-back cuff to a man's coat. The cuff frequently reached the bend of the elbow. The term "boot sleeve" was applied to one with a boot cuff. "These boot-sleeves were certainly intended to be the receivers of stolen goods" (1733, H. Fielding, *The Miser*).

Boot garters

(M)

Period: 18th century.

Straps fixed to the back of a riding boot and then passed round the leg above the knee, over the **breeches**, to keep the boot in position.

Boot hose

(M, rarely F)

Period: ca. 1450–18th century.

Stockings worn inside boots to protect the more elegant under-stockings or **nether stocks** from wear and dirt. Usually of coarse fabric, but in the late 16th and early 17th centuries some were very fine. "They have also boot-hose to be wondered at; for they be of the finest cloth that may be got" (1583, Stubbes, *Anatomie of Abuses*).

Period: 18th century.

They were called **boot stockings**.

Boot hose tops, tops

(M)

Period: 16th and 17th centuries.

A decorated upper border to **boot hose**; the tops might be of thread lace or gold or silver lace, ruffled linen, or fringed with silk. "For a quarter of an ounce of gold lace to laye on the toppes of those boot-hose" (1590, Petre Accounts, Essex Record Office).

Bootikin

(M)

Period: 18th century.

A soft boot of oiled silk or wool worn by sufferers from gout.

Period: 19th century.

A child's boot.

Boot jack

(M)

Period: 18th and 19th centuries.

An implement of wood or iron to hold the boot while the wearer withdraws his foot, an office previously performed by a servant. Used chiefly for removing any form of high boot.

Boots

(F & M)

Period: Early Anglo-Saxon onwards.

Footwear of leather or stout cloth extending up beyond the ankles and made in many varieties of height and style; they could be pulled on or fastened with laces or buckles.

Period: 15th century.

"Single boots" indicated unlined as opposed to lined boots.

Boot sleeve

See Boot cuff.

Boot stocking

See Boot hose.

Bopeeper

(M)

Period: 17th century.

A **mask**.

Borders

(F)

Period: 16th century.

Another name for the **billiments**, upper and nether, of the **French hood**. Also, the bands of decorative fabric or goldsmith's work which could be applied to the front edges and hems of gowns. "To my Ladie Scudamore a pair of Borders of Golde of the beste, to mrs. Goringe a paire of Borders with pearle…" (1594, Will of Lady Dacre, Essex Record Office).

Borel, burel

Period: 14th and 15th centuries.

A coarse woollen cloth and the plain garment made from the cloth.

Bosom bottles

(F)

Period: ca. 1750 to early 19th century.

Small vessels of tin or glass holding water and worn by ladies to keep their bouquets fresh. "Bosom Bottles, pear-shaped, flat, 4 inches long, of ribbed glass for bouquets" (1770, *Boston Evening Post*).

Bosom flowers

(F & occasionally M)

Period: 18th century.

Artificial **nosegays** worn by women in full dress; also by macaronis (see **Macaroni suit**) in day dress.

Bosom friends

(F)

Period: Late 18th and early 19th century.

Chest protectors, of wool, flannel or fur, which also served as **bust improvers**. "The fashionable belles have provided themselves with *bosom friends* for the winter. Their province is to protect that delicate region from assault of every kind; and they may be had at all the furriers shops in town. A modern lady, with her feet in *a fur-basket,* and her *bosom-friend,* is as impregnable as the Rock of Gibraltar" (Dec. 26, 1789, *Norfolk Chronicle*).

"Some persons do not hollow out bosom friends but knit them square or oblong" (1838, *Workwoman's Guide*).

Bosom knot

Synonymous with **breast-knot**.

Bosses

(F)

Period: Late 13th to end of 14th century.

Decorative **cauls** of network or linen covering thick coils of plaited hair, generally artificially enlarged and arranged on each side of the head above the temples. Usually worn with a veil **coverchief**.

See Templers.

Botews

(M)

Period: 15th and 16th centuries.

Another name for **buskins**.

Bottine

(F)

Period: 16th century.

A knee-high riding boot. "Ryding botines lyned with cloth" (1503, List of boots and shoes for the Queen of Scots).

Boudoir cap

(F)

Period: 19th century onwards.

A cap which was worn by women in the privacy of their "boudoir"; not a simple **night-cap** but a lightweight, decorated cap which covered the hair before it was dressed for daytime activities.

Bouffant

(F)

Period: 19th century.

Term denoting a puffed-out part of a dress.

Bouffante sleeve

(F)

Period: 19th century.

A term used for named varieties throughout the century. A puffed-out shoulder sleeve for evening wear, distended to the elbow for day wear.

Bouffant mécanique

(F)

Period: 1828.

A spring attached to the top of the **corset** and projecting into the top of the sleeve to distend it.

Bouillon

(F)

Period: 19th century.

A puffed-out, applied trimming.

Bourbon lock

(M, sometimes F)

A love lock.

Bourgogne, Bourgoigne, Burgundy

(F)

Period: Late 17th century.

A lady's cap; "The first part of the Dress for the Head next the Hair" (1690, *Fop Dictionary*).

Bourrelet, burlet

(F & M)

Period: 14th and 15th centuries.

A French term for a padded roll at first found in female head-dresses and then absorbed into male headwear as a feature on **chaperons** and **hoods**.

(F)

Period: 19th century.

A pad inserted into a dress.

Bourse, burse

Period: 1440–18th century.

A large purse or bag. The form "bourse" was used until the mid-18th century when "burse" became more usual. Also, but rarely, an 18th-century term for the black silk bag of a **bag-wig**.

Boutique

Period: Mid-18th century onwards.

From the French term for shop or stall. In 20th- and 21st-century usage, a small, specialist shop or section within a larger store, often selling fashionable clothing. "It was agreed that if we could find the right premises for a boutique…we would open a shop. It was to be a bouillabaisse of clothes and accessories, sweaters, scarves, shifts, hats, jewellery and peculiar odds and ends" (1966, M. Quant, *Quant by Quant*, p. 35).

Boutonnière

Period: 19th century onwards.

A bud or small spray of flowers worn in a buttonhole (the literal translation of the French term).

Bowdy, bow-dye

Period: 17th century.

Scarlet; from the dye-house at Bow established in 1643, but later applied to goods dyed elsewhere with a similar hue.

Bowler

(M)

Period: 1860 onwards.

A hard felt hat with domed crown and narrow brim rolled up at the sides. The name derived from a hatter, William Bowler (ca. 1850–1860), but the shape was much older, being worn in the 1820s. Usually black, but brown and fawn were worn with **Norfolk jackets** in the 1880s. In the 20th century associated with civilian life after a period in military service and, post-1960, increasingly perceived as a symbol of traditional values.

Bow tie

(M)

Period: 19th century onwards.

A **necktie** worn with a bow in front, having a great many named varieties, some ready made-up.

Box bottoms

(M)

Period: 19th century.

The close-fitting extensions of breeches fastened below the knees and there stiffened with lining.

Box coat

(M)

Period: Late 18th to late 19th century.

A heavy, caped **overcoat**, the capes often multiple, worn by coachmen, travellers and those riding outside a coach.

Period: 20th century.

A fashionable style in the 1930s and 1940s, when the term described a loose-fitting coat with padded, square shoulders.

Boxer shorts

(M)

Period: 1940s onwards.

Loose-fitting cotton shorts with an elasticated waist worn as an undergarment; a front opening could be buttoned or just overlap the fabric. A wide variety of designs, plain and printed, and other fabrics were used over subsequent decades. A slightly sturdier version was worn as **swimwear**. They were based on the shorts worn by professional boxers which did not impede movement.

Boxes

(M)

Period: 17th century.

A form of **galoshes**; "…walk the streets with a dainty pair of Boxes neatly buckl'd on" (1676, Sir G. Etherege, *The Man of Mode*).

Box pleat

Period: Late 19th century onwards.

Two parallel folds of fabric turned in on themselves and pressed flat.

Braces, gallowses

(M)

Period: ca. 1787 onwards.

The term "gallowses" survived among country-folk to the mid-19th century, while the American term was **suspenders**.

Braces at first consisted of a pair of straps, often of morocco leather, passing over the shoulders and attached to a single button on each side in front and behind, to support the breeches or trousers.

From 1825 a double-tongued pattern, to attach to two buttons on each side in front, began to be used. Fancy designs in embroidered braces became fashionable. By 1850 the two straps were united at the point where they crossed under the shoulder blades and India-rubber braces were introduced. By 1860 "the plain elastic web with double sliding ends" had become the conventional mode.

In the 20th century brightly coloured and patterned braces were introduced, usually of an elastic construction, and occasionally worn by women.

Brael

(M)

Period: 14th century.

A girdle or belt to hold the breeches in place. There were many different spellings, including braie-girdle, **breech girdle**, bregirdle and braygirdle.

Braie-girdle, bregirdle, braygirdle

Alternative spellings for **breech girdle**.

Braier

(M)

Period: Medieval.

The French equivalent to **braie-girdle**, used for pulling in the waist of the **braies** and tied in front.

Braies, brèches

(M)

Period: Medieval–15th century.

A primitive form of male **drawers** which, having been in Saxon times an outer garment, became concealed from the mid-12th century by the Norman **tunic** and so converted into an undergarment. The legs were wide, loose and short, and the garment was pulled in by the **braie-girdle**, a running string which emerged at intervals from the deep hem at the waist. By the mid-13th century the legs were tied at the knees with strings; by the 15th century braies had shrunk to mere **loin cloths** and in 1500 they resembled **shorts**.

Brandenbourg, Brandenburgs

Period: 18th century onwards.

Trimming of transverse cording and tassel in the military style used on clothing of both genders. Especially fashionable for female dress from ca. 1870–1910.

Brandenburg

(M)

Period: 1674–ca. 1700.

A long, loose **overcoat** for winter wear, generally trimmed with cord and fastened with frogs, i.e. with loops and frog-buttons – olive-shaped **olivettes**.

Bra slip

(F)

Period: 1960s onwards.

A **petticoat** or **slip** with a **brassière** attached, thereby reducing the number of layers and offering a smoother line beneath clothing.

Brassard

(F)

Period: 19th century.

A ribbon bow attached to the outer side of the elbow of an evening-dress sleeve.

Brassière, bra

(F)

Period: 15th century.

The French term for a short jacket, similar to a **bolero**, usually of black silk or velvet and worn as an undergarment, but partly visible late in the century.

Period: Early 20th century onwards.

Term used to describe a bust support; this was a natural evolution from the late 19th-century **bust bodice**. Early versions were of lightweight fabrics, though later versions were boned and/or used elasticated fabrics. The first brassière was patented by Caresse Crosby (Mary Phelps Jacob) in America in 1914. By the 1930s cup sizes had been invented and the usage "bra" became popular.

See Wonderbra.

Bra-top

(F)

Period: Late 20th century onwards.

A top which was supportive like a bra but worn alone as an outer layer.

Also a style of dress in which the top was intentionally designed to look like a bra.

Bratt, bratte

(F & M)

Period: 10th century onwards.

A makeshift outer garment such as a cloak; often a rag. Also, an **apron** or pinafore for a child or a woman.

Brayette

(M)

Period: Late 14th century.

A narrow **braie-girdle** buckled in front.

Breast-hook

See Stay hook.

Breast-kerchief

(F, sometimes M)

Period: Late 15th to mid-16th century.

A **kerchief** wrapped about the shoulders and folded across the breast for warmth. Worn under the **doublet** or **gown**.

Breast-knot, bosom knot

(F)

Period: 18th and early 19th century.

A ribbon bow or bunch of ribbons worn at the breast of a woman's gown.

Breast pocket

(M, later F)

Period: 1770 onwards.

An inside pocket in the lining of the right breast of a man's coat. Also, a horizontal slit pocket outside the left breast of a man's coat; fashionable, off and on, from ca. 1830.

In the 20th century descriptive of a square pocket on the front of a shirt worn by both men and women.

Breasts

(M)

Period: 18th century.

Tailor's term, commonly used in bills, for waistcoat buttons; usually combined with "coats", for coat buttons.

Breech, breeches

(M)

Period: Early Medieval.

The term "breech" corresponded to **braies**.

Period: End of 14th to early 16th century.

The upper part of the long hose which then combined **stockings** and **breeches** in the form of tights.

b

Statuary.

The sculptor from The *Book of English Trades*, 1823 edition. The text states that he can "live like a gentleman, and mix in the first societies", and this can be seen in his clothing. He wears a **cravat**, **waistcoat**, **frock coat** and **breeches**, and his **stockings** are striped rather than plain, but the important **apron** to protect the clothing covers the front of the garments. Private collection.

Period: 16th century.
The breech was usually of a different colour and fabric from the rest of the hose. "A payre of hosen, black, with purple breche embroidered and underlayd with cloth of silver" (1521, *Inventory of Henry, Earl of Stafford*, Camden Society). The waist belt of the breech, when this was the upper portion of the joined long hose (in the form of tights), was then known as the **breech belt**.

Period: End of 16th century onwards.
An outer covering for the legs ending just above or more usually just below the knees; the terms "breeches" and "**hose**" were interchangeable until ca.1660 when hose began to signify stockings. In the 17th century breeches might be closed or open at the knee. A large number of named varieties were known.

See Cloak-bag breeches, Knee breeches, Galligaskins, Slops, Petticoat breeches, Spanish hose, Venetians.
The front had a vertical opening down the midline closed by buttons, a method which lasted as long as the front was concealed by a long waistcoat descending over the thighs. As the waistcoat shortened, ca. 1760, exposing the front of the breeches, the vertical opening was replaced by **falls** which remained in fashion for evening-dress breeches to ca. 1840, and for riding breeches until the end of the 19th century. The **fly-front** opening was used for evening-dress breeches after ca. 1840. The introduction of **braces** ca. 1790 led to a change in construction of breeches; previously cut very full in the seat they hung on the hip-bones, with the waistband tightened by strings at the back of the waist. When held up by braces the general fit was closer, but the waistband was no longer drawn in as tightly.

Period: 20th century onwards.
Breeches were retained for certain types of formal wear, ski-ing outfits in the 1930s, and for golf and other country pursuits. Women wore them for outdoor or service activities during war time and occasionally as fashionable clothing.

Breech belt
See Breech.

Breech farthingale
(F)
Period: 1580–1620s.
An unusual term for the **roll farthingale** which extended the gown's skirt at the back and sides.

Breech girdle
(M)
Period: 13th–15th century.
A girdle threaded through the wide hem at the top of the breech to secure it about the waist or, more usually, just below.
See Braier.

Bretelle
(F)
Period: 19th century onwards.
A strap-shaped trimming on a bodice; usually sections of ornamental fabric across each shoulder beginning and ending at the waist at back and front.

Breton hat
(F)
Period: Late 19th century onwards.
A style of straw or felt hat with a close-fitting, round crown and a deep brim which was rolled up all the way round.

Bridal veil
See Wedding veil.

Bride-lace
Period: 16th and 17th centuries.
A length of blue ribbon binding sprigs of rosemary

used as wedding favours. In the 16th century such sprigs were tied to the arm, but later worn in the hat. The bride of Jack of Newbury (mid-16th century) "was led to church between two boys with bride laces and rosemary tied about their sleeves". "With nosegay and bride laces in their hats" (1603, Heywood, *A Woman killed with Kindness*).

Brides

(F)

Period: 1830s and 1840s.

A term for the broad ribbon-strings attached inside the brim of the open bonnet and occasionally the broad-brimmed hat of the period, and allowed either to float free or tied loosely under the chin. A rosette of ribbon was often used to cover the point of attachment.

Bridge coat

(F)

Period: 20th century.

A loose, open jacket of brocade, lace, velvet or similar, worn over an afternoon or evening dress.

Bridles

(F)

Period: 18th century.

The strings for tying a **mob cap** under the chin.

See Kissing-strings.

Briefs

(F & M)

Period: 1930s onwards.

A pair of very short, close-fitting knickers or trunks; sometimes called "scanties" by women; particularly useful at a time when clothing was sleekly fitted.

Brigadier wig

(M)

Period: 1750–1800.

This was identical with the **major wig**, a military style with a double **queue**. "Brigadier" was the name used in France, but seldom in England. "Hence we hear of the Brigadier or the Major for the Army" (1782, James Stewart, *Plocacosmos*).

Brilliantine

(M, occasionally F)

Period: Late 19th century onwards.

A type of hair oil which held the hair in place and ensured a glossy, smooth finish.

Bristol diamond, Bristol stone

Period: ca. 1590 to end of 18th century.

Rock crystals found at Clifton, near Bristol, and used as imitation diamonds in jewellery.

See Paste.

British warm

(M)

Period: ca. 1900–1950s.

The British Service warm was a short, double-breasted **overcoat** of comfortable fit made from Melton cloth. By the end of World War I it had replaced the standard officer's greatcoat but was also, due to ex-army surplus, worn outside of the services.

Broad beard

(M)

Period: 16th and early 17th centuries.

Identical to a **cathedral beard**.

Brodekin, brodkin, brotiken

(M)

Period: 15th to late 17th century.

A **boot** reaching to the middle of the calf or just below the knee. The name is chiefly Scottish, though used in English accounts; the English form was **buskin**.

Brodequin

(F)

Period: 1830s.

Boots of velvet or satin, trimmed with a fringe round the top edge.

Brog, brogue

(M)

Period: Late 16th–19th century.

Long breeches or trousers worn by the Irish.

Brogues

(M & F)

Period: 16th–19th century.

Rough shoes of undressed leather with the hair side out, tied on with thongs. Worn by the poor in the wilder parts of Ireland and the Scottish Highlands.

Period: Late 19th century onwards.

A sturdy leather shoe worn for country pursuits; adapted from a traditional Scottish design for a walking boot with punched-leather decoration. A variant of the early 1900s had a fringed tongue covering the laces and was worn with Scottish dress.

Brooch

(F & M)

Period: Medieval onwards.

One of the earliest forms of fastening, which developed into a decorative piece of jewellery. A face of metal behind which a pin was placed; the pin passed through a cloak, cap or mantle and was held within a secure twist or channel of metal; acquired the name "brooch" from the medieval English "broche". Brooches were made in all shapes and sizes and of all materials, from precious metal and gemstone stomacher brooches in the late 17th and 18th centuries, to bakelite novelties in the 20th century. Increasingly a female ornament from the 18th century and sometimes found within a **parure** of matching pieces of jewellery.

Brooks Brothers

Period: 1818 onwards.

Originally a New York-based clothing company which sold ready-made clothing to male customers; it became a subsidiary of the British company Marks & Spencer in 1988.

Brooks Brothers had often looked to the UK for ideas, such as button-down collars on shirts, Madras fabric for shirts, Harris tweed and Shetland sweaters. It also extended its range to include casual wear, e.g. **Bermuda shorts** and clothing for women. Its comfortable **classic styles** of clothing were worn by **Ivy League** and **preppie** customers in America.

Brown George
(M)
Period: Late 18th century.
Colloquial term for a brown **wig** said to resemble a loaf of coarse brown bread.

Brummell bodice
(M)
Period: 1810–1820.
A whalebone corset worn by dandies of the Regency period; named after George "Beau" Brummell (1778–1840).

Brunswick gown, Brunswick sack, German gown
(F)
Period: 1760–1780.
A **sack**-backed gown of variable length with a buttoned false-bodice front and tight sleeves to the wrists.

Brutus head, Brutus wig
(M)
Period: 1790–1820.
A cropped head of hair or a brown, unpowdered wig, both dishevelled in appearance; inspired by the French Revolution. The wig became associated with the Prince Regent, later George IV, but the hairstyle was also popular with young women; "I wonder if the pretty Misses go in *self* coloured drawers…and brutus Heads with you as they do here" (1798, H. L. Piozzi, *Letters*).

Bubble cut
(F)
Period: Late 1950s onwards.
Hair cut short and teased into tight curls; this effect was later achieved by a bubble permanent wave in the early 1980s, when some men adopted this style alongside women.

Bubble dress
(F)
Period: 1957.
The French designer Pierre Cardin (b. 1922) introduced short dresses and skirts with stiffened linings to create a bubble shape.

Buck clothes
Period: 16th and 17th centuries.
Clothes taken in buck baskets to be washed, the domestic laundry being a bi-annual event. "One woman to wash their buck clothes" (1625, *Statutes of Uppingham Hospital*).

Buckingamo
(M)
Period: Mid-17th century.

A cap similar to a **Montero**. "When I must be covered I infinitely prefer the Buckingamo or Montero, lately reformed" (1661, J. Evelyn, *Tyrannus, or the Mode*).

Buckle
(M, later F)
Period: Medieval onwards.
A clasp consisting of a rectangular or curved rim with one or more movable tongues secured to the **chape** at one side or in the middle and long enough to rest on the opposite side. Used to fasten belts, straps, etc. or used as ornaments. Buckles for securing breeches or shoes were often highly decorative and made from base to precious metals and stones of every type.
See Artois buckle.
In the 20th century and later belt buckles were made from many materials including bakelite, plastic, etc.

Period: 18th century.
A secondary meaning is taken from the French *boucle*; a curl of hair associated with men's **wigs** of the 18th century.

Buckled wig
(M)
Period: 18th century.
A **wig** having tightly rolled curls generally arranged horizontally above or about the ears.

Buckskin
(M)
Period: 15th–19th century.
A term meaning gloves of buckskin.

Period: ca. 1790–ca. 1820.
Occasionally, breeches of buckskin.

Budget
Period: 17th century.
A wallet. "A budget or pocket to hang by their sides to put their nails in" (1677, Moxon, *Mechanick Exercises*).

Buff coat, buff jerkin, leather jerkin
(M)
Period: 16th and 17th centuries.
A military garment adopted by civilians; a jacket made of ox-hide (originally buffalo hide) and very strong. It was worn over the **doublet** and followed the fashion shape of the day; sometimes sleeveless having **wings** only.
In the 17th century it might have sleeves of fabrics other than leather, and longer skirts.

Buffins, pair of buffins
(M)
Period: 16th century.
A North Country term for a pair of wide breeches such as **slops**, or possibly **round hose**. Buffin was a coarse cloth used for a variety of garments.

Buffon, buffont
(F)
Period: ca. 1750–1790.
A large, diaphanous neckerchief of gauze or fine linen

swathed round the neck and shoulders and puffed out over the bosom. "A large buffont of white gauze carried up near the chin" (1787, *Ipswich Journal*).

Bugles

Period: 16th century onwards.

Tubular glass beads, generally black but also white or blue, very popular in the 16th century for decorating women's dresses, cloaks, hats and hair. Less popular in the 17th and 18th centuries, but much used from 1870 on in a wider range of colours.

Bulgare pleat

(F)

Period: 1875.

A form of pleating used on skirts, being a double box pleat, narrow at the waist and expanding downwards, the folds being kept in place by strips of elastic sewn on the under-side.

Bull head, bull-tour

(F)

Period: ca. 1670–1690.

A female coiffure with a forehead fringe of thick curls. "Some term this curled forehead a bull-head from the French Taure, a bull. It was the fashion of women to wear bull-heads or bull-like foreheads, anno 1674 and about that time" (R. Holme, *Armory*).

Bullion-hose

(M)

Period: 16th century.

Trunk hose with full pleats in the upper section of the garment. Also called "Boulogne hose".

See French hose.

Bully-cocked

(M)

Period: 18th century.

A hat cocked in the style favoured by the bullies of the period; generally a broad-brimmed hat. (The Oxford Smart) "easily distinguished by…a broad bully-cocked hat" (1721, Amherst, *Terrae Filius*).

Bum-barrel

(F)

Period: ca. 1550 to early 17th century.

A padded roll for distending the skirt at the hips.

Bum roll, bum

(F)

Period: ca. 1550 to early 17th century.

Similar to **bum-barrel** but the more usual term.

Burberry

(F & M)

Period: 1856–1900.

A firm founded in England by Thomas Burberry (1835–1926), with a specific association with a proofed, cotton fabric called gabardine which was used for rainproof clothing. A London-based business was started in 1891 and the various garments produced were aimed at country and leisure pursuits.

Period: 1900 onwards.

Two trademarks were registered in 1902 and 1909, gabardine and The Burberry respectively, the latter referring to the coats it manufactured. The military coats of the 1914–18 war included the distinctive **trench coat**, a **classic style** much copied and worn in civilian life.

In the latter part of the 20th century the distinctive, checked lining was used for accessories including bags, hats and scarves, and the company enjoyed a revival with new fashion lines in the late 1990s.

Burdash, berdash

(M)

Period: Late 17th and early 18th centuries.

A fringed **sash** worn round the waist over the coat; the term was also linked to a type of **cravat**.

Burka, burkha, burqa

(F)

Period: Late 20th century onwards.

A long, loose outer garment worn in public places by Muslim women to shield them from the gaze of men and strangers. It is a traditional garment in certain countries in the Middle East but has appeared in Western countries relatively recently. It can incorporate veiled holes for the eyes and was, infamously, forced upon all women in Afghanistan by the Taliban during their regime.

See Chador, Hijab, Jilbab, Niqab, Veil.

Burlet

(M)

Period: 15th century.

A circular padded roll worn as a head-dress or as part of the **chaperon**.

See Bourrelet.

Burnet

(F & M)

Period: 17th century.

"A hood or attire for the head" (1616, John Bullokar, *An English Expositor*).

Burn-grace

Synonym of **bongrace**.

Burnouse, burnous

(F)

Period: 1830s–1860s.

An evening wrap of cashmere, usually knee-length, fastened at the neck; sometimes with a small hood, or imitation of one, attached. The **Algerian burnouse** of 1858 was of wool with broad satin stripes. Both styles owed their name and shape to the hooded cloak worn by Arabs and Moors and much recorded in words and illustrations from the 17th century onwards.

Burrail collar

(M)

Period: 1832.

A collar of a **greatcoat** made "to stand up or fall down at pleasure" (*Gentleman's Magazine of Fashion*).

Burse

See Bourse.

Bush, bush beard, bush-wig

(M)

Period: Late 16th century and 17th century.

Jocular synonyms for a thick mop of hair or full **beard**.

Busk

(F, sometimes M)

Period: 16th to early 20th century.

"Buc, a buske, plated (pleated) bodie or other quilted thing worne to make or keepe the bodie straight" (1611, Cotgrave). Occasionally, in the 18th and 19th centuries, it meant to dress, deck with clothing.

However, the usual meaning of the word was the stiffened front of a bodice; the busk being a flat length of bone, whalebone, wood or, in the 17th century,

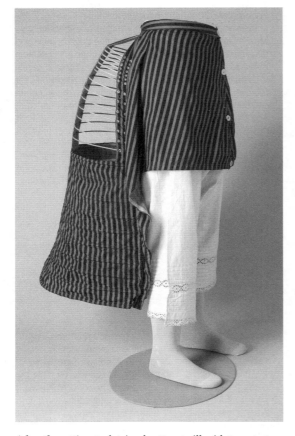

A **bustle** petticoat of striped cotton twill with twenty-two half **hoops**, ca. 1872–74; worn over white cotton **drawers** edged with **broderie anglaise**, ca. 1870. Copyright the Olive Matthews Collection, Chertsey Museum.

sometimes horn, attached to the front of a bodice or the **stays** to render it inflexible. In the 18th century the busk was sometimes carved with emblems and worn pushed down into a busk sheath in front of the bodice. By the 19th and early 20th centuries stay busks were often of steel.

Buskins

(F & M)

Period: 14th to end of 17th century.

High boots sometimes reaching to the knees. In the earlier period often made of silk in various designs; in the 16th century those worn at court might be of silk or cloth. Leather buskins were mainly riding boots. Women's buskins, worn for travelling, were of velvet, satin or Spanish leather.

Period: 18th century onwards.

The term was also applied to quasi-historical boots used for theatrical performance (they were associated with tragedians especially), **fancy dress** and **masquerade costume**.

Busk point

(F)

Period: Late 16th to early 18th century.

A tie for securing the **busk**.

Bust bodice

(F)

Period: 1889–ca. 1930.

A support for the breasts, based upon the camisole, usually of white **coutil**, laced front and back with bones on each side of lace holes. Worn above the corset. It was the prototype of the modern **brassière**.

Bustier

(F)

Period: Late 1970s onwards.

An item of underwear which combined a **brassière** and a **camisole**; not dissimilar to a 19th-century, boned **bust bodice**, it became a fashionable item of outer wear for young women and was often strapless. The American singer Madonna wore them as stage costumes.

Bust improver

(F)

Period: 1840 onwards.

Bosom pads of wool and cotton. Various structures were introduced, such as a patent of 1860 – "an improved inflated undulating artificial bust to improve the female figure". In 1896 flexible, celluloid bust improvers were advertised. In the 20th century soft, foam-rubber pads became available.

Bustle

(F)

Period: 14th century onwards.

The term "bustle" was not used until ca. 1830; this is now a usual description for a device for thrusting out the skirt at the back of the waist. Innumerable forms and materials have been adopted through the centuries, from foxes' tails (1343) to kitchen dusters (1834, Mrs Carlyle), from down cushions to wire cages. Until the 19th century, padded rolls were the usual form.

See Bum roll, Bearers, Rump-furbelow, Cork rump.

19th-century versions included:

Period: 1806–1820.

A small pad or narrow roll, sometimes known as a **Nelson**.

Period: 1815–1819.

An outside bustle called a **frisk** helped to produce the **Grecian bend**; this was more a French than an English fashion.

Period: 1830–1850.

A bulky, wool-stuffed pad, spreading from the back round the sides of the waist.

Period: 1865–1876.

Bustles of steel half-hoops known as **crinolettes**.

Period: 1882–1889.

Bustles were fashionable again and at their maximum in 1885; the shape projected backwards like a shelf and varied in structure. At this time the bustle was known as a **dress improver** or **tournure**, before finally disappearing in 1889.

Period: 20th century onwards.

Small pads or larger extensions were used by fashion designers for emphasis, but rear display was usually limited to extra pleating of fabric, a large bow, or a modest structure beneath the skirt.

Butcher's boy cap
(F & M)

Period: 1960 onwards.

A wide cap with a deep brim and peak, named after the tradesmen's caps of earlier periods that they resembled, but fashionable in various fabrics such as wool tartan, cotton corduroy, etc. intermittently from this period.

Butterfly bow sleeve
(F)

Period: 1895.

An evening-dress sleeve with pleats on the outer side forming wings.

Butterfly cap, fly cap
(F)

Period: ca. 1750–1770.

A small lace cap wired into the form of a butterfly and worn perched above the forehead. **Lappets**, jewels and flower trimming were sometimes added for court wear.

Butterfly head-dress
(F)

Period: ca. 1450–1500.

A 16th-century term for the head-dress of the previous century, which had consisted of a wire frame supporting a gauze veil spreading out above the head on each side, like a pair of diaphanous wings, with a V-shaped dip over the forehead. It was fixed to a small ornamental cap, cone-shaped, worn on the back of the head. "These were called by some "Great Butterflies" from having two large wings on each side resembling those of that insect" (1591, Paradin).

Butterick
Period: 1860s onwards.

The American tailor Ebenezer Butterick (1826–1903) created the first graded or sized clothing patterns for the domestic sewing market in response to his wife's request. After some experiments he settled upon paper for the patterns and quickly developed styles for adults and children. The popularity of such patterns was immense and the Butterick brand was publicized through magazines and response to user correspondence. Throughout the 20th century the firm continued to develop, acquiring other labels, such as Vogue patterns, and using the latest technology to refine its products and meet new and changing demands.

See Sewing machine.

Button
(F & M)

Period: 13th century onwards.

These were fastenings or dress ornaments in the form of a knob or disc sewn or affixed to a garment to fasten it by passing through a buttonhole.

See Basket button, Death's head button, Dorset thread button, High-tops, Leek button, Olive button, Snail button, Stalk button.

Button boots
(M)

Period: 1837–1860s.

(F)

Period: 1830s to early 20th century.

Short boots fastened up the outer side with buttons, usually black japanned; the mother-of-pearl buttons used in the 1830s were ornamental. Light jack boots.

See Jack boot.

Buttoned cap
(M)

Period: 16th century.

A cap with a round or square, close, beret-shaped crown, and a button on the top for securing the side flaps when present.

Buttoned handkerchief
(F & M)

Period: 1590–1700.

A pocket **handkerchief** trimmed at the corners with buttons acting as tassels.

Buttoner
(F & M)

Period: 14th century.

A close row of buttons down the front of the **houppe-lande**, serving as an ornament.

Button hook

Period: 19th century.

A metal hook on a handle; used to place the buttons of tight **gloves** or boots into their respective buttonholes.

Button-hooks

(M)

Period: 1865 onwards.

These were metal eyelet hooks replacing punched eyelet holes up the fronts of boots. The boot-laces were caught in the hooks and criss-crossed from side to side, thus fastening the boot. In 1897 they became brass, oval hooks called **lacing studs**.

Button stand

Period: 19th century.

Tailor's term for a separate piece of cloth carrying the buttons and buttonholes of a coat, usually double-breasted, or a waistcoat and seamed on to the margin of the **forepart**. A device supposedly invented by King George IV around 1820.

Byron tie

(M)

Period: 1840s and 1850s.

A small, narrow **necktie**, such as "a bit of *mousselaine de laine* a few inches long or a bit of broad shoe-string".

C

Caban

(M)

Period: 14th and 15th centuries.

A loose cloak with arm-holes.

Period: 1840s.

A loose **wrapper** with a turned-down collar and wide enough to be worn without using the sleeves. Sometimes in the form of a **paletot-sac**. Also known as a **templar cloak**.

Cabbage-ruff

(M)

Period: Early 17th century.

A large **ruff** with informal convolutions not in the organ-pipe style. "Hiss cabbage Ruffe of the outragious sise, Starched in colour to beholders eyes" (ca. 1620, S. Rowlands, *A Roaring Boyes Description*).

Cabbage shoe-string

(M)

Period: ca. 1610–1680.

A large, cabbage-shaped rosette or **shoe-rose**.

Cable hatband

See Hat-band.

Cable knit/stitch

Period: Late 19th century onwards.

Any embroidery stitch or knitted design which resembles the twisted strands of a metal or rope cable.

Cabriole, capriole head-dress

(F)

Period: 1755–1757.

A head-dress in the shape of "some kind of carriage". "Those heads which are not able to bear a coach-and-six...make use of a post-chaise" (1756, *The Connoisseur*).

Caddie

(M)

Period: 1890s.

A hip-pocket, i.e. a cross-pocket at the back of the hip of trousers.

Cadogan

(F & M)

Period: Late 18th century.

Rare term for **catogan** or **club wig**.

Caftan, kaftan

(F & M)

Originally described as a traditional style of full-length, long-sleeved tunic, held at the waist by a sash or belt and worn in Turkey and other Middle Eastern countries.

(F)

Period: 1844.

An outdoor garment "between a Paletot and a Mantle".

(F, occasionally M)

Period: 1950s onwards.

The French designer Christian Dior (1905–1957) produced a caftan without a sash in the mid-1950s. Other designers followed suit and the style with a slit or narrow V neckline, usually in cotton or silk with simple embroidery at the edges became a popular informal evening style.

Cage

(F)

Period: 1856 to late 1860s.

Short name for the **artificial crinoline** composed of a coarse petticoat distended with graduated hoops of whalebone, wire or watch-spring.

Cage-Américaine

(F)

Period: 1862–1869.

A cage petticoat of which only the lower half was covered with fabric, the upper half being in skeleton form to reduce the weight.

Cage Empire

(F)

Period: 1861–1869.

A cage for wearing under a ball-dress; the cage slightly trained and composed of 30 steel hoops increasing in width downwards.

Cage petticoat, cage crinoline, artificial crinoline

(F)

Period: 1856–1868.

A structure composed of hoops, at first of whalebone but after 1857 of wire or watch-spring, joined together at intervals by vertical bands of tape or braid. The hoops increased in size from the waistband down, forming a dome-shaped petticoat resembling a cage, to be worn under a wide skirt to distend it to the required size. The cage was tied round the waist in front and below the ties a short gap in the hoops enabled the cage to be put on. The number of hoops, their size and shape varied.

At first dome-shaped, becoming by 1860 pyramidal; by 1866 the front was flattened with the main projection behind; by 1868 the cage shrank and became the **crinolette**.

Cagoule

(F & M)

Period: ca. 1950 onwards.

A lightweight, waterproof, hooded jacket, not dissimilar to an **anorak**. Originally worn by climbers, it became a popular garment for many outdoor activities.

Cake hat

(M)

Period: 1890s.

A soft, felt hat with a low, round crown slightly depressed circularly; similar to the Alpine hat. "A blue cake hat" (1895, *The Babe,* B.A.).

Calash, calèche

(F)

Period: 1770–1790; revived 1820–1839.

A large, folding, hooped hood, built up on arches of whalebone or cane covered with soft silk; named after the hood of the lightweight French carriage called a *calèche*. Worn out of doors to protect the fashionable, high head-dresses and hairstyles. Its original French name was a *Thérèse*.

Calcarapedes

(M)

Period: 1860s.

"Self-adjusting **galoshes**" of rubber (1861, *Our Social Bees*).

Calico button

Period: 1840s onwards.

A flat button consisting of a metal ring covered with calico and sewn on by piercing the calico; some had two metal eyelets in the centre. Both types appeared about the same date. Used for underclothing until gradually replaced by plastic buttons in the 20th century.

Calotte, callot

(M)

Period: 17th century.

An under-cap. "An ordinary callotte or cap which we wear under our hats" (1670, Lassels, *Voyage to Italy*). Also a plain **skull-cap**.

In later centuries used to describe the skull cap worn by Roman Catholic clergy.

Calves

See False calves.

Calypso chemise

(F)

Period: 1790s.

A **round gown** of coloured muslin worn with a loose robe over it.

Camail

(F)

Period: 1842.

A waist-length or three-quarter-length cloak with armholes and a small, falling collar. Rounded or pointed below and lined with silk in summer or wadded cashmere, satin or velvet in winter.

Camargo

(F)

Period: 1879.

A day-jacket, the **basques** of which were rounded off and arranged into **paniers** on the hips; worn over a waistcoat. Named after Marie Camargo (1710–1770), a celebrated French dancer.

Camargo hat

(F)

Period: 1836.

An evening-dress hat, small, with the brim raised in front.

Camargo puff

(F)

Period: 1868.

Formed by looping up high the back of the overskirt of a **panier** dress.

Cambridge coat

(M)

Period: 1870 to early 20th century.

A **lounge** coat, single- or double-breasted, usually a **three-seamer** with central back vent. Made with three buttons, but at first "cut sharply off from the 1st or 2nd button producing an opening at the waist".

From 1876 made closer and longer with four **patch pockets** having buttoned flaps. By 1880 it was identical with the single-breasted **reefer**.

Cambridge paletot

(M)

Period: 1855.

A large and full knee-length **overcoat** with wide sleeves having immense turned-back cuffs; wide cape-collar and broad lapels descending nearly to the hem.

Cameleons

(F)

Period: 1859.

Women's boots and shoes having the uppers perforated with ornamental holes revealing coloured stockings.

Cami-knickers

(F)

Period: Late 19th century onwards.

A combined undergarment uniting a **camisole** with a pair of **drawers** which buttoned at the crotch, but shorter and more streamlined than the two worn separately. Originally made from light cotton fabrics, they later were made of silks and synthetics and came in many colours. Also known as "knicks" and "step-ins". The 1920s' **teddy**, fashionable again in the 1980s, was a variant of this style.

Camise, cames, kemes, kemse

See Chemise.

Camisia

(F & M)

Period: Medieval.

A **shirt** or **smock**.

Camisole

(F)

Period: 1820s–ca. 1920.

A short-sleeved or sleeveless under-bodice of white long-cloth, worn over the stays to protect the tight-fitting dress. Sometimes called a **waistcoat** and, by 1890, a **petticoat bodice**.

Gradually replaced by **cami-knickers** or **brassière**, **panties** and **petticoat**.

Campaign coat

(M)

Period: 17th century.

A long military coat worn by civilians from ca. 1667. "Campaign-coat, originally only such as soldiers wore, but afterwards a mode in Cities" (1690, B.E., *Dictionary of the Canting Crew*).

Period: 18th century.

A term used for any old, tattered coat worn by beggars and gipsies to arouse compassion.

Campaigne wig, travelling wig

(M)

Period: ca. 1675–1760.

A bushy **wig** with short side locks with knotted ends and a very short **queue** behind. The side locks were sometimes tied back for travelling. It was a popular wig for the elderly and still worn, though old-fashioned, after 1760.

Camp shirt

(F & M)

Period: 1950s onwards.

An American informal shirt, loosely cut with a soft collar, buttoned front and elbow-length sleeves, which can be worn outside shorts and trousers and comes in a range of colours and patterns.

See Hawaiian shirt.

Cane

(M, occasionally F)

Period: Early 16th century onwards.

The stem of a plant similar to bamboo and used as a walking-stick, the finer kinds usually carried under the arm. The fashionable periods for canes (as distinct from sticks) were the 17th and 18th centuries. Canes were of very variable length; in the second half of the 18th century they were often very long and carried by women as well as by men. Named types included Malacca or "Clouded" cane and Rattan, a species of palm from the East Indies. "...a little black rattoon painted and gilt" (1660, *Diary of Samuel Pepys*).

Canezou

(F)

Period: 1820s–1850s.

In the 1820s this was a white, sleeveless **spencer**. In the 1830s it became a short, pointed cape covering the front and back but not the arms. By 1850s the canezou had become an elaborate **fichu** of muslin, lace and ribbons covering the front and back of the upper body.

Canezou-pelerine

(F)

Period: 1830s.

A canezou with long **pelerine** extensions down the front.

Canions

(M)

Period: ca. 1570–1620.

Thigh-fitting extensions from **trunk-hose** to the knees or just below, and often of a different colour and fabric from the trunk-hose. Stockings were drawn up over them.

Cannons, canons, port canons

(M)

Period: ca. 1660–1700.

Wide decorative frills to the tops of stockings worn with **petticoat breeches** or breeches not confined at the knee.

These borders were turned down over the garters and fell in a broad flounce below the knee. "He walks in his Portcannons like one that stalks in long grass" (ca. 1680, Samuel Butler, *Genuine Remains*).

Cannon sleeves, trunk sleeves

(F)

Period: 1575–1620.

Gown sleeves, moderately wide above and sloping to be closed at the wrist. They were made rigid with padding, and sometimes distended with reed, wire or whalebone sewn into a lining of fustian or holland, thus producing their cannon shape.

Cantab hat

(F)

Period: 1806.

A day hat of straw, with a rectangular crown, flat on the top, and a narrow rolled brim.

Cap

(M)

Period: Medieval period onwards.

A small head-covering, usually of soft fabric and often fitting more closely than a hat. In the 16th century the cap began to imply social inferiority, as in the servant, apprentice or schoolboy.

See Statute cap.

Period: 19th century.

When elite men began to wear a cap in the country or for outdoor sports, they made it a rule never to wear it "in Town". The cap with a stiff visor was an improvement of the 1880s; the hook-down cap, in which the front of the crown hooked on to the top of the visor, appeared in the 1890s and was especially favoured for tennis and golf.

Period: 20th century onwards.

Caps for many activities, such as golf, riding, sailing and skiing, appeared alongside the simple, soft cap worn by many workmen. Later, foreign styles such as **baseball caps** were adopted by all classes and age groups.

(F)

Period: ca. 1500 to late 19th century.

The domestic cap was worn indoors and came in many named varieties, such as the **caul**, **lettice cap**, **cornet**, **rail**, **fontange**, **round-eared cap**, **pultney cap**, **mob cap**, **butterfly cap**, Marie Stuart cap, **babet bonnet**, **Charlotte Corday cap**, etc.

The wearing of caps began to decline in the 1850s, and in 1857 "young married ladies need not wear caps until they have acquired the endearing name of "Mother". By 1880 "young women no longer wear caps", and by the 1890s they were worn only by the elderly and by female domestic servants.

Capa pluvialis, chape a pluie

(F)

Period: Medieval.

A large cloak, generally hooded, for protection from the rain.

Cape

Period: 12th–14th century.

Known as a **cope**.

Period: 15th to late 18th century.

A turned-down collar, whether large or small. Also, a short shoulder-cloak. However, the former meaning (of turned-down collar) remained as a tailor's term in the 19th century.

Cape coat

(M)

Period: 17th century.

An **overcoat** with a cape collar.

Capeline

(F)

Period: 1750–1800.

A woman's hat adorned with feathers.

Period: 1863.

A light hood with attached cape, usually of cashmere or barege; for country wear.

Cape-paletot

(M)

Period: 1859 onwards.

A sleeved cloak with a deep cape; known as the **Inverness**.

Cape sleeve

(F)

Period: 20th century onwards.

An excessively flared short sleeve.

Cap-hood

See Capouch.

Capot, capote

(M)

Period: 18th century.

A loose coat. "Wrapped in their thick capots or loose coats" (1775, R. Chandler, *Travels in Asia Minor*).

Capote

(F)

Period: Mainly 1830s.

A bonnet with a soft crown shaped to the head and having a rigid brim round the face.

Capote anglaise

(F)

Period: 1830s.

See Bibi bonnet or English cottage bonnet.

Capouch, capuche

(F & M)

Period: 17th century.

A hood attached to a cloak. "His Hood or Capuch (which was part of the Cloak) and served to cover the Head" (1658, J. Cleveland, *Rustick Rampant*).

Caprice

(F)

Period: 1846.

A loose, sleeveless evening jacket sloped away behind to a rounded point below the waist.

Capri pants

(F)

Period: 1950s onwards.

Close-fitting trousers reaching to just above the ankle, not dissimilar to **leggings**, but usually of a sturdier fabric. An American style popularized by the film star Audrey Hepburn (1929–1993) in various films, such as *Roman Holiday* (1953) and *Funny Face* (1957).

Cap sleeve
(F)
Period: Late 19th century onwards.
A small sleeve literally as a cap extending from the armhole at the top of the bodice of a dress or shirt.

Capuche
(F)
Period: 1852.
A muslin sun-bonnet lined with silk.

Capuchin, capuchon
(F)
Period: 16th to late 18th century.
A soft hood worn out of doors. In the 18th century it was known as a riding hood and was worn in the country and when travelling by coach. It had a coloured lining and a deep cape.

Capuchin collar
(F)
Period: Late 18th and early 19th centuries.
A roll collar following a V-neckline of the high-waisted dress.

Capuchon
(F)

Period: 1837.
A waist-length evening **mantelet** with a hooped hood and long sleeves; worn out of doors.
See Capuchin, Carmeillette.

Period: 1877.
A **bonnet** composed entirely of flowers mounted on a slight foundation, covering only a small part of the head.

Caracalla wig
(M)
Period: Late 18th and early 19th centuries.
A black wig.

Caraco
(F)
Period: ca. 1750 to early 19th century.
A thigh-length, waisted jacket, either fitting at the waist or with a **sack-back**. A variant of this, called a short-gown, had a cross-over front and was the usual jacket for working women. It emerged as an informal style for fashionable French women in the late 1760s and in England it was close-fitting, three-quarter-length, closed jacket with the back occasionally longer than the front and made of printed cotton or linen. In the 1840s a style of jacket bodice, sometimes called a **caraco corsage**, appeared, usually worn with a matching skirt.

Caraco corsage
(F)
Period: 1848–1870.

The bodice of a day dress made to resemble a jacket.

Caracul
See Karakul

Caravan
(F)
Period: 1765.
A small and early form of the **calash**. "It consists of whalebone formed in large rounds, which at a touch throws down over the face a blind of white sarcenet" (1764, *Universal Magazine*).

Carcan, carcanet
(M)
Period: 16th century.
A heavy collar-like necklace, usually of gold and gemstones.

Car coat
(F & M)
Period: 1940s onwards.
A loose-fitting, thigh-length coat worn over other travelling clothes and easily removed. Much less bulky than the motoring coats of the early years of the century.
See Motoring dress.

Cardigan
(M)
Period: 1850s to early 20th century.
Originally associated with the Earl of Cardigan (1797–1868) and his officers in the Crimean War, this was a short, close-fitting, knitted jacket of Berlin wool or English worsted; no collar or a velvet one; by 1896 some versions had a short roll collar.

(F & M)
Period: Late 19th century onwards.
A knitted woollen jacket without a collar, either buttoned to the neck or with a V-neck. Worn informally and available in ready-made versions or with patterns for home knitters; it could be matched with a short-sleeved jumper.
See Twin set.

Cardigan suit
(F)
Period: 1920s onwards.
Attributed to the French fashion designer Coco Chanel (1883–1971), the use of soft, jersey fabric for a loose, cardigan-style jacket with a matching skirt revolutionized comfortable but chic women's day clothes. Variants might include a blouse or jumper, but the combination continues to be produced, often in mix-and-match colours and patterns.

Cardinal
(F)
Period: 18th and 19th centuries.
In the 18th century the term referred to a three-quarter-length hooded cloak, usually of scarlet cloth. By the 1840s the term described a shorter cloak, ending about waist-level and without hood or collar.

Cardinal pelerine
(F)
Period: 1840s.
A deep lace **bertha** divided at the centre front and worn with evening dress.

Cardows
(M)
Period: Late 16th and early 17th centuries.
The tasselled cords of a ceremonial robe.

Careless
(M)
Period: 1830s.
A loose overcoat with a large, full cape and spreading collar; without a seam at the waist.

Cargo pants
(M, sometimes F)
Period: 1950s onwards.
An American style of informal, lightweight trousers, often of cotton, with one or more large pockets on the outside of each leg. A variant allows a section of the lower leg to be unzipped to provide shorts.

Carmeillette
(F)
Period: 1830s.
See Capuchon.

Caroline corsage
(F)
Period: 1830s.
An evening corsage having a narrow fall of lace and drapery forming a V in the shape of a **pelerine**.

Caroline hat
(M)
Period: 1680s to mid-18th century.
A hat made of Carolina beaver; the fur imported from Carolina and, owing to the climate, inferior to the Canadian fur known as "French Beaver". Caroline hats were therefore usually worn by servants and generally black. "Two Caroline hats for the servants" (1742, *Purefoy Letters*).

Caroline sleeve
(F)
Period: 1830s.
A day-dress sleeve, very full to the elbow; thence close-fitting to the wrist.

Carpet slippers
(M)
Period: 1840 onwards.
Bedroom slippers, the uppers made either of German wool woven like carpets, or worked by hand in the cross-stitch designs of **Berlin work**.

Carriage dress
(F)
Period: 19th century.
A dress, or dress and cape or cloak, depending on the season or climate, worn when riding in a carriage; the dress was suitable for paying calls; "Carriage or visiting dress..." (1869, 17 July, *Harpers Bazaar*).

Carrick
(F)
Period: 1877.
A long dust-cloak with triple capes; a type of overcoat. *See* Ulster.

Carthage cymar
(F)
Period: 1809.
A fancy **scarf** of silk or net with gold embossed border; worn with evening dress, attached to one shoulder and hanging down the back to about knee-level.

Cartoose collar
(M)
Period: 17th century.
A standing collar with small **pickadils** about its upper edge on which the **ruff** was supported. A term possibly related to the architectural one, cartouse, meaning a bearer or support.

Cart-wheel hat
(F)
Period: Late 19th century onwards.
A hat with a wide, circular brim similar to a cart-wheel.

Casaque
(F)
Period: 1855–1860s.
A close-fitting jacket buttoned up to the neck with a deep **basque** forming an overskirt.

Casaque bodice
(F)
Period: 1873.
A close-fitting bodice with a deep **basque** in front.

Casaquin bodice
(F)
Period: 1878.
A tight-fitting day bodice, shaped like a man's **tail coat** and buttoned down the front; some with a waistcoat, "actual or simulated". Worn with a "short skirt", untrained and two inches off the ground. Usually **tailor-made**.

Casaweck
(F)
Period: 1836 to ca. 1850.
A short, quilted outdoor **mantle** with sleeves and a close-fitting collar of velvet, satin or silk. A trimming of fur, velvet or lace bordered the garment.

Cascade waistband
(F)
Period: 1860s.
A waistband fringed with jet pendants arranged in **vandykes**.

Cased body
(M)
Period: ca. 1550–1600.

A sleeveless **jerkin** worn over the **doublet**, fitting it closely.

(F)
Period: 1810–20.
A bodice with a series of transverse pleats or **gauging** across the front.

Cased sleeve
(F)
Period: 1810–1820.
A long sleeve divided into "compartments" by bands of insertion.

Casquette
(F)
Period: 1863–1864.
A straw hat shaped like a **Glengarry**, the brim low in front and behind; trimmed with black velvet and an ostrich feather.

Cassock
(F & M)
Period: 16th century.
Originally a term for a long, loose gown worn by both sexes. Later it became the long, loose overcoat buttoned down the front, sometimes with cape collars; often worn by soldiers. Described at the time as "a horseman's coat"; in a shortened version it was worn by farmers and countrymen. Also a term for a closed or open-fronted child's coat.

Period: 17th century onwards.
An additional meaning described the floor-length, high-collared, front-buttoned garment worn by Anglican clergy, similar to a Catholic soutane.

Cassock mantle
(F)
Period: 1880s.
A cloak with short sleeves and reaching to below the knees; gathered on the shoulders and down the centre of the back. In 1880 it was recorded that, "Nothing could be more peculiar or unbecoming".

Cassock vest
(M)
Period: 1850s.
A new form of clerical waistcoat, at first fastened on the right shoulder; later, nearer the midline. Worn by Tractarian High Church clergy and so thought to savour of "Popery"; hence its nickname, the "Mark of the Beast" or "M. B. waistcoat". Worn with a white **dog collar** fastened behind.

Castor
(F & M)
Period: 17th–19th century.
A beaver hat, but towards the end of the century the castor was often made of other materials. "The Castor… is made of Coney wooll mixt with Polony wooll" (1688, R. Holme, *Armory*).
See Demi-castor.

Casual wear, casuals
(F & M)
Period: 1930s onwards.
Informal clothing, usually as an alternative to clothing for work or for formal events. A term that first appeared in America and was then adopted elsewhere as a description for clothing that is also, but later, called **leisure wear**.

Catagan
(F)
Period: 1870–1875.
A **chignon** of ringlets or plaits of hair hanging at the back of the head, tied above with a wide ribbon and forming a resemblance to the male **catogan** of the 18th century.

Catagan head-dress
(F)
Period: 1889.
The hair plaited behind and turned up with a wide ribbon bow; a style suitable for older schoolgirls.

Catagan net
(F)
Period: 1870s.
A hair-net frequently used to contain the plaited **catagan**.

Cater-cap
(M)
Period: 16th and 17th centuries.
The four-cornered, square cap worn by academics at universities.

Cathedral beard
(M)
Period: 16th and early 17th centuries.
A broad, long **beard**.

Catherine wheel farthingale
(F)
Period: 1580 to ca. 1620.
A **farthingale** producing a tub-shaped hang of the skirt. "A short Dutch waist with a round Catherine wheel fardingale" (1607, Dekker and Webster, *Northward Hoe*).
See wheel farthingale.

Catogan, club wig
(M)
Period: 1760–1800.
A wig with a broad, flat **queue** turned up on itself and tied round the middle with black ribbon.

Cat suit
(F)
Period: 1960s onwards.
An amalgam of **leotard** and **leggings**; an all-in-one garment of close-fitting cut and flexible fabric with various permutations. "Miss Odell wears a "cat-suit" which is sleeveless, low-cut, tight around the shanks and everywhere else" (1960, *The Guardian*, 16 November).

Caudebec hat
(M)

Period: Late 17th and 18th centuries.

A felt hat imitating a **beaver**; said to have originated from Caudebec in Normandy. Known in England as a cawdebink or **cordyback hat** hat. "For a black Cawdebink hat" (1680, W. Cunningham, *Diary*).

Caul

(F)

Period: 14th–17th centuries.

A trellis-work **coif** or **skull-cap** of silk thread or gold-smith's mesh, sometimes lined with silk. More often worn by unmarried girls; wives usually wore **veils**. The medieval caul was generally called a **fret**.

Period: 18th and 19th centuries.

The soft, pliable crown of a bonnet or cap.

(M)

Period: Late 17th and 18th centuries.

The network foundation on which the wig was built. "To the foretop of his Wig…Down to the very net-work, named the caul" (1786, Peter Pindar).

Cauliflower wig

(M)

Period: 1750–1800.

A closely curled **bob-wig**, commonly worn by coachmen.

Cavalier sleeve

(F)

Period: 1830s.

A day sleeve, full down to the elbow, thence half-tight to the wrist; closed along the outer side by a series of ribbon bows.

Caxon

(M, rarely F)

Period: 18th century.

A tie-wig, usually white or pale-coloured but occasionally black. Worn with "undress", chiefly by the professional classes.

"Some wives there are… / Invade man's province, bluster and look big; / Nor wear the breeches only but the wig; / The red-hair'd lass, to hide her golden nob / Tucks up her tresses in a nut-brown mob, / And full-blown dames, thro' time a little flaxen, / Conceal that outrage by a coal-black caxen" (1798, Thomas Morton, *Secrets worth Knowing*).

Ceint, seint

(F & M)

Period: 14th and 15th centuries.

A **girdle**.

Ceinture, cincture

(F)

Period: Late 16th century until 1900.

The French term for a girdle, belt or sash in its original and anglicized version; an intentionally antiquated form used in literature in the 19th century.

Ceruse

Period: 16th to end of 18th century.

A cosmetic used by both sexes to whiten the face. Originally made of white lead.

Chador

(F)

Period: Late 20th century onwards.

An enveloping outdoor robe similar to the **burka** worn by some Muslim women and seen increasingly in Western countries in the last 30 years, though worn as traditional dress well before this. The chador leaves the face uncovered.

See Jilbab, hijab, niqab, veil.

Chaffers

(F)

Period: 16th century.

The embroidered lapels of the English gable-shaped hood.

Chain buckle

(M)

Period: Mid-18th century.

A variety of curled wig; **buckle** meaning curl.

Chain-hole

(M)

Period: 1879 to mid-20th century.

An additional hole, for the watch-chain, resembling a buttonhole, placed vertically between two buttonholes of the waistcoat. First mentioned in 1879 but common from 1888, and general in **lounge suits** from 1895.

Chambard mantle

(F)

Period: 1850s.

A three-quarter-length sleeved **mantle** with hood or collar and deep, hollow folds at the back.

Chammer, chimer, chimere, chymer, shamew

(M)

Period: Late 14th to early 19th century.

A rich, sleeved gown worn open in front. "A chammer of black satin with three borders of black velvet and furred with sables" (1517, Wardrobe Inventory of Henry VIII).

Other meanings and applications are associated with clerical dress, such as a loose gown with lawn sleeves attached for bishops.

Chancellor

(M)

Period: 18th century.

A variety of **wig**, possibly the **full-bottom** form.

Chape

Period: Medieval onwards.

The section of metal used on a buckle or on the scabbard of a sword. "A Chape . . . holdeth the Tongue of the Buckle in its proper place" (1688, Randle Holme, *Academy of Armory*).

Chapeau bras

(M)

Period: ca. 1760–1840.

A dress hat made to be carried under the arm. In the 18th century it was a flat **tricorn**; in the 19th century it was a flat, crescent-shaped hat, usually carried under the arm but occasionally worn with the peaks pointing fore and aft. By the 1830s it was generally called an **opera hat**.

(F)
Period: 1814.
A satin **calash**, small enough when folded flat to be carried in a handbag.

Chaperon

(M)
Period: 14th century.
The Anglo-French term for a hood with **gole** or cape and pendant **liripipe.**

Period: 15th century.
The chaperon, derived from the hood, was a head-dress consisting of a circular roll or **burlet**, a liripipe or **tippet**, sometimes left suspended, sometimes twisted round the head, and surmounted by the cockscomb-like, flopping crown.

Chaperone

(F)
Period: 17th century.
A small, soft **hood** for informal wear.

Chaplet

(F & M)
Period: Anglo-Saxon–16th century.
Originally a term applied to a garland of flowers for the head; it was worn by both sexes on festive occasions such as May Day, Whitsun and weddings. By the 15th century the chaplet of flowers was worn by the bride only.

Period: 14th to early 16th century.
A circlet set with gems, also called a "coronal of gold-smithry"; worn by both sexes on festive occasions, and in the 16th century by brides.

Period: Late 14th and 15th centuries.
A wreath of twisted silk or satin, or an ornamental pad-ded roll, not confined to festive occasions and worn

Left centre detail from the Devonshire Hunting tapestries, *The Boar and Bear Hunt*, ca. 1425–30. This detail from a southern Flemish tapestry of ca. 1425–30 depicts a group of elite hunt-ers, their admiring female compan-ions and a couple of attendants. The rich colours, including **mi-parti hose,** furred **gowns, chaperon** head-dresses for most of the men, high hairdressing with false hair (top left) or complex ar-rangements of **veils** (lower right) for the women, offer evidence about the luxurious elite clothing of this period. Photo © Victoria and Albert Museum, London.

by women and occasionally men. "White and blod (red) taffata and red tartryn for chaplets for the Earl of Derby's daughters" (1397, Duchy of Lancaster Records; white and red were the livery colours of the House of Plantagenet).

Period: 17th century.
A term used to describe a short rosary or set of beads. "A chaplet hanging down on her neck" (1653, H. Cogan, *Pinto's Traveles,* ed. 1663).

Charlotte Corday bonnet
(F)
Period: 1870–1890.
An outdoor head-dress with an upstanding crown of soft material, drawn to a narrow, frilled brim, the join covered by broad ribbon band with pendant strings behind. In 1889 there was a version with a flattened crown.

Charlotte Corday cap
(F)
Period: 1870s.
An indoor day cap with a small puffed muslin crown gathered under a ribbon band with a lace frill below. Small lace **lappets** behind and long dangling ribbons.

Chatelaine
(F)
Period: 1840s to early 20th century.
An ornamental chain attached at the waist, usually with a hook, from which hung various articles of domestic use, such as scissors, penknife, tape-measure, thimble-case and button hook. In the 1840s it was usually made of cut steel; in the 1870s of oxidized silver, steel or electroplate.

Chatelaine bag
(F)
Period: ca. 1870–1890.
A small bag suspended from a belt in the manner of a **chatelaine**. Often of leather with metallic decoration.

Chausons
The equivalent of the English **braies**.

Chausseambles, chauuxsimlez, chasembles, cashambles
(M)
Period: Medieval.
Taken from a French term, these were **hose** with leather or whalebone soles stitched under the feet to obviate the need for boots or shoes which, by ca. 1350–1450 were in general use by the nobility.

Period: ca. 1450 to early 17th century.
They were garments proper to the Robes of the Order of the Bath. "Cloth stockings soled with white leather called Cashambles but no shoes" (1610, British Museum, Harl. MS 5176).

Chausses
(M)
Period: Medieval.

An Anglo-French term for medieval hose, but as soon as Anglo-French gave way to English as the language of knighthood and nobility, in the 15th century the word "chausses" was abandoned in favour of **hose**, which had been in use since the 11th century. Later uses of the term were found in the context of armour.

Chav
(F & M)
Period: From mid-1990s onwards.
A youth style, originally found in southern England, and perceived as cheap and nasty despite the wearing of "designer" labels; "...council-estate chic – man-made fabrics, fake labels and lots of eight-carat gold..." (2004, *The Sunday Times*, 15 August).

Cheats
(M)
Period: 17th century.
Waistcoats with rich front panels but with cheap fabric at the back.

Period: 19th century.
A term sometimes applied to a shirt-front with collar attached, worn as a **dickey**.

Check
See Cut-in.

Checkered-apron men
Period: 16th century.
See Apron.

Cheeks and ears
See Coif.

Cheek wrappers
(F)
Period: ca. 1750–1800.
The side flaps of the **dormeuse** or **French night-cap**.

Chelsea boots
(M)
Period: Late 1950s onwards.
Also known as elastic-sided boots, these ankle-length boots were designed to accompany the tapered trousers then fashionable. "Be up-to-date and completely "with it" in these elegantly styled black leather Chelsea boots with smart chisel toe shape, elastic side gussets, rubber top-piece heels" (1963, *Freeman's Mail Order catalogue*).

Chemise, camise
(F, occasionally M)
Period: Medieval to 15th century.
Called kemes or kemse in medieval English, this garment was worn next to the body. It was usually of linen and worn by both sexes in the early medieval period. From the 13th to early 14th centuries the chemise and **smock** were often recorded together as distinct garments. "Hire chemise smal and hwit...and hire smoc hwit" (ca.1200. Trinity College Homilies, 163). At that date the chemise was sometimes coloured and

worn over the smock. Subsequently, the chemise was known as a smock when worn by a woman and a **shirt** when worn by a man. From the early 14th century, the term chemise disappeared until imported from France in the late 18th century as a polite name for a smock or **shift**.

Period: 19th century.

The chemise was made of linen, homespun or cotton; it was voluminous and knee-length, oblong in shape, with short sleeves and untrimmed. Until ca. 1850 the square neck often had a front flap which fell over the top of the corset. In 1876 pleated gussets were introduced to allow for the shape of the breasts. Subsequently it became elaborately trimmed with frills, tucks and lace. In the 1890s it was gradually replaced by **combinations**.

Period: 20th century onwards.

Often a shorthand term for a **chemise dress** rather than an undergarment.

Chemise dress, chemise gown, chemise robe
(F)

Period: 1780 to ca. 1810.

A lightweight, unstructured dress not dissimilar to the undergarment; always made of thin muslin, cambric, or coloured silk and made with the fashionable waist-line of the time.

In the late 18th century the top was drawn in round a low neck and always worn with a sash; it had long, tight sleeves. The English chemise gown, known as the "Perdita Chemise", was closed down the front from bosom to hem with buttons or a series of ribbon bows; a sash was essential.

In the early 19th century the neckline might be drawn in high with a falling frill or cut low. Buttons down the front were usual, and a small train was optional. Sleeves were short and melon-shaped; no sash was worn.

Period: 20th century onwards.

The chemise dress of 1918 was a style which combined a bodice and tunic, and could be pulled over the head and worn with an underskirt; it needed no fastenings. Subsequently the term was used for a light, often sleeveless, unfitted dress.

Chemisette
(F)

Period: 19th century.

In the first half of the century, a high-necked and sleeveless, white muslin or cambric fill-in to the bodice of a day gown, cut low in front. By the 1860s, a long-sleeved blouse.

Period: 20th century.

Lace or fabric insert into the décolletage of a low-cut dress.

Cheongsam
(F)

Period: 1950 onwards.

A traditional Chinese one-piece dress with a high **mandarin collar** fastened asymmetrically across the chest, slim-fitting with slits at both sides of the skirt; usually made of a brocaded silk. It became popular as a style of cocktail dress amongst non-Chinese women in the mid-1950s and today can be bought in a number of variants in sleeve and skirt length and even with an open back.

Chesterfield
(M, occasionally F)

Period: 1840 onwards.

An overcoat, named after the 6th Earl of Chesterfield (1805–1866), a leader of fashion in the 1830s and 1840s. A slightly waisted overcoat, single- or double-breasted, having a short back vent and centre back seam but no seam at the waist, or side vents. A velvet collar was usual, as were side-flapped pockets and an outside left-breast pocket. By 1859 a small ticket-pocket was added above the pocket on right side. Fastened by four or five covered buttons to waist-level, occasionally under a fly.

In the 1850s this form of overcoat was known in France as a **twine** and corresponded to the **pardessus**. Often known in tailors' parlance as a Chester.

By the early 20th century this had become a **classic style** of overcoat for both men and women.

Chevesaille

Period: Medieval.

Taken from the Old French term *chevecaille,* this rare term described the border round the neck of a garment. It was used by Chaucer in *Romaunt of the Rose,* ca. 1400.

Cheveux-de-frise

Period: 18th century.

A **vandyked** frill or edging.

Chevrons
(F)

Period: 1826 to late 19th century.

"A new form of trimming above the hem of a skirt", applied in a zigzag pattern.

Chicken-skin gloves
(F)

Period: Late 17th to early 19th century.

"Some of chicken-skin at night
To keep her Hands plump, soft, and white" (1690, J. Evelyn, *Mundus Muliebris*).

Though retaining the name, the gloves were frequently made of other leathers; "The name induced some to think they were made from the skins of chickens; but on the contrary they are made of a thin strong leather which is dressed with almonds and spermaceti" (1778, From a shop bill of Warren the Perfumer).

See Limerick gloves.

Chignon
(F)

Period: ca. 1750 onwards.

Term denoting a mass of hair arranged at the back of

the head. The "chignon flottant" of the 1790s was made up of loops of hair or ringlets arranged to hang down from the back of the head over the neck.
See Banging chignon.

The chignon reached its maximum size in the late 1860s and 1870s, when it was composed mainly of artificial hair and formal rows of curls (marteaux) pinned down. "False hair is worn in incredible quantities and chignons are made of these marteaux all ready to be fastened on with a comb" (1866).

"Chignons often weigh five or more ounces" (1868).

In the 20th century chignons were considered old-fashioned when hair was bobbed or permed but a classic chignon, using natural or artificial hair, returned to fashion, worn high on the crown of the head, in the late 1960s.

Chimney-pot hat
(M)

Period: 1830s to end of the 19th century.

A high-crowned hat with narrow brim, replacing the high-crowned **beaver hat** previously fashionable.

"The surface covering being of silk faced with a felting of rabbit hair which has received a smooth satin-like surface" (1862, Mayhew, *London Labour and the London Poor*).

Synonyms: **Pot hat**, **Top hat**, **Topper**, **Silk hat**, **Plug hat**.

Chin cloak, chin clout, chin cloth, chinner
Period: 1535–1660s.

Synonyms for **muffler**.

Chinese slipper
(F)

Period: 1786.

See Kampskatcha slipper.

Chinese spencer
(F)

Period: 1808.

A very short jacket or **spencer** with two long points in front.

Chinos
(M)

Period: 1940 onwards.

An American term taken from the word "chino" which described a cotton, twilled fabric with a surface sheen and applied to informal trousers made from this fabric, worn in summer by American servicemen. Originally khaki-colour, chinos are now produced in various colours, paler and darker in hue.

Chin stays
(F)

Period: Late 1820s to ca. 1840.

Frills of tulle or lace added to the insertion of bonnet strings, forming a frill round the chin when tied.

See Mentonnières.

Chiton
(F & M)

Period: ca. 480–323 BCE.

The ancient Greek garment formed from one piece of cloth wound round the body and held by a pin at the shoulder, or two pieces of cloth fastened along their top edges at the shoulders and down the arms. Both types could be held by a girdle below the breasts or round the waist.

The depiction of this garment has inspired later designers and makers; the **chemise dress** and Fortuny's **Delphos dress** owe much to this style.

Chitterlings
(M)

Period: 16th–19th century.

Popular term for ruffs and the frills down the front of a shirt and their manner of ornamental pleating.

Chlamys
(M)

Period: ca. 480–323 BCE.

A rectangular cloak or **mantle** of wool cloth. Originally worn by soldiers, first as a **loin cloth** and then as an asymmetrical cloak, and then absorbed into general use and possibly worn over the **chiton**.

Choker
(M)

Period: 19th century.

A large white **handkerchief** worn high around the neck by waiters and clergymen; similar to a **cravat**.

(F)

Period: Late 19th century onwards.

A band or ribbon or a jewelled band worn high and close around the throat, usually for evening wear.

Choli
(F)

Period: 20th century onwards.

A close-fitting bodice of cotton or silk, usually worn under a **sari** by Indian women. Some reveal the midriff, and variants are made from a variety of non-Indian fabrics and worn by western women for exercise and leisure activities.

Chopine, chopin, chapiney
(F)

Period: 16th and 17th centuries.

An over-shoe consisting of a toe-cap fixed to a high sole of cork or wood, variously decorated. Rare in England except in the theatre; but "there are many of these chapineys of a great height, even half a yard high" (1611, T. Coryate, *Crudities*).

Choux
(F)

Period: Late 17th century.

A lady's **chignon**. "The great round boss or bundle (of hair) resembling a cabbage" (1690, J. Evelyn, *Mundus Muliebris*).

Chukka boot
(M)

Period: 1930s onwards.

A boot of suede or reversed calf-leather, originally worn by polo players. It reached to the ankle and was tied together through two or three eyelet holes. A similar style was known as a "desert boot" but the latter is sturdier, higher, and was originally worn by American troops.

Ciclaton, cinglaton, syglaton

See Cyclas.

Cigarette pants

(F)

Period: 1950s onwards.

Trousers cut to taper and fit closely towards the ankle; a longer version of **Capri pants**.

Cinema (influence of)

(F & M)

Period: 20th century onwards.

Seeing the clothing worn by others, how it looked on different shapes and sizes of person, and how it looked in movement, offered crucial information to audiences. Performers in films quickly overtook stage performers in significance, and magazines from the pre-World War I period onwards offered details about the clothing and beauty secrets of the new stars. From the 1920s the fashions, hair styles, make-up and mannerisms of performers were imitated, and garments with names like "Studio Styles" could be found in department stores and home dressmaking pattern books; mail-order catalogues were equally influential in offering the styles of the stars. British tailoring, American leisure wear, teenage fashions, biker and hippie clothes all found international audiences through the cinema.

Circassian bodice

(F)

Period: 1829.

A bodice with cross-over folds descending from the shoulders and crossing at the waist.

Circassian wrapper

(F)

Period: 1813.

A loose day wrap cut like a night-chemise; made of muslin and lace, with the sleeves of muslin and lace in alternating strips.

Circlet, serclett

Period: 15th and 16th centuries.

A term denoting a decorative, circular head roll or chaplet of goldsmith's work. "For a serclett to marry maidens in" (1540, Church-wardens' Accts., St. Margaret's, Westminster).

Circular skirt

(F)

Period: 1895.

A tailor-made, gored skirt with sewn-down pleats over the hips and back; the hem 18 feet round.

Circumfolding hat

(M)

Period: 1830s.

A round dress-hat, the crown moderately low and made to fold flat for carrying under the arm.

Clarence

(M)

Period: 19th century.

A style of boot, made with a triangular gusset of soft, folded leather and eyelet holes for lacing across it; a forerunner of the **elastic-sided boot**.

Clarissa Harlowe bonnet

(F)

Period: 1879.

A large **bonnet** of Leghorn straw, the brim brought forward on the forehead; lined with velvet. Named after the eponymous heroine of Samuel Richardson's novel published in 1747.

Clarissa Harlowe corsage

(F)

Period: 1847.

An evening-dress style, with neckline off the shoulders and folds caught in at the waist with a band of ribbon; short sleeves with two or three lace falls.

Classical dress

The detailed discussion of the terminology of classical dress is outside the remit of this dictionary. However, references to the clothing of the Greco-Roman world, more especially the period when Greek culture was at its zenith (ca. 480–323 BCE) which then influenced Roman culture up to ca. 300 CE, is found in later ecclesiastical, literary, pictorial and theatrical contexts, and also enters the visual vocabulary of fashion and fashion designers. Basic terms useful to dress historians are therefore included in the appropriate place.

See buskins, chiton, chlamys, cothurnus, himation, palla, pallium, peplos, stola, toga, tunica.

Classic style

(F & M)

Period: 20th century onwards.

Items of clothing that are timelessly elegant; they never look old-fashioned and, although subtly reworked from time to time, retain discerning purchasers. Such garments include **trench coats**, cashmere jumpers, tweed jackets and **brogue shoes**.

Cloak

(M & F)

Period: Anglo-Saxon onwards.

A loose outer garment of varying length, falling from the neck over the shoulders. There are many named styles, which are found under their respective headings.

Cloak bag, portmanteau

(M)

Period: 16th century onwards.

A receptacle in which a valuable cloak could be packed for travelling, usually on horseback.

From the 18th century the term meant a receptacle for

clothing, often of leather and hinged to open into two sections.

Cloak-bag breeches

(M)

Period: Early 17th century.

Breeches that were full and oval in shape, drawn in above the knee; encircled with decorative **points**, either metal-tipped laces or ribbons, or closed below the knee with a ribbon rosette or bow on the outer side.

Cloche, clocher

Period: Late 13th–15th century.

A travelling cloak.

See Bell.

Cloche hat

(F)

Period: ca. 1920 onwards.

A bell-shaped, close-fitting hat pulled well down over the forehead and eyes; fashionable in the 1920s and occasionally later.

Clock

Period: 16th century onwards.

A gore or triangular insertion into a garment to widen it at that point, as with collars, stockings, etc.

"Of a band (collar) the clocks (are) the laying in of the cloth to make it round" (1688, R. Holme, *Armory*).

In the 16th century the cape portions of some of the hoods worn by women were with or without clocks. Also, since the seams forming the triangular insertion began to be embroidered, the term clock was transferred to this form of embroidery and the clocks of **stockings** came to mean embroidery at the ankles, whether gored or not.

Clogs

(F & M)

Period: Medieval onwards.

Wooden-soled over-shoes to raise the wearer above the dirt. Until the 17th century the term was synonymous with **pattens**. The shape followed the fashion of footwear of the day. "Clogges or Pattens to keepe them out of the durt" (1625, Purchas, *Pilgrimage*).

Period: 17th and 18th centuries.

The term was applied to ladies' leather-soled over-shoes with merely instep-straps, and generally matching the shoe. (On arrival of the guests) "the Gentlemen were to put their hats and sticks in one corner and the Ladies their clogs in another" (1780, *The Mirror,* no. 93).

All-wooden shoes worn by country-folk were also known as clogs.

Period: 20th century onwards.

Term applied to any form of footwear which replicated the practical shape of a clog in a combination of materials, including synthetics such as plastic.

Close coat

(M)

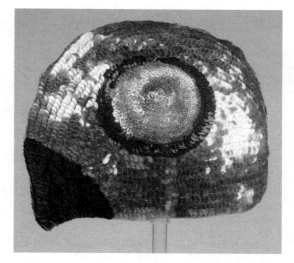

Cloche hat in the form of a bird's head with overlapping **sequins**, ca. 1925–30. Copyright the Olive Matthews Collection, Chertsey Museum. Photograph by John Chase.

Period: 18th and 19th centuries.

Term for a coat worn buttoned up; "...dress'd in a drab colour'd close Great Coat" (1757, Dec., *Norwich Mercury*).

Clot, clout-shoen

(M)

Period: 15th century.

A heavy shoe shod with thin iron plates; worn by labourers.

Clothes, clothing

(F & M)

Period: Medieval onwards.

Providing the naked body with cloth or articles of **apparel** or **dress** made from simple or complex fabrics, which are constructed to cover, disguise or enhance the human form.

Clothes rationing

(F & M)

Period: 1941–1950.

In World War I there were shortages of fabrics and clothing and the ill-received attempt to introduce a **National Standard Dress** in 1918, but it was only in World War II that the British government introduced clothes rationing alongside other rationing of crucial resources. Everyone had a ration book which contained the annual allocation of coupons. Adult males had 66 coupons, not many when a suit used 26 and a pullover 5, so there was a thriving black market and encouragement to "make do and mend", a recycling exercise not dissimilar to that

of World War I. In America and elsewhere there were regulations about use of fabrics and the method of making clothing simpler and more practical.
See Utility Scheme.

Cloud
(F)
Period: 1870s.
A long scarf worn as an outdoor head-covering, with evening dress. "…in a swans-down cloak with a white cloud" (1888, R. Kipling, *Plain Tales from the Hills*).

Clout
(F & M)
Period: Medieval onwards.
Various meanings, including old clothing, patches and the fabric used for them; also baby's nappies.

Club
(M)
Period: Medieval onwards.
A heavy stick; fashionable instead of a cane in the 1730s and ca. 1800–1810, but also carried as an aggressive or protective weapon by criminals.

Period: 18th century.
An alternative name for the **catogan** wig. "In an undress, unless you have a club as thick as both your double fists, you are not fit to be seen" (1769, G. Colman, *Man and Wife*).

Clutch bag
(F)
Period: 1950s onwards.
A new name for a **pochette**, namely a small handbag which can be held in the hand or under the arm, invariably without handles and made from a wide variety of natural or manmade materials.

Cly
Period: 16th century onwards.
Slang for a pocket.

Coat
(F & M)
Period: 13th century.
The everyday loose tunic; the main garment worn by both sexes, though a **kirtle** was more usual for women.

(M)
Period: 14th and 15th centuries.
The term was largely replaced by **gipon** or **doublet**.
See cote, cote-hardie.
Period: 16th century.
A short-sleeved or sleeveless jacket or jerkin worn over the doublet.

Period: Mid-17th century.
The term was beginning to acquire its modern meaning, that of a sleeved body garment, varying in style according to the fashion of the period and worn as a body coat or as an upper garment.

Period: 18th century.
Distinguished from the **frock** by having no turned-down collar; towards the end of the century the formal coat had a stand collar. By that date the day coat and the frock merged into the **frock coat** and the **dress coat** for day or evening wear, and began to replace the former coat.

Period: 19th century onwards.
A shorthand term for a variety of coats worn in the daytime and as overcoats.

(F)
Period: 16th to end of 18th century.
The name "coat", shortened from "petticoat", was the term commonly used either for the under-petticoat or for the skirt of the gown.

Period: 19th century onwards.
A term for a variety of styles of outer garment, such as **jacket**, **overcoat**, etc.

Coat-bodice
(F)
Period: 1880s.
A day bodice made with long **basques** and pleated at the back like a man's **frock coat** with two hip buttons; cut high in the neck, having outside pockets and fastened all down the front. Sometimes made in a double-breasted version. Usually **tailor-made**.

Coat dress, coat frock
(F)
Period: ca. 1914 onwards.
A semi-formal garment resembling a dress but with certain stylistic features similar to a single- or double-breasted coat, especially in the weight of fabric; a useful spring or autumn garment. "The coat-dress has an assured future. It can be worn over a waistcoat, petticoat or princess slip" (1915, *Vogue*).

Coat-hanger
(M)
Period: 19th century onwards.
The early name for the loop attached within the neck of a coat by which it could be hung up; the device was used from 1830. Chain coat-hangers were introduced from ca. 1850.
Also a term for a wooden or metal structure, sometimes padded, which fits into a garment, with a curved top to hang on a **wardrobe** rail.

Coatlet
(F)
Period: 1899.
A short coat of velvet or fur with a fan-shaped spreading collar and large revers. Some were of cloth, frogged and braided.

Coats
Period: 18th century.

A tailor's term for coat-buttons.

See Breasts.

Coat shirt

(M)

Period: 1890s.

A shirt opening all down the front and closed by buttons, a device to avoid having to put the shirt on over the head; an American novelty, becoming later the **tunic shirt**.

Coat-sleeve

(F)

Period: 1864 onwards.

Cut like the sleeve of a man's coat, straight and tubular, with a slight curve about the elbow and slight narrowing towards the wrist. Used for women's bodices and jackets. In the early 1870s a **mousquetaire cuff** was often added.

Cock, cocked hat

(M)

Period: Late 17th to early 19th century.

The turn-up of the brim of a hat; various named forms, such as the **Denmark cock**, the **Monmouth cock** and the **Dettingen cock**.

Later the term was used to denote the angle at which the hat was worn, and also the term was adjusted to "cocked hat".

Cockered cap

(M)

Period: 16th century.

A cap with a turned-up brim.

Cockers, cokers, cocurs

(M)

Period: 14th–16th century.

A knee-high boot of rough make, worn by labourers, shepherds and country-folk.

Period: 17th century.

A type of sea-boot. "Fishermen's great boots with which they wade into the sea, are called cokers" (1695, Kennet, *Par. Antiq. Gloss.*).

On dry land the term was generally applied to leggings buckled or buttoned at the side and strapped under the foot.

See Oker.

Cockle

(F)

Period: 17th century.

A curl or ringlet. "Instant she sped

To curl the Cockles of her new-bought head" (1608, Sylvester, *Du Bartas*).

Cocktail dress

(F)

Period: ca. 1920 onwards.

Cocktails or mixed drinks were an American invention which was exported to Europe in the mid-19th century.

At cocktail parties in the 20th century, usually held in the early evening, a new form of clothing was worn, smarter than a day dress but not as formal as a dinner or evening dress. Cocktail pyjamas and cocktail suits were similarly devised for this purpose.

Cod

Period: Medieval–16th century.

A bag.

Period: 18th century.

A cant term for a purse.

Codovec

(M)

Period: 17th century.

A fancy tradename for a **castor**.

Codpiece

(M)

Period: 15th century.

The front flap forming a pouch at the fork of the long hose. "A kodpese like a pokett" (ca. 1460, *Townley Mysteries*).

Period: 16th century.

When worn with **trunk-hose**, the codpiece was padded and very prominent and tied to the hose with **points**.

Period: 17th and 18th centuries.

When the projecting pouch was discarded the term was often applied to the front fastening of the breeches, and, in the 18th century, occasionally to the front **fall** of the breeches.

Cod-placket

(M)

Period: 16th–18th century.

Term denoting the front opening of the breeches.

Codrington

(M)

Period: 1840s.

A wrapper or loose overcoat, double- or single-breasted, somewhat resembling a **Chesterfield**. Named after the British Admiral, the victor of Navarino in 1827.

Coggers

(M)

Period: 18th and early 19th centuries.

Gaiters of stiff leather or cloth, buttoned up the side with a strap under the instep.

See Cockers.

Coif

(M)

Period: End of 12th to mid-15th century.

A close-fitting plain linen cap, resembling a baby's bonnet, covering the ears and tied under the chin.

Period: 16th century.

Worn by the learned professions or the aged, as under-caps or alone, for warmth; sometimes made of black cloth.

(F)

Period: 16th–19th centuries.

In the 16th century the coif was worn as an under-cap and later, in the 16th and in the early 17th centuries, it was often embroidered in coloured silks, the sides made to curve forwards over the ears (popularly known as "cheeks and ears") and often worn with a **forehead cloth**. In the 18th century the term was sometimes applied to indoor caps, particularly the **round-eared cap**.

Coiffure

(F, occasionally M)

Period: 17th century onwards.

From the French *coiffer*, to dress the head and arrange the hair. A term mainly used to describe the hair-styling or type of head-dress worn by women.

Coin de feu

(F)

Period: 1848.

A short coat with wide sleeves and closed at the neck. Made of velvet, cashmere or silk, and generally worn indoors over a "home dress".

Cointise, quaintise

Period: 13th and 14th centuries.

Term denoting the curious or extravagant in fashion. Also used in connection with 14th-century armour and the favours or devices associated with it.

Collar

Period: ca. 1300 onwards.

A piece of fabric attached to the neck opening of a garment or added separately, to form a covering for the neck. In the second half of 16th and throughout the 17th century the more usual term was **band**.

The significance of the collar restricting the free movements of the neck and thus symbolizing class distinctions persisted through several centuries.

See Prussian collar, Masher collar, Stand-fall collar, Rosebery collar, Eton collar, Dux collar, Piccadilly collar, Polo collar.

Collar of Esses, SS collar

Period: ca. 1360–16th century.

The **livery** collar of the House of Lancaster instituted by John of Gaunt, Duke of Lancaster, ca. 1360 and in the 15th and 16th centuries worn by adherents of the Tudor dynasty.

Collections

Period: 16th century onwards.

The assembling of groups of artefacts by elite collectors created cabinets of curiosities and these presaged the later public collections, often known as galleries or museums. Specific collections of clothing and/or textiles were formed by royal dynasties in Denmark, Russia and Sweden in the 17th century, and artists assembled garments which were painting props, while theatres also acquired garments from elite patrons to eke out wardrobe stock for performers.

The 20th century saw an explosion of museum collecting of every type of clothing, from high fashion to folk and regional dress. Permanent displays and temporary exhibitions informed visitors about the continuum of dress, past and present, and were increasingly used as inspiration by fashion designers.

Private collectors included C. W. and P. E. Cunnington, whose collection of clothing and associated material, including fashion plates and photographs, was acquired by Manchester in 1947 and formed the nucleus of what is now the Gallery of Costume. This is just one of many internationally significant collections found in cities and towns around the world.

See Vintage.

Colleen Bawn cloak

(F)

Period: 1861.

A cloak of white grenadine with a large cape caught up in the middle of the back with two rosettes. Named after Dion Boucicault's eponymous melodrama.

Collegians, Oxonians

(M)

Period: 1830s.

Short boots with "a wedge cut out from each side of the top so as to enable the boot to be pulled on easily".

Colley-westonward

(M)

Period: 16th century.

A term denoting "worn awry", and applied to the **mandilion**, a form of jacket fashionably worn sideways with one sleeve hanging down in front and the other behind.

Colour

A particular hue or tint distinguishing the natural colour of a fibre or a dye, natural or synthetic, which creates a new shade on the fibre or on the woven textile by a process of weaving or printing.

Names describing colours before 1800 will be found in the Obsolete Colour Names glossary.

Coloured shirt

(M)

Period: 1840s onwards.

Developed from the **aquatic shirt**, pink being a common colour. In 1860 French printed cambrics in various coloured patterns were made into shirts for informal wear. By 1894 coloured shirts had become "perfectly good form even with frock coats", provided that the collar was white. "Solid colours are barred; neat stripes in pink and blue are favourites."

In the post-1960 period a wide variety of colours and patterns, e.g. check, Paisley and spot, were used for shirts with matching collars.

See Arrow shirts.

Comb

(F)

Period: 19th century onwards.

Alongside the practical purpose of a comb to disentangle hair, there emerged decorative combs, often several inches high and made of tortoiseshell or of metal, with the straight or curving upper edge pierced or inlaid with gems, paste, pearls or similar. Especially popular during decades when hairstyles were vertical, such as the late 1820s and the early 1900s. "The new real tortoiseshell combs, set with "Whitlock" diamonds (replicas), are a pleasing addition to the coiffure, and these may be had from a guinea each" (1904, *The Lady's Realm*). In the 20th century inexpensive plastic combs, often in pairs, were worn to hold the hair away from the face.
See Diadem comb.

Combinations
(M)
Period: Mid-19th century to ca. 1950.
Although children had worn one-piece undergarments in the late 18th century, the adult version of **vest** and **drawers** constructed from one piece of woollen fabric was patented in 1862; it became commonly worn from the 1880s.

(F)
Combinations for women, chemise and drawers in one, were introduced in 1877. Sometimes they were made with high necks and long sleeves, for day wear, and made from linen, merino, calico, nainsook and washing silks. By 1885 they were made of natural wool, introduced by Jaeger & Co., and in the 1890s became more elegant, with lace trimming, and the neck was sometimes drawn in with coloured "baby-ribbon". "Ladies natural or white merino combinations" (1914, *Gamages General Catalogue*).

Comforter
(M)
Period: 1840s onwards.
A woollen scarf for wrapping round the neck in cold weather.
See Muffler, Scarf.

Comforts
(F)
Period: 1800.
Double-soled sandals.

Commode
(F)
Period: Late 17th and early 18th centuries.
Initially the wire frame which held up the head-dress of the 1690s, but by the beginning of the 18th century the actual head-dress."The Commode is a frame of Wire cover'd with silk, on which the whole Head Attire is adjusted" (1690, J. Evelyn, *Fop-Dictionary*).
The 18th century commode was composed of a linen cap, lace-edged, with layers of pleats raised above the head and supported by the wire frame. Two lappets, often of lace, were either pendant or pinned up.

Compass cloak
(M)
Period: 16th and 17th centuries.
One style of the **French cloak**, being circular in cut. The "Half Compass Cloak" was semicircular.

Confidants
(F)
Period: Late 17th century.
"Smaller curles next the eares" (1690, J. Evelyn, *Mundus Muliebris*).

Constables
(M)
Period: 1830–1840.
"Very small canes without handles, the top covered with gold plate" (1830, *Gentleman's Magazine of Fashion*).

Conversation bonnet
(F)
Period: 1806.
A **poke bonnet** with one side of the brim projecting beyond the cheek, the other side being turned back from the cheek.

Conversation hat
(F)
Period: 1803.
Similar to the **conversation bonnet** but with brim complete at the back.

Coolie hat
(F)
Period: 20th century onwards.
A broad, conical shaped hat, often of straw and used as a sun hat. The term was appropriated from the headwear worn by some East Asian labourers.

Cope
(F & M)
Period: Medieval onwards.
Originally, and throughout the medieval period, a voluminous semicircular cloak with a hood and open down the front. Worn by both sexes as a protection against cold and rain. Distinguished from the **mantle** which had no hood. "A route of ladies…in kirtles and in copes riche…. The cloth when fresh and new may make either a cope or a mantle, but in order of time it is first a cope – when it becomes old it is beheaded, and being beheaded it becomes a mantle" (1393, Gower, *Confessio Amantis*). Also, the cope is a monastic and ecclesiastical garment, still in use.

Copotain, copintank, copatain, coppintanke, copytank, coptank
(F & M)
Period: 16th and 17th centuries.
First mentioned in 1508 but very fashionable from 1560 to 1620. A hat with a high, conical crown and moderate brim often rolled up at the sides. Revived between ca. 1640–1665 as the **sugarloaf hat**.

Copped hat, copped cap

(M)

Period: 16th and 17th centuries.

Similar to a **copotain**. "Sometyme men were coppid cappis like a sugar lofe" (1519, Horman, *Vulgaria*).

Copped shoe

(M)

Period: ca. 1450–1500.

A **piked shoe**.

Coral currant button

(M)

Period: 1850s.

A coral button shaped like a red currant and used on waistcoats.

Corazza

(M)

Period: 1845 to early 20th century.

A shirt made to button down the back, cut to the shape of the body, with narrow sleeves; of cambric or cotton.

Cordyback hat

See Caudebec hat.

Co-respondent shoes

(M)

Period: ca. 1918 onwards.

Term used to describe shoes using two different coloured leathers, usually black and white or tan and white.

Cork

(M)

Period: 15th century.

Apparently identical with the early **galosh** and **patten**, except that the sole was made of cork and not aspen.

Cork rump, rump

(F)

Period: Late 18th century.

A **bustle** in the form of a large, crescent-shaped pad stuffed with cork.

Cork shoe, corked shoe, cork-heeled shoe

(F & M)

Period: 16th and early 17th centuries.

Shoes with wedge-shaped cork heels. Also worn for swimming.

Cork soles

(F & M)

Period: 16th and 17th centuries.

Shoes with cork soles and heels.

Period: 19th century.

Thin soles of cork for inserting into men's boots; patented in 1854. Also thin soles of cork lined with wool for inserting into women's boots in cold weather and worn from 1862.

Cork wig

(M)

Man's **co-respondent shoes**; brown and white buckskin **brogues**, possibly originally sports shoes; made by Austin Reed, ca. 1930–40. The French couturier Jean Patou (1880–1936) was photographed in a lounge suit wearing a similar pair in the 1920s. Copyright the Olive Matthews Collection, Chertsey Museum. Photograph by John Chase.

Period: 1760s.

Cork was one of the many materials used for making **wigs**. "John Light, peruke maker, has brought to great perfection the best method of making Cork Wigs, either smooth or in curls; and also Cork-Bag-wigs in the neatest manner" (1763, *The Salisbury Journal*).

Corned shoe

(M)

Period: 1510–1540.

The fashionable, broad-toed shoe. "So many garded hose, such cornede shoes…" (1529, Skelton).

Cornet, cornette

(F)

Period: 16th and 17th centuries.

The cornet was similar to the **bongrace** and generally made of dark-coloured velvet when worn with a **French hood**; otherwise of lawn. "Cornet, a fashion of shadow or Boongrace" (1611, Cotgrave).

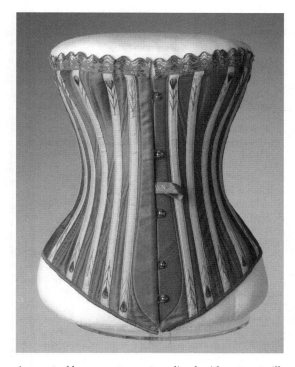

A **corset** of brown cotton **sateen** lined with cotton twill; metal spoon shaped **busk** and steel "bones" within the boning channels. The lining is printed with the equivalent of a promotional **label**, "The Y&N Corset Regd, The Y&N Diagonal seam trademark, Awarded Three Gold Medals", ca. 1885–95. Copyright the Olive Matthews Collection, Chertsey Museum. Photograph by John Chase.

In the late 17th century the term was applied to a lace or lawn day cap with **lappets** falling about the ears and sometimes a pendant flap behind.

Period: ca. 1800–1850.

A cornette was a bonnet-shaped cap with rounded or slightly pointed back, which tied under the chin.

Cornet skirt, French skirt

(F)

Period: 1892.

A day skirt made with a seam at each side and slightly trained; the front piece slightly gored to measure 40 inches at hem diminishing to 20 inches, and shaped with darts at the waist; the back cut on the cross in one piece, 20 inches at the hem diminishing to 10 inches at the waist, the train being a segment of a circle. No foundation skirt was worn under it.

Coronet, cronet

(F & M)

Period: 14th century.

The open crown of nobility, also called a coronal.

Corsage

(F)

Period: 19th century onwards.

The upper or bodice portion of a woman's dress; from the French term denoting the upper or bodice section of a dress, primarily in the 19th century.

Also a small arrangement of flowers and leaves usually pinned to the front of a bodice or to one shoulder; an American term originally.

Corsage en fourreau

(F)

Period: 18th century.

A style in which the bodice was cut in one section with the skirt by means of a central panel at the back. Used occasionally in the first half of the century, but more usual after ca. 1750.

Corse

See Baldric.

Corselet

(F)

Period: 1860s onwards.

A deep form of **Swiss belt**. In the early 1900s a corselet skirt extended several inches above the waist.

Corset, corse

(F & M)

Period: 14th and 15th centuries.

A close-fitting sleeveless bodice, often very decorative.

(F)

Period: Late 18th century to mid-20th century.

A change of usage encompassing corset and **stays** and applied to an undergarment with whalebone or steel ribs encircling the chest and compressing the natural waist. The French word "corset" was beginning to be used as a refinement for "stays" at the close of the 18th century, but both terms were in common use. "Neat stays and corsets" (1800, advertisement, *Ipswich Journal*).

Amongst the many styles were the following, in date order:

Period: 1800–1810.

The long corset: this supported the breasts, covered the hips and was laced up the back.

Period: 1820s.

The demi-corset: eight to ten inches long with light whalebones, worn by day for domestic duties.

Period: 1820s.

The short corset: metal-bound eyelet holes were introduced to the back-lacing. "Stays are bound with iron in the holes through which the laces are drawn, so as to bear the tremendous tugging which is intended to reduce so important a part of the human frame to a third of its natural proportion" (1828).

Period: 1867.

The glove-fitting corset: front fastened, held by a spring latch; front fastening for all corsets of a better quality became usual after ca. 1851.

Period: 1899.

The skeleton corset: a belt corset with a few crossed straps. In the course of the 19th century, despite the attempts of reformers to abolish tight corsetry, it was not unusual, as in *Harpers Bazaar* for 1870, to see illustrations of corsets for children as young as one to two years alongside formidable adult versions. Training corsets pre-figured training bras by over a century.

Period: 20th century onwards.

Corsetry of the rigid variety gradually disappeared, though boning was found in **brassières** and **swimwear**; elasticated corsets were called **girdles**.

See Corset cover, Stays, Swanbill corset.

Corset cover

(F)

Period: 19th and early 20th centuries.

The corset was sandwiched between two washable layers – the chemise or shift worn next to the body, and the corset cover which was worn over the corset and under a blouse, bodice or dress. Usually shaped to fit smoothly over the corset, there were many variants, from high-necked to off-the-shoulder; they also came in sets with matching petticoats.

Corsican necktie

(M)

Period: 1830s.

See Napoleon necktie.

Cosmetics

(F, occasionally M)

Period: 17th century onwards.

A preparation which beautifies or enhances the body, face and hair; often used specifically to describe potions and powders for the face and bosom in the earlier period. By the 20th century cosmetics included a wide range of preparations, e.g. foundation, powder, eye shadow, rouge, lipstick in many colours, suited to different skins and made by many different companies throughout the world.

See Ceruse, Pomatum.

Cossacks

(M)

Period: 1814–ca. 1850.

Trousers pleated into a waistband and tied round the ankles with a ribbon drawstring. Inspired by the Cossacks accompanying Tsar Alexander I of Russia at the Peace celebrations of 1814. At first very baggy, but becoming less so in 1820, when the drawstrings were usually omitted; double straps under the instep were added in 1830 and from ca. 1840 a single strap, when the garment began to be called simply "pleated trousers".

Costume

(F)

Period: ca. 1800 onwards.

Clothing suitable for a specific event or time of year; usually applied to fashionable dress.

Period: 1860s–1890s.

A dressmaker's term denoting a day dress of one cloth designed for outdoor activities; by 1868 also applied to afternoon dresses with long trains.

Period: 1890s onwards.

A term used to describe a jacket and skirt, rather than a **suit**.

(F & M)

Period: 19th century onwards.

A term used to indicate the appearance, i.e. clothing, hairstyle and other decorations, which distinguished a particular class, nation or historic period. Thus "costume collections" and "costume history".

Also used to denote the theatrical clothing worn by performers in order to represent a character in a ballet, opera or play, and in the 20th century on film or TV.

Costume jewellery

(F, occasionally M)

Period: 20th century onwards.

The term was first used in the *New Yorker* magazine in 1933. There had been much earlier experiments with glass, non-precious metals, such as pinchbeck and Berlin ironwork, and paste, but it was only when designers saw how well innovative jewellery could be used that it became important. So it is jewellery designed and made to complement a specific fashion but using non-precious materials, such as beads, perspex, wood, etc. and it often marks a partnership between fashion designer and jewellery designer.

Costume rasterre

(F)

Period: 1870s.

A walking dress of which the skirt just brushed the ground.

Costumière

(F)

Period: Late 19th and early 20th centuries.

A **dressmaker** given a quasi-French connection; a marketing term to attract customers who wanted the latest French designs.

Cote, cotte

(F & M)

Period: 14th and 15th centuries.

A French term used in English for a garment worn over the **chemise** and below the **robe**. Women's cotes were laced at the centre front of the bodice and had short sleeves to which more elaborate false sleeves could be attached. The male cote lost its importance towards the end of the 14th century but was revived as a tighter inner robe ca. 1480.

See Coat.

Cote-hardie, cote-hardy

Period: 14th and 15th centuries.

(M)

The cote-hardie was probably a close-fitting, knee-length overgarment buttoned down the front to a low waist with elbow-length sleeves with a tongue-shaped extension behind. After ca. 1350 the garment short-ened and the elbow flap lengthened into a long, narrow, hanging band known as a "tippet". Tippets and skirts were often dagged. A belt was worn at hip-level.

(F)

A garment with the modesty of the robe allied to the tight bodice of the cote; however it lacked the cote's visible front lacing, but did have matching long sleeves.

Cothurnus

(M)

Period: Greco-Roman.

A thick-soled boot, usually reaching to mid-calf; the height of the sole could be up to 12 inches. It was worn by tragedians in late-period Hellenistic and Roman drama. It was supposedly invented by Sophocles (ca. 496–406 BCE) but this seems unlikely.

See Buskins.

Cottage bonnet

(F)

Period: 1808–1870s.

A close-fitting straw bonnet, the brim projecting beyond the cheeks. Modified through these decades and in the 1870s the brim was rolled upwards and there was a lining of pleated satin.

Cottage front

(F)

Period: 1800–1820.

A day bodice made with a gap in front and fastened by lacing across from one edge to the other over a **habit shirt**.

Couched

Period: Medieval.

Trimmed or embroidered.

Coudières

See Tippet, Cote-hardie.

Counter-fillet

(F)

Period: Late 14th and early 15th centuries.

The **fillet** securing the **veil**.

Courrèges boots

(F)

Period: 1960s.

A simplified style of flat boot with open sections just below the top edge; often white and made from plain or patent leather. Designed and manufactured to complement the clothing of the French designer André Courrèges (b. 1923).

Court dress

(F & M)

Period: Medieval onwards.

All cultures within which a hierarchical system obtained and usually required certain styles of clothing to be worn in the presence of the ruler. This both upheld the status quo and provided custom for those clothing the ruling elite and their immediate circle, and encouraged indus-tries such as lace making, silk weaving, etc. Regulations about what was to be worn, according to the status of the wearer, were usually written down and provided guidance for those attending court occasions and for those who made the garments. The provision of this specialist clothing was usually divided between court dressmakers, whose clientele might include royal and elite women, and tailors and robemakers who made formal and state robes and the suits and uniforms for elite men.

Courtepy

(F & M)

Period: 14th and 15th centuries.

An upper garment akin to a coat or cloak; of a thick or rough fabric. The male garment was often described as short.

Court shoe

(F)

Period: 20th century onwards.

A plain, low fronted shoe with a medium to high heel, occasionally with some decoration at the front; a **clas-sic style** of footwear.

Also, and earlier, a shoe worn at court as part of the required dress or uniform.

Coutenance, countenance

(F & M)

A Lady in full Dress for the Drawing Room, in June 1777

This **fashion plate** shows "full dress for the Drawing Room", in other words, **court dress**. The woman's elevated hair would have needed false hair to provide such bulk and height; the cap perched on it is a **dormouse** with the **lappets** pendant rather than tied under the chin. The closed robe is worn over a **hoop** and has a long **train**. The deep sleeve **ruffles** are of **lace** and probably matched the lappets, 1777. Copyright the Olive Matthews Collection, Chertsey Museum.

Period: Late 16th and early 17th centuries.
A small **muff**. "A snuff kin or muffe" (1611, Cotgrave).

Couture
(F)
Period: 20th century onwards.
A French term meaning sewing or needlework which was applied to the design and making of fashionable women's clothing. "Haute couture" is descriptive of the work of the most celebrated and skilful fashion designers.

Couturier, couturière
(M & F)
Period: 20th century onwards.
The French terms for the man or (couturière) woman whose output is described as "haute couture"; in English- language countries the term "fashion designer" is often preferred.

Coverchief
(F)
Period: Medieval–16th century.
The Norman term for the Saxon **head rail** or **veil**. A draped head-covering, made of various fabrics and colours and varying in size, worn by all classes but largely discarded by the higher ranks from the 15th century or worn with other head-dresses. In the 13th century coverchiefs worn by royalty or nobles were of silk or cloth of gold.

Covert coat, cover coat
(M)
Period: 1880s onwards.
A short, **fly-fronted** overcoat with strapped seams, made with a whole back, no centre back vent, but short vents in the side seams. Popular "with horsey young gentlemen" and at first designed for riding, but soon adopted for general wear. In 1897 made with **Raglan sleeves** and known as a "Raglan Covert".
Period: Late 20th century.
In the late 20th century worn by young men characterized as "young fogies", i.e. traditionalists in dress and social attributes but unusually young for such tastes.

Cowboy styles
(M, sometimes F)
Period: 1950s onwards.
Items of working clothing worn by American cowboys, such as **bandanas**, hats, shirts, **jeans** and boots. These were bought and worn by non-cowboys or influenced fashion designers, who produced versions of some of these items. The boots with their Cuban heels, pointed toes and decorative leather have become a design **classic**.

Cowl
(M, later F)
Period: Medieval onwards.
Originally descriptive of the collar or hood of a monk or friar's habit, designed to cover the head and shoulders; differing according to the particular religious order.
Later applied to a style of enlarged, softly draped collar on dresses, jumpers, etc.

Coxcomb, cockscomb
(M)
Period: Late 16th and early 17th centuries.
A professional fool's hood with its apex in the shape of a cock's comb.

Cracowes, crakows, crawcaws
(F & M)
Period: 1360, 1390–1410, 1450–1480.
Long **piked shoes**, later called **poulaines**.
Cran
(M)
Period: 1830s onwards.
The V-shaped gap between the turned-over collar and
the lapel of a coat.
Crants, craunce, graundice
(F)
Period: Medieval to late 18th century; occasionally 19th
century.
A **chaplet** or garland of flowers or of goldsmith's work
and gems. "The Funeral Crants" was a symbolic garland
carried at the funeral of a virgin (Hamlet, V, i). These were
sometimes made of paper flowers and a framework of
linen or iron to which the flowers, real or sham, were
attached. Subsequently the Crants were hung over the
deceased's seat in church or chancel, together with her
collar, girdle and one white glove.
Cravat
(M)
Period: 1660 to late 18th century.
A neckcloth of lawn, muslin or silk, folded round the
neck, the ends tied in a knot or bow in front, first mentioned in 1643.

Period: 19th century onwards.
The cravat was often starched and supported on a
"stiffener". From ca. 1840 the large form covering the
shirt-front above the waistcoat was called a scarf, the
smaller a **necktie**. From the later 19th century onwards
it was worn infrequently and coloured and patterned silk
versions were associated with informality.

(F)
Period: From 1830s onwards.
Worn with sporting clothing such as **riding habits**.
Cravate cocodes
(F)
Period: 1863.
A large bow cravat worn with a **habit shirt** and stand
collar.
Cravat strings
(M)
Period: 1665–1680s.
A length of coloured ribbon passed round the two ends
of the cravat and tied in a bow under the chin. Later it
was often a made-up stiffened bow with several loops,
fixed on behind the cravat which was loosely tied, the
ends falling over the centre of the bow.
Crepine, crepyn, crippen, crespine
Period: 16th and 17th centuries.
A crimped or pleated frill. "Crespine, the crepine of a

French hood" (1611, Cotgrave). The word "crepine"
was revived at the beginning of the 16th century; spelt
in 1532 "crispyne", apparently a crimped fabric.
Crêve-coeur
(F)
Period: End of 17th century.
Curled locks at the nape of the neck.
Crewel cap
(M)
Period: 17th century.
"The crewel cap is knit like hose
For them whose zeale takes cold i"th" nose;
Whose purity doth judge it meete
To clothe alike both head and feete" (ca. 1620, *The
Ballad of the Cap*).
Crew neck
(F & M)
Period: 20th century onwards.
The high, round, close-fitting neckline of a garment, usu-
ally associated with **jumpers** or **sweaters**. Originally an
American term.
Cricket shoes
See Spiked shoes.
Crinolette
(F)
Period: 1868–ca. 1873.
A small form of **cage crinoline** hooped behind only;
"of steel half hoops with horsehair or crinoline flounces
forming a bustle".
Crinolette petticoat
(F)
Period: 1870 revived 1883.
A petticoat plain in front, with half-circle steel hoops
round the upper part behind and flounces below.
Crinoline
(F)
Period: 1829 onwards.
Originally a term for a textile which by 1840 was made of
horsehair warp and wool weft and used for making stiff
under-petticoats to expand the skirt. The textile quickly
became synonymous with the actual petticoat. In 1856
the **artificial crinoline** or **cage petticoat** appeared
with whalebone hoops added, replaced in 1857 by
watch-spring hoops.
Henceforth the name crinoline was applied to this
cage petticoat. The number of hoops varied and also
the shape; in 1857–9 it was domed, then pyramidal.
By 1862 the size began to diminish; in 1866 the front
became flat and the back projected, merging by 1868
into the **crinolette**. Named varieties included **cage-
Américaine**, **cage empire**, **ondina**, **panier** and
sansflectum.
Crinoline hat
(F)

Period: 20th century.

A broad-brimmed hat made from crin, a mixture of horsehair and vegetable fibre, or also from the fibres of a palm, the *crin végétal*.

Crisp
(F)

Period: 16th century.

A **veil**.

Period: 17th century.

A curl of hair.

Crispin
(M)

Period: 1839.

A cloak for evening dress; with very large floating sleeves, lined with silk, wadded and quilted.

(F)

Period: 1842.

A short mantle, occasionally sleeved, fitting close round the neck, with a small **pelerine**. Cut on the cross, made of cashmere, satin or velvet, and often wadded.

Crispin cloche
(F)

Period: 1842.

A bell-shaped **crispin**, knee-length.

Crochet

Period: 14th century.

A hook; by the 15th century used for fastening a shoe.

Period: 16th and 17th centuries.

Attached at the waist of a woman's dress for suspending a pomander. The crochet was often an article of jewellery.

Crochet work

Period: 19th century onwards.

A type of knitting using a hooked needle and cotton thread or wool.

Crocs
(F & M)

Period: 2002 onwards.

Moulded plastic clogs worn for sailing and other leisure and work activities.

See Deck shoes.

Cromwell collar
(F)

Period: 1880s.

A deep turn-over collar, the front nearly meeting edge to edge. Worn with morning dress.

Cromwell shoes
(F)

Period: 1868.

Leather shoes with a large buckle and tongue covering the instep. "The favourite for croquet parties." Revived in 1888 as a day shoe with high-cut front and a large bow. Also worn in the early 20th century.

Crop
(M)

Period: 17th century onwards.

Term denoting short, as in **crop-doublet** (1640) and "crop-scratch wig" (1806). "The Bedford Crop", a style of short hair favoured by the Duke of Bedford and his political friends in the 1790s, was a protest against the tax on hair powder.

(F)

Period: 1950 onwards.

A short, boyish style of haircut favoured by women.

Crop-doublet
(M)

Period: 1610.

A short-waisted **doublet**.

Croquet boots
(F)

Period: 1865.

Boots of morocco leather often with fancy toe-caps and side springs and described as "rising to a point in front and back with tassels, and laced with coloured ribbons".

Crosscloth, forehead cloth
(F)

Period: 16th and 17th centuries.

A triangular piece of fabric worn with a **coif** or **caul**, its straight border over the forehead, with the point behind; tied on under the chin or at the back of the head. Often embroidered to match the coif with which it was worn.

(F & M)

Period: 16th–18th century.

Plain crosscloths worn in illness or in bed to prevent wrinkles. "Many weare such cross-clothes or forehead cloathes as our women use when they are sicke" (1617, Fynes Moryson).

See frontlet.

Cross-dressing
(M)

Period: 18th century onwards.

Although the adoption of female clothing by men can be traced back much further, especially in the performing arts, this pattern of behaviour is identified and commented upon more openly from this period onwards.

Cross-gartering
(M)

Period: ca. 1550 to early 17th century.

A manner of wearing a sash garter placed below the knee in front, the ends crossed behind the knee and brought forward to be tied in a bow above the knee, either centrally or on the outer side. Common with stockings worn over **canions**.

Cross pocket

Period: 18th and 19th centuries.

A pocket with a horizontal opening.

Cruches

(F)

Period: Late 17th century.

Small forehead curls.

Cuban heels

(F & M)

Period: ca. 1904 onwards.

A sturdy, stacked, leather heel, reasonably straight and medium high. Male use is often associated with boots or shoes that add height.

Cue

Period: 18th century.

An English variant of the French term **queue**; the pendant tail of a **wig**. It first appeared as a civilian fashion ca. 1720.

Cue-peruke

Period: 18th century.

A **wig** with a **cue**.

Cuff, cuffe

(F & M)

Period: 15th century onwards.

A variant of the medieval English term "coffe", this is the turned-back part, actual or sham, of the sleeve of a garment so as to give an extra cover to the wrist, either for warmth or ornament. Originally it could be turned down over the hand, for warmth. A fur cuff was frequently added to women's gowns in the 15th century.

Men's cuffs have more usually been a feature of display, such as the detachable lace cuff in the form of a reversed funnel-shape, commonly worn with a falling-band from the mid-16th to mid-17th centuries, or a ruff. "Holland to make yor Lordship Cuffes…1 laced ruff and 2 payer of Cuffes" (1632, Viscount Scudamore Accounts at Holme Lacy). Replaced later by the ruffled end of the shirt or chemise sleeve.

The cuff of the man's coat sleeve became a striking feature in the 18th century until ca. 1770, the cuff being either open behind, up to ca. 1750, or closed and known as a closed cuff.

See Boot cuff, à la marinière cuff.

The closed cuff of the 1750s was wide and winged, falling away from the sleeve on the outer side; it gradually diminished, becoming small and close by ca. 1770. In the 19th century the male **French cuff** and female **Amadis sleeve** were popular styles.

In the 20th century the rolled back or turned back cuff, either held by a button or informally positioned, became a feature of summer clothing for both men and women.

Cuff-button, sleeve button, cuff link

Period: Late 17th century onwards.

Two discs, usually of metal, connected by a link, used to close the vent in the wristband of a shirt; replacing the earlier **cuff strings**. "A Cuff Button with a Diamond…" (1684, *London Gazette*). "Four Turkey Stone Sleeve Buttons set in Gold and Enamell'd" (1686, *London Gazette*).

The term "Links" is mentioned in Aris' *Birmingham Gazette,*1788. Cuff strings, however, remained in general use until the 19th century when a small mother-of-pearl button at the base of the cuff served to close it. Cuff links, often jewelled, inserted close to the edge of the cuff, so as to be visible, became fashionable ca. 1840. By the 20th century many variants of cuff link were made, from the jewelled to the knotted silk or thread ones.

Cuffie, cuff

(F & M)

Period: 14th century.

A term for a **cap** or **coif**.

Cuff string, sleeve string

(M)

Period: 17th–19th century.

The tie for the shirt sleeve at the wrist. "A pr. of cuffs strings" (1688, James Masters' Expense Book),

Cuirasse bodice

(F)

Period: 1874.

A very long, tight day bodice, boned, descending over the hips; often made of a different fabric from the dress, the sleeves matching the trimming. "It moulds the figure to perfection."

Cuirasse tunic

(F)

Period: 1874.

A plain, tight tunic worn with a **cuirasse bodice**.

Cuker

(F)

Period: 15th century.

Part of the horned head-dress.

'She is hornyd like a kowe…for syn

The cukar hynges so side now, Furrid with a cat skyn" (c. 1460, *The Towneley Mysteries*, Surtees Soc.).

Culottes

(F)

Period: Early 20th century onwards.

Term taken from the French meaning breeches and applied to divided skirts worn by women; usually full enough to suggest a skirt rather than knee breeches.

Cumberland corset

(M)

Period: 1815–1820s.

Corset worn by the fashionable dandies. "Ordered a pair of Cumberland corsets with whalebone back" (1818, *Diary of a Dandy*).

Cumberland hat, hat à la William Tell

(M)

Period: 1830s.

A tall hat with an 8-inch crown tapering upwards and a narrow brim turned up at the sides.

Cummerbund

(F & M)

Period: 17th to late 19th century.

A type of **sash** or **girdle** worn around the waist; from the Anglo-Indian term.

Period: 1893 onwards.

A wide sash of coloured silk or drill wound twice round the body by men in lieu of a waistcoat, and fastened on one side sometimes by ornamental buttons, or tucked in. Worn at first as a black waistband with evening dress; later, as coloured sash by day in the summer. In the 20th century a feature of evening dress in black or colours.

Cupee

(F)

Period: 17th century.

"A pinner that hangs close to the head" (1690, Evelyn, *Mundus Muliebris*).

Cupola coat

(F)

Period: 1710–1780.

Contemporary name for a **bell hoop** or **petticoat**. A domed, hooped petticoat distended with whalebone or cane hoops to the fashionable size. "The cupola-coat allows all the freedom of motion…the compass of the coat serves to keep the men at a decent distance and appropriates to every lady a spacious verge sacred to herself" (1747, *Whitehall Evening Post*).

Curricle cloak

(F)

Period: 1801–1806.

A half- or three-quarter-length cloak shaped in at the waist, the front borders curving away from midline; edged with lace or fur.

Curricle coat

(F)

Period: 1808.

A long coat with lapels, fastened at the bosom only, then sloping away towards the back. Very long sleeves. Sometimes called a "gig coat" in the 1820s.

(M)

Period: 1840s.

New name for the **box coat** or driving coat, with one or more capes.

Curricle dress

(F)

Period: 1794–1803.

A **round dress** worn with an over-tunic or **half robe**, usually of net. The tunic short-sleeved, open in front, and thigh-length; the low neck sometimes filled in with a **habit shirt**.

Curricle pelisse

(F)

Period: 1820s.

A **pelisse** with three capes.

Cushionet, quissionet

(F)

Period: 1560–1630s.

A form of **bustle** worn with a **farthingale** to give it an upward tilt at the back. "A varingale and quissionet of fustian in Apres" (1566, Will of Wm. Claxton of Burnehall).

Cushion head-dress

A 19th-century term for the circular padded roll worn by women in the first half of 15th century.

See Chaplet.

Cutaway coat

(M)

Period: 1876.

"Formerly called the Newmarket."

See Newmarket coat.

Cut-fingered gloves

(F & M)

Period: End of 16th century.

The fingers of the glove were slashed to reveal the underlying rings:

"But he must cut his glove to show his pride
That his trim jewel might be better spy'd" (1597, Hall's *Satire*, IV).

Period: ca. 1700–1750.

The tips of the fingers were cut open, a fashion confined to women. "Half a dozen of cut-fingered gloves" (1719, Earl of Thanet Accounts, Kent Record Office). "2 pair of fine white thread gloves that are open-fingered" (1740, Purefoy Accounts).

Cut-fingered pumps

(M)

Period: 16th century.

Pumps slashed over the toes. "'Tis as good to goe in cut-finger'd pumps as corke shoes, if one wear Cornish diamonds on his toes" (1591, T. Nashe, Introduction to Sidney's *Astrophel and Stella*).

Cut-in, check

(M)

Period: 19th and early 20th centuries.

The more or less horizontal cut-back of the cloth of a dress coat at the level of the waist.

Cut-out dress

(F)

Period: 1960s onwards.

A term for a dress on which a cut-out section forms part of the design, e.g. a circle on the midriff to reveal the flesh beneath.

Cut steel buttons

(M)

Period: ca. 1770 onwards.

Buttons of steel, the face chased and polished.

Cut-wig

(M)

Period: 18th century.

A small plain **wig** without a **queue**.

Cut-work, dagging

Period: ca. 1340–1440.

The ornamental cutting in fantastic shapes, such as flames, leaves, etc., of the edges of fashionable garments; introduced, according to the Chronicle of St Albans, ca. 1346.

Period: 16th and 17th centuries.

Decoration made by cutting out portions of the fabric and crossing the spaces with geometrical designs in **needlework**. "White woorkes, alias cutwoorkes made beyond the seas."

Found in Italy ca. 1579, but by 1620 also in England.

Cyber fashion

(F & M)

Period: 1960s onwards.

The origins of this can be traced back to the superheroes in comic books of the 1930s, Superman for instance, and later, in the 1960s, space travel as depicted in a film like *Barbarella* (1967) or the *Star Trek* series of a year earlier. However, the term "cyber" when used for clothing is now associated with futuristic concepts, virtual reality and a technological alternative world and is much influenced by computer games and films.

Cyclas, ciclaton, cinglaton

(F & M)

Period: 13th century.

A rich gown worn on ceremonial occasions, e.g. at the coronation of Henry III and his Queen.

See Glossary of Fabrics and Materials.

Cycling pants, cycling shorts

(F & M)

Period: 1980s onwards.

Figure-hugging legwear, made of Lycra or spandex; designed to assist speed for professional cyclists, but also worn by amateurs.

D

Dag, dagges, dagging, jags, jagging

(F & M)

Period: 14th to late 15th centuries.

Dagging was introduced ca. 1346; it was also called **cut-work**. The term applied to the slashing of any border of a garment into tongues, scallops, leaves or **vandykes**, called "dagges", as a form of decoration.

Dalk

Period: ca. 1000 to late 15th century.

Usually a pin, but also a brooch clasp or buckle.

Dalmatic

(M)

Period: ca. 300 CE onwards.

A long, T-shaped, tunic-like garment with wide sleeves and a slit at either side of the skirt. Possibly derived from the classical tunic, it was worn as an ecclesiastical vestment and by rulers on solemn occasions such as coronations.

Dandizette

Period: 1816–1820.

The female **dandy** conspicuous for her **Grecian bend**; the name did not survive more than a few years.

Dandy

(M)

Period: ca. 1816 onwards.

A name for an exquisitely fashionable man, as represented by Lord Petersham. "The made up male doll who, when wig, dyed whiskers, stiff cravat, padded breast, paint and perfume are taken away, sinks into nothing" (*The Hermit in London,* ed. 1822).

By 1829 "Dandy has been voted vulgar and Beau is now all the word" (Disraeli, *The Young Duke*).

Count D'Orsay was described as "The last of the Dandies" whose logical heirs were the **heavy swell** of the 1860s, and the **masher** of the 1880s and 1890s.

Danish trousers, open bottom trousers

(M)

Period: 1870s.

For boys; the legs reaching just below the knees and the bottoms open; worn with a jacket.

Dannock

(M)

Period: 19th century.

"Dannocks, Darnocks, hedgers' gloves" (Forby, *Vocabulary of East Anglia,* ca. 1825).

Dart

A narrow, dart-shaped piece cut out and the edges sewn together to improve the fit of a garment. **Fish** was the corresponding term applied to male garments until the mid-19th century.

Davy Crockett cap, Davy Crockett hat

(M, occasionally F)

Period: ca. 1955.

The great success of the TV and film versions of several Davy Crockett stories based on the life of the 19th century American fur-trapper and scout led to huge demands for fur hats like those worn by the hero. The original was raccoon, circled the head, and had a tail pendant at the back, but fashionable copies were made of any fur, real or synthetic, that looked like the original.

Day dress
(F)

Period: Late 19th century onwards.

Term which describes any and every sort of dress or suit worn in the daytime rather than the evening. Early in the 20th century there were still many variants meeting the need to change two or three times, after World War II one type of daytime outfit, often literally a dress or **frock**, might suffice.

D-B

Period: 18th century onwards.

Tailor's term for double-breasted, the front of a coat or jacket which has sufficient fabric to overlap and allow two vertical sets of buttons.

Death's head button
(M)

Period: 18th century.

A domed button covered with a thread of metal twist or mohair, forming a pattern of four quarters.

Deck shoes
(M, occasionally F)

Period: Late 19th century onwards.

A shoe which does not slip on the deck of a boat or ship. In the UK deck shoes were similar to plimsolls – flat, rubber-soled canvas shoes – and could be bought for 12s 6d in 1879. However, the 20th-century versions are those developed in North America – lightweight, quick-drying shoes with slip-resistant soles and leather uppers, often two tones in colour, lacing through two holes on each side, and with a decorative lace encircling the upper around the sides and back. In 2002 the brightly coloured plastic shoes known as **Crocs** were invented, in America, to be a comfortable shoe for sailing and other activities and were hugely successful.

Décolletage
(F)

Period: 1890s onwards.

The low neckline of a woman's dress; the exposure of neck and shoulders, at first for evening wear but later for beach wear and similar during the 20th century.

Deconstructionists
(F)

Period: 1990s onwards.

Term applied to a group of European designers who experimented with drab fabrics, exposed zips, and seemingly unfinished seams and so forth, thereby challenging ideas about the role of design and fashion in the construction of clothing. They were much influenced by the innovative Japanese designers who emerged in the 1980s.

Deer stalker
(M)

Period: 1860s onwards.

A tweed cap with ear-flaps worn tied together over the crown; for country wear. It became internationally known as a result of the illustrations by Sidney Paget (1860–1908) for the Sherlock Holmes stories.

Delphos dress, Delphos gown
(F)

Period: ca. 1907–ca. 1950.

A style of dress created by the Spanish artist and designer Mariano Fortuny (1871–1949). It paid homage to the simplicity of **classical dress**, using a method of pleating thin silk, which was patented in Paris in 1909, and weighting and holding the dress together with thin cords and glass beads. The silk was coloured with natural dyes. These dresses were worn by artists, musicians and performers as a form of artistic or **aesthetic dress** and enjoyed a revival when they became desirable acquisitions for collectors in the 1970s and later.

Demi-castor
(F & M)

Period: 17th and early 18th centuries.

A **beaver hat** made partly of coney (rabbit fur) and therefore considered inferior to the **castor**.

Demiceint, demysent, dymyson girdle, demi-girdle, demison
(F)

Period: ca. 1450–ca. 1550.

A **girdle** with front ornamentation only. "A half girdle or one whose forepart is of gold or silver and hinder of silk" (1611, Cotgrave).

Demi-coronal
(F & M)

Period: 16th and early 17th centuries.

A tiara, i.e. half a **coronet**; a half-sized coronal.

Demi-gigot sleeve
(F)

Period: 1825–1830; also 1891.

A sleeve full at the shoulder, narrowing to the elbow, thence tight to the wrist.

Demi-gown
(M)

Period: Late 15th and 16th centuries.

A short gown, especially popular from 1500–1560; often worn on horseback. "My short rydinge gown of worsett" (1548, *Wills and Inventories of Northern Counties*).

Demi-habillement, half-robe, half-gown
(F)

Period: 1794–ca. 1800.

A low-necked, thigh-length **tunic** with short sleeves, worn over a **round gown** and pulled in at the waist by a narrow ribbon belt.

Demi-riding coat
See Just-au-corps.

Demi-sleeve, demi-maunch

(M)

Period: 16th century.

A wide sleeve ending at the elbow.

Demi-surtout

(M)

Period: 1818.

A light, fitting **overcoat** with a low collar.

Demob suit

(M)

Period: 1945–1947.

Although British soldiers were issued with a civilian suit when they left the army after World War I, it was only after World War II that the term "demob suit" was widely used. The suits were conservative in cut, using various standard designs and cloths, and some non-**Utility** features were offered, such as flaps on side pockets, an outside breast pocket and cuff buttons.

Demysent

See Demiceint.

Denmark cock

(M)

Period: ca. 1750–1800.

A **tricorne hat** with its brim "cocked", i.e. turned up high at the back and lower in front.

Department store

Period: 1840 onwards.

An enlarged shop within which various sections or departments specialized in distinct and different types of goods. Department stores concerned with appearance would contain all aspects of clothing and toiletries for men, women and children, carefully demarcated.

See Liberty & Co.

Derby

(M)

Period: 1860s onwards.

An American name for the **bowler** hat.

Period: 1890s.

A **necktie** usually called a **four-in-hand**; the tie was straight-sided with a slightly narrower centre and one end longer than the other; tied in a knot presenting a free edge above and below.

Derby shoe

(M)

Period: Late 19th century onwards.

A variant of the **Oxford shoe**.

Déshabillé, dishabille

Period: 1713–19th century.

Dressed in a negligent or careless manner or a style of dress indicative of such casual attitudes. "We have a kind of sketch of dress, if I may so call it, among us, which as the invention was foreign, is call'd a Dishabille. Everything is thrown on with a loose careless air" (Sept. 1713, *The Guardian*).

Period: Late 19th century.

A term meaning an **undress** style for wearing on informal occasions.

Designer labels, designer logos

Period: Mid-19th century onwards.

An identifying mark of a maker or designer; within clothing this was often a small, unseen label with the name of the firm and possibly an abbreviated address and/or city.

See Label.

In the late 20th century the discreet label was also accompanied by the outer signifying "logo" – printed initials, interlocked initials, patterns exclusive to a particular maker or designer which, supposedly, guaranteed authenticity.

Detachable sleeves

(M)

Period: 15th and 16th centuries.

Doublet sleeves which might be tied to the arm-hole by **points** (ties) and were removable at will.

(F)

Separate sleeves were made for partlets.

Dettingen cock

(M)

Period: 18th century.

A **tricorne hat** with high equal cocks, front and back.

Dhoti

(M)

Period: 20th century.

A **loin cloth** worn by Hindus, associated in western minds with the late Mahatma Ghandi (1869–1948). A long, cotton cloth wound around the body, passed between the thighs and tucked under the waistband at the back of the waist. Known in the west since the early 17th century.

Diadem

(F & M)

Period: Medieval onwards.

A crown or a headband, plain or jewelled, worn as a mark of sovereignty.

Also a wreath of flowers and/or leaves worn as a mark of distinction.

Diadem bonnet

(F)

Period: 1869.

A bonnet of lace and velvet forming an upright diadem above the forehead; tied on by a ribbon passing under the **chignon** and ruched strings loosely knotted under the chin.

Diadem comb

(F)

Period: 1830s.

A wide, curved comb with a high, ornamental gallery in the shape of a diadem; worn as a head decoration with evening dress.

Diadem fanchon bonnet

(F)

Period: 1869.

A shallow border, 1 inch wide, covered with tulle or ruching, trimmed with an **aigrette** of feathers or flowers; short, ruched lappets fastened in front under a satin bow beneath the chin.

Diana Vernon bonnet

(F)

Period: 1879.

A large bonnet with low crown and wide brim.)

Diana Vernon hat

(F)

Period: 1859.

A straw hat with shallow crown, the brim wide in front and curved up on one side; with rosettes and broad ribbon strings placed under the brim. For country or seaside wear.

Dickey, dicky

(F)

Period: Late 18th and early 19th centuries.

A woman's under-petticoat.

(M)

Period: 19th century.

A shirt-front with attached collar, of starched linen, worn over a flannel shirt. Known at the end of the 18th century as a "Tommy". "Never worn by a gentleman" (1840) but only by "a Two-shirts-and-a-dicky sort of man" (Surtees).

The term was also used for a shirt collar in America and, regionally, as a covering to protect clothing in every form from a leather **apron** to a child's **bib**.

Diffusion line

Period: 20th century onwards.

A term for a less expensive line produced by a well-known designer or brand.

Dildo

(M)

Period: Late 17th and 18th centuries.

A sausage-shaped curl of a **wig**.

Dinner jacket, dress lounge

(M)

Period: ca. 1888 onwards.

Introduced as "dress lounge" in 1888, the term "dinner jacket" was used from 1898 on. A jacket for informal evening wear; at first with a continuous roll collar and lapels turning low to waist-level; faced to the edge with silk or satin. One or two buttons, but always worn open. From 1898 one button only. The back cut whole, sleeves finished with cuffs. It was made in various fabrics, such as cheviot, corkscrew or velvet.

In the 20th century known colloquially as a DJ or "penguin suit".

See Tuxedo.

Directoire bonnet

(F)

Period: 1878–1880.

A square, moderately high-crowned bonnet, the brim fitting over the ears, spreading out above the forehead.

Directoire coat

(F)

Period: 1888.

The bodice of a day dress in the form of a double or single-breasted coat cut across horizontally above the waist-line in front, falling vertically at the sides and from a gathering at the back of the waist, to the ankles. Tight sleeves with cuffs. Worn with a wide, folded sash round the waist. If double-breasted worn with a **habit shirt**; if single-breasted, worn open with a **shirt** blouse.

Directoire hat

(F)

Period: 1888.

Similar to the **directoire bonnet** but larger.

Directoire jacket

(F)

Period: 1888.

A similar bodice of a day dress but without the skirt portion of the **directoire coat**.

Directoire skirt

(F)

Period: 1895.

A day skirt made with seven gores, the four at the back being fluted. It was lined and stiffened with horsehair and measured thirteen to eighteen feet round the hem.

Directoire styles

(F)

Period: Late 1880s–ca. 1910.

The revival of directoire styles was inspired by Sardou's drama *La Tosca,* as played by the French actress Sarah Bernhardt in 1887. The narrow, sleek lines and higher waistline recalled the fashions worn in France in the last years of the 18th century, though the corsetry and silhouette was unmistakeably of the later time.

Directoire swallow-tail coat

(F)

Period: 1888.

The back of a **directoire coat**, cut into tails with a deep central vent between; an afternoon dress style.

Dirndl

(F)

Period: 20th century onwards.

The fitted bodice and full gathered skirt, usually decorated with colourful folk embroidery and applied braids associated with Alpine peasant styles. A variant of this style became identified with ideals of German womanhood during the Third Reich.

Dishabille

See Déshabillé.

Dittos

(M)

Period: Mid-18th century.

Term denoting a suit of one cloth throughout.

Divided skirt

(F)

Period: 1882.

Introduced by Lady Harberton, President of The Rational Dress Society; this was a short, kilted skirt cut so that when the wearer was standing still the division of the two legs was concealed. Worn for bicycling.

See Culottes.

Divorce corset

(F)

Period: 1816.

A padded metal triangle, the point of which projected up between the breasts to thrust them apart.

Doctor Martens, 'Doc' Martens, DMs

(M, later F)

Period: 1960 onwards.

Originally a substantial walking boot with a cushioned sole, worn by workers who needed comfortable, protective footwear. It was the result of collaboration between Dr Klaus Maertens of Munich, who invented the cushioned sole, and R. Griggs & Co. Ltd of Northampton. The original boot was made of smooth, oxblood-red leather with eight sets of lace-holes, a black sole and yellow welt stitching. Once they were discovered by skinheads and **punks** in the 1960s and 1970s they evolved into an **alternative fashion**, with the range and colours enlarged.

Doctor Scholl's

See Scholl's.

Dog collar

(M)

Period: 1860s.

A plain, shallow stand collar encircling the neck and overlapping in front. A successor to the **all-rounder**. Later, the name was given to the clerical collar buttoning behind.

Dolly Varden bonnet

(F)

Period: 1881 to early 20th century.

A wide-brimmed bonnet with wide ribbons crossing it to be tied under the chin. The name was taken from the heroine of Charles Dickens's novel, *Barnaby Rudge*, published in 1849 but set in the late 18th century.

Dolly Varden cap

(F)

Period: 1888.

"A little bit of gathered lace with puckered crown and a few short ribbons"; worn with a **teagown**.

Dolly Varden hat

(F)

Period: 1871–ca. 1875.

A straw hat with small, low crown and very wide brim; slight trimming of flowers or ribbon. Worn at a forward tilt and tied on by ribbon under the **chignon**.

Dolly Varden polonaise

(F)

Period: 1871.

A **polonaise** dress based on the polonaise gown of ca. 1780 but made of chintz or cretonne. Worn with a bright silk petticoat – plain, flowered or quilted. In winter the Dolly Varden might be of flannel or cashmere printed with a chintz pattern. A fashion popular amongst the middle classes.

Dolman

(F)

Period: 1870s and 1880s.

A **mantle** with a sleeve cut all in one, with the side piece and hanging loose; sometimes made in the form of a sling. In the **bustle** period the front had hanging mantlet ends and the back a full **basque** tied to form a puff over the bustle. A cape was sometimes added.

Dolmanette

(F)

Period: 1890s.

A crocheted **dolman** tied at the neck with a large ribbon bow; also "if liked, sew a ribbon at the back to tie round the waist".

Dolman sleeve

(F)

Period: 1930s onwards.

A sleeve cut all-in-one with the bodice almost to the waist, giving a deep arm-hole but narrowing into the wrist; also called a **batwing sleeve**.

Domino

(F)

Period: 17th century.

"A veil used by some women that mourn" (1611, Cotgrave).

(F & M)

Period: 18th century.

A lightweight, full-length cloak, often black, worn with a mask at masquerades in preference to choosing to wear an historical or other distinctive costume.

Donarière

(F)

Period: 1869.

A round hood with attached **pelerine** and sleeves; of quilted satin.

Doncaster riding coat

(M)

Period: 1850s.

A loose form of **Newmarket coat**.

Donkey jacket

(M)

Period: 20th century onwards.

A **fashion illustration** depicting a man in **masquerade dress** wearing a "French **Domino**", a **mask** and a **feather** at the front of his hat, ca. 1777. Copyright the Olive Matthews Collection, Chertsey Museum.

A sturdy, sometimes waterproof coat buttoned to the neck and worn by workmen. Appropriated by intellectuals and students from the 1950s onwards.

Donna Maria sleeve
(F)
Period: 1830s.
A day sleeve, immensely full from shoulder to wrist, but caught in by a loop along the inner side of the forearm from elbow to wrist.

Dorelet, dorlet
(F)
Period: Medieval.
A hair-net embroidered with jewels.

Dormeuse, dormouse, French night-cap
(F)
Period: ca. 1750–1800.

An indoor, undress, white day cap with a puffed-up crown and edged on each side with curving flaps trimmed with lace and called **wings**; popularly known as **cheek wrappers**. These wings curved back from the temples, leaving the forehead and front hair exposed. The crown was decorated with ribbon. In the 1770s the dormeuse was sometimes tied under the chin by **lappets** attached to the cap.

Dorothy bag
(F)
Period: Late 19th and early 20th centuries.
A drawstring bag made from fabric or soft leather and drawn closed with a ribbon or thin chain just below the top edge, leaving a short frill above.

D'Orsay coat
(M)
Period: 1838.
An overcoat in the form of a **pilot coat** but made to fit in at the waist by having a long **fish** or dart taken out below the arm-hole; plain sleeves with three or four buttons of horn or gambroon and a shallow collar. Slashed or flapped pockets in the skirts, but no pleats, folds or hip buttons; the skirts cut to hang over the knees.

Dorset thread button
Period: 18th century to ca. 1830.
A button made on a brass wire ring covered with white cotton threads radiating from the centre and kept flat. Used on underclothes from ca. 1700.

Double
Period: 16th century.
A term often denoting lined, e.g. "double gloves" meant lined gloves.

Double bouffant sleeve
(F)
Period: 1832–1836.
A short, puffed, evening-dress sleeve, the puffing divided into two by a transverse band.

Period: 1855.
Revived for day wear, the sleeve to the wrist and the puffs being unequal; the division made just above the wrist, with a lace ruffle added.

Double-breasted
(M, later F)
Period: 18th century onwards.
Describes a garment, usually a **coat** or **waistcoat**, which has an overlapping front panel allowing for two vertical rows of fastening with **buttons** or **frogs**.

Double ruff
(F & M)
Period: 1600–1650.
A **ruff** with a double row of flattened convolutions.

Double sleeve
(F)
Period: 1854; revived 1891.

A loose over-sleeve reaching half-way down the upper arm over a long, tight sleeve to the wrist; both made of the same fabric as the dress. For day wear, chiefly in summer.

Doublet, gipon, pourpoint

(M)

Period: 14th century to ca. 1670.

The term "doublet", though used in France in the 14th century, was not general in England for civilian wear until the 15th century. It was a padded jacket worn next to the shirt; close-fitting and waisted but not usually belted unless worn without an over-garment. Doublet skirts varied from non-existent or very narrow to covering the hips, according to changing fashions. In the 17th century the skirts consisted of a series of tabs of varying depth.

In the late 15th and early 16th centuries the front was widely open, requiring a **stomacher** or **partlet** fill-in.

The 14th-century dancing doublet was often heavily embroidered.

(F)

Period: 1650–1670.

Female doublets following the male style were sometimes worn by women on horseback.

"Doublets like to men they weare
As if they meant to flout us,
Thrust round with poynts and ribbons fayre…" (Will Bagnall's Ballet, *Musarum Delicoe*).

Douillette, donnilette

(F)

Period: 1818–1830s.

At first a quilted **pelisse** for winter wear; in the 1830s it was winter dress in the form of a **redingote**, made up of a caped **pelerine** of merino, cashmere or stamped satin; with wide sleeves. To be worn over a cambric or silk walking-dress.

"She was wrapped up in a…figured satin douillette or wadded pelisse" (1825, Harriette Wilson, *Paris Lions and London Tigers*).

Downy calves

(M)

Period: 18th century.

False calves woven into the appropriate part of the stockings to produce manly-looking calves; patented in 1788.

See False calves.

Dragon's blood cane

(M)

Period: Early 18th century.

A fashionable cane made from the frond stems of the dragon palm, a rattan palm from Malaysia.

Drainpipe trousers

(M, then F)

Period: 1950s onwards.

Narrow, close-fitting trousers with straight legs and no crease; often made of **denim**. Worn by men in the 1950s and women in the 1960s.

Draped clothing

(F)

Period: 20th century.

The use of graceful folds of drapery to create a fashionable style of clothing. A particularly notable feature of the work of the French designer Madame Grès (1903–1993) was her skilful use of drapery. She worked as Alix Barton from 1934 and as Grès from 1942. She created sinuous, draped dresses in jersey, silk and wool and was also noted for her carefully pleated evening dresses. She retired in 1986 but many designers since have tried to emulate her draped clothing.

Drawers

(M)

Period: 16th century onwards.

The term "drawers" was loosely applied, in the 17th and 18th centuries to any garment – such as breeches – which could be drawn on, but essentially the term describes an undergarment and, until the 19th century, usually of linen. There were various styles:

Short drawers were knee-length drawers or trunks cut full and square, tied in front with ribbon and pulled in behind by tapes over a short vent. They were worn to the end of the 19th century.

Long drawers reached the ankle; some had feet or stirrup-bands passing under the instep. In the 19th century both types were known as trousers or long pants. Early in the 19th century the waistband had holes through which the tongues of the braces passed, but from ca. 1845 loops of tape were substituted for these holes. The vent at the back was filled in with a puff which could be reduced by tightening the lacing across it. From the late 18th century drawers were made of cotton flannel or wool stockinette.

(F)

Period: 19th century onwards.

Occasionally mentioned in earlier centuries but generally thought of as an immoral and European habit; Samuel Pepys was worried when he thought his wife, who was French, might be wearing drawers in 1663. The 19th-century ones were similar in cut to the male garment, but each leg was separate or merely attached to the waistband. In 1806 "muslin drawers" were spoken of and in 1807 "patent elastic woollen drawers of stockinette" for riding. In 1813 drawers with attached feet for cold weather were available. Silk drawers were worn by some elite women, but the usual fabrics through the first half of the 19th century were long-cloth, cotton or merino, and the garment was very full, reaching below the knee. In the 1840s broderie anglaise trimming might be added.

Drawers of scarlet flannel were fashionable under crinolines and often exposed to view. Sometimes they were replaced by knickerbockers of that fabric, or in the 1890s of grey flannel. From 1870 on the garment became elaborately trimmed with lace, embroidery, tucks and frills, the legs much widened.

See Combinations.

Drawn-work

Period: 16th and 17th centuries.

A form of decoration produced in a fabric by drawing out some of the threads of the weft and warp to form a pattern, with the addition of needlework to hold the pattern.

Dress

(F & M)

Period: 16th century onwards.

Visible **clothing**, **costume** or wearing **apparel** that can indicate a particular style or fashion and reflect prevailing customs about physical appearance.

Also, and increasingly from the 19th century, a female garment made in one piece, rather than consisting of a separate bodice and skirt.

Dress clip

(F)

Period: 1925 onwards.

One, but more usually two, clips fastened by a clip mechanism rather than a pin to the collar of a dress or coat; often of diamanté, but other stones and finishes were used.

Dress clip, page

(F)

Period: 1840s.

A metal hook, in a decorative form, attached at the waist; from this was suspended a chain with a clip at the end; used for clipping the hitched-up skirt when walking.

Dress clothes

(M)

Period: 19th century onwards.

A term applied in the first half of the century to the clothing for formal social functions in the day as well as in the evening. For both, the essential feature was a **tail coat** with foreparts cut in, the day-dress coat closely resembling that of the evening except that the former was often cut so that the foreparts could be buttoned together (never possible in the latter) and made single- or double-breasted. The evening-dress coat was always single-breasted. The waistcoat opening was always deeper in the latter than in the former.

While day-dress clothes might present a mixture of colours and fabrics, e.g. a brown cloth coat, blue silk waistcoat and lavender moleskin trousers in 1829; evening-dress clothes were subdued by ca. 1840, with the coat black or dark blue, the waistcoat tending to become white or black, with black trousers, pantaloons

or breeches. Breeches and **pantaloons** ceased to be part of evening dress after ca. 1850.

By ca. 1850 the term "dress clothes" gradually became applied only to evening costume; the day-dress coat, known for a few years as **half dress**, soon became relegated to the **livery** of the indoor upper servant. By 1860 "The Walking Dress Coat is much adopted in France, there called the "Habit frac", synonymous with our "half dress", a style not in general wear in England" (*The Gentleman's Herald of Fashion*).

Dress coat

(M)

Period: 19th to mid-20th centuries.

A formal **tail coat** with a cutaway front, usually worn only in the evening.

Dress frock coat

(M)

Period: 1870–1890.

A double-breasted **frock coat** opening low, with long, narrow lapels faced with silk to the edge; often made with a narrow velvet collar. Worn with two pairs of its buttons fastened. The opening exposed more of the shirt-front than did the ordinary frock coat.

Gradually replaced in the 1880s replaced by the **morning frock**.

Dress holder

(F)

Period: 1870s.

An elaborate form of **dress clip** with two pendant chains and clips.

Dress improver

(F)

Period: 1849; 1883–1889.

A term used as a polite name for a **bustle**.

Dressing-gown

(M)

Period: 1770s onwards.

The term was rare in the 18th century but described a loose-sleeved gown reaching the ground, often of elaborately patterned silk. In the 1850s and 1860s it had a broad rolling collar and was tied round the waist with a sash or girdle. Generally worn with a tasselled **skull-cap**. Until ca. 1850 worn informally indoors, as for breakfast; subsequently it became a bedroom garment and a garment in which to visit the bathroom.

In the 20th century often a warm, practical garment until the introduction of central heating, when lighter fabrics and towelling became usual in various colours, patterns and lengths.

(F)

Period: Late 18th century onwards.

In the first half of the 19th century it was usually of white cotton or cambric or wool, and very voluminous. After 1857 coloured and patterned dressing-gowns of a closer shape were worn; it was always a bedroom garment. In the 20th century many styles, lengths and weights of fabric were worn.

See Négligée, Peignoir.

Dress lounge

(M)

Period: 1888–ca. 1920.

A jacket for informal evening wear; at first only in the absence of ladies. The early name for a **dinner jacket**.

Dressmaker

(F)

Period: Early 19th century onwards.

In essence, a woman who follows as a profession or business the making of dresses for her own sex; the term co-existed briefly with that of **mantua maker**, the previous description of this type of activity. An advertisement "To Milliners and Dress-makers" appeared in the *Morning Herald* in February 1803, and a century later "the assistance of a sewing-maid or a working dressmaker" was taken for granted in *The Lady's Realm* of 1904.

Dress protector, dress shield

(F)

Period: 1840s onwards.

A crescent-shaped piece of absorbent or waterproof fabric sewn into the arm-holes of a dress to prevent staining from sweat. At first made of chamois leather; in 1881 Canfield's "Arm-pit shields of India rubber" were patented and by 1902 stockinette dress shields were available.

Dress reform

Period: Mid-19th century to ca. 1940.

There were a number of efforts in Europe and North America to make dress more comfortable, hygienic and practical. Women were especially engaged in trying to find garments more suitable for an active way of life, and dress reform is often associated with suffrage movements. Mrs Amelia Bloomer, Dr Gustav Jaeger and his woollen underclothing, Lady Harberton and her divided skirts for cycling, all espoused the idea of reform alongside experiments with artistic dress, but the last real group was the Men's Dress Reform Party (1929–1940) in the UK.

See Aesthetic dress, Bloomers, Knickerbockers.

Dress Wellington

(M)

Period: 1830–1850.

An evening-dress boot made to resemble an evening slipper and stocking, reaching to below the knee; made in one and worn within the dress trousers or **pantaloons**.

'Driza-Bone'

(F & M)

Period: 1898 onwards.

An Australian firm which produces oilskin coats, jackets and hats. The coat has a distinctive cape which was developed to suit the climatic conditions in Australia, for those riding and working on the land in stormy and wet weather. As Australians travelled, the usefulness of these garments was recognized in many other countries, and alongside the original garments many others have been developed for wear in towns and for leisure pursuits.

Drop waist

(F)

Period: 1920s onwards.

The natural waistline is challenged periodically by fashion designs and the drop waist, which is below the natural line, was a feature of 1920s clothing and was occasionally revived at later dates.

Dry cleaning

Period: 19th century onwards.

The process of cleaning clothing and other forms of textile without using water. Although various methods were used in previous centuries, it was only in the mid-to-late 19th century that highly flammable solutions of paraffin and similar solvents became commercially available. The use of dangerous solvents (flammable or carcinogenic) gradually disappeared during the first half of the 20th century, and the introduction of small dry-cleaning machines into laundrettes offered inexpensive dry cleaning. All textile items, including clothing, carry symbols which indicate whether dry cleaning is necessary.

See Laundry.

Du Barry corsage

(F)

Period: 1850.

An evening-dress style "en chemisette", with ruching from the shoulders curving down to form an under-stomacher.

Du Barry sleeve

(F)

Period: 1835.

A large day sleeve with two bouffants, the dressmaking term for puffed-out fabric or silhouette, one to just above the elbow, the second to just above the wrist.

Duchess, dutchess

(F)

Period: Late 17th century.

A ribbon bow, worn high, with the **Fontange** cap.

Duchesse pleat

(F)

Period: 1875.

A pleating at the back of a skirt, consisting of four **box pleats** on each side of the midline or placket opening.

Duck-bills

(M, occasionally F)

Period: 19th century onwards.

Term used by authors, such as J. R. Planché, to

describe the broad-toed footwear worn in the period between ca. 1490 and 1540.

Duck-hunter

(M)

Period: 1840s.

"A striped linen jacket of that species sometimes denominated a "duck-hunter" (1841, *Heads of the People*). Worn by waiters.

Ducks

(M)

Period: 19th century.

Trousers of the heavy canvas or linen called **duck**.

Dudes

Period: 16th century.

Slang term for clothes.

Duffle bag

Period: ca. 1914 onwards.

Originally an American term for a military-issue, cylindrical-shaped canvas bag pulled together with a cord at the top and carried across the back or over the shoulder. Later the style was adapted for use by students. Fashionable versions in leather and other fabrics have enjoyed popularity.

Dunce's cap

(M)

Period: 19th and early 20th centuries.

A cone-shaped cap worn by a dunce at school, often marked at the centre front with a D.

The name is derived originally from Duns Scotus, a Scottish academic and theologian (d. 1308).

Dungarees

(M)

Period: 19th century onwards.

Working overalls with a bib and adjustable straps, of tough cotton fabric; from "dungaree", a cheap Indian calico; often worn by sailors or workmen.

(F)

Period: Mid-20th century onwards.

Worn for work, but also informally, and made from a variety of fabrics including corduroy, cotton and denim.

Dust coat, duster, dust cloak

(M)

Period: 1870s.

A short summer overcoat of Melton or cheviot.

(F)

Period: 1880s.

A summer overcoat or "dust cloak", sometimes caped and belted like an **Ulster**, and long to the skirt hem. Made of alpaca or silk. The "Sling Duster" was a light, loose-fitting **dolman**.

Period: Early 20th century onwards.

A lightweight, loose coat worn to protect the clothing beneath. A popular style in the early days of motoring and retained later for other forms of travel.

Dust gown

(F)

Period: 18th century.

Term used for a **safeguard**; "A kind of Dust Gown or upper garment worn by women, commonly called a Safeguard" (1706, Phillips, ed. Kersey).

Dutch cloak

(M)

Period: Late 16th and early 17th centuries.

A short cloak with wide sleeves generally lavishly guarded, i.e. trimmed with bands.

Dutch coat

(M)

Period: Late 14th and 15th centuries.

A short jacket, later called a **jerkin**.

From the 14th to early 16th centuries "Dutch" meant German; in the 16th century, however, the word "Dutch" was generally replaced by "Almain".

Dutchess

See Knot.

Dutch waist

(F)

Period: ca. 1580–1620.

The square-cut waist of a woman's bodice, worn with a **wheel farthingale**, the usual deep point being unsuitable. "A short Dutch waist with a round Catherine wheel Fardingale" (1607, Dekker and Webster, *Northward Hoe*).

Duvillier wig

(M)

Period: ca. 1700.

A very long and high dress-wig named after a famous French wig maker of the period; also known as a "Long Duvillier", and a "Falbala" or "Furbelow" wig.

"A long Duvillier full of powder…"; "Huge Falbala periwigs" (1709, R. Steele, *The Tatler*).

Dux collar

(M)

Period: 1860s–ca. 1900.

A shallow **stand collar** with the corners turned down in front.

Dyes

All were of vegetable origin until the introduction of aniline dyes in 1859; the two first used in textiles for women's dresses were Magenta (1859), nearly resembling the modern Raspberry, and Solferino (1860), resembling the modern Fuchsia. Both were named after battles in the Franco-Austrian war of 1859.

E

Ear-ring, earring
(F & M)
Period: Early Saxon.
A ring worn in the lobe of the ear as an ornament but then abandoned for several centuries.

Period: ca. 1350.
Rings of gold for women's ears, mentioned in *The Romaunt of the Rose,* were a foreign fashion which was uncommon in England owing to the shape of the head-dresses of that period.

Period: Late 16th century to ca. 1660.
Rings were worn by women in both ears, while by men in one ear only.

Period: Late 17th century onwards.
Earrings of various types were mainly worn by women, but also by sailors, until the later 20th century when men often wore one or more small rings or studs in the ears.

Ear-string
(F & M)
Period: Late 16th century to ca. 1640.
A short length of ribbon or a few strands of black silk, worn as an ear-ring, tied and allowed to dangle from one ear only, usually the left.
"What! Meanst thou him that walks all open-breasted, Drawn through the eare with ribands" (1598, Marston, *Satires*).

Earthquake gown
(F)
Period: 1750.
Following two nocturnal earthquakes in London in March 1750 a third was foretold, causing many to flee to the countryside against the predicted night of disaster. "This frantic terror prevails so much that within these three days 730 coaches have been counted…with whole parties removing into the country.…Several women have made earthquake gowns; that is, warm gowns to sit out of doors all night…" (April 4, 1750, Horace Walpole).
A precursor of the **siren suit** of two centuries later.

Echelles
(F)
Period: Late 17th to late 18th century.
A **stomacher** trimmed down the front with ribbon bows arranged like the rungs of a ladder.

Ecossaise hat
(F)
Period: 1865.
A type of bonnet associated with Scotland.
See Glengarry.

Edge, neyge, age, oegge, egge
Period: Late 15th and 16th centuries.
A term used for a border or edging of goldsmith's work as a trimming for a head-dress.

Eelskin masher trousers
(M)
Period: 1884–1885.
Excessively tight trousers favoured by **mashers** and considered "utterly mashy".

Eelskin sleeve
(F)
Period: 17th century onwards.
A tight-fitting sleeve. "An eeleskin sleeve lasht here and there with lace" (1602, Middleton Blurt, *Master Constable,* ii). "Jersey jackets and eel-skin dresses" (1881, Miss Braddon, *Asphodel*).

Eel skirt
(F)
Period: 1899.
A day skirt very tight over the hips and slightly flared from below the knees, touching the ground all round. The fabric cut on the cross and gored, having a front panel, two side and two back panels, all except the front piece having circular hems; fastened in front or at the side or, rarely, behind. No placket hole for the inside pocket.

Egham Staines and Windsor
(M)
Period: Early 19th century.
Nickname for a **tricorn** hat, "from the triangular situation of those towns" (1824, *Spirit of the Public Journals*).

Eisenhower jacket
(M)
Period: 1945 onwards.
An olive-green US Army uniform jacket made popular by Dwight D. Eisenhower (1890–1969), the World War II military commander and later President of the USA. Also a non-military version of this style.

Elastic round hat
(M)
Period: 1812.
Patented in that year. The crown was fitted inside with a steel spring by which it could be flattened at will and carried under the arm. The forerunner of the **Gibus**.

Elastic-sided boots
(F & M)
Period: 1837 onwards.
Boots with gussets of India-rubber fabric inserted into each side; patented in 1837 by James Dowie.

e

(M)
The term was revived in the 20th century for a specific style called **Chelsea boots**.

Elbow cloak

(M)
Period: Late 16th and early 17th centuries.
An alternative name for the short cloak of those years.

Elbow cuff

(F)
Period: ca. 1700–1750.
The turned-back cuff of the elbow-length sleeve of a woman's gown. It spread round the point of the elbow but was very narrow at the bend.

Elephant sleeve

(F)
Period: 1830.
A very large sleeve of a day dress in light fabrics; the bulk of the fullness hanging down from the shoulder to the closed wrist "in the shape of an elephant's ear". The name was also given in 1854 to the pendulous cape of the **Moldavian mantle**.

Eleven-gore ripple skirt

(F)
Period: 1895.
A day skirt of eleven gores, very narrow above and hanging in flutes; the hem twenty feet round; lined and stiffened at the bottom with horsehair.

Elliptic collar

(M)
Period: 1853.
A patent collar made with the fronts cut higher than the back; to be fastened in front or behind and detachable from the shirt.

Embroidery

The craft of stitching onto fabric with threads of metal, silk and wool to create designs or patterns, often pre-drawn or occasionally freehand. Embroidered fabrics for clothing have been produced in domestic and professional settings over many centuries. Also called **needlework**.

Emperor shirt

(M)
Period: 1850–1870.
A shirt of red flannel; worn by gentlemen in the country.

Empire bodice

(F)
Period: 1889.
An evening bodice attempting to revive the Empire style of the early 19th century and made to appear short-waisted by an arrangement of silk scarves variously draped across the front and tied behind or on one side. *See* Directoire.

Empire bonnet, Empire cap

(F)
Period: 1860s.

A small, close-fitting, outdoor bonnet in the shape of a baby's bonnet.

Empire jupon

(F)
Period: 1867.
A wide-gored petticoat with two or three steels round the bottom, replacing the cage-crinoline. Worn with the so-called Empire-style dress of that date.

Empire line

(F)
Period: ca. 1800–1820.
The term is usually applied to the high-waisted, narrow and sinuous dresses worn by fashionable women throughout Europe during this period, and associated with the period of Napoleon's rule in France as First Consul and Emperor.
Later revivals in the 1890s and in the 20th century, and its regular appearance in films and on television, have given it a **classic** status.

Empire petticoat

(F)
Period: Late 1860s.
Another name for the **Empire jupon**.

Empire skirt

(F)
Period: 1888–1890s.
A day skirt gathered at the waist, with a full-gathered flounce above the hem. There were no "steels", i.e. half hoops, at the back in the lining, as was usual at this date. The evening-dress version, ruched at the hem and embroidered with flowers, was slightly trained. In 1892 the Empire skirt for day wear had two straight panels front and back and two triangular gores each side; slightly trained.

Empress petticoat

(F)
Period: 1866.
An evening-dress petticoat closely gored at the waist, spreading out to a circumference of eight yards at the hem, with a train "nearly a yard on the ground". Trimmed with a deep flounce from above the knee. Worn as a substitute for the **cage crinoline**.

Enamelled button

Period: 18th and 19th centuries.
Very fashionable for men's coats in the 1770s, and sometimes for men's waistcoats in second half of the 19th century. Also used on women's dresses in the 1860s.

Enbraude

Period: Medieval.
Term for embroider.

Engageantes

(F)
Period: Late 17th to mid-19th century.
In the 17th and 18th centuries, this French term indicated ruffles. "Engageantes, double ruffles that fall over

the wrist" (1690, *The Ladies' Dictionary*).

From ca. 1840 they were detachable, white under sleeves, edged with lace or embroidery. They ceased to be worn ca. 1865.

English chain

(F)

Period: Early 19th century.

An early form of **chatelaine**. "Chain also denotes a kind of string or twisted wire; serving to hang watches, tweezer-cases, and other valuable toys upon. The invention of this piece of curious work was owing to the English; whence in foreign countries it is denominated the English chain" (1819, Abraham Rees, *Cyclopaedia*).

English farthingale

(F)

Period: 1580s–1620s.

A roll farthingale, producing a tub-shaped hang of the skirt without any flattening in front.

See French farthingale.

English hood

(F)

Period: ca. 1500–1540s.

A hood wired up to form a pointed arch above the forehead. The early form hung in thick folds to the shoulders behind, with the facial borders continued into long lappets, called **chaffers**, in front. An under cap was worn, but the smooth, parted hair was visible under the gable until ca. 1525. After that date the back drapery was replaced by two long pendant flaps, sometimes pinned up, and the front lappets were shortened, turned up and pinned in place. The front hair was concealed in silk sheaths, often striped, and crossed over under the gable point.

Also described by 19th-century writers as the **gable** or **pediment** head-dress.

English nightgown

(F)

Period: 18th century.

An unboned, loose dress worn for comfort and usually informally. "It was four o"clock…Mrs Darner…in an English nightgown" (1769, *Letters of Lady Mary Coke*).

See Nightgown.

English work, opus Anglicanum

Period: Medieval.

Very fine Anglo-Saxon embroidery worked by ladies from the 7th to the 14th century. This pictorial style of work was particularly suited to ecclesiastical vestments and was so excellent that it was not only prized in England but celebrated abroad.

English wrap

(M)

Period: 1840s.

A double-breasted **paletot-sac** resembling a loose **Chesterfield**.

See Twine.

Engreynen

Period: Medieval.

To dye in the grain, i.e. to dye in the thread before weaving.

En tablier

See Tablier skirt.

Envelope bag

(F)

Period: Mid-20th century onwards.

A small, hand-held bag which has a flap fastening similar to an envelope.

Epaulettes

(F)

Period: 19th century onwards.

Ornamental shoulder pieces, very popular in the 1860s. Subsequently revived in the 20th century.

Equipage

(F)

Period: 18th century.

An etui or ornamental metal case slung by a chain from the waist and containing knife, scissors, tweezers, thimble, etc.

Esclavage

(F)

Period: Mid-18th century.

Necklace composed of several rows of gold chains falling in festoons over the bosom.

Espadrille

(M & later F)

Period: 1920s onwards.

A canvas shoe with twisted rope soles, originally worn in Spain, but popular for beach and sports wear for visitors to Spain and France from the 1920s. Expensive designer versions have been made, but the original style, impractical in wet weather, is the disposable summer footwear of choice for many Europeans.

Estaches

(M)

Period: ca. 1350–1400.

French term for strings for attaching the **hose** to the **doublet**.

See Points.

Ethnic dress

Period: 1950 onwards.

A loosely defined term in the context of dress, but usually meaning textiles and styles of dress from non-western countries, e.g. African or Indian, which are absorbed into or influence western fashions.

Etiquette

(F & M)

Period: 18th century onwards.

Originally concerning correct behaviour, dress and precedence at royal courts, by the 18th century travellers wrote about the differing national views on the etiquette of correct clothing. George Lucy, an Englishman on

An Indian **tie-dyed**, crinkle effect silk **shawl**, hand-printed; a **shoulder bag** of cotton velour with **tambour embroidery** from Mongolia and a Chinese **fan** with printed paper leaf and wooden sticks. All acquired ca. 2000–7 and indicative of the many non-European or **ethnic** sources of influence on western fashion. Private collection.

the Grand Tour, remarked upon the formality of Italian society, "…(they) dress much and I have been obliged to daub myself all over silver, accompanied by a sword and bag wig" (1755, quoted in J. Ashelford, *The Art of Dress*). British snobbery about correct and incorrect forms of dress generated many column inches in journals and etiquette books from the 19th century onwards, aimed at the newly affluent entrepreneurs and their families. By the 1830s, it was decreed that "It is in bad taste to dress in the extreme of fashion; and in general, those only do so who have no other claim to distinction – leave it in these times, to shopmen and pickpockets" (1834, *Hints on Etiquette*). Only after World War II did etiquette about clothing diminish, but vestiges of it are found on invitations which require "black tie" or "lounge suit".
See Court dress, Livery.

Eton collar
(M, occasionally F)
Period: 19th century onwards.
A broad, stiff, white collar worn outside the jacket by Eton schoolboys in earlier times, but also a collar of this style worn by women.

Eton crop
(F)
Period: Mid-to-late 1920s.
A closely cut, boyish hairstyle worn by women, which complemented the narrow androgynous outline of 1920s fashions.

Eton jacket
(F)

Period: 1892 to early 1900s.
A day bodice cut like the boy's jacket of that name and worn open over a waistcoat; the fronts sometimes rounded in 1898, braided and frogged.

Eton jacket bodice
(F)
Period: 1889.
A fitted jacket with large revers and flap pockets on each side; worn with a double-breasted, fancy waistcoat with revers and a large **cravat**.

Eton suit
(M)
Period: 1798 onwards.
Worn by junior schoolboys; comprising a short jacket, the fronts cut square or slightly pointed with a shallow, turned-down collar and wide lapels turning nearly to the bottom. The back with a slight point in the centre. Sleeves without cuffs. The foreparts cut back so that the jacket cannot be buttoned up. Worn with a single-breasted waistcoat having a narrow turned-over collar and buttoned high. Trousers of a lighter colour, commonly grey.
Originally the jacket was blue or red, becoming black in 1820 in mourning for George III. At first white **ducks** or nankin **pantaloons** were worn; at Eton College the Oppidans took to trousers in 1814, but the Collegers continued to wear **knee breeches** until ca. 1820. An essential feature of the outfit was the starched, white **Eton collar** turned down over the coat collar; worn with a white shirt and a black tie. In the correct form of Eton suit the bottom button of the waistcoat was left unfastened and the bottoms of the trousers turned up. "Harrow Eton jackets have no point" (1898, *The London Tailor*).

Etui
Period: 1611 onwards.
A term describing a small, often decorative, case to hold bodkins, needles, tweezers or similar.
See Equipage.

Evening dress
(F & M)
Period: 20th century onwards.
A generalized term for the more formal styles of clothing worn to evening functions, **dinner jackets** and long dresses for instance.

Exercise wear
(F & M)
Period: Late 20th century onwards.
Any type of garment designed and marketed for taking any form of physical exercise, including **track suits**, running clothes, etc.

Eyelets, oilets
Period: Medieval onwards.
"Oilets" was the 14th-century term replaced in the 17th century by "eyelets". The term describes holes for the

passage of a lace, cord or tape, to join garments or parts of garments. Until ca. 1828 these holes were bound with silk or thread; from 1828 they might be

strengthened by a metal ring, as used in corsets by ca. 1830, but not in the back-lacing of waistcoats until 1839.

F

Fabala, falbala
See Furbelow.

Fabric
See Glossary of Fabrics and Materials.

Faggoting
An openwork embroidery technique in which a number of threads are drawn out of a piece of fabric and tied together at regular intervals.

Also a means of joining two edges of fabric by the creation of lace-like, embroidered stitches.

Fair Isle
One of the Shetland Islands which has given its name to a style of knitted pattern found on jumpers, gloves, etc. Traditional forms and colours were originally used for local use, but a wider range developed from the mid-19th century onwards as the designs became fashionable beyond the island.

Faldetta
(F)

Period: 1850.

A short, waist-length **mantle** of coloured taffeta edged with deep lace round the hem, and wide sleeves.

Fall, falling band
(M)

Period: 1540s–1670s.

A turned-down collar, at first attached to the shirt but from ca. 1585 a separate item, the size and shape varying with the fashion; generally lace-edged. Worn as an alternative to the **ruff** and sometimes worn with a ruff, between 1580 and 1615, and entirely replacing the ruff from ca. 1640.

(F)

Period: 17th century.

Falling bands were occasionally worn by women but were very uncommon at an earlier time. The term could also mean a wrist ruffle, late in the century, but was rarely used in this sense. "Falls or long Cuffes to hang over the Hands" (1688, R. Holme, *Armory*).

Fal-lal
Period: 17th century onwards.

Any slight but noticeable decoration added to clothing. "His dress, his bows, and fine fal-lals" (1690, J. Evelyn).

Falling ruff
See Ruff.

Falls
(M)

Period: 1730 onwards.

A buttoned flap to the front of breeches and, later, of **pantaloons** and trousers. Whole falls was the name given to a flap extending from one side seam to the other; small or split falls was a narrow central flap. In each style the flap buttoned up to the front of the waistband. *See* Spair.

False calves
(M)

Period: 17th–20th century.

Pads worn inside the stockings to improve the shape of the legs. "They say he puts off the calves of his legs with stockings every night" (1601, B. Jonson, *Cynthia's Revels*). Still occasionally used in stage costumes.

False hips
(F)

Period: 1740s–1760s.

A pair of side **hoops** producing the excessive widening of the skirt on each side over the hips.

"I furnish'd her...with three pairs of hips" (1705, Sir J. Vanbrugh, *The Confederacy*).

See Oblong hoop.

False sleeves
See Hanging sleeves.

Falsies
(F)

Period: 1940s onwards.

Padded **brassières** or pads to insert into them to enhance the size and shape of the breasts. Originally associated with performers, but quickly copied by other young women.

Fan
Period: Mid-16th to late-18th century.

In common use by women, but until ca. 1580 the principal form was that of a rigid fan with feathers, silk or straw fixed to a decorative handle and variously shaped. After ca. 1580 the folding fan came into use, and both styles were popular until the 18th century when folding fans became the rule. The size varied considerably. In

Folding **ostrich feather fan**; the feathers dyed yellow. Sticks and guards of amber coloured **plastic**, ca. 1920–30. Copyright the Olive Matthews Collection, Chertsey Museum. Photograph by John Chase.

the 18th century the fan was an essential to a fine lady's toilet.

"It's shake triumphant, it's victorious clap,
It's angry flutter and it's wanton tap…" (1730, Soame Jenyns, *The Art of Dancing*).

Period: 19th century.
Fans of ivory were common in the early decades; painted fans in mid- century, and in the 1880s fans decorated with animals, such as cats' heads the size of furry toy cats, were fashionable. In the 1890s large, folding ostrich-feather fans with frames of ivory, mother-of-pearl or tortoiseshell were fashionable.

Period: 20th century onwards.
Advertising fans of paper or card were popular early in the century, alongside more formal varieties. As the century progressed fans were less popular, but in hot weather inexpensive paper versions and small battery-driven plastic fans could be bought.

(M)
Period: Late 16th century.
Fans were carried by foppish men in the late 16th century – "When a plum'd fan may shade thy chalked face" (1597, Hall's *Satire,* addressed to the fops of the day). They were also carried by some of the dandies of the late 18th century.

Fanchon
(F)
Period: 1830s–ca. 1900.
A small **kerchief** for the head, but the term was chiefly used for the lace trimming falling about the ears of a day cap or outdoor bonnet.

Fanchon cap
(F)
Period: 1840s–1860s.
A lace or tulle cap with side pieces covering the ears, or sloping down to them.

Fancies
(M)
Period: 1650s–1670s.
Ribbon trimming for suits worn with open-legged breeches and also **petticoat breeches**.
"I"ve a new suite and Ribbons fashionable yclept Fancies" (ca. 1652, Richard Brome, *Mad Couple,* Prologue).
The amount of ribbon used was commonly 72 yards; but up to 250 yards was not unknown.

Fancy dress
(F & M)
Period: Medieval onwards.
Denotes the wearing of clothing of a different place or time for the purposes of entertainment, usually at masquerades in the 18th century, and fancy-dress balls, pageants and parties from the 19th century onwards. Although dress for such events could often be hired from theatrical costumiers, fancy dress and theatrical dress are different in intention if not in form.
See Domino, Masquerade costume, Vandyke.

Fanfreluche bodice
(F)
Period: 1888.
A day bodice with gathers from neck and shoulders sloping to a point just above the top of the **corset**.

Fan hoop
(F)

Period: 1700–1750.

A hooped petticoat, pyramidal in shape, but compressed front and back to form a fan-shaped structure over which the skirt fell with a curve up on each side. Mentioned as early as 1713, but especially fashionable in the 1740s and 1750s.

Fan parasol

(F)

Period: 1790s–1850.

A small **parasol** with a hinge in the stick near the cover, by which it could be tilted upright and then used as a fan.

Fantail hat

(F & M)

Period: 1775–ca. 1800.

A **tricorne hat**, the front cocks sloping down towards the back; the brim behind semicircular in shape and vertically cocked resembling an open fan. Fashionable for riding and sometimes worn by women on horseback.

Fantail wig

(M)

Period: Early 18th century.

The **queue** of a **wig** hanging loose in a number of small curls.

Farthingale, vardingale, verdyngale

(F)

Period: 1545–1620s.

A structure, variously shaped, using hoops of rushes, wood, wire or whalebone, for expanding the skirt of a gown under which it was worn. There were several named styles: English, French, Italian, Scotch, Spanish, also the roll, pocket and demi- or semi-circular farthingale and **wheel farthingale**.

In Spain and Portugal the farthingales continued as formal court wear; the Portuguese Princess Catharine of Braganza, who married Charles II, and her attendants wore them on their arrival in England in 1662, causing much mirth.

Farthingale sleeves

(F & M)

Period: Late 16th and early 17th centuries.

Trunk sleeves or **bishop sleeves** distended by wire, reeds or whalebone.

Fascinator

(F)

Period: Late 19th century onwards.

A head shawl made of a light fabric or crocheted; originally an American term. In the late 20th century this came to mean a lightweight confection of feathers, flowers, ribbons and net which was worn on the head in lieu of a hat.

Fashion

Period: Medieval onwards.

From the French *façon*, denoting the process of making something, creating a particular shape or style.

Amongst various applications and meanings, it became increasingly associated with clothing and the constant shifts and changes in personal adornment. "Fashions crosse the Seas as oft as the Packet Boat" (1654, R. Whitlock, *Zootomia*). Later, changes were celebrated, "But to return to the magnificent fashions of the moment, for "magnificent" is the only word to express the sumptuousness of the fabrics, the beauty of the laces and embroideries, and the costliness of the furs now in use" (1904, *The Lady's Realm*).

Fashion designer

Period: 20th century.

The various terms describing professional designers and makers of female clothing range from **couturier** at the most expensive and exclusive Paris-based end of the business to local **dressmakers**, whose more derivative work could be afforded by many more customers. The term "fashion designer" is a hybrid, suggesting originality alongside a degree of exclusivity. As French couture was increasingly challenged by American, British and Japanese designers in the post-World War II period, the name "fashion designer" became usual as an Anglophone description of couturier. An early use of the term is: "The very red about which fashion-designers are decided" (1909, 15 March, *The Westminster Gazette*).

Fashion doll

Period: 14th to late 18th century.

Carefully dressed miniature figures rather than playthings, these advertisements for the latest fashions and fabrics were carried throughout Europe and to the New World to demonstrate changing personal appearance, from hairstyles to footwear. **Dressmakers** and **milliners** paid to acquire the latest "doll" to show to their customers, and only the regular and increasingly sophisticated journals of the late 18th century replaced them as a source of information. Miniatures continued to be made as part of an apprenticeship or for advertising a whole system, as with the "*poupées mondaine*" of *Le Théâtre de la Mode*, exhibited in Paris in 1945, which publicized the work of forty couturiers and went on tour to America in 1946.

Fashion illustration, fashion plate

Period: 16th century onwards.

Interest in the clothing of other nations prompted artists to produce printed illustrations in book form or as single sheets. 16th-century versions were produced in France, Germany and Italy and copied each other in accuracy and mistakes. They recorded known appearance rather than changing styles of dress, and this persisted into the 17th century when the Bohemian artist Wenceslas Hollar (1607–1677) produced a series of plates of female English styles from different social groups in the 1640s. In the 1670s in France, engravings began to depict new and changing fashions seasonally and annually, in order to promote the luxury trades such as silk weaving and lace making. The emergence of pocket books and magazines in the 18th century offered regular plates and details of fashions monthly, and in the 19th century weekly journals and newspapers all offered information about and engravings of fashionable garments. From the early years of the 20th century photography overtook fashion illustration in recording the ideal as well as the affordable in visual terms.

Fashion waist
(M)
Period: 19th century.
A tailoring term indicating the length from the base of a coat collar to the waist seam.

Fausse montre
(M)
Period: Late 18th century.
It was fashionable for a man to wear two watches, and often one of them was a sham, being perhaps a snuffbox disguised as a **watch**.

Favourites
(F)
Period: 1690–ca.1720.
"Locks dangling on the temples" (1690, *The Fop-Dictionary*).

(M)
Period: 1820–1840.
"Favourite" was a small tuft of hair worn under the chin.

Fax, facts, feax
Period: Medieval to ca. 1610.
The hair of the head.

Fearnothing, fearnothing jacket
(M)
Period: 18th and early 19th centuries.
A jacket resembling a sleeved **waistcoat** made of a thick, woollen cloth called "fearnothing", "fearnought" or "dreadnought". Worn by seafaring men, sportsmen, labourers and apprentices; "…that J. Tospill have cloaths with a fearnothing and stockings" (1725, Stoke-by-Nayland Records).

Featherbrush skirt
(F)
Period: 1898.
A day skirt of a light fabric having a series of overlapping flounces below the knees.

Feather pelts
Period: 14th to mid-17th century.
Skins of various birds with the feathers attached, used for trimming garments in place of furs. Especially those of the swan, ostrich, drake, crane and vulture. "A furre of drakes" necks for facing and furring his Lordship's gown" (1550, Revels Accounts).

Feathers
(M)
Period: Mid-14th century onwards.

Worn as ornaments, mainly on hats, from the mid-15th century in the UK, in Europe from the mid-14th century; thence off and on until the end of the 18th century, and after that as a modest trimming or with formal uniforms. Chiefly feathers were of ostrich; sometimes in the 15th century peacock, and at the end of 16th century pyed feathers, "figaro feathers". In the early 17th century spangled feathers were fashionable.

(F)
Period: End of 16th century onwards.
Worn from the time when hats came into fashion and usually attached to a hat or bonnet but also, from the end of 18th century, plumes were worn ceremonially in the hair. Ostrich, grebe and other feathers were used in 18th and 19th centuries for dress trimmings, **boas**, **mantles**, **pelerines**, **muffs** and fans. Even when hats began to disappear from general wear in the 20th century, **fascinators** often included feathers.

Feather-top wig
(M)
Period: ca. 1750–1800.
A wig with a **toupee** made of feathers, usually drake's or mallard's. Worn by parsons and also sportsmen. "Gentlemens" perukes for sporting made of drakes' tails" (1761, *Ipswich Journal*).

Fedora
(M, occasionally F)
Period: After 1882.
A soft felt hat with a medium curled brim and a crown with a crease from front to back. Very popular in the USA, but originally seen in Sardou's play *Fédora* produced in Paris in 1882. A classic style since the early 20th century.

Felt
(M)
Period: Mid-15th century onwards.
This term, when used alone, indicated a felt hat. "And on his heade a felt" (ca. 1450, Merlin). In the 17th century the word was often loosely used for any kind of hat, whether felt or not.
See Glossary of Fabrics and Materials.

Fent
Period: 15th century.
With the same meaning as **vent**, both being used in the 15th century, but subsequently "fent" was discarded in favour of "vent", a functional slit in a garment. "Fente of a clothe, fibulatorium" (ca. 1440, *Promptorium Parvulorum*).

Fermail, fermayll
Period: 15th century.
A buckle or brooch. Later used in heraldry.

Ferronière
(F)
Period: 1830s.

A narrow gold or jewelled band worn low round the head and crossing the forehead. Worn with day or evening dress.

Fetishist fashion

(F & M)

Period: 1950 onwards.

The psychological state of finding satisfaction by focusing upon a physical fetish, such as underclothing, leather, rubber or shoes, was extended into a system of clothing using those elements, along with chains, plastic or PVC, **body piercing** and **tattooing**, to create alternative forms of dress including so-called **bondage** clothing.

Fez

See Tarboush.

Fichu

(F)

Period: 1816 to early 20th century.

A term replacing the **handkerchief** or **neckerchief**, being a length of usually flimsy material worn round the neck and shoulders.

Fichu Antoinette

(F)

Period: 1857.

For summer wear, a morning fichu of fine muslin trimmed with black lace and narrow velvet ribbon, fastening with a small bow behind, the long ends floating at the back. It covered the shoulders like a **shawl** and crossed in front at the waist.

Fichu-canezou

(F)

Period: 1820s.

A form of deep collar, sometimes made with a small **ruff** and falling over the front and back of the dress bodice, but not covering the arms or sides.

Fichu Corday

(F)

Period: 1837.

A fichu of grenadine gauze with a broad hem run through with a ribbon; crossing over the bosom, it was tied behind; for day wear.

Fichu la Vallière

(F)

Period: 1868.

A fichu with the fronts not crossed but meeting edge to edge and fastened by a button.

Fichu-pelerine

(F)

Period: 1826 to early 20th century.

A large covering for the shoulders, generally of white fabric, and often having a double cape and turned-down collar. The front having fichu ends carried down beneath the belt to knee-level.

Fichu Raphael

(F)

Period: 1867.

A fichu of white tulle or lace, cut square over the shoulders and upper part of the bodice. Worn with a high-necked bodice to "give a dressy effect".

Fichu-robings

(F)

Period: 1820s.

A flat trimming from the shoulders to the waist to give the effect of a fichu.

Figaro jacket, signorita

(F)

Period: 1860s; revived 1892.

A figure-fitting jacket, curving away from the midline at the sides; tight sleeves with **epaulettes**; worn over a waistcoat. A variant of the **Zouave jacket**.

Fig leaf

(F)

Period: 1860s and 1870s.

A small ornamental **apron** of black silk, without a bib. "Known by the ladies as their fig-leaves."

Fillet

(F)

Period: 13th–17th century.

In medieval English also known as a "filet" or "felet", this was a narrow band to tie around the hair of the head. In the 13th and 14th centuries the fillet was a stiffened circlet of linen worn with a **barbette** or **fret**, or both.

Period: 18th century.

The term was sometimes used to mean a hair-net covering the whole head, worn at night. "…take a very large fillet which must be big enough to cover the head…" (1782, Stewart, *Plocacosmos*).

Period: Early 19th century onwards.

A fillet of satin and pearls spirally twisted round the head was sometimes worn with evening **coiffure**, or a simpler narrow ribbon at later periods.

Filleting

Period: 17th century.

A narrow tape.

Film

See Cinema.

Fish

(M)

Period: 1800–1850.

A tailoring term for a **dart**, a narrow dart-shaped piece of material cut out and the edges then joined together to improve the fit of a garment. The dictum "Where there is a crease there take out a fish" is attributed to George IV.

Fitchet

(F)

Period: 13th to mid-16th century.

A French term for a vertical placket hole in the skirt of a gown.

Fitzherbert hat

(F)

Period: 1786.

A modified form of the **balloon hat**, the wide brim oval in shape, the crown of puffed fabric slightly raised.

Flandan

(F)

Period: Late 17th century.

"A Flandan is a kind of Pinner (lappet) join'd with a Cornet (day cap)" (1694, *The Ladies' Dictionary*).

Flannels

(F)

Period: 18th and early 19th centuries.

The large flannel gown or wrap worn by bathers at the seaside and at spa towns such as Bath.

"Oh! 'Twas pretty to see them all put on their flannels And then take the waters like so many spaniels" (1766, C. Anstey, *The New Bath Guide*).

(M)

Period: 1850 onwards.

Cricketing or boating costume. "Beautifully dressed in white flannels" (1895, E. F. Benson, *The Babe, B.A.*). By the 20th century the term applied to casual trousers for men, made of flannel in various subdued colours. "All wool flannel trousers. White and three shades of grey" (1928, Harrods).

Flares

(F & M)

Period: Late 1960s–1970s.

An American fashion for trousers which fitted closely to the body and upper leg and then widened or "flared out" from knee to ankle.

See Loon pants.

Flat cap

(M, sometimes F)

Period: 16th century into the 17th century.

A cap with a flat crown spreading over a flat, narrow brim. By 1570 it was being worn only by citizens and apprentices and known as the "City Flat Cap".

Such caps continued to be worn by young men, and sometimes young women, when at work and, much later, was associated with working men of all ages before the **baseball cap** replaced it.

Flea-fur

(F)

Period: 16th century.

Popular name for a fur **stole** of marten or sable.

Fleece

(F & M)

Period: 1990s onwards.

A jacket or **sweater** lined with fleece, usually a synthetic fabric with a smooth outer layer and fleece-like inner layer. A style originally found in ski-wear and adopted by non-skiers.

See Glossary of Fabrics and Materials.

Flipe, flepe

Period: 16th century.

A fold or flap, as in the flexible brim of a hat or cap. "I tourne up the flepe of a cap" (1530, Palsgrave).

Flip-flops

(F & M)

Period: Late 1950s onwards.

A plastic- or rubber-soled **sandal** with a post between the big toe and the second toe to which two thin straps are attached and held on the sole towards the ankle. Possibly based on a similar but sturdier Japanese style.

Flockard

(F)

Period: 15th century.

This article was often listed in pairs for flockards were **veils** or **lappets**. "Item...for a pair of flokkardes for my Lady..." (1481, Howard Household Expenses).

Flocket

(F)

Period: 16th century.

A loose garment, possibly a **gown** with long sleeves. "In her furred flocket / And gray russet rocket" (1529, Skelton, *Elynour Rummyng*).

Florentine button

Period: 19th century.

A name for a covered button.

Flounce

(F)

Period: Early 18th century onwards.

A deep, gathered or pleated frill used as a trimming to women's garments.

Flounce à disposition

(F)

Period: 1852 onwards.

A flounce woven with the same border pattern as the dress material.

Flourish

Period: 16th century.

To ornament profusely; a garment "flourished with pearls" meant one lavishly decorated with them.

Flower bottle

(M)

Period: 1865.

A small glass bottle for flowers, worn in the buttonhole which at that date was sometimes worked in the left-hand lapel of a morning coat for that purpose. A piece of broad ribbon was put under the turn to hold the flower bottle in place.

Flower hole

(M)

Period: 1840s onwards.

A slit hole in the left lapel of a coat through which a flower stem could be inserted.

See Boutonnière.

Flower-pot hat, turf hat

(M)

Period: 1830s.

"Of grey felt, low crown like a flower-pot upside-down, the very large brim looped all round" (i.e. rolled over) (1830, *The Gentleman's Magazine of Fashion*).

Flowers

Fresh and artificial flowers have been used to decorate items of clothing across many centuries. Artificial flower-making was one of the notorious "sweated labour" industries in the 19th century. It was usual until recently for women to buy plain hats and decorate them with ribbons and flowers.

Flow-flow

(F)

Period: 1885.

The name given to a graduated cascade of coloured ribbon loops decorating the front of a bodice of an afternoon or evening dress "to brighten it up".

Fly cap

See Butterfly cap.

Fly-fringe

(F)

Period: 18th century.

A fringe of fine cord with knots and bunches of floss silk attached. Used to decorate gowns.

Fly-front fastening

Period: 19th century onwards.

A device for concealing a row of button fastenings by extending an overlap of the fabric over them. Used infrequently in the 18th century for waistcoats. Introduced for trousers ca. 1823; for breeches ca. 1840. Also often used for overcoats, e.g. **Chesterfields**. In the 20th century the fastening often concealed a **zip** rather than buttons.

Flying suit

See Jumpsuit.

Fly suit, fly-away suit

(F)

Period: 18th century.

A loose négligée dress. "Apparell for my Daughters. Two flye Sutes...." (1723, *Diary of Nicholas Blundell,* Univ. Press, Liverpool, 1952).

Fob pocket

(M)

Period: 17th to mid-20th century.

A horizontal pocket in the front of the waistband of breeches, **pantaloons** or trousers, usually one on each side.

Fob ribbon

(M)

Period: 1740s–1840s.

A short ribbon attached to the **watch** in the fob pocket and dangling outside, suspending seals and watch-key. Worn with breeches or **pantaloons** only.

Fogle

(M)

Period: 19th century.

Slang term for a silk handkerchief.

Foil button

Period: 1774.

Silk pasted on paper and applied to the underside of a glass button, as a foil; patented in 1774.

Folk costume, folk dress

(F & M)

Period: 19th century onwards.

Increased travel led to the acquisition of certain types of clothing found in surrounding countries or further away. In Europe Magyar dress and **Tyrolean** items became fashionable in the 19th century; **dirndls**, **espadrilles**, Afghan coats, etc. in the 20th century. Other cultures and their forms of dress also influenced major European and American designers.

Folly bells

(M)

Period: 15th century.

A form of decoration composed of small bells suspended by chains from the **girdle**, the shoulder belt or a neckband.

Fontange

(F)

Period: ca. 1690–1710.

An indoor linen cap with a small, flat crown behind and a tower of lace or lace and linen frills in front, kept erect by the **commode**, a tall wire frame. Two long lace or linen streamers called **lappets** hung down at the back or were sometimes pinned up to the crown. The front hair was arranged in curls mounting up from the forehead in front of the fontange elevation.

Period: 1850.

A term used for ribbon gathered along the centre as ruching and used to edge a day **corsage**.

Football shirt

(M)

Period: 1895 to late 20th century.

A cotton shirt with attached **Shakespere collar**, superseding the earlier knitted football **jersey**.

Football strip

(M, occasionally F)

Period: Late 20th century onwards.

A term usually applied to the team colours worn by players of football (not American football). Teams usually have home and away strips, and national sides also have two strips. Subtle annual changes have ensured that supporters will constantly buy new shirts, scarves etc. and these items are often worn even when not attending matches.

Foot-mantle, fote-mantel

(F & M)

Period: 14th to early 18th century.

Probably a protective garment worn to keep clothing from becoming soiled; associated with riding. "A foot mantel aboute hir hippes large" (ca. 1386, Chaucer, *Prologue, Canterbury Tales*).

See Safeguard.

Footwear

(F & M)

Period: 20th century onwards.

A generalized description for any type of **boot**, **sandal**, **shoe**, whether formal or casual.

Fop

(M)

Period: Late 17th century onwards.

The medieval meaning of the word was "fool", and its later use in respect of clothing is indicative of undue interest in or vanity about dress and grooming.

See Beau, Dandy.

Forage cap

(M)

Period: 1800–1850.

A cap adapted from the military and worn by small boys; it comprised a circular, flat crown, its border stiffened with cane; a tassel hanging from the centre; a visor in front and sometimes held in place by a japanned leather strap passing under the chin.

Period: 19th century onwards.

An undress cap of soft fabric worn by soldiers.

Forebody

(F & M)

Period: 17th and 18th centuries.

The front part of the garment covering the chest, namely the **bodice** or **doublet**. "A doublet whose forebodie is fine stuff and the backe course" (1611, Randle Cotgrave, *A Dictionarie of the French and English Tongues*).

Forehead cloth

See Crosscloth.

Forepart

(F)

Period: 16th century to ca. 1630.

Term applied to the decorative, triangular-shaped panel, mounted on a plain underskirt, which filled in the front opening of some styles of skirt.

(M)

Period: 19th century.

The fronts of a coat or waistcoat covering the chest.

Fore sleeves, half sleeves

(F & M)

Period: Late 14th to mid-17th century.

"A foresleeve of a garmente which Kevereth the arme from the elbow downwarde" (1538, Elyot, *Dictionarie*). The sleeve covering the forearm was often of richer fabric, the upper-arm portion being hidden by an overgarment. Fore sleeves were sometimes separate items. "A doublet of yellow satin and the foresleeves of it of cloth of gold" (1523, Inventory, Dame Agnes Hungerford's husband).

Fore-stocks

(F)

Period: 1500–1550.

A term meaning **fore sleeves** and listed with a **plackard**. Those matching the plackard were separate items. "Item. Pd. for makyng of a payer of forestockes and placard" (1525, Lestrange Household Accounts).

Foretop

(F & M)

Period: 13th to end of 18th century.

The hair of the head or of a wig immediately above the forehead. In the 18th century called **toupee** or merely **top**.

Forked beard

(M)

Period: 14th century; occasionally 17th century.

A **beard** trimmed in two peaks. "A marchant was there with a forked beard" (ca. 1386, Chaucer, Prologue, *Canterbury Tales*).

Foundation

(F)

Period: 1885–ca. 1914.

An underskirt forming a foundation and giving substance to the overskirt, both being joined together at the waist to form one garment; worn with day dresses.

Foundling bonnet

(F)

Period: 1880s.

A bonnet with a small, stiff brim, soft crown, usually of plush, and tied under the chin "like the Quaker headgear".

Fouriaux

(F)

Period: ca. 1100–1150.

Silk sheaths enclosing the two long, pendant plaits of hair worn by ladies of high rank. These sheaths were usually depicted white with red circular stripes.

Four-in-hand

(F & M)

Period: 1890 onwards.

Also known as a **Derby**. A **necktie** knotted in front, the knot presenting a free edge above and below, thus differing from the **sailor's reef knot** with its free edges on each side. Also worn by women with a morning blouse. In the 20th century worn more in North America.

Fourreau dress

(F)

Period: 1864.

A **princess** style dress, that is with no seam at the waist, "now beginning to be called by an old name "fourreau". It was buttoned all down the front and frequently worn with a **peplum** fastened round the waist.

Fourreau skirt

(F)

Period: 1864.

A skirt sufficiently gored to fit the figure and spread over the **crinoline**, without pleats at the waist; a morning-dress style.

Fourreau tunic

(F)

Period: 1865.

The upper skirt, that is the tunic, cut in one with the bodice and measuring about six yards round the hem. A double skirt for evening dress.

Fraise

(F)

Period: 1836.

A piece of embroidered muslin edged with **ruching**, folded across the bosom and secured by an ornamental pin; worn instead of a **cravat** with carriage dress.

Frelan, freland, frelange

(F)

Period: Late 17th century.

"Frelan…Bonnet and Pinner together" (1690, *The Fop-Dictionary*).

French bearer

(M)

Period: 19th century.

The **bearer** band of breeches or **pantaloons** made with **falls** and cut very narrow.

French boa

(F)

Period: 1829.

A long, round **tippet** of swansdown, fur or feathers; very fashionable again in the 1890s.

French bottoms

(M)

Period: 19th century.

Trouser legs cut somewhat wider at the bottom of the leg than above.

French cloak

(M)

Period: 16th and 17th centuries.

A cloak that was long, circular or semicircular in cut and described as **compass** or half-compass. Generally having a square, flat collar or a shoulder cape; sometimes plain.

French cuff

(M)

Period: 19th century.

A coat cuff with a side slit which was closed by buttons.

Period: 1850s onwards.

The name was also applied to a wide shirt cuff fastened by a link near the lower margin and by a button higher up at the wrist.

French farthingale

(F)

Period: 1580s–1620s.

This gave the same outline as the **wheel farthingale**, producing a tub-shaped hang of the skirt, but with wider curves at the sides and a flattening in front. "My wife…is underlayed not with a Frenche fardingale, whiche strottethe out by the sydes, But withe an English bumbaste wiche beareth out before" (1588, Letter from John Adams, Lord Middleton's MSS).

French frock

(M)

Period: 1770s–1800.

A French version of the **frock**, the closely-fitted, buttoned coat with a turn-down collar worn by fashionable men. This was the only elegantly cut, embroidered and "full trimmed", formal, dress form of the frock.

French gigot sleeve

(F)

Period: 1890–1897.

A sleeve with the cuff prolonged over the back of the hand; a fashion introduced by the French actress Sarah Bernhardt (1844–1923).

French gores

(F)

Period: 1807.

Gores introduced into the skirt of a day dress to eliminate gathers at the waist.

See Gored skirt.

French heel, Pompadour heel

(F)

Period: 1750–1790.

A high heel curving into a narrow base; named for Madame de Pompadour (1721–64), mistress of Louis XV of France.

"…Her tott'ring form Ill propp'd upon French Heels" (1784, Cowper, *The Task*).

French hood

(F)

Period: 1521–1590; unfashionably to ca. 1630.

A small bonnet made on a stiff frame, worn far back on the head, the front border curving forward on each side to cover the ears. This border was usually trimmed with an inched edging, behind which was the nether **billiment** of goldsmith's work; further back, arched over the crown, was the upper billiment. Behind this, falling down the back of the neck, was fabric in formal pleats or, more often, a stiffened flap which could be turned up and worn flat on the crown, the straight edge projecting over the forehead and known as a **cornet** or **bongrace**.

The English variation of the French hood (1525–1558), associated with Queen Mary I, was flattened across the head, projecting wide of the temples, then turned in at an angle to cover the ears, otherwise the same.

French hose

(M)

Period: ca. 1550–1610.

Round or oval **trunk-hose**, usually with **panes**, and with **canions** after 1570. Synonymous with **bullion-hose**.

French jacket

See Petenlair.

French lock

See Love lock.

French night-cap

See Dormeuse.

French opening vest

(M)

Period: 1840s onwards.

One with the **waistcoat** fronts cut low to expose much of the shirt-front.

French pocket

(M)

Period: 17th century.

The early form of horizontal slit pocket with the opening covered by a flap. "A straight bodied Coat with French pockets" (1675, *London Gazette*).

French ruff

(M)

Period: 1580–ca. 1610.

The very large cartwheel **ruff**, as mentioned by John Stowe.

French skirt

See Cornet skirt.

French sleeves

(M)

Period: ca. 1550–1600.

Sleeves, probably detachable and with **pinking** or **panes**. "A pair of French sleeves of green velvet" (1547, Inventory of Wardrobe of Henry VIII). "Sleeves of cambric and calico for plucking out of French sleeves" (1553, Inventory of the Palace of Westminster, Hatfield Papers).

French vest

(M)

Period: 1860s.

A **waistcoat** with short lapels cut on and not turned; buttoned high.

French work

(F)

Period: Early 19th century.

Insertions of embroidery let into the front of a bodice.

Fret, frette

(F, rarely M)

Period: 13th to early 16th century.

From the Old French word *frete*, this was a trellis-work **coif** or **skull-cap** made either of goldsmiths' work or fabric. "A frett of goold sche hadde next hyre her" (ca. 1385, Chaucer, *Legend of Good Women*, Prologue).

In 16th century it could mean trellis-work ornamentation on a garment.

Frileuse

(F)

Period: 1847.

A **pelerine** wrap of quilted satin or velvet, fitting into the waist behind, and having long, loose sleeves. For wearing over the shoulders "by the fireside or at the theatre".

Frill

Period: 16th century onwards.

An edging gathered to produce a rippled surface. "Their flaunting ruffes…their borowed frilles and such like vanities" (1591, R. Turnbull).

Frilling

(F)

Period: ca. 1850–1900.

A gathered edging of stiff white muslin, worn at the wrists and neck, especially on the dress of widows in the 1870s and 1880s.

Fringe

Period: Medieval onwards.

An ornamental border of pendant threads of various makes. In the medieval period used mostly for ecclesiastical garments but rare for lay dress before the 15th century. "Fringe of silke, yelowe, grene, rede, white, and blue" (1480, Wardrobe Expenses, Edward IV).

Fringed waistcoats, with fringe along the bottom of the **foreparts**, were fashionable between ca. 1710 and ca. 1730.

Also, a hairdressing term from the late 19th century onwards.

Frisette

(F)

Period: 19th century.

A crimped **fringe** of hair over the forehead, sometimes artificial. In the 1860s it denoted a pad over which the back hair was rolled.

Period: 1869.

The term extended to padding used in underskirts.

Frisk

(F)

Period: 1815–1818.

A **bustle** worn outside helping to produce the **Grecian bend**.

Frizze

(F)

Period: 17th century onwards.

Closely curled or crimped hair. "Her hair brown of a natural Frizze or curl about the forehead" (1685, *London Gazette*).

Frizzle

Period: 17th century.

A **frizz-wig**.

Also, a small **ruff**.

Frizz-wig

(M)

Period: 17th to mid-19th century.
A wig closely crimped all over.

Frock

(M)

Period: Medieval.
The term was first used for the monastic habit, but also began to denote a loose, sleeved outer garment of coarse material worn by farm-workers, carters and drovers, and later called a **slop** frock; in the 19th century it became a **smock-frock**.

Period: 16th century.
A loose jerkin or jacket made to be comfortable; sometimes called a "frocked jacket".

Period: From ca. 1720.
See Frock coat.

(F)

Period: 16th and 17th centuries.
The term was occasionally used for an informal gown, but more usually it denoted children's dresses, including those worn by small boys before they were breeched. "Instead of green sey that was wont to be used for children's frocks, is now used painted and India stained and striped calicoes" (1678, *The Ancient Trades, etc. by a Country Tradesman*).

Period: Late 18th and 19th centuries.
The word "frock" was used for a back-fastening dress of thin fabric. This usage continued into the 20th century but was superseded by the use of frock as an alternative to dress.

Frock coat

(M)

Period: 18th century to ca. 1815.
A sporting and informal coat which appeared in fashionable circles in the 1720s. That version had a small, turned-down collar and sleeves with narrow cuffs or slits. By the last quarter of the 18th century it had become acceptable formal wear.

Period: ca. 1816–ca. 1823.
It became a formal, waisted and close-fitting coat, at first single-breasted with roll or **Prussian collar** and no lapels; buttoned to the waist-level. It had a full skirt hanging vertically in front, the back with a vent, side pleats and hip-buttons.

Period: 1823 to early 20th century.
It acquired a seam at the waist, collar and lapels, and pockets on the hips under flaps. With minor variations this remained the basic style for the rest of the century; it was often called a **morning** frock coat in the 1870s and 1880s to distinguish it from the **dress frock coat**.

Frock great coat, top frock

(M)

Period: ca. 1830 to early 20th century.

One cut like a **frock coat** but often longer and usually double-breasted; for outdoor wear when it could be worn without an under-coat.

Frock jacket

(M)

Period: 1840s.
A very short, single-breasted **frock coat** just covering the buttocks. By the 1860s the name was applied to a jacket without a seam at the waist or a back seam; collar, and lapels small and cut in one with the **forepart**.

Frog, frogging

Period: 18th century onwards.
An ornamental loop-fastening for a coat, used with a **frog-button**; associated with **Brandenbourgs**.

Frog-button, olivette

Period: 18th century onwards.
A spindle-shaped, braided button to pass through frog fastenings.

Frog pocket

(M)

Period: 19th century.
A pocket in front of the side seam of breeches, and cut with a rectangular flap, the point secured by a button.

Front

Period: 17th to early 20th century.
A term applied to a forehead **fringe** of false hair.

Frontlet, frontel, frontayl

(F)

Period: Medieval.
A decorative band worn across the forehead, usually under a veil or **coverchief**, but by the late 15th century often a band of black velvet worn across the brow.

Frock Coats.

Plate depicting **frock coats** from T.H. Holding, *Coats*, 1902. These variants, including a clerical one, also present the correct headwear, a **top hat**, **wing** or **standing collars** to the shirts, **cravats** or thin **ties**, patterned **waistcoats** and **trousers** of striped or checked cloth. Private collection.

Period: 16th and early 17th century.

Worn with a bonnet, **caul** or **coif**. "Frontayle for a woman's head, Some call it a fruntlet" (1552, Hulock).

Period: 18th century.

A frontlet was synonymous with a **forehead cloth** or **crosscloth**, a band smeared with cream and bound round the forehead to remove wrinkles.

"In vain, poor nymph, to please our youthful sight
You sleep in cream and frontlets all the night" (1722, T. Parnell, *Elegy to an Old Beauty*).

Frose paste, Frows paste, Froes paste

Period: ca. 1527–1560s.

Possibly the quilled or crimped border to the front of a **French hood** with which pastes were associated in wardrobe accounts of the period. When French hoods went out of fashion, references to pastes vanished. The paste was "fine pasted paper such as paste-wives made womens paste of" (1570, Billingsley, *Euclid*). This was the foundation for the border of velvet, lawn or other rich material, sometimes decorated with gold or jewels.

Frou-frou dress

(F)

Period: 1870.

A day dress with a low corsage covered with a short muslin tunic, the skirts rounded off in front and worn over a light, silk underskirt trimmed with innumerable small, pinked flounces. Named from the 1869 comedy by Henri Meilhac and Ludovic Halévy.

Frounce

(F)

Period: Mid-14th century to ca. 1610.

A pleated or gathered frill, a flounce; adapted from its original meaning a wrinkle of the brow, a frown. The skirt over the **wheel farthingale** was often frounced to avoid the hard line produced by the understructure.

Frouting

Period: 17th century.

Rubbing perfumed oil into a garment to sweeten it.

Frouze, fruz

Period: Late 17th and early 18th centuries.

A term implying crimped false hair or a wig worn to cover up baldness. "This woman…has adorned her baldness with a large white fruz" (1678, Sir G. Etherege, *The Man of Mode*).

See Frizz-wig.

Full bottom, full-bottomed wig, French wig

(M)

Period: 1660 to early 18th century.

A massive wig with a centre parting and close curls framing the face, and extending all round on to the shoulders. Later in the 18th century it was worn on formal occasions and by the learned professions only.

Fun fur

Period: 1960s onwards.

Either cheap fur, such as rabbit skins, or synthetic furs dyed in bright colours and worn in place of expensive traditional furs.

Funnel sleeve

See Pagoda sleeve.

Fur

Period: Medieval onwards.

The short, fine, soft hair of various animals, from inexpensive pelts such as rabbits, to expensive ones such as sables, used to line and trim garments and later to form the outer layer.

Furbelow, below

(F)

Period: 18th century.

"Plaited or ruffled trimming for women's petticoats and scarves" (1730, Bailey, *Dictionary*). Furbelows were usually flounces of the same fabric as the garment, or of lace, and were also used on **gowns** and **aprons**. The French term, often used, was *falbala*.

G

Gabardine, gaberdine

(M, occasionally F)

Period: Early 16th to early 17th century.

A long, loose overcoat with wide sleeves, worn with or without a **girdle** at the waist. After the 1560s it ceased to be a fashionable garment but remained popular among the poor and was defined as "a cloake of felt for raynie weather", and also as "a horseman's cloak or coat".

See Glossary of Fabrics and Materials.

Gable bonnet, gable hat

(F)

Period: 1884.

A bonnet whose front brim rose "like the angle of a thatched roof forming a point over the face".

Gable head-dress

See English hood.

Gabrielle dress

(F)

Period: 1865.

A day dress of which the bodice and front breadth of the skirt were cut in one; three large **box pleats** at the back, or one each side and one behind; all widths gored.

Gabrielle sleeve

(F)

Period: 19th century.

One very full to the elbow, thence narrowing to mid-forearm and finished at the wrist with a deep cuff. Used for **spencers** in 1820, for day dresses from 1830 to 1835. Between 1859 and 1869 the term was applied to a sleeve made up of a series of puffs from shoulder to wrist.

Gadroon

(F)

Period: 19th century.

An inverted pleat or fluting used as a trimming on caps and cuffs, and popular for skirts of dresses in the 1870s.

Gainsborough bonnet

(F)

Period: 1877.

A close-fitting bonnet with a high front brim and a broad crown sloping off abruptly behind: generally of velvet trimmed with roses.

Gaiter

(M)

Period: Late 18th to 20th century.

A covering for the ankle or with it the small of the leg, and spreading out over the upper of the shoe or boot, with a strap passing under the instep. Generally buttoned up on the outer side.

(F)

Fashionable for women from the 1820s–1840s and also in 1890s. Usually made of silk, cashmere or elastic fabrics.

Gaiter bottoms

(M)

Period: ca. 1840–1860.

Term indicating the cut of the bottom of the trouser legs; "whole gaiter-bottoms" had the side seams brought forward 4" from the heel, the fronts being 5" wide and the backs 12½"; "half gaiter-bottoms" had the seams brought forward 1½", making the fronts 8" and the backs 11" at the ankles.

Galatea comb

(F)

Period: 1890s.

A decorative hair-comb with a few long prongs set in a curve with an ornamental, looped handle.

Galatea hat

(F & M)

Period: 1890s.

A hat of Chinese or Japanese plait, made with a sailor crown and turned-up brim; worn by small children in summer.

Galligaskins, gally-gas-coynes, gaskins

(M)

Period: ca. 1570 to end of 17th century; rare after 1620. Knee-breeches, either wide or bombasted round the buttocks, or "sometimes close to the buttocke like the Venetian gallicascoyne" (1610, S. Rowlands, *Martin Mark-all*).

Period: 19th century.

The term was applied to leather **gaiters** worn by sportsmen.

Gallislops, gallyslops, gally hose, gally breeches

(M)

Period: 17th century.

The same as wide **galligaskins**.

Gallo-Greek bodice

(F)

Period: 1820s.

A bodice with narrow, flat trimming descending from the shoulders, without quite meeting at the waist.

Gallowses

(M)

Period: 18th and 19th centuries.

Braces, unfashionable before the 1780s. "Contrivances made of cloth, and hooks and eyes, worn over the shoulders by men to keep their breeches up" (1730-6, Bailey, *Dictionary*).

Galosh, golosh

(F & M)

Period: 14th to early 20th century.

A generic term for a protective over-shoe, though the nature varied. There were many spellings, including galoche, galage, galoss, galossian, galloses, galloshoes and gallotives. In the 14th century they were buckled overshoes; in the 15th and 16th centuries they were the same as **pattens**, i.e. wooden soles secured by latchets.

In the late 16th and early 17th century they were wooden-soled, low over-boots, buckled and worn by all classes. In 1607 Prince Henry had sixteen gold buckles, "with pendants and tongues to buckle a pair of galosses" (Wardrobe Accounts).

In the late 17th century "galloshoes are false shooes or covers for shooes" (1688, R. Holme, *Armory*). In the 18th century they were usually called **clogs**. Rubber galoshes were introduced and patented in 1842.

Gamashes

(M)

Period: 1590s–1700.

Loose, long, cloth **leggings**, often buttoned. "Gamashes or upper stockings" (1598, Florio). In the 17th century they acquired soles. "Gamashes, high boots, buskins or start-ups" (1688, R. Holme, *Armory*). They were worn on horseback or by pedestrians as a protection against the dirt.

Gambado, gamada, gambage

(M)

Period: ca. 1650–1750.

"A kind of leather instrument attached to the saddle in place of stirrups" (1656, Blount, *Glosso-graphia*). The gambado resembled a large boot open on the outer side.

Gamine

(F)

Period: 1900 onwards.

A French term descriptive of a pert, elfin-featured, slender young woman, often with a short hair style. Particularly associated with the French dancer Zizi Jeanmaire (b. 1924) and the film actress Audrey Hepburn (1929–1993), and the clothing worn in *Jules et Jim*, the 1962 French film, boyish styles – cap, **knicker-bockers**, etc. with a feminine twist.

Gamp

Period: 19th century.

Popular name for an **umbrella**; so-called from Dickens's character, Mrs Gamp, in *Martin Chuzzlewit* (1843).

Gangsta style

(M)

Period: Late 1980s onwards.

An African-American term applied to young members of street gangs. The popularity of gangsta rap musicians ensured that their style of clothing – loose T-shirts, baseball caps worn at an angle, unbelted jeans worn low on the hips and an excessive quantity of heavy gold jewellery – was widely emulated throughout the world, often by white youths.

Garçonne look

(F)

Period: 1922.

The publication of Victor Marguerrite's novel *La Garçonne* offered a descriptive term for the young, emancipated women of the post-World War I period, with their androgynous clothing and cropped hair. The clothing choices of these women, often known as flappers and later as **gamines**, was suggestive of the black and white dress of French waiters – *garçons*.

Garde-corps

(F & M)

Period: 13th and early 14th centuries.

A voluminous, unbelted **super tunic** with hood and long, wide sleeves often worn as **hanging sleeves**, the arm passing through a vertical slit in the upper half. A garment for winter wear.

See Herigaut.

Garibaldi blouse, Garibaldi shirt

(F)

Period: 1860 into 1880s.

Worn in place of a bodice, with any style of day skirt, this blouse was originally of scarlet merino trimmed with black braid. Full sleeves or plain "coat sleeves" gathered into a wristband with small **epaulettes** on the shoulders; small collar and black **cravat**; sometimes worn with a **Zouave** jacket. The blouse usually overhanging the skirt and worn with a waist-belt.

Garibaldi bodice, Garibaldi vest

(F)

Period: 1860s.

A day bodice made loose and falling over the waistband or confined with narrow tucks from neck to waist; worn with or without a jacket. Also known as **Russian vest**. Garibaldi's visit to England in 1863 gave enormous popularity to anything named after him, from a blouse to a biscuit.

Garibaldi jacket

(F)

Period: 1860s.

An outdoor jacket, short and square-cut, without **basques**; made of scarlet cashmere with military braiding.

Garibaldi sleeve

(F)

Period: 1860s.

A sleeve that was full and gathered into a wristband. Worn with morning or afternoon dresses of thin fabrics.

Garment

Period: 14th century onwards.

Any item of clothing for the body.

Garnache

(M)

Period: 13th to mid-14th century.

A long, loose **super tunic** with short, cape-like sleeves cut in one with the body and falling over the shoulders. The side seams were sometimes left open or joined at the waist-level or from waist to hem.

In the 14th century a characteristic feature was two tongue-shaped lapels at the front of the neck; these were paler than the garment itself and often faced with fur.

See Tabard.

Garniture

Period: 17th century, rare after ca. 1900.

"The trimming of a suit with Ribbons, precious stones etc., as Garniture of Diamonds" (1706, Phillips, edit. Kersey).

Garter

(F & M)

A tie or band to keep the stocking in place on the leg, and placed above or below the knee. For the significance of "ungartered", see **love**.

(M)

Period: Medieval to late 16th century.

Garters were usually ties; subsequently ties or buckled bands.

Period: 17th and 18th centuries.

Some garters were like small decorative scarves, with fringed ends and tied in a bow on the outer side of the knee. Others were decorative bands with ornamental buckles, always placed below the knee. Garters might be of wool, worsted, crewel, list, or ribbon, taffeta, cypress and net. "2 yards of ribband for garters" (1522, Le Strange Accounts). "A pair of silver garters buckled below the knee" (1711, *The Spectator*).

(F)

Period: Late 17th and 18th centuries.

Garters, worn above or below the knee, were often very decorative and sometimes woven with mottoes addressed to young men who sought them as trophies. "Great quantities of silk garters are bought by the ladies with the following motto NO SEARCH" (1739, Pilborough's *Colchester Journal*).

Period: 19th century.

The garter was usually a long, narrow strip of knitted wool wound round the leg above the knee, or more elegant forms were of silk enclosing fine brass springs and having metal clasps. From ca. 1830 India-rubber woven elastic began to appear, becoming general by ca. 1850. From 1878 garters were replaced by **suspenders**.

Gascon coat, Gaskyn coat

See Jupe.

Gascon hose

Another term for **galligaskins**.

Gather

Period: 16th century onwards.

To draw a length of fabric into a shorter length by means of a thread; a basic sewing skill.

Gaucho pants

(F)

Period: 1920s onwards.

The style of wide-skirted, calf-length riding breeches worn by South American cowboys and made popular by Rudolph Valentino in *The Four Horsemen of the Apocalypse* (1921). The style was worn by women and became fashionable again in the 1960s.

Gauging, gaging, shirring

Period: 19th century.

A term applied to a series of close, parallel running stitches, so that the fabric in between is fixed in gathers. A form of decoration extremely popular in bonnets of the 1840s and in dresses of the late 1870s and 1880s; also found in traditional **smocking**.

Gauntlet

(M)

Period: Mid-15th to late 17th century.

Until the abandonment of armour this term was applied to a glove-like defence of the hand.

(F & M)

The term was also given to a glove with a cuff spreading up the wrist.

See Gloves.

Gemmews, jemews

(M)

Period: 15th century.

The jaws of a bag working on pins at the side, or a mere strengthening of leather or velvet round the jaws.

The Squire of Alsatia from a series of engravings called *The Cryes of London* by Marcellus Laroon II, ca. 1687–8. The name comes from a play by Thomas Shadwell and the "squire" was based on a real person. He is the epitome of fashion with a French style asymmetrical **wig** under a hat curling into a shape which will soon become a **cocked hat**. His **coat**, **waistcoat** and **breeches** are the beginning of the eighteenth century **suit**. A lace **cravat**, fringed **gauntlet gloves**, **cane** and sword are the **accessories** of a gentleman; a status assumed not real so this is dressing-up to mislead and for **theatrical** performance. Private collection.

Gender-blurred fashions

(F & M)

Period: 20th century onwards.

Not cross-dressing, but the adoption of clothing which defies usual gender categories, such as **jeans**, **T-shirts**, leather jackets, biker boots, and so forth.

See Unisex.

Geneva hat

(M)

Period: Late 16th and early 17th centuries.

A broad-brimmed, high-crowned hat, sometimes un-trimmed, worn by Puritan ministers and others.

Geneva print ruff, Geneva-set ruff

(F & M)

Period: 17th century.

A small **ruff** of Puritanical design modelled on that of the Genevan Calvinists. "In print as Puritan ruffes are set" (1613, Mynshul, *Essays*); "A little Geneva-set (ruff)" (1633, T. Adams).

Genoa cloak

See Spanish cloak.

German gown

See Brunswick gown.

Ghillie

See Gillie.

Ghutra, gutra

See Keffiyeh.

Giboun

(M)

Period: 1844.

A loose wrap in the form of a small shoulder cape with wide sleeves, resembling the **caban** of the period, but the fronts falling straight like a cloak without fastenings.

Gibus, Gibus hat

(M)

Period: 1840s onwards.

A **top hat** with a collapsible crown, the sides of which contained concealed within the lining a metal "lazy tongs"; when flat the hat could be carried under the arm. Worn with evening dress and replacing the earlier **elastic round hat**. Named after its inventor.

Gig coat

(F)

Period: 1820s.

See Curricle coat.

Gigot sleeve, leg-of-mutton sleeve

(F)

Period: 1824–1836, 1862 and 1890–1896; ca. 1960–1980.

A day sleeve, very full at the shoulder, diminishing in size towards the elbow and gradually becoming tight at the wrist. In 1827 the upper portion was sometimes distended with whalebone hoops. In 1862 used only for summer dresses. In 1895 the gigot was "monstrous", requiring 2½ yards of material. It collapsed abruptly in 1896 but was revived in the 1960s and 1970s.

(M)

Period: 1820s and 1860s.

A minor male fashion.

Gilet

(F)

Period: 19th century onwards.

A sleeveless bodice shaped to imitate a man's **waistcoat**.

Gillie, ghillie

(F & M)

Period: 19th century onwards.

A form of footwear worn with traditional Scottish dress and named for the attendant on a Highland chieftain. It is a leather shoe with an open front, with lacing from side to side through tabs and up around the ankle. It was and is made in various weights and variants of the style, to suit everything from dancing to stalking.

Gills, shirt-gills

(M)

Period: 19th century.

Colloquial name for the upstanding points of the shirt-collar.

Gimp, guimple

See Wimple.

Gingham

Period: 19th century.

A colloquial name for an **umbrella**, the cheaper kinds being made of that material.

See Gamp.

Ginglers

(M)

Period: Late 16th and early 17th centuries.

Spurs with one or two metal drops hung in an eye on the rowel-pin, which rattled against the rowel when the wearer walked. Very fashionable at the period indicated. "I had spurs of mine own before but they were not gin-glers." (1599, B. Jonson, *Every Man out of his Humour*). "You that weare Bootes and Ginglers at your heels" (1604, S. Rowlands, *Swaggering Ruffian*).

Gipon, jupon

(M)

Period: 14th century.

A military term adapted for civilian use and taken from the French term *jupon*. The gipon was a close-fitting, waisted and padded garment worn over the shirt. It ended near the knees at first, but was much shortened in the second half of the century. Buttoned or laced down the front, the sleeves long and tight with buttons up to the elbows on the outer side. No belt unless worn without an overgarment. The gipon was the forerunner of the **doublet** and was so-called towards the close of that century.

Gipser, gipcière

Period: 14th and 15th centuries.

A purse or pouch.

"A gipser al of silk Heng at his girdle…" (ca. 1381, Chaucer, *Canterbury Tales,* Prologue).

Gipsy, gypsy styles

(F)

Period: 20th century.

Low-cut blouses, wide colourful skirts, flowing scarves and gold jewellery, associated with both real and stage gipsies, entered the design vocabulary at several points in the 20th century.

Gipsy bonnet

(F)

Period: 1871.

A small, flat bonnet only covering the crown of the head; trimmed with lace and feather.

Gipsy hat

(F)

Period: 1800–1830s.

A straw or chip hat with wide brim, always with ribbons passing from the crown over the brim and tied in a bow under the chin.

Giraffe comb

(F)

Period: 1874.

A very high, ornamental hair-comb of tortoiseshell, worn in the day as well as with evening dress.

Girdle

(F & M)

Period: Medieval onwards.

A cord or band, tied or buckled, encircling the waist or hips. In the medieval period it confined the flowing garments at the waist, or was used to suspend various objects, or sometimes it was purely decorative.

"And by hire girdel heng a purs of lether

Tasseled with grene and perled with latoun" (ca. 1381, Chaucer, *Miller's Tale*).

See Knightly girdle.

(F)

Period: 1920s onwards.

An American term for an elasticated, rather than a boned, **corset**.

Girdle glass

(F)

Period: 17th century.

A hand mirror hanging from the waistband.

Girdlestead

(F & M)

Period: Medieval–17th century.

The waist-line.

Gite

(F, occasionally M)

Period: 14th–16th century.

A type of dress or gown.

Gladstone overcoat

(M)

Period: 1870s.

A short, double-breasted overcoat with a shoulder-cape and borders trimmed with astrakhan.

Glaudkin, glawdkin

(M)

Period: Early 16th century.

A term for a wide-sleeved, flowing gown.

Glauvina pin

(F)

Period: ca. 1820–1840.

An ornamental pin with a large, detachable head, often tasselled; used to secure an elaborate **coiffure**.

Glengarry, Glengarry bonnet

(F & M)

Period: 1860s.

"A Scotch bonnet higher in front than at the back" (1858, *Simmonds's Dictionary*). Generally decorated with a small feather and pendant ribbons behind; worn by certain Scottish regiments and with traditional Highland dress but, in this context, as a fashionable head-covering.

Glove-band

(F)

Period: ca. 1640–1700.

A band of ribbon or plaited horsehair tied at the elbow over a long glove to keep it in place.

Gloves

(M)

Period: Medieval to late 17th century.

Either covering the hand and ending at the wrist, or made with deep, spreading cuffs as **gauntlet** gloves. In the 16th century gloves were made of leather from stag, sheep, horse, kid, suède, doe, also satin, velvet, knitted silk and worsted, variously coloured. Some were slashed to show a finger ring. Long gloves were rare for men but occasionally worn by the ultra-fashionable in the 17th century, and often elaborately decorated, fringed and scented.

"He is indeed a pattern of modern foppery. He was yesterday at the play, with a pair of gloves up to his elbows" (1676, Etherege, *The Man of Mode*).

Period: 18th century.

"*Gants à l'anglaise*" ended at the wrist, having a short slit on the back or a narrow, turned-back cuff, sometimes embroidered. From 1600 until 1800 gloves were made from similar materials to earlier centuries though Spanish leather, cordovan, was very fashionable.

Period: 19th century onwards.

Invariably short and until ca. 1870 often coloured for day, with white for evenings and lavender for weddings. In the 20th century plain leather and knitted gloves were worn in town and country; there were specialist gloves for driving, golf, riding and other activities.

g

(F)

Period: Medieval to ca. 1800.

As for men, until ca. 1640 when elbow-length gloves, close-fitting, of fine leather or silk, and often white, sometimes embroidered, began to be fashionable and essential for full dress. In the 18th century elbow-length gloves were universal except with **riding habits** and, towards the end of the century, with long-sleeved dresses.

Period: 19th century.

Either short to the wrist or long to the elbow; coloured during the day, but white in the evening. A short evening glove was fashionable from 1830–1865; subsequently it lengthened and by the 1890s spread up beyond the elbow.

Period: 20th century onwards.

Many types and colours until the post-World War II period when gradually gloves became less essential, except for winter warmth.

See Berlin gloves, Limerick gloves, Woodstock gloves, York tan gloves, Chicken-skin gloves, Cut-fingered gloves, Mittens.

Glove-string

(F)

Period: 18th century.

Similar to a **glove-band**, made of ribbon or horsehair and tied or buckled at the elbow over a long glove. "Diamond buckles to the glove-strings" – for full dress (1783, *Lady's Magazine*).

Godet pleat

(F)

Period: 1870s onwards.

A hollow, tubular pleat, narrow above and expanding downwards to give a fluted effect to the skirt.

Godet skirt

(F)

Period: 1895.

A day skirt with godet pleats at the back and sides often sustained by fine steel in the hem and in the lining. "A labyrinth of black elastic to keep the flutes in place".

Goffered veil, nebula head-dress

Period: 19th century.

Terms used in the 19th century for a head-dress worn by women from ca. 1350–1420. The head-dress, made of linen, was draped over the head with a broad, goffered frill surrounding the face and ending at the temples or chin. The back drapery fell to the shoulders, sometimes having a goffered border.

Goffering

Period: 17th century onwards.

The use of heated goffering irons or tongs to create a decorative, fluted edge to cotton or linen used in clothing. Later it referred to a fabric with a permanent crimped appearance.

Gole, golet

(M)

Period: 14th and 15th centuries.

The cape portion of the hood or **chaperon**. "Golet" was the 15th-century term.

Golf vest

(M)

Period: 1894.

A single-breasted waistcoat without a collar; having two side pockets and watch-pocket. Of scarlet knitted wool bound with braid.

Golilla

(M)

Period: 17th century.

A Spanish term sometimes used for the semicircular collar or **band** curving round the back of the head with the straight border under the chin. Very fashionable from 1605–1630.

Gonel

(M)

Period: 14th century.

A gown, sometimes worn over armour.

Gored bell skirt

(F)

Period: 1893.

The front panel of this skirt was gored with three to five side gores; the back panel cut on the cross, keeping the fullness behind; the hem was 10–16 feet in circumference, lined with a footing of muslin or crinoline 9 inches deep.

Gored skirt

(F)

Period: 14th century onwards.

A constructional method of cutting the material into pyramidal-shaped panels, narrow above, to produce a close fit at the waist, avoiding gathers or pleats. Much used in the 19th century, especially the 1820s, late 1860s and mid-1890s, when it reached the highest degree of technical skill. Also found in the 20th century, especially on 1930s skirts.

Gorget, gorgette

(M)

Period: 14th and 15th centuries.

The cape portion of hood or **chaperon**.

See Gole.

Period: 15th–17th century.

A military steel or plate-armour collar covering the neck and upper chest and worn as a mark of distinction by civilians.

(F)

Period: 12th to early 16th century.

A neck covering. The more usual term was **wimple**; by the late 16th century it meant the small **ruff** of a **smock**.

Period: 17th to early 18th century.
A deep, falling, cape-like collar, generally called a **whisk**.

Goth

(F & M)

Period: 1980s onwards.
A follower of a particular post-Punk cult of music and appearance, the latter involving black hair, exaggerated black and white make-up, and black clothing often ripped or with aspects of **bondage style**, such as chains.

Gothic cap

(F)

Period: 1834.
An indoor morning cap with a very small crown; trimmed with ruching framing the face.

Gowce

Period: 14th and 15th centuries.
Term meaning a gusset.

Gown

(M)

Period: Medieval to ca. 1600.
A loose, long, upper garment of a formal nature, varying in design but generally with wide and often **hanging sleeves**; a **demi-gown** or half-gown reached the knees; a side-gown or long gown reached the ankles.

Period: ca. 1600 onwards.
Mostly worn by the learned professions and officials.

(F)

Period: Medieval–18th century.
A term indicating a woman's dress.

Period: 19th century onwards.
Usually implied a dress of uniform fabric fastened in front, as opposed to a **frock** which fastened behind. However, by the 20th century the term "dress" was more usual.

Grande-assiette sleeves

(M)

Period: Mid-14th to mid-15th century.
A type of sleeve sometimes made for the **gipon** and early **doublet**; the sleeve cut so as to form a circular, plate-like seam when inserted, thus overlapping the front and back of the body; rare in England.

Grannie skirt, Victoria skirt

(F)

Period: 1893.
Supposed to be a revival of the skirt of the 1830s; cut in a circular shape from double-width material, the hem sixteen to eighteen feet round; made with flounces and tucks from knee level, with a velvet band facing the hem; a pocket, if present, was behind in the **placket** hole.

Granny bonnet

(F)

Period: 1893.

Drawing by Hans Holbein of Henry VIII (foreground) and his father Henry VII, ca. 1536–7. This compare and contrast image depicts Henry VII in a simple **cap** with a turned-up brim decorated with a **brooch** and a long furred **gown** with a **slashed sleeve** to reveal the **doublet** beneath. Henry VIII's cap is covered with jewelled brooches and his wide shouldered gown is worn over a U-front **jerkin** over a side-fastening doublet; the doublet front and sleeves have **shirt** fabric pulled out between jewelled clasps and the **cod-piece** is an emphatic statement of masculinity. National Portrait Gallery, London. http://www.npg.org.uk.

"A huge erection with wide and flaring brim and pot-like crown and decorated with feathers." A homage to 1830s fashions.

Granny style

(F & M)

Period: 1960s and 1970s.

Clothing and accessories which suggested an earlier period; round wire-framed spectacles, collarless shirts, long skirts or similar. The quasi-Edwardian clothing designed by the British designer Laura Ashley (1925–1985) in the early 1970s was especially evocative of this referencing of past styles.

Graundice

(F)

Period: 16th century.

An ornament for the head; a variant of **craunce** or **crants**.

Greatcoat

(F & M)

Period: 18th century onwards.

An outdoor **overcoat** varying in style according to the fashion of the day.

Greatcoat dress

(F)

Period: Late 18th century.

A fashionable style of the 1780s; either a closed robe buttoned to the hem or, more often, just closed to the waist with the overskirt falling away to reveal the **petticoat**. The wrist-length sleeves fitted closely and the caped collar and contrasting revers of the male greatcoat were copied.

Grecian bend

(F)

Period: 1815–1819; 1868–1870.

A fashionable stance consisting of a forward stoop from the waist, the effect increased by a **bustle** and in the later period by a puffed-out overskirt.

Grecian sleeve

(F)

Period: 1852.

An **under sleeve** slit open at the side and closed with buttons.

Grecque

(M)

Period: ca. 1750–1800.

A style of dressing the hair of the **wig**. "Some people wear it cut short before and comed up en brosse very high upon the top of the head; it's called à la greque and is very pretty when well done" (January 1766, Lady Sarah Bunbury to Lady Susan O"Brien, *The Life and Letters of Lady Sarah Lennox*, J. Murray, 1902).

By 1787, "The hair is dressed in 2 long curls on each side and a Grecque behind, divided like a horseshoe, inclining a little forward en coque" (*Ipswich Journal*).

In 1788, " The hair is dressed in four curls on each side,

three below and one above, and a grecque en dos d"âne turned off at top behind in the form of a horse-shoe and tied behind in a long queue" (*Ipswich Journal*). The side curls were arranged horizontally, framing each side of the face.

Grecque corsage

(F)

Period: 1850.

An evening-dress bodice, low off the shoulders and square, with vertical pleats sloping down to a point in front.

Gregorian

(M)

Period: Mid- to late 17th century.

A **wig** called after "one Gregory a barber in the Strand" (1670, Blount, *Glossographia*).

Gregs

See Galligaskins.

Grelot

Period: 1860–1900.

Small metallic balls or bells used on a fashionable trimming for dresses.

Gretchen

(F)

Period: 1890s onwards.

Term describing a style associated with young German women, such as plaits wound around the head or peasant-style blouses with their distinctive round necklines and embroidery.

Grunge

(F & M)

Period: Late 1980s onwards.

Loose-fitting, layered clothing, ripped jeans and heavy boots worn by subcultural band members and copied by their followers. Perceived as a junk shop or charity shop approach to dressing, rejecting commercialism in favour of recycling. One of many movements in the 20th century which seemed to reposition fashion as a street-influenced business.

G-string, gee-string

(F)

Period: 20th century.

Term originally referring to a **loin cloth** but appropriated to describe the modest fabric triangle and strings worn by exotic dancers and strippers in night-clubs. From the 1990s a form of minimal underwear for women.

See Thong.

Guard-chain

(M)

Period: 1825 onwards.

A long chain of small links worn round the neck and attached to the **watch**, replacing the fob-chain.

Guards

(F & M)

Period: 16th to mid-17th century.

Decorative bands of rich material, plain or embroidered, used as borders to conceal seams on garments. "A jacket guarded with velvet" meant one trimmed with guards. Also a term used in heraldry.

Guernsey
(M, later F)
Period: Early 19th century onwards.
Worn much earlier by local fishermen (Guernsey is one of the Channel Islands), these thick, knitted, oiled-wool, close-fitting sweaters with their distinctive rib and rope patterns became increasingly popular in the 19th century, either in the original deep blue/black or in other colours. Their warmth and waterproof qualities ensured that they became a **classic** garment in the 20th century.

Guimpe
(F)
Period: 1890s.
A term used in America for a **chemisette** worn with a low-necked dress.

Gwimple
See Wimple.

Gym-slip
(F)
Period: Early 20th century onwards.
A sleeveless woollen tunic with a deep, square-necked yoke from which the garment reached to knee level or just below in wide **box pleats**; the waist usually held by a sash or belt and worn over a long-sleeved blouse. The term derives from gymnasium clothing but quickly became a school **uniform** for girls, rather than athletic wear. Hugely popular by the 1920s, the garment was also called a gym-dress or gym-tunic and often worn with gym knickers (long and baggy) and gym shoes. The style has been used as inspiration for fashion designers and is also appropriated for fetishist purposes.
See Pinafore dress.

Gypsy
See Gipsy.

H

Habit
(F & M)
Period: Medieval onwards.
Fashion or style of clothing, often used for the distinctive dress of a particular rank or profession, especially of religious orders.

(F)
Period: 18th century onwards.
The dress or suit worn on horseback, as riding habit.

Habit bodice
(F)
Period: 1877 onwards.
A long **cuirasse bodice** with long **basques** or with the back of the basque cut into short tabs or coat-tails similar to those found on a postilion's coat behind. The bodice open in front and worn with a waistcoat.

Habit d'escalier
(F)
Period: Late 18th and early 19th centuries.
A full evening dress with **half robe** and short sleeves slit open from below and joined by ribbon ties resembling the rungs of a ladder.

Habit glove
(F)
Period: 18th century.
A lady's riding **glove**; some of these were of grey kid, some of York tan; usually short and resembling men's.

Habit-redingote
(F)
Period: 1879.
A **princess polonaise**, the overskirt as long as the underskirt behind and closed down to the knees in front.

Habit shirt
(F)
Period: 18th century.
Worn as part of a riding costume; it was a linen garment about 15" deep in front and 11" behind, and tied round with tape. It had a **stand collar** and ruffled shirt front, buttoned with two buttons; the sleeves frilled at the wrist. It was worn under a waistcoat.

Period: 19th century.
Worn as a fill-in for a day dress. In 1815 a **ruff** was added to the neck; often of cambric or muslin. A habit shirt was often called a **chemisette**.

Hacking jacket
(F & M)
Period: Late 19th century onwards.
A full-skirted, single-breasted jacket, with a long skirt and either a centre back vent or two side vents. Usually made in tweed and worn for riding.
Later, in the 20th century, it became a fashionable riding jacket.

Hair-band
(F)

Period: 15th–17th century.
A ribbon or **fillet** for binding the hair.

Period: 20th century onwards.
A structured band of stiffened fabric or plastic, of various widths, which held the hair back from the face.
See Alice band.

Hair cap
(F & M)
Period: 17th–19th century.
A travelling **wig**.

Hair colour
(F & M)
Period: Medieval onwards.
There were always preferred hair colours at certain periods and methods, both primitive and subtle, of achieving them; coloured wigs, powdered hair, and dyestuffs including henna and peroxide were used until, in the second half of the 20th century, sophisticated colour ranges for home or professional application became widely available.

Hair-do
(F)
Period: 1930s onwards.
An American term for a method of arranging and styling the hair.
See Coiffure.

Hair lace
Period: 16th century.
A synonym for either a **hair-band** or a **crosscloth**, the purpose of the latter being "to keep the wrinkles out of their foreheads" (1698, Fryer, *East India and Persia*).

Hair pieces
(F)
Period: 16th century onwards.
Usually lengths of hair or sections to add bulk to curls, ringlets or similar. Made of human hair until synthetic hair became available in the 20th century. A late-20th-century variant was extensions, to add length and bulk to women's hair.

Hair style
(F & M)
Period: Medieval onwards.
The manner in which hair was cut, curled or straightened; its length and arrangement on the head. Often involving trained barbers or hairdressers, though across the centuries the cutting, washing, colouring and arranging of hair has often taken place within the domestic setting.
See Coiffure.

Half boots
(M)
Period: Late 18th to early 20th century.
A name given to boots reaching to just below the calf of the leg.

Half dress
(F & M)
Period: Late 18th and 19th centuries.
A term denoting the costume worn at day functions and at informal evening ones.

Half-gaiters
See Spats.

Half handkerchief
(F)
Period: 18th century.
Half of a square of fabric cut diagonally across; usually decorative, and in the 18th century it was worn usually on the head or round the neck.

Period: 1800–1830.
An evening cap of triangular shape pinned to the crown, with the point behind and the straight side curving round the head. From the 1830s this style is generally known as a **fanchon**.

Half hose
(M)
Period: 19th century.
A tradename for socks.

Half kirtle
See Kirtle.

Half robe, half gown, demi-habillement
(F)
Period: 1794 to early 19th century.
A low-necked, thigh-length **tunic** with short sleeves, worn over a **round gown** and pulled in at the waist with a narrow ribbon tie or belt.

Half shirt
(M)
Period: 16th and 17th centuries.
A short shirt with decorative front, intended to be worn over a full-length plain shirt or one that had become soiled.

Period: 18th century.
Sometimes called **shams**. "Half-shirts or shams of coarse linen" (1772, Nugent, *History*).

(F)
Period: 18th and 19th centuries.
Half shirts of a coarse fabric were occasionally worn by countrywomen.

Half sleeves
See Fore sleeves.

Halter neck
(F)
Period: 20th century onwards.
A method whereby a bodice is supported by a band of fabric passing round the top of the neck but revealing the rest of the back and shoulders. It can be high or low-cut at the front and the halter can be tied or buttoned in place.

Handkerchief of white **calico** printed in indigo with various motifs including actors and actresses in **theatre costume**. Although probably produced with snuff-takers in mind; printing disguised hard to launder stains, this one was embroidered with a name and date "Susanna Pearce July the 9 1774". She was possibly an admirer of David Garrick, the great actor-manager or his various acting colleagues depicted here. Copyright the Olive Matthews Collection, Chertsey Museum. Photograph by John Chase.

Hammercut beard
(M)
Period: ca. 1618–1650; rarely to 1660.
This combined **beard** and **moustache**, the small straight or, rarely, twisted tuft under the lower lip forming the handle of the hammer; the moustache, waxed horizontally, forming the cross-piece. "Some with hammercut or Roman T" (1621, J. Taylor, *Superbiae Flagellum*).

Handbag
(F & M)
Period: 19th century onwards.
A term originally descriptive of a small travelling bag of the sort made famous by Lady Bracknell in Oscar Wilde's *The Importance of Being Earnest*, first performed in 1895. More usually, by the late 19th century, a British term for a woman's bag of the type that is suspended by handles from the hand or, later, the shoulder.

Hand cloth
See Handkerchief.

Hand cuff
See Hand fall.

Hand fall
(F & M)
Period: 17th century.
A turned-back, spreading **cuff**, sometimes double, trimmed with lace and starched. It might be worn with a standing or falling **band**, with a falling **ruff** and occasionally with a standing ruff. "12 rouffe bands and 8 payre of handefalles £1.10" (1604, Inventory of Wm. Spicer, Exeter Records).

Handkerchief
(F & M)
Period: 16th to late 18th century.
Although its history goes back much earlier, it was in the 16th century that the handkerchief became especially popular. Often distinguished as a **pocket handkerchief**, this was a square of linen or silk, often edged with lace, carried about the person and used for wiping the face or nose; the more elegant styles being used for display only, e.g. "five handkercheves wrought with golde and red silke" (1556, Nichols, *Gifts to Queen Mary*).
See Buttoned handkerchief, Tasselled handkerchief.
Souvenir handkerchiefs date back to the 17th century and include printed maps, performers, unusual events, etc.; if used they were often acquired by snuff-takers. In the 19th century, alongside the black-edged handkerchiefs carried by both sexes for mourning, at the death of notable people huge mourning or commemorative handkerchiefs were produced, printed with the portrait of the deceased and details of his life.

Period: 19th and early 20th centuries.
(M)

Men's handkerchiefs were always larger than women's, often coloured for day use, with black for mourning (1804) or, later, with a black border up to an inch wide. "Generally of silk, cotton not being known among the middling ranks since the duty has been taken off silk" (1830). India coloured silk and foulard bordered with a white stripe were fashionable in the 1830s.

See Bandana, Belcher.

By 1840 a white silk handkerchief, often embroidered and edged with lace, was fashionable for evening wear. By ca. 1870 the plain white cambric was correct for day and evening, the former carried in the outside breast pocket, the latter in the tail-pocket.

In the 1890s there was a fashion, borrowed from the military, of wearing the day handkerchief in the cuff of the left sleeve. At the close of the century a red silk handkerchief was often worn tucked into the opening of the evening-dress waistcoat.

(F)

Women's handkerchiefs, for day use, were of white cambric, linen or cotton; for evening, they were often of lace or edged with lace or embroidery; about the middle of the 19th century the corners of the handkerchief were rounded. By the 1890s the diminutive "hanky" was being used.

(F & M)

Period: Early 20th century onwards.

The distinction between the size remained; men's handkerchiefs were silk for breast pockets, and cotton in white, colours or patterns for actual use. Women's were similarly silk for display, often patterned, and plain white or edged with lace or embroidered in one corner. Towards the end of the century paper handkerchiefs became usual and were made in several sizes.

Handkerchief dress
(F)

Period: 1880s.

A dress composed of pieces of fabric resembling large **bandanna handkerchiefs**. "Two compose the tunic, the point of the lower reaching nearly to the hem of the skirt which is plain in front, the back kilted. The point of the upper handkerchief shews beneath the deep basqued jacket-bodice, which is plain, coat-shaped with revers and worn with a waistcoat."

Handkerchief points
(F)

Period: Early 20th century onwards.

An overskirt, or layered sections of fabric making-up a skirt, creating a loose, floating, zigzag effect like an assemblage of handkerchiefs with angled points.

Hand ruff
(F & M)

Period: 1560–1630s.

A small wrist-ruff. A "pair of ruffs" meant hand ruffs only.
See Ruffles.

Hand sleeve
Period: 16th century.

The term for the wrist portion of a sleeve and not a separate item.

Hanger
See Coat-hanger, Shoulder belt.

Hanging sleeves
(F & M)

Period: ca. 1400–1560.

Wide, long, tubular sleeves with a slit in the upper half through which the arm could emerge, leaving the sleeve pendant. Some nearly reached the ground. Worn with **gowns**, **houppelandes**, jackets and **jerkins** and sometimes with women's dresses of the **French farthingale** style.

Period: ca. 1560–1640.

Sham or false hanging sleeves were worn by both sexes. Men's garments had pendant streamers attached to the back of the arm-hole; the remains of a true hanging sleeve had become merely ornamental. Worn sometimes with jerkins.

Women's sham hanging sleeves corresponded to those worn by men.

(F)

Period: 17th and 18th centuries.

Another form of a sham hanging sleeve was represented by the **leading strings** worn by children, and remained, as a sign of youth, for girls and young women. "Carry my wedding suits to Mrs. Arnold and tell her she has forgot the hanging sleeves to the gowns" (1754, S. Richardson, *The History of Sir Charles Grandison*).

Hanselin, hanslein, henselyns, haunseleynys, hense lynes
(M)

Period: Late 14th and early 15th centuries.

The extremely short **doublet**, also called a **paltock**, which was fashionable. Also spelt "hanslet" or "anslet".

Haori
(M)

A Japanese term for a traditional style of short, loose, open coat worn over a kimono. Usually of silk and decorated with emblems or other designs.

Harem pants, harem skirt
(F)

Period: ca. 1909 onwards.

Another style associated with the arrival of the **Ballets Russes** in Paris in 1909. These loose, wide-legged trousers gathered into the waist and ankles were worn in the evening and were popular at various times later in the century.

The skirt was a modest variant at a time when few women wore any form of trousers and was not dissimilar to a **hobble skirt**.

Hare pocket
(M)

Period: 19th century

A large pocket inside the skirts of a shooting jacket or coat.

Harlot, herlot

(M)

Period: Late 14th century.

This usage is problematic but might, conceivably, be connected to one medieval meaning of "harlot" which is buffoon and one meaning of "herlot" which is acrobat. The Cunnington and Beard definition is of a garment for the lower limbs in which the hose legs (like stockings) and the breech were combined to form one, resembling modern "tights". Previously separate hose legs had been worn and presumably the term "harlot" was used for this new fashion, which by many was considered indecent (see Chaucer, *The Parson's Tale*).

Harvest gloves

(M)

Period: 15th–18th century.

See Dannock, Hedger's gloves.

Hasp

(M)

Period: 17th and 18th centuries.

An ornamental **hook and eye** fastening for coats instead of buttons. "A set of gentlemen who take the liberty to appear in all public places without any buttons on their coats, which they supply with little silver hasps" (1711, *The Spectator*).

Hat

(M)

Period: 10th century onwards.

A head-covering generally consisting of a crown and brim; always designed to draw attention to a man's head, emphasizing the social class of the wearer; contrasting with the insignificant, close-fitting **cap** of the working man. Worn indoors as well as out until ca. 1680, and in church until that time.

(F)

Period: Medieval onwards.

Hats were rarely worn by women until the late 16th century, except for travelling, and usually considered frivolous; hence in the 19th century hats were considered less proper than **bonnets** for women to wear on Sundays or in church, until ca. 1875.

Hat à la Reine

(F)

Period: 1863.

A hat of Italian straw with a shallow brim turned down all round a small, flat crown with a narrow ribbon hat-band, the fringed ends of which hung down behind.

Hat-band

(F & M)

Period: 14th century onwards.

A length of gold, silver or coloured silk or ribbon, bound about the base of the crown of a hat as an ornament.

In the late 16th century these were very elaborate, often of goldsmith's work and enamelled, set with gems and pearls, or formed of a string threaded with buttons of precious metal. In the late 16th century the absence of a hat-band, together with a dishevelled appearance, was said to indicate that the wearer was in love.

See Love.

The cable hat-band, a late-16th-century fashion, was made in a twisted design resembling rope. "I had a gold cable hat band, then new come up; it was a massie goldsmith's work" (1599, Ben Jonson, *Every Man out of his Humour*).

See Mourning band.

Hat cap

(M)

Period: 17th century.

The hat cap was part of the military equipment for the English Foot sent to Ireland in 1601.

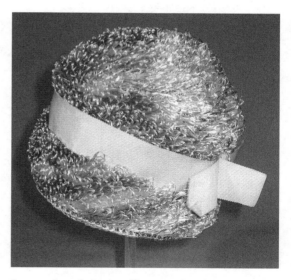

Summer **hat** of plastic **raffia** rimmed with **grosgrain** ribbon; **label** "Hand Made in Italy", ca. 1960. Copyright the Olive Matthews Collection, Chertsey Museum.

(F)

Period: 18th century.

A term for a day cap worn under a hat.

See Under cap.

Hatire

See Attire.

Hat pin

(F)

Period: Late 19th century onwards.

With the shift from **bonnet** to **hat** it was necessary to ensure the latter did not move from its fashionable position on the head or blow away, and hat pins became a decorative accessory for most women. They were at their longest, up to 14 inches with ingeniously styled heads, in the period between 1900 and 1914. The width and height of hats was supported on "transformations" (pads of false hair) into which the pin could be pushed without scratching the scalp.

Hat-screw

(M)

Period: Late 18th and early 19th century.

An implement, usually of boxwood, consisting of a screw-shaft with a curved, horizontal piece at each end; used to stretch the cylindrically shaped crown of a **beaver hat** into an oval to fit the wearer's head. "The natural shape of the common hat which, by its being made on a perfectly round block, requires to be brought to the oval shape by means of a screw…liable when exposed to rain to get soft…and return to its round form.…"

The need for a hat-screw was abolished in 1817 by the invention by Messrs Dando & Co. of the "Improved Oval-shape Beaver Hat, being finished upon an oval block, nothing can cause it to lose its shape…" (1817, Advertisement, *Ipswich Journal*).

Haute couture

Period: 19th century onwards.

A French term describing the highest form of fashionable design and dressmaking, initially found in Paris and later elsewhere in the world.

Hawaiian shirt

(M)

Period: 1950s onwards.

A loose, brightly coloured shirt printed with bold patterns of flowers, birds, etc. found in Hawaii and taken back to mainland America as tourist souvenirs and copied by other shirt-makers.

Hawk-glove, hawking glove

(M)

Period: 13th century onwards.

A short glove worn on the left hand as a protection when the hawk was being carried on the wrist. In the 16th century some of these gloves were lined with velvet and some embroidered. "Hawking glove" is the later term.

Head

(F)

Period: Late 17th and 18th centuries.

Often called a **tête**. The shortened term for head-dress, generally indicating an indoor cap, but by the end of 17th century it often included the whole arrangement of the **coiffure**. "Lost, a Head with very fine looped lace" (1700, *The Protestant Mercury*).

See Quadrille head.

Head band

(F & M)

Period: 16th to early 18th century.

Synonymous with **crosscloth**, although separately named in technical documents. Like the crosscloth, it was supposed, when medicated, to induce sleep. "To promote sleep take common roses with the white of an egg well beaten…and make an Head band or fillet of it" (1725, Bradley, *Family Dictionary*).

Head cloth

(F)

Period: Medieval.

Synonymous with **kerchief**.

Head-dress, head-dressing

(F)

Period: 16th century onwards.

A descriptive term for what was worn on the head.

See Head.

Headgear

(F & M)

Period: 16th century onwards.

Any form of head covering.

Head kerchief

Period: 17th century.

A large **handkerchief** folded cornerwise and worn on the head.

Head rail

(F)

Period: 16th and 17th centuries.

A large form of **kerchief** or **veil** worn on the head and flowing down behind; generally edged with lace; sometimes starched and sometimes wired up over the head between 1590 and 1620. "For mendinge, washinge and starchinge of a heade raille of fine sipers edged rounde aboute with white thred bone lace" (1588, Egerton MS).

Head scarf

(F)

Period: 20th century onwards.

A **scarf** worn as a head covering instead of a **hat**. In previous centuries scarves and shawls were often worn by poorer women in place of a **cap**, **bonnet** or **hat**. In the 20th century a square or length of fabric could be tied around the head in several combinations which were practical or fashionable. They were much worn during World War II and after. Chic brands compete to produce silk scarves for elite women.

Head suit

Synonymous with **head-dress**.

Heart breaker

(F)

See Crève-coeur

(M)

See Love lock.

Heart-shaped head-dress

(F)

Period: ca. 1420–1450.

A descriptive term applied later to the **bosses** or **templers** covering the ears and extending upwards above the head, together forming a U-shaped dip above the forehead. These were secured by a decorative circlet and draped with a **veil** falling at the back.

Heavy swell

(M)

Period: 1860s.

Term applied to ultra-fashionably dressed young men. A "rank swell" was a flashily dressed person drawing attention to himself.

Hedger's gloves, hedging gloves

(M)

Period: 16th–19th century.

A countryman's **mittens**.

See Dannock.

Helmet cap

(F)

Period: 1810.

A day cap domed and shaped like a helmet, generally made up in stripes of lace and embroidery and tied under the chin with ribbons.

In the 1960s the term was applied to a sleekly elegant cap designed by Pierre Cardin (b. 1922).

Helmet hat

(M)

Period: 1870s.

A hat with a helmet-shaped crown and narrow brim, made of cloth; chiefly worn at the seaside.

Hemispherical hat

(M)

Period: 1850s and 1860s.

A hard felt hat with bowl-shaped crown and narrow, flat brim. By 1858 it had developed a knob on the crown, and was sometimes called a **Bollinger**; replaced by the **bowler** in the 1860s.

Henley boater

(M)

Period: 1894 onwards.

A blue or drab felt hat in the shape of a straw **boater**.

Hennin

(F)

Period: 1450–1500.

French term for the steeple-shaped head-dress; very rare in England. Generally worn with "loose kerchiefs atop hanging down sometimes as low as the ground".

Henri deux cape

(F)

Period: 1890s.

A variation of the **Tudor cape** but having a square yoke; the name refers to Henri II of France (1519–1559).

Henrietta jacket

(F)

Period: 1890s.

A three-quarter-length, loose jacket with a deep collar falling over the chest in front; lined with quilted satin or merv.

Herigaut, herigald, heregaud, gerygoud, herigans

(M, rarely F)

Period: Early 13th to early 14th century.

A gown-like garment of three-quarters to full length with full, generally **hanging sleeves**.

See Garde-corps.

Heroin chic

(F)

Period: 1990s.

The use of slender, waif-like models with angular bones and pale, exhausted make-up to promote **lingerie**, skinny **T-shirts** and other forms of clothing. The association with drugs was, supposedly, that this was how some models ensured that their tiny bodies did not put on weight. This movement was the start of the dangerous fad for ever thinner and ever younger models, leading to the public debate about the impact on the impressionable young.

Hessians

(M)

Period: 1790s–1850s.

Short riding boots, calf-length behind and generally curving up to a point in front to below the knee-cap, and there decorated with a tassel. Made of black leather, sometimes bound round the top with a narrow border of coloured leather.

Heuse, huseau, housel, houseau

(M)

Period: 1240s to late 15th century.

A long riding boot reaching to mid-thigh and fitting the leg by means of buttons, buckles or straps on the outer side of the leg. "Heuse" is the earliest form of the word.

High-head

(F)

Period: Early 18th century.

Synonym for the **fontange**.

Highlows

(M)

Period: 1750–1800.

Boots reaching to the calf of the leg and laced up in front; made of stout leather. Worn in the country and by those little interested in fashion. "Dressed in…a pair of Highlows" (1757, *Norwich Mercury*).

Period: 19th century.

Boots reaching just above the ankle. "A pair of polished high-lows secured across the instep with a strap and buckle" (1841, Arthur Armitage, *Heads of the*

h

People). Eventually becoming more elegant; "High-lows pass as patent-leathers" (1878, W. S. Gilbert, *H.M.S. Pinafore*).

High-tops

See Top button.

Hijab

(F)

A long, rectangular, black cloth or scarf which is wrapped around the head and shoulders, covering the hair and flesh and held by safety pins. Usually worn by Muslim women for cultural or religious reasons, often with the **jilbab** and sometimes with the **niqab**.

Himation

(M)

Period: Classical Greece.

The outer garment worn over the **chiton**, described as "an oblong piece of cloth thrown over the left shoulder, and fastened either over or under the right" (Liddell & Scott, *Greek-English Lexicon*).

Hip bags

(F)

Period: 1883.

A popular slang phrase for the pannier folds "known in England as the Pompadour" and in America as the "curtain drapery", which were draped across the hip region.

Hip-buttons

(M)

Period: Late 17th century to ca. 1900.

The pair of buttons at the back of a skirted coat, heading the pleats on each side of the back vent; in the 19th century generally at waist-level, and after 1823 on the seam at the waist. There is no evidence that these buttons were ever functional.

Hippie style, hippy style

(F & M)

Period: 1950s.

A term appropriated from the hipsters of the early 1950s. This was an alternative approach to fashion espoused by the young and demonstrated through their choice of clothing, which mixed recycled but colourful old clothing with patchwork, psychedelic colours, and some **ethnic** elements such as Indian fabrics and Afghan coats. Often long, wild hair styles, beards and bare feet were part of the look.

Hip-pocket

(M)

Period: 1890s onwards.

A **cross pocket**, with or without a flap, placed at the back of the hip of trousers.

See Caddie.

To be distinguished from the tailoring phrase "pockets on the hips", meaning outside pockets over the hip region in a skirted coat.

Hipster

(F & M)

Period: Late 1960s onwards.

A pair of trousers or a skirt cut to fit from the level of the hips rather than the waist.

Historical shirt

(M)

Period: 17th century.

A shirt embroidered in religious subjects.

"Sure you should not be

Without a neat historical shirt" (ca. 1619, J. Fletcher & P. Massinger, *The Custom of the Country*).

See Holy work.

Hive

(F)

Period: Late 16th to mid-18th century.

A high-crowned, hive-shaped hat of plaited straw with narrow or no brim. "Upon her head a platted hive of straw" (1597, W. Shakespeare, *Lover's Complaint*).

"...the hive, the milkmaid's chip hat, were rescued for a time from old women and servant girls to adorn heads of the first fashion" (1754, *The Connoisseur*).

H-line

(F)

Period: 1954.

The name given by the French designer Christian Dior (1905–1957) to his autumn collection which Vogue described as "the tapering figure of a young girl" by increasing the distance between hips and bust.

Hobble skirt

(F)

Period: ca. 1909–1915.

A style attributed to the French designer Paul Poiret (1879–1944). The skirt narrowed towards the hem and was sometimes held beneath the knees with a decorative band of fabric. Probably influenced by the designs for the **Ballets Russes** which were first seen in Paris in 1909.

Hodtrene

(F)

Period: 1500–1550.

Probably the draped fabric or pendant **lappets** at the back of a hood, as in the **English hood** or **French hood**.

Hogger

See Oker.

Hollow lace

Period: 16th century.

A form of braid **lace** used for edging.

Hollywood style

(F & M)

Period: 1920s onwards.

The increasing dominance of American **cinema** throughout the world from the post-World War I era had an impact on clothing. What was worn on the screen quickly became desirable, and the appearance of everything from men's suits to women's evening dresses and hair styles were imitated accordingly.

See Capri pants.

Holy work, hollie work

Period: Late 16th and 17th centuries.

Lace, **cut-work** and **embroidery** representing religious subjects, used in the ornamentation of **shirts**, **smocks**, **bands** and domestic linen. "Collars of Hollie work" appear in an inventory of Mary Queen of Scots in 1578, but the fashion was spread by Puritan ladies towards 1620.

"She works religious petticoats; for flowers
She"ll make church-histories. Her needle doth
So sanctify my cushionets! Besides my smock sleeves have such holy embroideries
And are so learned, that I fear in time
All my apparel will be quoted by
Some pure instructor" (1631, Jasper Mayne, *City Match*).

See Religious petticoat, Historical shirt.

Homburg hat

(M)

Period: 1870s onwards.

A stiff felt with a dent running from front to back in the crown, the brim braided and slightly curved up at the sides. A style made fashionable by the Prince of Wales, later Edward VII, who frequented the German spa town of Homburg.

Home dressmaking

Period: 19th century onwards.

At much the same time that professional dressmaking was moving in several different directions, namely exclusive shops with well-known owner/makers, small local dressmaking businesses and sections within department stores offering readymade and couture garments, there was an increased surge in home dressmaking. This was assisted by the invention of the **sewing machine** and the sized pattern, both becoming generally available in the 1860s.

See Butterick.

Hood

(F & M)

Period: Medieval onwards.

A term usually indicating a loose, soft covering shaped to fit over the head; worn as a separate garment or sometimes attached to an outdoor garment such as a cloak, etc.

The name often loosely applied to other kinds of women's head coverings, such as the **French hood**.

See Chaperone, Capuchin, Long hood, Pug hood, Short hood.

Hoodie

(F & M)

Period: Late 1980s onwards.

A British term for a hooded **fleece**, **sweatshirt** or similar. Also, pejoratively, as a description of a loutishly dressed youngster wishing to conceal their identity.

Hooker chic

(F)

Period: Late 20th century onwards.

Various meanings based on the slang term for a prostitute, a style of discreet disguise unexpected from such a profession; a style of dress encouraging inappropriate sexual interest, i.e. short, tight and revealing too much flesh, found on women, on dolls and impacting upon the type of clothing worn by pre-pubescent girls.

Hooks and eyes

Period: Early 17th century onwards.

Known in the 14th century as **crochets** and loops, but as hooks and eyes from 1620 on. "The needle lance Knights…put so many hookes and eyes to every hose and doublet" (ca. 1626, Egerton MS., Duke of Devonshire). They were made of iron hammered flat; in the 18th century often of copper, sometimes tinned; early in the 19th century of brass; by 1840 of wire (brass or of japanned iron) and in the 20th century of stainless steel.

See Hasp.

Hoop, hoop petticoat

(F)

Period: 1710–1780, to 1820 for court wear.

An under-petticoat variously distended with cane, wire or whalebone hoops. For the different shapes see **bell hoop** or **cupola coat**, **fan hoop**, **oblong hoop** or **square hoop**, **pocket hoop**. Also, the term "hoop" was occasionally applied to the farthingale of the 16th century. "The hoopes that hippes and haunch do hide" (1596, Gosson, *Pleasant Quippes for Upstart Newfangled Gentlewomen*).

Horn button

Period: 18th and 19th centuries.

A button of moulded horn.

Horned head-dress

(F)

Period: ca. 1410–1420; rarely to 1460.

A head-dress worn with wide **templers** and wired up to resemble horns from which a pendant veil curtained the back of the head. "She is hornyd like a kowe…for syn" (ca. 1460, *The Townley Mysteries*, 312, Surtees Society).

Horns

(F)

Period: 14th century.

Originally identical with **bosses** and so named because the spirally lapped bosses began to resemble rams' horns.

Horsehair petticoat, crinoline petticoat

(F)

Period: 1840s–1850s, 1868–1870.

An under-petticoat made of crinoline, a fabric with a horsehair warp and wool weft. The petticoat might be six feet round the hem, which was often stiffened with lines of piping. Used to distend the skirt, but replaced by the **cage crinoline** and revived for a few years when the cage was going out of fashion.

Horse-shoe cap

(F)

Period: Mid-18th century.

A small day cap with long **lappets**.

Horse-shoe collar

(F)

Period: 1950s.

A deep, U-shaped **roll collar**, in the shape of a horse-shoe, found on some fashionable clothing of this decade.

Hortense mantle

(F)

Period: 1849.

A three-quarter-length **mantle** with a falling collar and lapels, and a square-cut, fringed cape descending to the waist. Named after Queen Hortense (1783–1837), the mother of Napoleon III.

Hose

(M)

Period: Medieval to 15th century; after ca. 1660.

The word meaning leg-wear or covering, with long, tailored stockings being united at the fork and carried up over the buttocks forming **tights**. These were known as **long-stocked hose**. In the 16th century the upper portion was expanded and this was variously termed **trunk-hose**, **round hose**, or **upper stocks**, the lower stocking portion called **nether stocks**.

(F)

Period: Medieval onwards.

Hose meant **stockings**. "Her hosen weren of fine skar-let redde, Ful straite y-tyed" (ca. 1387, Chaucer, *The Wife of Bath*).

Hosiery

Period: Late 18th century.

A collective term for all goods sold by a hosier; any items frame-knitted, from **stockings** to waistcoats. In the 20th century more usually socks, stockings and **tights**.

Hotpants

(F)

Period: 1970.

American term applied to very tight, brief shorts worn as a fashion statement rather than for leisure activities; often made of colourful and luxurious fabrics.

Hounds ears

(M)

Period: ca. 1660–1690.

A popular name for the rounded corners of the large coat-cuffs with a deep turn-up and open behind.

Houppelande

(F & M)

Period: Mid-14th and 15th centuries.

A term introduced in France around the time that "goun" or "gown" appeared in England. It was a volumi-nous upper garment fitting the shoulders and generally falling in tubular folds. The length varied from reach-ing the thighs to trailing on the ground (in ceremonial costume). Earlier forms had high, bottle-neck collars expanding round the head; in later forms the collar varied. Sleeves very wide, expanding to a funnel shape below; **bagpipe sleeves** were common in the 15th century. A belt was usual but optional. After 1450 the term **gown** was more usual, but the term **pellard** was also applied to a houppelande, according to Ducange in the late 16th century, and this was picked-up by later dress historians.

House coat

(F)

Period: Early 20th century onwards.

"A superior type of dressing gown worn at home in the evening, or for breakfasting" (1973, Mansfield & Cunnington, *Handbook of English Costume in the Twentieth Century 1900–1950*). Possibly a variant of the **house dress** or **teagown**.

House dress

(F)

Period: 1877 onwards.

A plain **princess robe**, sometimes with a **Watteau** back, trained, worn without **corsets** informally at breakfast and indoors during the morning. By 1890 it had become a close-fitting **teagown**.

Housemaid skirt

(F)

Period: 1884.

A plain skirt with five or six tucks round the lower part; worn informally by young women.

Houvette

See Howve.

Howling bags

(M)

Period: Mid-19th century.

Slang term for **trousers** with a loud pattern.

Howve, houve

(F & M)

Period: 14th century.

A hood.

See Houvette, Huvet.

Hoxter

(M)

Period: 19th century.

Slang term for an inside pocket of a coat.

Huke, hewke, heyke, huque, hewk, hyke, heuque

(F & M)

Period: ca. 1400–1450; rare later.

Mentioned in French literature in the 13th century, this was a short overgarment of tabard design with front and back panels; occasionally with sleeves and generally belted, probably also a form of cloak.

(F)

Period: 16th and 17th centuries.

A large **head rail** or **veil** enveloping the wearer to knees or ankles. It was known to English travellers from its use by women in the Low Countries, although it originated in Spain, where it later became the **mantilla**. It is doubtful if it was ever worn in England, though the expression "to huke", meaning to veil, was used here.

Hungarian cord

(F)

Period: 1860s.

A substantial silk cord used to border the hem of a trained skirt, in place of the conventional braid; particularly popular in 1867/8.

Hungerland band

(F)

Period: 17th century.

A kind of **lace** sometimes used for making **bands**, i.e. collars; presumably "point de Hongrye", a lace made at Halle of a style and pattern accepted as being Hungarian.

Hunting belt

(M)

Period: 1820s.

A belt of whalebone worn by the **dandy** in the hunting field.

Hunting necktie

(M)

Period: 1818–1830s.

A very broad necktie worn high round the neck, with three creases each side verging towards the centre in front; the ends brought forward and crossed over and concealed under the coat; secured by a pin.

Hunting stock

(M)

Period: 1890s onwards.

A large **scarf** of cellular cloth, folded and tied twice round the neck, concealing the absence of a collar. "But few there are who can wear a hunting-stock and still look like a gentleman" (1898, *The Tailor& Cutter*).

Huntley bonnet

(F)

Period: 1814.

A style of **bonnet**, also known as a "Scotch bonnet", made in twilled plaid sarcenet and trimmed with a rosette and three feathers.

Hure

(M)

Period: Late 13th to 17th century.

The shaggy hair of a man's head. "A staring, horrid, unkembed, or ill-kept pate of hair" (1611, Cotgrave).

Also a cap of the skin of an animal with the hair on; later, possibly, a cap of piled felt or thrummed material; and still later, a round-topped felt cap.

Hush Puppies

(F & M)

Period: Late 1950s onwards.

Brushed pigskin, patented as shoe leather in America in 1957 and used to make a classic, brown-suede, Oxford-style, laced shoe. This style was launched with the brand name, Hush Puppies. These were comfortable, low heeled, lace-up shoes and were popular when fashionable shoes were narrow and uncomfortable. In the 1960s **Mods** wore them, and over successive decades many different styles and colours were introduced into the range.

Husky

(F & M)

Period: Second half of 20th century onwards.

A sturdy, quilted jacket often made from quilted nylon, sometimes with a contrasting turn-down collar of leather or needle cord. Devised to cope with cold and damp conditions in the country, it became a design **classic** for town amongst certain social groups in Europe. Variants include the use of other fabrics and a body warmer or waistcoat version.

See Puffa.

Hussar boots, buskins

(M)

Period: Late 18th century to 1820s.

Calf-length boots with a dip at the centre front top edge and a tassel on either side.

Hussar jacket

(F)

Period: 1880s.

A short jacket, braided and **frogged**; worn with a waistcoat to form the bodice portion of a day dress. From 1887 worn as an outdoor jacket.

Hussar point

(M)

Period: 1820s.

A feature appearing in the cut of waistcoats, the bottoms of the foreparts shaped to produce a beak-like point in the centre curving downwards when the garment was buttoned up. The sides of the foreparts "hollowed", i.e. cut with a slight curve over the hips.

Huvet

See Howve.

Hydrotobolic hat

(M)

Period: 1850s and 1860s.

A hat with the crown ventilated by having a small hole in the centre protected by wire gauze. "Becoming very general" (1851, *Punch*).

h

I

Imbecile sleeve, sleeve à la folle

(F)

Period: 1829–1835.

A day sleeve very full down to the wrist and there gathered into a narrow cuff. No stiffening but "falls down in all its amplitude". Named after the sleeve of the "straight-waistcoat" worn by lunatics.

Imperial

(M)

Period: 1829 onwards.

Term describing a loose, fly-fronted **paletot** overcoat. Also, a narrow tuft of beard below the lower lip.

Inchering

Period: 18th century.

Measuring a person in inches for making a garment. "Pd. for Inchoring the girls 2d" (1729, Walthamstow Records).

Incroyable bows

(F)

Period: 1889.

Huge bows of **lace** and **mousselaine de soie**, worn at the throat with **Directoire**-style garments.

Incroyable coat

(F)

Period: 1889.

A coat with long coat-tails and wide lapels, worn with a lace jabot and waistcoat for afternoon dress; intended to resemble the **swallow-tail** coat of the Directoire period of French history (1794–1799). A fashion attributed to Lillie Langtry in a play of 1886 and also to Sardou's play *La Tosca* (1887).

Indian necktie

(M)

Period: 1815–ca. 1840.

A muslin **cravat**, the ends brought round in front and secured by a sliding ring. In 1818 it was called a "Maharatta".

Indian nightgown, Indian gown

(F & M)

Period: 17th and 18th centuries.

A synonym for a **banian** or banyan.

Also a term occasionally used for a woman's **négligée** attire. "Contented…instead of a variety of new gowns and rich petticoats, with her deshabillie or flame-colour gown called Indian" (1673, Wycherley, *The Gentleman Dancing Master*).

India rubber

Period: 19th century onwards.

An elastic or flexible material taken from the sap of rubber trees and processed to form various types of product. A patent for its use was registered in 1823. "A recent discovery substituting India rubber for elastic wires" (1831).

Previously brass-wire springs covered with cloth had been used.

Indispensable

(F)

Period: 1800–ca. 1820.

A small handbag of soft fabric such as silk or velvet, often square or lozenge-shaped, drawn in with a running string; suspended from the arm or hand by a length of ribbon.

See Ridicule.

Ineffibles

(M)

Period: 19th century.

One of the many euphemisms for breeches or trousers. "Our lower garments or Ineffibles sit but awkwardly" (1823, *New Monthly Magazine*).

Inexpressibles

(M)

Period: Late 18th and early 19th centuries.

A euphemism for breeches or trousers.

See Unmentionables.

Intarsia

Period: 19th century onwards.

Term applied to inlaid, patterned motifs of glass, stone, etc. set into metal as jewellery.

Also used in knitting to describe patterns created in two or more coloured wools.

Inverness

(M)

Period: 1859 onwards.

"The new name for the Cape Paletot." A large, loose **overcoat**, about knee-length, with a fitting collar and deep arm-length cape. In the 1870s the cape was usually incomplete behind, being sewn to the side seams. By the 1880s the sleeves were often omitted, the cape being sufficient and then called "Dolman cape sleeves". However, between 1890 and the early 20th century there were very large arm-holes under the cape, which were faced with a sling or "arm-rest" to support the forearms.

Irish mantle

Period: 15th century.

Term used for a cloak, or a blanket.

See Bratt.

Irish polonaise

(F)

Period: 1770–1775.

A day gown with a close-fitting, low, square-cut bodice fastened close down the front and fitting behind. The bodice had an overskirt pleated to it, this overskirt being bunched up behind and open in front. The underskirt, called a **petticoat**, was worn short. This style of polonaise was also called "Italian", "French" or "Turkish".

Isabeau corsage

(F)

Period: 1846.

The bodice resembled a jacket descending to just below the hips where the edges were rounded off. The front, open at the bottom, was trimmed across with bands of galloon and silk buttons. The neck was cut high with a falling collar; the sleeves nearly wrist-length with an open **mancheron** below each shoulder. A style of dress for morning wear.

Isabeau sleeve

(F)

Period: 1860s.

A triangular-shaped sleeve, the apex at the shoulder and widely open below; made with an inner and an outer seam. Used for dresses, often with an under sleeve or **engageante**; also used for the **pardessus** and the **Maintenon cloak**.

Isabeau-style dress

(F)

Period: 1860s.

A day dress, the bodice and skirt in one, shaped to the figure by goring, without a seam at the waist. A line of buttons or rosettes all down the front.

Italian cloak

(M)

Period: 16th and 17th centuries.

A short, hooded cloak; the same as the **Spanish cloak** or **Genoa cloak**. "He wears a short Italian hooded cloak" (1590, Marlowe, *Edward II*).

Italian farthingale

The same as the **wheel farthingale**.

Italian heel

(F)

Period: 1770s onwards.

A small, peg-top heel with slender waist, placing the heel forward under the shoe with wedge extension under the instep. The heel was made of wood covered with kid of a colour different from that of the shoe, generally white or cream.

Italian hose

(M)

Period: ca. 1600.

Synonym for **Venetians**.

Italian nightgown, Italian robe

(F)

Period: 1770s.

A day dress of a semi-formal nature (see **Nightgown**). The bodice, with low neck and elbow sleeves, was boned and joined to a long overskirt open in front. The underskirt, called the **petticoat**, was of a colour different from the rest of the gown. The overskirt could be hitched up like a **polonaise** by "loops to two small buttons on the hips", or by running strings in the lining which were fixed to the hem, emerging at the waist with a large tassel at each hip, "by which they draw up the robe to dance country dances".

Italian polonaise

(F)

Period: 1770s.

Synonymous with **Italian nightgown** or **Italian robe**.

Ivy League

(F & M)

Period: 1930s onwards.

Term describing styles of clothing worn by American students at wealthy and long-established East Coast "Ivy League" colleges. Traditional rather than innovative, and not dissimilar to the conservative dress of the previous generation. Sometimes called "preppie".

J

Jabot

(F)

Period: 19th century onwards.

A made-up **cravat** of lace or similar fabric, worn at the neck and sometimes frilling down the front opening of a bodice or **blouse**.

Jack

(M)

Period: Late 14th century.

A short **jacket**; also a military garment and the term continued in use until late in the 17th century.

Jack boot

(M)

Period: ca. 1660–18th century.

A boot made of hard leather and worn for riding.

Heavy jack boots of "bend leather", i.e. hardened by boiling or by applications of pitch paint, in the 17th century had expanding bucket tops to enclose the knees and deep, square heels and square toes. In the 18th century the style was less cumbersome.

Light jack boots were of softer leather and sometimes laced or buttoned on the outer side. In the 18th century the front of the boot extended above the knee, the back being scooped out to allow for the bending of the knee. Half jack boots; see **Jockey boots**.

Jack chain
(M)

Period: 17th century, also 19th century.

A form of decoration; a chain made up of links each in the figure of eight and joined at right angles. Considered a trumpery ornament.

Jacket
(M)

Period: 1450–ca. 1630.

A short body garment varying in use, sometimes only for boys, sometimes also for men. As an upper garment it was worn over the **doublet** or occasionally alone with a **plackard** or **stomacher**; subsequently, until ca. 1630, it was worn over the doublet and was often sleeveless, and usually called a **jerkin**.

Period: 18th century.

The jacket was the main body garment "in use among Country people" (1706, Phillips) and was also worn by labourers, apprentices, seafarers, postillions and sportsmen. In the 18th century elite men used it only when powdering.

Period: 19th century.

It began to be acceptable ca. 1840 as part of a gentleman's suit, replacing the coat, for informal occasions and acquired specific associations, e.g. **hacking jacket**, **Norfolk jacket**, **smoking jacket**, etc.

Period: 20th century onwards.

An informal coat for both summer and winter wear, made of various weights and types of fabric but retaining earlier connotations and acquiring new ones, such as the sports jacket: "Sports lounge model. Two styles of jacket" (1922, Harrods).

(F)

Period: 16th century onwards.

The woman's jacket was an alternative kind of bodice, being then an essential part of the gown. It was sometimes called a **waistcoat** in the 16th century.

Period: 19th century.

It was worn as an upper garment, mainly for sports wear, or as a part of the **tailor-made** costume, especially in the 1890s.

Period: 20th century onwards.

Jackets were often matched to a dress as well as being a popular separate garment for day-time wear. They were made in a wide variety of weights and fabrics. *See* Blazer.

Plate depicting **lounge coats** from T.H. Holding, *Coats*, 1902. The most important coat or **jacket** in the twentieth century and shown here in single and double breasted versions, matching the cloth of **trousers** and **waistcoats** in some instances. Although **gloves** and **cane** are basic **accessories** the headwear is less prescriptive; a **bowler**, a **boater**, a **trilby** or a **homburg hat** was all acceptable. Private collection.

Jack Tar suit
(M)

Period: ca. 1880–1900.

A **sailor suit** with **Jack Tar trousers**; worn by small boys.

Jack Tar trousers
(M)

Period: 1880s.

Trousers having the legs cut without a side seam, close-fitting above, expanding below to 22 inches round the ankles. Made with **whole falls**, and worn for yachting.

Jaeger underclothes
(F & M)

Period: 1880s onwards.

Introduced by a German, Dr Gustav Jaeger (1832–1917), this underclothing of natural wool was constructed on hygienic principles so as to envelop the whole trunk and limbs. George Bernard Shaw was an early advocate. Gradually the company diversified into a number of lines of pure wool garments until the 1920s when it expanded into other, more fashionable ranges of clothing.

Jags, jagging

See Dag.

Jambee cane

(M)

Period: Early 18th century.

A knotty bamboo walking-stick.

Japanese hat

(F)

Period: 1867–1869.

A circular, plate-shaped hat without a crown, the straw brim sloping slightly downwards from a small, central knob; trimmed with ribbon and tied on with ribbon passing under the chignon.

Jasey, jazey

(M)

Period: Late 18th and 19th centuries.

A **wig** made of Jersey yarn.

"Jasey, a contemptuous name for a wig or even a bushy head of hair, as if the one were actually as the other is apparently made of Jersey yarn" (1825, Forley, *Vocabulary of East Anglia*).

Hence a slang name for a judge: "the cove with the jazey".

Jean de Bry

(M)

Period: 1790s–ca. 1820.

A double-breasted coat with high stand-fall collar and low-turning lapels. Sleeves greatly padded and gathered at the shoulders; the coat-tails short and scanty. A style named after Jean-Antoine-Joseph de Bry (1760–1834), a leading member of the National Convention and a regicide during the French Revolution.

Jeanette

(F)

Period: 1836.

A **necklace** made up of a narrow tress of hair or velvet ribbon, suspending a small cross or heart.

Also, a fabric similar to **jean** cloth.

Jeans

(M)

Period: 1810 onwards.

A twilled cotton cloth, **jean**, similar to fustian and used for trousers made of this fabric, thus jeans. Later conflated with **denim**, as blue jeans.

(F)

Period: 20th century onwards.

Term often used for cotton or denim informal trousers before proprietary brands, such as Levis, etc., were introduced.

Jellies

(F & M)

Period: 1970s onwards.

Term for jelly sandals or jelly shoes, a colourful rubber or plastic item of footwear, originally found on beaches but later worn more widely.

Jellybag

See Night-cap.

Jemmy

(M)

Period: 19th century.

A shooting coat, being a short **frock coat** with multiple pockets.

Jemmy boots

(M)

Period: 18th century.

Light riding boots, a smart form of **jockey boots**.

Jemmy cane

(M)

Period: 18th and early 19th centuries.

A little switch carried under the arm, most fashionable in the 1750s and 1760s.

Jemmy frock

(M)

Period: 18th century.

A smart **frock**; "The jemmy frock with plate buttons" (1756, *The Connoisseur*).

Jerkin, jerking

(M)

Period: 1450–1630.

A **jacket** worn over the **doublet** and following the same pattern, with slightly longer skirts; sometimes made with **hanging sleeves**. In the 16th and 17th centuries jerkins were often sleeveless, having **wings** only.

Jersey

(M)

Period: 1860s onwards.

A knitted, sleeved body garment, generally made with horizontal stripes; worn for football in the 1870s and later also worn by boys as a winter garment. "Begin your jerseys" (November 1863, Mrs Charles Darwin to her son).

In the 20th century the jersey was not wholly a sporting garment and was also described as a **jumper**, **pullover** and a **sweater** – all terms for hand- or machine-knitted garments intended for casual wear.

(F)

Period: Late 19th century onwards.

Jerseys for women were often made as **cardigans** and, once the machine-knitted fabric was used by Coco Chanel (1883–1971) for cardigans and skirts, it became ultra-fashionable in the 1920s and later. Women also wore jumpers and sweaters.

Jersey costume

(F)

Period: 1879.

A blue or red knitted silk or wool **jersey**, fitting the figure and reaching to thigh level; worn above a serge or flannel kilted skirt. A style popularized by Mrs Lillie Langtry, the "Jersey Lily" (1853–1929), actress and mistress of Edward VII.

The island of Jersey had long been known for the quality of its knitted goods.

Jessamy gloves, jasmine gloves

(F & M)

Period: 17th century.

A description of gloves heavily perfumed with jasmine, but a variety of scents were used. It was a custom to give a supply as a wedding present both to the bride and to the bridegroom. Thus a prospective mother-in-law wrote: "I could not get so many woman's Jessamy gloves as she wrote for, they being a prohibited and scarce commodity; and at last I was fained to pick upon cordinent (i.e. the Spanish leather, cordovan) for men and perfumed kid for women; I had them perfumed better than ordinary that they might give content" (1661, The Gurdon Papers, *East Anglian Notes & Queries*).

Jet buttons

(F)

Period: 19th century onwards.

Worn in 1818 by women on **half boots** buttoned at the sides; also popular for black clothing or as a contrast on paler hues. Jet was much used for jewellery, both in its original form and as the glass imitation, French jet.

Jewellery

(F & M)

Period: Medieval onwards.

Precious or other stones set into metals and worked into various forms, bracelets, brooches, buttons, **earrings**, necklaces, etc. Often a gift with symbolic or other significance, or a memento of foreign travel. Inexpensive items were known as **costume jewellery**; the latter might use base metals, glass and plastic instead of expensive settings and stones.

Jigger button

(M)

Period: 19th century.

A small, concealed button, usually brass, fastening back the point of a wide lapel or the wrap-over of a double-breasted waistcoat. In washing waistcoats this button was of mother-of-pearl.

Jilbab

(F)

One of the three garments worn by Muslim women who prefer traditional styles of dress for cultural or religious reasons. This is a full-length, long-sleeved, black robe, often front-fastening (modern ones have zips), with which the **hijab** and **niqab** is worn.

Jim Crow hat

(M)

Period: 19th century.

A felt hat with a very wide, flapping brim; named after the Negro plantation song as performed by the American Thomas D. Rice (1808–1860) in the 1830s.

Jingle spur

See Ginglers.

Joan

(F)

Period: 1755–1765.

Sometimes called the "Quaker cap", this was a close-fitting, indoor cap shaped like a baby's bonnet, tied under the chin and trimmed round the face, with a muslin or lace frill.

Joan-of-Arc bodice

(F)

Period: 1875.

A tight day bodice, known as a **cuirasse bodice**, shaped like a pair of **stays** reaching to the hips, and covered with jet or steel beads; tight sleeves frilled at the wrists.

Jocelyn mantle

(F)

Period: 1852.

A **mantle**, knee-length, double-skirted and with three capes each fringed; with arm-holes but no sleeves.

Jockey

(F)

Period: 1820s onwards.

A flat trimming applied over the outer part of the shoulder of a dress and having the lower border free.

Jockey boots, half jack boots

(M)

Period: 1680s to late 18th century.

A boot ending below the knee with turned-down top of softer and lighter-coloured leather. Pulled on by leather or string loops on each side. After 1780s called **top boots**.

Jockey cap

(M)

Period: Late 17th and 18th centuries.

A peaked cap of black velvet or cloth with a **hat-band** buckled at the front above the peak and worn for riding and other sports.

Period: 19th century.

A light silk, coloured jockey cap came into favour for racing.

See Riding hat.

Jockey sleeve

(M)

Period: Late 17th century onwards.

A close-fitting sleeve with small, close cuff.

Jockey waistcoat

(M)

Period: 1806 to late 19th century.

A straight waistcoat buttoned high, with a low **stand collar** cut off square in front leaving a deep gap under the chin. A fashion revived in 1884.

Jodhpurs

(M)

Period: Late 19th century onwards.

From the Indian for trousers cut loose at the top but close-fitting below the knee; the term was applied to riding breeches, full at the upper but tighter below the knee, with a gaiter-like structure.

(F)

Period: 1920s onwards.

Worn by women in preference to the riding skirt.

Jogging suit

(F & M)

Period: 1960s onwards.

Clothing designed for wearing when warming-up for, or cooling down after, this type of aerobic running. Usually a zip-fronted, loose jacket and trousers with elasticated

Quilted waistcoat or **jump**, ca. 1720–30. Silk with floral motif embroidery; the lining of two types of printed cotton **calico**. Copyright the Olive Matthews Collection, Chertsey Museum. Photograph by John Chase.

waist and ankles in a washable fabric.

See Track suit.

Joinville

(M)

Period: 1844–1855.

A **necktie** worn as a broad, wide-spreading bow with square, fringed ends. The name was revived in the 1890s for an American scarf tie filling the space above the waistcoat opening.

Joseph

(F)

Period: Mid-17th to early 19th century.

Initially a cloak in the 17th century; the term was applied to a **greatcoat** or a riding coat which buttoned at the front from the early 18th century. It seems often to have been made of green cloth.

Josephine bodice

(F)

Period: 1879.

An evening-dress bodice with a very low, round **décolletage** and a wide silk or satin belt draped round in folds.

Jub, jube

(M)

Period: 17th century.

A short, sleeveless coat or jacket.

Juive tunic

(F)

Period: 1875.

A **princess** style over-bodice and skirt; the bodice with wide arm-holes, a V-opening in front and behind; the skirt portion falling in a point to hip level and continued into a train behind. The tunic worn over a dress constituted a **costume** for outdoor wear without additional covering.

Juliet cap

(F)

Period: Late 19th century onwards.

An open-mesh cap, often of metal threads and decorated with beads or seed pearls. Worn in the evening or by brides. Named after the style of cap worn by the heroine in Shakespeare's *Romeo and Juliet*.

Jump, jumpe, jump-coat

(M)

Period: 17th century.

In the early part of the century, a soldier's coat. "A Colonel in beaten Buff with a scarlet Jump" (1639–1660). Later, a civilian coat. "Jumpe...extendeth to the Thighs, is open or buttoned down before, open or slit up behind half way; the sleeves reach to the wrist" (1688, R. Holme, *Armory*).

(F)

Period: Late 17th and 18th centuries.

Usually in the plural, as "jumps"; a loose, unboned

bodice worn instead of **stays** for comfort or during pregnancy. "Bought my wife a new pair of jumps instead of stays" (1716, *Marchant Diary*).

Jumper
(F & M)
Period: 19th century onwards.
A variety of meanings, in part deriving from the loose upper garment or shirt worn by sailors and other workers. Thus, a loose-fitting blouse, a pinafore dress, and a long-sleeved, woollen sweater.

(M)
Period: 1861–1880.
A loose, single-breasted **Tweedside** jacket, the fronts cut straight with three buttons. The fit was improved by the introduction of **side bodies**. Also known as an **Oxonian jacket**.

Jumper coat
(M)
Period: 1880s.
See Beaufort coat.

Jumpsuit, jumpersuit
(F)
Period: 20th century onwards.
The idea seems to have been derived from a child's **romper suit**. This adult version is all-in-one garment, with long sleeves and ankle-length legs, which is usually zipped at the front. It is similar to the **boiler suit**.

Jupe, jupon
(M)
Period: 1290–1400.
See Gipon.

(F)
Period: 16th and early 17th centuries.
A riding coat generally worn with a safeguard (i.e. a protective over-skirt). "A safeguard with jhup or gaskyn coat of faire cullored satten" (1588, Nichols, *Progress of Queen Elizabeth*).

Juppo, juppa, jippo
(M)
Variants of **jump**; often implying one of meaner quality.

Just-au-corps, justacorps, justico, justacor, chesticore, juste
(M)
Period: 1650 to early 18th century.
A close-fitting coat worn over a **waistcoat**. "His justaucorps brac'd to his body tight" (1705, Elsbob, *Hearne Collecteana*).

(F)
Period: 1650–1700, late 18th century.
A riding coat; in the 17th century shaped like a man's coat; in the 18th century made with short **basques** and often called a **demi-riding coat**.

K

Kaftan
See Caftan.

Kall, kelle
A woman's **caul**.

Kampskatcha slipper, Chinese slipper
(F)
Period: 1786–1788.
A slipper made with a pointed toe turned up at the tip; the vamp moderately high, and a low French heel. "… perfectly adapted to the winter season; they are made of fine black Spanish leather and turned up at the toes in the Chinese taste; and securely guard the feet of the wearer from cold by being lined with white or fox-coloured fur which is brought over the edge and forms the binding" (1787, *Ipswich Journal*).

Kate Greenaway costume
(F)
Period: 1880s and 1890s.
A style of dress for small girls made popular by the artist of that name in her illustrations of children's books. A frock in the style of an **Empire** dress with high waist and puffed shoulder-sleeves, the skirt trimmed with a narrow flounce; made of light fabric patterned with flowers.

Keffiyeh
(F & M)
Period: Late 20th century.
The square **head scarf** folded in triangular fashion and held in position by a cord, worn by many Arab men and associated by many westerners with the late Yasser Arafat (1929–2004), the Palestinian leader. Traditionally made of a cotton and wool mix, sometimes patterned with black or red checks and with tasselled corners, the scarf was appropriated by western supporters of both sexes and worn around the neck to show solidarity with the Palestinian cause.

Kelly bag
(F)
Period: 1930s onwards.
Hermès, the French firm established in 1837, produced a classic handbag inspired by saddle bags in 1935. A

smaller version of this achieved worldwide publicity in 1956 when Princess Grace of Monaco (1929–1982), formerly Grace Kelly, appeared holding one on the cover of *Life* magazine. After that this style was always known by her maiden name and came in a wide range of leathers and colours. Named bags were unusual until the 1990s; for instance, Chanel's quilted shoulder bag with its leather and gilt chain strap was called 2.55 because it first appeared in February 1955.

Kemes, kemise, kemse
See Chemise.

Kennel
(F)
Period: 1500–1540s.
A 19th-century term for the gable-shaped head-dress or **English hood**.

Kerchief, kercher, kercheve, karcher
(F)

Japanese cockade **fan**, the leaf painted with pairs of figures in traditional dress including **kimonos**; the guards and stick of ivory with metallic bird and tree motifs on the guards, ca. 1890–1910. Copyright the Olive Matthews Collection, Chertsey Museum.

Period: Early Medieval to late 18th century.
A draped covering for the head.
See Coverchief.
In the 16th century "kerchief" was often loosely used for **neckerchief**, a similar covering for the neck. Occasionally the term also applied to a **handkerchief**.

Kersche
Period: Medieval.
Term for a **kerchief**.

Kevenhuller cock, Kevenhuller hat
(M)
Period: 1740s–1760s.
A large felt **tricorne hat**, the front brim cocked high, forming a peak. "A laced hat pinched into what our Beaux have learnt to call the Kevenhuller Cock" (1746, *The British Magazine*).

Key chain
(M)
Period: 1890s onwards.
A chain attached to a bunch of keys in a trouser pocket; the other end of the chain attached to a **braces** button on the trousers.

Kick pleat
(F)
Period: 1940s onwards.
A short inverted pleat inserted into the lower back or side seam of a tightly fitting skirt to allow easier movement.

Kicksies
See Unmentionables.

Kilt
(M)
Period: Late 18th century onwards.
One item within Highland dress for men is a kilt, a length of woollen cloth, usually of a checkered or tartan pattern, fitting around the waist and descending to the knee, with closely overlapping pleats and a plain wrap-over panel at the front held by straps and buckles and a decorative pin.

(F)
Period: 20th century onwards.
Kilts began to be worn by women, though often their construction was lighter, involving a shorter yardage of cloth but the principles of the male kilt were retained. Fashion designers often used variants of the style, the fabric or both in the 1970s.

Kimono
(F & M)
Period: Late 19th century onwards.
Kimono is the modern Japanese term for the kosode, a T-shaped garment, of cotton or silk, often brightly patterned, with wide, rectangular sleeves and overlapping front sections held in place by an **obi**, a wide sash. The style became popular in western countries as a result of widespread artistic interest in Japanese art and culture.

It was an artistic alternative to the **teagown**. In the 20th century the style became popular for **dressing-gowns**.

Kimono sleeve

(F)

Period: Late 19th century onwards.

The wide, rectangular sleeve found on the traditional **kimono** was used on various other items of clothing, blouses, coats and dresses.

Kirtle

(M)

Period: 9th to late 14th century.

A sleeved, knee-length body garment, the same as the **tunic**. In the 13th and 14th centuries it was commonly worn with a **courtepy**, probably a type of **surcoat**. "A kertil and a courtepy" (1362, Langland, *Piers Plowman*).

(F)

Period: 10th to late 15th century.

An inner garment worn over the **smock** but beneath the **gown**. The term kirtle replaced **tunic** at about the turn of the 14th and 15th centuries, though the purpose of the garment, which was to provide an early form of corseting, remained the same. In the 14th century it might be worn without an overgarment, especially by unmarried women. "Damoselles two right young and full semelyhede In kirtels and none other wede...." (Chaucer, *Romaunt of the Rose*).

Period: Late 15th century to ca. 1650.

The kirtle was usually worn under the gown. A "full kirtle" was bodice and skirt; a "half kirtle" was skirt only. From ca. 1545 onwards the kirtle meant the skirt or **petticoat**; subsequently as the name kirtle was dropped, petticoat replaced it.

Period: 18th and 19th centuries.

The term was occasionally applied to a short jacket. "Kirtle, a kind of short jacket" (1706, Phillips); "Kyrtle, a kirtle or short coat without laps or *skirts*") 1828, Craven, *Dialect*).

It was also a **safeguard**;"Kirtle, an outer petticoat to protect the other garments from dust, etc. in riding" (1825, Forby, *Vocabulary of East Anglia*).

Kissing-strings, bridles

(F)

Period: 1700–1750

Strings for tying the **mob cap** under the chin.

Kiss-me-quick

(F)

Period: 1867–1869.

Popular name for the very small bonnet then fashionable.

Kitten heel

(F, rarely M)

Period: 1959 onwards.

A relatively low, pointed heel on a shoe or boot.

Knee-band

(M)

Period: End of 17th century onwards.

The band closing the **knee breeches** below the knee.

Knee breeches

(M)

Period: ca. 1570 onwards.

Breeches closed below the knee, the usual leg-covering of the 18th century but rarer in the 19th century except for formal evening, court and ecclesiastical wear. Even rarer in the 20th century except for certain uniforms and sports wear.

See Knickerbockers.

(F)

Period: From 20th century onwards.

Intermittently popular for sports and more rarely as fashionable garments.

Knee buckles

(M)

Period: Late 17th century onwards.

Buckles securing the breeches knee-band below the knee; rare after 1920 except for **court**, etc.

Knee cuffs

(M)

Period: Mid-17th century.

Probably a synonym for **port cannons**. "One paire of scollopp lynnen knee cuffs worth three pounds" (1659, Middlesex Session Rolls).

Knee-fringe

(M)

Period: 1670–1675.

The hanging fringe of ribbons about the bottom edge of the open breeches.

Knee-piece

(M)

Period: 17th century.

The top portion of **boot hose**.

Knee-string

(M)

Period: 17th and 18th centuries.

The ties for drawing-in of breeches below the knee.

Knickerbockers

(M)

Period: 1860 onwards.

A loose form of breeches of tweed, etc., fastening with a band below the knee; introduced at first for the voluntary militia, and then used by civilians for country pursuits; "cut three inches wider in the leg and two inches longer than ordinary breeches" (1871, *The Tailor & Cutter*). Usually worn with a Norfolk or other type of sports jacket for golf, etc. The name derived from the fictional Dutch founders of New York as depicted by Washington Irving in his *History of New York by Dietrick Knickerbocker* (1808).

(F)

Period: 20th century onwards.

A country style of dress; also an intermittent fashion.

Knickers

(F)

Period: 1890 onwards.

An undergarment similar to **knickerbockers** but usually made of flannel or longcloth, and worn instead of **drawers** and often without a petticoat.

In the 20th century a term denoting any form of female drawers or panties, but usually large, baggy, elasticated versions often worn at girls' schools.

Knife pleat

Period: Late 19th century onwards.

Similar to an **accordion** pleat but with all pleats facing in one direction; the actual pleats could be of any width.

Knightly girdle

(F & M)

Period: ca. 1350–ca. 1420.

A decorative belt comprising metal clasps joined together and fastened in front by an ornamental buckle or clasp. Always worn encircling the hips, not the waist, over the **gipon** or **cote-hardie**, and only by the nobility.

Knitted spencer

See Spencer.

Knitted vest

(M)

Period: 1880s.

A home-made, knitted **waistcoat** in fancy colours, often with a **fly-front fastening** and worn with a velvet **lounging jacket**.

Knitting

Period: 16th century onwards.

A method of producing a fabric by interweaving thread or wool using hand-held needles or, later, a machine.

Knitwear

Period: 20th century onwards.

A generic term for all items of clothing produced by hand or machine knitting.

See Jersey.

Knop

Period: Medieval onwards.

A button or tassel, generally decorative in character.

Knot

(F)

Period: 17th to mid-18th century.

A ribbon bow for decorating the head or gown; feather knots were also used. Named varieties included: the "bosom knot" worn at the breast; the "duchess", "a knot to be put immediately above the tower" (1694, *Ladies' Directory*), i.e. above the raised curls of the **fontange** coiffure; a "suit of knots", a set of bows for the gown and sometimes also for the head; the "top knot", a large bow or bunch of ribbon loops worn on the top of the head, usually known as a **pompon** in fashionable circles in the 18th century.

Period: 19th century onwards.

Name given to the hair when it was twisted into a "bun" at the back of the head.

Kurta

(F & M)

A loose shirt or tunic made from cotton or silk and reaching to the knees; worn over churidars or shalwars (both styles of trousers, the former tight-fitting, the latter looser) in Bangladesh, India and Pakistan, and abroad by those who live in Europe, North America or other parts of the world.

See Shalwar kameez.

L

Label

(M)

Period: 15th century.

The turned-back, tongue-shaped **lapel** of the **tabard**.

Period: 19th century onwards.

The small strip of fabric attached on the inner surface of a garment bearing the name of the owner, or maker, or both. The earliest example of a label on a man's coat, 1822, was concealed under the yoke lining and was of parchment bearing the owner's name. Paper labels were occasionally used, on **bespoke** coats and waistcoats until ca. 1870, sometimes with the owner's measurements as well as name, together with the tailor's name.

This was placed under the yoke lining or within a back pleat; towards the close of the century it was placed on the lining of the inside breast pocket.

Cotton or silk fabric labels with the tailor's name and address woven on them began to appear by 1850, but were uncommon until the 1880s; from ca. 1870 the tailor's name might be woven on to the coat-hanger loop. On waistcoats the name was often attached to the lacing tabs at the back, from ca. 1840.

(F)

The dressmaker's name woven on a label attached to the inner surface of the bodice or waistband became usual from ca. 1870.

Black cotton Chantilly **lace parasol** cover with a picot edge and a mixture of floral and scalloped motifs on a net ground, ca. 1860–80. Copyright the Olive Matthews Collection, Chertsey Museum.

(F & M)

During the course of the 20th century brand and makers labels including country of origin became usual and, gradually, extra labels with laundering or dry-cleaning details were also inserted in every type of garment and accessory.

Lace

Period: Medieval onwards.

A tie for fastening or pulling together opposite edges, as for boots, stays, etc.

Period: 16th century onwards.

Braid used for trimming, now found mostly on ceremonial uniforms.

Period: 16th century onwards.

An openwork trimming of many patterns; both handmade and machine-made.

See Glossary of Laces.

Laced

Period: 17th century onwards.

Tightened or closed with cord or tape, etc. "One pair of new Laced shooes" (1697, *The London Gazette*).

Period: 17th century to ca. 1900.

Trimmed with braid or lace; this meaning was discarded for general use but retained for uniforms after 1900.

Lace-ups

(F & M)

Period: 19th century onwards.

A shorthand description of boots or shoes that are laced rather than fastened with buttons or straps or have elastic sides. Usually applied to sturdy, front-lacing, leather footwear rather than the lighter, side-laced boots worn by women in the 19th century.

Lacing studs

(M)

Period: 1897 onwards.

Oval brass hooks for criss-cross lacing-up of men's boots and later, in the 20th century, women's hiking boots, to avoid having to thread through eyelet holes.

See Button-hooks.

Lamballe bonnet

(F)

Period: 1865.

A very small, saucer-shaped bonnet of straw, worn flat on the head, curving down slightly on each side, and tied under the chin with a large ribbon bow. Some were made with a very small **bavolet** behind; others with lace **lappets** on each side of the **chignon**.

Langet, langette, languette

(F & M)

Period: Late 14th–16th century.

The term "langette" was used to describe tongue-shaped decorative beads, of amber, jet, etc.

Period: 15th–17th century.

A "langet" was a type of thong for tying hose, or a strap or lace for tying shoes in the 17th century; also spelt "langot".

(F)

Period: ca. 1818–1822.

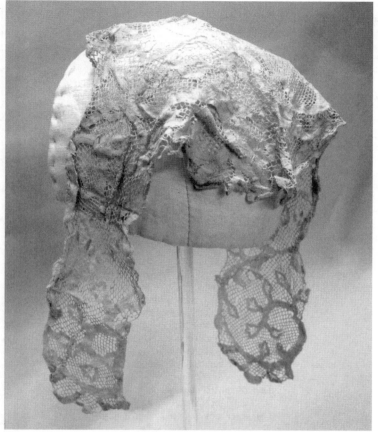

Woman's **cap** with **lappets** of **Milanese bobbin lace**; the lace tinted at a later date, ca. 1700–20. Copyright the Olive Matthews Collection, Chertsey Museum.

A "languette" was a flat, tongue-shaped, applied trimming, a common decoration for skirts and **pelisses**.

Langtry hood

(F)

Period: 1880s.

A detachable hood to any outdoor garment; resembling an academic hood displaying a coloured lining and attached by hooks or short ends crossing in front.

Lapel

(M, later F)

Period: 19th century onwards.

The turned-back upper part of the front of a coat or waistcoat, known in the second half of the 19th century as "the turn".

Lap-mantle

(F & M)

Period: Late 16th and early 17th centuries.

A covering for the knees; a rug.

Lappets

(F)

Period: 18th and 19th centuries.

Pendants from an indoor head-dress, hanging at the sides or behind, and made either plain or trimmed with lace.

Lasting boots

Period: Late 19th century.

Boots of which the uppers were made of black cashmere.

Latchet

(M, later F)

Period: Medieval onwards.

A strap to fasten a shoe or clog.

Laundry

Period: Medieval onwards.

The washing of clothing was a lengthy and physically arduous activity, but it was not necessarily a frequent occurrence. In fact, it was a sign of wealth that a household had many changes of **shirts**, **smocks** and other washable body linen, bed linen and towels. All of these items were white until comparatively recently and needed soaking and washing before being hung out to dry. Elite households had dedicated laundry areas, close to water supplies, and it was a sign of social mobility to be able to afford to take laundry to professional laundresses.

However, by the 19th century various items of machinery had improved considerably, such as mangles to squeeze out water and early washing machines. Early domestic machines were still expensive and were designed to look like a piece of kitchen furniture rather than an appliance; "An ingenious but simple combination of Mangle, Wringer, Washing Tank and Table, eminently suitable for flats and small houses, where space is limited" (1914, *Gamages General Catalogue*). A series of inventions before and after World War I in America led to washing machines that were electrically powered and undertook several processes efficiently. Automatic machines were made by the late 1940s, and in launderettes and individual homes they ensured that laundry was no longer an arduous chore.

See Dry cleaning.

Laveuse costume
(F)

Period: 1876.

A day dress with an overskirt, called a tunic, turned up "like a washerwoman's" and draped round the sides, gathered behind and there buttoned.

Layering
(F)

Period: Mid-20th century onwards.

Term used to describe clothing which requires layers of different construction, length and weight to create an effect; found in **hippie style** clothing of the 1960s and 1970s. Also used to mean clothing which suits changeable weather by layering unstructured items, such as **T-shirts**, **shirts**, **sweaters**, **coats**, etc., which are lightweight and easily removable.

It also describes a method of cutting hair.

Leading strings
(F & M)

Period: 17th and 18th centuries.

A term applied to children's clothing. Long, narrow strips of fabric forming sham **hanging sleeves** were attached to the back of the arm-holes and used to control the child's efforts to walk. "Buy me a pair of leading strings for Jak (aged 4); there is stuff made on purpose that is very strong" (1715, *Verney Letters*).

Leaf
See Stand-fall collar.

Leefekye, lyfkie
(F)

Period: 16th and early 17th centuries.

A bodice.

Leek button
Period: 1842.

A button with a metal shell or mould of pasteboard with a metal edge applied to it, covered with silk or other fabric, and having a flexible shank made of "woven wire cloth". Made at Leek in England and patented in 1842.

Legging, leggin
(M)

Period: 18th century.

An extra covering for the leg from ankle to knee and sometimes higher, usually of cloth or leather.

(F)

Period: 1960s onwards.

A fashionable form of leg covering, often close-fitting and of elasticated fabric; adopting a style worn by dancers.

See Leg warmers, Tights.

Leghorn hat
(F)

Period: Early 18th century onwards.

A summer hat made from an Italian plaited straw. The hat was associated with Livorno in northern Italy and anglicized to "Leghorn". A particular type of wheat was cut when green, bleached and plaited, offering a flexible material for hat-making. Many imitations were attempted, but this name for a wide-brimmed straw hat was retained.

Leg-of-mutton sleeve
See Gigot sleeve.

Leg warmers
(F)

Period: 1970s onwards.

A style adopted from professional dancers, who wore long, knitted, foot-less stockings over their tights as they warmed up or cooled down in practice sessions. Within mainstream fashion these came in various weights of wool or synthetic, in many colours, and could be pulled up or concertinaed over tights and trousers for warmth.

Leicester jacket
(M)

Period: 1857.

A **lounging jacket** with **raglan sleeves**.

Leisure wear
(F & M)

Period: Mid- to late 20th century onwards.

An all-purpose term for clothing worn informally or for activities pursued when not working, e.g. **fleeces**, **polo shirts**, **T-shirts**, etc.

Leotard
(F & M)

Period: 1880s onwards.

A closely fitted, one-piece garment covering torso and

arms and made from a stretchable fabric; worn by ac-
robats, dancers and other performers. Named after J.
Léotard, a 19th-century French trapeze artist.

Le smoking

(F)

Period: Late 1960s onwards.

A **dinner jacket** or **tuxedo** suit for women introduced
by the French designer Yves Saint Laurent (1936–2008)
in 1966.

Lettice cap, lettice bonnet, ermine cap, miniver cap

(F)

Period: 16th century.

An outdoor bonnet covering the ears; triangular-shaped
above the head; made of lettice, the fur of the snow
weasel, or of the cheaper miniver or more costly ermine.

(M)

Period: 16th and 17th centuries.

A night-cap or house-cap made of lettice fur; in the 17th
century it was supposed to induce sleep. "Bring in the
Lettice cap. You must be shaved, Sir, and then how
suddenly we'el make you sleep" (1619, John Fletcher,
Monsieur Thomas).

Lettice ruff

(M)

Period: Early 17th century.

An error in spelling for "lettuce"; a ruff with flattened
convolutions resembling the crinkled leaves of a lettuce.
See Cabbage-ruff.

Levis

(M, later F)

Period: 1860s onwards.

A proprietary name for denim **jeans** and **dungarees**
manufactured by Levi Strauss in America in the second
half of the 19th century. From working garments these
evolved into highly fashionable styles in the second half
of the 20th century, and included named varieties such
as Levi 501s.

Levite gown, Levetes

(F)

Period: 1780s.

An **open robe**, often of linen, in which the back of the
bodice appeared pointed although continuous with the
overskirt; the bodice front was often closed by cross-
straps. It had long sleeves and could be worn with or
without an **apron**. Day wear.

Liberty & Co.

Period: 1875 onwards.

A London department store started by Arthur Lasenby
Liberty (1843–1917) in Regent Street. The store sold
goods imported from the Far East, including cashmere,
silks and satins. Its early customers were the artistic,
intellectual and progressive members of late Victorian
and Edwardian society. It was closely linked to the
Aesthetic movement and its workshops produced

artistic and quasi-timeless style of clothing, often with
arts-and-crafts-style embroidery; these included its
perennially popular **burnous** evening cloak. After a
period of stagnation in the post-World War I period it
was resuscitated by young designers in the late 1950s,
when its scarves, ties, printed lawns, and ranges of
clothing including shirts and blouses, repositioned it as
a fashionable store.

Liberty bodice

(F)

Period: 1908 to mid-1960s.

A waist-length, sleeveless undergarment of knitted cotton with vertical cotton bands offering support. Front-
fastening with buttons, originally bone, later rubber; suspenders for stockings could be buttoned to the bodice.
Designed for girls aged between nine and thirteen, it
became a classic item of underclothing for British girls
and in countries trading with the UK. It was produced by
the Leicestershire corsetry factory of Symington & Co.
and by the 1930s its success led to enlarged premises.
Various versions were produced, including an unsuc-
cessful nylon variant in the 1950s.

Lily Benjamin

(M)

Period: 19th century.

A colloquial term for the white overcoat much worn in
the first half of the century.

See Benjamin.

Limerick gloves

(F)

Period: ca. 1750–1850.

Long or short gloves made of very fine leather, said to be
made from the skins of unborn lambs. "Lymarick gloves
1 pr. 3/–" (1789, Biddulph Accts., Hereford Records).

Limousine

(F)

Period: 1889.

A long, circular evening cloak, gauged round the throat,
with the fullness falling in folds over the arms, as sleeves.

Linecloths

(M)

Period: 15th century.

A "pair of linecloths" were linen drawers or possibly
loin cloths. "A payre of lynclothys" (ca. 1474, Paston
Letters, Inventory of Servants' Clothes).

Lingerie

(F)

Period: ca. 1830s onwards.

A French term describing any linen items found in
women's **trousseaux** or wardrobes; later, in the 20th
century, usually articles of underwear and night wear.

Liripipe, tippet

(F & M)

Period: ca. 1350–ca. 1500.

The long, pendant tail of a **hood**. In the 15th century

it was suspended from the male **chaperon** or wound round it, turban-wise; also sometimes pendant from the female head-dress, added as an ornament.

List

Period: 18th and 19th centuries.

The border or selvage of cloth; strips of selvage, joined together, were used to make slippers. "Her quiet tread muffled in a list slipper" (1847, Charlotte Brontë, *Jane Eyre*).

Little black dress, LBD

(F)

Period: Mid-1920s onwards.

A novelty supposedly introduced by the French designer Coco Chanel (1883–1971). A simple, narrow, black dress, often knee-length in the 1920s, was worn at the newly fashionable cocktail parties. It offered simplicity and elegance and, instead of being a colour associated with servants or widows, black became chic. "An essential in every wardrobe is a black evening dress." (1926, quoted in Cunnington, *English Women's Clothing in the Present Century*).

In subsequent decades the continuing allure of the LBD can be attributed to the fact that black is a colour which magically makes its wearer look slimmer and taller and is acceptable at many types of social event.

Little Lord Fauntleroy suit

(M)

Period: 1886 onwards.

A style of dress for young boys, made fashionable by the eponymous hero of Frances Hodgson Burnett's novel. It comprised a velvet tunic and **knickerbockers** and a white lace collar falling over the shoulders, faintly reminiscent of 17th-century Cavalier clothing; with a wide sash round the waist and a bow with hanging ends on one hip.

The author described it as: "a black velvet suit with a lace collar and with lovelocks waving about…the face". The author was American and Oscar Wilde, on his visit to the USA in 1882, had declared the Cavalier costume to have been the most artistic male dress ever known, and had recommended its revival. He may, in part, have been responsible for the Little Lord Fauntleroy style of dress for boys. In the 20th century it became an outfit for **fancy dress** or performance rather than boy's clothing.

Livery

(F & M)

Period: 14th century onwards.

Amongst several meanings connected with clothing the central one is the provision of cloth and/or actual garments from a master to any degree of inferior who serves in her/his household. Initially it was perhaps one item – a badge, collar, hood or gown – but actual servants wore the colours and fabrics associated with a family, for instance the green and white of Henry VIII. The term also referred to the garments worn by members of livery companies and those in the armed services, though the latter tend to wear uniform which is, in many respects, a natural extension of livery. It was a form of identification of role and social grouping. "A Servant out of livery leaped from the box." (1841, E. Bulwer-Lytton, *Night and Morning*).

See Mandilion.

Loafer

(M, later F)

Period: 1930s onwards.

A casual, leather, slip-on shoe, originally worn in Norway. Similar to a **moccasin** but with a firm sole and low, wide heel. Below the front tongue was usually a decorative strap stitched into place. Other versions had top stitching, tassels or chains at the centre front. The distinctive Gucci loafers, produced from 1953, had a metallic horsebit or snaffle across the front.

Lock stitch

Period: ca. 1860.

A term referring to sewing by the lockstitch machine rather than the chainstitch machine. It began to be used by English dressmakers in the 1860s.

See Sewing machine.

Loden

(M, later F)

Period: 19th century onwards.

Term for both a fabric and a style of coat or jacket. Originally found in the Tyrol region of Austria, these traditional waterproof fabrics, at first made of sheep's wool and dyed in several colour ways, eventually evolved in the 20th century into an alpaca, camel hair and mohair mixture and ca. 1900 a dark green fabric was used for a simple, calf- or knee-length coat with button fastening often masked by a **fly-front**, a round collar and long back vent or inverted pleat. This gradually became a design **classic** within Europe, outpacing other loden garments such as capes and short jackets, both of which were edged with braid.

Loin cloth

(M, occasionally F)

Period: Greco-Roman onwards.

A long piece of cloth wrapped around the lower body, of variable length and sometimes worn passed between the legs to cover the genitalia. It is found in many different cultures where draping, folding and tying fabric is more usual than sewing it.

See Braies, Dhoti, Linecloths.

Long-bellied doublet

See Peascod-bellied doublet.

Long clothes

Period: ca. 1650 to early 20th century.

The conventional dress of the infant in arms, gradually replacing the former swaddling clothes. A long gown, some three feet or even more in length, fastening at the back, with short sleeves; the whole often richly ornamented with lace and insertion. The garment appears to have been adapted from the christening robe formerly only used on that particular occasion.

Long hood

(F)

Period: 18th century.

A soft hood made like the **pug hood** or **short hood**, but the portion surrounding the face was continued into two long strips for tying under the chin or for swathing round the neck.

Long johns

(M)

Period: 19th century onwards.

A combination undergarment uniting a long sleeved vest, usually buttoned at the front, with long, close-fitting drawers. Wool vests and drawers were a feature of male underclothes in cold weather or cold climates and this provided a streamlined version. "The long john is a homely woollen undergarment of rustic provenance" (1964, 14 February, *The Spectator*).

In the 20th century long johns were made in the new fabrics which were used for **thermal** underwear.

Long lock

See Love lock.

Long pocket

(M)

Period: 18th and 19th centuries.

A vertical pocket in coat or overcoat.

"...the two sorts of pockets – the long pocket with a plain or indented flap – the cross pocket with the round or the trefoil or scallop flap" (1715, John Harris, *Treatise upon the Modes*).

Long stock, long stocking

(M)

Period: 16th and early 17th centuries.

The long stocking portion of **trunk-hose** to which they were joined high up the thigh. "All the swarming generation of long stocks, short pain'd hose and huge stuff'd doublets" (1607, Beaumont and Fletcher, *Woman Hater*).

Long-stocked hose

See Long stock; also Hose.

Loo mask

(F)

Period: Mid-16th to 18th century.

A half-mask covering the upper part of the face only.

See Mask.

Loon pants

(M, occasionally F)

Period: Early 1970s.

Casual trousers, close-fitting to the knee and widening into a wide flare to the ankle; pairs were advertised with a circumference of up to 30 inches around the bottom. Derived from "looning", a mid-1960s term for teenagers dancing, lounging around, enjoying themselves

aimlessly. Probably connected to the much earlier usage of a clown or behaving like one.

See Flares.

Lorgnette

(F)

Period: Late 19th century onwards.

A pair of eyeglasses in a tortoiseshell frame with a long handle; for examining objects at a distance. "Nearly every smartly dressed woman wears a lorgnette." (1893) Less worn in the 20th century.

Louis heel

Another name for a **Pompadour heel**.

Louis XIII corsage

(F)

Period: 1850.

Day corsage of a **pelisse-robe**, closed at the neck and waist, with the centre open displaying a **chemisette** or cambric pleats or embroidery.

Louis XIV sleeve

(F)

Period: 1850.

A sleeve cut to widen from the shoulder downwards, and usually edged below with rows of fluted trimming. Worn with an under sleeve or **engageante**.

Lounge suit

(M)

Period: ca. 1860 onwards.

A suit made up of a **lounging jacket**, **waistcoat** and **trousers**, all of the same cloth; for informal wear.

From the mid 20th century onwards the waistcoat was often omitted.

Lounging jacket, lounge jacket

(M)

Period: ca. 1848 into early 20th century.

A short-skirted, single-breasted coat just covering the seat, slightly waisted and with or without a seam at the waist. Flapped pockets on the hips or slit pockets in the side seams, and outside pocket on the left breast; corners rounded. The style varied according to the fashions of the day.

See Albert jacket, Three-seamer.

Love and clothing

(M)

Period: 16th and 17th centuries.

It was correct to show by a nice disorder in his dress that a man was in love; e.g. to go without a hat-band and to appear unbuttoned (a symbolic gesture). "He taught me how to know a man in love. Then your hose should be ungarter'd, your bonnet unbanded, your sleeve unbuttoned, your shoe untied, and everything about you demonstrating a careless desolation" (1623, W. Shakespeare, *As You Like It*).

Apart from this example of love and melancholy, there are several terms which conjoin love and appearance: "love-badge" which was a rare mid-17th century usage;

Caricature ca. 1860. This pokes gentle fun at the invention of **aniline dyes**, first mauve and then magenta. The younger man (left) sports the monocle, **cane**, fashionable **lounge jacket** and pale **waistcoat** and **cravat** with a jewelled pin of the **dandy**; even his **top hat** is impractically pale and his tuft of **beard** emulates that of Napoleon III of France. His older companion is sedate apart from the matching magenta coat and nose. Private collection.

SCENE—COMMERCIAL ROOM.

Incipient Commercial to Crusty Old Traveller. "YOU'RE ALWAYS IN THE FASHION, I SEE. LAST TIME I HAD THE PLEASURE OF SEEING YOU, MAUVE WAS THE PREVAILING COLOUR, AND YOUR NOSE WAS MAUVE. NOW MAGENTA IS ALL THE GO, AND IT'S CHANGED TO MAGENTA."

"love-beads", the coloured beads worn by **hippies** in the 1960s; a "love curl", a term first used in the 1840s. A "love-favour", of a ribbon, **glove** or jewellery, was a custom originating in the 16th century but, through a "love-lace", can be traced back to the obscure 14th century gift of a **girdle**. A "love-hood" was connected with mourning, was often made of crape or gauze and appeared in the 17th century and continued into the 19th century, "The ladies to wear black silk, plain muslin or long lawn, crepe or love hoods" (1861, *The Times*, 19 March). Mourning also encompassed "love ribbons" of narrow gauze with satin stripes found in the 17th century and lasting until the 19th century and "love **veils**" of thin crape or gauze.

Love knots
(F)
Period: Early 15th century onwards.
Complex, decorative knots of hair, ribbon or silk worn as a sign of love. In the 16th century one form was ornamental ribbon bows tied across coloured puffs emerging from sleeves with a vertical slash down the front.

Love lock
(M, sometimes F)
Period: 1590s onwards.
A long lock of hair, usually curled, turned forward from the nape of the neck so as to fall over the chest in front, particularly associated with royalists during the reign of Charles I (1625–1649) but the term was applied to other versions. "Lovelocks as the sailors term the curls they wear on their temples" (1840, F. Marryat, *Poor Jack*).

Lunardi hat
See Balloon hat.

Lyons loops
(F)
Period: 1865.
The name given to the velvet straps used to loop up the **overskirt** in three or four places, when double skirts were in fashion.

M

Macaroni cravat

(M)

Period: 1770s.

A muslin **cravat** edged with lace and tied in a bow under the chin.

Macaroni suit

(M)

Period: 1770s.

Introduced by young men returning from Italy and the Grand Tour who founded the Macaroni Club in 1764. The special style of **suit** did not develop until the 1770s; it comprised a coat, somewhat short and tight; "their coat sleeves are so tight they can with difficulty get their arms through their cuffs…their legs are covered with all the colours of the rainbow. Their shoes arc scarce slippers and their buckles are within one inch of their toe" (1772, *The Town & Country Magazine*).

They favoured a very small **tricorne hat** and attached a very large **nosegay** of flowers to the left shoulder.

Mackintosh

(M and later F)

Period: 1836 onwards.

A short, loose overcoat using the patent India-rubber cloth invented by Charles Macintosh (1766–1843) in 1822. It had proof straps over the seams and the original colour was drab or dark green. The wearing of these garments met, at first, much opposition owing to "the offensive stench which they emit" (1839, *Gentleman's Magazine of Fashion*).

In the 20th century the term was loosely applied to any waterproof outer garment and the abbreviation "Mac" came into use.

Macramé

Period: Second half of 19th century onwards.

A fringe or trimming of knotted cord, string or thread; often an edging for soft furnishings. As macramé lace, a substantial edging for clothing. It was an amateur pursuit amongst other needleworking skills.

Made-to-measure

(M, occasionally F)

Period: 19th century onwards.

In tailoring terms, the method whereby an existing pattern is adapted to fit a customer's measurements and offers a range of cloths and colours. Less time-consuming than **bespoke** tailoring and less expensive, but offering a better fit than **ready-made**.

Madras turban

(F)

Period: 1819.

A turban made of a blue and orange Indian **handkerchief**.

Magenta

Period: 1860.

The first chemical dye to be used in dress fabrics. Hailed as "the queen of colours" and immensely popular for women's clothing. Named after the battle in 1859.

See Aniline dyes, Solferino.

Magyar dress

(F)

Period: Late 19th century onwards.

The colourful folk dress of Hungary (the home of the Magyar people) was made popular by the Empress Elizabeth of Austria (1837–1898) who identified closely with the Hungarian part of the Austro-Hungarian Empire and was depicted in elite versions of national dress. In dressmaking, the Magyar style of blouse in which the sleeves are cut as one piece with the body of the blouse and gathered tightly at the wrist was an easy style for amateurs to make.

Maharatta tie

See Indian necktie.

Mahoitres, maheutres

(M)

Period: Late 14th to late 15th century.

A term used in France from 1394, and in England from ca. 1450–1480, describing shoulder pads for broadening the shoulders of men's gowns and jackets.

Mail-coach necktie, waterfall necktie

(M)

Period: 1818–1830s.

A very large **neckcloth**, sometimes composed of a cashmere **shawl**, folded loosely round the neck and tied once in front in a common knot over which the folds spread down "like a waterfall". Generally white and worn by "professional swell drivers" and **dandies**.

Maillot

(F & M)

Period: After 1870 onwards.

There are three different meanings for this French term. The first is that of **tights** worn by dancers, circus artists and similar. The second is that of a close-fitting, one-piece **bathing suit**. The third meaning is that of the *maillot jaune*, the yellow **jersey** worn by the leader in the Tour de France bicycle race.

Mail order

Period: 1860 onwards.

Originally an American term for the supply of goods by postal service, usually from a newspaper advertisement

m

or a catalogue designed to promote a range of items, including clothing. For instance, the Gamages catalogue for 1914 runs to 191 pages, of which 16 advertise a limited range of garments and accessories, but additional information on washing and sewing machines, luggage, perfumery and haberdashery indicate that everything from pins to motor bicycles (*sic*) could be purchased by mail order.

In the 21st century this type of service has been increasingly challenged by online shopping via websites.

Maintenon cloak
(F)
Period: 1860s.
A very large, black velvet cloak with wide sleeves; trimmed with a deep, pleated flounce covered with black guipure lace; sometimes embroidered.

Maintenon corsage
(F)
Period: 1839 and 1840s.
A close-fitting evening bodice trimmed with ribbon knots down the centre front, with a fall of lace at the waist.

Major wig
(M)
Period: ca. 1750–1800.
A military style of **wig** worn by civilians; a wig with a **toupee** and two corkscrew curls tied together at the nape of the neck to form a double **queue** behind. "The two locks of my major perriwig" (1753, J. Hawkesworth, *The Adventurer*); "His peruke which is naturally a kind of flowing Bob, but by the occasional addition of two tails it sometimes appears as a major" (1754, *The Connoisseur*).
See Brigadier wig.

Make do, make do and mend
Period: 20th century.
Terms denoting improvisation and ingenuity by re-using existing resources when cash or resources were in short supply. Applied to re-making clothing, unpicking woollen garments and knitting anew, and so forth; encouraged by government propaganda during and just after World Wars I and II.

Make up
(F & M)
Period: 19th century onwards.
A description of how performers altered their facial appearance, and occasionally their hands, in preparation for any type of stage performance. The heavy preparations were often precursors to innovations in fashionable make-up for women.
See Cosmetics.

Malacca cane
(M)
Period: 18th century.
A **cane** made from the "clouded" or mottled stem of a Malacca palm; also called a "clouded cane".

Mameluke sleeve
(F)
Period: 1828–1830.
A very full sleeve with a deep cuff; for day wear and of thin fabrics.

Mameluke turban
(F)
Period: 1804.
A **turban** of white satin, the front rolled upwards like a hat-brim over a domed crown; trimmed with a large ostrich feather.

Mancheron
(F)
Period: 19th century.
A very short, ungathered over sleeve in the nature of an **epaulette**, worn with day dresses or sleeved outdoor garments. The name gradually became replaced by **epaulette** in the 1860s.

Manchette
(F)
Period: 1830s into 20th century.
A lace ruffle worn at the wrist for afternoon dress.

Mandarin coat
(F)
Period: 20th century onwards.
A long, embroidered silk coat with straight, narrow lines, designed to emulate those worn by elite Chinese men. Sometimes referred to as a "coolie coat".
See Mandarin jacket.

Mandarin collar
(F, sometimes M)
Period: 20th century onwards.
The narrow, standing collar, open at the front, which was found on the clothing of Chinese officials and others. Adapted for a variety of western uses on blouses, dresses and **jackets**.

Mandarin hat
(F)
Period: 1861.
A black velvet hat suggestive of that worn by mandarins; trimmed with feathers over the back of the flat crown. Associated with the Franco-British war with China which ended in October 1860.

Mandarin jacket
(F)
Period: 20th century onwards.
A straight jacket, buttoned at the front and with a narrow standing collar. Worn by Chinese officials and often originally of embroidered silk. Both imports and westernized copies in other fabrics became available in the post-1950 period.

Mandilion, Mandeville
(M)
Period: 1570s–1620s.
A loose, hip-length jacket with close sleeves (later,

sham) and open side seams. A garment often worn **colley-westonward**. In the 17th century the name "Mandeville" was preferred, and after ca. 1630 it was usually a **livery** garment.

Mannequin

(F)

Period: Mid-18th to mid-20th century.

From the French term meaning a lay figure or dummy, as used by artists. The term widened to include a young woman displaying clothing in the show-rooms of **couturiers** and fashion designers. Charles Frederick Worth (1825–1895) was the first couturier known to use mannequins, anonymous young women who often doubled as seamstresses or sales assistants, but the practice evolved in various different ways. Lucile (1863–1935), the English designer, had named mannequins and Paul Poiret (1879–1944) took his mannequins on tour and had them filmed. Training schools sprang up to offer gullible young women opportunities to enter this new, seemingly glamorous profession, which also encompassed photographic work. By the 1970s the term was almost obsolete in English, replaced by the term **model**.

Manon robe

(F)

Period: 1860s.

A silk day dress, the fronts cut in one, the back with a broad, double box-pleating flowing loosely down from under the collar to the hem in the style of the **Watteau pleat**. The hem was trimmed with a deep flounce.

Mant

See Mantua.

Manteau

(M)

Period: 16th century.

A man's cloak. The *manteau à la reître* or "French cloak" was either a **compass cloak**, namely circular, or a 'half compass", semicircular in shape.

(F)

See Mantua.

Manteel

(F)

Period: 1730s–1750s.

A scarf-like cape with long ends in front and usually a falling hood behind.

Mantelet, mantlet

(M)

Period: Medieval.

A short mantle or cape. "A Mantelet upon his shulder hangynge, Bretful of Rubies reede" (ca. 1386, Chaucer, *Knight's Tale*).

(F)

Period: 18th and 19th centuries.

"Mantlet, a small cloak worn by women" (1730, Bailey, *Dictionary*). In the following century it described a half-shawl, rounded at the neck, some with a falling hood or a small cape. Some had short, wide sleeves. Worn as an outdoor cloak.

Mantella, mantilla

(F)

Period: 1840–1860.

A small **mantle**, deep at the back, with long scarf ends in front; sometimes, confusingly, called a "mantilla" when made of lace.

Period: 16th century onwards.

The spelling "mantilla" denotes a long lace scarf or veil worn over the head and shoulders, especially associated with Spanish women.

Mantle, mantil

(F & M)

Period: 12th century onwards.

The word was reintroduced from France in the 12th century; in Old English the word was *mentel* and there are many other variants descriptive of this long, voluminous, cloak-like outer garment reaching to the feet and made without a hood. An everyday garment until the 14th century, then generally ceremonial and for men, and usually fastened on the right shoulder with three large buttons, giving free play to the right arm. Tied in front for women.

Period: 16th century.

A "double mantle" meant a lined mantle.

Period: 17th and 18th centuries.

A large wrap for infants in arms. "The uppermost garment that nurses wrap up young infants in before they coat them" (1735, Dyche and Pardon, *Dictionary*).

Period: 19th century.

The length varied and some mantles had capes or a cape, and some had sleeves.

Mantua, manteau, manto, manton, mantua gown

(F)

Period: Mid-17th to mid-18th century.

A loose gown, the bodice unboned, joined to an overskirt which was open in front exposing a decorative underskirt called a **petticoat**. The distinctive feature was the elaborate arrangement of the back drapery of the overskirt, which in its final form in the 1730s consisted of a narrow train. It was worn on all social or formal occasions. "A long trailing mantua sweeps the ground" (1712, J. Gay, *Trivia*).

Mantua hose

Period: Early 17th century.

Knitted silk **stockings** made at Mantua in northern Italy. Mantua provided rich fabrics, often silk, imported from the 16th century, and in the 18th century damasks and paduasoys are mentioned.

Mantua maker, mantua woman

(F & M)

Period: 17th to early 20th century.

A person who made mantuas, later known as a **dress-maker**. The term "mantua woman" is less used and not beyond the 18th century.

Mao style

(F & M)

Period: After 1949.

The westernization of Chinese clothing began under the government led by Sun Yat-sen (1866–1925). The basis was a simplified military or safari-style jacket, first seen in Japan with a buttoned front, four pockets, and a **stand collar**, later modified to a narrow turn-down collar worn with trousers. Mao Zedong wore this style from ca. 1927. Another influence was the simplified style worn by Soviet students in the 1920s and 1930s. When Mao came to power he recognized the economic and cultural impact of clothing and always wore a version of the Sun Yat-sen suit. There were two subtly different variants, but always made in black, blue, grey or khaki (the last for the military) which the entire population were encouraged to wear. The term "Mao" is associated with the soft cap, the collar, the jacket, suit and trousers, which actually were introduced by a predecessor. The simple styles and limited palette influenced western designers in the 1960s and 1970s.

Marcel wave, Marcelle wave, marcel wave

(F)

Period: 1872 onwards.

A method of forming deep waves in the hair with a type of reverse curling tongs; invented by the Frenchman François Marcel Grateau (d. 1936) in 1872, this method of transforming straight hair was overtaken by the **permanent wave** in the 1930s. The terms "marcel wave" or "marcelling" continued in popular usage long after the method disappeared.

Marie-Antoinette skirt

(F)

Period: 1895–1900.

A day skirt with seven gores, one in front, two on each side, and two behind, box-pleated; 12–18 feet round the hem.

See Gored skirt.

Marie-Antoinette sleeve

See Marie sleeve.

Marie sleeve

(F)

Period: 1813–1824–1829, and 1872.

A sleeve full to the wrist but tied into compartments by a series of ribbons. Revived in 1872 under the name **Marie-Antoinette sleeve**.

Marie Stuart bodice

(F)

Period: 1828.

An evening bodice, tight and boned down the front to a deep, pointed waist.

Marie Stuart bonnet

(F)

Period: 1820s–ca. 1870.

A bonnet having the front brim curled with a dip in the centre over the forehead. A style often worn by widows.

Marie Stuart hat

(F)

Period: 1849.

An evening-dress hat of tulle, having a stiff brim curled up with a central dip over the forehead.

Marin anglais bonnet

(F)

Period: 1870s.

Resembling a child's **sailor hat**, ornamented with flowers, feathers and ribbon; worn at the back of the head and tied under the chin with a ribbon bow.

Mariner's cuff

See À la marinière cuff.

Marino Faliero sleeve

(F)

Period: 1830–1835.

A large, hanging sleeve caught in at the elbow by a ribbon band. Called after Lord Byron's 1820 drama of that name.

Marlborough hat

(F)

Period: 1882.

A large, flat hat of lace and Tuscan straw, trimmed with long, shaded feathers and worn slightly on one side.

Marmotte bonnet

(F)

Period: 1832.

A very small bonnet with narrow brim round the front, like a small **Bibi bonnet**.

Marmotte cap

(F)

Period: 1833.

A half-handkerchief placed far back on the head and tied under the chin. Worn by day indoors.

Marquise bodice

(F)

Period: 1874.

An evening bodice with a frilled edge; the front heart-shaped.

Marquise mantle

(F)

Period: 1846.

A short taffeta **mantlet** with short sleeves and pulled in to fit the waist behind; trimmed with flounces and lace.

Marquisetto, marquisotted beard

(M)

Period: 1550–1600.

A close-cut **beard**.

Mary cap, Mary Queen of Scots cap, Marie Stuart cap

(F)

Period: 1750s and 1760s.

An indoor cap curved up on each side above the forehead with a central V-shaped dip; made of black cypress or gauze and edged with French beads. "As the cap was made of black gauze and saved washing; it had too much housewifery in it ever to be immense taste" (1762, *London Chronicle*).

Period: Late 1840s and late 1860s.

The Marie Stuart cap for day wear enjoyed a revival.

Mary Janes

(F)

Period: 1927 onwards.

An American style of children's shoe which gained popularity with adults. A smooth or patent-leather, round-toed shoe with a narrow strap across the ankle, and buttoned at one side; the heel flat or slightly raised.

Mary Stuart cap

See Mary cap.

Masher

(M)

Period: 1870–1900.

The elaborately dressed **dandy** of the period; also known in the 1890s as a "Piccadilly Johnny".

Masher collar

(M)

Period: 1870s and 1890s.

A very high, all-round **stand collar**, worn by **mashers**.

Masher dust wrap

(M)

Period: 1880s.

A close-fitting **Inverness** with large arm-holes covered by the cape, which was incomplete behind.

Mask, whole mask

(F)

Period: 1550 onwards.

A covering for the face to which it was shaped and pierced opposite the eyes, nose and mouth. The lighter masks had, at the mouth, a bead which was held by the wearer in the mouth. Masks were worn to conceal identity, to protect the skin from the sun, wind and rain when riding, and by ladies at the theatre. A **vizard** or vizard mask was a whole mask; a **loo mask** was a half-mask. "She's mask'd and in her riding suit" (1611, Lord Barry, *Ram-Alley*).

(M)

Occasionally worn by fashionable men, especially in Italy when attending masked balls or carnival.

Masquerade costume

(F & M)

Period: 18th century.

There is a long tradition of wearing disguises and **masks** to celebrate festivals and great events, and in Catholic countries there were lively entertainments during carnival, the season between late December and Lent. In Italian cities there was street theatre and balls which encouraged masking and disguise as a form of anonymity. Similar masquerades, held in palaces, pleasure gardens and theatres swept through European cities, London in 1708, Paris in 1715 and into Austria, the German states and Russia. The simplest form of disguise was a **domino** worn over ordinary clothing, and a mask and veil or three-cornered hat, but various forms of historical dress and Turkish or other exotic styles became popular and were copied and adapted and published. In the 20th century the reintroduction of carnival in Venice encouraged a bold, modern interpretation of disguise and masks.

See Fancy dress, Vandyke dress.

Maternity wear

(F)

Period: Medieval onwards.

Evidence about what was worn is limited. The looser garments prior to the 16th century probably accommodated pregnancy by the means of not using a belt. The sleeveless gowns and unstructured embroidered jackets of the 16th and 17th centuries were an attractive and practical alternative to tightly laced bodices. Corsets may have been replaced by **jumps** in the later 17th and 18th centuries, and the **sack** in its closed form was an ideal style for this purpose.

In the 19th century letting out standard styles, adding a loose front panel, using short jackets, shawls, **teagowns**, in fact a range of relatively unstructured garments, indicated ingenuity but there is little information, apart from advertisements for a "gestation stay" in the 1880s and a maternity corset in the early 20th century.

Full, unstructured dresses and smocks, loose from a high yoke to hips were a mainstay of early to mid-20th-century expectant mothers. Specialist brands, like Mothercare in the UK, trading from the early 1960s, offered everything for the mother-to-be and signalled a lively business opportunity. Although specific clothing is produced in many styles, young women often customize fashionable clothing or just buy it in larger sizes.

See Nursing dress.

Matildas

(F)

Period: 19th century.

Velvet ornamentation round the hem of a dress.

Also, in the 1840s, a term applied to a bunch of flowers worn in the hair.

Matinée

(F)

Period: 1851.

A hooded **pardessus** made of jacconet or muslin and worn outdoors over a morning dress.

Maud

(F)

Period: 1855.

A plaid, fringed **wrapper**, swathed round the shoulders and waist.

Maxi coat, maxi dress, maxi skirt

(F & M)

Period: Late 1960s.

A term coined to describe an unusually long garment at a time when **mini skirts** were still fashionable. Usually ankle-length, these garments were popular with the young for several years; the coats were often worn over mini dresses and the innovative French designer Pierre Cardin (b. 1922) included maxi dresses worn with ankle boots in his 1969 collections. The influence of Edwardian styles, due to the work of Laura Ashley amongst others, ensured a wide range of maxi styles.

Mazarin hood

(F)

Period: ca. 1675–1699.

A **chaperon** style named after the niece of Cardinal Mazarin (1602–1661), chief minister of Louis XIV.

M. B. waistcoat

See Cassock vest.

M-cut collar

(M)

Period: 19th century.

A notch cut in the shape of an "M", between the turned-over collar and the turned-back **lapel** of a coat; it first appeared in 1800, ceasing for day coats ca. 1850, but still used for many evening coats until ca. 1870.

Mecklenburg cap

(F)

Period: 1760s.

A "turban roll" worn as an indoor cap, dating from the marriage of Princess Charlotte of Mecklenburg-Strelitz to George III in 1761.

Medici collar, medicis

(F)

Period: 18th to early 20th century.

A collar, generally of net or lace, upstanding round the back of the neck, sloping down to nothing on the front of the bodice. "A broad medicis of Dresden lace" (1778, Sir N. Wraxall, *Memoirs of the Court of Berlin*).

Medici dress

(F)

Period: 1870s.

A trained **princess dress** with short sleeves and **tablier** front.

Medici sleeve

(F)

Period: 1830s.

A day sleeve puffed out to the elbow, thence tight to the wrist.

Medusa wig

(F)

Period: 1800–1802.

A **wig** made up of "a mass of snake-like curls hanging down".

Melon sleeve

(F)

Period: 1809–1815.

An evening-dress sleeve distended and shaped like a melon, either round the shoulder or elbow length. Often worn with a transparent long sleeve as an extension to the wrist.

Melote

(M)

Period: Medieval to early 16th century.

Originally a sheepskin garment; later a cloak of any coarse fur, principally, if not solely, worn by monks or friars at their work.

Mentonnières, chin stays

(F)

Period: 1820s and 1830s.

Quillings of tulle or lace sewn to the insertion of bonnet strings and tied under the chin, forming a white frill round the lower part of the face.

Mermaid's tail

(F)

Period: 1875–1882.

Nickname given to the train of a tie-back skirt.

Merry Widow hat

(F)

Period: 1907–1910.

A memorable example of the fashion for wide, lavishly decorated hats, the original was designed by Lucile (1863–1935), the English designer, and worn by the actress Lily Elsie (1886–1962) in the Franz Lehár operetta in its first London production in 1907. This style of hat was black, often made of a dull straw such as chip; it had a deep crown which was smothered in black tulle or feathers. It was often worn with a white or pale dress. This was an era when fashions on the stage were hugely influential.

Metal clothing

(F, occasionally M)

Period: 20th century onwards.

Metal threads were woven into fabrics or used in embroidery for many centuries, and in the 20th century fabrics such as **Lurex** had periods of popularity. However, actual metal, although made into buttons, zips, etc., was rarely used as a material for clothing before the work of the Spanish designer Paco Rabanne (b. 1934). His work as a jeweller led him to experiment with metal discs, chains, aluminium, etc. to fabricate clothing in the 1960s. Metal was also used within **alternative** styles.

Metal eyelets

Period: 1823 onwards.

Eyelet holes with metal surround for use in stays, boots, etc., in place of the stitched lace-holes; the patent dates from 1823.

Micro skirt

(F)

Period: 1960s onwards.

A particularly short version of the **mini skirt**, more like a pelmet than a skirt. The style has been revisited in the early 2000s.

Midi skirt

(F)

Period: Late 1960s and early 1970s.

A calf-length skirt, worn in its original form with high boots. Later, this length became usual for fashionable clothing.

Milan bonnet

(M)

Period: 1500–1550.

A **cap** with a soft, beret-shaped crown and rolled-up brim, often slit at the sides. The **bonnet** was sometimes slashed with decorative "pullings out" or trimmed with **aglets**. "Myllaine bonetes of crimosyn sattin drawen through with cloth of golde" (1542, Halle, *Chronicle*). Black was the more usual colour.

Milan coat

Period: 16th century.

Light armour; possibly mail.

Military folding hat

See Opera hat.

Military frock coat

(M)

Period: 19th century.

Worn by civilians from 1820. A **frock coat** without flapped pockets, the fronts often braided. The early style made with a **Prussian collar** or **roll collar** but without **lapels**.

Military stock

(M)

Period: Mid-18th to mid-19th century.

Worn by civilians. A made-up **neckcloth** stiffened with paste-board in the 18th century or leather in the 19th century and tied or buckled behind. In the 18th century it was always black for military men, white for civilians, and was commonly made of corded silk edged with kid. George IV abolished the white stock for civilians and William IV attempted unsuccessfully to restore it.

Milkmaid hat

See Bergère hat.

Milkmaid skirt

(F)

Period: 1885.

A plain skirt in striped fabric of two colours with an overskirt gathered at the waist, turned up on one side to show the lining and drawn through a loop of cord. Worn by day only.

Milliner

Period: 16th century onwards.

Someone who sells fancy goods and fashionable accessories; the term derives from Milan in Italy and the fact that many of these items originated in that city. By the late 17th century some informal garments were sold alongside accessories and trimmings, such as **fans**, **gloves**, ribbons and **lace**. The association with selling headwear is found from the late 19th century onwards. "There is no doubt that the lady milliner has raised her craft to a fine art, and that the pleasant and refined atmosphere of the "private upstairs show-room" gives a totally new tone to that most important of all dress matters, the choice of a new hat" (1904, *The Lady's Realm*).

Mini dress

(F)

Period: ca. 1965–1970, revived in the 2000s.

A dress with a short skirt ending well above the knee

Fashion plate advertising the services of Payne, **Milliner**. The **evening dresses** are simple and it is the millinery – the **caps** with their exuberant **feathers**, **ribbons** and swathed fabric of contrasting textures which are the important element in this plate; 1802. Copyright the Olive Matthews Collection, Chertsey Museum.

and worn by young girls and women. At its original introduction it was "much disapproved of by older people"
(1968, J. Ironside, *A Fashion Alphabet*).

Minimalism

Period: 1920s onwards.

Various movements in art, design, literature, music and
philiosophy which rejected excess, reduced expendi-
ture, and used unadorned simplicity to obtain results.
The term was not much used in respect of clothing, but
the 1920s and 1930s can be construed as minimalist.
The most obvious examples are found in the 1990s in
which sobriety of tonal palette and rejection of superficial effects appeared in the work of designers reacting
against the excesses of the 1980s.

Mini skirt

See Mini dress.

Mi-parti

(M)

Period: 14th and 15th centuries.

A description of the manner in which a garment was
divided visually into two sections, with the right side
having one colour or pattern and the left a contrasting
colour or pattern. This was especially fashionable between ca. 1320 and 1370, but was retained for men's
hose until the end of the century and for **livery** garments well into the 15th century. Later, the term was
used in regard to heraldic colour schemes. The term
"motley" was sometimes used, but is usually applied to
clown's and jester's clothing rather than to fashionable
apparel.

Mistake hat

(F)

Period: 1804.

A hat of straw or chip with a tall, flat-topped crown, the
front brim, with a blunt point, turned sharply up, the
back brim turned down. Worn on the back of the head.

Mitre head-dress

(F)

Period: ca. 1420–1450.

See heart-shaped head-dress; both were descriptive
terms applied by 19th-century authors.

Mitt

(F)

Period: ca. 1750–ca. 1870.

An abbreviation of **mitten**, a fingerless **glove**.

Mitten, metteyn, mytan, meting

(M)

Period: 13th century onwards.

A glove with a single covering for fingers and one for
the thumb. The palm was sometimes slit horizontally, to
allow the fingers to protrude without having to remove
the mitten. Often worn by countrymen for warmth.

(F)

Period: Mid-16th to late 17th century.

Fingerless gloves with an open thumb, usually decorative; of various fabrics, often embroidered.

Period: 18th century.

Mittens were usually elbow-length and the fingers
emerged together through one opening covered along
the back by a prolongation of the mitten into a pointed
flap, which usually had a decorative lining, visible when
the flap was turned back. These mittens were made of
kid, cotton, silk or – in plainer styles – worsted.

Period: 19th century onwards.

Long or short mittens were usually of net or openwork.
In the 1830s and 1840s, short black mittens were worn
with morning dress and long mittens with evening.
These were revived for evening wear in the 1870s. In
the 20th century, light mittens and heavier woollen ones
were occasionally worn.

Mitten sleeve

(F)

Period: 1891.

"The new mitten sleeve of lace, etc. fitting the arm
closely and reaching the knuckles; for dinner and theatre dresses."

Moab

(F)

Period: 1865–1870.

Wrist-length black net fingerless **mittens**; all-over
spot motif and **elastic** around the wrists, ca. 1840–45.
Copyright the Olive Matthews Collection, Chertsey
Museum. Photograph by John Chase.

A turban hat with a bowl-shaped crown; nicknamed from the phrase: "Moab is my washpot".

Moabite turban

(F)

Period: 1832.

A **turban** of crêpe arranged in multiple folds with an **aigrette** on one side. Worn tilted up off the face.

Mob cap

(F)

Period: 18th and 19th centuries.

A white indoor cap of cambric or muslin with puffed **caul** and frilled border. Until 1750, bonnet-shaped with side **lappets** hanging loose or tied under the chin and called **kissing-strings** or **bridles**.

After 1750 the cap was usually not tied and fitted loosely over the head, the frilled border surmounted by a ribbon band. The size varied, being very large in the 1780s, subsequently smaller. Plain 18th-century mob caps were worn in bed and called **night-caps**.

See Ranelagh mob.

Moccasins

(F & M)

Period: 20th century.

A type of shoe originally worn by North American Indians, in which the leather of the uppers is wrapped around the foot from underneath; usually a soft, heel-less, casual shoe.

See Loafer.

Mockador, mocket, mocheter, mokadour, moctour, moketer

Period: 15th–17th century.

A **handkerchief** for the nose, or a child's **bib**. "For eyen and nose the nedethe a mokadour" (Early 15th century, Lydgate, *Minor Poems* "Advice to an Old Gentleman").

See Muckinder.

Mod

(F & M)

Period: Late 1950s to mid-1960s.

Term applied to a group of youngsters in the UK whose appearance and tastes in clothing and music differentiated them from **rockers**, the latter closer in style to **Teddy boys**. These early sub-cultural movements were a sign of the growing independence and buying power of teenagers. Mods admired both beatnik and American college fashions. All mods were clean and neat with short, well-cut hair. The young men wore bright-coloured, button-down, collared shirts and ties, **blazers** and narrow trousers or Italian-style mohair suits, **winkle-picker shoes** or **Hush Puppies** (a trade name for a soft suede laced shoe). The young women favoured **twin sets**, modest narrow skirts or **ski-pants** and **shift dresses** in the summer. Their preferred outerwear was a long, zipped **parka**. Although they denied being mods, at the beginning of their career in the early 1960s, the Beatles wore suits which were typically mod.

Model

(F)

Period: Mid-20th century onwards.

Previously known as **mannequins**, the young women who were employed to wear clothes for fashion houses and for photographic spreads in magazines and newspapers became known as "models" in the period after ca. 1960. The aloof beauties of earlier eras were overtaken by stylish but idiosyncratic young women whose personal fashion sense mattered as much as their ability to display **couture** clothing advantageously. By the late 1980s a new, internationally powerful group of young women whose ability to sell products from clothing to **cosmetics** and perfume appeared; they were called "super models" (a term first coined in the 1940s) and were instantly recognisable by name, appearance and international coverage of their work and private lives.

Although men and children model clothing, they are usually differentiated as *male* models or *child* models.

Modesty piece

(F)

Period: 18th century onwards.

A strip of lace or lace-edged linen pinned to the **corset** in front to cover the "pit of the bosom" in a low décolletage.

Moldavian mantle

(F)

Period: 1854.

A long **mantle** with a deep cape falling the full length and falling over the arms on each side to form what were known as "elephant sleeves".

Monkey jacket

(M)

Period: 1850s onwards.

A short, unwaisted **pilot coat**.

Monmouth cap

(M)

Period: 1570s–1625.

A knitted cap with a tall crown and no brim or turn-up. Worn by Welshmen, soldiers, sailors and others for comfort. Made at Monmouth and also at Bewdley, Worcs.

See Bewdley cap.

Monmouth cock

(M)

Period: 1650–1700.

A hat with a low, round crown and a broad brim which could be "cocked", i.e turned-up; when cocked behind the head and given this name, this was fashionable among young men, especially from the late 1660s.

Monogram buttons

(M)

Period: 1870s.

Buttons of composition with owner's monogram in

colour on a black background; fashionable for coats and waistcoats.

Montague curls

(F)

Period: 1877.

An evening-dress **coiffure**, the front hair arranged in a crescent-shaped fringe of curls gummed to the forehead.

Montero, mountera, mountere, mountie cap

(M)

Period: Early 17th century onwards.

A peaked cap with flaps which could be let down each side and tied or buttoned under the chin. "…a montero or close hood wherewith travellers preserve their face and heads from frost biting and weather heating in summer" (1611, Cotgrave).

Montespan corsage

(F)

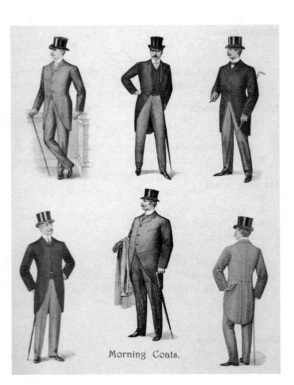

Plate depicting **morning coats** from T.H. Holding, *Coats*, 1902. There are subtle differences between each coat from the "normal three-button" type to the one button and also in the cloth chosen for trousers. The **accessories** include a **top hat**, a stiffened or **wing collar**, cravat, **bow tie** or narrow **tie**, **gloves**, a **cane** and in the case of the stouter model, an **umbrella** and **raincoat**. Private collection.

Period: 1843.

An evening-dress bodice, tight-fitting, with a very low, square-cut décolletage and deeply pointed waist, front and back.

Montespan hat

(F)

Period: 1843.

A small, round, velvet hat, the front brim turned up and trimmed with a plume. Worn with evening dress.

Montespan pleats

(F)

Period: 1859–ca. 1870.

Large, flat, double or treble **box pleats** in series, sewn to the waistband of a skirt made of heavy cloth.

Montespan sleeve

(F)

Period: 1830.

A day sleeve, the upper half full, caught in to a band at the elbow, then falling in a **vandyked** ruffle over the upper forearm.

Mont-la-haut

(F)

Period: Late 17th century.

Same as the **commode**. "Montla-Haut, a certain wier that raises the head-dress by degrees or stories" (1694, *The Ladies' Dictionary*).

Montpensier mantle

(F)

Period: 1847.

A **mantle** falling low behind with the fronts descending to a point, but slit up each side towards the shoulders, leaving the arms free.

Moon boot

(F & M)

Period: 1970s onwards.

The Italian firm Tecnica produced the first moon boots and licensed the name in the early 1970s. Inspired by the footwear worn by astronauts on moon walks, they designed a boot for cold, snowy, wet weather. It had a deep sole, a heavily insulated lining, and was produced in bright colours and edged with fur. They were already popular for après-ski wear in the mid-1970s and many versions have been produced since.

Moppet

Period: 18th century.

A doll dressed in the latest French fashion and sent over to England to serve as a miniature model for dressmakers to show to customers.

Moravian work

Period: Early 19th century.

A kind of cotton embroidery known later, ca. 1850, as **broderie anglaise**. Originating from Moravian refugees expelled from Bohemia near the end of the 18th century.

Morning coat

(M)

Period: 19th century onwards.
Originally a riding coat or **Newmarket coat**. The fronts sloped off from the bottom button near the waist, and the skirt at the back had a vent up to the waist-level with two hip-buttons; a turned-down collar and short lapels. Usually single-breasted; pockets in skirt lining, but after 1850 pockets in pleats; also flapped hip-pockets and one outside on the left breast.

Period: 1860–1880.
Commonly called a **shooting coat**, single- or double-breasted, with a ticket pocket above the flapped pocket on the right.
In the second half of 19th century the **morning coat** tended to replace its rival, the **frock coat**, for formal wear, especially when the fashionable waist level was low.

Period: 20th century.
Increasingly worn for special occasions of a formal nature.

(F)
Period: 1895.
A **tailor-made** version of the male morning coat adopted by women as a development of the day jacket; worn over a **waistcoat** with masculine collar and **necktie**.

Morning gown
(M)
Period: 18th century to ca. 1830s.
A long, loose coat tied at the waist with a **sash** or **girdle** and worn indoors as a form of négligée.
See Nightgown, Dressing-gown, Banian.

Morning walking coat
See Riding coat.

Mortar
(M)
Period: 17th century.
A cap resembling a mortar in shape. "I"ll go to him with a mortar" (1623, Middleton and Rowley, *The Spanish Gipsy*).
Also, as "mortar-board", an academic cap with a rigid, square top.

Moschettos
(M)
Period: Early 19th century.
Similar to the **pantaloons** of the period, but made to fit over the **boots** like **gaiters**.

Moscow wrapper
(M)
Period: 1874.
A loose **overcoat** hanging full, with **pagoda sleeves**, **fly-front fastening** up to the neck, with a narrow, turned-down collar of astrakhan fur which also trimmed all the edges.

Mother and daughter dresses
(F)
Period: Early 20th century.
A term describing adult and child versions of fashionable styles of dress. Made popular by the French fashion designer Jeanne Lanvin (1867–1946), amongst others.

Mother Hubbard cloak
(F)
Period: 1880s.
A three-quarter-length cloak of plush, velvet, brocade, satin or cashmere, lined and quilted; fitting round the neck with a high collar and there tied; gauging over the shoulders with loose sleeves. After 1882 the side seams had vents allowing the back to be gathered up with a ribbon bow, to be draped over the bustle.

Mother-of-pearl buttons
Period: 1770–1800.
The hard, opalescent layer which forms inside certain shells was used to make large buttons used on outer garments worn by both sexes.

Period: 1800 onwards.
Small mother-of-pearl buttons were used on underclothes from ca. 1800; on men's shirts ca. 1820. Such buttons were also used as decoration on accessories.

Motoring dress
(F & M)
Period: ca. 1900–1930s.
Described as a "passing craze" in 1900, the ownership and/or driving of early motor cars was seen as an outdoor hobby or sporting activity requiring protective clothing. Both men and women drove cars or were passengers and there was relatively little difference in their clothing. Long, fur-lined, leather coats or heavy cloth coats were worn in winter, with caps and goggles for men and wide, veiled hats or **hoods** with goggles for women. In the summer **dust coats** of linen or alpaca were still combined with sensible head-coverings and goggles. As open-top cars became a choice rather than standard, the clothing reduced in weight and quantity; however, leather motor coats retained their popularity into the 1930s. By the immediate post-World War II period, thigh-length overcoats, "jeep coats", became the precursors of the car coats of the 1950s and later. In the later 20th century only driving gloves provide a link with the specialized garments of the early days of motoring.

Mouche
(F, occasionally M)
Period: ca. 1595 to end of 18th century.
A black **patch** worn as an ornament on the face.

Moulds, mowlds
(M)
Period: 1550–1600.
Drawers stuffed with horsehair, etc., to produce the fashionable bombasted shape, over which the ballooned

m

breeches were worn. "For black cotton to make a pair of mowldes 2/. For heare for them 12d."; "To lyne a pair of vellet breeches to draw upon mowldes…" (1569, Petre Accounts, Essex Record Office).

Mourning attire
(F & M)
Period: 14th and 15th centuries.
Black was correct for all classes. "In clothes black dropped all with tears" (ca. 1386, Chaucer, *Knight's Tale*).

Period: 16th century.
Black was usual, but in court circles white was permissible and was commonly worn by royal widows.

Period: 17th and 18th centuries.
Purple was worn by royalty, but black was usual for other social groups.

Period: 19th century onwards.
Various forms of full, half and limited mourning were devised for women, ranging from complete black to pale mauve and grey; the impact of Queen Victoria's widowhood was felt throughout fashionable circles, but after her death in 1901 the rules gradually relaxed, despite the losses of both world wars.

Mourning band
(M)
Period: 17th century.
A scarf-like **hat-band** of black cypress worn by those following the hearse. "The other men that follow the Herse have…hatt bandes of black sipres hanging down behynde called Trawerbandes, that is, mourning bands" (ca. 1618, Fynes Moryson, *Itinerary*).
This custom survived until ca. 1880, the trailing hatbands of male mourners being white when the deceased was a virgin. The black hat-band of the **top hat** was deepened during the period of mourning, sometimes covering the sides nearly to the top, the depth indicating the degree of mourning; a tradition surviving to the end of the 19th century.
The mourning arm-band, of black cloth worn round the left upper arm, originally a military style, came to be adopted by civilian men ca. 1820 and gradually became a "correct" symbol of mourning, the width of the band regulated by the relationship to the deceased. Three to four inches was not unusual. The custom survived into the 21st century.

Mourning garland
(F & M)
Period: 17th century.
A garland of willow or a **hat-band** of willow worn by such "who have lost their love" in death or desertion.

Mourning gloves
(F & M)
Period: 18th and 19th centuries.
Black kid gloves, worn by all at funerals and by the

Black **crepe mourning bonnet** with a pleated white cotton edging and a double layered **veil** of **silk voile**, ca. 1860. Copyright the Olive Matthews Collection, Chertsey Museum.

bereaved subsequently for varying periods.

Mourning handkerchief
(F & M)
Period: 18th and 19th centuries.
See Handkerchief.

Mourning knot
(M)
Period: 18th century.
A bunch of black ribbon attached to an armlet worn on the left arm. "Officers to wear…a mourning knot on the left arm" (1708, *British Apollo*).

Mourning posy
(F & M)
Period: 17th century.
A bunch of rosemary carried by mourners and finally cast upon the coffin.

Mourning ribbons
(M)
Period: 17th century.
Black ribbon worn on the hat.

Mourning scarf
(M)
Period: 17th and 18th centuries.
A scarf of armozeen or lawn, up to 3¼ yards long; given, with **hat-bands**, to the principal mourners at a funeral.

Mourning tire
(F)
Period: 17th century.
A mourning **veil**.
See Love and clothing.

Mousquetaire cuff
(F)
Period: 1873.
A large, turned-back cuff on a day sleeve.

Mousquetaire gloves
(F)
Period: 1890.
Gloves with gauntlets embroidered and scalloped.

Mousquetaire hat
(F)
Period: 1857–1860.
A brown straw hat, mushroom-shaped, with a pendant edging of black lace all round the brim.

Mousquetaire mantle
(F)
Period: 1847.
A black velvet **mantle** edged with braid, with short, loose sleeves, outside pockets and quilted satin lining.

Mousquetaire sleeve
(F)
Period: 1853, revived 1873.
A full sleeve with a turned-back cuff cut into deep points.

Moustache, mustache, mustachio, mouchado
Period: 16th century onwards.
"A mostache is the berde of the upper lyppe" (1551, W. Thomas, trans. of Barbard's *Travels in Persia*).
Very seldom worn in the 18th century; considered in the 19th century a military appendage until the Crimean War (1853–1856) encouraged civilians to adopt it and versions have been worn throughout the 20th century and beyond.

Muckinder, muckender, muckiter, muckinger
Period: Early 15th to early 19th century.
A **handkerchief** for wiping the nose and eyes. "Wipe your nose…where's your muckinder your grand-mother gave you?" (1607, Marston, *What you will*).
"Be of good comfort; take my muckinder and dry thine eyes" (1633, B. Jonson, *Tale of a Tub*).
Also a child's **bib** or a table napkin.
See Mockador.

Muff
(F)
Period: ca. 1550 onwards.
A covering for both hands as a protection against cold, though also used as an elegant accessory. Tubular or flat, varying greatly in size; made of fur, feathers, fine fabrics, and padded within. In the 18th century a woman's muff and **tippet** were usually made to match. A pocket for a card-case and purse was introduced in ladies' muffs of the 1880s.

(M)
Period: ca. 1600–ca. 1800.
"Lost – a large sable tip Man's Muff" (1695, *London Gazette*). Less usual.

Muff bracelet
(F)
Period: ca. 1650–1700.
A small muff worn round the wrist.

Muffetees
(F & M)
Period: 18th and 19th centuries.
Small wrist **muffs** made in pairs, worn for warmth or to protect the wrist ruffles when playing cards.
Also, small muffs closed at one end and worn over the hands for warmth; some with a separate compartment for the thumb. "Pray buy my mother a pair of black silk French muffetees for the hands…they must be with thumbs to them." (1748, *Purefoy Letters*).
In the 19th century they could be a coarse kind of **mitten**, "either of leather or of knitted worsted, worn by old men" (1808–1818, Jamieson).
Revived in 1877 as a wrist muff for women, called "muffatee".

Muffin hat
(M)
Period: 1860s.
A round hat with a flat crown surrounded by a narrow, upright brim; made of cloth, for country wear.

Muffler
(F)
Period: 1530s–1660s.
A square of fabric folded diagonally and worn over the mouth and chin and sometimes the nose, to protect from cold air and sometimes as a disguise.
See Chin clout.

(F & M)
Period: 16th century onwards.
A **scarf** worn round the neck for warmth.

Muff's cloak
(M)
Period: Late 16th and early 17th centuries.
A sleeved German cloak, the same as the Dutch cloak; "muff" also being a derogatory term for a foreigner, especially German or Swiss.

Muff string
The ribbon suspending the **muff** from the neck; occasionally used.

Mules, moiles, moyles, mowles
(F & M)
Period: 16th century onwards.
A light indoor shoe with only a front section, either flat-soled or high-heeled. "A slipper without heel-piece or quarter."
See Pantofles.

Muller-cut-down

(M)

Period: 1870s.

The popular name for a hat resembling a **top hat** cut down to half its height; named after the murderer in 1864 whose cut-down hat led to his identification.

Mushroom hat

(F)

Period: 1870s and 1880s.

A mushroom-shaped straw hat plentifully trimmed over the small crown with ribbon, flowers or, in the 1880s, a bird.

Mushroom sleeve

(F)

Period: 1894.

A short sleeve for evening dress; pleated round the arm-hole and edged with a lace frill.

N

Nabchet, nab-cheat

Period: 16th and 17th centuries.

Slang for **hat** or **cap**.

Napkin

Period: 16th–18th century.

A **handkerchief** for wiping the nose; often a regional term. Other meanings include a piece of fabric used as a table napkin, a **neckerchief** and a small towel.

Napkin-cap

(M)

Period: 18th century.

A plain **night-cap** or house-cap to cover the bald head when the **wig** was removed. "He then took off his bag (i.e. wig), coat and waistcoat…and after some trouble put on a napkin-cap" (1746, H. Walpole, *Letters*).

Napkin hook

(F)

Period: 17th century.

A hook for suspending the **handkerchief** from the waistband. A common form of gift or "fairing" from young men to girls.

Napoleon necktie

(M)

Period: ca. 1818.

A somewhat narrow, violet-coloured **necktie** surrounding the back of the neck, the ends brought forward and crossed in front without tying, and then fastened to the **braces** or carried under the arms and tied on the back. This style was said to have been worn by Napoleon on his return from Elba in 1815. By ca. 1830 this was becoming known as the **Corsican necktie**.

Napoleons

(M)

Period: 1850s.

New name for long military boots reaching above the knee with a scoop out behind to allow flexion. Worn by civilians on horseback. The name was a compliment to the Prince, later Napoleon III (1808–1873).

Napron

Period: ca. 1300–1450.

Term denoting an **apron**, taken from the Old French *naperon*, a diminutive of *nape* or *nappe*, a tablecloth. From ca. 1460 "appurn" or **apron** became the usual name.

National Standard Dress

(F)

Period: 1918

This was an experiment to introduce a simple, multi-purpose dress at a time of shortages. It did not need **hooks and eyes** or a metal belt buckle and was intended to be made of silk so that it could be worn as "outdoor, housegown, rest gown, teagown, dinner gown, evening dress and nightgown" (1918, quoted in Cunnington, *English Women's Clothing in the Present Century*). A paper pattern offered three variants, all of which look feasible for the home dressmaker. This idea may have influenced **utility dress** in World War II.

Neapolitan bonnet

(F)

Period: 1800.

A bonnet of **leghorn** trimmed with straw flowers and straw-coloured ribbons fastened to the crown and tied loosely on the bosom.

Nebula head-dress

(F)

Period: 1350–1420.

A descriptive term used by 19th-century writers for a woman's head-dress.

See Goffered veil.

Neckatee

Period: Mid-18th century.

An unusual term for a **neckerchief**.

Neck button

(M)

Period: Mid-17th century.

An ornamental button worn at the neck of the

fashionable shorter **doublet**. This button, with a loop, closed the doublet at the top while below it was often left open to reveal the **shirt**.

Neck-chain

(M)

Period: Medieval to mid-17th century.

A gold or gilded brass chain worn as an adornment by men. Sometimes worn by medieval travellers as portable wealth; a few links cut from it could serve as money. In the 17th century it was usually called a **jack chain**.

Period: Late 20th century.

Chains, especially gold ones, became fashionable for some men, such as sportsmen, performers, etc.

Neckcloth

(M)

Period: ca. 1660 to mid-19th century.

A general term for any kind of **cravat** or neckwear swathed round the neck, as distinct from a **collar**. Prior to 1660 the term neckcloth indicated a woman's **neckerchief**.

Necked bonnet

(M)

Period: ca. 1500–1550.

A **cap** with a deep flap fitting round the neck at the back. Double or single, that is lined or unlined.

Neckerchief, neckercher, neck-kerchief

(F)

Period: Late 14th to late 19th century.

Any square or strip of linen or other material folded round the neck. "On his (a child's) shoulder about his neck a kercheff fyne must be" (ca. 1460, Russell, *Boke of Nurture*).

The term "neckercher" was regional usage in the 18th and 19th centuries.

See Kerchief.

(F & M)

Period: 19th century.

The term occasionally applied to a large silk **cravat**.

Neck handkerchief

(M)

Period: 18th and 19th centuries.

Synonym for **cravat** or **necktie**. "To buy Cravats or Neck- Handkerchiefs" (1712, Steele, *The Spectator*).

Neckinger

(F)

Period: 16th–19th century.

A corrupt form of **neckercher**, used regionally.

Necklace

(F)

Period: 16th century onwards.

A string of beads, gemstones, metal links or similar worn around the neck as a decoration.

See Neck-chain.

Also, in the 17th and 18th centuries, a ribbon or lace band worn around the neck.

Neckline

(F)

Period: Early 20th century onwards.

Term used in conjunction with other descriptions (high, low, boat-shaped, etc.) for the area between the neck and **décolletage** of a blouse, dress or similar. "Necklines always make headlines" (1968, J. Ironside, *A Fashion Alphabet*).

Necktie

(M)

Period: 19th century.

A term coming into use about 1830, but not entirely displacing the earlier name **cravat**. A band of varying width and fabric wound round the base of the shirt collar.

Neck-wear

(M)

Period: ca. 1870 onwards.

An American term for a **necktie** and in general usage by the late 20th century.

Négligée, négligé

(F & M)

Period: 18th century.

A term used for describing someone dressed in an informal manner, both in and out of doors, and also a term for a loose female gown and a male informal garment worn in domestic settings.

Period: 19th century onwards.

Usually a term describing a women's light **dressing-gown** of flimsy or revealing fabrics.

Secondary usage includes a type of male **wig** of the 1750s devised in Paris.

Also, a mourning **girdle** of jet with a nine-inch pendant end; worn by women as part of public mourning at the death of Princess Charlotte in 1818.

Nehru jacket

(M, occasionally F)

Period: 1960s onwards.

The style of jacket, based on a longer indigenous garment, worn by the Indian politician Jawaharlal Nehru (1889–1964); this was a long-sleeved, hip-length, front-buttoned, linen or cotton jacket with a high, round collar, which successfully synthesized traditional clothing for Indian men with a quasi-European style. It became fashionable in the late 1960s for both sexes in western countries and continues to be worn in India.

Nelson

(F)

Period: 1819–1820.

A bustle worn to enhance the effect of the **Grecian bend** stance of the time.

See Frisk.

Nelson hat

(F)

Period: 1895.

A straw hat, the brim sharply turned up, front and back,

n

with a plume in front and ribbon bows at the peaks each side.

Neoclassical dress

(F & M)

Period: Late 18th and early 19th centuries.

Rejection of the highly decorative rococo forms in favour of simplicity and regularity of design. Informed by archaeological excavation and renewed interest in classical art, the clothing of this period offered a narrow silhouette and an interpretation of the appearance of certain aspects of the dress of classical antiquity.

Nether integuments

See Unmentionables.

Nether stocks

(M)

Period: ca. 1515 to late 17th century.

The lower or **stocking** portion of **hose**, the upper portion being variously called the **breech**, **upper stocks** and, later, **trunk-hose**.

The term was sometimes used for women's stockings at the end of the 16th century.

New Age

Period: Late 20th and early 21st centuries.

Specifically the Age of Aquarius; this, in astrological terms, is supposed to introduce improved spiritual awareness and collective understanding. Ecological methods, an eclectic simplicity, and a stronger ethical approach to the origins and production of clothing are aspects of this approach, as is recycling. New Age travellers typified this practicality, but it is a diverse movement in constant flux.

See Ethnic dress, Hippie style, Grunge.

Newgate fringe

(M)

Period: 19th century.

Colloquial term for a fringe of **beard** under the jaw.

New Look

(F)

Period: 1947.

Term applied by an American journalist to the "Corolle" fashions introduced by the fashion designer Christian Dior (1905–1957) in that year. The ultra-feminine silhouette which emphasized the bosom, a narrow waist and offered long, full skirts (containing up to 20 yards of fabric) provided an antidote to the privations of World War II and looked back to the neo-Victorian styles of the late 1930s.

Newmarket coat

(M)

Period: 1838–ca. 1900.

Previously called a **riding coat** and from 1750–1800 called a **Newmarket coat** which was a riding coat (see **frock**).

The Newmarket coat was a **tail coat**, single- or double-breasted, the fronts sloping away from above the waist level and often worn open. The skirts were short with rounded corners; sleeves with cuffs; often with flapped **hip-pockets**. By 1850 it was generally called a **cutaway coat**, and by 1870 it was merging into the **morning coat**.

Newmarket jacket

(F)

Period: 1891.

A close-fitting jacket, single- or double-breasted, made hip-length; with a turn-over collar and silk-faced lapels cut on masculine lines. The characteristic Newmarket feature was flapped pockets (real or sham) on the hips; close sleeves ending in a cuff or buttoned slit. Often part of a **tailor-made** costume of tweed. For day wear.

Newmarket overcoat

(M)

Period: 1881.

Resembling a single-breasted **frock** overcoat cut short in the waist, very long in the skirts. Velvet collar and cuffs common; usually made of homespun or shepherd's plaid.

(F)

Period: 1889.

A **tailor-made**, single- or double-breasted coat, closed to the waist, the long skirts left open to reach nearly to the ground. Flapped pockets on the hips; close sleeves. Velvet collar, lapels and cuffs. Made of heavy cloth for winter wear and still worn in the early 20th century.

Newmarket top frock

(M)

Period: 1895.

An overcoat resembling a **frock coat** with a broad velvet collar; pockets on the waist seam; skirts to 4 inches below the knees. Made of a rough cheviot, the body lined with silk or satin, the skirts with check fabric.

Newmarket vest

(M)

Period: 1894.

A **waistcoat** of a plaid or check pattern cloth and cut to button high; made with or without flapped pockets. Worn especially by sportsmen.

New Romantic

(F & M)

Period: Late 1970s to mid-1980s.

A term applied to someone associated with the fashion and music sub-cultural movement of this period, which had begun as a reaction against **punk** styles and resuscitated the glam rock styles of the early-to-mid-1970s. Colourful hair, distinctive make-up, and androgynous but consciously glamorous clothing were epitomized by Boy George and the Pirate and New Romanticism collections of the British designer Vivienne Westwood (b. 1941).

Nifels, nyefles

(F)

Period: 1450–1500.

A woman's **veil**.

Night-cap

Period: 14th to mid-19th century.

(M)

A form of skull-cap constructed from four conical sec-tions of fabric with a close, upturned brim, often decora-tive; a very common form from the 16th century and worn indoors for comfort, replacing the wig, when that was in fashion.

Also a plain washable cap worn in bed from the earliest time. In the 19th century it was often called a "jelly-bag" from its shape, usually of knitted silk with a tassel on the top.

See Biggin.

(F)

Period: 18th and 19th centuries.

A **mob cap** tied under the chin and worn in bed.

Night-cap wig

(M)

Period: Early 18th century.

A **bob-wig** with roll curls circling the back of the head from cheek to cheek.

Night-clothes

(M)

Period: 16th century onwards.

Until the 16th century men slept naked or in a day-shirt; subsequently a night-shirt, varying in quality, was worn in bed. Nobles in the 16th century wore embroidered shirts or "wrought night-shirts". By the 19th century the night-shirt resembled a day-shirt with a loose, turned-down collar, or a loose, ankle-length **nightgown** was worn.

(F)

Period: 16th century onwards.

Informal morning or evening attire. "My lady Castlemaine who looked pretty in her night-clothes." (1667, *Pepys' Diary*)

Like men, until the 16th century women slept naked or in day-shifts; subsequently in a night-chemise.

See Nightgown.

Night coif

(F)

Period: 16th and 17th centuries.

A woman's **coif** worn as **négligée** or in bed. The coif was often embroidered and generally worn with a **fore-head cloth**. "A night coyf of cameryck cutworke and spangils with a forehead cloth" (1577–1578, Nichols, *Progress of Queen Elizabeth*).

Nightgown

Period: 16th to late 18th century.

(M)

Man's white linen **night cap** embroidered with silk and metal threads and **spangles**, ca. 1600–10. Copyright the Olive Matthews Collection, Chertsey Museum. Photograph by John Chase.

A loose gown or long coat, sometimes fur-lined, cut to the contemporary fashion, worn as négligée indoors and informally out of doors for morning visits, in the 17th and 18th centuries.

See Banian, Indian nightgown, Morning gown.

(F)

An unboned, comfortable but often very elaborate dress, worn indoors and out, and sometimes on for-mal occasions as at weddings. Also called a "Morning Gown", although worn at any part of the day. Similar to and probably the precursor of the mantua.

Period: 19th century onwards.

A loose gown of cotton, linen or silk, worn in bed only; often known as a "night dress".

Night-kercher

(F)

Period: 16th century.

A **neckerchief** worn at night.

Night-mask

(F)

Period: 17th century.

"Here be fine night-masks, plaster'd well within, To sup-ple wrinkles and to smooth the skin" (1627, M. Drayton, *The Muses' Elysium*).

See Ceruse.

Night rail, night rayle

(F)

Period: 16th to late 19th century.

A cape of lawn, holland, silk or satin falling to the waist or hips; worn before dressing or after undressing. "When we was packing your few traps and your Mis'ess's night rail and dressing things" (1891, T. Hardy, *Tess of the d'Urbervilles*).

Night-shift

(F)

Period: Late 17th century onwards.

A **chemise** worn in bed only; a night dress or gown.

Night-shirt

(M, later F)

Period: 16th century onwards.

A **shirt** worn in bed only. Occasionally worn in the 20th and 21st centuries by women as well as men.

See Pyjama.

Night slippers

Period: Late 16th century onwards.

Slippers worn in the bedroom. From the 20th century more usually known as "bedroom slippers".

Niqab

(F)

One of the three elements of dress that can be worn by Muslim women to shield themselves from the gaze of strangers. This is a black face veil, a square or rectangle of fabric with a narrow slit to allow the eyes to be used, though in some circumstances this is covered by a decorative mesh. If worn with the **jilbab**, **hijab** and with the hands covered, this constitutes the full **veil**.

Nithsdale

(F)

Period: 1715–1720.

A long, hooded riding cloak. "It is called a Nithsdale since Fame adorned a Countess with that name" (1719, D"Urfey, *Pills to purge Melancholy*).

The Countess of Nithsdale (1680–1749) had rescued her husband, a supporter of the Jacobite rebellion, from the Tower by disguising him in her cloak and hood in 1715.

Nivernois hat

(M)

Period: 1760s.

A **tricorne hat** with broad, spreading brim rolled over a flat crown; known as the "Nivernois cock". "He wears this large umbrella-like hat. This is the Nivernois." (1765, *London Magazine*)

Also called a "waterproof hat" because of its umbrella-like protection.

Norfolk jacket

(M, sometimes F)

Period: 1880 onwards.

A modification of the **Norfolk shirt**. A lounge jacket of mid-thigh length, made with a **box pleat** to each forepart and a central box pleat behind, large bellows pockets on the hips and a vertical slit pocket in the left breast;

a belt of self-material. In 1894 a yoke was often added, the box pleats starting from the yoke. Commonly made of Harris tweeds and homespuns.

Norfolk shirt

(M)

Period: 1866–1880.

The forerunner of the **Norfolk jacket**. A short **lounging jacket** with box pleat down the centre of the back and down each forepart; collar and wristbands made in the style of a shirt. Flap pockets in the front skirts; belt of same cloth; always worn buttoned up. Of rough tweeds for country wear.

Norma corsage

(F)

Period: 1844.

An evening bodice with a loose fold in the centre, caught in with a gold ornament.

Nosegay

Period: 15th century onwards.

A small bunch of sweet-smelling flowers or herbs, the latter as an antidote to infectious diseases. In the 16th and 17th centuries they were worn in the hat at weddings. "A nosegay bound with laces in his hat, Bridelaces, Sir, and his hat all green" (1599, Henry Porter, *The Two Angry Women of Abingdon*).

Notch

(M)

Period: 19th century onwards.

The term for the gap cut out between the collar of a coat or waistcoat collar and the lapel. It varied in shape, a mere slit being called by tailors a "light"; the "M-notch" was shaped like the letter M; a rectangular cut back was called a "step".

Nouch

See Ouch.

Nursing dress

(F)

Period: Early 19th century.

A dress constructed so that the wearer could suckle her infant without having to remove the bodice when this was fastened up the back by hooks and eyes; over each breast a small slit opening, closed by a button, was concealed under a **robin** or pleated folds of the bodice fabric. Such dresses were in use between ca. 1820 and 1850.

Nycette, niced

(F)

Period: Late 15th and early 16th centuries.

A light wrapper for the neck.

See Kerchief.

Nylons

(F)

Period: 1930 onwards.

Shorthand for nylon **stockings**.

O

Oatland village hat

(F)

Period: 1800.

A day hat, the brim curved up in front and behind, the crown dome-shaped with a ribbon round it. Of straw, twist or leghorn. Named after the country house of the Duchess of York.

Obi

Period: Late 19th century onwards.

A long sash worn around the waist to secure a garment in Japan, e.g. a **kimono**. The style became well known in the west in the 19th century and was referenced by 20th-century fashion designers.

Obi hat

(F)

Period: 1804.

A straw or chip hat for walking; the high crown with flat top, a narrow brim rolled back in front; tied under the chin with ribbon strings passing over the brim from the crown which was also trimmed round with ribbon. Named after a character in a pantomime.

Oblong hoop, square hoop

(F)

Period: 1740s–1760s.

An undergarment variously constructed, projecting out horizontally from the waist on each side, the front and back being flattened to give enormous breadth to the hips. Some were hinged, allowing the wearer to fold the overskirt under the arms when passing through a too-narrow doorway. It was required for **court dress** and in a modified form continued until 1820.

Octagon tie

(M)

Period: 1860s to early 20th century.

A made-up scarf, the front arranged in four tabs above the tie-pin with a neck-band fastened behind by a hook and eyelet hole.

Oes, owes

(F, rarely M)

Period: 16th and 17th centuries.

Small rings or eyelets sewn to the material of a garment to form decorative designs. "Vaile of net lawne embroidered with Oes" (1616, Chapman, *Masque of the Inns of Court*).

See Spangles.

Off-the-peg

(F & M)

Period: 1850 onwards.

Clothing that could be bought from shop stock rather than being **made-to-measure**. Often carried connotations of being cheap and nasty in terms of fabric and fit until the 20th century.

Off-the-shoulder

(F)

Period: 20th century onwards.

A style of neckline which leaves the neck, shoulders and upper arms uncovered; often used for formal evening dresses.

Oilets

Period: 18th and early 19th centuries.

The early term for **eyelets** or lacing holes.

Oker, hogger, hoker, coker

(M)

Period: 16th century.

"Boots for ploughmen called Okers" (1552, Hulcot).

Oldenburg bonnet

(F)

Period: 1814.

A very large bonnet with wide, projecting brim in front and a flat crown draped with ostrich feathers; ribbon ties under the chin. Named after the Duchess of Oldenburg, sister of Tsar Alexander I and, with him, a visitor to the Peace celebrations of 1814.

Olive button

Period: Mid-18th century onwards.

A long, oval button covered with silk.

Olivet, olivette

Period: Mid-18th century onwards.

An olive-shaped button of wood covered with silk or braid and used to fasten a **brandenburg**.

See Frog-button.

Ondina crinoline

(F)

Period: 1860s.

A cage crinoline with the hoops arranged in "wave-like bands".

Op Art

Period: Mid-1960s onwards.

A movement which used bold, abstract designs, often in strongly contrasting colours such as black and white. It had a considerable impact on fabric design and clothing in the late 1960s and in subsequent revivals ca. 2000.

Open robe

(F)

Period: 19th century.

A style of dress in which the skirt is open in front from the waist down, revealing a decorative underskirt or **petticoat**. It was chiefly fashionable, for day and evening, during the 1830s and 1840s.

Although this form of construction was used from the

16th century onwards, it does not appear to have been called an "open robe" until the 19th century.

Opera cloak

(F, sometimes M)

Period: Early 19th century onwards.

A full-length evening cloak, often of a rich fabric.

Opera hat

(M)

Period: ca. 1750–1800.

A small, flat, three-cornered hat made for carrying under the arm and also called a **chapeau bras**.

Period: 1800–1830.

A crescent-shaped hat with a soft crown which could be compressed between the crescent-shaped side brims, and carried under the arm, as the chapeau bras. Also called a **military folding hat** or **cocked hat**. After 1830, except for full dress: the opera hat was the **circumfolding hat** and later the **gibus**.

McCALL PRINTED PATTERNS

MANNISH SUITS GIVE UP THEIR COLLARS

Two designs for women's **suits** issued by McCall's dressmaking **patterns**. The hat to the left is a **Tyrolean** style, and hats with **gloves** and **handbags** were always part of an outdoor **outfit**. "Mannish suits give up their collars" suggest that these pared-down suits despite the decorative **handkerchiefs** in each **breast pocket** are intended to meet **clothes rationing** and/or **Utility regulations**, ca. 1942. Copyright the Olive Matthews Collection, Chertsey Museum.

Orange-blossom wreath

See Wedding veil.

Orientalism

Period: 1600 onwards.

The impact upon western dress and fashions of the clothing and customs of oriental nations across many centuries; Turkish, Indian, Chinese and Japanese fabrics and forms of dress influenced western ideas of design and construction.

Orphrey, orfrey, orfray, orfries, orphrieis

Period: 13th century onwards.

Embroidery with gold thread. From the early 13th century the term was applied to narrow bands of gold embroidery decorating the borders of garments, especially ecclesiastical vestments. Later it came to mean narrow strips of any kind of embroidery, such as orphreys of blue, red and green, also plain velvet.

Orrelet, orilyet

(F)

Period: ca. 1550–1600.

Adapted from a French term *oreillet* which described the ear guards of a helmet, these were the side pieces of a woman's **coif**, covering the ears; also called "cheeks and ears".

Osbaldiston tie, barrel knot

(M)

Period: 1830s and 1840s.

A **necktie** tied with the centre knot in the form of a barrel.

Ouch, nouch

Period: 13th–15th century.

A jewelled clasp or buckle, or a collection of jewels.

See Pontificals.

Ourle, orle

Period: 13th and 14th centuries.

A border of fur. "Orle" is the later form.

Out-coat

(M)

Period: Late 17th and 18th centuries.

An overcoat for outdoor wear.

Outfit

(F & M)

Period: 19th century onwards.

A set of clothing designed or selected to be worn together, and often including accessories such as jewellery, shoes, etc.

Oval beaver hat

(M)

Period: 1817.

A hat made on an oval block, an improvement on the round block previously used, which required a "hat screw" to stretch it to the shape of the head.

Overalls

(M)

Period: 19th century.

Loose trousers of white cord or leather, worn for riding; adapted by civilians from those worn by the cavalry in early 19th century. "To a Baragon Stable Jacket & overalls £1:13" (1840, domestic bill).

Period: 19th century onwards.
A garment which protected the clothing of workers, e.g., a smock or long coat of coarse, washable fabric, or trousers with a bib and straps across the shoulders.

Overcoat
(M & later F)
Period: 18th century onwards.
A coat worn out of doors over an indoor suit, or over a dress by women after ca. 1780.
See Greatcoat.

Overskirt
(F)
Period: Mid-19th century onwards.
An extra skirt worn over the skirts of a dress, often of a lighter fabric, shorter or open at the front or sides; decorative or protective.

Overslop
(M)
Period: ca. 950 to late 14th century.
Term for a loose overgarment; also a stole, cassock or surplice.

Overstocks
See Stocks.

Over-vest
(F)
Period: Late 20th century onwards.
Another item of **leisure wear** developed originally to be worn over a sports bra, but now worn as an informal sleeveless alternative to a **T-shirt**.

Oxford bags
(M)
Period: 1920s.
A mainly British style of excessively wide-legged trousers worn by some students at Oxford University.

Oxford button-overs
(M)

Period: 1860s.
"Oxonian shoes which cover the instep and are closed by being buttoned instead of being stringed" (1862, Mayhew Bros., *London Life and London Poor*).

Oxford gloves
(F & M)
Period: Mid-16th to mid-17th century.
Gloves often scented with the Earl of Oxford's perfume.

Oxford shoe
(M)
Period: Late 19th century onwards.
A shoe which laces at the front, with the vamp stitched on top of the facings which carry the laces.
See Oxonian shoe.

Oxford tie
(F & M)
Period: 1890s.
A narrow, straight **necktie**, having the same width from end to end. Worn by men with a **lounge suit** and by women with a morning blouse.

Oxonian boots, collegians
(M)
Period: ca. 1830–1850.
A short boot, later black-japanned, having a wedge-shaped piece cut out from each side at the top to enable the boot to be pulled on easily.

Oxonian jacket, Oxford coatee
(M)
Period: 1850s and 1860s.
A "real Oxford bang-tail coatee, bright blue with only two buttons and button-holes and all sorts of jolly pockets in original places" (1855, F. Smedley, *Harry Coverdale's Courtship*).
See Jumper.

Oxonian shoe
(M)
Period: 1848.
"Laces up in front with three or four holes. The vamp comes well above the joint [i.e. ankle]. Seam across the instep" (Sparkes-Hall).

P

Padded shoulders
(F & M)
Period: 18th century onwards.
The use of padding or pads to extend the shoulder line in width or height in blouses, coats and jackets.
See Power dressing.

Paddock coat
(M)
Period: 1892 onwards.
A long overcoat without a seam at the waist, made double- or single-breasted with a **fly-front fastening**. A seam descended from the arm-hole to the top of the

flapped pocket on the hip, to give better fit, in contrast to the old-style **paletot**, otherwise resembling it in that there was a side-body. This was revived in 1893 and was then called by some the "new paletot'.

Both styles had deep side pleats concealing a back vent; pockets were plentiful.

Page bonnet
(F)

Period: 1874.

Identical with the **Charlotte Corday bonnet**.

Page boy
(F)

Period: 1920s onwards.

A haircut which emulated the style worn by pages in Renaissance paintings; usually chin-length, curving around the face, with a deep fringe over the forehead.

Pages
See Dress clips.

Pagoda parasol
(F)

Period: 1790s–1830s.

A parasol with the cover shaped in an ogee curve up the stick; when expanded it was said to resemble the roof of a pagoda.

Pagoda sleeve
(F)

Period: 1849–1860s.

A sleeve with one seam on the inner side and cut so as to expand widely at the elbow where it was caught up at the bend, but falling on the outer side nearly to the wrist. Some were made with a slit up in front, which by 1857 extended almost the whole length. By 1859 the name was being replaced by **funnel sleeve**. Worn with **engageantes**.

Period: 20th century.

A long, narrow sleeve opening about six inches above the wrist with a small under sleeve or detachable short sleeve.

Palatine
(F)

Period: 1840s.

A neck **tippet** with long, flat ends reaching in front below the waist.

See Pallatine.

Palatine royal, victorine
(F)

Period: 1851.

A fur **tippet** with a quilted hood and short ends in front.

Palazzo pants
(F)

Period: 1960s.

Loose **trousers** with wide legs, usually for informal wear; "palazzo pyjamas" were a two-piece variant.

Pale

Period: Late 14th to early 16th century.

A vertical stripe or one of a series of stripes of contrasting colours.

"But what art thou that sayest this tale That warest on thy hose a pale" (ca. 1384, Chaucer, *House of Fame*).

See Mi-parti.

Paletot
(M)

Period: 1830s–ca. 1900.

A French term used to describe a short **greatcoat** made without a seam at the waist, and often having a whole back, but always side seams; no side pleats in many versions. The back vent, if present, was very short.

(F)

Period: 1839 to end of 19th century.

A three-quarter-length cloak hanging in stiff pleats from the shoulders and having a short, stiff cape; the arm-holes guarded with flaps. By 1843 it had three capes, a velvet collar and loose sleeves.

Period: 1860–1890.

The "short paletot" or **yachting jacket** was worn as an outdoor jacket.

Period: 1865–1884.

The "long paletot" was usually a figure-fitting outdoor coat reaching below the knees, with tight sleeves and often trimmed with lace; in the 1870s some were sleeveless and made with a **Watteau pleat** or in the **casaque** shape.

Period: Early 20th century.

Term used to describe a long, fitted **overcoat**.

Paletot-cloak
(M)

Period: 1850s.

A short cloak scarcely covering the buttocks, fastened in front and single- or double-breasted with arm-hole slits; no sleeves.

Paletot-mantle
(F)

Period: 1867.

A three-quarter-length cloak with a cape and hanging sleeves.

Paletot-redingote
(F)

Period: 1867.

An outdoor long coat cut to fit the figure, without a seam at the waist; made with revers at the top and sometimes with circular capes. Buttoned all down the front.

Paletot-sac
(M)

Period: 1840s and 1850s.

A short, straight paletot, single- or double-breasted, and often having a hood instead of a collar.

Palisade

(F)

Period: ca. 1690–1710.

A wire frame for supporting the high **fontange** coiffure. "Palisade, a wire sustaining the Hair next the Dutchess or first knot" (1690, J. Evelyn, *The Fop Dictionary*). *See* Commode, Mont-la-haut.

Palla

(F)

Period: ca. 100 BCE to ca. 300 CE.

A loose outer garment or wrap, long and worn out-of-doors; like the male **toga**, it could be drawn-up over the head.

Later the term was used for an altar-cloth or chalice cover.

Pallatine

(F)

Period: ca. 1680 to early 18th century.

A sable shoulder wrap or **tippet**. "That which used to be called a "sable tippet" but that name is changed to one that is supposed to be finer, because newer and à la mode de France" (1694, *Ladies' Dictionary*).

Pallium

(M)

Period: Greco-Roman.

A large, rectangular cloak or mantle, similar to a **himation** and almost certainly made of wool.

The term was later applied to a church vestment.

Palmerston wrapper

(M)

Period: 1853–1855.

A single-breasted **sac overcoat**, the fronts hanging loose and wrapped across. Sleeves wide at the hands; no cuffs; wide collar and lapels, faced up to the edge of the button stand and with four button-holes; side-flapped pockets. Named after the British politician Lord Palmerston (1784–1865).

Paltock, paltok, paultock

(M)

Period: 14th to mid-15th century.

A **gipon** or **doublet** to which the **hose** were tied.

Pamela bonnet

(F)

Period: 1845–1855.

A small straw bonnet, the narrow brim open round the face and sloping back to be continuous with the crown, flat behind, and having a small curtain. Trimmed with ribbons and sometimes flowers. Named after the eponymous heroine of Samuel Richardson's novel of 1741.

Pamela hat

(F)

Period: 1845.

A small **gipsy hat** of coarse straw.

Panama hat

(M)

Period: 1830s onwards.

A hat made from the plaited fibres of the toquilla leaf, which originated in Ecuador and became popular in Europe for summer wear. Twentieth-century versions include travelling styles which can be rolled and placed into luggage, and the original fibre is often replaced by substitutes of plaited straw.

Panel skirt

(F)

Period: 1894.

A day skirt consisting of an overskirt two inches shorter than the underskirt and open on the left side to expose a contrasting decorative panel.

Panes

(M, occasionally F)

Period: 1500–ca. 1660.

Various designs by French **couturiers**, ca. 1936. **Hats** are essential **accessories** whether close-fitting (left) or wide-brimmed straw trimmed with artificial flowers (right). **Gauntlet gloves**, **court shoes** and small **handbags** are typical at this date. The man wears a **panama hat** and a light summer **jacket**. Copyright the Olive Matthews Collection, Chertsey Museum.

A decoration produced by slashing the material into long, ribbon-like strips or by using ribbon lengths set close and parallel, joined above and below. Through the gaps part of the shirt or sleeves might be pulled out, or a contrasting coloured lining might be drawn out. For instance, a "gown of crimson velvet with French sleeves lined with tynsell" (1523, Inventory of Dame Agnes Hungerford). This device was also common with **trunk-hose**.

Panier

(F)

Period: 18th century onwards.

The French term for side hoops or **false hips**. The word was not used in England in the 18th century, **hoop** being preferred.

In the late 19th and early 20th century it described a drapery style of the skirt or overskirt when bunched upon the hips, and could be spelt as "pannier".

Panier anglais

(F)

Period: 18th century.

The French name for the **hoop petticoat**; a term rarely used in England.

Pannier crinoline

(F)

Period: 1870s.

Thomson's Pannier Crinoline combined a **cage crinoline** and a **bustle**, the upper portion extending round the back and sides.

Pannier dress

(F)

Period: 1868.

A day dress with a double skirt, the upper bunched out round the back and sides by means of a draw-string below, the underskirt trained, and trimmed with a flounce.

Pantalettes

(F)

Period: ca. 1812–1840s.

The feminine version of **pantaloons**. An undergarment of long, straight-legged, white drawers reaching to below the calf and there trimmed with lace or tucks. Visible below the skirt, with children, until ca. 1850; a mode surviving into the 1840s for ladies' riding costume.

Pantaloons

(M)

Period: 1660–1680.

The same as **petticoat breeches**, "…the pantaloons which are a kind of Hermaphrodite and of either sex" (1661, J. Evelyn, *Tyrannus or the Mode*). "A paire of new fashion'd rideing panteloons" (1662, Sir Miles Stapleton, *Household Books*).

Period: 1790–ca. 1850.

Close-fitting tights shaped to the leg and ending just below the calf until 1817; then at the ankles, usually with short side-slits, strapped under the foot and known as **tights**, ca. 1840.

(F)

Period: 1812–ca. 1840s.

An undergarment in the form of long, straight-legged drawers; a term not often used before 1820. In the 1830s often called trousers. "With short dresses those who have not handsome legs generally wear pantaloons" (1822).

Pantaloons appearing below the skirt went out of fashion before 1840, except for children.

See Pantalettes.

Pantaloon-trousers

(M)

Period: ca. 1815–ca. 1830.

A hybrid garment – tight-fitting, but moderately loose from the calf down, and without side-slits. The bottoms were cut square or with the fronts hollowed out over the insteps.

Panteen collar

(F)

Period: 1880s.

A high **stand-fall collar**, common with ladies' **tailor-made** jackets and coats.

(M)

Period: 19th century.

A white, turned-down collar worn by the clergy until replaced by the **stand collar** and the **Prussian collar** in 1860–1870; the style favoured by evangelical and nonconformist ministers.

Pantie girdle, panty girdle

(F)

Period: 1960s.

A combination of the lightweight, elasticated, unboned **girdle** and panties, of varying length and designed to be worn with **tights**.

Panties, pants

(F & M)

Period: 20th century onwards.

Term for short **underpants**.

Pants is also an American term for **trousers**; an abbreviation of the earlier **pantaloons**.

Pantihose, pantyhose

(F)

Period: 1960s onwards.

An American term for women's **tights**.

Pantile

(F & M)

Period: 1640s–1665.

A popular name for the **sugarloaf hat**. There was a 19th-century slang term "tile", meaning hat.

Pantofles, pantables, pantacles, pantobles, pantibles

(F & M)

Period: Late 15th to mid-17th century.

Over-shoes in the form of mules. Very common from 1570.

Pants suit

(F)

Period: Late 20th century onwards.

An American term for a **trouser suit**.

Paper dress

(F)

Period: 1960s.

A dress not strictly of paper but of bonded or non-woven fibres, often synthetic; Vilene is a typical example. Such garments were cheap and disposable, but improved versions were flame-proof, did not tear, and could be washed for a few times before disintegrating.

Paper pattern

Period: Mid-19th century onwards.

The template for many styles and sizes of garment; pinned to fabric, cut-out and sewn; this allowed domestic dressmaking to develop into a sophisticated form from the 1860s onwards.

See Butterick.

Paper underwear

(F)

Period: 1960s.

A temporary novelty, supposedly offering disposable panties and slips for holiday wear.

Papillotte

(F & M)

Period: 18th century.

A screw of paper used to make a curl of hair.

Papillotte comb

(F)

Period: 1828.

A decorative comb of tortoiseshell, three or four inches long, used to raise the hair at the sides.

Paquebot capote

(F)

Period: 1830s.

The same as the **Bibi capote**.The inside of the brim was trimmed with ribbon and blonde lace.

Parachute hat

See Balloon hat.

Parasol

(F)

Period: ca. 1800–ca. 1860.

A light, ornamental **umbrella** carried by women as a shield against the sun. The pagoda shape was usual; some, however, were small and hinged so that the cover could be turned upright to act as a fan; see **Fan parasol**. The telescopic stick of steel appeared by 1811; the small parasol with a folding stick for use in the carriage from ca. 1838 on. From that time the parasol became more elegant, with carved ivory handles in the 1830s and 1840s and fringed borders, the covers of coloured silk and lace, black Maltese lace being fashionable in the 1860s.

Period: 1860–1900.

By 1867 "the pagoda shape has entirely disappeared; handles are longer; covers in stripes, brocade and satin". In the 1880s a domed shape was usual, with linings in bright colours; handles with a large crystal or china knobs; ribbon bows near the point and handle appeared in 1886; 1888 saw sticks "as long as alpenstocks" with knobs as large as billiard balls. By 1890 there were covers of chiffon or crêpe-de-chine with deep flounces or puffed all over; handles of Dresden china were fashionable in 1896, and in 1899 covers of fancy silk in broad, coloured stripes were popular.

Period: 20th century.

Highly decorative parasols were fashionable until ca. 1914. Japanese paper sunshades and short-handled parasols suitable for motoring signalled a simpler style for the post-World War I period, and gradually the combination of sunglasses with a wide-brimmed hat mostly replaced parasols.

Parchment calves

(M)

Period: 1750–1800.

Parchment shapes worn inside the stockings to improve the shape of the legs.

See False calves.

Pardessus

(F)

Period: 1840s onwards.

Generic name for any outdoor garment of half or three-quarter length, with sleeves and shaped into the waist; often with rounded cape or **pelerine**; trimmed with lace or velvet.

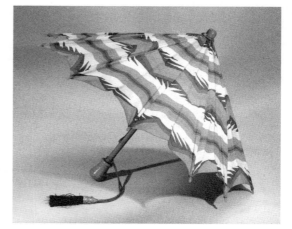

Printed cotton **parasol** or sunshade with a short wooden stick and tassel decoration; the print suggestive of **Art deco** design, ca. 1925. Copyright the Olive Matthews Collection, Chertsey Museum.

p

Pardessus redingote

(M)

Period: 1850s onwards.

The French name for the **frock coat**.

Pareo, pareu, parou

(F, occasionally M)

Period: 1960s onwards.

Originally the description of a wraparound garment made of bark cloth and worn in French Polynesia and other Pacific islands with French connections. Later, a sarong or, for men, a loincloth made of brightly printed cotton and adopted for beachwear beyond the original islands.

Parka

(M, later F)

Period: Late 19th century onwards.

The origins of the word are found in Russian and describe a hooded, thigh-length garment similar to an **anorak** but front-fastening, and often with a fur lining. This type of garment is windproof and used for outdoor activities, including winter sports, and it is frequently issued to military personnel. It became the favourite outdoor wear of the **Mods**, who found their parkas in **army surplus** stores, opting for those which were longer and loosely cut; these they customized with a variety of badges. Many firms began to produce parkas from the 1960s onwards in a variety of colours and finishes, and the modern range is huge.

Parrock

(M)

Period: 15th century.

A loose cloak with arm-holes. "Parrock or Caban" (ca. 1440, *Promptorium Parvulorum*).

Parti-coloured hose

(M)

Period: Mid-14th to mid-15th century.

Hose in the form of footed, long stockings reaching above the fork as tights, the legs coloured differently or striped. "Their hose are of two colours or pied with more" (ca. 1413, *Eulogium*, Anon.).

See Mi-parti.

Partlet, patlet

(M)

Period: 1500–1550.

A sleeveless jacket or merely a covering for the upper part of the chest and neck left exposed by a low-cut doublet, then fashionable. Partlets were often very decorative. "A straight sleeveless jacket made like a partlett" (1523, Letters and Papers, Henry VIII).

(F)

Period: 16th and 17th centuries.

A fill-in, like a **chemisette** for a low décolletage and made with a high collar from the 1530s. "He cannot make a standing collar for a partlet without the measurement for her neck" (1533, Letters and Papers, Henry VIII).

See Detachable sleeves.

Parure

(F)

Period: Late 18th century onwards.

A set of matching jewellery usually worn together. The set might include a bracelet, a brooch, a necklace and ear-rings; an optional extra might be a tiara. A "demi-parure" was two matched pieces, e.g. ear-rings and necklace.

Pashmina

(F, occasionally M)

Period: Late 1990s onwards.

An especially lightweight cashmere **shawl**. The term *pashm* is a Persian word denoting the finest underbelly fibres of Himalayan mountain goats, and the word "pashmina" was known in the UK in the mid-19th century as both the woven fabric and a shawl made from it. Modern versions, often with a warp of silk and a weft of cashmere, became popular in the late 1990s and are produced in many colours; some are embroidered and cheaper copies use cotton or viscose.

Pass

(F & M)

Period: 17th century.

The front of a man's or woman's hat.

Passe

(F)

Period: 1864.

The bridge of flowers or trimming under the brim of a bonnet.

Passementerie

See Glossary of Fabrics and Materials.

Paste

Period: Mid-17th century onwards.

A hard, vitreous composition similar to glass, used for making imitation gemstones.

Patches

(F)

Period: 1590s to late 18th century.

Small spots of black velvet or silk, variously shaped and applied with mastic as ornaments on the face. At some periods, e.g. the early 18th century, the arrangement of the patches on the face served to indicate the wearer's political party.

(M)

Period: 18th century.

The wearing of patches by men was rare.

Patch pocket

Period: 19th century onwards.

A pocket formed from a piece of fabric sewn onto a garment, usually square or rectangular and not dissimilar to patches used for repairing worn clothing.

Patent lace

See Glossary of Laces.

Patent-leather boots

(M)

Period: 1870s onwards.

Ankle-length, buttoned boots with patent-leather uppers, worn for day and also evening dress. In the 20th century, when boots were no longer worn, patent-leather evening shoes replaced them.

Patrol jacket

(M)

Period: 1878.

A close-fitting, hip-length jacket, single-breasted, closed by five buttons; with a **Prussian collar**; cross pocket on each hip and on the left breast. Of military cut and worn with tight knee breeches for bicycling on the high "penny farthing" machine.

(F)

Period: 1889.

A close-fitting, hip-length jacket, the back without a centre seam, the front trimmed across with military braiding; tight sleeves with close cuffs and a **stand collar**. A military style inspired by a military campaign in Egypt.

Pattens

(F & M)

Period: 14th to mid-19th century.

Over-shoes consisting of wooden soles, secured by leather straps and worn with boots or shoes to raise the wearer above the dirt when walking. The shape varied according to the period. Usually for country wear, but very fashionable in the 15th and 18th centuries; until the 17th century the term was synonymous with **clogs**. From ca. 1630 pattens were raised on iron rings: "The women leave in the passage their pattins, that is a kind of wooden shoes which stand on a high iron ring. Into these wooden shoes they thrust their ordinary leather or stuff shoes when they go out" (1748, Pehr Kalm's *Account of his Visit to England*, Stockholm, 1753. Trans. J. Lucas, 1892).

Countrywomen continued to use pattens until the mid-19th century.

Patti jets

(F)

Period: 1869.

Balls of polished jet hanging from a ribbon necklace, with similar ear-rings; for morning wear. Jet, a form of polished lignite or fossilized coal, had been used for many centuries but was especially prized in the second half of the 19th century.

See Jet buttons.

Pautener

(M)

Period: Medieval to 17th century.

The bag hanging from the **girdle**.

Pea jacket, pilot coat

(M)

Period: 1830s onwards.

Worn either as an overcoat or as a short, closed coat, and made of pilot cloth or mohair. Double-breasted with wide lapels and velvet collar, the skirts closed behind. As an overcoat, made loose and sack-like, the corners cut square, and ending above the knees.

Pair of **pattens** with silk **brocade** uppers and wool lining; ties holes but no fastening laces or ribbons, ca. 1730–40. Copyright the Olive Matthews Collection, Chertsey Museum. Photograph by John Chase.

In the 1850s it was given huge buttons and often a short back vent. From ca. 1860 it became known as a **reefer** and both terms associate the coat with its naval use, when sailors and officers wore shorter and simpler, navy, wool versions differentiated by the buttons, plain or brass. Its 20th-century popularity owes much to **army surplus** stores. However, as a design **classic**, it is now made in other colours and cloths.

Peaked shoe
See Piked shoe.

Pearls
(F, occasionally M)
Period: Medieval onwards.
Individual or strings of pearls decorated garments and formed items of jewellery. A pearl is the smooth, hard, silvery white seed found within an oyster, formed around an irritant such as sand within the shell. Cultured pearls were introduced by the Japanese in 1914. Seed pearls, real or of coated glass, were used in embroidery.

Peasant skirt
(F)
Period: 1885.
A full, round tennis skirt made with two or three wide tucks and a fall of lace.

Peasant styles
(F, sometimes M)
Period: 20th century onwards.
The folk dress or regional styles worn in many European countries across several centuries were adopted/adapted for use within fashionable circles to indicate a simpler approach to clothing. Colourful head scarves, embroidered blouses with full sleeves, **dirndl** skirts or complete outfits, lederhosen (southern German leather trousers), and **Tyrolean** hats were all worn at various times.

Peascod-bellied doublet
(M)
Period: ca. 1570s–1600.
A term used by Bulwer in 1653 describing the fashion for padding the front of the doublet at the point of the waist to produce a bulge overhanging the girdle. Originally a Dutch style. Also called **long-bellied doublet**.

Pectoll
(M)
Period: 16th century.
The breast of a shirt.

Pedal pushers
(F)
Period: 1950s onwards.
Close-fitting trousers ending at mid-calf, often of a sturdy fabric. Designed for riding a bicycle; the length ensuring that trousers did not catch on the pedals.

Pediment head-dress
(F)
A 19th-century term for the 16th-century English hood.

Peeper, peepers
(F & M)
Period: Late 17th century and 18th century.
A term applied in the singular to a spy-glass or a looking glass, and in the plural as slang for a pair of spectacles. "Peeper, a spying glass" (1785, F. Grose, *Dictionary of the Vulgar Tongue*).

Peep-toe
(F)
Period: Mid-1930s onwards.
A term used to describe shoes designed to reveal one or more toes.

Peg-top skirt
(F)
Period: 1950s onwards.
A skirt shaped literally like a wooden peg, with a narrow waist, fuller hips and narrowness at the hem.

Peg-top sleeves
(M)
Period: 1857–1864.
Sleeves cut wide above and narrowing towards the hand; a modified revival of the **gigot sleeve** of the 1820s.

Peg-top trousers, Zouave trousers
(M)
Period: 1857–1865.
Trousers with the legs cut wide at the hips, a low crotch, and sloping inwards to a close fit at the ankles. For day wear only and never a universal fashion. A modified revival occurred in 1892.
In the 20th century this style was occasionally revived in France and elsewhere in Europe.

Peigne giraffe
See Giraffe comb.

Peigne Josephine
(F)
Period: 1842.
A high comb surmounted by small balls, often gilt; worn at the back of the head with evening dress.

Peignoir
(F)
Period: Late 18th century onwards.
A loose wrapper of light fabric, worn as a day **négligée** or informal morning wear. The bodice was unboned and in 1840 made with **bishop sleeves**. "She…let down her peignoir from her shoulder" (September 1780, *Gentleman's & London Magazine*).

Pelerine
(F)
Period: 1740 to end of 18th century.
A short cape with long, pendant ends in front, often worn crossed over the bosom, passed round the waist, to be tied behind.

Period: 19th century.

A cape-like collar, but from 1825 it reverted to the style of the 18th century; it was often made of cambric or muslin, often embroidered or trimmed with lace.

Period: 20th century.
In the early years of the century – "Pelerines falling completely over the shoulders are becoming very fashionable" (1903, quoted in Cunnington, *English Women's Clothing in the Present Century*).

Pelisse, pellice
(M)
Period: Early 18th century onwards.
A fur-lined cloak or mantle, usually waist-length, as an element in the uniform worn by Hussar regiments.

(F)
Period: 18th century.
A three-quarter-length cloak with shoulder-cape or hood and arm-hole slits. Lined and trimmed with silk, satin or fur. "A pellice of rich brocade lined with sables" (1718, *Letters of Lady Mary Wortley Montagu*).

Period: 1800–1810.
Three-quarter-length with or without sleeves; subsequently ankle-length, sleeved and figure-fitting, often having one or more shoulder capes.

Period: 1880s.
A long winter **mantle**, often of velvet, silk or satin, gathered on the shoulders and having large, loose sleeves.
Throughout the 19th century a pelisse for infants in arms was a long, caped cloak, generally of cream-coloured cashmere, though bright colours (blue or scarlet) were also made.

Pelisse-mantle
(F)
Period: 1838–1845.
A three-quarter to full-length cloak with a cape reaching the waist and draped round the arms to form hanging sleeves. In the 1840s this mantle was drawn-in at the waist behind.

Pelisse-robe
(F)
Period: 1817–1850.
A day dress in the form of a pelisse fastened all down the front with ribbon bows or concealed hooks and eyes. After ca. 1840 it became known as a **redingote**.

Pelisson
(F & M)
Period: 14th to early 16th century.
A furred over-gown or **super tunic**; identical with a **pilch**.

Pellard
See Houppelande.

Pembroke paletot
(M)
Period: 1853–1855.

Fashion plate advertising the services of Wingman, **Dressmaker** in Hanover Square, London. Both women are in day wear; the woman to the left carries a **parasol** with a marquise hinge allowing it to be tilted vertically, the woman to the right is wearing a **pelisse**; 1802. Copyright the Olive Matthews Collection, Chertsey Museum.

A long-waisted, double-breasted **overcoat** reaching the calf; wide lapels, two rows of four buttons, vertical breast pocket, two flapped side pockets; easy sleeves with turned-back cuffs.

Penang lawyer
(M)
Period: 19th century.
A walking-stick with a bulbous head, made from stem of a palm from Penang.

Pencil skirt
(F)
Period: 1930s onwards.
A narrow skirt, completely straight from hip to knee or below, according to length.

Pendicle
(M)

Period: Late 15th to 17th century.

A pendant ornament; a drop ear-ring of the style when only one was worn by men.

Pentes

(F)

Period: 1886.

Pyramidal panels of silk or velvet, in graduated stripes, forming a full-length panel of an underskirt, with the overskirt or tunic draped so as to expose it.

Peplos

(F)

Period: ca. 480 BCE to ca. 300 BCE.

A garment constructed from a long, rectangular section of linen or wool, later of cotton or silk. It was folded vertically and passed round the body, and distinguished from the **chiton** by an overfold of fabric over the bust and back, held by pins or brooches at the top of the shoulders, and belted at the waist or below the bust. Female peploi were ankle-length for women unless depicted worn by goddesses or mythological characters, when they were knee-length. In an annual ritual a richly embroidered example was presented to the statue of Athena in Athens.

Peplum

(F)

Period: 1866, revived in 1890s.

A short tunic or overskirt, cut away front and back, and hanging in points at the sides. For day dress.

Period: 20th century onwards.

An overskirt cut away to hang in points; an extended basque to give a partial overskirt effect.

Peplum basque

(F)

Period: 1866.

A peplum-shaped **basque** attached to a waist belt and worn with a day or evening bodice.

Peplum bodice

(F)

Period: 1879.

An evening bodice with long side panels forming **paniers**.

Peplum dolman

(F)

Period: 1872.

A **dolman** with long points on the sides.

Peplum jupon

(F)

Period: 1866.

A gored under-petticoat with three steels round the bottom and a deep, pleated flounce, replacing the **cage crinoline**.

Peplum overskirt

(F)

Period: 1894.

Drapery of decorative fabric, pleated into the waistband behind and there short, but descending in ripples to the hem towards the front, and caught in along the whole length of the side seams of the front breadth, which is left uncovered.

Peplum rotonde

(F)

Period: 1871.

A waist-length, circular cloak with back vent and fringed borders.

Perdita chemise

(F)

Period: 1783.

A day dress with a close-fitting bodice, a V-neck and a deep falling collar, single or double. The gown closed in front from bust to hem by buttons or ribbon ties, and long, tight sleeves buttoned at the wrist. A broad sash at the waist tied behind and flowing down the back of the skirt.

Perfume

Period: 16th century onwards.

Originally fragrant fumes or vapour, later a term applied to an aromatic liquid which can be applied to the body or its clothing. Natural ingredients and synthetic ones are used; the best-known early synthetic one is Chanel No. 5. Also known as "fragrance" or "scent".

See Jessamy gloves.

Periwig

See Wig.

Permanent wave

(F, rarely M)

Period: 20th century onwards.

A process, using lotions, curling devices and heat, which transforms straight hair into curls and/or waves.

See Marcel wave.

Peruke

See Wig.

Peruvian hat

(F)

Period: Early 19th century.

A hat made of plaited strands of the leaves of the Cuban palm. "Fraser's Patent Peruvian Hats…not injured by rain" (1816).

Petal collar

(F)

Period: After 1950.

A collar constructed from overlapping ovals of fabric emulating the look of petals.

Petenlair, pet-en-l'air, French jacket

(F)

Period: ca. 1745–1770s.

A French fashion which appeared earlier and was adopted in other countries before it became fashionable in Britain. It was a thigh-length, or sometimes knee-length, jacket-bodice with sack-back, short elbow sleeves, and often a **stomacher** front. Worn with a plain skirt, called a **petticoat**.

"Inspir'd by thee, the skilful engineer Lopp'd half the sack and form'd the pet-en-l'air" (1751, "Hymn to Fashion", *The Gentleman's Magazine*).

Peter Pan collar
(F)

Period: ca. 1909 onwards.

A neat, turn-down collar inspired by the play and book by J. M. Barrie. "Collarless bodices in daytime are only becoming to the very young…as also are the Peter Pan and Claudine collars" (1911, *The Woman's Book*).

Petersham Cossacks, Petersham trousers
(M)

Period: 1817–1818.

An excessively loose form of **Cossacks**, spreading out widely round the ankles and over the foot, or drawn in leaving a flounce round the ankle. Named after the Regency dandy, Charles, Viscount Petersham (1780–1851).

Petersham frock coat
(M)

Period: 1830s.

A frock coat made double-breasted with a broad velvet collar, lapels and cuffs, and large, flapped pockets aslant on the hips. No side bodies.

Petersham great coat
(M)

Period: 1830s.

A great coat made with a short shoulder-cape.

Petit bord
(F)

Period: 1835–1850.

A form of head-wear for evening dress; at first a small-crowned hat with a halo brim, trimmed with ribbon and aigrettes. In the 1840s it was much smaller, becoming a **toque** hat, usually of velvet, with narrow upturned brim. The petit bord was always worn at the back of the head, often with a sideways tilt.

Petticoat
(M)

Period: ca. 1450–ca. 1600, but rare after 1520.

An under-**doublet**, usually padded and worn for warmth; subsequently called a **waistcoat**. "In wynter next your shert use you to wear a pettycott of scarlet" (1577, Andrew Borde, *Regyment*).

(F)

Period: 16th–19th century.

Before the 19th century, the term "petticoat" was applied to the skirt of a dress, being part of the **gown** and not an undergarment. It could be of a contrasting or matching fabric, and sometimes was **quilted** or decorated with embroidery, braid, etc. However, as an undergarment it was often called an "under-petticoat", until the term acquired its modern meaning.

Period: 16th to end of 18th century.

Usually of inferior material and tied to the body of the dress by laces or **points**. Often made of white flannel, but in the 18th century also of cambric; worn under the hoop and sometimes called a **dickey**.

Period: 19th century.

The petticoat gradually became more elaborate and in the 1840s several were worn, the under most usually of flannel. In the 1860s white cotton petticoats were often bordered with broderie anglaise. By the 1890s petticoats were often of silk or satin, lavishly flounced, frilled, and bordered with ribbon and lace, producing a "seductive frou-frou" sound, in walking.

Period: 20th century onwards.

Petticoats were made in various styles and could be full- or half-length. Artificial fibres were used to create imitation silks and satins, but generally the line was sleek, and by the end of the century petticoats were not an essential undergarment, though **bra slips** were a useful combination of **brassière** and petticoat.

Petticoat bodice
(F)

Period: 1815 onwards.

A petticoat with a sleeveless bodice to it, joined with a seam at the waist, by gores or gathers, thus contrasting with the **princess petticoat**. At first usually made with a low stomacher front; after 1825 buttoned up behind.

In the 1890s the term was applied to a bodice covering the stays.

See Camisole.

Petticoat breeches
(M)

Period: 1660s–1670s.

Breeches immensely wide in the leg and pleated or gathered on to a waistband, falling like a divided skirt to the knees or just above. Some had a lining forming baggy under-breeches gathered into a band above the knee. Always trimmed with ribbon loops at the waist and usually also down the outer side of the legs.

See Fancies, Rhinegraves, Pantaloons.

Petticoat breeches continued to be worn as the livery of running footmen until the mid-18th century.

Pewter buttons

Period: Late 17th century onwards.

Hollow pewter buttons were patented in 1683. They were an inexpensive coat-button worn by the working classes in the 18th century. Pewter was an alloy of tin and lead, or sometimes copper, and was a deep grey colour.

Photography and fashion

Period: Late 1830s onwards.

The process of capturing an accurate likeness with a camera had a swift and long-lasting impact on recording personal appearance. Many more people could afford a

A man in the short open **doublet** and a **cloak** of ca. 1670 in an engraving by Romeyn de Hooghe, a Dutchman working in Paris. The emphasis in this **fashion illustration** is on the **petticoat breeches**, the full **wig** and the quantities of **ribbon** trimming every garment. The **falling band** has a deep **lace** edge. Private collection.

visit to a photographic studio than have an artist draw or paint how they looked. Although there were early attempts at artistic photography, it is the millions of photographs taken by amateurs and generalist professionals that provide a detailed visual survey of clothing worn by different social groups, at various times of year and in many countries and contexts. These offer rich evidence of non-idealized appearance across more than 150 years. As the process became less cumbersome, illustrating fashion by photography became feasible. Early and influential practitioners included Baron de Meyer (1868–1946), George Hoyningen-Huene (1900–1968), Cecil Beaton (1904–1980) and Richard Avedon (1923–2004). *Vogue* was the first magazine in which fashion photography was the norm rather than the exception, and de Meyer was an early contributor. By the 1920s fashion photographers were recording **mannequins**, **couturiers** and elite women from around the world in

every type of fashionable garment. Succeeding generations of fashion photographers include Lord Snowdon, David Bailey, Terence Donovan and Mario Testino, all of whom add to the sophisticated record of fashionable glamour in newspapers, journals, on TV and in film.

Phrygian cap

(M)

Period: 9th to end of 12th century.

A descriptive term used from the 18th century as applied to a pointed cap with the apex turned over slightly towards the front. A common form of headwear in the classical era and also in early medieval times, it is now associated with the cap of liberty worn during the French Revolution.

Physical wig

(M)

Period: ca. 1750–1800.

Worn by the learned professions, replacing the **full-bottomed wig**. It resembled a large form of the longer form of the **bob-wig**, swept back from the forehead, with or without a centre parting, and standing out in a "bush" round the back of the head, often hanging below the nape of the neck. "What wags call a lion or a pompey" (1761, *Gentleman's Magazine*).

Picards

(F)

Period: 17th century.

"New shoes of the French fashion" (J. Evelyn, *Ladies' Dictionary*).

Piccadilly collar

(M)

Period: 1860s onwards.

A shallow **stand collar** separate from the shirt, fastened to it by a button at the back of the neck and a stud in front. But in 1895 "a deep stand-fall collar cut so as to leave free passage for the band of the scarf".

Piccadilly weepers

(M)

Period: 1870s and 1880s.

Long, combed-out whiskers.

Pickadil, pickardil, piccadilly

(M)

Period: 16th century.

A tabbed or scalloped border, as a form of decoration; commonly used for doublet skirts, said to be "wrought in pickadils".

(F & M)

Period: Late 16th century to ca. 1630.

The term was now transferred to a tabbed and stiffened support for the back of a ruff or collar ("band"). "How his band jumpeth with his pecadilly" (1617, Henry Fitzgeffery, *Notes from Blackfryers*).

Pickdevant, pique devant

(M)

Period: 1570s–1600.

A short, pointed beard, usually worn with a brushed-up moustache.

Picture hat

(F)

Period: 1890s onwards.

A large, wide-brimmed hat of straw or light material, brightly coloured and trimmed with strongly contrasting colours. Named after Gainsborough's 1787 portrait of the Duchess of Devonshire. In the first half of the 20th century this type of hat was often trimmed with ribbons and artificial flowers and worn in the summer at garden parties, racing events, etc.

Piedmont gown, robe à la Piémontèse

(F)

Period: ca. 1775.

A variation of the **sack**-back gown, in which the box pleats were detached from the back of the bodice so as to form a bridge from the shoulders to the hips, where the pleats again merged into the overskirt.

Pierrot

(F)

Period: 1780s–1790s.

A close-fitting, low-necked jacket-bodice with short basques. Generally worn with a flounced, matching skirt **petticoat**; for day wear.

Pierrot cape

(F)

Period: 1892.

A three-quarter-length cloak with shoulder-cape and satin Pierrot ruff.

Pierrot collar

(F)

Period: 1880s onwards.

A soft, floppy ruff in the style associated with the theatrical character with his loose white costume and whitened face. Pierrot and Pierette (the female version of the character) costumes were popular disguises for **fancy dress**.

Pierrot ruff

(F)

Period: 1892.

A ruff bordered with fur, on capes for outdoor wear.

Pifferaro bonnet

(F)

Period: 1877.

A felt bonnet with a blunt-pointed crown and narrow brim slightly turned up; feather trimming.

Pifferaro hat

(F)

Period: 1877.

A hat with a short, chimney-pot crown trimmed with an **aigrette** in front.

Pigeon-winged toupee

(M)

Period: 1750s and 1760s.

A toupee with one or two stiff, horizontal roll curls projecting above the ears, with the foretop and sides smooth and plain. Worn with various **queues**.

See Aile de pigeon.

Pigtail wig

(M)

Period: 18th century.

A wig with a long **queue** spirally bound or interwoven with black ribbon and generally tied above and below with black ribbon bows.

Piked shoe, peaked shoe

(F & M)

Period: 14th and 15th centuries, mainly ca. 1370–1410 and 1460–1480.

Shoes with long spear-like points extending beyond the toes; the same shape applied to **pattens** of the period.

See Copped shoes, Cracowes.

Pilch, pilche

(F & M)

Period: 14th to early 16th century.

A close-fitting over-gown lined with fur and worn by both sexes in winter and by the clergy for warmth in cold churches.

Period: Late 17th century onwards.

An infant garment or wrapper worn over a napkin, "now used for flannel cloth to wrap about the lower part of young children" (1694, *Ladies' Dictionary*).

Pillbox

(F)

Period: 1950s onwards.

A hat in the form of the small, cylindrical box used for holding pills. Made fashionable by Jacqueline Kennedy Onassis (1929–1994) when her husband was President of the USA in the early 1960s.

Pillion

(M)

Period: Late 14th to mid-16th century.

A round hat or cap, mainly worn by ecclesiastics and scholars.

Pilot coat

See Pea jacket.

Pinafore

Period: Late 18th century onwards.

A child's washable covering of the front of the frock to protect it from becoming soiled; similar to an **apron**.

Pinafore costume

(F)

Period: 1879.

A tennis dress with a tunic having a bib-pinafore front and waistband, worn over a **princess dress** with a kilted skirt; the tunic made of fancy material such as Pompadour sateen.

Pinafore dress

(F)

p

Period: 20th century onwards.

A sleeveless dress, originally with a bib front but later with various styles of opening, but usually worn over a blouse or sweater. The "pinafore gown" was introduced in 1906, but pinafore dresses became popular in the 1930s.

Pinchbeck buttons

Period: From 1770 onwards.

The metal for these buttons was an alloy of copper and zinc, invented by Christopher Pinchbeck, an English watchmaker ca. 1700. Much used to simulate more expensive gilt buttons.

Pinking, pouncing

Period: Late 15th–17th century.

A form of decoration consisting of small holes or very short slits cut or punched in the material or in the finished garment, or on shoes, and arranged so as to form a pattern.

"For one thousand and a halfe pynkes for a kyrtell…" (1580, Egerton MS).

"This pair of shooes…pinckt, with letters for thy name" (1600, Dekker, *The Gentle Craft*).

Period: Mid-17th century onwards.

Pinking, in the modern sense of the word, means an unhemmed border cut into minute scallops or angles. Pinking shears were developed for this purpose.

Pinner

(F)

Period: 17th to mid-18th century.

The lappet of an indoor cap, the lappets being often pinned up. From ca. 1680s the term transferred to the indoor cap itself. "A lady's headdress with long flaps hanging down the sides of the cheeks…. Some term this sort of long-eared Quoif by the name of a Pinner" (1688, R. Holme, *Armory*).

In the 18th century the lappets were often omitted, the pinner being a flat, circular cap with a frill.

Period: 17th century.

The term was sometimes used for a **tucker**, but more usually for an apron with a bib, a **pinafore**, and this usage remains.

Pins

Period: Medieval onwards.

A thin, usually cylindrical length of metal with a sharp point and round, wider head for fastening clothing. A type with the heads hammered on round the end of the shank were used until ca. 1830, when they were replaced by the pin with head and shank in one.

See Safety pin.

Pinson, pinsnet, pinsonet

(F & M)

Period: 14th to end of 16th century.

A light, indoor shoe, the earlier ones often furred. In the 16th century often worn with a protective over-shoe. "A pumpe or pinson to weare in pantofles" (1599, Minsheu). In the 17th century the term was being replaced by **pump**.

Piped seams, piping

(F)

Period: 1820s onwards.

Ornamentation by means of narrow cord enclosed in pipe-like folds along the seams of a garment. A construction occurring first ca. 1822 in muslin dresses and becoming a very general fashion in the 1840s; imitated in men's coats and waistcoats by a narrow edging of cord.

Pipes

(M)

Period: 17th and 18th centuries.

Small rolls of pipe clay used, when heated, for tightening the curls of wigs.

See Roulettes.

Pipkin, taffeta pipkin

(F)

Period: ca. 1565–1600.

A small hat with a flat crown drawn in and pleated into a narrow, flat brim; usually having a narrow, jewelled hatband and feather trimming.

Piquets

(F)

Period: 1878.

Ornamental sprays decorating evening lace caps worn by mature women.

Plackard, placart, placcard, placcate

(M)

Period: Late 15th to mid-16th century.

A stomacher or chest-piece covering the V- or U-shaped gap of the low-fronted doublet or jacket.

(F)

Period: Mid-14th century to ca. 1540.

The front panel or **stomacher** portion of a side-less **surcoat**, often embroidered or trimmed with fur. Also a stomacher to wear with a gown or **kirtle**.

Placket

(F)

Period: 16th century onwards.

A short opening or slit near the top of a woman's skirt or petticoat. In the 19th century "the opening at the back of a skirt or petticoat extending from the waist downwards, designed to enlarge the aperture made at the waistband to allow for passing the skirt over the head and shoulders" (1882, *Dictionary of Needlework*).

In the 20th century generally found at the back or side waist of a skirt or dress; also found from the neck of a bodice. Usually concealed by a right-over-left fastening.

Plaid

(F & M)

A long piece of twilled woollen cloth usually woven with a chequered or tartan design in a variety of colour ways; worn as the outer or top layer of Highland Dress.
See Arisaid, Kilt.

Plain bow stock
(M)
Period: 1830s.
A straight-sided stock of black silk with a bow in front.

Plastron
(F)
Period: 19th and early 20th century.
Taken from the French term for a breast plate, this described the front panel of a bodice of a different colour and material from the rest of the bodice.

Plated buttons
(M)
Period: 18th century.
The term usually denoted buttons that were silver-plated as distinct from gold-plated, known as "gilt". Until ca. 1750 the surface of silver was obtained by French plating, later by Sheffield plating. Very fashionable for use on men's coats.

Platform soles
(F)
Period: From 1940 onwards.
A thick, built-up sole of cork, rubber or composition, covered with leather.

Platoff cap
(F)
Period: 1814.
An evening cap of pale pink satin, the front scalloped; trimmed with a row of pearls and a pearl tassel from the crown. Named after the Cossack General Matvei Platov (modern spelling) who attended the Peace celebrations in London in 1814.

Playsuit
(F)
Period: 1930s onwards.
A style of **beachwear** comprising a pair of shorts attached to a bodice or a pair of shorts with matching shirt.

Pleat
Period: 16th century onwards.
A fold of cloth or drapery held in place along one edge by ironing or other pressure, or stitched into place along part or all of an edge.

Pleated shirt, plaited shirt
(M)
Period: 1806–1870s.
At first a day shirt with narrow, vertical pleats down the bosom and no frill, the front closed by three buttons. From 1840 also worn with evening dress, the front being closed by ornamental studs.

Pleated trousers
See Cossacks.

Plimsolls
(F & M)
Period: Mid-19th century onwards.
A rubber-soled, canvas sports shoe.
See Pump.

Pluderhose
(M)
Period: 1550–1600.
A German and Swiss form of **trunk-hose** characterized by broad **panes** and wide gaps bulging with silk linings often overhanging the panes below.

Plug hat
(M)
Period: ca. 1830s onwards.
American term for a **top hat**.

Plummet
Period: 17th century.
A drop ear-ring. "To clog the ear with plummets" (1617, H. Fitzgeffery, *Satyres*).
See Pendicle.

Plumpers
(F)
Period: Late 17th to early 20th century.
Small balls or pads of various materials to plump out the cheeks of those with few teeth.
"Certain very thin, round and light balls (of cork) to plump out and fill up the cavities of the cheeks" (1690, J. Evelyn, *The Fop's Dictionary*).
"Mrs. Button who wears cork plumpers in each cheek and never hazards more than six words for fear of shewing them" (1780, Mrs Cowley, *The Belle's Stratagem*).
"Having been upset [carriage accident] Rosabella lost her plumpers" (1825, Harriette Wilson, *Paris Lions and London Tigers*).

Plus fours
(M, occasionally F)
Period: 1920s onwards.
A variant of **knickerbockers** made especially long and wide; the name derived from the extra four inches of fabric which created the overhang.

Plymouth cloak
(M)
Period: 17th century.
A slang term for a cudgel or cane. "With Plymouth cloaks in our hands" (1677, Aphra Behn, *The Rover*).

Pochette
(F)
Period: 20th century onwards.
A flat, oblong handbag like an envelope; without handles or with a strap-handle on the back through which the hand was placed. Also produced in versions for men after ca. 1975.

Pocket
(M)
Period: 15th to mid-16th century.

A small pouch independent of the garment and used for carrying money, etc.

Period: Mid-16th to late 17th century.
A small pouch built into **trunk-hose**, into **breeches** from the end of the 16th century, and into coats from the early 17th century, e.g.: "The keys of my counting-house are in the left pocket of my coat" (1633, W. Rowley, *A Match at Midnight*, Act 3).

Period: Late 17th to late 19th century.
Pockets were protected by flaps from ca. 1690. and were placed in **waistcoats** from the 18th century.
See named varieties: Bellows pocket, Breast pocket, Caddie, Cross pocket, Fob pocket, Hip-pocket, Long pocket, Salt-box pocket.
Descriptive terms need interpretation, for instance a **hip-pocket** has to be distinguished from a "pocket on the hips", the former being in the back of the trousers, the latter being on the outside of a skirted coat over the hip region.
A "pocket in the pleats", i.e. at the back of the skirt of a coat with opening under a pleat, has to be distinguished from a "pocket in the skirt", with its opening in the lining of the skirt.
A "slash pocket" had a slit opening on the surface of a coat, the edges of the slit usually strengthened by welting. A "pocket in the seam" of a skirted coat meant a horizontal slit (not welted) in the waist seam, placed at the side; a common form of ticket pocket.

Period: 20th century onwards.
Various styles were associated with particular garments, but the range was a wide one and visible, as with breast and patch pockets, and hidden, such as poacher's pockets, ticket and watch pockets and similar.

(F)
Period: 18th century.
The pocket was a separate article in the form of a small, flat bag or a pair of such bags attached together by a tape. "I keep in my pocket, ty'ed about my middle next to my smock" (1701, J. Swift, *Mrs Harris' Petition*). These pockets, tied on round the waist under the dress, were reached through the placket hole. They were frequently ornamented with coloured needlework patterns.

Period: 19th century.
For the first twenty years of the century these tied-on pockets ceased to be worn, being replaced by the **indispensable** or **reticule** carried in the hand. However, the tied-on pair of pockets continued to be used when travelling and became known as "railway pockets".
A built-in pocket in the skirt, accessible through a pocket hole at the back, became usual ca. 1840, when a watch pocket was added, hidden in the folds of the bodice in front of the waist; a few years later this watch-pocket was transferred to the waistband. A patch-pocket placed low down on the back of the skirt of princess and polonaise dresses in 1876 was a fashion welcomed by pick-pockets. A novelty of 1899 was a pocket for the handkerchief placed in the lining of the skirt or in the border of the petticoat just above the hem.

Period: 20th century onwards.
Pockets were often omitted if they spoiled the line of a garment, but full skirts, coats, jackets, etc. offered options for pockets inserted into side seams or on the outside of a garment.

Pocket book
(M)
Period: Late 17th century onwards.
A folding case or wallet carried in the pocket to contain papers or money; now mostly American usage.

(F)
Period: Early 19th century onwards.
A purse or small handbag. A term chiefly used in America.

Pocket handkerchief
(F & M)
Period: 16th century onwards.
Elegant handkerchiefs made from cotton, linen or silk, edged with lace or embroidered, were often carried in the hand rather than concealed in a pocket. Men's handkerchiefs were always larger than women's, and in the 19th century were often coloured for day-time use. Mourning handkerchiefs might be entirely black during the Regency period; later they were white with a black border, its depth depending on the degree of mourning.
See Handkerchief, Mockador.

Pocket hoop
(F)
Period: ca. 1720s, also 1770s.
"Hoops of the smallest size, commonly called Pocket-Hoops", were mentioned in the regulations at Bath Assembly Rooms, and again when the size of hoops was beginning to be reduced. For instance, undress fashions for July 1774: "Light brown night gowns and coats (i.e. petticoats) with small pocket hoops..." (*The Lady's Magazine*).

Pointed sleeves
See Raglan sleeves.

Points
(M)
Period: 15th to mid-17th century.
Silk or leather ties tipped with **aglets** and either functional or decorative. Functional points attached hose, trunk-hose or breeches to the **doublet**; until ca. 1630 they attached detachable sleeves to the doublet, and fastened the front of the doublet or **jerkin**. As decoration they were used in bunches or separate bows to

adorn male or female garments in the 16th and 17th centuries.

Poke
(F & M)
Period: ca. 1300 onwards.
A pouch or sack-like bag, now often a paper bag. In the 16th and 17th centuries the term was synonymous with **pocket**.

Poke bonnet, poking bonnet
(F)
Period: 1799 to end of 19th century.
A bonnet with an open brim projecting forward over the face. The term was applied to a large variety of styles, the "poke" often very slight.

Poking sticks
Period: 16th century.
Sticks of wood or bone, heated, for setting the pleats of a ruff. By 1574 some were made of steel.

Back view of a cream silk **gown** and **petticoat** embroidered with floral motifs. The skirt of the gown has loops and buttons to create the fashionable **polonaise** effect when the skirt is raised; worn as a **wedding dress**, ca. 1780. Copyright the Olive Matthews Collection, Chertsey Museum. Photograph by John Chase.

Pokys sleeves
See Bagpipe sleeves.

Policeman's cape
(F)
Period: 1895.
A cape cut in one piece from a circle.

Polish boots
(F)
Period: 1860s.
Tall boots with pendant tassels and high, coloured heels.

Polish greatcoat
(M)
Period: 1810.
A long, close-fitting coat, the collar, cuffs and lapels of Russian lambskin; closed by loops and **frogs**. Worn with evening dress.

Polish jacket
(F)
Period: 1846.
A waist-length jacket with masculine revers and collar. Sleeves square and slit open to the elbow along the inner side. Made of cashmere, lined with quilted satin, and worn at the seaside or in the country.

Polish mantle
(F)
Period: 1835.
A knee-length mantle with **pelerine** cape; of satin edged with fur.

Polka
(F)
Period: 1844.
A short, shaped **mantle** or jacket with loose sleeves; made of cashmere or velvet lined with silk. An outdoor garment, a variety of the **casaweck**.

Polo coat
(F & M)
Period: Late 19th century onwards.
A loose coat worn at sporting events such as polo matches; usually of camel hair. Polo cloth was a loose, woven mix of camel hair and wool and appeared at much the same time. The American firm of Brooks Brother (founded 1818) introduced a polo coat of white cloth for wearing over riding clothes in 1910; later it was made of camel hair.

Polo collar
(M, later F)
Period: ca. 1899.
A starched, white, stand-fall collar, the fronts sloping apart.

Period: 20th century.
American usage; similar to **polo neck**.

Polonaise, polonese
(F)
Period: 1750s.
A small, hooded cloak.

Period: 1770s–1870s.
A dress with an overskirt bunched up behind and completely uncovering the underskirt, which was usually ankle-length or sometimes trained.

Period: Early 20th century.
The term was occasionally used to describe a style of tunic or overdress.

(M)
Period: 1773.
A "Polonese Frock" was worn by gentlemen.

Period: 1830s.
The name "Polonaise" was commonly used for a military style **redingote**, usually of blue cloth, as worn by civilians.

Polonaise pardessus
(F)
Period: 1840s.
A short, half-length **pardessus** buttoned down the chest and then sloping away from the midline to reveal the dress. Some with a short, square **pelerine** cape.

Polo neck
(F & M)
Period: Early 20th century onwards.
A high, round, turned-over collar on a dress or **jumper**.

Polonia, Polony heel
(F & M)
Period: 17th century.
The high heel of boot or shoe which became fashionable in that century, causing the wearer to stagger in walking. "Mounted Polonially till he reels…" (1617, H. Fitzgeffery, *Notes from Black Fryers*).

Polo shirt
(M, later F)
Period: Late 19th century onwards.
A sports shirt, originally of white, woven cotton with a turn-over collar, two or three buttons to the neck, and short sleeves. Later variants included many different colours, longer sleeves, and a manufacturer's logo on the chest.

Polverino
(F)
Period: 1846.
A large, wrapping, silk cloak, unlined, with or without a hood.

Pomander
(F)
Period: ca. 1500–1690s.
A receptacle made of goldsmith's work, containing perfume or ingredients thought to protect against infection. The form was usually a circular, flat box or ball-shaped, with perforations. The pomander was suspended from the girdle in front. A variety of recipes for the contents were in use and these were loosely known

as "pomanders", e.g. "make a pomander under this maner…" (1542, A. Boorde, *Dyetary of Helth*).
Pomanders were occasionally carried by fops.

Pomatum
(F & M)
Period: 16th century onwards.
Originally a term for an ointment for face and hands but gradually the usage shifted to a scented ointment for the hair. Also described as a "pomade"; both meanings indicate that an original ingredient was apples.

Pompadour
(F)
Period: 18th century.
See Pompon.

Period: 1870s to early 20th century.
A pad over which the natural hair was rolled back from the forehead, or an artificial piece simulating the same style.

(M)
Period: 1880s onwards.
An American term descriptive of a hair style with the hair swept back from the forehead without a parting.

Pompadour bodice
(F)
Period: 1870s.
A day bodice with a square opening over the bosom and tight elbow sleeves finished with deep frills. Common with **polonaises**.

Pompadour heel, French heel
(F)
Period: 1750s–1760s.
A high, slender heel, waisted and curving to a small base.

Pompadour pardessus
(F)
Period: 1850s.
A **pardessus** of coloured silk, fringed, with demi-long sleeves; often hanging loose and fastened at the neck only. For summer wear.

Pompadour polonaise
(F)
Period: 1872.
A **polonaise** of black foulard figured with large, brightly coloured flowers; worn with a plain skirt.

Pompeian silk sash
(F)
Period: 1860s.
A wide, black, silk sash woven with mythological subjects; worn with a summer dress, generally a white jacket, bodice and coloured skirt.

Pompey
See Physical wig.

Pompon, pompom
(F)

Period: 1740s–1790s.

An ornament constructed from many elements, including ribbons, placed on the hair or cap. "The ornament worn by ladies in the middle of the forepart of their head-dress. Their figures, size and composition are various such as butterflies, feathers, tinsel, cockscomb, lace, etc." (1748, *The London Magazine*).

The word was short for **Pompadour**, which was sometimes used.

Period: Later 19th century onwards.

A round, fluffy ball of wool or similar tufted trimming for a hat, coat or other article of clothing.

Poncho

(M)

Period: 1850s.

A double-breasted, cape-like overcoat with very wide pagoda sleeves; also called a **talma**. Not the same as the **talma cloak** or **talma mantle**.

(F)

Period: 1860s.

A loose, three-quarter-length cloak, buttoned from neck to hem; with a small **stand collar**; full sleeves contracted at the wrist, the sleeves covered by a cape.

(F & M)

Period: 20th century onwards.

A blanket-shaped, sturdy garment with a slit in the centre to pass the head through. Originally South American, but absorbed into casual dress via the USA.

Pontificals

(M)

Period: 16th century.

Brooches, clasps or buckles, often ornamental; though more often rings. "A peyre of ouches otherwise call'd pontificalles of silver and gilt" (1508, Will of Joan Hampton, Somerset Wills).

See Ouch.

Ponyet, poynet

(M)

Period: 14th–16th century.

The **fore sleeve** of a **doublet** and made of a different material. "Doublet…with foresleeves of velvet called in those days poynettings of a doublet" (1555, T. Marshe, *Institution of a Gentleman*).

Period: 17th century.

"Little bodkins" (1611, T. Cotgrave), worn with decorative **points**.

Poodle cut

(F)

Period: Mid-20th century.

A tightly curled, short hair style, cut to resemble the appearance of a French poodle.

Pop Art

Period: 1950s onwards.

An artistic movement which used imagery and themes taken from modern popular culture and the output of mass media, transforming it into clear, brightly coloured images akin to photography. Two of its most celebrated exponents were the English artist Peter Blake (b. 1932) and the American Andy Warhol (1928–1987). Their ideas and images filtered into fabric design, onto **T-shirts** and into mainstream fashion. Some critics see their work as a precursor to the impact of **minimalism** on fashion in the 1990s.

Pop music

Period: 1950s onwards.

As with Pop Art, the shortened term "pop" stands for popular, and although popular music has a long history (folk song, spirituals, jazz, crooners, etc.), it was only in 1952 that Top Twenty charts were introduced in the UK, signalling the growing importance of recording stars in the lives of young people, at much the same time as they had money to spend on clothing that was aimed at them. The clothing worn by American, British and international artists influenced the young people of the 1950s onwards in the way that clothing worn by film stars had influenced their parents. Individuals like Elvis Presley, groups like the Beatles and the Rolling Stones, Tamla Motown stars, and boy and girl bands were defined by their appearance and widely copied.

Popover

(F)

Period: 1940s onwards.

An American term for loose, casual items of clothing easily slipped on and off. It often described a type of wraparound dress or tunic. "Sunbound popover, to be paired with pants,…loosely string-tied and loosely kimono-sleeved" (1968, *New York Times*, 3 December edition).

Pop socks

(F)

Period: Late 1960s onwards.

An English term for nylons or thicker socks, elasticated at their upper edge which reached the knees. They became fashionable at the time of the first **mini skirts** and have remained popular for use under trousers or longer skirts. The American term for them is descriptive – "knee-highs".

Porcelain buttons

Period: Late 18th century.

Patented in 1785 these were a fashionable ornament on gentlemen's coats and waistcoats.

Pork-pie hat

(F)

Period: 1860s.

A hat with a low, flat crown of straw or velvet, with a narrow brim turned up close all round.

Port cannons

See Cannons.

p

Porte-jupe pompadour

(F)

Period: 1860s.

A belt with eight suspenders, worn under the dress and used for hitching up the skirt when walking.

Portmantua

See Cloak bag.

Portuguese farthingale

(F)

Period: ca. 1662, briefly.

A **farthingale** flattened front and back with considerable lateral expanse; a fashion brought over by Catherine of Braganza on her marriage to Charles II, but not adopted in England, the farthingale having ceased to be fashionable from ca. 1630.

Postboy hat

(F)

Period: 1885.

A small straw hat with a high, flat crown and a narrow brim sloping down all round. A plume of feathers in front. Worn perched on the top of the head.

Pot hat

See Top hat.

Pouch

(M)

Period: 12th to early 16th century.

A bag or wallet slung from the girdle or attached to the belt of a gentleman, and generally worn with a knife or dagger stuck through the supporting strap.

Pouf

(F)

Period: Late 18th century.

An elaborate form of head-dress.

Period: Late 19th century onwards.

A pad or roll of hair, false or natural, to bulk out a hair style.

Also, a dressmaking term defining an element which has fabric gathered-up to create an effect, such as a "pouf sleeve". The French designer Christian Lacroix (b. 1951) produced a puff-ball-shaped, short skirt described as "le pouf" soon after setting up his own label in 1987.

Poulain, poulaine, pullayne

(F & M)

Period: 1395–1410, 1460–1480.

A French term for **piked shoes**; a term rarely used in England.

See Cracowes.

Pouncing

See Pinking.

Pourpoint

See Gipon.

Powdering jacket, powdering gown, powdering dress

(M)

Period: 18th century.

A loose, wrap-over garment, ankle-length, or shorter when the term "jacket" was used, worn to protect the clothes while the wig was being powdered.

Power dressing

(F)

Period: 1980s.

A term applied to the appearance of business women in tailored suits with wide **padded shoulders**, high-heeled shoes, sleek make-up and back-combed hair. Revived in 2009.

Pregnant stay

(F)

Period: 1811.

A corset enveloping the body from the shoulders to below the hips and elaborately boned, "so as to compress and reduce to the shape desired the natural prominence of the female figure in a state of fruitfulness".

See Maternity wear.

Preppie, preppy

(F & M)

Period: Mid-20th century onwards.

The term, derived from "preparatory", is descriptive of conservative, wealthy, young American students whose choice of clothing is neat and **classic**. Young men in crisp shirts, corduroy slacks or **chinos**, **blazers** or seersucker jackets worn with **loafers**; young women in pleated skirts or **kilts**, white blouses with frilly collars, **Fair Isle** sweaters, cashmere cardigans and simple leather shoes were typical of the tastes of this group.

"The pair of loafers my sons refuse to own because they"re too preppy" (1978, *New York Times*, 6 May).

See Ivy League.

Prêt-à-porter

The French term for **ready-to-wear**.

Prince of Wales' jacket

(M)

Period: 1868.

A loose version of the **reefer**, with three pairs of buttons instead of four.

Prince Rupert

(F)

Period: 1896.

A long, figure-fitting coat of velvet or plush, worn with a blouse and skirt.

Princess dress

(F)

Period: 1840s to mid-20th century.

Also known as **Agnes Sorel**, **Fourreau** and **Gabrielle dress**. A dress made without a seam at the waist, the bodice and skirt being cut in one and the skirt gored. A style popularly associated with the Princess of Wales, later Queen Alexandra, when it was very fashionable ca. 1878–1880.

In the 20th century the style was often known as a **princess line** dress.

Prince's sleeve

(M)

Period: 1830s.

A sleeve with a pointed gore inserted into the seam at the wrist.

Princess line

(F)

Period: 20th century onwards.

Derived from the 19th century **princess dress**, this describes a style which follows the natural outline of the body, with darts providing the shape but without a seam at the waist; the skirt usually wider than that of a **sheath dress**.

Princess petticoat, princess slip

(F)

Period: 1840s onwards.

A petticoat worn as an undergarment with a bodice made in one with the skirt, without a seam at the waist. Popular in the 1870s, when it was buttoned down the back. In 1882 it was buttoned down the front with box pleats behind, which were made to stand out like a bustle by means of tapes attached to side seams underneath and tied together.

In the 20th century a petticoat and bodice in one piece became known as a **slip**.

Princess polonaise

(F)

Period: 1870s.

A polonaise dress made in the princess style. The French term was *petit casaque*.

Princess robe

(F)

Period: 1848.

A day dress made in the princess style without a seam at the waist, the skirt very gored. Trimmed all down the front with buttons and descending lines of ribbon on each side. The sleeves to below the elbows, open and worn with **engageantes**. A style rare at that date.

Protective clothing

(F & M)

Period: 20th century onwards.

Too important to be influenced by fashionable dictates, protective clothing, i.e. garments, accessories and allied equipment that ensure physical wellbeing, improved considerably as a result of man-made fabrics, **space exploration**, and a culture in which health and safety became paramount in some, but not all, countries. The earliest, pre-20th-century protective clothing was designed for warfare, and later, although primitive, for firefighting and surviving in alien environments. Lightweight body armour and flame-retardant fabrics are part of a continuum which, in domestic situations, encompasses PVC aprons, rubber gloves and waterproof coats, which benefited from innovations in protective wear.

Prudent

(M)

Period: End of 18th century.

Thought to have been a winter wrap. "Gentlemen begin to throw off their furs and prudents" (1774, *Westminster Magazine*).

Prussian collar

(M)

Period: 19th and early 20th centuries.

A high, turn-over or **stand-fall** coat collar, usually rather shallow, with the ends nearly meeting in front.

Psychedelic

Period: 1960s.

A term applied to the brilliant colours and combinations of clothing which were a tangible expression of the state of mind of those experimenting with hallucinatory drugs. *See* Hippie style.

Pudding sleeve, puddle sleeve

(M)

Period: 18th century.

A large, loose sleeve, especially of a clergyman's gown. "About each arm a pudding sleeve" (1709, J. Swift, *Baucis and Philemon*); "Recd, for altering a puddle sleve gown into a master sleve…" (1755, Domestic bills, Suffolk Record Office).

Puff

(M)

Period: 19th and early 20th centuries.

A gore of thin fabric filling in a V-shaped gap made in back of the waistband of breeches or trousers; the sides of the gap having lacing holes and a lace so that they can be drawn in to fit, producing a "puff" between.

Puffa

(F & M)

Period: 1975 onwards.

A proprietary name for a quilted garment with a soft, downy filling. This British firm originally produced jackets and reversible gilets, but now provides an extended range of garments for equestrian and fashion wear. The term is often used to describe any type of similar, quilted coat or jacket.

Puffs, pullings out

Period: ca. 1500–1650s.

The effect produced by the drawing out of material, whether shirt or bright-coloured lining, through slashes or panes; a purely decorative device. *See* Panes.

Puff sleeves

(F)

Period: 20th century onwards.

A short sleeve which is especially full at the shoulder, the fabric often gathered into a band. Originally worn by young girls.

Pug hood

(F)

Period: 18th century.

The same as a **short hood**; a soft, limp hood made with pleats radiating from a central point at the back of

the head; with or without a cape. Usually black with a coloured lining turned back to frame the face; tied under the chin with ribbon matching the lining when present.
See Long hood.

Pullings out
See Puffs.

Pullover
(F & M)
Period: 20th century onwards.
A garment for the upper body, usually knitted, without fastenings, and pulled over the head.
See Jumper, Sweater.

Pultney cap
(F)
Period: Mainly 1760s.
A day indoor cap wired up in two curves with a dip in the centre over the forehead. Two optional short **lappets** behind.

Pumps
(F & M)
Period: Second half of 16th century onwards.
Shoes with thin soles and soft uppers, generally of Spanish leather, and flat heels. "Pumps are shooes with single soles and no heels" (1688, R. Holme, *Armory*). Dancing pumps were worn by children.

(M)
Period: 19th century.
Pumps with short quarters and low sides, trimmed with a ribbon bow until ca. 1890; subsequently the tie was omitted. Worn with full evening dress into the 20th century, until replaced by shoes.

(F)
Period: 20th century onwards.
Term used for **plimsolls**; also, in America, for women's **court shoes**.

Punge
(M)
Period: Medieval.
A purse.

Punk fashions
(F & M)
Period: 1970s onwards.
An **alternative** way of dressing espoused by disaffected and unemployed British young people in the mid-1970s, this movement was taken up by mainstream designers. Improvised "deconstruction" was an aspect of the look – black plastic bin liners became garments, lavatory chains, **safety pins** and razor blades parodied jewellery, hair was gelled and coloured, and cosmetics were dark and ghoulish. As with many other sub-cultural groups, the clever re-use of second-hand and surplus-store clothing, often dyed and customized, offered financially hard-pressed youngsters a punk look. Punk and **Goth** styles are closely allied.

Purfle
Period: ca. 1400–18th century.
A decorative border or trimming for a garment; it might be embroidered, have a deep fringe or a fur edge.

Purfled
Period: 16th century.
Edged or bordered with trimming.

Puritan bonnet
(F)
Period: 1893.
A small, flat bonnet without a crown, being oval or triangular with the point in front; trimmed with lace or an **aigret**.

Purl
Period: 16th and 17th centuries.
A pleat or fold of a ruff. "I have seen him sit discontented a whole play, because one of the purls of his band was fallen out of his reach to order again" (1618, N. Field, *Amends for Ladies*).
Also, a kind of silk, gold, silver or metal lace for edging clothing or accessories.

Purse
Period: Medieval onwards.
At first a pouch, but from 14th century a small bag without metal attachments, for carrying money, and capable of being cut free; the cutting of purses by thieves was mentioned in 1362.
Throughout the centuries the shape changed and in the 18th century the knitted "stocking purse" was popular. In the 19th century metal fastenings became general, and from the middle of that century the "sovereign purse", a metal, tubular container with internal springs, holding sovereigns at one end and half-sovereigns at the other, was fashionable. In the 20th century purses were made from many different fabrics and in many sizes and shapes, but leather became usual, often with several internal compartments to carry coins, notes, credit cards, etc.

Pussy-cat bonnet
(F)
Period: 1814–1818.
A bonnet made of catskin, fashionable in those years.

(M)
Also slang for a cheap variety of male silk hat.

Pygostole
(M)
Period: 1860s and 1870s.
A long form of **surtout**, worn with the "mark of the beast" waistcoat.
"The least irreverent of names for the peculiar M.B. coats worn by Tractarian curates."
See Cassock vest.

Pyjama, pyjama suit
(M & F)

Period: 1880s onwards.

Originally loose cotton or silk trousers, tied at the waist and worn by both sexes in Asian and Middle Eastern countries. By the last quarter of the 19th century allied to a loose top, often a jacket-style, the word denoted a sleeping suit made in various colours and often striped; displacing the night-shirt. "The doom of the sleeping shirt is written. Those possessed of any ought to preserve them carefully so that they can show to succeeding generations the wonderfully and fearfully made garments their forefathers slept in.... The pyjama sleeping suit is to take its place…of oriental origin, of silks, etc., generally striped" (1897, *Tailor & Cutter*).

In the 20th century the term was used in conjunction with others, but usually described either the traditional

sleeping outfit for both sexes or lounging pyjamas for women. The latter were worn for evening and casual day-wear from the late 1920s onwards.

Pyramids
(F)
Period: 1858.
Day-skirt trimmings of triangular panels, the base below; the panels were of different colour and material from the dress and were sometimes alternating in two colours.

Pyramid style
(F)
Period: 1845.
A day-skirt trimming of a series of horizontal bands of a fabric such as velvet, diminishing in width from below upwards.

Q

Quadrille head
(F)
Period: Late 18th century.
A fashionable style of cap. "The ladies now wear the lappets to their gauze heads worked with aces of spades, hearts, diamonds and clubs, and call them Quadrille Heads" (1792, *Northampton Mercury*).

Quail-pipe boot
(M)
Period: Late 14th to early 17th century.
A high boot of soft leather which, when worn, fell into folds down the leg and was considered very fashionable. Possibly the, "High shoes that are wrinkled like a quail-pipe" (ca. 1400, Chaucer, *Romaunt of the Rose*). "A gallant that hides his small-timbered legs with a quail-pipe boot" (1602, T. Middleton, *Blurt, Master-Constable*).

Quaker cap
See Joan.

Quaker hat
(M)
Period: 18th century.
A three-cornered **tricorne hat** with a fairly tall crown and an open cock. In the 19th century this was replaced by a wide-brimmed, round hat with a low, flat crown.

Quartered cap
(M)
Period: Mid-18th to mid-19th century.
Worn by boys, a cap with flat, circular crown, the material divided into segments; on a stiff head-band with or without a small visor. "Boys Satin Quarter'd Caps" (1757, *Norwich Mercury*).

Querpo, cuerpo
(M)

Period: 17th century.
The term, from the Spanish word for "body", used to denote a man without a cloak or upper garment; i.e. in body clothing only.
"By my cloak and rapier, it fits not a gentleman of my rank to walk the streets in querpo" (1647, Beaumont and Fletcher, *Love's Curl*).
See Upper garment.

Querpo hood
(F)
Period: 17th century.
A plain, soft hood.

Queue
(M)
Period: Late 17th century onwards.
The pendant tail of a **wig**.

Quilling
Period: 19th century onwards.
Small, round pleats made in lace, tulle or ribbon lightly sewn down, the edge of the trimming remaining in open, flute-like folds. Used for trimming dresses.

Quilted petticoat
(F)
Period: 1710–1750.
Rare before or after. Worn as the skirt of a gown having an overskirt when the petticoat was exposed in front, but essentially part of the dress and not an undergarment.

Period: Early 18th century and after 1850.
An undergarment used in the 18th century to distend the skirt and in the 19th century mainly for warmth; made of satin or alpaca lined with wadding or eiderdown.

Quilted petticoat, ca. 1760 and a detail of the quilting. Copyright the Olive Matthews Collection, Chertsey Museum. Photograph by John Chase.

Quilting

Lines of running stitches made in any material threefold in thickness, i.e. the outer or right side of good material, the under often of wadding, and the third a lining. The stitches made diagonally to form diamonds or a fanciful design, very common in the 18th century, but also later.

Quizzing glass

(F & M)

Period: 18th and early 19th centuries.

A monocle dangling from a neck-chain – a very fashionable accessory; in the 1820s dandies often had the glass fixed into the head of their canes.

Quoif, quafe

See Coif.

R

Rabagas bonnet

(F)

Period: 1872.

A small high-crowned bonnet with a narrow brim turned up all round; the crown trimmed with feathers, flowers or ribbon cascading down behind; tied under the chin with a large ribbon bow. Named for the French dramatist Sardou's political satire of that name.

Radical chic

(F & M)

Period: 1970s onwards.

The styles of dress associated with the fashionable adoption of radical, left-wing ideas and views. Slogan **T-shirts**, recycled clothing and fair trade goods emerged from this movement.

Raglan boot

(M)

Period: Late 1850s.

A boot of soft black leather reaching to mid-thigh and worn when hunting. Named after Lord Raglan (1788–1855), the Crimean War general.

Raglan cape

(M)

Period: 1857 to early 20th century.

A loose sac-like overcoat, single-breasted, often fly-fronted; no vents. Distinguished by the cut of the sleeves at their insertion, first called **pointed sleeves** and later, **Raglan sleeves**. The sleeves of the Raglan cape were very wide at the hand; the pockets without flaps. Often made of waterproofed fabric.

Raglan covert coat

(M)

Period: 1897.

A **covert coat** with Raglan sleeves.

Raglan overcoat

(M)

Period: 1898.

A revival of the **poncho** of the 1850s but with **Raglan sleeves**; full and long; side vents with two buttons. Fly front fastening; generally of waterproof material, replacing the **mackintosh**.

Raglan sleeve

Period: 1857 onwards.

Instead of being inserted into a round arm-hole the sleeve was carried up into a point on the outer seam which ran up to join the collar seam, eliminating a separate shoulder seam, thus preventing the entry of rain. *See* Pointed sleeve.

Rah-rah skirt, Ra-ra skirt

(F)

Period: 1960s onwards.

A short frilly, layered skirt worn by cheerleaders. Popular among young women as a new variant of a **mini skirt** in the 1980s and subsequently.

Rail, Rayle

(F)

Period: Late 15th to late 17th century.

A neckerchief folded and worn shawl-wise round the neck. "The gathered piece of cloth which women throw about their necks when they dress them, is called a Rail" (1678, *Phillips Dictionary*).

See Head rail, Night rail.

Railroad trousers

(M)

Period: ca. 1837–1850.

The name given to trousers with vertical stripes, and soon applied also to trousers with horizontal and vertical stripes.

Railway pockets

(F)

Period: 1857 to early 20th century.

Flat bags with a side opening worn under the dress and tied on with tapes round the waist. When worn with a crinoline dress this was designed to protect valuables from pickpockets.

Raincoat

(F & M)

Period: 20th century onwards.

A coat which is waterproof or water resistant made from natural or synthetic fabrics; of various weights, as thick as a lined winter coat or as light as a thin plastic coat. *See* Mackintosh.

Ramillies wig

(M)

Period: 18th century.

Worn by officers of the Guards and those civilians affecting a military air. A wig with a long **queue** diminishing in size, of plaited hair tied with black ribbon bows above and below or sometimes only below. From 1780 the plait was sometimes turned up and bound by a ribbon tie at the nape of the neck or looped up high and secured by a comb to the back of the wig.

Rampoor-chuddar

(F)

Period: 19th century.

A fine twilled woollen **shawl** from India; in various colours especially red and white. Fashionable in the second half of the century.

Ranelagh mob

(F)

Period: 1760s.

A gauze or fine mignonette bobbin lace **handkerchief** folded diagonally, worn over the head, the point behind; tied under the chin, the two ends then turned back and pinned behind and allowed to hang down the neck.

Copied from the silk handkerchiefs which market-women tied over their ears. A fashionable form of **undress**.

Ranelagh or Rattlesnake tippet

(F)

Period: ca. 1775.

A lightweight lace **tippet**. Made "of fine blond stuck with flowers" (1775, *Lady's Magazine*).

Rasta style

(F & M)

Period: 1930s onwards.

The colours of red, yellow, green and black became the symbol of the Rastafarian movement which began in Jamaica in the mid-1930s. A well known advocate several decades later was the singer Bob Marley (1945–81). Along with long hair woven into dreadlocks an enduringly distinctive aspect of this style is the knitted cap or beret in circles of the symbolic colours. **T-shirts**, **baseball caps**, **trainers**, luggage etc. are also decorated in the familiar colours.

Rational dress

(F)

Period: ca. 1880–1900.

r

One of several attempts to offer greater comfort and ease of movement to women encased in **corsets** and layers of bulky garments. The notable successes were in the adoption of **knickerbockers** for cycling and more practical blouses and simple skirts or suits for travel and business.

Rationals
(F)

Period: 1890s onwards.

A popular name for the knickerbockers worn by young women when bicycling.

See Bloomers.

Rationing
(F & M)

Period: 20th century.

During World War I there was informal rationing of clothing and fabrics, due to shortages. In World War II rationing was systematic in both Britain and the USA with economical items of clothing designed and points allocated to many garments.

See Clothes rationing, National Standard dress, Utility scheme.

Rattan
Period: 17th and 18th centuries.

A cane made from an East Indian palm.

Ready-made clothes
(M)

Period: Late 17th century onwards.

From the 1660s onwards such garments as cloaks, nightgowns and riding habits could be bought in London. Suits, ready-made, for the working classes were being advertised by the middle of the 18th century, e.g.: "Mens and Boys ready made broad and narrow Cloth Cloathes, Ratteen and Frieze Suits… Fustian Cloaths of all Sorts, Everlasting Waistcoats and Breeches, Velvet and Shag Waistcoats and Breeches, Russia Drab Frocks of all sizes, Fearnought and Duffle Coats and Waistcoats…" (1758, May 13 Advertisement, *Norwich Mercury*).

In the 19th and 20th centuries the range widened as homemade garments became less and less common and the term was gradually supplanted by the term **ready-to-wear** which applied to clothing for men and women, though ready-made is still used for men's suits.

Ready-made dresses
(F)

Period: 18th century.

Ready-made dresses for the working classes were being advertised in muslin, calico and gingham, when those materials were popular at the close of the 18th century.

Period: 19th century.

For the middle classes the custom began, in the 1840s, of buying the skirt ready-made with material sufficient for making the close-fitting bodice. By 1865 some ready-made morning dresses of fabrics such as gingham or mohair, were being advertised but so long as the tight-fitting bodice remained fashionable it was impossible to be "in the fashion" without personal fittings by a dressmaker. However throughout the second half of the century considerable progress was made towards persuading women of the qualities of ready-made dresses, though many might have agreed with the opinion that, "Dresses bought ready made in shops are apt to exhibit a distressing similarity" (ca. 1875, *How to Dress Well on a Shilling a Day*).

Period: 20th century onwards.

The simplicity of dresses from the post-World War I period onwards and the growth of department and chain stores and mail order catalogues enabled ready-made dresses to be purchased by all members of society.

Ready-to-wear
(F & M)

Period: Mid-20th century onwards.

The English term for **prèt-â-porter**; the inexpensive collections designed by fashion houses throughout the world. However, the term is often applied to all ready-made clothing.

See Diffusion lines.

Rebato
(F)

Period: ca.1580–1635.

A white collar wired to stand up round the neck of a low-necked bodice to which it was pinned. "Three rebateres of whight loome worke. Rebating wiers" (1589, Essex Record Office).

In the 17th century the term was transferred to the wired support of a collar or ruff. "These great ruffes which are borne up with supporters and rebatoes" (1631, Dent, *The Plaine Man's Pathway to Heaven*).

Redingote
(M)

Period: 1830.

Also called a **polonaise**, this was a greatcoat in military style, of blue cloth buttoned across with silk frogs; sloping flapped pockets on the hips and a fur collar.

(F)

Period: ca.1790–1820

A light overcoat fastening across the bosom. (The bride) "was all over Lace and then put on a plain gown and a silver Redingote for her journey" (1799, *The Jerningham Letters*, ed. E. Castle, 1896).

Period: 1820, commonest from 1835 to 1860s.

A variation of the **pelisse-robe**, a gown derived from the **pelisse**; close-fitting and fastened down the front to the hem. In the 1840s the skirt was often *en tablier* and by 1848 the name had replaced pelisse-robe. By then the bodice and skirt were sometimes separate garments but previously the distinguishing features of the redingote were that it should have the appearance of being a front-opening dress and be close fitting, with lapels.

Period: 1890–ca. 1914.
The name was applied to an outdoor coat with fitted back and semi-fitting front.

Redingote dress
(F)
Period: 1869.
A day dress in the **princess** style with a double-breasted bodice having velvet revers or open over a waistcoat buttoned up to the neck.

Reed hat
(F)
Period: 1879.
A hat of woven reeds capable of assuming any shape; worn for tennis or when bathing.

Reefer
(M)
Period: 1860 onwards.
A very short double-breasted jacket with three or four pairs of buttons, low collar and short lapels; no back seam but short vents in the side seams; the fronts cut square. Sometimes worn as an overcoat; in the 1890s it was only fashionable when so worn.
See Pilot coat, Pea jacket, Yachting jacket.

Reefer jacket
(F)
Period: 1890s.
An outdoor double-breasted jacket of blue serge, resembling the male garment.

Re-enactment costume
(F & M)
Period: 1960s onwards.
Groups and societies who organize and promote certain historical periods by, for instance, fighting battles wearing garments that are carefully researched and made as similar as possible to surviving originals in private and public collections. An important movement in Europe, North America and the UK which has contributed considerable practical knowledge to dyeing, spinning, weaving and making clothing following archival evidence. The American Civil War, the Napoleonic wars in Europe and the English Civil War of the 17th century are especially well represented and such groups are used by film and TV companies and add a degree of authenticity with their scrupulous copying of past fashions and military kit. Galleries, heritage centres, museums and stately homes use re-enactors as practical educators; such groups and individuals often discuss how the clothing is made, how it feels, its impact on movement and so forth.

Regatta shirt
(M)
Period: ca. 1840.
A striped shirt of cambric or Oxford shirting for informal outdoor wear in the summer. The front without pleats or frill.

Regency hat
(F)
Period: ca. 1810.
A fur hat with turned-up brim and a gold hat-band.

Reister clok, Reiter cloak
(M)
Period: 1570s–1670s.
A full knee-length cloak sometimes with a flat square falling collar; sometimes caped.
See French cloak.

Religious petticoat
(F)
Period: 17th century.
Petticoats, in the sense of skirts, embroidered with religious stories by Puritan women. "She works religious petticoats…" (1631, Jasper Mayne, *The City Match*).

Resort wear
(F)
Period: 20th century.
An American term for the range of clothing worn for holidays at fashionable resorts; including beach wear, swim wear etc.

Reticule, Ridicule
(F)
Period: ca.1800–1820s.
A lady's **handbag**, commonly lozenge-shaped or circular, of velvet, satin, silk, red morocco or made of coloured beads and drawn in with a running string. It contained a handkerchief, purse, scent-bottle, etc., and was much used in the absence of dress pockets in this period.
See Indispensible.

Retro
Period: Late 20th century.
Looking back at earlier styles of dress, though usually within living memory, and incorporating actual items of clothing and forms of presentation into current fashions.
See Vintage.

Revers
Period: 14th century onwards.
Initially the term meant facings or borderings to a garment, generally of fur. Subsequently the term meant the turned-back edge of coat, waistcoat or bodice. From the 20th century onwards it often meant the **lapel**.

Reversible clothing
Period: 19th century onwards.
An item of clothing, often a coat or jacket which can be turned inside out and worn displaying a different colour or fabric. Discussing housebreakers' night-time

r

WALKING DRESS.

English **fashion plate**, hand coloured ca. 1805. The **accessories** are the main focus with a **feather** trimmed **bonnet**, a short **mantle** with trailing points trimmed with tassels, plain buff **gloves** and a modest **reticule**, the small bag which replaced pockets when dresses became narrower. Private collection.

behaviour a journalist wrote, "On such occasions they often wear "reversibles", or coats which may be worn inside out; one side being of a bright, the other of a dark colour" (1863, *Cornhill Magazine*).

Rhinegraves
See Petticoat breeches.

Rhinestone
Period: Late 19th century onwards.
An imitation diamond of glass or **paste** originally used in the theatre but taken up by mainstream jewellers; it was especially popular in the first half of the 20th century.

Riband, Ribbon
Period: 14th and 15th centuries.
The border of a garment.

Period: 16th century onwards.
A narrow band of silk or decorative fabric used on clothing and accessories.

Ridicule
See Reticule.

Riding boots
Period: Medieval onwards.
In many forms and styles across the centuries but usually of sturdy leather and usually knee-length, sometimes higher.

Riding coat
(M)
Period: 1825–1870s.
A term applied to a short-skirted coat, the fronts slanting away from the waist level, with pockets in the pleats; later, flapped pockets on the hips were added. The corners of the skirts were rounded. The slope away from the midline in front steadily increased, starting above the waist level, producing a series having distinctive names:

Period: 1830s.
Also called a **Morning walking coat** but by 1838 becoming known as the **Newmarket coat**.

Period: 1850–1870.
Known in the 1850s as a **cutaway coat** but in the 1860s evolving into the **shooting coat**.

Period: 1870s.
It now became "the **morning coat**" the latest adaptation of the old Newmarket Riding coat" (*The Tailor & Cutter*).

Period: 20th century onwards.
The term riding coat is often applied to long, knee-length or longer waterproof coats such as **Drizabone**.

Riding coat dress
(F)
Period: 1785–ca.1800.
A dress resembling a greatcoat with deep collar and large lapels; buttoned all down the front and slightly trained; long tight sleeves.
See Greatcoat dress.

Riding dress-coat
(M)
Period: 1800s–1860s.
A coat with **cut-ins** at the waist, resembling a shortened **tail-coat** with corners rounded. Worn for riding in town.

Riding dress frock coat
(M)
Period: 1820s.
A **frock coat** with deep collar and large lapels; for wearing on horseback in town.

Riding habit

(F)

Period: 18th century.

An outfit specially designed for women riding side-saddle on horseback. It consisted of coat and waistcoat modelled on the male garments, together with a skirt, called a petticoat, made without a train, until 1780 when a train was added. The **riding coat dress** was also worn.

Period: 19th century.

At first the riding habit was a gown resembling the **riding coat dress** and often trimmed with **brandenburgs**; subsequently it was made in the **redingote** style, and by 1840 a jacket and long trained skirt became the usual style. By 1860 the skirt was now cut so as to fit over the pommel and in the 1870s trousers were worn under the habit skirt. Around 1890 skirts began to be made without trains.

Period: 20th century.

Early in the century **apron skirts** were worn over breeches and, for riding astride divided skirts were usual or ankle-length coats over breeches. By 1920 jackets and breeches without skirts were depicted in fashion magazines and by 1930 breeches and boots or jodhpurs had almost superseded the traditional riding habit amongst the young.

Riding hat

(F & M)

The concept of a style of hat specifically worn for riding is associated with horse racing which required jockeys to shield their eyes from bright light and keep their hair away from the face. A soft-crowned peaked cap was worn in the late 17th century but it was more usual for both sexes to wear three cornered hats in the 18th century. In the 19th century shortened versions of the top hat, with a veil for women, were popular and only in the 20th century did it become usual for a hard-crowned version of the jockey cap with a narrow brim to be worn by men and, later, by women.

See Jockey cap.

Riding hoop

(F)

Period: 1720s.

A small hoop sometimes worn on horseback. "Riding habits £4:17:0. Riding Hoop-petty-coats, two, 17/–" (1723, *Blundell's Diary and Letters*).

Rigoletto mantle

(F)

Period: 1835.

A knee-length mantle with pelerine cape; of satin edged with fur.

Ring

(F & M)

Period: Medieval onwards.

Apart from the "Ladies in the Dress of 1794" this plate also depicts a small boy in a **skeleton suit**. The woman to the left is wearing a **riding habit** while her companion is in day or morning dress. Copyright the Olive Matthews Collection, Chertsey Museum. Photograph by John Chase.

Normally an item of jewellery worn on one or more fingers. Often connected with rites of passage, engagement, marriage and so forth when initials or a simple message is inscribed within the ring, but also used to indicate role (bishop), status (signet ring) or wealth when precious stones of considerable size are set in precious metal. **Costume jewellery** includes rings made from glass, plastic and other non-precious materials. Rings have also been worn on the toes and inserted into the nose and other areas of the body.

See Body piercing.

Riveling, Rilling

(F & M)

Period: 12th–14th century.

A shoe of raw hide with the hair on the outside.

See Brogues.

Robe

(M)

Period: Medieval.

From the French meaning a gown; a term which came to be used for ceremonial wear. A secondary meaning was of a loose outer garment later a more usual term for a **dressing gown**.

See Gown.

(F)

Period: 18th century.

A rare term unless describing a French style of dress.

Period: 19th century.

Descriptive of a woman's dress consisting of an under-dress or skirt with an over-dress; the skirt being open in front and usually long behind, but the term was also loosely used for a gown.

The term was sometimes used for an outdoor garment or **pelisse** which developed into the **pelisse-robe**.

Robe de chambre

(F & M)

Period: Early 18th century onwards.

A style of **dressing gown** often made from a luxurious fabric.

Robe de soir

(F)

French term for evening dress.

Robe de style

(F)

Period: 1920s.

French term for the style of dress with a longer, fuller skirt which contrasted with the narrow chemise outline preferred for much of that decade.

Robe à l'Anglaise

(F)

Period: 18th century.

A fitted gown especially popular in Britain. It had various styles of bodice including the stomacher front, the but-toned front (*compère*) which was a false waistcoat sewn to the inner lining of the bodice, and the closed front. In the 1770s it assumed a hybrid form combining the fitted bodice back of the **mantua** with the back pleats of the **sack** but these were so reduced in size that they became seams. The **fourreau** back was also found in the 1770s but in the 1780s there was a division at the waist.

Robe à la Piémontèse

See Piedmont gown.

Robin, Robings

(F)

Period: 18th and 19th centuries.

Broad flat trimmings decorating a gown round the neck and down the front of the bodice, and sometimes con-tinued down the borders of an open over-skirt to the hem.

Robin front

(F)

Period: 19th century.

A bodice trimmed with **robings** descending from the shoulders to meet at the waist, forming a deep V-point.

Rockers

(F & M)

Period: 1960s.

The antithesis of **Mods** but always listed with them due to the stand-offs between both groups in the early 1960s. Although they were keen fans of rock music they were much less interested in fashion than the Mods. Rockers, male and female, had long hair, scruffy **jeans** and leather jackets as a tribute to their devotion to powerful motor bikes and their idol Marlon Brando (1924–2004) in *The Wild One* (1954). In many respects, Rockers are the precursors of later biker groups, tough, leatherclad and indifferent to fashion.

Rocket, Rochet, Roket, Roget

(F & M)

Period: 14th and 15th centuries.

A woman's gown, usually of white linen. Also worn by the clergy.

Period: 16th and 17th centuries.

A cloak of any colour. "A scant cloak without a cape" (1688, R. Holme, *Armory*).

Roguelo dress

(F)

Period: 1807.

A bodice close fitting in front and trimmed with **rob-ings**, but the back loose like a **sack**; a low collar with a triangular cape.

Roll

(M)

Period: 15th century.

The circular pad of the **chaperon** when the hood is converted into a cap or hat. The roll was often of a dif-ferent colour, e.g.: "a hode of skarlet with a rolle of purpill felwet…item, 1 gret rollyd cappe of sangweyn greyred" (1459, *Fastolfe Inventory*).

Roll, Rolls, Rowles

(F)

Period: 16th and 17th centuries.

Pads over which the front hair was turned to raise it from the forehead. "The heare of a woman that is laied over her foreheade, gentyl women did lately calle them their rolles" (1548, Elyot, *Dictionary*).

Roll collar

Period: 19th century onwards.

The turn-over of a coat or waistcoat collar rolled in a curve and without a notch between it and the lapel. After ca.1840 the name persisted for such a collar al-though it was laid flat.

Roll farthingale
See Bum roll.

Rollio
Period: 19th century.
A trimming of material rolled into a very narrow tubular shape.
See Rouleaux.

Roll-on
(F)
Period: 1930s onwards.
A lightweight elasticated **corset** without fastenings.

Roll-up breeches
(M)
Period: Late 17th to mid-18th century.
Breeches worn with roll-up stockings and therefore buttoned and not buckled at the knee. "Roule up breeches made buttoned downe the sides" (1679, The Isham Accounts).

Rollups, Rollers, Roll-up stockings, Rolling stockings or hose
(M)
Period: Late 17th to mid-18th century.
Long stockings drawn up over the knee of knee-breeches and then turned over in a broad flat roll. (Stolen) "½ doz. pair of Roll stockins and 18 pair of short stockins" (1697, *London Gazette*).

Roman dress
Period: 100 BCE to ca. 300 CE.
Clothing worn by citizens of Rome and its empire. Derived from classical Greek garments they allowed fluidity of movement with their simple, practical shapes and constructions.
See Tunica, Toga, Palla, Pallium, Stola.

Roman T-beard
See Hammercut beard.

Romantic dress
(F & M)
Period: Early 19th century.
At a time when there were distinctive qualities identifiable in art, literature, music which were opposed to the tenets of classicism, the softening of outlines, the revival of late medieval and renaissance edges and decorative elements were found in clothing, especially that of women.
See Medici collar, Vandyking.

Romper suit
(F & M)
Period: 20th century onwards.
Colloquially called rompers and descriptive of a child's all-in-one outfit for play. Also, an informal garment worn by young women. Used by the army as slang for all or part of battle dress.

Roquelaure, Roculo, Roccelo, Rocklo
(M)
Period: 1700–1750.

A knee-length cloak with a single or double cape-collar, and buttoned down the front; a back vent for wearing on horseback. "Lost, Blue Cloak or Roculo with brass buttons" (1744, *Boston News Letter*).

Rosebery collar
(M)
Period: 1894.
A white linen detachable collar, standing nearly three inches high behind, the points in front rounded off. Named after the British Prime Minister Lord Rosebery (1847–1929).

Roses
(F & M)
Period: ca. 1610–1680.
Large decorative rosettes of ribbon or lace, often jewelled or spangled, mainly for shoes but also used on garters and hat-bands.

Rotonde
(F)
Period: 1850s.
A short circular mantle, generally of the same fabric as the dress.
See Talma mantle.

Rouleaux
(F)
Period: 19th century onwards.
Lengths of material loosely puffed into a tubular shape, and used for trimmings of dresses, especially the bottom of skirts, in the 1820s. Used intermittently at later periods as a decorative feature on various articles of clothing but usually made as long narrow tubes of fabric cut on the cross.

Roulettes
See Pipes, Bilboquets.

Round dress or gown
(F)
Period: Late 18th to mid-19th century.
A term indicating a dress with joined bodice and skirt, the latter closed all round rather than open in front to expose an underskirt. In the 18th century it was occasionally made with a slight train. During the 19th century there was no train; the term actually meant a dress without a train.

Round-eared cap
(F)
Period: 1730s–1760s.
A white indoor cap curving round the face to the level of the ears or below. The front border with a single or double frill, generally with a small ruffle and "pinch" in the centre. The back of the cap without a frill and drawn together by a running string. The back of the cap was shallow, exposing much of the back hair.
Side lappets were optional, and single or double, attached to the lower borders of the front frills. Single lappets were often pinned up to the crown or loosely

r

tied under the chin, a style common with servants. From ca.1745 the frill at the sides widened and was starched and later wired to stand away from the face as "vast winkers". At the same time the top of the cap narrowed with a small V-shaped pleat in the centre – "a pinched cap", and lappets became less usual. The fabrics used included cambric, lace, gauze, and net, often with a bright silk lining; there were optional trimmings of ribbons, feathers or small artificial flowers. Occasionally called a **coif**.

Round hat
(M)
An informal hat which began to replace the tricorne in the 1770s.

Round hose
(M)
Period: 1550s–1610.
A form of trunk-hose padded and distended to resemble the shape of an onion.
See French hose and Trunk-hose.

Roundlet
(M)
Period: 17th century
A term for the **roll** of the **chaperon** of the 15th century.

Roxalane bodice
(F)
Period: 1829 onwards.
A low-necked bodice trimmed with broad bands of pleated folds across the top, sloping down to the centre and there meeting at an angle. The bodice always had a central bone down to the waist.

Roxalane sleeve
(F)
Period: 1829 onwards.
A bouffant sleeve for evening dress; puffed out above and below the elbow and there confined just above the bend by a fringed band. Worn with or without a **manchette** of white blonde lace.

Roxburgh muff
(F)
Period: 1816
A swansdown muff caught in by a series of bands of white satin.

Royal George stock
(M)
Period: 1820s–1830s.
A stock of black Genoa velvet and satin, the satin sloping down across the velvet and tied in a bow in front.

Rubens bonnet
(F)
Period: 1872.
A small bonnet with brim turned up on one side; trimmed above with a bow and a feather.

Rubens hat
(F)

Period: 1870s and 1880s.
A hat with a high crown and brim turned up on one side; many variations were made.

Ruche, Rouche
Period: Early 19th century onwards
Usually a narrow frill of a gathered or pleated lightweight fabric such as gauze or lace to trim a garment or accessory.

Rucksack
(F & M)
Period: Late 19th century onwards.
A bag carried on the back and held by two straps over the shoulders; made from various materials including canvas and leather. Originally used for hiking and walking, later for other uses.

Ruff
(F & M)
Period: 1560s–1640s.
A circular collar of cambric, lawn or similar fabric, in the form of a starched and **goffered** frill radiating from the neck; at first attached to the shirt collar band but by 1570 it had become a separate article. It was usually closed all round for men, but also worn by both sexes with a gap under the chin.

The tubular folds were known as **sets** and formed by moulding them by means of setting sticks. Ruffs were tied with tasselled **band-strings**.

Named varieties included the **falling ruff** worn ca. 1615–1640. This was gathered without being set into formal pleats, and was sewn to a high neckband from which it fell down to the shoulders. The **short ruff** was a small version favoured by Puritans during the early 17th century. The **oval ruff**, worn ca.1625–1650 was a female fashion only. It comprised a "large closed Ruff set in formal tubular pleats spreading laterally over the shoulders"; it was often worn with a beaver hat with a spreading brim. During the 17th century women's ruffs sometimes had a small neck-frill of gauze or lace added to the inner border of the ruff.

Period: 18th century onwards.
Revived on a small scale for women from the 1740s–1830, and again from 1874–1900. Also occasional use in the 20th century.

Ruffled shirt
(M)
Period: 18th to mid-19th century.
A shirt with a **goffered** frill down the chest; worn for day and evening dress but from ca.1840 becoming gradually limited to evening only. The frill, which projected forward, varied in width up to three inches.

Ruffles
(F & M)
Period: ca. 1550 to late 17th century.

A somewhat rare term in the 16th century but synonymous with **hand ruff**, attached to the shirt sleeve. "Very unseemly ruffles at their hands" (1571, MS. Letter, Library of Corpus Christi College).

(M)
Period: 17th to early 19th centuries, later 20th century. The frilled front of men's shirts.

(F)
Period: ca.1690–ca. 1800.
Deep flounces of lace or cambric, worn with elbow-length sleeves; often multiple with scalloped edges.

Period: 1800 onwards.
A frilled edge to a collar, cuffs and a decorative finish to other garments.

Rullion
Period: 17th century.
A shoe made of undressed hide, possibly Scottish in origin.

Rump, Rump-furbelow, False rump
(F)
Period: 18th century.
A small crescent-shaped hip pad placed beneath the dress at either the back or sides; very prominent between 1770 and 1790 but later, if worn, very small.
See Cork rump.

Running clothes
(M)
Period: Late 17th to mid-18th century.
The clothing worn by a Running Footman; a type of **livery**. "Francis Robinson, running footman…running clothes…drawers, stockings, pumps, cap, sash, and petticoat-breeches" (1720, Wages, Duke of Somerset's Servants, *Gentleman's Magazine,* lxi).

Russian blouse
(F)
Period: 1890s.
A loose tunic-bodice falling to the knees in front and a little longer behind, and confined at the waist by a belt. Revived in the 20th century.

Russian fur hat
(F & M)
Period: 20th century.
Also called a Cossack or Zhivago hat, both terms indicative of the original inspiration and its popularity outside Russia. A fur hat, often of **astrakhan** or a thick, dense fur, with no brim and a medium height crown.

Russian jacket
(F)
Period: 1865.
A short sleeveless jacket worn over a sleeved waistcoat.

Russian vest
See Garibaldi bodice.

S

Sabot sleeve
(F)
Period: 19th century.
A variation of the **bouffant**; a single or double puffed-out extension above the elbow, worn with evening dress from 1827 to 1836 and for day wear from 1836 to 1840, then becoming the **Victoria sleeve**.

Sac, sack, sacque
(F)
Period: 16th to late 17th century.
A loose gown, possibly for country wear. "Frumpton's wench in the frieze sack…at the milking time" (1599, George Peele, *Sir Clyomon*).

Period: Late 17th and 18th centuries.
"My wife this day put on first her French gown call'd a Sac" (1669, *Pepys' Diary*).
This was an informal gown and in its earliest form it hung loose at both back and front, descending from shoulder to hem in a pyramid shape. This style retained

its popularity in the first half of the 18th century as **maternity wear**.

In its fashionable form in the early 18th century, it had loose, unstitched pleats at front and back, and the front was stitched from waist to hem or left open revealing a petticoat.

In the 1730s the pleats became more structured, set into two double box pleats and the bodice was fitted closer to the body. By the 1750s the sack, worn as an open robe, had almost replaced the **mantua** as the preferred style for formal dress. During the 1770s it became unfashionable, but was retained for certain court events. From 1770s the box pleats were sometimes sewn down to the waist, as in the **robe à l'Anglaise** or cut loose as in the **robe à la Piémontèse**.

Sack-back jacket
(F)
Period: 1896.
A short, loose jacket, often edged with fur.

Sack dress

(F)

Period: 1960 onwards.

A loose, short dress, often shaped into a narrower hemline. Designed by the Spanish couturier Cristóbal Balenciaga (1895–1972), it was copied by other designers and makers.

Sac overcoat

(M)

Period: 1840s to ca. 1875.

A loose overcoat reaching nearly to the knees; with four button-holes in front; cross-pockets with narrow welts also at the front. Its large sleeves were also wide at the wrist. Made with a whole back having a short slit at the bottom. The edges bound or double-stitched. In the 1860s it buttoned high; a very narrow collar and lapels with three or four button-holes in front; pockets were optional. Some styles had velvet collar, lapels and cuffs.

Safari jacket, safari suit

(M, later F)

Period: 19th century onwards.

Clothing created for cross-country expeditions in the 19th century, especially in East Africa. Suitable clothing for Europeans had to be both sturdy and lightweight and included a pith-helmet-style hat or solar topi, the former made from dried pith, the latter an Indian term for any European hat protecting the head from the sun. Other items included a shirt, jacket and trousers of sturdy cotton, often pale coloured, boots and puttees, strips of protective leather or fabric wrapped around the legs. The style of jacket with its belt, vented back, pleated outside pockets with flaps and buttoned front was not dissimilar to the **Norfolk jacket**. The apparently glamorous locations used in 20th-century films as a backdrop to these rugged garments ensured that versions of such styles inspired fashion designers.

Safeguard

(F)

Period: Early 16th to late 18th century.

An overskirt worn when travelling on horseback or riding, to protect from dirt or cold. Occasionally in the form of a large apron. Usually worn with a cloak or a **jupe**. Also a term for infant bands, "A safe-guard, a sort of swathing band for a young child" (1706, Phillip's *World of Words*, ed. J. Kersey).

See Foot-mantle.

Period: 1745–1790.

In the West of England known as a **seggard** but with its earlier use.

(M)

A coloured stuff apron, also protective; worn by bakers, etc.

Safety pin

Period: 1878 onwards.

The Danish safety pin, with wide protective sheath covering the point, came into use and was subsequently made in various sizes and types of metal.

Sailor blouse

(F)

Period: 1890s.

Worn by school-girls; a white linen blouse with blue cuffs and turned-over collar, imitating that worn in the Navy.

Sailor collar

(F)

Period: Late 19th century onwards.

The wide, flat collar derived from sailors' uniforms appeared on coats, jackets, blouses, etc. and was especially popular during World War I and World War II.

Sailor hat

(F)

Period: 1860s.

A crinoline hat with low, flat crown and wide, drooping brim; ribbon and feather trimming.

Period: 1880s.

A straw **boater** with slight variations in depth of crown and width of brim.

(M)

Period: 1880s.

A popular form of headgear for small boys; a straw hat with wide, évasé brim and ribbon round the base of the crown, often embroidered with the fanciful name of a ship.

Sailor's reef knot tie

(M)

Period: 1870s onwards.

A popular form of tying the necktie, the central knot presenting vertical borders at the sides, the ends flowing loosely, often with a gap between. Most fashionable in the 1890s and rivalling the **four-in-hand** tie. Made with square and with pointed ends in the 20th century.

Sailor suit

(M)

Period: ca. 1870.

A popular style of dress for small boys, comprising at first a sailor's blouse worn with either a baggy pair of **knickerbockers** or **Danish trousers** with open bottoms and reaching just below the knees.

Period: ca. 1880 onwards.

The suit developed a wide, turn-over, white collar and the knickerbockers acquired closer-fitting legs. An alternative form was Jack Tar trousers with **bell bottoms** of ankle length. Usual accessories were a lanyard and boatswain's whistle. Made of blue serge trimmed with braid and worn with a **sailor hat**.

Sailor trousers

(F)

Period: 20th century onwards.

Trousers designed to fasten in the traditional naval man-ner, with a fall front which buttons at the top and sides.

Salopettes
(M, later F)
Period: 20th century onwards.
The French term for workmen's overalls with a high waist, bib-style front, and shoulder straps which, when adapted to fit closely around the ankles, became a favoured item of ski-wear in the post-1950 period. Waterproof versions were recommended to beginners.

Salt-box pocket
(M)
Period: ca. 1790.
A popular name for the rectangular, flapped waistcoat pocket which had replaced the scalloped flap.

Sandal
(M)
Period: Medieval to 16th century.
A term applied to an item of footwear consisting of a sole attached by straps variously arranged over the foot.

Period: 1600 to early 20th century.
Worn by monastic orders and pilgrims.

(F & M)
Period: 1920s onwards.
Various forms of lightweight and more substantial san-dals were introduced for beachwear and, eventually for general summer use.
See Birkenstock sandals.

Sandal-shoes, sandal-slippers
(F)
Period: 1790 to end of 19th century.
Thin-soled slippers cut low over the foot, with flat heels; tied on by criss-cross ribbons over the instep and round the ankle. For indoor and evening wear.

Sanitary ball dress
(F)
Period: 1890.
A ball dress with an under-bodice of cream or pink kid to protect the chest against the influenza epidemic of that year.

Sansflectum crinoline
(F)
Period: 1860.
A washable **cage crinoline**, the hoops covered with **gutta-percha** and others fitted with a detachable flounce.

Santon, sautoir
(F)
Period: 1820s.
A coloured silk **cravat** often worn with a small **ruff** which it served to support.

Sardinian sac
(M)
Period: 1856.

A loose, single-breasted sac overcoat, the collar cut square, without lapels; full, bell-shaped sleeves "which are not used but allowed to fall loosely". Fastened by a cord and tassel in front.

Sari, saree
(F)
A length of cotton or silk arranged around the body and passed across one shoulder; the principal item of dress of Hindu women.

Sarong
(F, occasionally M)
A Malay term meaning "sheath" and descriptive of a long strip of cloth worn around the waist or under the arm-pits. Traditional dress for Malay and Javanese of both sexes, but appropriated for beachwear by western women and, rarely, men from the mid-20th century onwards.

Sarpe, serpe
(M)
Period: 15th century.
A decorative collar worn round the neck and lying on the shoulders, as distinguished from a chain.

Sash
(F & M)
Period: 16th century onwards.
A band or scarf of soft material, the ends tied but not buckled or otherwise fastened; worn round the waist or over the shoulder for ornamental purpose.

(M)
Period: 16th–18th century.
Sashes were used as part of uniform and in non-military contexts with informal dress.
See Burdash.

(F)
Period: 16th century onwards.
Worn with négligé garments until the 18th century, when sashes were worn with dresses and varied in width. Subsequently they appeared from time-to-time, of vari-ous styles and fabrics.

Sashoon, sashune
(M)
Period: Late 17th century.
A leather pad worn on the leg and inside a boot. "Stuffed or quilted leather to be bound about the small of the leg of such as have long heels, to thicken the leg, that the boot may sit straight and be without wrinkles" (1688, R. Holme, *Armory*).

Saucer-collar
(F)
Period: 1898.
The high, splayed-out collar worn on fashionable day dresses.

Sautoir
(F)

Period: 20th century onwards.

A long necklace of pearls or a long gold chain set with gemstones.

See Santon.

Saxon embroidery

See English work.

S-B

(M)

Period: 19th century.

Tailor's term for **single-breasted**, as descriptive of a coat or waistcoat.

S-bend

(F)

Period: Late 1890s and early 1900s.

A term applied to the curving silhouette created by the corsetry of the time.

Scabilonians, scavilones

(M)

Period: 1550–1600.

Apparently a new fashion of **drawers**, possibly of Muscovite origin. "Nayler put off hys nether stockes and so bare foote and bare legged save his silke scavilones to the ankles – came in" (1571, *Holinshed's Chronicle*).

See Barrel hose.

Scalings, scaling hose

(M)

Period: 1550–1600.

Possibly a new fashion in knee-breeches resembling **Venetians**. "For a lace to drewe his skalinge hose together benethe the knee" (1566, Sir Philip Sidney's Accounts).

Scallop

An ornamental border indented with segments of a circle so as to resemble the edge of a scallop shell.

Scalpette

(F)

Period: 1876.

"A false front of invisible net to which luxuriant tresses are attached." Worn across the front of the crown of the head to cover thinning hair; an American invention.

Scanties

(F)

Period: 1920s onwards.

A term for particularly short **panties**.

Scarborough hat

(F)

Period: 1862.

A hat with a deep, turned-up brim in front, sloping to a point behind; much worn at that time, though considered by many to be "rather vulgar".

Scarborough Ulster

(M)

Period: 1892.

An **Ulster** with a cape and a hood but without sleeves.

Scarf

(F & M)

Period: Mid-16th century onwards.

A narrow strip of fabric worn for warmth or show round the neck and/or over the shoulders. Sometimes in the 16th and 17th centuries worn by men like a **baldrick**. However, the term increasingly became applied to a scarf as understood in the 20th century.

See Muffler.

(M)

Period: 1830 to early 20th century.

A very large **cravat** spreading over the shirt-front and usually held in place by a decorative tie-pin. By the end of the 19th century the term was being applied within the trade to any pendant **necktie** with ends much wider than the middle.

Scarf drapery

(F)

Period: 1870s.

Trimming consisting of fabric draped across the front of a skirt, the fold or "scarf" trimmed with flounces, frills and ribbons variously arranged.

Scarf veil

See Veil.

Scholl's

(F & M)

Period: 1959 onwards.

The original Dr Scholl's exercise sandal was introduced in 1959 and became a world-wide favourite. It had a beechwood base for the foot, with an adjustable leather strap across the foot and a rubber sole. It offered support and exercise and was one of many footwear products and treatments devised by Chicago-born Dr William Scholl, through a career which started in 1904 and only ended with his death in 1968.

Scissoring

See Slashing.

Scoop neckline

(F)

Period: 1950s onwards.

A rounded, low-cut neckline on any female garment, either revealing flesh or another garment, such as a blouse beneath a jumper when the latter has a scoop neckline.

Scotch farthingale

(F)

Period: Late 16th and early 17th centuries.

Apparently similar to a **wheel farthingale**. "A Scottish farthingale…prithee fit, fit it…. Is this a right Scot? Does it clip close and bear up round?" (1605, Marston and Chapman, *Eastward Hoe*).

Scratch bob, scratch wig

(M)

Period: 1740–1800.

A **bob-wig**, sometimes with one curl, covering only the

S

back part of the head, the natural hair being brushed up over it in front. "The one-curled Scratch" (1764, *The Oxford Sausage*).

Scrip

Period: Medieval.

A **pouch** or wallet.

Scrunchie

(F)

Period: Late 20th century onwards.

An American method of holding the hair in a pony tail or similar style drawn away from the face. An elasticated band is covered by a loose, encircling layer of fabric; sometimes decorative effects involving beads or flowers are used. The first appearance was in the late 1980s and the style spread swiftly.

Scye

(M)

Period: 19th century.

Tailoring term for the curved lower segment of the arm-hole of a coat.

Sea cap

(M)

Period: Late 15th to early 17th century.

Probably similar to a **Monmouth cap**.

Sea coat

(M)

Period: Late 15th to end of 17th century.

A lined and hooded coat mostly worn by seamen.

Sea-gown

(Possibly M)

Period: Late 15th to early 17th century.

A **wrap** worn at sea.

Sealskin coat

(F)

Period: 1880s.

Especially fashionable at that time, it was a coat full at the back and, from ca. 1882 to 1888, trimmed with a broad, flat bow over the **bustle**.

Seamstress, sempstress

(F)

Period: 16th century onwards.

A woman who does plain sewing, as opposed to providing the more complex skills required within the cutting and making of garments. "To the Old Exchange, and there, of my pretty seamstress, bought four bands" (1665, Pepys' *Diary*, 8 April).

Second-hand clothing

(F & M)

Period: 17th century onwards.

Clothing was constantly recycled and remade, and throughout history it seems likely that alongside clothing handed over to family and friends and remodelled, there was always a thriving market in dealing in such clothing. Certainly in the 1830s, in the UK, second-hand clothiers had to be licensed. In the 20th century the development

of charity shops added a new dimension to this trade.

See-through clothing

(M)

Period: 1930s.

Male swim suits without upper sections covering the chest caused comment in the 1930s but gradually became accepted.

(F)

Period: 1960s onwards.

The American designer Rudi Gernreich (1922–1985) introduced a topless swim suit for women which caused considerable scandal in 1964, but by 1968 Yves Saint Laurent (1936–2008) had included a see-through blouse in his collections. In later decades, transparent fabrics

Old Cloaks, Suits or Coats from Laroon's *Cryes of London*, ca. 1687/8. This is the poor street tradesman's scruffy, pared back version of the squire of Alsatia's clothing. He deals in **second-hand clothing**. He cannot afford a wig or coat but wears a skimpy **cloak** over a **sleeved waist-coat** and **breeches**. Even his shoes are unmatched and his wares are old fashioned. Private collection.

and increasingly skimpy clothing became acceptable in Europe and North America.

Seggard

See Safeguard.

Seint

(F & M)

Period: Medieval.

A girdle.

See Ceint.

Selvage

Period: 14th century onwards.

The edge of a piece of fabric so woven as to prevent unravelling.

Semicircled farthingale, demi-circled farthingale

(F)

Period: ca. 1580–1620.

See French farthingale.

Sempstress bonnet

(F)

Period: 1812.

A bonnet tied on with very long, broad ribbon strings crossed under the chin and then brought up to the summit of the crown and there tied in a bow.

Señorita

(F)

Period: 1860s.

A short muslin jacket shaped like a **bolero**, with elbow sleeves, worn over a dinner dress.

Sequin

Period: 1880s onwards.

From the Italian term *zecchino* meaning a gold coin, the sequin was similar to the pierced metal **spangles** of an earlier period which were sewn to clothing and accessories. From the 20th century they were usually made of light composition, often plastic, and produced in many colours and several sizes and shapes.

Serge

Period: 19th century.

Term used to describe a kind of over-sewing often used on the raw edges of seams to prevent unravelling of the cloth.

See Glossary of Fabrics and Materials.

Serpent, dragon

(F)

Period: 18th century.

A long, hanging lock of hair rolled back upon itself. "These serpents or dragons are seldom worn but at Court balls or by actresses on the stage" (1768, G. Bickham, *The Ladies' Toilet*).

Sets

See Ruff.

Settee

(F)

Period: Late 17th century.

The double lappets of a woman's indoor cap.

Sewing machine

Period: ca. 1790 onwards.

After many experiments in Europe and North America, using various stitches, I. M. Singer patented his lock-stitch machine in 1851 and his firm soon dominated the international market. This machine revolutionized domestic and professional making of clothing, and many competitors invented or refined the original concept, but Singer and sewing machine became synonymous from the mid-19th century onwards until challenged by other makers in the 20th century.

Shade

(F)

Period: ca. 1750 to early 19th century.

A transparent section of net, gauze or lace worn to shade the bosom of a very low-necked gown. The shade sometimes had a small, attached ruff at the neck. A fashion which was at its height in the 1750s.

Shadow

(F)

Period: ca. 1580–1640.

Similar to a **bongrace** but not part of a hood. Made of velvet, linen or lawn edged with lace. "A French shadow of velvet to defend them from the sunne" (1617, Fynes Moryson, *Itinerary*).

Shag-ruff

(F)

Period: 17th century.

A **ruff** with a shaggy or irregular outline.

Shakespere collar

(M)

Period: 1860s onwards.

A shallow turn-over collar, the points projecting downwards onto the shirt-front.

Shakespere vest

(M)

Period: 1876–1877.

A **waistcoat**, single- or double-breasted, of which the turn-over collar had wide points directed downwards, with a notch to a short, narrow lapel.

Shalwar kameez

(F & M)

Period: 1820s onwards.

"Shalwar" comes from Persian and refers to the loose trousers worn by both sexes in certain south Asian countries. The "kameez" is the knee-length shift with long sleeves worn with the trousers. This combination was known in Europe for several centuries before it became a well-known inspiration to designers.

Shamew

See Chammer.

Sham hanging sleeves

See Hanging sleeves.

Shams

See Half-shirt.

A rectangular woollen **shawl** with the distinctive pine cone motif; often called a Paisley shawl after a major centre of production, ca. 1835. The Indian and Persian motifs found on shawls were copied by many European manufacturers throughout the nineteenth century and the shawl became a major **accessory** for women of all social groups. Copyright the Olive Matthews Collection, Chertsey Museum. Photograph by John Chase.

S

Shaving hat

(M)

Period: Early 18th century.

A hat made of finely plaited wood-shavings instead of straw (1723, "Elizabeth Robinson, Shaving Hatmaker", *London Gazette*).

Shawl

(F & occasionally M)

Period: Mid-18th to 20th century.

A square or oblong **wrap** to cover the shoulders and upper part of the body, made in various sizes and fabrics. Used by women chiefly as an indoor **accessory**; by men as a protection in travelling by coach in the first half of the 19th century. It was made of wool, silk or cotton in mixtures or plain; the designs woven, printed or embroidered. From the 20th century synthetic fabrics of various compositions were also used.

Well-known types included cashmere shawls, originally made in Kashmir from the hair of the mountain goat and imported into Europe in the late 18th century. They were being made in England by 1818 and in Edinburgh of Australian wool in 1826. French shawls imitating Kashmir patterns, in silk warp and woollen weft were produced from 1804. After 1815 they were often of

flowered silk with deep borders; up to 2½ yards square. Norwich shawls, introduced in 1803, were woven with a silk warp and woollen weft in "fill-over" patterns; they were often a yard square. Paisley shawls, made in Scotland, appeared from 1808, made of silk or cotton warps and woollen or cotton wefts, or wholly of silk. By 1830 they often used "Botany worsted", Australian wool. They were very fashionable in the 1840s and 1850s, in the pine cone or buta pattern. "Reversible Paisley shawls", with the same pattern on both sides, were introduced in 1860. The size of fashionable shawls increased with the expanding size of the skirt, reaching in the **crinoline** period up to 12 feet long.
See Rampoor-chuddar.

Period: 20th century onwards.
Although popular in the early decades of the century, shawls were replaced by cardigans and light jackets until the revival of interest in Paisley in the 1960s and the introduction of the feather-light **pashmina** in the 1990s.

Shawl collar
(M)
Period: 1820s onwards.
A term denoting a broad turn-over collar of a coat or waistcoat, continuous with the lapels and without notches. After 1850 the name was gradually replaced by the **roll collar**.
In the 20th century shawl collars were found on garments designed and worn by both men and women.

Shawl waistcoat
(M)
Period: 19th century.
A term denoting either a waistcoat made with a shawl collar or a waistcoat of fabric having a shawl design. Waistcoats made from actual shawls were rare.

Sheath dress
(F)
Period: 1920s onwards.
A tightly fitting dress which closely hugged the curves of the body. A style popularized by American films and their glamorous stars of the golden age of the cinema.

Sheepskin coat, sheepskin jacket
(F & M)
Period: 20th century onwards.
Although sheepskins had been used from the earliest times as cloaks, etc. the fleece was often worn outside. However, the idea of making structured garments like jackets and coats from cleaned and processed skins, with the skin outside and the fleece inside, developed in several parts of the world in the 19th century. They were less expensive than many fur coats and suited to travel, early motoring and other outdoor activities. As fashionable clothing, they became popular in the 1960s and an embroidered Afghan variant was brought back by **hippies** from their travels.

Shell
(F)
Period: 18th century.
A loosely knotted curl of hair forming a bow.

Period: Late 20th century onwards.
A lightweight, closely fitted top, worn beneath a jacket.

Shell suit
(F & M)
Period: 1980s onwards.
A brightly coloured variant of a **track suit** worn in place of trousers and shirts by men and women who preferred comfort to style.

Shift
(F)
Period: 18th century.
The term which gradually replaced the term **smock** for the undergarment known in the 19th century as a **chemise**. It was worn next to the skin and made of homespun, linen or cotton.

Shift dress
(F)
Period: 1960s onwards.
A simple dress which skimmed the contours of the body rather than emphasized them; often short-skirted and sleeveless.
See Mini dress.

Shingle
(F)
Period: 1920s.
A short, tapered hair style cut so that all the ends are exposed like roof shingles.

Ship-tire
(F)
Period: Late 16th and early 17th centuries.
Term denoting a high style of coiffure. "Thou hast the right-arched beauty of the brow, that becomes the ship-tire" (1598, W. Shakespeare, *The Merry Wives of Windsor*).

Shirring
Period: 20th century onwards.
Rows of gathers similar to **gauging**. From around 1940 very fine elastic thread was often used to create this effect.

Shirt
(M)
Period: Early Medieval onwards.
The garment worn next to the skin until the introduction of the **vest** ca. 1840. A neckband appeared in the 14th century and an upright collar in the 15th. Side vents were added in the 16th century and from then onwards such parts of the shirt as were exposed to view became variously decorated with embroidery, pleating, frills and lace. Coloured shirts for day wear were introduced in the 19th century and detachable collars were replaced by attached collars of same or contrasting

colour. 20th-century shirts came in all colours, weights and styles and short-sleeved shirts were worn in hot weather.

See Aquatic shirt, Arrow shirts, Corazza, Hawaiian shirt, Historical shirt, Pleated shirt, Ruffled shirt; also Chitterlings, Half shirt.

(F)
Period: 1890s.
A name applied to the summer blouse worn by women.

Period: 20th century onwards.
The term describing the female version of the male shirt, though female versions might have darts at the bust, in all other respects, apart from buttoning, they mirrored the male cut.

Shirt-drawers
(M)
Period: 1890.
The shirt extended to reach the middle of the calf "and the slits are in the centre of front and back instead of at the side; the shirt thus dresses the leg". Thus drawers as a separate garment were not required.

Shirt dress, shirtwaist dress
(F)
Period: 1930s onwards.
A style of dress with front-buttoned bodice, collar and revers which looked like an elongated shirt; a practical style which has become a **classic** garment.

Shirt pin
(M)
Period: 19th century.
"A shirt pin made of jeweller's gold wire" (1825, T. Hook, *Sayings*). Worn in the bosom of the shirt.

Shoe
(F & M)
Period: Medieval onwards.
A covering for the foot; usually a leather sole and leather or fabric upper, the shape varying greatly through the centuries according to function and fashion.

Shoe-buckle
(F & M)
Period: Mid-17th century to ca. 1790.
A metal **buckle**, rectangular or oval in shape, attached to the front of the upper to hold the shoe in place; becoming highly ornamental and large ca. 1770. "Formerly, indeed, the buckle was a sort of machine intended to keep on the shoe; but the case is now quite reversed, and the shoe is of no earthly use but to keep on the buckle" (1777, R. B. Sheridan, *A Trip to Scarborough*).

Period: 1800 onwards.
Decorative buckles appeared on shoes alongside small practical buckles, but integral to the shoe rather than detachable.

Shoe-horn, showing horn
Period: 16th century onwards.

A semi-tubular implement with curved sides, of metal or horn, and in the 20th century of plastic, used to assist the foot to slip into a tight boot or shoe. "A showing horn of iron" (1576, City of Exeter Records).

Shoe-laces
Period: 19th century onwards.
Laces for tying the sides of the uppers together; usually of braided mohair, but ribbons were used for women's shoes. In the 20th century cotton or nylon cord replaced the earlier materials.

Shoe-rose
See Roses.

Shoe-strings
Period: 17th to mid-19th century.
Ties for securing shoes; the strings commonly of ribbon. "But he does not get his shoe-strings ironed" (1825, Harriette Wilson, *Paris Lions and London Tigers*).

Shoe-tie necktie
(M)
Period: 1850s.
A very narrow **necktie** "not half so broad as a watch-ribbon", tied in a bow in front or passed through a ring, the ends dangling.
See Byron tie.

Shooting coat
(M)
Period: 1860s–1880s.
The name commonly given at that period to the **morning coat**.

Short-coat
Period: 16th–19th century.
The term for the clothing for an infant when it could start to crawl; before that it wore long clothes, often swaddling bands.

Short hood
See Pug hood.

Shorts
(M)
Period: 1820–ca. 1850.
The name occasionally given to evening-dress **breeches**.

Period: 20th century onwards.
An American term for **underpants**.

(F & M)
Period: 1930s onwards.
Short trousers, usually to the knee or higher worn for sports, hiking and outdoor holidays. Increasingly worn in place of trousers for casual summer occasions.

Short spatterdashes
(M)
Period: 18th century.
These resembled **spats** but were not called by that name. They were chiefly worn by country folk.

Shotten-bellied doublet
(M)

Period: 1560–1580 and 1600s.
The short-fronted as opposed to the **peascod-bellied doublet**.

Shoulder bag
(F, occasionally M)
Period: 1940s onwards.
Plain bags with long straps which passed over the shoulder were so popular that they were issued to the women's services in the UK; they became less fashionable in the late 1940s, but reappeared in many styles and sizes in the 1980s.

Shoulder belt
(M)
Period: 17th century.
Previously the term used was **baldrick**; indicating a diagonal belt passing across the body from the right shoulder to the left hip or lower, over the doublet, for suspending the sword or rapier. After 1680 it was gradually replaced by the waist belt and frog, worn under the coat and waistcoat; and in the latter part of 18th century by the cut-steel hanger with its chains.

Shoulder heads, shoulder straps
(F)
Period: 17th century onwards.
"The straps passing over the shoulders and connecting the back to the front of a woman's dress" (1688, R. Holme, *Armory*).

Shoulder knot
(M)
Period: ca. 1660–1700.
A bunch of ribbon loops, cord or lace, sometimes bejewelled, worn as an ornament on the right shoulder. In the 18th century it became part of **livery** and "a knight of the shoulder knot" meant a footman.

Shoulder pad
(F & M)
Period: 1940s onwards.
An insertion of padding into the upper shoulder of a coat or dress to emphasize the width of the shoulders; often detachable, though some were placed between the fabric of the garment and its lining.
See Power dressing.

Shrug
(F)
Period: Early 21st century.
A lightweight, short-bodied and short-sleeved **bolero** designed to be worn with sleeveless dresses, literally to shrug on or off.

Sicilian bodice
(F)
Period: 1866.
An evening-dress bodice with a low square décolletage; attached to the bodice was a tunic in the form of two knee-length panels in front and two behind "as four sash ends".

Side
Period: 15th and 16th centuries.
The term then meaning "long", e.g. "side sleeves", "side gown".

Side body
(M)
Period: 1840s onwards.
Tailoring term for a separate panel inserted into a coat from below the arm-hole down to the waist-seam, to give a closer fit.

Side edge
(M)
Period: 19th century.
A scalloped flap inserted into the back vent of a skirted coat and projecting from inside the pleat so as to resemble the flap of a narrow, vertical pocket. This ornamental addition, unknown before 1810, first appeared then in some greatcoats; soon after 1820 frock coats and by 1829 day-dress coats were often trimmed with side edges, which were revived in the 1840s and again in 1873 on some **top frocks** and **Oxonian jackets**. Side edges also survived in certain **livery** coats.

Sideless surcoat
(F)
Period: ca. 1360–1500, and as state apparel until ca. 1525.
A low-necked, sleeveless and long overgarment, widely open at the sides from shoulders to hips, revealing the sleeves and bodice of the kirtle. The front panel, variously decorated, was known as the **plackard**.

Side piece
(F)
Period: 19th century.
Panel in women's coats corresponding to the **side body** in men's.

Silk hat
(M)
Period: 1797 onwards.
Invented by John Hetherington, a London haberdasher, and first worn by him on 15 January 1797, thereby provoking a riot, for which he was charged "with a breach of the peace for having appeared on the Public Highway wearing upon his head a tall structure having a shining lustre and calculated to frighten timid people" (*St James' Gazette*, 16 January 1797). This rival to the **beaver hat** became the **top hat**, the headwear of the gentleman from ca. 1830 onwards; its surface of silk with a satin-like gloss on a felting of rabbit hair.

Single-breasted
(F & M)
Period: Late 18th century onwards.
Describes a garment which fastens at centre front with one row of buttons and without the overlapping layer of cloth used for **double-breasted** coats, jackets etc. "Single breasted lounge suits. One, two

or three buttons, from £6.8.6" (1925, Army and Navy Stores).

Singlet

(M, later F)

Period: 18th century onwards.

In the 18th and early 19th centuries this term was used for an unlined (thus, single, not double) **waistcoat**, often of a woollen, knitted or woven cloth. Later, it became closely-fitted to the body and was used as a type of **vest**. In the 20th century it became associated with sporting activities and was worn by both sexes and benefited from man-made fabrics. It is now usually sleeveless with a scoop neckline and is similar to a sleeveless **T-shirt**.

Siphonia

(M)

Period: 1850s and 1860s.

A long, weatherproof overcoat. The "Pocket Siphonia" was a short, thin variety capable of being rolled up and carried.

Siren suit

(M)

Period: 20th century.

A term for an all-in-one, shirt-and-trousers garment, usually buttoned at the front and made from a sturdy fabric.

See Boiler suit.

Skeleton suit

(M)

Period: ca. 1790–ca. 1830.

A boy's suit consisting of a tight jacket having two rows of buttons on the front ascending over the shoulders; ankle-length trousers buttoned to and over the jacket round the waist; the trousers made with split **falls**. The suit was often made of **nankeen**.

Skin-coat

(M)

Period: 16th century.

A leather jerkin worn by peasants and shepherds.

Skin-head

(M)

Period: Late 1960s and 1970s.

A member of a working-class subculture identified by closely cropped or shaven heads, **T-shirts**, short **jeans** held-up by **braces** and heavy boots such as **'Doc' Martens**. Skin-heads were connected to **Mods** and later were linked to the **punk** movement. Like many of the post-World War II subcultures in the UK, they reinvented clothing for young people, especially young men, by imposing their ideas and ignoring mainstream fashion. Inevitably they did influence fashion and the popularity of the shaved head in the 21st century owes much to their "hard-man" prototype.

Skinny-rib sweater

(F)

Period: Mid-1960s and 1970s.

A hand- or machine-knitted jumper which fitted tightly to the contours of the body; executed in rib stitch. Occasionally revived.

Ski-pants

(F & M)

Period: 20th century.

Close-fitting trousers of a flexible fabric, with straps under the foot to keep them in place. Originally worn for ski-ing but later appropriated, especially by women, for general wear in place of looser trousers.

Skirt

(M)

Period: 17th century onwards.

That part of a man's coat below the waist; varying greatly in length according to the fashion of the day.

(F)

Period: Medieval–19th century.

A term occasionally used for the lower part of a woman's dress from the waist to the hem. Until the 19th century the more usual term was **petticoat**.

Period: 20th century onwards.

Separate skirts were increasingly important alongside the attached skirt of a dress. Named varieties include the **mini skirt**.

Skirt ruff

(F)

Period: 1880s.

A thick ruching of material attached to the inside of the hem of a day skirt to make it stand out.

Ski-wear

(F & M)

Period: 1920s onwards.

Clothing, usually a high-necked jacket closely fitted at neck and wrists, trousers, caps, mittens and boots, designed for warmth and ease of movement when using skis. Fabrics which included elasticity or were made of man-made fabrics such as nylon, or later Lycra, were used in special collections of ski-wear for both professional and amateur use.

See Après-ski wear.

Skull-cap

(M)

Period: 17th to early 20th century.

A round-topped or flat cap fitting the head; worn as a **night-cap** or, in the 19th century, as a "smoking-cap".

Slacks

(F & M)

Period: 1920s onwards.

Loosely cut, full-length trousers for informal wear.

Slammerkin, trollopee

(F)

Period: ca. 1730–1770.

A loose, unboned morning gown with a trained

S

LES NEIGES

Costume pour les sports d'hiver, en " agnella " de Rodier

Gazette du Bon Ton. Nº 9. — Planche 65

Fashion plate from *Gazette du Bon Ton*, 1920. The female skier is depicted in a close-fitting **cap** and a **wraparound coat** and high **boots**. The coat was made from "agnella" a fabric created by the French firm of Rodier whose winter-white cloths of wool and cashmere were one of many innovations in a history of producing new woollen and mixed fabrics. **Ski-wear** was a variant of fashionable apparel not yet a separate form of clothing. Private collection.

sack-back and short **petticoat**. As négligée it could be worn without a **hoop**.

Slap-shoe

(F)

Period: 17th century.

A mule, generally high-heeled. "Slap shooes or Ladies shooes are shooes with a loose sole" (1688, R. Holme, *Armory*).

Slashing, scissoring

Period: ca. 1480s–1650s.

The making of slits of varying lengths in any part of a garment, but often hose and sleeves, as a form of decoration. The slashes were symmetrically arranged and the gaps filled in by pulling out puffs of a white

undergarment, such as the shirt, or, after 1515, of a bright lining of a contrasting colour.

Slash pocket

(M)

Period: 19th century.

A horizontally cut pocket without a covering flap, in a man's coat.

Slavin, sclaveyn, sclavin

(M)

Period: Late 13th to late 15th century.

A pilgrim's mantle.

Sleeve

(F & M)

Period: Medieval onwards.

The section of a garment which encloses all or part of the arm and is attached to the arm-hole of an upper-body garment by ties or stitching. Many variants in size and style are found, e.g. **gigot sleeve**.

Sleeved waistcoat

(M)

Period: ca. 1660s–1750s.

See Waistcoat.

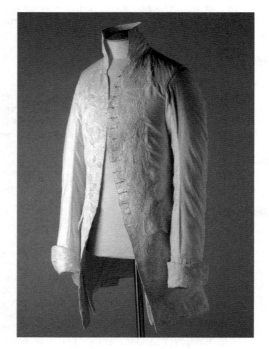

A man's **sleeved waistcoat** of white **linen** embroidered in **white work** with a front fastening of fifteen buttonholes and eyelets from which detachable **buttons** have been removed, ca. 1740–50. Copyright the Olive Matthews Collection, Chertsey Museum. Photograph by John Chase.

Sleeve hand
Period: 17th century.
The open end of a sleeve through which the hand is thrust, whether the sleeve ends at the wrist or higher up.

Sleeveless spencer
Period: 1800–1801.
See Spencer.

Sleeve string
See Cuff string.

Sleeve tongs
(F)
Period: 1890 onwards.
Ornamental metal tongs for drawing down the large dress sleeves through the sleeves of the jacket or overcoat.

Sling backs
(F)
Period: 1930s onwards.
A style of sandal or shoe with a strap around the back of the heel, usually punched and with a small buckle to allow adjustments to fit.

Sling duster
(F)
Period: 1886.
A **dust cloak** with **sling sleeves**; often of silk in black and white checks.

Sling sleeve
(F)
Period: 1885.
A sleeve made from the cape of a dust cloak or mantle, the cape being attached horizontally on each side just above waist level with an arm-hole above, supporting the arm as if in a sling.

Sling-sleeve cloak
See Bernhardt mantle.

Slip
(M)
Period: 1888–ca. 1939.
White piqué edgings buttoned into each side of the waistcoat "V" and slightly protruding; perhaps to prevent soiling of the shirt or possibly the vestigial remains of an under-waistcoat. The fashion is said to have originated with King Edward VII. Correctly worn only with a **morning coat**.

(F)
Period: 17th century.
An undergarment serving as a foundation to a dress especially when the latter is of semi-transparent material. (Payment for) "woorking slips for my Lady 2/–" (1620, Lord William Howard of Naworth, *Household Books*).

Period: 18th century.
The term for a kind of corset-cover. "Mrs. Lawson's loose slip altered and made fit to the new stays" (1756, The Lawson Family, *Domestic Accounts*).

Period: 20th century onwards.
A shorthand term for a light, unstructured petticoat, either full-length or waist-length.

Slip-on, slip-over
(F & M)
Period: 1930s onwards.
A jumper or **pullover** worn over a blouse or shirt, usually knitted. "Sleeveless slip-ons (for men) in two-colour pattern in blues, greys, fawns and browns, 16/6" (1935, Army and Navy Stores catalogue).

Slipper
(F & M)
Period: 16th century onwards.
The word "Slype-Shoe" was used by Anglo-Saxons. A generic name of a light form of low shoe easily slipped on and off; generally with short uppers. But the word **shoe** was frequently used for slipper until the 19th century.

Slip-shoe
(M)
Period: 16th to mid-18th century.
A mule with a flat heel. "They use a maner of slippe-shoes that may be lightly putte of and on" (1555, Watreman, *Fardle of Facions*).
The term "slip-shod", when first coined ca. 1570, meant the wearing of slip-shoes in which the wearer had to walk with a shuffling step.

Slit
(F)
Period: Late 13th century onwards.
An opening in a garment, sometimes suggestive of a pocket.

Slit pocket
(M)
Period: 19th century.
A vertically cut pocket in a coat or overcoat.

Slivings, slivers, slives, sleevings
(M)
Period: Late 16th and early 17th centuries.
Wide breeches often likened to **slops**.

Sloane Ranger
(F)
Period: Late 1970s onwards.
Term coined by Anne Barr and Peter York to describe young, well-connected women who lived and worked in London during the week and shopped in or around Sloane Square in Chelsea. Their style of dress was distinctively **classic**. The archetypal Sloane Ranger, prior to her wedding in 1981, was Lady Diana Spencer who married the Prince of Wales.

Slop
(M)
Period: Late 14th and early 15th centuries.
A short jacket worn over a doublet.

S

(F & M)

Period: Late 15th century to ca. 1550.

A slipper, then a cloak or a nightgown. "Sloppe – a nightgown" (1530, Palsgrave).

(F)

Period: Late 16th and early 17th centuries.

A woman's **cassock**. "A slope is a morning cassock for Ladyes and gentill Women, not open before" (Late 16th century, *Book of Precedence*, Queen Elizabeth's Academie).

(M)

Period: Late 16th and early 17th centuries.

This was the principal use of the word, namely to denote very wide knee-breeches, also called **slivings**. The term was also used occasionally for paned trunk-hose, especially the voluminous styles, such as **pluderhose**.

The official name – Great Sloppes – was used in various **sumptuary** regulations forbidding tradesmen to wear such garments. For instance, "Richard Bett, taylor, uses and has his calligas [i.e. footwear] with great sloppes contrary to the proclamation and form of the Statute. Fined 4d" (October 1565, Essex Sessions Records).

"A German from the waist downwards, all Slopes" (1599, W. Shakespeare, *Much Ado about Nothing*); "In a pair of pain'd (paned) slops" (1600, B. Jonson, *Cynthia's Revels*).

See small slops for a similar restriction affecting university students, but the date of the latter –1585 – suggests a reference to knee-breeches while the date of the Essex Sessions Record – 1565 – suggests a reference to bombasted trunk-hose, not to breeches.

Period: Late 18th and early 19th century.

Name often used for the labourer's Smock. "...Wearing a light-coloured Coat, a Waistcoat and a Slop betwixt them and a pair of leather breeches" (1774, *Norwich Mercury*). "A light half-straight coat over a brown slop and brown fustian breeches" (1815, *Bury and Norwich Post*).

Slop-hose

(M)

Period: 15th–18th century.

Sailors' breeches. "A sort of wide-kneed breeches worn by seamen" (1736, *Bailey's Dictionary*).

Sloppy Joe

(F & M)

Period: 1950s.

A very large, loose-fitting sweater; often a woman "borrowing" the garment of a larger, bulkier, male friend.

Slops

Period: 19th century.

Cheap, ready-made or old clothes, or a combination of all three.

Slouch hat

(F & M)

Period: 18th and early 19th centuries.

A hat with a flopping or uncocked brim.

Small clothes

(M)

Period: 1770 to mid-19th century.

A euphemism for **breeches**.

Small falls, split falls

See Falls, Spair.

Small slops

(M)

Period: ca. 1585–ca. 1610.

Short breeches with open legs not covering the knees. "...Nor to weare anye Slop but the plaine small Slop, such as is not to be lett downe beneathe the knee..." (Regulations for the apparel of university students at Cambridge in 1585).

Smock

(F)

Period: ca. 900–1290.

A woman's undermost garment worn next to the skin – loose, T-shaped, with a gathering thread or tape at neck and sleeve edges; usually knee-length or longer.

Period: Late 13th–17th century.

Fashionable smocks of finest linen were often embroidered with gold thread or coloured silks.

Period: 17th and 18th centuries.

Smocks acquired large balloon sleeves edged with ruffles and, in the 18th century, slightly bell-shaped sleeves, until ca. 1740 when the ruffled border ceased to be visible.

At various times the fabrics used were **linen**, **cambric**, **Holland**, occasionally silk; for the less well-to-do, usually **lockeram**.

See Shift.

Smock-frock

(M)

Period: 18th and 19th centuries.

The term was interchangeable with **smock** and denoted a loose gown of homespun or cotton worn by country workers. It was about knee-length; some with a **sailor collar**; some made with a yoke. Generally smocked or **gauged** in front in various patterns associated with the locality of the owner.

(F)

Period: 1880s.

An informal garment worn by women influenced by the **Aesthetic** Movement. "No artistic dresser would be without a Smock cut exactly like a farm labourer's, with square turned-down collar, gatherings front and back, gathered full sleeves, worn over a **habit shirt**, and looped up over an underskirt with a belt at the waist" (1880).

Also worn by small children, especially girls, in the late 19th and early 20th centuries.

S

Smocking

(F)

Period: 1880 onwards.

A form of needlework producing honeycomb ornamentation of which the basis is close gathering of fabric with a variety of stitched patterns holding the gathers in place.

Smock petticoat

(F)

Period: 17th century.

An under-petticoat. "2 smock petticoats of worsted" (1627, Lismore Papers).

Smoking jacket

(M)

Period: 1850s onwards.

A short, round jacket, single- or double-breasted, of velvet, cashmere, plush, merino or printed flannel, lined with brightly coloured material and commonly ornamented with **brandenburgs**, **olives** or large buttons. Worn informally in the home, but less frequently in the 20th century.

Snail button

Period: 18th century.

A covered button trimmed with French knots. Used on men's coats and waistcoats.

Snake

(M)

Period: 17th century.

The name commonly given to **love locks**. "The yard long snake he twirls behind" (1676, J. Dryden's Epilogue to Etherege's *The Man of Mode*).

Sneakers

(M, later F)

Period: Late 19th century onwards.

An American term for soft-soled shoes, often canvas with rubber soles; often synonymous with **trainers** in the late 20th century.

Snood

(F)

Period: 20th century onwards.

In a much earlier usage, a ribbon or hair-band, but now generally associated with the fine cord or mesh net retaining a chignon or other styles of rolled-up hair. Worn outdoors with or without a hat. Also made of fabric and attached to a hat.

Snoskyn, skimskin, snowskin, snufkin, snuftkin

(F)

Period: Late 16th and early 17th centuries.

A small muff for the hands.

Socks

(M)

Period: 8th to late 15th century.

The name was sometimes applied to a slipper or light shoe.

(F & M)

Period: Early 14th century onwards.

A short stocking; in the medieval period it was worn with footless hose but in the 16th century men often wore them with **boot hose** and stirrup hose; from 1790 they were worn with **pantaloons** and, in the 19th century, with trousers. Men's socks were kept up, from ca. 1890, by elastic **suspenders**.

Period: 20th century.

An increasingly wide range of socks were made, using traditional fibres or synthetic ones, and they were produced in all lengths, from ankle to knee, in many colours and patterns and for various leisure activities.

Sock suspenders

See Suspender.

Soled hose

(M)

Period: Saxon, 13th to end of 15th century.

Stockings of thick wool or thin leather, with leather sole attached, and worn without shoes.

In the 15th century **long-stocked hose** were added forming an early type of **tights**; these might also be soled with leather.

Solferino

Period: 1860.

One of the two first aniline dyes used for dress fabrics; corresponding to the modern fuchsia colour. Named after the battle of June 1859 in the Franco-Austrian War. *See* Magenta.

Solitaire

(M)

Period: 1730s–1770s.

A black ribbon worn over a stock and usually with a **bag-wig**. A broad solitaire was draped round the neck and either tied in a bow under the chin or tucked into the shirt-front, or pinned into place, or loosely knotted and allowed to dangle. A narrow solitaire was worn close and tied in a stiff bow in front.

(F)

Period: 1835.

A narrow, coloured scarf worn round the neck, loosely knotted in front, with the ends hanging to the knees. Worn with a white day dress.

(F & M)

Period: 19th century onwards.

The name given to a single gem set in a brooch or tie-pin.

Sombrero

(M, occasionally F)

Period: Late 18th century onwards.

A broad-brimmed hat shading the face, worn originally in Spain and Latin American countries, though it was worn by others: "He [Alfred, Lord Tennyson] would always wear his great Spanish cloak and sombrero, which excited much interest" (Sir Charles Tennyson, *Alfred*

S

Tennyson, pub. 1949, p. 425). Its increased popularity can be attributed to its use in American films from the early 20th century onwards.

Sorti, sortie
(F)

Period: Late 17th century.

"A little knot of small ribbon peeping out between the pinner and the bonnet" (1690, J. Evelyn, *Mundus Muliebris*).

Sortie de bal
(F)

Period: 1850s–1870s.

An evening, hooded cloak, generally of silk, satin or cashmere, with a quilted lining.

Soufflet sleeve
(F)

Period: 1832.

An evening-dress sleeve, very short, with full puffs vertically arranged.

Sou'wester
(M, occasionally F)

Period: 19th century onwards.

A waterproof hat with a brim deeper at the back to cover the collar; worn by sailors and fishermen.

Space exploration
Period: 1960 onwards.

Various fabrics and types of streamlined garments developed for use in space exploration had an impact on mainstream clothing.

See Moon boots.

Spaier, spere, speyer
Period: Medieval to late 16th century.

A term used for any vertical slit in a garment.

Period: Late 16th and 17th centuries.

The opening of a garment.

Spair
(M)

Period: 1840s to late 19th century.

A name sometimes given to the **falls** of breeches. "The Spair or Fall-down, called by some erroneously, the Fold" (1843, J. Couts).

See Falls.

Spangles
Period: Late 15th to late 19th century.

Small discs of shining metal, often pierced and sewn or stuck onto fabric as a trimming.

In the 16th century they were used on the clothing of both sexes and on hats and stockings. In the 17th century they were applied to garters, **pantofles** and **shoe-roses**. They were used on men's coats and women's fans in the 18th century, and in the late 19th century were occasionally applied to women's bonnets, and to evening dresses.

See Oes, Sequins.

Spanish breeches, Spanish hose
(M)

Period: 1630–1645, revived 1663–1670.

High-waisted, long-legged breeches. Somewhat full in the seat with a few pleats into the waistband, the legs narrowed down the thighs to end below the knees, where they were either closed by ribbon rosettes or bows, or left open to overhang the stockings; the margins usually trimmed with ribbon bows. Often trimmed with braid or buttons down the outside leg. The revived version, as described by R. Holme (1688, *Academie of Armory*) "…are stret and close to the thigh and are buttoned up the sides from the knee with about 10 or 12 buttons, anciently called Trowsers".

Spanish hose were hooked to the **doublet** lining and closed by buttons, not concealed by a **fly-front**.

Spanish cloak
(M)

Period: 16th and 17th centuries.

A short, hooded cloak.

Period: 1836 to early 20th century.

A short, round, evening cloak shaped to the shoulders and lined with a bright-coloured silk.

Spanish farthingale
(F)

Period: ca. 1545–1600.

An underskirt distended by circular hoops of rushes, wood, wire or whalebone, and formed to produce a funnel-shaped, domed or bell-shaped skirt. Some **farthingales** had a single hoop at the hem only. The underskirt itself was made of mochado, fustian, buckram or woollen stuff; the more costly ones of silk or velvet.

Spanish hat
(F)

Period: 1804–1812.

A large hat of velvet, satin or sarcenet, the brim turned-up at the front, trimmed with feathers. For evening or promenade dress.

Spanish jacket
(F)

Period: 1862.

A short, outdoor jacket fastened down the chest in front and then sloping away to the back which ended at waist-level, with or without a small **basque**.

Spanish kettledrums
(M)

Period: 1555–1570s.

Colloquialism for **trunk-hose**, in particular for the **round hose** style.

Spanish sleeve, slashed sleeve
(F)

Period: 1807–1820.

A short, evening-dress sleeve, puffed at the shoulder

and slashed at the sides over a silk lining.

Spats, spatts

(M)

Period: 1800–ca. 1939.

"A small sort of spatterdashes that reach only a little above the ankle; called also half-gaiters" (1802, *James' Military Dictionary*).

They were short **gaiters** reaching just above the ankle, buttoning on the outer side with a strap going under the foot, but not adapted for civilian use until the mid-19th century. In 1860 spats were worn with trousers and made of the same fabric. By 1878 they were fashionable with the **morning coat**, but incorrect with the **frock coat** until 1893, and made of box-cloth or canvas cloth in white, grey or fawn. In the 20th century they were worn infrequently after World War I.

Spatterdashes

(M)

Period: 1670s onwards.

Leggings of leather, canvas, cloth or cotton, generally reaching above the knee and laced, buckled or buttoned down the outer side. In the 18th century there was sometimes an extension over the foot and a stirrup strap beneath. "A sort of light boot without soles" (1736, *Bailey's Dictionary*).

Spectacles

(M, later F)

Period: Late 13th century onwards.

Single or pairs of lenses to correct long or short sight were probably a European invention and a pair is recorded in Venice in the late 13th century. The diarist Samuel Pepys thought he was losing his sight and recorded, "I this evening did buy me a pair of green spectacles, to see whether they will help my eyes or no" (1666, 24 December, *The Diary of Samuel Pepys*).

Bi-focals were invented by Benjamin Franklin in the mid-1770s and tri-focals were made in the 1820s. The term "specs" as a diminutive is known by ca. 1807. Women seem to have preferred **lorgnettes** to the plain and practical metal or tortoiseshell frames of the 19th century. The idea of spectacles as fashionable belongs to the second half of the 20th century, when plastic lenses replaced glass and frames of different shapes and colours were designed. By the 1960s multi-focal lens were available and designers had begun to add spectacle frames, with logos, to their ranges of accessories.

See Sunglasses.

Speedo

(F & M)

Period: Early 1930s onwards.

The patented name for an Australian brand of **swimwear**. The name was first used in 1928 and became famous due to the success of a Swedish swimmer who set a world record in the new brand. More usually associated in recent decades with short, close-fitting, male swimming trunks, but a wide range of swim and leisure wear is designed for adults and children.

Spencer

(M)

Period: 1790–ca. 1850.

A short, waist-length jacket with a stand-fall collar or roll collar and cuffed sleeves; buttoning down the front, and worn out of doors as a protection for the chest, generally in the country or by sportsmen. "Young Gentleman's Spencer or Tunic suit from £1:15:0" (1838, *The Globe*, advertisement).

(F)

Period: 1790–1820s.

A short jacket ending at waist-level or just above and worn as an outdoor garment or indoors for evening wear, and then very ornamental and often sleeveless. The form followed the fashion of the dress-bodice with which it was worn.

See Chinese spencer, Canezou.

Period: Late 19th century.

A flannel or knitted, sleeveless spencer was worn under the jacket for extra warmth by the elderly or infirm.

Spencer cloak

(F)

Period: 1804.

A cloak of worked net with short, elbow-length sleeves.

Spencerette

(F)

Period: 1814.

A spencer "tight to the shape", closed over the bosom, but with the neck cut low and edged with a lace frill.

Spencer wig

(M)

Period: 18th century.

A style of **wig** worn in the first half of the 18th century. Sometimes referred to simply as a "Spencer".

Spiked shoes

(M)

Period: 1861.

Shoes with spikes permanently attached to the soles; for cricket; patented in March 1861.

Spit-boot

(M)

Period: 18th to mid-19th century.

A boot combining shoe and **gaiter**, closed down the outer side by a series of interlocking fastenings, the last of which, at the ankle, was in the form of a sharp iron "spit" or spike which was inserted into an iron socket. Mainly worn in the north of England. "A pair of spit-boots" (1707, *N. Blundell's Diary*).

Split falls, small falls

See Falls.

Splyter-hat, splinter hat

Period: 16th century.

A straw hat made of braided strips of split straw called "splints", as opposed to tubular, whole straws.

Spoon back

(F)

Period: 1885.

Name given to the circular folds of drapery at the back of the tunic or over skirt of a woollen walking dress.

Spoon bonnet

(F)

Period: 1860–1864.

A bonnet with a narrow brim close to the ears, then rising up vertically above the forehead in a spoon-shaped curve, and sloping down behind to a small crown edged with a **bavolet**.

Sports jacket

(M)

Period: 20th century onwards.

Term describing a jacket worn for informal occasions. "Sports lounge model. Two styles of jacket" (1922, Harrods).

Sportswear

(F & M)

Period: 20th century onwards.

A portmanteau description of the many types and styles of garment worn for sporting activities.

See Ski-wear, Track suits, Trainers.

Spring boots

(M)

Period: 1776.

Boots made with a whalebone spring inside the back seam to check wrinkling.

Square

(F)

Period: 16th and 17th centuries.

A form of head-covering. "As women weare on their heads being sicke" (1611, G. Florio, *A Worlde of Wordes*).

Period: 16th–18th century.

The panel of embroidered linen or cambric forming the breast of the woman's shift. Also, in the early 16th century, an edging of jewels around the square neckline.

Period: Late 19th century onwards.

A square piece of fabric used as a cravat or scarf.

Square hoop

See Oblong hoop.

Stalk button

Period: ca. 1700–1750.

A button with the shank made of catgut.

Stand collar

(M)

Period: 19th century onwards.

An upright collar of a coat or waistcoat, made without a turn-down.

Stand-fall collar

(M)

Period: 19th and early 20th centuries.

A turned-over shirt collar, the inner layer called the "stand", the outer or turned-over parts the "**cape**".

Standing band

See Band.

Starch

Period: 16th century onwards.

First used in England ca. 1560s, for stiffening ruffs, collars, etc. It was sometimes coloured yellow or blue; other colours were used in European countries.

Starcher

(M)

Period: 19th century.

A starched **cravat**.

Startup, startop, styrtop, stertop

(M, sometimes F)

Period: Early 16th to early 19th century.

A term found as early as 1517 and descriptive of a high shoe reaching above the ankle, sometimes laced or buckled up, sometimes loose-fitting, and then called a **bagging shoe**.Worn by country folk and for sport; usually made of raw leather. A woman's startup might be more elegant. "Her neat, fit startups of green velvet bee flouresht with silver" (late 16th century, Sylvester's trans. of Du Bartas). The term continued as a description for country footwear into the 19th century, when it often meant a short style of **gaiter**.

Statute cap

(M)

Period: 1571–1597.

A knitted woollen **cap** which the English Statute of 1571 (repealed 1597) ordered all persons below a certain rank to wear on Sundays and Holy days on pain of a fine of 3/4. "Better wits have worn plain statute caps" (1588, W. Shakespeare, *Love's Labour's Lost*).

Stay hook, crochet

(F)

Period: 18th century.

A small hook attached to the front of the **stays** from which was hung the **watch**. They were often decorative. "Silver stay hooks with fine stones" (1743, *Boston Gazette*). They were sometimes known as Breast Hooks. "Gold and stone sett Breast Hooks…" (1762, *Boston News Letter*).

Stays

The earlier name for **corsets**.

Steeple head-dress

See Hennin.

Steinkerk

(M, sometimes F)

Period: ca. 1692–1730, unfashionably to ca. 1770.

A long **cravat**, generally edged with lace, loosely knotted under the chin and the ends either threaded through a buttonhole of the coat or pinned to one side, or sometimes left dangling. A fashion and name derived from the battle of Steenkerque, August 1692.

Women wore the Steinkerk with a riding habit.

Step-ins

(F)

Period: 1930s onwards.

An American term for elasticated corsets. Also used for other garments which did not need to be put on over the head.

Stepped collar

(M)

Period: 20th century onwards.

A collar meeting the lapel with a plain V-notch.

Sticking plaster dress

(F)

Period: 1893.

A name given to a tight, black, satin evening dress.

Stiffener

See Cravat.

Stiletto heels

(F)

Period: 1950s onwards.

The high, tapered heel of a shoe or sandal, thought to resemble the sharp narrow blade of an Italian dagger known as a "stiletto".

Stirrup hose, stirrup stockings

(M)

Period: 17th century.

Long over-stockings with an under-instep strap instead of a sole; worn as a protection to finer stockings when riding; serving the same purpose as **boot hose**.

Stirrup pants

(F)

Period: 20th century onwards.

A term for close-fitting trousers, often of a flexible fabric with a strap under the foot, not dissimilar to **ski-pants**.

Stock, stocks

(M)

Period: ca. 1400–1610.

The leg portion of hose, appearing as "tights", and after 1550 the leg portion of **trunk-hose**, often called **nether stocks**, the seat part being known as **upper stocks** or **overstocks** or "the breech", before ca. 1550.

From ca. 1590 "stock" was occasionally used for **stocking**.

Period: ca. 1735 to end of 19th century.

A high, made-up neckcloth, often of linen or cambric, stiffened with a frame of pasteboard and buckled or tied behind. The black military stock of the 18th century was often adopted by fashionable civilians and from 1820 was correct wear at the British court by civilians. A hunting stock of cellular cloth, tied twice round the neck and worn without a collar, became fashionable from ca.

1890 for hunting and riding; this style was retained into the 20th century.

Stock buckle

(M)

Period: 18th to mid-19th century.

The buckle fastening the stock at the back of the neck. In the 18th century, although frequently concealed by the **wig**, the buckle was often ornamental, being plated, or of gold, silver or pinchbeck worked or plain, or set with jewels, real or imitation.

Stock-drawers

Period: 17th century.

A rare term meaning **stockings**.

Stockings

(F & M)

Period: ca. 1550 onwards.

A close-fitting covering for the foot and leg. Although worn from Saxon times they were called by other names (**hose**, **nether stocks**, **stocks**) until the mid-16th century. "For two lambes skynes to make a paier of stockings 16d. For silke to stitche the clockes 2d. For cloth to sole them 2d" (1570, Petre Accounts, Essex Record Office).

"Stocking of hose" in the early 16th century indicated the stocking portion of **trunk-hose**, the leg portion of that garment rather than a separate item. Stockings for men and women might be knitted in the late 16th century. The materials and colours varied: wool, cotton, thread and silk, plain or embroidered, a tradition which lasted well into the 20th century for female stockings, even after nylon revolutionized their appearance in the 1940s.

(M)

Period: ca. 1830 onwards.

Men began wearing socks unless wearing breeches.

(F)

Period: 1960s onwards.

Tights began to supplant stockings for many younger women, but seamed stockings and hold-ups, the stockings designed to stay in place without suspenders, also attracted loyal customers.

Stola

(F)

Period: ca. 100 BCE–300 CE.

A sleeveless gown worn over a **tunica** and covered with a **palla**. These were the three layers of clothing worn by elite Roman women.

Stole

(F)

Period: 16th century onwards.

A medieval ecclesiastical term adapted to designate a fur or warm shoulder-scarf worn by women.

Stomacher

(M)

S

Stomacher, ca. 1730. Linen and silk with embroidery in silk and metal threads with gold thread lacing across the central section. The structural shape and tabs at the base are similar to the front of **stays** of this date. Copyright the Olive Matthews Collection, Chertsey Museum. Photograph by John Chase.

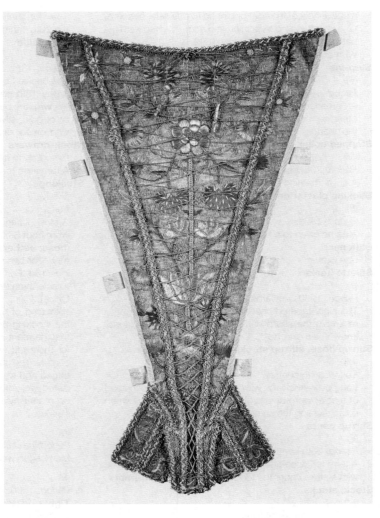

Period: Late 15th and early 16th century.

A chest-piece, often very ornamental, covering a V- or U-shaped gap of a doublet cut low in front.

(F)

Period: Late 16th century to 1770s.

A long, ornate panel forming the front of an open, low-necked bodice. The stomacher descended to a sharp or rounded point at the waist and the upper horizontal border formed the limit of the décolletage. For "high stomacher" and "low stomacher", see stomacher-front dress.

Stomacher bodice

(F)

Period: 1820s.

A bodice with revers called **pelerine** lapels, sloping down from the shoulders to a V at the waist, the enclosed space filled in with **gauging** or pleating, the upper edge defined by a **tucker**.

Stomacher-front dress

(F)

Period: 1800–1830.

A type of construction inherited from the mid-18th century and describing a form of front fastening to a woman's dress. There were two types: the "high stomacher", in which the upper third of the skirt is split down the sides forming a sort of tethered apron or inverted flap, to which is fastened the front of the bodice like an apron bib. This is pinned up at shoulder level. A draw-string at the waist tied behind secures the skirt flap, and the join might be covered with a belt or sash; and the "low stomacher" version, in which the skirt flap does not include the front of the bodice, which is closed by a wrapping front with cross-over folds or by a **robin front**, a **cottage front** or a **waistcoat-bosom**.

Stote, stoat

Period: 19th century.

A method of sewing two edges of cloth together so that there is no visible seam; used especially with thick fabrics.

Straight English skirt

(F)

Period: 1890.

A day skirt, ankle-length, the fullness at the back made by gathers or flat pleats, the front and sides shaped to the waist by darts. The front flat or slightly draped above; with a stiff lining 12 inches from the hem or pleated muslin **balayeuse**.

Straights

(F & M)

Period: Medieval–ca.1900.

A term applied to footwear before boot and shoemakers evolved the technique of creating a left and right sole. Men's footwear preceded women's in forgoing straights.

Straight trousers

(M)

Period: 19th century onwards.

Trousers in which the legs are cut the same width all the way down.

Straight waistcoat

(M)

Period: 19th century.

A tailoring term denoting a single-breasted waistcoat without lapels; with or without a stand collar.

Strapped pantaloons

(M)

Period: ca. 1819–1840s.

Pantaloons in which each leg was held taut by a strap under the instep.

Strapped trousers

(M)

Period: 1820s–1850, unfashionably to 1860.

Trousers in which each trouser leg was held down by a strap or a pair of straps under the instep.

Street style

(F & M)

Period: 1960s onwards.

A term coined to describe the impact on fashion created by ingenious young people with imagination but little income, who searched for clothing in unusual places such as charity shops, adapted it and mixed old and new fabrics and garments. These styles were cannibalized by major fashion designers, creating a new "trickle-up" effect.

String tie

(M)

Period: 1896.

A very narrow bow tie.

String vest

(M)

Period: 1930s onwards.

A sleeveless **vest** edged with tape but loosely structured, like netting; usually worn in warmer months, and in the early 21st century becoming less popular.

Strips

(F)

Period: 1650–1700.

Straight bands of fabric, plain or bordered with lace, worn crossing the shoulders to meet in a V in front, and serving as an edging and fill-in to a low-necked bodice.

Strossers, straser

(M)

Period: Late 16th and early 17th centuries.

Sometimes called **trousers** but essentially an informal garment, knee or ankle-length; possibly of linen cut on the cross to give a close fit.

Stud

(M)

Period: ca. mid-18th century onwards.

A button on a short neck with a broad base, used to fasten parts of a garment together by inserting it through complementary eyelet holes. In the 18th century its only use was occasionally to secure the shirt sleeve at the wrist. Studs were used to secure the front of the shirt from ca. 1830, and in the 1840s three ornamental studs attached together by small chains, known as "tethered studs", were commonly worn in evening dress. With the separate collar, coming into fashion for day wear ca. 1860, a stud was introduced in the back of the neckband of the shirt.

For evening wear, studs with coloured stones, pearls, diamonds, etc. were fashionable until ca. 1870, when they were gradually replaced by plain gold ones.

(F)

Period: 20th century onwards.

Term occasionally used for small, round or flat **ear-rings** for pierced ears.

Style width

(M)

Period: 19th century onwards.

A tailoring term for the horizontal measurement from the midline seam on the back of a coat to the nearest margin of the arm-hole.

Sugarloaf hat

(F & M)

Period: 1640s.

A similar style to the **copotain**, but the brim was usually broader than that of the earlier copotain.

S

Suit, sute

(F & M)

Period: 17th century onwards.

Term generally denoting a complete costume made of one fabric throughout, for example the wedding costume of the Princess of Wales in 1736, "Dressed in a suit of rich silk" (*Read's Weekly Journal*).

Increasingly from the 19th century onwards a suit referred to a man's **lounge suit**.

Suit of apparel

(M)

Period: 16th and 17th centuries.

A suit of clothes consisting at least of **doublet** and **hose**, both being indispensable parts of such a "suit".

Suit of knots

See Knots.

Suit of night-clothes

(M)

Period: 18th century.

A colloquial expression denoting the **night-cap** and **night-shirt**. "Whip a suit of Night-Clothes into your pocket and let's march off" (1703, Colley Cibber, *She Wou'd and She Wou'd Not*).

Suit of ruffs

(F & M)

Period: ca. 1560–1640.

A neck **ruff** with matching hand ruffs.

Sultana scarf

(F)

Period: 1854.

A loose scarf of oriental colours, worn over a **canezou**, tied below the waist with the ends left dangling.

Sultana sleeve

(F)

Period: 1859.

A large hanging sleeve slit open in front; the usual style of sleeve with a **casaque**.

Sultane

(F)

Period: Late 17th century, also 1730s and 1740s.

In 1690 described by Evelyn as a gown trimmed with buttons and loops. In the 18th century it was an informal gown with short **robings** and a **stomacher** and a plain back, sometimes trimmed with fur and obviously thought to show some Turkish influence. "My lady will travel in her sultane, I suppose?" (1734, J. Gay, *The Distress'd Wife*).

Sultane dress

(F)

Period: 1877.

A day dress in the **princess** style, with a **scarf** elaborately draped to fasten at one side.

Sultane jacket

(F)

Period: 1889.

A man's **suit** of **coat**, **waistcoat** and **breeches**; grey ribbed silk embroidered with floral motifs in coloured silks, ca. 1780. Copyright the Olive Matthews Collection, Chertsey Museum. Photograph by John Chase.

A sleeveless **Zouave jacket** "scarcely reaching below the shoulder blades".

Sultan sleeve

(F)

Period: 1830s.

A large hanging day sleeve caught up in the middle of the arm and forearm.

Sumptuary legislation

Period: Medieval onwards.

Religious or secular laws determining consumption, including what fabrics could be bought and how they might be made and then worn by different groups in society. Most legislation applied to women and young girls and was difficult to enforce. Essentially it was a means of reinforcing hierarchies within a region or country, and the last vestiges can be found in the bands of ermine on state robes and similar abstruse details. In the 19th century, long after most legislation was forgotten, etiquette manuals fulfilled a similar role, indicating what was and was not acceptable clothing for the socially mobile.

Sunglasses

(F & M)

Period: Late 19th century onwards.

Glasses tinted to protect the eyes from the glare of bright sunshine were made in Germany in the 1880s. In the 20th century they became an ever-changing and fashionable accessory, often embossed with the logo of a well-known designer and acquired the nickname "shades".

Sunray pleats

Period: Late 19th century onwards.

Pleats radiating out from a central point to the edge of a garment, usually a skirt.

Sunray skirt

(F)

Period: 1897.

A circular day skirt made from two lengths of wide material joined to form a square; the skirt then being cut in a circle with a hole in the centre for the waist and shaped to fit; the forerunner of the flared skirt.

Supertotus

Period: Medieval.

A sleeved and hooded cloak worn by travellers.

Super tunic

(F & M)

Period: 9th to end of 14th century.

Generally called a **surcoat** or **surcote** in the 13th and 14th centuries. The term continued in use in the context of garments worn at coronations.

(M)

A loose garment put on over the head and worn over the tunic or cote. The shape varied and by the 14th century was closer fitting. It was long if ceremonial; otherwise knee-length. The sleeves were wide to the elbow or wrist; less commonly, close-fitting and long.

See Garnache, Garde-corps, Tabard.

(F)

A long, loose garment worn over the tunic or kirtle with long, loose sleeves, tubular or bell-shaped and, in the 12th century, sometimes with pendulous cuffs. From the 13th to mid-14th century some versions were sleeveless.

See Sideless surcoat.

Supportasse, underpropper

(F & M)

Period: ca. 1550–1650.

A framework of wire generally whipped over with gold, silver or silk thread, and fixed at the back of the neck to support a large, starched ruff or band (collar). "To beare up the whole frame and body of the ruff from falling" (1583, Stubbes, *Anatomie of Abuses*).

See Pickadil, Rebato.

Surcoat, surcote

(F & M)

Period: Medieval–17th century.

A rich outer garment of variable style. It seems to have gradually evolved into a ceremonial garment worn by heralds or by nobility as part of their state robes.

See Super tunic.

Surkney, suckeny

(F & M)

Period: Medieval.

A coarse, loose frock or **gabardine** worn by country people.

Surplice bodice

(F)

Period: 1881.

A day bodice made in full gathers from the neck over the shoulders and bust.

Surrealism

Period: Early 20th century.

This artistic and literary movement, which expressed the ideas of the subconscious mind, found its major proponent in the world of fashion in the work of the designer Elsa Schiaparelli (1890–1973) who was close to the artist Salvador Dali (1904–1989).

Surtout

(F & M)

Period: Late 17th century.

Synonymous with the **Brandenburg** overcoat. For women it was a type of mantle with a hood.

Period: 18th century.

Mainly worn after ca. 1730 in the form of a long, loose overcoat with one or more spreading collars called "capes". Also called a **wrap-rascal**.

Period: ca. 1820s–1840s.

Often called a **surtout** greatcoat, being a single- or double-breasted overcoat made like a frock coat and the forerunner of the **top frock**.

(F)

Period: Late 18th century.

A caped overcoat. "Mrs. Cholmeley's surtout lapelled, high stand-up velvet collar, and three scalloped capes, of fine mixt beaver, velvet sleeves" (1785, Cholmeley Papers at Bransby).

Suspender belt

(F)

Period: 1878 onwards.

An elastic suspender, attached to the border of the corsets and clipping on to the top of the stocking, began to be used by women. By 1882 garters "are almost things of the past, suspenders having superseded them; the suspender is made in satin and elastic with gilt mounts and clips, with a shaped belt fitting the corset".

Period: Early 20th century onwards.

Alongside clips on corsets various other styles emerged, the most usual being a lightweight, elasticated belt from which two front and two back pendant straps with metal and rubber clip fasteners were suspended to grip the stockings.

Suspenders

(M)

Period: 19th century onwards.

A term for the braces which supported trousers. "…A British sailor walking up the High Street with suspenders to his trousers…the suspenders crossed each other over his shoulders" (1825, *Ackermann's Repository*).

It remains the usual name for **braces** in America and – in the trade – as an alternative in England.

Period: 1895 onwards.

The sock suspender was a device for preventing socks from slipping down; introduced in the form of a garter of elastic round the calf, with a pendant piece terminating in a metal and rubber clip to grip the top of the sock. This was obviously adapted from the female style and initially unpopular for that reason. In the 20th century, when elasticated sock-tops became the norm, this type of support became rare.

Swaddling bands, sweath-bands

Period: Medieval to late 18th century.

Long bandages for wrapping round the body and limbs of an infant to form the limbs, giving it the appearance of a mummy. The infant usually remained thus swaddled until it was weaned. "Bought a Blanket and Swadler for her child" (1785, Essex Records).

Among the elite classes, swaddling was being replaced by **long clothes** early in the 18th century.

Swagger coat

(F)

Period: 20th century onwards.

A loose top coat with a flared shape from the shoulders, making it useful to wear over a suit or similarly bulky clothing. Known as a "topper" in the USA.

Swallow-tail

(M)

Period: ca. 1850.

A coat with the fronts cut away at the waist, leaving only tails below the waist at the back. The description began to be applied to the evening-dress coat.

Swanbill corset

(F)

Period: 1876.

A long, back-lacing corset with a long metal busk in front shaped to curve over the lower abdomen.

Swatch

(F & M)

Period: 1980s onwards.

The trade name of a style of fashionable **watch** with many seasonal and limited-edition versions using popular imagery, bright colours and flexible plastic for straps.

Swathe

Period: 19th century.

A baby's binder.

Sweater

(M)

Period: ca. 1890 onwards.

A loosely knitted jersey reaching below the hips and worn outside the top of the **knickerbockers**. At first with a stand-up edge round the neck; for golf a **polo collar** was added in 1894. Cyclists continued to wear the earlier form, but "no man can wear it as it now stands without looking like a bounder" (1900, *Tailor & Cutter*).

In the 20th century sweaters continued to be worn for sporting activities, but also more generally.

(F)

Period: Early 20th century onwards.

Popular for sports and informal wear, but gradually becoming an essential part of clothing. "All kinds of knits: sweaters, cardigans, woolly shirts, blouses and boleros…" (1940, *Vogue*).

Sweater dress

(F)

Period: Mid-20th century onwards.

A closely-fitting dress resembling an elongated sweater.

Sweatshirt

(F & M)

Period: 20th century onwards.

An informal, loose-fitting, long-sleeved top often worn for sporting activities; of washable cotton with a fleecy lining; became a mainstream informal style in the late 20th century.

Sweetheart neckline

(F)

Period: 20th century.

A fairly wide, square neck descending into a curved V and resembling the top of a stylized heart-shape.

Swimsuit, swimwear

(F & M)

A portmanteau term for anything worn for swimming: bikinis, bathing costumes, etc.

Swire, sworl, swyrell

Period: Medieval.

A twist or convolution used in embroidery or decoration of garments.

Swiss belt

(F)

Period: 19th century.

Fashionable 1815 and 1816; again in 1860s, 1880–1900. A waistband broadening in front to a lozenge shape, pointed above and below. From the 1860s it might be laced across the front, becoming a **corselet**.

Swiss bodice

(F)

Period: 1867.

A velvet bodice combining a **Swiss belt**, and worn with a sleeved **chemisette**.

Sword

(M)

Period: 16th century to end of 18th century.

All men from families entitled to coats of arms (armigerous) could wear a sword; therefore it was perceived as an essential element in a gentleman's outfit.

System

See Toque.

T

Tabard

(M)

Period: Late 13th and 14th centuries.

In the late 13th century it was a circular **mantle** of moderate length; in the 14th century it was an overgarment, one form being the **garnache**. Also at this period it was a clerical-academic garment. Subsequently it became ceremonial and heraldic and is still worn by heralds in the early 21st century.

Tabi

(F & M)

Period: Early 17th century onwards.

Japanese, thick-soled, cotton ankle socks, often white, with one section for the big toe and one for the other toes. Intended to be worn with sandals and **kimonos**, but also worn within a house as both sock and footwear. Known in the west for several centuries, they became readily available in the late 20th century.

Tablet

(F)

Period: 16th century.

A rare term for an **apron**, anglicized from the French *tablier*.

Tablier skirt

(F)

Period: 1850s and 1870s.

A skirt with the front breadth defined by descending trimmings on each side of it, suggesting a decorative apron or separate panel. The term was occasionally used in the 20th century, and the French term *en tablier* is an elegant way of describing an apron or a feature which copies the look of an apron.

Tablier tunic

(F)

Period: 1875.

An overskirt triangular in shape, with one corner descending nearly to the hem of the skirt in front, the others fastened under the **basque** of the jacket-bodice.

Tache

Period: 15th–17th century.

A brooch, clasp, buckle or hook.

Tackover

(M)

Period: 18th century onwards.

The overlap of the pleat at the top of the back vent of a skirted coat.

Taffeta-pipkin

See Pipkin.

Taglioni

(M)

Period: 1839–ca. 1845.

A double-breasted **greatcoat** with a very large collar lying flat on the shoulders, very wide lapels reaching over the breast; collar, lapels and cuffs of quadrilled satin, velvet or "a new silk material resembling fur". The coat defining the waist, the skirts full and short without back or side pleats. A central back vent with a three-cornered **tackover** at the top. Cross or slit pocket on each side. Sleeves with turned-back cuffs. The whole bound with a twilled binding. The waist seam through the foreparts only.

Named after the celebrated ballet-master Filippo Taglioni (1777–1871), the creator of the ballet *La Sylphide.*

Taglioni frock coat

(M)

Period: ca. 1838–1842.

A single-breasted **frock coat**, the skirts short and full, often without hip-buttons. Made with a very broad collar and one large cape; slash or flapped pockets on the hips; back vent without pleats but a tackover.

Tail

See Train.

Tail clout

Period: Late 16th–17th century.

A baby's napkin.

Tail coat

(M)

Period: Mid-19th to early 20th century.

A colloquial usage in the 1850s for the formal male coat with tails, especially **cutaway** or **morning coats** or **swallow-tail** coats.

t

The Duchess of Kent. The Queen. Prince Albert.
The Last & Newest London & Paris Fashions 1843. Morning & Evening Dresses

Fashion plate with Queen Victoria, her mother the Duchess of Kent and her husband Prince Albert. This busy image includes four evening hairstyles; a daytime **bonnet** for the duchess who is wearing morning dress and holding a fur **muff**. The queen is depicted in **evening dress** holding a **fan** with her **Paisley**-patterned shawl to one side. The prince, in day dress, has closely fitting **pantaloons**, a version of the **Taglioni frock coat**, a short **waistcoat**, a high cravat and a neat **moustache**, 1843. Copyright the Olive Matthews Collection, Chertsey Museum.

Tailleur

(F)

Period: Late 19th century to ca. 1970s.

A French term for a tailor or, in this instance, a **tailor-made** suit for female customers. The British tailor John Redfern (1853–1929) was a distinguished exponent of this style from the mid-1880s onwards. His clients included international royalty and other elite women.

Tailor-made

(F)

Period: 1877 onwards.

A woman's costume for morning and country wear; usually of one fabric throughout and that a cloth; in the 1890s two materials were sometimes used.

The essential feature was that the costume was made by a tailor and not by a dressmaker, and that it was constructed on masculine lines, and often imitating the fashionable male cut of the day.

Until the late 17th century women's formal garments were made by tailors, and the **riding habit** was always made by tailors, but it was a significant step when Charles Worth (1825–1895) set up as a dressmaker in Paris in 1858, and in 1867 "a London tailor has recently set up dressmaking".

Various outdoor garments for women, such as cloaks and **ulsters**, began to be made by tailors, but the outfit which became known as a tailor-made dates from 1877. *See* Tailleur.

Tallien redingote

(F)

Period: 1867.

"Worth has produced an extremely pretty covering for outdoor use called the "Polonaise" or "Tallien Redingote" (1867). Made with a heart-shaped opening in front and a full back; trimmed with a sash and a large bow behind, and sash ends carried down each side terminating in bows; the sash was of the same fabric as the dress or of black silk.

By increased puffing at the back this garment developed into the 19th-century **polonaise**.

Talma

See Poncho.

Talma cloak

(M)

Period: 1850s.

A knee-length cloak with a wide turn-over collar, often quilted, and a silk lining. Worn with evening dress. Named after the French actor François Joseph Talma (1763–1826) who reintroduced the **toga** to classical dramas.

Talma lounge

(M)

Period: 1898.

A **lounge jacket** made with **raglan sleeves**, straight fronts, and curved or slanting pockets.

Talma mantle

(F)

Period: 1850s, 1870s, 1890s.

In the 1850s, a long cloak with a hood or tasselled falling collar; shortened in 1854 and called a **rotonde**. In the 1870s, a similar style but made with sleeves. Revived in the 1890s as a loose-sleeved **overcoat** of ground length, with a deep velvet collar or a lace cape.

Talma overcoat

(M)

Period: 1898.

A **raglan overcoat** with very wide arm-holes. "It is fashionable to go about in a Talma with the hand thrust in the side in the trouser pocket" (1899, *The London Tailor*).

Tam-o'-Shanter

(F)

Period: 1880s.

This Scottish cap, named after a poem by the Scottish poet Robert Burns (1759–1796), became fashionable with women in the 1880s, though it was much worn by boys and men in Scotland.

The fashionable version was a soft, round, flat hat without a brim, having a bobble in the centre of the crown. It came in velvet, plush, cloth or crochet work and was worn well into the 20th century. It was also called a "Tam" or "Tammie".

Tango fashions

(F)

Period: ca. 1913 onwards.

The tango was introduced as a ballroom dance into Europe and North America from Argentina. Men could wear their usual day or evening suits but, at a period when **hobble skirts** were tight and constricting, women's dresses or skirts had to have a slit at one side of the leg to allow for the dance steps. It also changed underwear: "The tango and the pegtop fashion between them are responsible for a completely new form of skirt-knickers. The characteristic of the new garment is that it is formed entirely of one length of material falling from the waist in front to the knees and up again to the waist at the back, with slits at the sides for the legs" (1913, Quoted in C. W. Cunnington, *English Women's Clothing in the Present Century*).

Tango shoes were introduced in 1884 but were relatively unseen until skirts shortened ca. 1910. They had a high back, a moderate heel, and were fastened across the instep with buckles or ties, and ribbons or tapes were criss-crossed up the leg.

The tango enjoyed a new lease of life in the 1920s as a result of Rudolph Valentino's film *The Four Horsemen of the Apocalypse* (1921) in which he electrified audiences with his tango. By then shorter dresses, shoes with instep straps, and less cumbersome underwear meant that only true aficionados who wished to dress like Argentinian dancers needed specific clothing.

Tank top

(F & M)

Period: 1960s onwards.

A short, close-fitting, sleeveless **pullover**, often with a scoop or V neckline, and usually knitted in various colours and patterns.

Tarboush

(M)

Period: Early 18th century onwards.

A cloth or felt cap with a conical, upright crown, worn either separately or as part of a turban head-dress in Muslim countries. The cap was often red and had a pendant silk tassel, usually blue. The Ottoman Turkish form, banned by Kemal Atatürk (1881–1938) during his dress reforms in the 1920s, was called a "fez".

Tasselled handkerchief

(F & M)

Period: 16th century.

A pocket handkerchief trimmed with tassels at the corners and often having a fringed border.

See Buttoned handkerchief.

Tater

(M)

Period: 15th century.

Phonetic spelling for "tetour" – a hood. "With long taters down to the ars behynde" (i.e. hood or chaperon with long liripipes) (ca. 1490, *A Treatise of a Gallant*).

Tattersall vest

(M)

Period: 1895 onwards.

A sporting waistcoat in fancy materials with small checks; made single-breasted with six buttons, no collar and four flapped pockets.

Tatting

Period: Early 19th century onwards.

An edging lace consisting of knots and loops worked with an ivory or metal shuttle, using a strong thread. Another variant uses a needle rather than a shuttle.

Tattoo

(M, later F)

Period: Early modern period onwards.

Sailors often acquired tattoos during their travels; these were indelible patterns or messages in the skin effected by means of inks inserted into punctures. Blue or indigo was traditional, but other colours were used.

In the late 20th century tattoos became increasingly fashionable amongst both men and young women, including film stars, etc.

Taure

See Bull head.

T-bar shoes

(F, occasionally M)

Period: 1920 onwards.

A shoe with a central bar from vamp to buckled strap just below the ankle, thereby forming a T-shape. More popular in the 1930s, when they also appeared on sandals as well as shoes, and occasionally on male sandals.

Teagown

(F)

Period: ca. 1877–ca. 1940.

A loose dress worn without corsets and at first by married women only. "The teagown arose from the habit of ladies having tea in the hostess's boudoir and donning smart dressing-gowns. Now that gentlemen are admitted to the function peignoirs have developed into elegant toilettes of satin, silk, etc." (1877).

Its style followed contemporary fashions, but from 1889 a high-waisted, **Empire** style was favoured, with long, hanging sleeves and trimmings of yards of lace. A lace and muslin mob cap was worn with it. Gradually in the 1880s this clinging style became "permissible for young

t

ladies", though it was particularly useful for married women in pregnancy.

See Maternity wear.

In the 20th century the name persisted but the styles overlapped with long, more structured dresses and shorter outfits worn for taking tea outside the home.

Tea jacket

(F)

Period: 1887 onwards.

Often replacing the **teagown**. A jacket, close-fitting behind, loose in front, with tight sleeves; trimmed profusely with lace. It might be worn to replace the tailor-made bodice at afternoon tea.

Teddy, teddie

(F)

Period: 1970s onwards.

A type of lightweight undergarment; in one piece with the skimpy bodice attached to panties and fastened beneath the crotch with buttons, etc. Usually of silk or an artificial alternative.

Teddy boys

(M, sometimes F)

Period: 1950s onwards.

Young men wearing an approximation of the fashions of the Edwardian period (1901–1910). Their female equivalent wore less exaggerated coats and shoes, but back-combed their hair into something akin to the fullness of the earlier period.

Tee

Another term for a **T-shirt**.

Telescope parasol

(F)

Period: 1811.

The stick or handle of this style of parasol was a steel tube which could be lengthened by being pulled out like a telescope.

Templar cloak

See Caban.

Templers, templettes, temples

(F)

Period: 1400–1450.

Ornamental bosses of goldsmith's work or fine needlework worn over the temples and enclosing the hair. They were supported by a connecting fillet crossing above the forehead, or by the rest of the head-dress.

See Bosses.

Tennis shoes

(M, much later F)

Period: 16th century onwards.

Shoes with soft soles. "For sooling of syxe paire of shooys with feltys to playe in at tennys" (1536, Wardrobe Accounts, Henry VIII).

For lawn tennis, shoes with india-rubber soles appeared in 1878, and in the 20th century women also began to wear tennis shoes which became firmer and more supportive as sporting footwear evolved.

Tent dress

(F)

Period: 1950 onwards.

The term describes a dress or coat fitted at the shoulders and widening towards the hem. Attributed to the Spanish designer Balenciaga (1895–1972), it, alongside the **sack dress** and the bell and trumpet shapes appearing in America, Europe and the UK, changed the emphasis from the constrictions of the **New Look** into a form which reached its apogee in the body-skimming **mini dress** of the 1960s.

Terai hat

(F, sometimes M)

Period: 1880s to mid-20th century.

A riding hat worn by Englishwomen in tropical countries. Made of fur or wool felt in the form of two hats sewn together at the edge of the brim. A red lining within and a metal vent fitted through the crown. The crown generally somewhat squat and the brim three to five inches wide. "She used to trot up and down Simla Mall…with a gray Terai hat well on the back of her head" (1888, R. Kipling, *Plain Tales from the Hills*).

Teresa, Thérèse

(F)

Period: 1770–1790.

A light, gauze scarf worn on the head, sometimes tied over the indoor cap.

Terrier overcoat

(M)

Period: 1853.

It resembled a **pilot coat**. "Black and tan colour with large china buttons" (*Punch*).

Tête

See Head.

Tête de mouton

(F)

Period: 1730–ca. 1755.

A head of false curls worn "curled all over behind or tete de mouton" (1782, *Plococosmos*).

"We have imitations of it that will do as well; both sides of a fashionable head are now curled out to the best advantage" (1731, *Weekly Register*).

Textiles

Generic term for any type of woven cloth. A usual way of denoting the separation between collections within museums, i.e. between costume/dress/fashion collections and textile collections which include soft furnishings as well as clothing.

Theatre costume

(M, later F)

Period: Medieval onwards.

Clothing was an essential tool for performers, whether in dance, opera, play or, much later, film and TV. It offered characterization ahead of gesture or voice, and certain characters, clowns and melancholics for instance, were instantly recognized when they appeared in traditional clothing for such roles. Courtly entertainments, which included masques, operas and plays in which major roles might be taken by royals and courtiers, were observed by few, but travelling players and the emergence of theatre buildings in towns and cities from the mid-18th century onwards allowed expensive, fashionable clothing to be observed alongside stock wardrobe items. Ahead of film stars, stage performers were admired and emulated. Ellen Terry in costumes designed by Doucet and Lillie Langtry in Worth designs captured new audiences for the work of major couturiers, as did less mainstream styles; Lena Ashwell in a "…simple robe of soft white silk, which might for all the world be one of Liberty's latest productions, and which is pretty enough to be copied by any modern maiden with a taste for artistic dress…" (1895, *The Sketch*) are all examples from the 1890s.

The actor-manager Sir George Alexander appeared in Pinero's *His House in Order* in 1906 wearing soft collars and **lounge suits**, thereby offering approval of this less formal style of menswear. English tailoring and French couture were worn by subsequent generations of British and European performers until the more leisurely styles of American clothing became dominant as a result of the influence of **cinema**.

See Fancy dress, Masquerade costume.

Theodore hat

(F)

Period: 1787.

"The crown exceedingly high with two rows of gauze and trimmed with fine blond net; bordered with blue satin. A large bouquet of poppy-coloured flowers in front, and behind deep lappets of gauze reaching to the waist" (December 1787, *Ipswich Journal*).

Thermal clothing

(F & M)

Period: 20th century onwards.

Keeping warm in cold climates has been a challenge throughout history, but technological developments in man-made and natural fibres provided fabrics which could be made into underwear such as combinations, vests, Long Johns, gloves, socks, etc., and similar fabrics were used as linings for outer garments. Silk is now used alongside other fibres in the creation of attractive thermal underwear and outerwear. Layers of clothing are often worn in extreme conditions: "In addition to long johns, thermal socks and two caps, Harwell wore a tee shirt" (1978, 16 April, *Detroit Free Press*).

Thong

(F, occasionally M)

Period: ca. 1975 onwards.

Similar to a **G-string**, this skimpy, V-shaped cover for the genital area, held by elasticated straps across the lower hips, became popular as both a way of avoiding a visible panty line and as a provocative item of underwear for women and some men. Thong briefs and tangas became marginally more substantial variants for both sexes in the late 20th century.

Three-decker

(F & M)

Period: 1877 to early 20th century.

An **Ulster** with three capes.

See Carrick.

Three-fold linen button

Period: 1841 into 20th century.

Introduced in that year by John Aston; a button covered with three layers of linen.

Three-piece suit

(M)

Period: 18th century onwards.

A term used occasionally in the 18th century to describe coat, **waistcoat** and **breeches** when worn together. In the 20th century it usually referred to a **lounge suit** and waistcoat.

Three-seamer

(M)

Period: 1860 onwards.

A round jacket with a central seam down the back and two side seams; as contrasted with the coat having side bodies giving five seams.

Three-storeys-and-a-basement

(F)

Period: 1886.

The popular name given to fashionable hats which had very high crowns.

Thrum, thrummed

(F & M)

Period: 16th to early 18th century.

"Felts are of two kinds – bare or thrummed" (1547, Statutes at Large).

Thrums were the waste ends of warp threads left unwoven and attached to the loom. Various forms of headwear – bonnets, caps, hats and night caps – were made from these or with thrums inserted into another fabric; "thrum caps" were mentioned regularly.

Tibi

(M)

Period: 1840 onwards.

A loop fastening button to button across the top of a coat, instead of button to buttonhole.

Ticket pocket

(M)

Period: Late 1850s onwards.

A small pocket for a railway ticket generally placed above the right-hand flapped pocket of the overcoat. In 1875 it was inserted just above the left cuff of the **Inverness** overcoat. In the 1890s a ticket pocket was added to the **lounge** jacket, above the right-hand pocket; and by 1895 a similar one was introduced in the **morning coat**.

Tie

(M, occasionally F)

Period: From mid-1950s onwards.

The usual term for a **necktie**.

Tie-back skirt

(F)

Period: 1874–1882.

A day or evening skirt, trained, with a series of tapes sewn to the side seams within; by tying these tapes together the back of the skirt was bunched out and the front flattened. By this means was produced an extreme narrowing of the skirt in front of the tapes, thus creating a form of **hobble skirt**.

Tights

(M)

Period: 19th century.

A term sometimes used for **pantaloons**, especially those worn for evening dress. The term was also used, in the context of circus or theatrical performance, for closely fitting stockings of stretch fabric which incorporated knickers and extended to the waist and were worn by performers of both sexes.

(F)

Period: Mid-1960s onwards.

Nylon tights were introduced as an alternative to **stockings** and quickly became available in various weights, colours and patterns.

Tight-slacks

(M)

Period: 1881.

Trousers very tight at the knees and slack at the bottoms.

Tilbury hat

(M)

Period: 1830s.

A small hat with a high, tapering crown, flat-topped and with a narrow, round brim.

Tippet

(F & M)

Period: Medieval.

Pendant streamers from the sleeves of the **cote-hardie**. The term was also used for a **liripipe**.

(F, occasionally M)

Period: 16th century onwards.

A short shoulder-cape.

Titus hair, Titus wig, hair à la Titus

(M)

Period: 1790–1810.

A cropped head of hair, or a wig resembling it, intentionally dishevelled.

See Brutus head.

Toby ruff

(F)

Period: 1890.

A neck-frill of chiffon or lisse gathered in two or three layers and tied at the throat with ribbon; for day wear.

Tog

Period: Medieval.

A coat, from the Latin **toga**.

Period: 16th century.

Becoming a popular word for clothes. "I cut the Child's strings (leading strings) off from her coats and made her use togs alone" (1617, *Diary of Lady Anne Clifford*).

Period: 16th century onwards.

A slang term for finery. "Togged out" meaning dressed in finery.

Toga

(M)

Period: ca. 100 BCE–ca. 300 CE

The Roman citizen's formal garment worn over the tunic and arranged in folds around the body and across the shoulders. It was revived for theatrical use in the late 18th century.

Toggle

Period: 20th century onwards.

A device for fastening a garment whereby a short section of bone, plastic or similar passes through a loop or hole and when adjusted from horizontal to vertical remains in a fixed position. An alternative to a button and found on **duffel** coats.

Toile

Period: Late 19th century onwards.

A French term for the cloth used for creating the pattern for a couture or made-to-measure garment; usually stiffened muslin which can be cut, pinned and adjusted without losing its structure.

Toilet, twillet

(M)

Period: 17th century.

A loose linen wrapper worn about the shoulders of a man while being shaved. "The barber, after he had cast the linen toilet about his shoulders (asked) how shall I trim your majesty" (1684, J. Phillips, translation of Plutarch).

(F)

Period: 18th century.

The term denoted the loose wrapper worn by ladies while having their hair dressed.

Toilet cap

(M)

Period: 17th century.

A plain **night-cap** worn by men while being barbered.

Toilette

(F, occasionally M)

Period: 18th century onwards.

Style or way of dressing; thus a dress, suit, etc.

Top

See Toupee.

Top boots

(M)

Period: 1780s to early 20th century.

Previously called **jockey boots**. Boots reaching to just below the knees with turn-over tops of a lighter or different colour, e.g. brown over black. Loops for pulling on and also boot garters or strings. In the 19th century a button and strap kept them in position.

Top button

A button of which the face alone was gilded. When the under-surface was also gilded it was known as an "all-over". By the mid-19th century this type of button was known as a **high-top**.

Top coat, overcoat, greatcoat

(M)

Period: 18th century onwards.

Terms used for any form of coat worn over the suit when out of doors. "Top coat" and "**greatcoat**" were names in use in the 18th century, while "**overcoat**" came into use by the mid-19th century.

"Greatcoat" implied a garment of heavy material suitable for travelling; "top coat" indicated a fitting garment of lighter cloth, suitable for walking; "overcoat" was a similar garment but suitable for travelling by train.

Top frock

(M)

Period: 1830 to early 20th century.

An overcoat cut like a **frock coat** but usually somewhat longer and generally double-breasted. It was intended to be worn without an under-coat while looking like an overcoat.

See Upper garment.

Top hat

(M)

Period: 19th century onwards.

A tall, high-crowned hat, resembling a chimney-pot, with a narrow brim usually slightly rolled up at the sides but at some dates, e.g. ca.1840, with a brim almost flat. The shape appeared at the end of the 18th century before the name. Until ca. 1830 it was a high-crowned **beaver**, but this was subsequently replaced entirely by the **silk hat**. This reached its extreme height ca. 1850, with a crown some eight inches high. By the end of the century this was reduced to five inches.

The top hat was usually black, but sporting varieties might be grey or brown; white was the fashionable colour for sportsmen from ca. 1820 and was the colour generally worn by all gentlemen in the 1830s and 1840s.

See Chimney-pot hat, Pot hat, Silk hat, Plug hat.

(F)

Period: 1830s onwards,

Top hats might be worn by women riders but were gradually replaced by **riding hats** in the 20th century.

Top knot

See Knot.

Topless

(F & M)

Period: 20th century onwards.

Literally going without any garment from head to waist. Usual for men at the seaside, but less so for women until topless sun-bathing became acceptable in the later 20th century.

Topper

"His white topper" (1820, *Sporting Magazine*).

Also an American term for a shortened version of a **swagger coat**.

See Top hat.

Toque, toocke, tock, tuck

(F)

Period: 16th and early 17th century.

A woman's head-kerchief or **coif**.

Period: ca. 1815–1820.

"A sort of triangular cushion or edifice of horsehair called, I believe, a toque or a system, was fastened on the female head…and upon and over this system the hair was erected and crisped and frizzed" (1817, Maria Edgeworth, *Harrington*).

Period: 19th century.

A close-fitting, turban-like hat without a brim, worn by day out of doors and sometimes also with evening dress. Made of a variety of materials, silk, satin, straw, and fashionable from 1817 to the end of the century, except in the 1850s.

Period: 20th century.

A close-fitting, high-crowned hat without a brim, often made from soft fabrics and sometimes trimmed with a feather or brooch; fashionable in the 1920s and associated with Queen Mary, consort of George V.

Toquet

(F)

Period: 1840s.

A small **toque** of satin or velvet with a shallow, turned-up brim in front and trimmed with an ostrich feather. Placed far back on the head and worn with evening dress. In 1867 the term was used as "a more elegant phrasing for the pork pie hat".

Toque-turban

(F)

Period: 1840s.

A **turban** in the form of a **toque**; for evening wear.

Toreador hat

(F)

Period: 1890 to early 20th century.

A circular hat with a flat, shallow, circular crown; made of felt or straw and worn aslant. A fashion inspired by

Bizet's opera *Carmen* (1875) and Emma Galvé"s performance of the name part.

Toreador pants
(F)

Period: Mid-20th century.

Close-fitting trousers laced at the knee; similar to those worn by Spanish bull-fighters.

Torsade
(F)

Period: 1864.

A twisted or plaited **coronet** of velvet or tulle with long **lappets**; worn with evening dress.

Tote
(F)

Period: 20th century onwards.

A very large **handbag** or shoulder bag, made of various materials and often lightweight, as it might carry heavy loads; "Tote Bags – Great for knitting supplies, shopping" (1969, 24 September, *Daily Colonist*).

As bags increased in size in the early 21st century the term was applied to chic and expensive designer-label bags, alongside practical canvas or nylon versions.

Toupee, toupet, foretop, top
(M)

Period: 1730 to end of 18th century.

The roll back from the forehead of the hair of a wig; before 1730 the wig had a centre parting.

Period: 19th century onwards.

A piece of false hair or a small wig to blend in with the natural hair.

(F)

Period: Late 19th century.

A fringe or forehead frizz of false hair.

Tournure
(F)

Period: 1882–1889.

Taken from the French for "form" or "shape" and used as a polite term for a **bustle**.

Tower, tour
(F)

Period: 1670s–1710.

False curls added to the front hair up above the forehead; a coiffure generally worn with the **fontange**.

Track suit
(F & M)

Period: Mid-20th century onwards.

A loose, two-piece garment, elasticated at ankles and wrists, worn by athletes while warming-up or after competing. Absorbed into the wardrobe of the non-athletic as casual clothing.

See Shell suit.

Trafalgar turban
(F)

Period: 1806.

An evening-dress **turban** embroidered with the name of the British Admiral, Lord Nelson (1758–1805), who won the sea battle but lost his life.

Train, tail
(F & M)

Period: Medieval onwards.

An elongation of the bottom of a dress, gown or robe at the back so that it trailed over the ground. A "demi-train" was a short train produced by having the back of a gown made somewhat longer than the front.

A common feature of the ceremonial gown worn by men, e.g. at coronations, was that the length of the train depended on the rank of the wearer, such as those worn by high judicial and similar functionaries.

Trains were worn by elite women from the earliest times, the most singular being a train *in front* as well as behind, as indicated in a Book of Precedence of 1440: "A surcoat is a morning garment made like a close or straight-bodied gowne, which is worn under the man-tell; the same for a countess must have a trayne before, another behind. For a baroness no train. The trayne before to be narrow, not exceeding the breadth of 8 inches and must be trussed up under the girdle or borne upon the left arm" (Harl. MS 6064).

Trainers, training shoes
(F & M)

Period: 1960s onwards.

A soft shoe without spikes worn by athletes and other sporting persons when training. Named brands, of which there are many, include the American "Converse" brand which in a history of over 90 years produced a **classic** trainer, originally for basketball players and only in black canvas with a thick rubber sole, but from the 1960s in other colours. Trainers were adopted by the non-athletic as a casual, lightweight item of footwear, especially by the young.

Trapeze line
(F)

Period: 1958.

Short for "trapezium", this line was planned by Christian Dior (1905–1957) but launched by Yves Saint Laurent (1936–2008) in his first season as Dior's successor. It was a wide, rigid, full-skirted and knee-length, tent-like silhouette, fitted to a high bust at the front but with a loose back falling from the shoulders.

Trawerbandes
Period: 17th century.

Mourning bands.

Trench coat
(M, later F)

Period: Late 19th century onwards.

A quasi-militaristic style adapted for optional wear by officers serving in the trenches during World War I. It was a long, belted coat with flapped pockets, usually waterproof, with an optional cape for protection across the shoulders. It became a **classic** overcoat for both sexes from the 1920s onwards. Both **Aquascutum** and **Burberry** promoted the style; Aquascutum in the 1850s and Burberry in 1901.

Trencher hat
(F)
Period: 1806.
A silk hat with a triangular brim rising to a point above the forehead.

Tressour
(F)
Period: 14th century.
A **chaplet** of goldsmith's work or fabric worn on the head.

Tricorn, tricorne hat
(M, occasionally F)
Period: 1690 to end of 18th century.
The 19th-century name for a three-cornered cocked hat worn by men, and occasionally women, when riding.

Tricot
See Glossary of Fabrics and Materials.

Trilby hat
(M, occasionally F)
Period: 1895 onwards.
A soft, black, felt hat with shallow brim and indented crown, similar to the **Homburg** style. Named after the play in which Sir Herbert Beerbohm Tree (1853–1917) played Svengali in a hat of that description.

Trollopee
(F)
Period: 18th century.
"I did not wear one of their trolloping sacks" (1733, Duchess of Queensberry).
See Slammerkin.

Trolly cap
(F)
Period: ca. 1750–1800.
An indoor cap trimmed with **trolly lace**.

Trotteur
(F)
Period: 1890s into 20th century.
A French term for the type of woollen walking suit introduced by Redfern in the 1890s. It combined a masculine cut of jacket with an ankle-length skirt which allowed ease of movement.
See Tailleur.

Trouser press
Period: ca. 1890 onwards.
An appliance consisting of two flat boards between which a pair of trousers was laid and the boards then tightened together by means of thumb-screws; by this means the fashionable crease down the front of the trouser leg could be maintained. In the 20th century streamlined versions which were heated by electricity were introduced and became a feature in many hotels, as well as in the home.

Trousers, trowsers
(M)
Period: 1730 to end of 18th century.
A garment enclosing the legs and extending from the waist to the ankles. The legs were not shaped but varied in the degree of looseness. At this period the trowsers were wide-legged, ending just below the calf, made with a narrow belt buttoned in front; a front opening buttoned, but without a fly covering.
They were mostly worn by non-elite men in town or country and by sailors and soldiers. "A sea-faring man in…long trowsers" (1771, *Salisbury Journal*). "A regiment of cavalry who on foot wear trowsers" (1782, *The Torrington Diaries*).
More rarely they were worn by a country squire, though breeches were usual for all social groups: "In his best trowsers he appears, And clean white drawers" (ca. 1730, Wm. Somerville, *The Officious Messenger*).

Period: 1807 to early 20th century.
Trousers began to become fashionable for day wear and from ca. 1817 for evening, though not entirely replacing evening-dress breeches until 1850.
The closure was by **small falls**; from 1823 occasionally by **fly-front** closure, which became general after ca. 1840.
See American trousers, Cossacks, Eelskin masher trousers, French bottoms, Gaiter bottoms, Pleated trousers, Railroad trousers, Straight trousers, Zouave trousers, Tight-slacks.

Period: 20th century onwards.
The basic shape was fixed but the width, the addition or not of turn-ups, and the actual cloth with which trousers were made developed over the decades. The gradual introduction of **zip fasteners** after the mid-1930s, and the option on casual trousers of elasticated waists, changed perceptions of comfort.
See Flannels, Oxford bags, Jeans.

(F)
Period: 19th century.
Trousers were worn by women on horseback, under the voluminous skirt of the **riding habit**. These took the form of strapped **pantaloons** of coutil cloth in the first half of the century or, in the 1830s, of white florentine. In the 1850s they were sometimes chamois leather with black feet. From 1860 onwards they were made of black or dark cloth, with a strap and buckle at the back of the waist and an opening down the left hip; the seat lined with chamois leather or cotton.
Although trousers for women were illegal in 19th-century France, they were worn under short skirts as part of the regimental uniforms allowed to *cantinières*; these styles predated **bloomers** by several decades. The name

"trousers" was also applied to the long drawers with frilled lower edges visible below the hem of the skirts, as worn by young girls ca. 1830–1860.

Period: 20th century onwards.

Experiments with knickerbockers for cycling in the late 19th century were followed by the gradual adoption of trousers in many forms and styles from World War I onwards. By the late 20th century many women preferred jeans or trousers to skirts.

See Trouser suit.

Trouser stretcher

Period: ca. 1880.

An appliance for stretching the legs of trousers to remove "bagginess". Two types were in general use; the first was a long steel loop bent into an H shape; inserted into the legs of a pair of trousers when not in use, thus preserving their shape by stretching the cloth.

The second type employed a wooden frame which gripped each end of the garment and extended it by means of a screw action; this was often combined with the boards of a **trouser press**.

Trouser suit

(F)

Period: Late 19th century onwards.

The combination of jacket and **knickerbockers** preceded the occasional use, in artistic circles usually, of women wearing a jacket and trousers similar to those worn by men. The German actress Marlene Dietrich (1901–1992) popularized such suits in the 1930s, but they really became widespread after the 1960s, the decade in which Saint Laurent introduced the female tuxedo, **le smoking**.

Trouses, Trowses

(M)

Period: 16th and 17th centuries.

The name commonly given to the **drawers** worn by men beneath **trunk-hose**. "Walks up and down in his gown, waistcoat, and trowses" (1625, B. Jonson, *Staple of News.* Stage direction: the young man awaits his tailor to bring his suit of clothes).

Trousseau

(F)

Period: 19th century onwards.

In previous centuries young women sewed and embroidered a variety of textile items, garments and soft furnishings in preparation for marriage, but the concept of an identifiable number of pieces of clothing being available for purchase appeared in the 19th century. For instance, in 1867 it was possible to spend £100 or, in 1868, £20 depending upon means. The garments were mainly underwear and nightwear; **chemises**, **nightgowns**, **petticoats**, stockings and handkerchiefs. By 1900 the fashionable bride was thought to need eighteen of each trousseau item.

In the 20th century the term widened to encompass outer wear acquired to wear after the wedding, but it is rarely used in the 21st century.

Trunk-hose, trunk slops, trunk breeches, round hose, French hose

(M)

Period: ca. 1550–1610.

The upper portion of men's leg-wear, from the waist around the seat; this trunk part was variously distended, often paned (see **panes**) and joined to the stocking portion near the crotch, or half-way down the thigh. The style with **canions** continued to 1620.

Trunks

(M)

Period: 19th century.

Short, tight-fitting drawers or pants worn by athletes and swimmers; the term may be derived from theatrical trunks or short breeches, a usage found earlier in the century.

Period: 20th century.

"Trunk drawers", a type of short, close-fitting item of underwear, possibly derived from swimming trunks.

Trunk sleeves

See Cannon sleeves.

Truss

(M)

Period: Late 14th century to ca. 1630.

A verb used in the sense of to tie up. The words "to truss the points" meant to fasten with **points** long, tailored stockings and, later, **trunk-hose** to the **doublet**.

(F & M)

Period: 16th and 17th centuries.

A form of close-fitting bodice or waistcoat. "A truss with satin sleeves" (1606, Surrey Wills, The clothes of Mary Parkyn's husband).

Trusses

(M)

Period: 1570s to early 17th century.

A name sometimes used for tight **Venetians**. "…others straight trusses and devil's breeches" (1592, Nashe, *Pierce Penilesse*).

T-shirt

(M, later F)

Period: 20th century onwards.

A term originally applied to a simple, short-sleeved, round-necked, cotton jersey **vest** worn below other garments. Possibly European in origin, the T-shirt became popular with American servicemen in World War I who recognized how useful it was in different climates and conditions. Its versatility led to it being produced in colours and patterns and worn as a casual lightweight top by men, women and children from the mid-20th century.

Also called **Tee**.

T-shirt dress

(F)

Period: 1960 onwards.

An elongated version of the **T-shirt**; often a simple, short dress.

Tube

(F)

Period: 1960 onwards.

A simple, unshaped garment of varying length. The most well-known being the "boob tube" – a strapless, often elasticated top worn informally.

Tubular necktie

(M)

Period: Patented 1852.

A **necktie** of various materials woven in the form of a tube, eliminating a seam.

Tucked skirt

(F)

Period: 1895.

A day skirt with a broad box pleat in front and pleats behind, stiffened at the waist with horsehair, and side fullness given by a series of vertical tucks down the hips.

Tucker

(F)

Period: 17th century.

"A Pinner or Tucker is a narrow piece of cloth, plain or laced, which compasseth the top of a woman's gown about the neck part" (1688, R. Holme, *Academie of Armory*).

Period: 18th and 19th centuries.

A white edging, usually frilled, of lace, lawn, muslin or a soft fabric, to a low-necked bodice. In the 19th century also an accessory to evening dress. When it was turned over to hang down over the front of the bodice it was called a "Falling Tucker".

Tudor cape

(F)

Period: 1890s.

A circular cape with a pointed yoke at front and back, and a velvet **Medici collar**; usually of embroidered cloth.

Tuft

(M)

Period: 15th century.

A tassel.

Period: 17th–19th century.

A small section of hair on head or chin distinctively shorn.

Period: 18th century.

The name was applied to the tassel pendant from the centre of mortarboards worn at British universities.

Tunic, cote

(M, rarely F)

Period: 9th to early 14th century.

A loose body garment of varying length, equivalent to the **kirtle**.

(M)

Period: 1660–1680.

Tunic or **surcoat**, a loose coat hanging to just above the knees, buttoned down the front and having "commodious sleeves". Always worn with a vest, i.e. a loose under-coat. The tunic and vest were introduced by Charles II in 1666.

Period: 1840–1860.

A garment worn by small boys; a form of jacket, close-fitting to just below the waist, with a gathered or pleated skirt to just above the knees; sleeves long or ending well above the wrists to reveal white shirt sleeves. Fastened down the front. Worn with trousers to the ankles or to just below the knees.

Tunica

(F & M)

Period: Greco-Roman.

A T-shaped garment resembling a shirt; the basic, first-layer garment worn by Greek and Romans in the classical era. Usually made of wool and with long or short sleeves. Its form continued throughout the history of dress, evolving into shirts and shifts and allied items of clothing.

Tunic dress

(F)

Period: 19th century.

A dress with an overskirt, this being the tunic. It varied in length and design but was usually closed all round.

Period: 20th century.

A narrow overdress made fashionable by the French designer Paul Poiret (1879–1944) and others in the pre-1914 period. Also popular in the 1960s over a skirt or trousers, and intermittently fashionable ever since.

Tunic shirt

(M)

Period: Patented 1855.

A shirt open all down the front, so that it did not require to be put on over the head; the original of the modern shirt.

Tunic skirt

(F)

Period: 1856 onwards.

A double skirt. In the 1850s a popular form for ball dresses, the upper skirt or tunic trimmed with lace, the underskirt with a deep flounce. In 1897 day skirts were sometimes double, and known by this name. In the early 20th century they were worn narrow, especially in the 1920s and 1930s.

Turban

(F)

Period: 1760s–1850s.

A head-dress of fabric folded round the head or made up into that design and adapted from non-European versions. Worn for dress or undress until the 19th century, when it became mainly a form of evening headwear.

Period: 20th century.

Particularly fashionable in the first half of the century for day wear. "Turban of smocked nappa in black, with royal jersey swathe. Also other colours. 5 gns" (1942, Harrods).

Turf, tyrf, tark

Period: 15th century.

The turn-up or facing of a hood or sleeve.

(M)

Period: 16th century.

The turn-up of a cap, usually at this date called a **bonnet**. "A black Milan bonnet, double turfed" (1526, Papers, etc. Henry VIII).

Turf hat

(M)

Period: ca. 1830.

A hat with a tall, slightly tapering crown, flat-topped and with a broad brim turned up on each side.

Turkey bonnet, Turkey hat

(M)

Period: 15th and 16th centuries.

Any tall, cylindrical, brimless hat. "To weare Powle's steeple for a Turkey hat" (1566, John Heywood, *The Spider and the Flie*).

One of many foreign fashions then in demand: "The Spanish codpeece on the bellye; the Itallyan waste under the hanch bones; the Dutch Jerkin and the Turkie Bonnet; all these at the first we despised and had in derision. But immediately we do not onlye reteyne them but we do so farre exceede them that of a Spanish codpeece we make an Englishe footeball…and of a Turkie bonnet a Copentank for Caiphas" (1576, George Gascoigne, *Delicate Diet for Droonkardes*).

Turkey gown

(M)

Period: ca. 1525 onwards.

Supposed to be of Turkish origin and probably identical with the long Hungarian coat with long, narrow sleeves; the gown loose, or fastened down the front with loops or buckles and straps. This was regarded as the principal secular gown and later adopted by Puritan ministers who regarded the voluminous gown-sleeves worn by the established clergy as savouring of Popery. "Do not somme wear side gownes having large sleeves with tippets, whiche is not well liked of your secte; some of more perfection (i.e. the Puritans), Turkey gownes, gaberdines, frockes or nightgownes of the most laye fashion for avoiding of superstition" (1570…Harding, *Computation*).

A Turkey Gown of black velvet, bordered with silver and furred with lynx, having "77 round gold buttons, black enamelled" was made for Henry VIII.

Turkish trousers

(F)

Period: 20th century.

"…the Turkish trouser suits are really intended to be worn in the sanctity of one's own room, although full-length coats can at an emergency be slipped over them and worn for more occasions with decorum" (1926, Lady Angela Forbes, *How to Dress*).

See Bloomers, Harem pants.

Turnover

(F)

Period: 17th century.

A woman's **head kerchief**.

Turn-ups

(M, later F)

Period: Late 19th century onwards.

Term usually referring to the turned-up bottom of trousers. Usually associated with informality and lounge suits and never worn in the evenings. Woman's sporting wear copied this style, and in the later part of the 20th century turn-ups became fashionable from time-to-time but were not universally popular.

Turret bodice

(F)

Period: 1883.

A bodice with a **basque** cut into tabs.

Turtle neck

(M, later F)

Period: Late 19th century onwards.

An American term describing a close-fitting collar in height between a **polo neck** and a **crew neck**; often used in the context of sweaters.

Tutankhamen influence

(F)

Period: After 1922.

The discovery of the boy-king Tutankhamen's tomb and extensive relics in Egypt led to a vogue for Egyptian patterns and colours on garments and accessories.

Tuxedo

(M)

Period: 1898 onwards.

The American term for a **dinner jacket**, often closed with one button only.

Tweedside

(M)

Period: 1858 onwards.

A loose **lounging jacket**, single-breasted and buttoned high, often only the top button was used; mid-thigh length with a small collar and sometimes short lapels; patch or slit pockets. "One of the most ugly but fashionable garments it has ever been our duty to describe" (1859, *Gentleman's Herald of Fashion*).

t

Tweedside overcoat

(M)

Period: 1850s.

A knee-length form of the **Tweedside** jacket.

Twine

(M)

Period: 1840s.

"As the French call it", an **English wrap**. A double-breasted **paletot-sac** resembling a loose **Chesterfield**.

Twin set

(F)

Period: Late 1920s onwards.

A matching cardigan and jumper, the latter usually short-sleeved and from the 1990s sometimes called a **shell**. Often of knitted wool, but also found in cotton, rayon, silk or mixtures of natural and synthetic fibres.

Twist button

Period: 1860s.

A button covered with strong cotton twist.

Two-piece costume

(F)

Period: 20th century.

A description occasionally used for a suit of jacket and skirt; rarely a dress and jacket.

Tye

(M)

Period: 18th century.

A **wig** with a tied-back **queue**.

Tyes

(F)

Period: Late 19th century.

An American name for girls' **aprons**.

Tyrolean costume

(F & M)

Period: 1930s onwards.

The designer Elsa Schiaparelli (1890–1973) used forms and motifs from traditional Austrian folk dress during the 1930s. This, and increased travel, ensured the widespread popularity of such styles, which were also found in Bavaria and included embroidered blouses, close-fitting waistcoats, boiled wool jackets in bright colours, lederhosen (leather breeches for men) and Tyrolean hats *See* Tyrolese hats.

Tyrolese cloak

(F)

Period: 1809.

A shoulder cape sloping down to the knee-level in front, with rounded ends. Made of sarcenet edged with lace.

Tyrolese hat

(F)

Period: 1869.

A felt hat with a small, flat-topped, tapering crown and a narrow brim turned up slightly at the sides. Trimmed with a feather cockade on one side.

Period: 1930s.

Called a "Tyrolean hat" when the fascination with Austrian styles prompted a revival.

U

Ugg boots

(M, later F)

Period: Early 20th century onwards.

An Australian style of soft, sheepskin boot worn by sheep shearers in the 1930s and adapted for wider use in the 1950s and 1960s, when surfers began to wear them as a warm item of footwear after leaving the ocean. They reached America by the 1970s via the surfing fraternity and were worn as **après-ski** or leisure footwear. Their worldwide popularity was ensured when the actress Pamela Anderson wore them on *Baywatch* in the early 1990s. They are not a brand but a style; the term may derive from "ugly", and they are now made in many countries with different versions and colours other than the familiar, natural, light tan.

Ugly

(F)

Period: 1848–1864.

The popular name for an extra brim, resembling the front of a **calash**, worn round the front of a bonnet as a protection against the sun. Made of half-hoops of cane covered with silk, and when not in use could be folded flat.

Ulster

(M)

Period: 1869 to mid-20th century.

An overcoat with a waist belt either complete or as a strap across the back. At first it had a detachable hood, but in the 1870s a detachable cape was more usual; by 1875 a **ticket pocket** was inserted in the left sleeve just above the cuff.

It was made in single- or double-breasted versions with a buttoned front; in the 1890s a fly front was common. The length varied; in the 1870s the garment reached to the ankles.

u

(F)

Period: 1877–ca. 1940.

A long overcoat, sometimes trained; otherwise similar to the male garment, except for the "Three Decker" or **Carrick** variety in which there were two or three capes. Made of cloth or waterproof material.

Umbrella

(F)

Period: 17th century.

At first used chiefly as a sunshade by women, the shape being nearly flat. "There she lay flat spread as an umbrella" (1616, Ben Jonson, *The Devil is an Ass*).

Period: Early to mid-18th century.

Of oiled silk or linen, the ribs of whalebone or cane, the shape of the cover being pagoda-shaped or domed. Regarded as essentially an article for women only, its use by men being considered as eccentric. Colonel Wolfe in Paris observed in 1752: "The people here use umbrellas...I wonder that a practice so useful is not introduced into England". Jonas Hanway had ventured to do so ca. 1750.

(F & M)

Period: 19th century.

Between 1800 and ca. 1810 the term was used as a slang name for a very broad-brimmed man's hat of that date. "A large slouched beaver umbrella that wanted only a crape hatband to sanctify it for funeral" (1800, C. L. Lewes, *Memoirs*).

However, those using real umbrellas had pagoda-shaped ones, by 1800, on a frame of whalebone with metal stretchers. Patent tubular metal frames appeared ca. 1835. In 1848 alpaca covers were introduced, and in 1852 S. Fox patented metal ribs U-shaped on cross section. Cheaper forms were covered with gingham, which then became a popular name for the article itself. By the middle of the century it had become fashionable for gentlemen to carry umbrellas, "the great point seems to be to get one as long and light as a sunbeam" (1858, *Punch*). For the rest of the century it remained correct to carry one provided it was always rolled up. By 1895 "closely rolled umbrellas will be seen more frequently than ever before. Fashionable men are already wedded to them" (*Tailor & Cutter*).

Ladies' umbrellas of variously coloured silks preserved something of the elegance of the **parasol**, though on a larger scale.

Period: 20th century onwards.

Umbrellas continued to be popular with both sexes. New variants included umbrellas with transparent plastic covers, large colourful golfing umbrellas, and collapsible or telescopic versions.

Umbrella robe

Period: 18th century.

A long overgarment. "Paid for an Umbrella robe to be used in wet weather at funerals" (1768, Essex Records).

Umbrella skirt

(F)

Period: 1891.

A skirt of double-width material cut on the cross with only one seam down the back, concealed under box pleats. Shaped to the hips by darts and slightly trained. Lined throughout and tied back inside.

Under cap

(M)

Period: 16th century.

An indoor cap, usually in the form of a **coif**, sometimes like a **skull-cap** and worn under a hat, cap or bonnet; usually limited to old men. The under cap was sometimes called a **night-cap** and then worn alone.

(F)

Period: 16th to mid-19th century.

An indoor cap worn under an outdoor hat or bonnet. The shape varied throughout the centuries, but many approximated to the coif form.

Underclothes

(F & M)

Items of clothing worn below others, more especially those worn next to the skin, such as combinations, shift, vest, etc.

Underpants

(F & M)

Period: 20th century onwards.

Short, close-fitting knickers or **panties**.

Underpropper

See Supportasse.

Under sleeves

See Engageantes.

Undervest, vest

(F & M)

Period: ca. 1840s onwards.

This undergarment, on the hygienic principle of "wool next the skin", was usually of merino, thigh-length and sleeved; buttoned with a short vent at the neck. It replaced a flannel **under-waistcoat** and cheaper versions were of flannel. From 1875 women adopted coloured vests of washable silk, and gussets shaped for the breasts were then introduced.

In the 1890s vests of natural wool and lambs' wool, with ventilating perforations in the armpits, appeared; these, for men, were then called "undershirts".

In the 20th century vests became lighter, often made of cotton jersey or similar, and **string vests** became popular for men. Women gradually ceased to wear them except in thermal versions for extremely cold conditions.

Under-waistcoat

(M)

Period: ca. 1790–ca. 1850; revived 1888.

A sleeveless waistcoat, shorter than the over-waistcoat but extending a little above its upper edge; the visible portion of rich fabric contrasting in colour with that of the overgarment. Most fashionable ca. 1825–1840 when several under-waistcoats might be worn, one above the other; in the 1840s its use was becoming restricted to evening wear, ceasing to be fashionable after ca. 1850. Revived in 1888 in the form of a white **slip**.

Underwear

See Underclothes.

Undress, common dress

(F & M)

Period: 18th and early 19th centuries.

A term indicating informal styles of clothing, such as that worn for everyday purposes, especially morning dress.

Uniforms

(M, later F)

Period: Medieval onwards.

Any form of dress related to a role or occupation and which is worn by groups of people who need to be quickly identified. Those in convents and monasteries, servants in **livery**, soldiers with distinctive clothing and colours are all in uniform.

See Gym-slip.

Unisex

(F & M)

Period: 1960s onwards.

A term coined to describe styles of clothing or forms of hairdressing and footwear which can be interchangeably worn by men and women, e.g. **T-shirts**, **jeans**, **trainers**.

University athletic costume

(M)

Period: 1886.

A vest with half sleeves; **knickerbockers** to below the knees; a sash round the waist; ankle socks and laced shoes.

University coat

See Angle-fronted coat.

University vest

(M)

Period: 1872.

A double-breasted waistcoat with two pairs of buttons, the front corners sloping away from the bottom button; worn with a **university coat**.

Unmentionables

(M)

Period: 19th century

One of many euphemisms for a man's trousers or breeches; the expressions, ranging from the sublime to the ridiculous, began ca. 1800 with **inexpressibles**; later, **unwhisperables**, **nether integuments**, don't mentions, **bags** and **kicksies**.

Unwhisperables

See Unmentionables.

Upper garment

(M)

Period: 17th century onwards.

The extra outer garment which distinguished the elite male from the non-elite.

"Because we walke in jerkins and in hose,

Without an upper garment, cloake or gowne,

We must be tapsters, running up and down" (1613, S. Rowlands, *Knave of Hearts*).

No elite man would consider himself properly dressed, out of doors, unless he was wearing an upper garment, a cloak, cassock or gown, or was carrying a sword. Without such a garment he was in **querpo**.

Significantly, the embroidered Garter Star of the Order of the Garter was worn on an upper garment, whereas the Lesser George was attached to a ribbon around the neck and not always visible. When Pepys visited the Tower of London, a royal palace, he had to remove his sword at the gate, then he realised he was "improperly dressed" and had to retire to a tavern while he sent for his cloak (1662, *Diary*, October 30).

Traces of this etiquette survived to the end of the 19th century; a Victorian gentleman in the city had to carry a stick, in lieu of a sword, unless he was wearing an overcoat.

Upper stocks

See Stock.

Utility Scheme

(F & M)

Period: 1941–1949.

Clothing was rationed in the UK during World War II and "Utility clothing" was introduced in 1942. There were standard patterns for dresses, suits and top coats, which were produced by a committee of designers and then manufactured. The principal purpose was to minimize the use of fabric and any decorative features which used scarce resources. Even so, a man's Utility suit required 26 of the adult male's annual clothing ration of 66 coupons.

See Clothes rationing.

u

Platform shoes with **peep toes**, **ankle straps** and **wedge** heels. The upper of suede, the heel of contrasting bands of suede and alligator leather. A **Utility** mark is printed inside the shoe, ca. 1941–45. Copyright the Olive Matthews Collection, Chertsey Museum. Photograph by John Chase.

V

Vamp, vampey
Period: 15th century onwards.
A term taken from Old French *avantpied*. The upper front part of a boot or shoe.

Vandyke, vandyking
(F)
Period: 1750s onwards.
A term denoting a pointed border, either in lace or fabric, edging a garment, or an actual ruff itself, intermittently popular for fashionable dress as well as for fancy dress. "Circling round her ivory neck / Frizzle out the smart Vandyke; / Like the ruff that heretofore / Good Queen Bess's maidens wore" (1755, Francis Fawkes, *Odes*).
Also, a lace-bordered handkerchief. "This article has been lately revived and called a vandyck" (1769, *London Magazine*).

Vandyke dress
(M)
Period: 18th century.
A fashion for being painted in a **masquerade costume** resembling that of the 1630s when Anthony Van Dyck was in England; "I am drawn in the Vandyke dress… sleeves and breast slashed" (1770, *Diary of Silas Neville*).

(F)
Mrs Montagu was painted in the female version: "… my dress white satin, fine new point for tuckers, kerchief and ruffles, pearl necklace and earrings and pearls and diamonds on my head, and my hair curled after the Vandyke picture" (1747, Elizabeth Montagu, *Correspondence 1720–61*).

Varens
(F)
Period: 1847.
An outdoor jacket; short with loose sleeves, made of cashmere or velvet lined with silk. A variation of the **casaweck** and **polka**.

Vareuse
(F)
Period: 1950s.
A traditional, heavy cotton, Breton fisherman's smock which appeared in the collection presented by Christian Dior in 1957.

Vegetable ivory buttons
Period: 1862.
Buttons made in the shape of balls, from the seed of the South American palm tree.

Veil

(F)

Period: Medieval.

A **coverchief**.

Period: Late 18th century onwards.

A piece of transparent fabric, such as net, lace or gauze, worn with an outdoor bonnet or hat and arranged to cover part or the whole of the face, or sometimes draped behind as a form of trimming, and then often large and white or black, as in the 1820s and 1830s.

In the 1860s half veils were fashionable. The scarf veil of the 1870s entirely covered the face and was "long enough to be thrown round the neck as a scarf; worn at the seaside.

In 1889 and the 1890s large, spotted veils were worn, pulled in under the chin by a string "rather like a nose-bag".

In the 20th century veils became smaller and lighter, often rolled back from the front of the hat or omitted entirely. In the later years of the century the term was applied to complete covering such as the **burka** worn by Islamic women.

See Voilette, Wedding veil.

Venetian bonnet

(F)

Period: 1800.

A small straw bonnet trimmed with straw wreaths or flowers, the strings emerging from a bow at the back and tied loosely on the bosom.

Venetian cloak

(F)

Period: 1829.

A black satin cloak with a collar and cape and wide, hanging sleeves.

Venetians

(M)

Period: ca. 1570–1620.

Knee breeches, at their most fashionable in the 1580s. "Venetian hosen, they reach beneath the knee to the gartering place of the legge, where they are tied finely with silke points or some such like" (1583, Philip Stubbes, *Anatomie of Abuses*).

Venetians were usually pear-shaped, wide, and often bombasted round the hips and narrowing towards the knees, ca. 1570–1595. Some, however, were voluminous throughout and were called **Venetian slops**. Others were "close to the buttocke like the Venetian galligascoigne" (1610, S. Rowlands, *Martin Mark-All*). They were also called **trusses**.

Venetian sleeve

(F)

Period: 1858.

A day sleeve fitting at the arm-hole, then expanding widely to mid-forearm and slit up the front nearly to the shoulder. Worn with a large, puffed **engageante** having a close cuff.

Venetian slops

See Venetians.

Veney-a-moi, venez-a-moi, venze moy

See Assasin.

Vent

Period: 15th century onwards.

Term used for a vertical slit up, usually from the hem of

An engraving from Henry VI, Part I published by John Boydell in his Shakespeare series. Although this is unlikely to be a depiction of a scene from an actual production it does give a useful impression of **theatre costume**. At this date it was a mixture of styles, suggestive of the status of the performer, and of past history. Using **Vandyke** styles and quasi-historic **fancy dress** it did not bother unduly with historical accuracy, 1795. Copyright the Olive Matthews Collection, Chertsey Museum.

V

a garment, such as coat, shirt, etc., and made for ease of movement. "Item, 1 jakket of red felwet, the vents bound with red lether" (1422–83, Paston Letters).

Ventoye, ventoy

(F)

Period: 17th century.

A **fan** of the Italian type consisting of a short stem with a rectangular vane at the top.

Veronese cuirasse

(F)

Period: 1880.

A jersey bodice lacing at the back.

Veronese dress

(F)

Period: 1880s.

A day dress with a long, plain **princess** tunic of woollen cloth, knee-length, with deep points extending to the hem of the silk underskirt, made with deep box pleats.

Vest

(F & M)

Period: 17th century onwards.

A term at first used for an **under-waistcoat** worn for warmth. Later, an undergarment worn next to the skin. *See* Undervest.

(M)

Period: 1660s–1670s.

A knee-length coat with elbow sleeves, generally confined at the waist by a sash or buckled girdle, and always worn under a **tunic** or **surcoat**. This tunic and vest, mainly a court fashion in England, was the forerunner of the coat-and-waistcoat style and the origin of the man's suit.

Period: 19th century onwards.

Synonymous with **waistcoat**; the American term is still "vest".

(F)

Period: 1794 into 19th century.

A short, sleeveless bodice of varying design, worn with full evening dress.

Period: Early 19th century.

A term for the French long corset. "New invented Parisian vests…made of rich French Twillet, with double cased bones that will never break. The form of them is particularly elegant, by a Reserve on the peak…(which) has the pleasant and very essential effect of keeping the gores…in the proper position, and obviates that unpleasant rucking and chafing that is in all the long corsets that have been invented…" (Advert., July 3, 1802, *Norfolk Chronicle*).

Victoria bodice

(F)

Period: 1899.

A full evening-dress bodice with very low, square or round **décolletage** secured by shoulder straps. Generally trimmed with frills and ruchings of tulle.

Victoria bonnet

(F)

Period: 1838.

A bonnet of satin, the small crown without stiffening, the brim rather close and arching round the face to below the chin; there rounded and curving up towards the crown. The bonnet strings pass from this point under the brim to be tied under the chin. Interior of the brim often trimmed with flowers. A long full **bavolet** at the back.

Victoria mantle

(F)

Period: 1850s.

A knee-length **mantle** with shoulder-cape cut square and short in front, descending to below the waist behind, or merely **vandyked**. Wide, hanging sleeves.

Victoria pelisse-mantle

(F)

Period: 1855.

A double-breasted mantle buttoned down the front; knee-length, with flat collar and short, wide sleeves having reversed cuffs; side pockets.

Victoria skirt

See Grannie skirt.

Victoria sleeve

(F)

Period: 1838 and 1840s, revived in 1890s.

A day sleeve with a large volan (flounce) at the elbow and two smaller ones above; the forearm tight with a closed cuff.

Victorine

(F)

Period: 1849 and 1850s.

A narrow, flat neck **tippet** with short ends in front tied with ribbon at the throat and edged with fur.

Period: 1899.

A waist-length or ankle-length cloak with a high, fluted collar rising from a shaped fur flounce.

Vigone

(M)

Period: Mid-17th century.

A hat made of vicuna wool instead of beaver fur.

Vintage

(F & M)

Period: Late 20th century onwards.

In previous centuries the fashions of earlier generations were occasionally worn, for **fancy dress**, or an heirloom item such as a lace wedding veil or christening robe might reappear. However, the acquisition and regular re-use of every type of item, from accessory to entire outfit, is relatively recent. Wearing family items or seeking out admired styles from a particular period in

V

charity shops, auctions and specialist dealers began seriously in the 1970s. Stylists for celebrities made this trend newsworthy, and the pleasure of a couture piece at a fraction of modern couture prices appealed to innovative dressers in many countries.

Violin bodice
(F)

Period: 1874.

A day bodice with a piece of dark material, in the shape of a violin body, inserted down the back. This was prolonged into the skirt when made with a **princess dress**.

Virago sleeve
Period: ca. 1600–1650.

"The heavily puffed and slashed sleeve of a woman's gown, then fashionable" (1688, Randle Holme, *Armory*).

Visite
(F)

Period: 1845 to early 20th century.

A generic name for a loose outdoor garment ranging from a **pelerine**, mantle or cloak, to a caped **overcoat** in the 1880s. In the 1890s it was given a double cape and a high collar.

Vizard
A whole mask.

See Mask.

Voided shoe
(F & M)

Period: 16th century.

A shoe with short uppers, leaving only a toe-cap and instep strap. "Crepida, a low voyded shooe, with a latchet" (1565, Thomas Cooper, *Thesaurus*).

Voilette
(F)

Period: 1840s to early 20th century.

A fashionable style of diminutive **veil**.

Also a thin dress fabric.

See Voile in Glossary of Fabrics and Materials.

Volant
Period: 19th century.

A small flounce or frill commonly used as a trimming.

Volupere, voluper
(F & M)

Period: 14th century.

A cap or head-dress.

(F)

Period: 16th century.

A head-dress, possibly a **kerchief**.

Vulcanite buttons
Period: 1888.

Also known as ebonite, a hard form of vulcanised rubber, capable of being cut and polished; used as a substitute for jet.

Vulcanized rubber bands
Period: 1845 to early 20th century.

Patented in 1845 and used for garters and belts.

W

Wadded hem
(F)

Period: 1820–1828.

The hem of a skirt padded out with cotton wool.

Waistband
(M)

Period: 18th century onwards.

The band of material attached to the top of breeches, trousers, etc. At the centre of the back was a short vent with lacing holes on each side for lacing across; this vent, after ca. 1790, was generally closed by a **puff** of chamois leather. The waistband, inherited from the **trunk-hose**, ceased to be fashionable after ca. 1836, though it continued in **American trousers**.

(F & M)

Period: 19th century.

The name given to a detachable belt.

Period: 20th century onwards.

The band encircling the waist at the top of shorts, skirts, trousers and other garments with a defined waist.

Waistcoat
(M)

Period: 16th century to 1668.

A waist-length under-doublet, sometimes called a **petticoat**, i.e. a short coat, usually quilted and worn without or with sleeves which were detachable. Worn for warmth or, if for display, then of rich fabrics.

Period: 1668–ca. 1800.

An under-coat, at first cut on similar lines to the coat but without hip-buttons and pleats, the sleeves being discarded from ca. 1750, though occasionally worn by the elderly until ca. 1800.

Becoming shorter ca. 1775, when the front skirts were mere flaps which disappeared by 1790. Constructed as a **single-breasted** garment until the 1730s, with

The Calico Printer.

A calico printer from *The Book of English Trades*, 1823 edition. The clothing is that of the late eighteenth or early nineteenth century with a **shirt**, the sleeves rolled up covered by a high collared **waistcoat**, the breeches and **stockings** partly masked by the workman's sturdy **apron**. Cotton **calico** was often printed with one colour by roller with additional colours added by block printing as here. Printed cottons were very fashionable throughout the nineteenth century. Private collection.

the **double-breasted** form becoming common in the 1780s and usual by the 1790s.

Period: 1800 onwards.
Both single and double-breasted forms were fashionable at various times for day wear, the double-breasted form becoming permissible for evening dress in the 1890s.
See Jockey, Straight, Tattersall, Shawl, French vest.

Period: 20th century onwards.
Waistcoats remained an element of formal dress until World War II, but informally they were less essential or if worn could be knitted, or later of leather and suede alongside fabric versions.

(F)
Period: 16th and 17th centuries.
A close-fitting jacket-bodice worn with a **petticoat** or with a **bedgown** for extra warmth, often replacing the **plackard** or **stomacher**.

Period: 18th to early 20th century.
Cut on the same lines as the male garment and worn with a riding habit, or as a fill-in for an open bodice, when the waistcoat was sometimes sham, having sewn-in front panels only.

Period: 1800–1850.
A flannel waistcoat might be worn as an undergarment for extra warmth; it was replaced by the introduction of the **undervest**, ca. 1840.

Period: 1851.
A fashion for wearing elaborately embroidered waistcoats with carriage dresses; these were darted to fit the figure and were sometimes made from brocaded male waistcoats of the 18th century; this fashion was revived towards the end of the century.

Period: 1880 to early 20th century.
Waistcoats, cut on masculine lines, were common in the tailor-made costumes of those decades.

Period: 20th century onwards.
Waistcoats were occasionally fashionable and were made from a variety of fabrics; they were also knitted and made of leather or suede.

Waistcoat-bosom dress
(F)
Period: 1800–1810.
A dress made in the low-stomacher style with the bodice buttoned down the front.
See Stomacher-front dress.

Waist seam
(M)
Period: From 1823 onwards.
A horizontal seam uniting the body of a formal coat with its skirts.

Wallet
(F & M)
Period: Medieval to early 19th century.
A bag used when travelling, large enough to hold a variety of goods including clothing; similar to a pedlar's pack or a pilgrim's **scrip**.

Period: 19th century onwards.
An American term describing a flat bag or purse designed to hold documents and paper money; originally of leather, but later of various natural and man-made materials.

W

Wardle hat

(F)

Period: 1809.

A straw hat with a conical crown. The name recording a notorious scandal of 1809, exposed by Colonel Wardle in the House of Commons.

Wardrobe

Period: 15th century.

A room in which clothes and occasionally armour were kept. Also, from this period onwards, the clothes belonging to a particular person.

Period: Late 17th century onwards.

The stock of clothing and properties held by a theatrical company.

Period: 19th century onwards.

A piece of furniture, with pegs, rails and shelves or drawers for containing clothes.

Waspie

(F)

Period: Late 1940s onwards.

Abbreviation of "wasp-waisted" as applied to a short, tightly fitting, boned and elasticated **corset**. Worn under the **New Look** garments and later whenever a narrow, defined waist was required.

Watch

(F & M)

Period: Late 16th century onwards.

A small, portable time-piece. In the late 16th century it could be suspended from a chain or ribbon and was set into a variety of forms. England took the lead in the production of watches for much of the 17th century, but French watches were the first to incorporate a spring on the balance mechanism.

Watches in decorative cases were carried, suspended from belts and clothing, and watch chains for men began to be used during the 18th century. All watches were wound with keys until the 1840s when winding buttons were introduced. By then women's jewellery included bracelet and ring watches.

The first wrist watch was designed by Louis Cartier (1875–1942) for the Brazilian aviation pioneer Alberto Santos-Dumont in 1904 and went on sale to the public in 1911. Wrist watches were also made for women and gradually superseded pocket watches. The variety and forms of watch changed swiftly as the major Swiss makers competed for custom at luxury level and at popular level. In the late 20th century the name of the brand or maker – Cartier, Patek Phillippe, Rolex – was as important as that of a major fashion designer.

See Swatch.

Waterfall back

(F)

Period: 1883–1887.

The skirt of a morning or walking dress made with a series of flounces down the back from waist to hem so that with a projecting bustle "the skirt seems to pour itself over a precipice".

Waterfall neckcloth

See Mail-coach necktie.

Waterproof

Period: 1800 onwards.

A name beginning to be applied to many forms of outdoor garments of which the threads composing the fabric used had been rendered waterproof before weaving; thus distinct from those textiles impregnated with

A woman's gold fob **watch** with a green guilloche enamel back (shown on the right) with a central pearl. The watch face is edged with an outer rim of **pearls**. The watch is suspended from a bow-shaped gold and enamel **brooch**, ca. 1880. Copyright the Olive Matthews Collection, Chertsey Museum. Photograph by John Chase.

solution of india-rubber.

See Mackintosh.

In 1893 Burberry's patent waterproof material was composed of an outer layer of gabardine with an inner of soft tweed; in 1896 the Manchester firm of Joseph Mandleburg listed "silk striped proofing".

Waterproof cloak

(F)

Period: 1867.

A cloak with a small, tasselled hood of waterproof material.

Watteau

(F)

Period: 1870s.

A **polonaise** with a Watteau back, usually of white fabric strewn with flowers.

Watteau body

(F)

Period: 1853–1866.

A day **basquine** bodice with low, square neck, the fronts not meeting but filled in by a **chemisette** crossed by ribbon bows to the waist closing the bodice; elbow sleeves with deep lace ruffles. The name is derived from the style of dress found in the work of the French artist Antoine Watteau (1684–1721).

Watteau costume

(F)

Period: 1868.

A bodice with a **fichu** front and round skirt edged with deep pleating, and an over-dress looped up at the sides of the skirt, with a **Watteau pleat** behind from neck to hem.

Watteau pleat

(F)

Period: ca. 1850 to early 20th century.

A revival of the 18th-century **sack**-back. Worn occasionally, especially in the 1850s and 1860s for afternoon wear and, from the 1880s into the early 20th century, as a feature on **teagowns**.

Watteau robe

(F)

Period: 1850s.

A ball dress in the open-robe style with a **Watteau pleat** at the back and inset with lace.

Wearing sleeves

(F)

Period: 17th century.

Sleeves worn on the arms, as opposed to **hanging sleeves** which were usually sham. "Three gownes with wearing slevis and long slevis for three other gownes" (1612–13, Warrant to the Great Wardrobe on Princess Elizabeth's marriage).

Wedding dress

(F)

Period: 19th century.

Before the 19th century there was no set formula for this dress, except that it was often white or silver amongst elite families.

From 1800–1840 it was a semi-décolleté evening dress with short sleeves and long white gloves. From 1830 a wedding dress was usually white lace over silk or satin. From 1844 a white afternoon dress replaced the evening, low-necked gown, and in 1867 white book muslin was often used instead of silk or satin. From the 1880s the dress was always high-necked, but by then "a bride is often married in her going-away dress", a choice which was permissible throughout the century and was usual for women from humbler families.

Period: 20th century onwards.

Department stores provided ready-made wedding dresses. There were many **paper patterns** and an extensive range of fabrics for those able to sew or to find a dressmaker and, except for widows and older brides, white became usual. The length of dresses varied, short in the 1920s and 1960s, but mostly ankle-length with an optional train and a veil covering the head rather than a hat. By the late 20th century it was usual for younger brides to wear a strapless white evening dress, combining the style for the service with that worn at an evening party; the more discreet might wear a **shrug** or sleeved stole beneath the veil.

Wedding garter

(F)

Period: 16th–18th century.

This was generally blue; the colour associated with the Virgin Mary, but sometimes white or red. The bride's garters were trophies eagerly sought for: "…let the young Men and the Bride-Maids share Your garters; and their joints Encircle with the Bridegroom's Points" (1648, Herrick, *Hesperides*).

Fragments of them were then worn in the young men's hats.

Wedding gloves

(F & M)

Period: 16th and 17th centuries.

White gloves were distributed among the wedding guests. "Five or six pair of the white innocent wedding gloves" (1599, Dekker, *Untrussing of the Humorous Poet*).

Wedding knives

(F)

Period: 15th to end of 17th century.

A pair of knives contained in one sheath were given to the bride and then worn as a symbol of her married status. "See at my girdle hang my wedding knives" (1609, Dekker, *Match Me in London*).

Wedding suit

(M)

Period: 19th century.

In previous decades, for fashionable elite men, this had been merely a ceremonial full dress suit, often with white waistcoat and stockings. By 1820 a blue **dress coat** with gilt buttons, white waistcoat and black knee-breeches had become the convention; by ca. 1830 the breeches were commonly replaced by white trousers or **pantaloons**. In the 1850s the **frock coat** was beginning to replace the day-time dress coat. "Mr. P. consulted me about his wedding-coat whether it shall be a frock-coat, which I advised though I believe not quite correct with a bride's veil" (1853, *Lady Elizabeth Spencer Stanhope's Letter-Bag,* ed. A. M. W. Stirling). By 1860 the outfit had become a blue or claret-coloured frock coat, white waistcoat and lavender doe-skin trousers. In the 1870s the frock coat was being replaced by the **morning coat**, which by 1886 had become the rule, reverting in the 1890s to a black **frock coat**, a light-coloured, double-breasted waistcoat and grey striped cashmere trousers, with patent-leather **button boots**. A white buttonhole flower was worn from ca. 1850. A black silk **top hat**, replacing the **beaver**, became general by 1840. Light-coloured gloves; from ca. 1870 lavender-coloured were worn.

Period: 20th century onwards.
The frock coat with a pale waistcoat was worn until the 1920s, but after World War I a morning coat with striped trousers and a black or pale waistcoat was more usual for those who could afford formal wear; uniforms and lounge suits were worn by many men. The morning coat and its correct accompaniments continued to be worn throughout the century, but for the majority of men the **lounge suit** was the usual choice for civil and religious weddings.

Wedding veil, bridal veil
(F)
Period: ca. 1800–1900.
A fashion known in the 17th century, but rare before about 1800. From this date until ca. 1860 the veil was attached to the head and hung down the back almost to the ground. It was usually of white lace, especially of Brussels or Honiton in the 1840s, following the fashion set by Queen Victoria.
From ca. 1830 an orange-blossom wreath was added, and by 1860 onwards the new fashion was for the veil to hang over the face down to the waist or knee, though the earlier style survived into the 1880s. In 1892 one corner of the veil was arranged to hang over the face to knee level and "the fullness drawn back on either side with jewelled pins".

Period: 20th century onwards.
Lighter veils of silk net or tulle replaced lace, and **Juliet caps** with veils hanging behind were popular before and after World War I, with long veils in place of a dress

with a train, or short veils, often with coronet-style head-dresses, orange blossom chaplets. "…a little tricorne hat with yards and yards of veil sweeping behind you…" (1931, *Essex County Standard*).
Variants of these styles continued after World War II, with artificial net or tulle replacing silk, and with tiny caps, imitation tiaras and arrangements of flowers (real or artificial) or feathers being worn with shoulder-length or longer veils.

Wedgies, wedge-soled shoes
(F)
Period: 1930s onwards.
Although something not dissimilar to a wedge sole (the solid section of heel forming part of the raised sole) had been seen earlier, it was the Italian maker Salvatore Ferragamo (1898–1960) who introduced a wedge heel for shoes. This style became especially popular in America in the late 1930s and has been intermittently fashionable since that date.
Men's crepe-soled shoes of the 1950s, with no defined sole and heel, were a variant of the female style.

Weed, weyd, wede
Period: 9th century onwards.
A term for a garment of some type; surviving well into the 19th century in the description "widow's weeds", meaning mourning apparel.

Weepers
(M)
Period: 18th century.
Muslin arm-bands. "Mourners clap bits of muslin on their sleeves and these are called weepers" (1762, O. Goldsmith, *The Citizen of the World*).

Period: 19th century.
Broad muslin hat-bands tied round a mourner's hat, the two ends hanging down behind to the waist; worn at a funeral. Black was the general rule, but white was worn if the deceased was a virgin. Less common during the last quarter of the century.
See Mourning attire.

Welch wig
(M)
Period: ca. 1800–1850.
A worsted cap with a fluffy surface, worn by travellers and others. "The sexton's Welch wig which he wore at rainy funerals" (1849, Albert Smith, *The Pottleton Legacy*).

Wellesley wrapper
(M)
Period: 1853.
A short, sac-like wrapper, double-breasted and often bordered with fur. The front fastened with military **brandenburgs**.

Wellington boot
(M)

w

Period: 1817 onwards.

Similar to a **top boot** but without the turn-over top. The name of this and other items of clothing celebrate the Duke of Wellington, the great British general and politician who defeated the Emperor Napoleon I at Waterloo in 1815.

(F & M)

Period: 20th century onwards.

The term was transferred to rubber boots made in this style.

Wellington coat

(M)

Period: 1820–1830.

"A kind of half-and-half greatcoat and under-coat [i.e. frock coat] meeting close and square below the knees" (1828, *The Creevey Memoirs*).

Wellington frock

(M)

Period: 1816–1820s.

The forerunner of the Victorian **frock coat**; at first a single-breasted coat with roll or **Prussian collar** but no lapels; buttoned down to the waist; a full skirt to just above the knees. The fronts meeting without a cut-in; the back with a central vent, side pleats and hip-buttons. No waist seam.

In 1818 a horizontal dart was added at the waist-level to improve the fit; this **fish**, the tailor's term, became in 1823 extended into a seam at the waist. Flapped pockets in the skirt at the sides of the waist were usual.

Wellington hat

(M)

Period: 1820–1840.

A tall beaver hat "the crown 8 inches deep and over-spreading at the top" (1830, *Dissertatio Castorum*).

Wellington pantaloons

(M)

Period: 1818–1820s.

Pantaloons with side-slits from the calf down, closed by loops and buttons.

Welt

Period: 16th century onwards.

A strengthened border of a garment or part of one, and in the 16th century a decorative border synonymous with a **guard**. "Gownes welted with velvet" (1592, *Quips for an Upstart Courtier*).

The term used in the making of footwear means the narrow strip of leather sewn around the edge of the upper and insole, to which the sole is attached.

Wet look

Period: 1920s onwards.

The shiny, seemingly wet surface of a fabric, created by a chemical or other finish.

See Ciré in Glossary of Fabrics and Materials.

Whalebone

Period: Medieval onwards.

The ivory of the walrus or a similar mammal confused with a whale was often meant. The usual meaning describes the horny substance taken from the upper jaw of the whale and used to stiffen corsetry and garments. *See* Glossary of Fabrics and Materials.

Whalebone bodice, whalebone bodies

(F, also children)

Period: 16th and 17th centuries.

A bodice of a gown stiffened with **whalebone** strips; sometimes an under-bodice as a pair of **stays** and sometimes combining both, the front being decorative and the back, if covered by an over-gown, plain like a corset. "…the first time the child (a girl aged three) put on a pair of whalebone bodies…" (1617, *Diary of Lady Anne Clifford*).

Wheel farthingale, farthingale

(F)

Period: 1580–1620s.

A wheel-shaped structure made of wire or **whalebone** and covered with fabric, often silk. It was worn round the waist, with a slight tilt up behind. The skirt of the gown was carried out horizontally over this frame and then allowed to fall to the ground from the edge of the wheel. This was a variant of the **French farthingale** and gave the same tub-like appearance.

See Catherine wheel farthingale, Italian farthingale.

Whisk

(F)

Period: ca. 1625–1720.

A broad **falling band** or collar, generally trimmed with broad lace. "A woman's neck-whisk is used both plain and laced, and is called of most a gorget or falling whisk because it falleth about the shoulders" (1688, R. Holme, *Armory*).

Whittle

(F)

Period: 17th century onwards.

Various meanings but predominantly a large cloak, mantle or shawl, usually of flannel and worn by countrywomen, especially by a mother carrying a baby. "My whittle that is fringed" (1668, Will of Jane Humphrey, of Dorchester, MA, USA).

"A lying-in's expensive too, In cradles, whittles, …" (ca. 1730, W. Somerville, *The Yeomen of Kent*).

Whole backs

Period: 19th century.

A term denoting coats made without a central back seam.

Whole falls

See Falls.

Wide-awake

(M)

Period: 19th century.

POSVI DEVM ADIVTOREM MEVM

ELISABET D.G.ANGLIAE, FRANCIAE, HIBERNIAE, ET VERGINIAE REGINA, FIDEI CHRISTIANAE PROPVGNATRIX ACERRIMA. NVNC IN DÑO REQVIESCENS.

Engraving by Crispijn van der Passe after Isaac Oliver of Elizabeth I, ca. 1600. The **wheel farthingale**, long **hanging sleeves** and bulky sleeves attached to the **bodice** widen the silhouette. A lace edged **ruff** is open and pinned to the neckline and a long gauzy **mantle** attached to a halo collar focus attention on the head and face. The queen is probably wearing a **wig**, she owned many in various colours, and that and her clothing are covered in **pearls** or gemstone clasps or **brooches**. National Portrait Gallery, London. http://www.npg.org.uk.

A broad-brimmed, low-crowned hat of felt or **stuff**. For country wear.

Wig, periwig, peruke
(F & M)
Period: 16th century onwards.
An artificial covering of hair for the head; worn by men and women for decorative purposes or to conceal thin or non-existent hair.
Worn by men almost universally during the 18th century until ca. 1790, and by women especially from ca. 1795 to 1810. Named varieties include: **Adonis**, **bag-wig**, **bob**, **brigadier**, **campaigne**, **catogan**, **cauliflower**, **caxon**, **club**, **cue-peruke**, **cut-wig**, **Duvillier**, **major**, **pigeon-winged**, **pigtail**, **Ramillies**, **scratch**, **toupee**, **tye**.

Period: 20th century.
The use of natural hair for wig-making was gradually replaced by synthetic alternatives for whole wigs or partial pieces such as extensions.

Wimple
(F)
Period: Late 12th to mid-14th centuries, rare in the 15th century.
A long piece of white linen or silk draped over the front of the neck and swathed round the chin, the ends being pinned to the hair above the ears. It was worn with a **veil** or a **fillet** or both, or sometimes alone.

Period: 1809.
The name was used for a gauze covering of the head, worn with evening dress.

Wimpled
Period: 16th century.
A term with two meanings: firstly "disguised" and secondly "arranged in folds", as with a muffler which was worn like a wimple.
"Why are they wimpled? Shall they not unmask them?" (1590, *Three Lords and Ladies of London*).

Windbreaker, windcheater
(F & M)
Period: ca. 1950 onwards.
A type of short jacket with a fitted waistband, based on British RAF flying jackets. Versions have been made in wool, gabardine, and synthetic fabrics, and all types are usually waterproof and fasten with a front zip. Worn for outdoor sports and leisure pursuits.
See Anorak.

Wing collar
(M)
Period: 19th to mid-20th century.
A standing collar with the two front points turned down; it was also known as a "butterfly collar".

Wings
(F & M)
Period: ca. 1545–1640s.
Stiffened and generally decorative bands, often crescent-shaped, projecting over the shoulder seam of **bodices**, **doublets** and **jerkins**, and women's gowns. With detachable sleeves the wings hid the ties.

Period: 1750–1800.
The side flaps of an indoor cap thus constructed, such as the **dormouse** cap.

Winkers
(M)

W

Period: ca. 1816–1820.

The very high points of the shirt collar which, as worn by the ultra-fashionable, reached up to the corners of the eyes.

Winkle-picker shoes

(F & M)

Period: Early 1950s onwards.

As a distinct contrast to the suede, crepe-soled shoes worn by **Teddy boys**, this new style with its elongated toe acquired several names before becoming the "winkle-picker". Popular with **Mods** and later with **punks** and **Goths**, this style has always been a rock "n roll favourite with bands from the Beatles to the Kings of Leon. Often they were made of eye-catching materials such as pearlized crocodile skin. The female equivalent was often low-heeled with long narrow toes, or a combination of **stiletto heel** and "needlepoint toe" as the style was sometimes called.

Witchoura mantle

(F)

Period: 1808–1818, and the 1830s.

A **mantle** with a deep cape and fur trimming. In the 1830s the name was revived for a mantle without a cape but with a high **stand collar** and very large sleeves. Trimmed or lined with fur; always a winter garment.

Witch's hat

(F)

Period: 1800 onwards.

Similar to a **gipsy hat**. The essential feature being that the brim was bent down by ribbon strings passing over it from the crown, to be tied under the chin.

Wonderbra

(F)

Period: 1935 onwards.

A Canadian style of uplift **brassière** which was sold in America and Canada for several decades before it became a worldwide phenomenon in the early 1990s, when the British firm Gossard, making it under license from its American owners, repackaged it in 1991 as the ultimate "must-have" bra – with its under-wired uplift and divide enhancement of female breasts. Although the marketing campaign was aimed at men, women bought it by the million.

Woodstock gloves

(F & M)

Period: 18th century.

"Riding gloves made of fawn skin; got them at Woodstock where they are famous for making them" (1777, *Letters of Mrs. Graham*).

Woolward

Period: 16th century.

Clothed wholly in woollen materials; i.e. without a linen shirt. "I go woolward" (1590, *Love's Labours Lost*).

Wrap

(F)

Period: Early 19th century onwards.

A loose, unstructured garment to wear over a dress, often used as an interchangeable term for cloak or shawl. "Hoar-frost velour wrap, three-quarter lined heavy crepe-de-chine. Tastefully trimmed opossum fur, 13 gns" (1925, Rogers Brothers, Colchester).

Wraparound

(F)

Period: ca. 1950 onwards.

Any item of clothing that is wrapped around the body and tied, rather than fastened with buttons, **zips** or similar. The **sarong**-style wraparound skirt has been popular for beachwear and variants of this, with ties and waistbands, similarly with blouses and dresses, were produced by designers and manufacturers. The American designer Diane von Furstenberg (1946–) created a wraparound jersey dress in the 1970s which became a wardrobe **classic** for busy women.

Wrapper

(F)

Period: 18th century.

A term used for a woman's bedroom loose robe which might also be worn in bed. "My Lady generally was in Bed with nothing on but a loose Gown or Wrapper" (1744, Report of the Annesley Cause; evidence of the maid. *The London Magazine and Monthly Chronologer*). "Fine thick printed Cotton…to make two wrappers for my mother" (1739, *Purefoy Letters*).

(M)

Period: 1840–1860.

In the 1840s a name applied to various forms of loose overcoat, both single- and double-breasted and sometimes used for a **Chesterfield**. In the 1850s it was defined as a loose, thigh-length overcoat cut to wrap over the front, sometimes buttoned but more often held in place by the hand. The collar was a deep shawl type. Often worn with evening dress.

Wrapping front dress

(F)

Period: 1800–ca. 1830.

The bodice of a low, **stomacher-front dress** made to fasten in a cross-over manner.

Wrapping gown

(F)

Period: ca. 1700–1750.

A term applied to a dress having a bodice with a wrap-over front continuous with the upper part of the skirt.

Wrap-rascal

(M)

Period: ca. 1738–1850.

A loose form of overcoat; in the 19th century it usually applied to a countryman's coat or to the kind worn by those travelling on the outside of a coach. Generally made of heavy cloth.

w

X and Y

Yachting jacket, short paletot

(F)

Period: 1860–1890.

A short, square-cut, outdoor coat reaching to hip level. Made single- or double-breasted, with large buttons and loose sleeves.

Yankee neckcloth

(M)

Period: 1818–1830s.

See American neckcloth.

Yarmulke

(M)

A thin, rounded skull-cap worn by Orthodox Jewish boys and men and other males on religious occasions; usually held in place by a hair grip. Also known as a "kippah".

Yashmak

(F)

The substantial veil worn by Muslim women beneath their eyes to cover their faces for cultural and religious reasons.

Yeoman hat

(F)

Period: 1806–1812.

Hat with a full, deep, soft crown and close, up-turned brim or none, but the crown gathered into a broad band. For morning or walking dress.

Y-fronts

(M)

Period: 1935 onwards.

Patented by the American hosiery firm Coopers, these close-fitting underpants made from a cotton jersey fabric, with an elasticated waist and an inverted Y opening at the front, were originally thought too daring but eventually became the leading style until **boxer shorts** and **trunks** began to overtake them in popularity in the 1990s.

Y-line

(F)

Period: 1955.

The line designed by Christian Dior (1905–1957) which emphasized the neck and shoulders, with large collars but narrowing towards the hemline.

Yoke

Period: 19th century onwards.

The shaped sections across the upper body, between neck and bust or shoulders, to which the garment is sewn; a similar section was also found below the waistband of a skirt in certain styles.

Yoke bodice

(F)

Period: 1880s onwards.

A bodice or blouse made with a **yoke**. A similar yoke was often added to the **Norfolk jacket** from 1894.

Yoke skirt

(F)

Period: 1898 onwards.

A day walking skirt made with a pointed **yoke** joined to the lower part, which was cut from a circle. Worn with a foundation or under-lining attached at the waist only. Some were made with a flounce below the knees.

York tan gloves

(F & M)

Period: 1780–1820s.

Gloves, long or short, of fawn-coloured soft leather. "York tan gloves…the smooth surface inside, tied high above the elbows" (1788, *Mrs. Papendiek's Memoirs*). The male versions were wrist-length.

York wrapper

(F)

Period: 1813.

A high-necked morning dress, buttoned behind; made of jacconet muslin, the front decorated with alternate "diamonds" of lace or needlework.

Youth styles

(F & M)

Period: 1950s onwards.

Clothing for the adolescent young, "teenagers" in the term used by Americans and adopted elsewhere, had appeared in the late 1930s. In Europe teenage or youth styles followed in various waves, some specific to particular countries. The UK was particularly fruitful in this regard with **Teddy boys**, **Mods** and **Rockers**, **punk** styles, **New Romantics**, **Goths**, and so on. From the 1960s onwards these styles, sometimes described as **Street style**, were imitated and transformed by major designers looking for inspiration.

Yukuta

(F & M)

Period: 20th century onwards.

A lightweight, cotton **kimono** with a fabric covered in stencilled designs, originally worn after bathing but now used as a **dressing-gown** or house coat. Known in the west since the early 19th century, it became widely available in the 20th century.

x & y

Z

Zazou style
(F & M)

Period: 1940s.

The French version of the **zoot suit** clothing which originated in America. It was fashionable amongst a group of young men and women, many in Paris during the German occupation in the early 1940s. The men wore tight-fitting trousers with large, thigh-length jackets with a dropped shoulder-line. The women wore a loose-fitting jacket or square-shouldered fur coat with a short, pleated skirt and **platform** shoes.

Zip fastener, zip, zipper
Period: Late 19th century onwards.

Experimental fasteners appeared in America in the 1890s, but the interlocking metal-tooth version was developed just before World War I and used on **windcheaters** for the US navy in 1917. The term "zip" was not always used; this invention was described as a "Lightning plastic fastener" by Schiaparelli in 1935, but the term was usual by the 1920s: "Many of the new sports suits have zip-fasteners" (1927, *Daily Express*, 22 November).

Zone
(F)

Period: 1770s and 1780s.

A fill-in for an open bodice of a gown, the shape varying according to the shape of the exposed gap.

Zoot suit
(M)

Period: Late 1930s onwards, but rare after the 1960s.

A style of suit associated with African Americans but adopted by others as an expression of originality. A wide-shouldered, long jacket, narrow at the waist with a draped back, worn with peg-top, loose trousers which were narrow at the ankle, was complemented by a dangling key or watch chain, a broad-brimmed hat and colourful silk ties. All of these garments were often brightly coloured or patterned and influenced both alternative and mainstream designs.

Zouave coat, Oriental wrapper
(M)

Period: 1845.

A cloak-like coat with velvet collar and cuffs, lined and quilted throughout with silk. "Has the advantage of a coat and a cloak, can be worn as a riding or walking coat or opera cloak."

Zouave jacket
(F)

Period: 1859–1870 and the 1890s.

A jacket of silk, velvet or cloth, without a back seam, the front borders rounded off and fastened at the neck only.

Many variations, but all retaining the main features. The original design was adopted from the Algerian Zouave troops in the Italian war of 1859.

(M)

Period: 1860s.

A similar jacket, worn by little boys.

Zouave paletot
(M)

Period: 1840s.

A **paletot** of llama wool, waterproofed. "May be worn with or without an under-coat. One of the most gentlemanly and unassuming garments offered to the public."

Zouave trousers, Sarouel trousers
See Peg-top trousers.

Fashion plate from a supplement to *The Queen, The Lady's Weekly Journal*, 18 March 1863, depicting two young women in day wear. The one at the rear has "The **Zouave jacket** ... universally worn in braided cloth or velvet" over a bodice and skirt; a velvet one, as shown here cost 2 gns in 1863. Both women have full skirts supported by **crinolines**. The woman in the foreground wears a version of the **Marie Stuart bonnet** and **gloves** ready for paying visits while her companion has a lace and flower trimmed indoor **cap**. Copyright the Olive Matthews Collection, Chertsey Museum.

Glossary: Fibres, Fabrics, Materials

A

Abaca
Period: 19th century.
The native name for the palm which provides Manila hemp. The name is also applied to the fibre from which "the most exquisite textile fabrics and elegant Manilla hats are manufactured".

Acetate
Period: 1869 onwards.
A manufactured synthetic yarn and then fabric made from cellulose; a German invention used when a light, silky fabric was needed.

Acrylic
Period: 1947 onwards.
A synthetic fibre used as a substitute for wool and later given tradenames such as Acrilan and Orlon.

Adrianople
Period: 1878.
An unglazed cotton lining; in 1880, a red **calico** printed with arabesques.

Aerophane
Period: ca. 1820.
A fine, crimped **crepe**.

Aertex
Period: 1888 onwards.
Cotton cellular fabric invented in England; the Aertex Company was formed in 1888 and the fabric was used for underwear and sports clothes.

Alamode
Period: 17th century.
"A thin light glossy black silk" (Chambers); often spoken of as "Mode".

Albatross
Period: 20th century
Lightweight woollen fabric with a slightly creped surface finish.

Albert crape
Period: 1862.
A superior quality of black silk **crape** for mourning. In 1880 made of silk and cotton.

Alepine, alapeen, allopeen
Period: 18th century.
A mixed stuff of silk and wool or of mohair and cotton. In 1832 the name of a textile resembling **bombazine**.

Alexander
Period: Medieval.
A striped silk material.

Algerine
Period: 1840.
A twilled **shot silk**, green and poppy-red, or blue and gold.

Allejah, alajah
Period: Early 18th century.
Any kind of corded stuff; also a corded silk fabric from Turkestan.

Alliballi
Period: Early 19th century.
An Indian **muslin**.

Alpaca
Period: 1841.
A springy, shiny textile, of the wool of the Alpaca goat and silk; later, cotton. Originally created by Sir Titus Salt in 1838.

Alpago
Period: 1843.
"A stout satin delaine".

Amen
Period: 19th century.
A fine quality of figured **lasting**; also called **draft**.

Amice
Period: 16th century.
A kind of grey fur, possibly squirrel.

Amy Robsart satin
Period: 1836.
A satin "with white ground with white flowers traced in gold thread, or pale-coloured ones in silver".

Anabas
Period: Early 18th century.
A cheap cotton material.

Ancote vale velvet
Period: ca. 1840.
A cotton **velvet**.

Andalusian
Period: 1825.
A fine, open, washing silk with a **broché** pattern.

Anglo-merino
Period: ca. 1809.

A textile nearly as fine as muslin, manufactured at Norwich and made from King George III's flock of merino sheep.

Angola, Angora
Period: 1815.

"The new lama cloth", made from the hair of the llama goat, from the neighbourhood of Angora in Asia Minor. Originally imported as **mohair**. In 1850 it was woven with a warp of coloured silk under the name of "poil de chèvre".

Aniline dyes
Period: 1856 onwards.

Dyes derived from coal tar which transformed the range of colours available for fabrics. The first synthetic dye was discovered by William Henry Perkin (1838–1907) whose aniline purple, better known as mauve, was an instant success and led to further discoveries.

Anterne
Period: Early 18th century.

A **stuff** of wool and silk, or of mohair and cotton.

Applebloom, appleblue
Period: 14th century.

A cloth resembling in colour, and perhaps in pattern, apple-blossom.

Aquerne
Period: ca. 1200.

Squirrel's fur.

Aramid
Period: 20th century.

A manufactured fibre formed from synthetic polyamide (a type of nylon). Fabrics woven from aramid fibres are strong and resistant to high temperatures and extreme conditions. Such fabrics are often used for overalls, jackets, gloves and similar items which require considerable thermal protection.

Ariel
Period: 1837.

A woollen **gauze** quadrilled in white on coloured ground.

Armazine
Period: 18th century.

A strong **corded silk** used for ladies' gowns and gentlemen's waistcoats.

Armine
See Ermine.

Armoire
Period: 1880.

A very thick **corded silk**.

Armoise, armoisin, armozeen
Period: 16th century.

A **taffeta**, generally black. In the 19th century it was "a stout silk almost invariably black, used for hatbands and scarves at funerals" (1840, Perkins).

Armozeau
Period: 1820s.

"A silk similar to lutestring but not so thick."

Armure
Period: 1850.

A rich silk and wool fabric with an almost invisible design, such as a twill, a triangle or a chain, on the surface.

Armurette
Period: 1874.

A fancy silk and wool fabric.

Artificial silk
See Rayon.

Astrakhan
Period: 18th century onwards.

The skin of young lambs from this part of Russia resembled a silky fur; also known as "Persian lamb". A woollen fabric woven to resemble the lambskin was fashionable in the early 20th century.

Astrakine
Period: 1932.

Light, flexible velvet with a surface imitating Persian lamb.

Atlas
Period: 17th and 18th centuries.

A smooth, silk cloth imported from India; in England the term applied to tawdry silks woven with gold and silver threads. Also applied loosely to a gown of that material. "Ladies with tawdry atlasses" (1706).

Attaby
Period: 14th century.

A silk fabric; the name becoming later **tabby**.

Augusta
Period: 17th century.

A **fustian** made at Augsburg, Germany.

Avignon
Period: 19th century.

A silk **taffeta** used for coat linings.

Aylesham
Period: 13th and 14th centuries.

Usually linen, but also a woollen cloth, made at Aylesham in Norfolk.

Azure
Period: 16th century.

A blue cloth similar to **plunket**.

B

Badger
Period: Medieval.
The fur of the animal, but not used by elite groups.

Baft
Period: 16th century.
A coarse cotton fabric, red, blue or undyed, or printed in checks.

Bagdad
Period: 1872.
An Eastern silk fabric striped like **Algerine** but with wider lines and of thicker substance.

Bagheera
Period: Early 1900s.
A type of uncut pile velvet used for evening dresses; later imitations were made of **rayon** crepe.

Bag Holland
Period: 17th century.
A fine quality of linen used for shirts.

Baise, baize, bays
Period: 16th century.
A woollen cloth resembling a thin **serge** introduced by Walloon refugees from the Spanish Netherlands in 1561. One of the many "**New Draperies**".

Bakelite
Period: ca. 1907 onwards.
An invention of the Belgian Dr Leo Baekeland, who between 1907 and 1909 created a thermoplastic sub-stitute for shellac. It was the first synthetic, plasticized material which could be shaped when heated, mass-produced and formed in moulds. Its slogan was, "The Material of a Thousand Uses". It was used to make buttons, belt and shoe buckles, jewellery, clasps for handbags and similar.

Baldekin, baudekin
Period: Medieval.
A rich silk fabric with gold thread, of the nature of **brocade**.

Baleen
Period: 14th century.
The horny substance in the upper jaw of the whale, used in armour, and in dress from the 16th century when it became known as **whalebone**.

Balernos
Period: 1874.
A very soft and silky **mohair**.

Balzarine
Period: 1830s.
A cotton and worsted fabric similar to **barege**.

Balzerine
Period: 1889.
A narrow-striped **grenadine** with broad, silk crepe stripes.

Bambulo
Period: 1885.
A coarsely woven, slightly transparent, shot **canvas** cloth.

Bangal, Bengal
Period: 17th century.
Various piece goods imported from Bengal which may have included calico, gingham, silk, etc.

Banlon
Period: 20th century.
Name given to a process used to add weight and elas-ticity to synthetic fabrics; created by the American firm of J. Bancroft & Sons.

Barathea
Period: 1840s.
A black silk and worsted mixture used for mourning. Later, worsted fabrics in twill hopsack weave.

Barege
Period: 1819.
A semi-transparent, open-mesh fabric of silk and wool, the former thrown up on the surface. Sometimes of all wool.

Barege de Pyrenees
Period: 1850.
A barege printed with delicate foliage and brilliant flowers.

Barege-grenadine
Period: 1877.
A cotton and **jute** barege.

Barleycorns
Period: 18th century.
A checked fabric, sometimes scarlet; exact composition unknown.

Barlingham
Period: 14th century.
A **taffeta** woven at Burlingham, near Norwich.

Barmillion
Period: 17th century.
A variety of **fustian** made in Manchester (1641).

Baronette satin
Period: 19th century.
Sports fabric of silk fibre with cotton back; similar to **georgette** satin.

Barpour
Period: 1847.
A twilled silk and wool mixture.

Barracan
Period: Late 18th and 19th centuries.
A coarse, thick, corded stuff resembling **camlet**; the warp of silk and wool, the weft of Angora goat's hair. In the 18th century often watered.

Barragon
Period: 18th century.
Perhaps identical with **paragon**.

Barras
Period: 17th and 18th centuries.
A kind of **canvas** or linen imported from Holland and used for neckcloths.

Barratee
Period: 19th century.
A silk stuff, a variety of **barathea**.

Barrister's plaid
Period: 1850s.
A small-check pattern cloth used for trousers.

Basin de laine
Period: 1855.
A thick woollen **dimity**, the right side ribbed, the other with a long, soft nap.

Bath coating
Period: 18th and 19th centuries.
A thick, double-raised **baise** used for overcoats.

Batik
Period: 19th century.
A technique devised in Java for creating designs on textiles by covering the base fabric with wax within a distinct patterned area; the exposed areas were then dyed. The process could be repeated if several colours were required. This method reached the UK by way of Holland.

Batiste
Period: 1820s.
Dressed cotton **muslin** with a wiry finish.

Batiste de laine
Period: 1835.
"A new material of the Chaley kind but mingled with silk. It is striped with satin stripes which form squares, and is always in two colours strongly contrasted."
See Challis.

Baudekin
Period: Medieval.
A costly, imported, figured silk; some versions with a warp of gold thread and a weft of silk. By the 15th century these were **lampas** silks, plain or figured, woven in one or several colours.

Bauson skin
Period: 16th century.
The skin of the badger.

Bayadere
Period: 1840s.
A striped silk and wool fabric, the stripes being alternately plain and satiny.

Bazan, basen
Period: 13th century.
Sheepskin tanned in oak or birch bark.

Bearskin
Period: 17th century onwards.

As a dress fur, first mentioned in 1619. In the 18th century, a rough cloth used for working men's frocks.

Bearskin cloth
Period: 19th century.
A thick, coarse, woollen cloth with a shaggy nap; resembling **dreadnought**.

Beaudoy
Period: 18th century.
A worsted cloth used for stockings.

Beaupers
Period: 16th and 17th centuries.
Linen similar to **bunting**.

Beaver
Period: Medieval.
The fur of that animal used for gloves.

Period: Late 18th and 19th centuries.
A woollen overcoating with one face sheared, heavily milled and with a nap-raised finished; much used in the 19th century, when beaver leather was also used for **Woodstock gloves**.
Also, a hat cloth of felted wool and rabbit's fur, with a nap of beaver hair, for superior quality hats.

Beaverteen
Period: 19th century.
A cotton, twilled cloth in which the warp was drawn up into loops forming an uncut pile; mentioned in 1827.

Beche-cashmere
Period: 1848.
A woollen cloth "thicker than flannel and as soft as silk".

Bed
Period: ca. 1600.
Coarse, thin worsted similar to **say**.

Bedford cord
Period: 19th century.
A combination of plain weave and **whipcord**, the cords running in the direction of the warp; of all wool or cotton and wool. Used especially for riding breeches. Later, silk and cotton mixtures with similar ribbing acquired the same name.

Begin
Period: 14th century.
A rayed (striped) silk fabric.

Beige
Period: 1874.
A woollen **vicuna**, usually coffee-coloured; firm, thin worsted with a smooth twill.

Belgian linen
Period: 1879.
Thick, damask-like linen with coloured pattern on a cream ground.

Belladine, bellandine
Period: 18th century.
A fine, white, silk fabric from the Near East.

Bend-leather

Period: 17th and 18th centuries.

Leather from the back and flanks of an animal; used for the legs of jackboots.

Bengal

Period: 17th century.

A mixed fabric with cotton base from the East Indies: mentioned in 1680. Defined by Johnson (1755) as "a sort of thin slight stuff of silk and hair, for women's apparel". Striped varieties in cotton having "Bengal stripes" were popular.

See Bangal.

Bengaline

Period: 1869.

A very light **mohair**, self-coloured or brocaded with very small flowers.

Period: 1880.

Similar to a silk **barege**.

Period: By 1884.

"A new name for Sicilienne; a corded silk and wool fabric, the weft of wool."

Bengaline poplin

Period: 1865.

A **poplin** with a thick cord.

Bengaline Russe

Period: 1892.

A shot wool and silk flecked in contrasting colours.

Berlin canvas

Period: ca. 1820.

Canvas made of silk union yarns in various colours, the threads having a strong cotton core.

Berlin work

Period: 19th century.

The patterns and embroidery wools, originally imported from Germany and used to produce smaller items such as slippers, smoking caps, waistcoats and similar.

Besshe, bise, bice, bisshe

Period: 13th–16th century.

The fur of an animal, possibly a squirrel or similar creature.

Birdseye

Period: 16th century.

A silk fabric with light spots on a dark ground; popular for women's hoods.

Black-a-lyre

Period: 14th century.

A black cloth from Lire in Brabant.

Black elastic

Period: 1884.

A cloth resembling a **melton** "but as soft as a vicuna" (*Tailor & Cutter*).

Blackerybond

Period: 16th century.

Black-a-lyre in long, narrow ribbons. "Blackerybond

for gyrdells" (1550, Middleton MSS).

Blacks

Period: 17th century.

A common name for any black cloth used in mourning attire.

Black work

Period: 16th century.

Embroidery in black silk, generally upon linen. Often worked in an all-over, continuous, scrolling pattern. Popular for collars, smocks, wristbands and handkerchiefs. This and similar embroidery in red, called "Red Work", were sometimes known as "Spanish Work".

Blanket, blanket cloth

Period: Medieval–17th century.

A white woollen cloth with a pile raised by teazing. Used by the non-elite.

Blanket cloth

Period: 19th century.

A heavy, all-wool, West of England cloth with a raised finish. Much used for overcoats.

See Witney blanket.

Blaunchmer, blaundemer, blaundever, blauner

Period: 14th and 15th centuries.

A fur, the animal uncertain but possibly white and apparently costly.

Blue

Period: 15th century.

"Stafford Blue", a blue cloth woven in that county.

Period: 16th and 17th centuries.

"Coventry Blue", a blue cloth woven at that town.

Blueing

Period: 18th century.

A blue material. "For 3 yards of Blewin" (1715, Essex Records).

Boccasin

Period: 15th to early 18th century.

"A kind of fine buckram that has a resemblance to taffeta" (Cotgrave).

Boiled wool

Period: 20th century.

A process of hot washing or felting to produce a compacted woollen fabric.

Bokasyn

Period: 15th century.

A kind of **fustian**, according to Fairholt.

Bombazet

Period: 18th and 19th centuries.

A slight, twilled cloth of cotton and worsted, usually black and used for mourning.

Bombazine

Period: 16th century.

Introduced by Flemish weavers at Norwich in 1572. Of a silk warp and worsted weft; at first the natural colour and classed as "White Work"; from the 17th century onwards it was usually black and used for mourning. Its surface had a twilled appearance.

Bonéette
Period: 1877.
A wool and silk fabric having a **damask** pattern over it.

Book muslin
Period: 19th century.
A **muslin** with a hard finish, somewhat coarser than Swiss muslin.

Borato, boraton, burato
Period: 16th century.
A thin, light stuff of silk and worsted resembling **bombazine**.

Borsley
Period: 18th century.
A **stuff** made of combing wool.

Botany
Period: 19th century.
A worsted at first made of merino wool found near Botany Bay, Australia; imported from ca. 1830. Later, a term denoting the finest grades of worsted. "Shawls of Botany worsted" (1830).

Bouclé
Period: Late 19th century onwards.
Finish produced on any fabric woven or knitted from a yarn which has knots or loops in it, thus producing an uneven or curly surface.

Bouclé cloth
Period: 1886.
A cloth having knots and curls on the surface.

Bouracan
Period: 1867.
A kind of ribbed **poplin**.

Bourrette
Period: 1877.
A woollen cloth, twilled, having multi-coloured knots and threads of spun silk on it.

Boxcloth
Period: 19th century.
A heavily milled woollen fabric with a dress face resembling felt; originally used for driving coats.

Braid
Period: Medieval onwards.
A narrow band of various fabrics, woven by interlacing; used as an edging to garments.

Branched velvet
Period: 15th and 16th centuries.
Figured velvet.

Brawls
Period: 18th century.
A blue and white cotton fabric from India.

Brazilian corded sarcenet
Period: 1820.
A coloured **sarcenet** with a thick, white, satin cord running through it.

Bridgwater
Period: 16th century.
A **broadcloth** manufactured in that English town.

Brighton nap
Period: Early 19th century.
A woollen cloth resembling **baise** but with knots on the surface; made in Norwich.

Brillianette
Period: ca. 1790.
A glazed woollen cloth, striped and flowered; made in Norwich.

Brilliante
Period: 1840s.
A cotton fabric with a small, lustrous fleck.

Brilliantine
Period: 1836.
A very light fabric of silk and cashmere wool.

Brilliants
Period: 1863.
A silk fabric, the white ground having a small **damask** pattern.

Bristol red
Period: 16th century.
A West of England cloth dyed red at Bristol.

Britannia
Period: 17th century.
Linen imported from Brittany.

British cloth
Period: 17th century.
See **Britannia**, the name by which it was often called.

Broadcloth
Period: Medieval onwards.
A fine woollen cloth of plain weave.

Period: 19th century.
A cloth made of fine merino yarns in plain twill weave, heavily milled with dress face finish.

Brocade
Period: Medieval onwards.
A fabric with a pattern of raised figures (Beck). A silk interwoven with threads of gold and silver (Strutt). In the 18th century the raised figures were in coloured silks, formed by an extra weft which did not run from selvage to selvage but was contained within the patterned areas.

Brocantine
Period: 1898.
A fine woollen fabric brocaded with silk in monochrome pattern.

Brocatelle
Period: 19th century.
The term was used for a **linsey-woolsey** lining fabric in France; also a heavy satin and a heavy **corded silk** with a raised arabesque pattern in self-colour.

Broché
Period: 19th century.
A velvet or silk with a satin figure on the face.

Broderie anglaise
Period: ca. 1600 onwards.
Known in Europe as a type of fine white-on-white embroidery surrounding pierced holes; also called Swiss or Madeira embroidery and especially popular from the mid-19th century onwards as a decorative addition to underwear and children's clothing.

Broella
Period: Medieval.
A coarse cloth worn by countrymen and monks.

Brogetie
Period: 17th century.
Probably a coarse form of **brocade**.

Broglio-broglio
Period: 18th century.
A kind of **camlet**.

Brunswick cloth
Period: 15th century.
A linen cloth woven at Brunswick.

Brure
Period: 1912.
"A glorified Turkish towelling".

Brussels
Period: 14th century.
A cloth in various colours imported from Brussels.

Brussels camlet
Period: Mid-18th century.
"A stronger kind of Irish Poplin much worn for habits and coats."

Buckram
Period: 13th–19th century.
Term for fine linen or cotton, similar to **lockeram**; used for clothing and household items.

Buckram canvas
Period: 16th century onwards.
A coarse cloth of hemp or linen stiffened with gum and used for linings in coats and other garments.

Buckskin
Period: 15th century.
Leather from the hide of the buck, used for gloves. In the 18th century used for making leather breeches.

Buckskin cloth
Period: 19th century.
A closely woven, twilled woollen cloth of a cream colour, replacing the leather of that name; used especially for riding breeches.

Budge, boge, bogey
Period: Medieval.
White or black lambskin, with the wool dressed outwards and used as a trimming; usually imported.

Period: 17th century

Occasionally kidskin.

Buff, buff-leather
Period: 16th to 19th century.
Originally leather made from buffalo hide, but often applied to thick leather made of ox-hide, dressed with oil and with a rough surface, much used for military clothing. It was a dull, creamy-yellow in colour, and this colour was often called "buff".

Buffin
Period: 16th century.
An inferior form of **camlet**, used for gowns, doublets, etc., of the poorer classes.

Bugle
Period: 16th century onwards.
A tubular bead, commonly black; used to decorate clothing when threaded together.

Bulgarian cloth
Period: 1883.
A cream-coloured cotton fabric, plain or striped, worked in tinsel and coloured silk.

Bunting
Period: 1881.
A coarse kind of **nun's cloth**.

Burail
Period: 17th and early 18th centuries.
A "silk rash"; a stuff half silk, half worsted.

Burdet
Period: 18th century.
A mixed fabric of silk and cotton. "All sorts of half-silks such as English and Turkey burdets..." (1740).

Bure, buret
Period: 17th century.
"Stuff that's halfe silk and halfe worsted" (Cotgrave).
Period: 1874.
A coarse woollen stuff with a broad diagonal rib.

Burel
Period: ca. 1300 to 19th century.
A coarse woollen cloth of a dark red colour.

Buridan
Period: 1836.
A wide horizontally striped silk of two tones of one colour.

Burlap, borelap
Period: 17th century.
Coarse linen. Later, a coarse canvas.

Burnet
Period: 13th century.
A cloth of a brown colour.

Burracan, burragon
Period: 16th and 17th centuries.
A coarse cloth.

Bustian
Period: 15th century.
A kind of **fustian**.

Byssine
Period: 13th century.
A fine, silky, linen cloth.

Byzantine
Period: 1881.
A dull, semi-transparent fabric of silk and wool closely woven; used for mourning.

Byzantine granite
Period: 1869.
A dark brown, woollen cloth enriched with scattered threads of gold.

C

Cachemire
Period: 1876.
A fine wool and silk fabric, the patterns usually of Eastern shades.

Cachemire royal
Period: 1889.
Resembles rich cashmere with a silk back.

Caddas, caddace
Period: ca. 1400.
A floss silk, wool or flock used for padding.

Caddis
Period: 16th century.
A woven tape; also a coarse **serge**.

Caddis leather
Period: 16th and 17th centuries.
Leather from Cadiz in Spain.

Caffa
Period: 16th century.
A kind of coarse **taffeta**, according to Cotgrave.

Caffoy
Period: 18th century.
A fabric imported from Abbeville, possibly a **damask**; also found in Ireland, containing mohair.

Calaber, calabre
Period: Medieval.
The fur of the grey squirrel.

Calamanco, calimanco
Period: 16th century.
A woollen cloth, plain, striped or checked, and glazed.

Period: 18th century.
Of single **worsted**, glazed.

Period: 19th century.
A cotton and worsted fabric, highly glazed, plain or twilled.

Caledonian silk
Period: 1810–1820.
Similar to **poplin** but with a silkier surface, and having a chequered pattern on white ground.

Calico
Period: 16th century onwards.
Originally of Indian cotton, but from ca. 1600 to 1773 with a weft of cotton with a linen warp; since then entirely of cotton. Named from the town of Calicut on the coast of Malabar; hence sometimes known as "Calicut cloth".

Calicut cloth
Period: 16th century.
See **Calico**.

Calton
Period: 17th century.
A coarse, narrow cloth, made in the North of England, and similar to **frieze**.

Camayeux silk
Period: 1850.
Chiné silk fabric with colour on colour.

Cambaye
Period: 18th and 19th centuries.
A cotton cloth from India. "A coarse chequer cloth" (1727, A. Hamilton).

Cambresine
Period: 18th century.
Fine linen from Cambray and also from the Near East.

Cambric
Period: 16th century onwards.
A very fine quality of linen.

Cameleon
Period: 1830.
A silk figured in large bouquets on the outside and stripes on the reverse. In the 1840s a shot-silk of three colours. In the 1850s descriptive of a shot poplin.

Camel hair
Period: Late 17th century onwards.
Pure camel hair – soft, pale, wool-like hair in shades from creamy beige to light tan used for coats. From the 19th century onwards a mixture of wool and camel hair was used. A cashmere and wool mixture, dyed camel colour, was known as "camel hair cloth".

Camelina
Period: 19th century.
A **vicuna** cloth with very small basket pattern and loose, upstanding hairs on the face.

Cameline
Period: 1284.
A fabric or garment reputedly of camel hair. In the late 19th century, a printed fabric.

Camlet, chamlet
Period: 15th century.
Thought to have been at first a kind of camel hair or mohair; later woven in various mixed fibres. Camlets were woven in the UK from ca. 1600, and were warp-faced tabby cloths with a distinctive weft rib. They could incorporate metal thread and be patterned or watered. Sometimes "half silk, half hair" (1675). In the 18th century they could be wool or silk or hair, or mixtures; in the 19th century cotton or linen was added. Made plain or twilled.

Camletto, camletteen
Period: 18th century.
"A stuff of combing wool" (1739). "A sort of fine worsted camlets" (1730, Bailey).

Cammaka
Period: 14th and 15th centuries.
A costly fabric, probably of silk and camel hair, from the East, used for royal and ecclesiastical garments.

Camocho
Period: 16th and 17th centuries.
A silk fabric from Italy.

Camouflage
Period: 20th century onwards.
A fabric, cotton or synthetic, printed with the random blocks of colour which are perceived to offer disguise for troops. The colours are usually dark brown, olive green and sand, but vary according to the terrain within which they are worn.

Candlewick
Period: 14th century.
A cloth worn by servants.

Period: 20th century.
A soft cotton yarn used to create a tufted or ridged surface on a flat base.

Cantaloon
Period: ca. 1600.
A fancy name invented for a variety of worsted, a single **camlet**. In the 18th century a West of England cloth mentioned by Daniel Defoe; a worsted woven of fine, single yarns.

Cantoon
Period: 19th century.
A **fustian** with a fine cord on one side, and a satiny surface of yarns running at right angles to the cords on the other.

Canvas
Period: 16th century.
Coarse linen, generally imported. A superior quality woven with lines of thread, silk or metallic thread, and decorated with tufts at intervals, or stitched with quilting. Hence "tufted canvas".

Caracule, caracul
Period: 1892.

Similar to **astrakhan**, with a wide curl in the hair.

Caracule material
Period: 1894.
A crocodile mohair surface over a sort of flannel lining, giving the effect of black shot with colour.

Carda
Period: 14th century.
A cloth used in the making of surcoats, probably for linings.

Cardinal white
Period: Late 16th century.
A white, undyed, woollen **homespun**.

Carioca
Period: 1938.
Tradename used by the Colony Sales Corporation, New York for wool, cotton, silk and rayon fabrics.

Carmeline
Period: 1870.
A fine cloth similar to **vicuna**.

Carmelite
Period: 1890s.
An all-wool, plain-weave cloth similar to thin **beige**.

Carnagan
Period: 1820s.
A cloth used for trousers.

Carpmeal
Period: 15th to 18th century.
A coarse cloth used chiefly for linings; made in the North of England.

Carpmeal white
Period: 16th century.
"Commonly used for linings of hose."

Carrel, currelles
Period: Late 16th to early 18th century.
A cloth of silk and worsted.

Carrodary
Period: 18th century.
The original name of **cherryderry**, an Indian cotton fabric.

Cary
Period: 14th and 15th centuries.
A coarse cloth.

Casbans
Period: 19th century.
Cotton similar to **jacconet** but stouter; used for linings.

Cashmere
Period: 19th century onwards.
A fine, soft, woollen fabric first imported from Kashmir; imitated as "Thibet cloth" in Yorkshire and at Paisley in 1824. These were twilled fabrics of fine worsted. The original yarn was the wool of the Tibetan goat; now Himalayan and Mongolian goats also provide a source of wool.

Cashmere Syrien
Period: 1840.
A very fine twilled cashmere, more substantial than

mousselaine de laine but very soft and without a wrong side.

Cashmere twill
Period: 1890.
A cotton imitation of French cashmere.

Cashmerienne
Period: 1880.
A fine woollen cloth with twill on both sides.

Casimir
Period: 1877.
A thin, twilled woollen cloth of worsted warp and woollen weft in diagonal twill weave.

Casimir de soie
Period: 1853.
A silk and wool fabric having the appearance of shot silk.

Cassenet
Period: Early 19th century.
A dress fabric with diagonal twill, the warp of cotton, the weft of fine wool or of wool and silk mixed; for summer wear.

Cassimir, Cassimere
Period: 18th and 19th centuries.
A cloth patented by Francis Yerbury of Bradford-on-Avon, England, in 1766. According to Yerbury, "There were two species of my thin cloth distinguished by the name Cassimire; one is quilled in the weaving with a flat whale, the other with a round one ... the woof must not be spun in the same manner as for common cloth but drawn out into a much finer thread ..." This early cassimir has been described (R. P. Beckinsale, *The Trowbridge Woollen Industry*) as cloth "in which the woof and the warp were usually spun to much the same fineness and to which a diagonal ribbing was given in weaving", the cloth being heavily milled.
Until ca. 1820 only imported Spanish merino wool was used, but during the Napoleonic war years, when Spanish wool was in short supply, substitutes were used including cotton mixtures; in 1817 there was advertised "Patent Mohair Cassimere for waistcoats and trowsers".
From about 1820 German wools from Saxony and Silesia began to displace the Spanish, which had declined in quality. The German in turn were replaced, ca. 1850, by Australian merino wools. Before then the names cassimere and **kerseymere** had become confused and used often indifferently by writers; by the introduction of Australian merino the two fabrics themselves ceased to be distinguishable.

Catalapha
Period: 17th century.
A silk fabric listed in a charter of 1641.

Catalowne
Period: 17th century.
Supposedly identical with **buffin**; an inferior kind of camlet.

Catgut
Period: 18th century.
A material made from the intestines of sheep, was used to form the stalk of a certain kind of coat button.

Catling
Period: 17th century.
A variety of **lutestring**.

Catskin
Period: Medieval.
Only black or white skins were given this name; the tabby variety was classified as "wild cat".

Caungeantries
Period: 16th century.
A fabric of worsted warp and silk weft having a spot effect.

Caurimauri
Period: 14th century.
A coarse fabric probably identical with **cary**.

Cavalry twill
Period: ca. 1914 onwards.
A worsted or rayon twill cloth woven with a diagonal, raised cord; produced in khaki for use by cavalry regiments in World War I and later worn by civilians made into trousers of a buff/fawn colour.

Celanese
Period: 1921.
The proprietary name of an early synthetic fibre and fabric, "Celanese Artificial Silk", made in Britain.

Celes
Period: 1916.
Pure silk crêpe.

Celestrine
Period: Medieval.
A light blue form of **plunket**.

Cellulose
The insoluble carbohydrate derived from the cell walls of plants which is used in the production of many vegetable or natural fibres.
Also a major component in the production of manufactured or synthetic fibres such as **acetate**, **rayon** and triacetate.

Cendal
Period: Medieval.
A silk fabric resembling a coarse **sarcenet**.

Cendryn
Period: Medieval.
A grey cloth of a good quality.

Chadoe
Period: 17th century.
A printed cotton or cotton and linen fabric from the East Indies.

Chain lace
Period: 16th and 17th centuries.
A braid lace made of a single cord knotted upon itself.

Chaisel, cheisil
Period: Medieval.
Fine linen used for shirts and smocks.

Challis, chaley
Period: 1831.
A thin, twilled fabric of silk and worsted; originally of silk and camel hair. Printed in colours.

Challis barege
Period: 19th century.
A thin form of **challis**, sometimes corded or striped.

Chalon
Period: Medieval.
A cloth friezed on both sides (Chaucer).

Chambertine
Period: 1872.
A fabric of linen and wool; used for summer dresses.

Chamblette
Period: 17th century.
A fabric originally all silk; later, with worsted weft; woven in plain weave.

Chambray
Period: 1880s.
A thick, strong, coarse **zephyr**.

Chamlet
See Camlet.

Chamois
Period: 16th century onwards.
Soft, pliable leather originally made from the skin of the chamois antelope found in Asia and Europe. For several centuries the skins of sheep, calves, deer and goats have been substituted for the antelope. The creamy-buff shade of the leather also became a description of a popular colour.

Champeyn, champaigne cloth
Period: 15th century.
A fine linen cloth.

Changeable
Period: 15th century onwards.
Term used to describe fabric showing more than one colour.

Channon cloth
Period: 15th century.
A worsted cloth.

Charmeuse
Period: 1907.
A lightweight, soft, satin-like silk with a dull reverse. Later a term for any silk, cotton or rayon satin-weave fabric with a dull back and semi-glossy surface.

Chatoyante
Period: 1847.
A thin woollen of grey ground covered with broad, satin checks.

Check, checkery, checkers
Period: 15th century onwards.
A fabric woven or printed with intersecting crossed lines forming squares, as on a chess board. Named variants include "hound's-tooth check", an irregular design of broken checks.

Cheesecloth
Period: 20th century.
Loosely-woven, plain-weave cotton of thin weight, originally from India; popular in the 1960s and 1970s for clothing.

Cheklaton, ciclatoun
Period: 13th and 14th centuries.
Originally a scarlet textile; later, cloth of gold.

Chele
Period: Medieval.
Fur from the marten's throat.

Cheney
Period: 17th and 18th centuries.
A woollen or worsted stuff; probably a short name for **Philip and Cheney**.

Chenille
Period: Late 17th century onwards.
A fine, velvet-like cord with short threads of silk or wool standing out from the base; it was used as a trimming.

Cherryderry
Period: 18th century.
An Indian cotton fabric similar to **gingham**.

Cheveril
Period: Medieval.
Kid leather; used for gloves.

Cheviot
Period: 19th century.
A rough-finished fabric of strong, coarse wool, well milled; a form of Scottish tweed. In 1880 the name was given to a soft, woollen textile made in tiny hair stripes and checks; used for ladies' dresses.

Chevron de laine
Period: 1878.
A fine, diagonally woven cloth, of German make, each horizontal line being reversely twilled.

Chicorée
Period: 19th century.
Any fabric cut with its edge unhemmed.

Chiffon
Period: 1890.
A delicate silk fabric, almost translucent.

Chiffon taffeta
Period: 1906.
"Resembles sarcenet".

China crepe
Period: 19th century.
A **crepe** made of raw silk, gummed and twisted; thicker than ordinary crepe.

China damask
Period: 1879.
Cotton **damask** in two shades with palm pattern.

China gauze
Period: 1878.
A **gauze** in light colours sprinkled with tufts of floss silk.

China grass
Period: 1870.
A plain-weave fabric spun from China grass; used for summer waistcoats.

Chinchilla
Period: 19th century onwards.
The fur of a small South American animal of this name, used for luxurious coats and small accessories.

Chiné silk
Period: 1820s.
A silk of which the pattern has the appearance of having "run".

Chintz
Period: 17th and 18th centuries.
A glazed **calico** of cotton and linen, having printed patterns in colours. Originally imported from India.

Chip straw
Period: Late 18th century onwards.
A wood or similar fibre made into thin strips which could be woven into bonnets and hats.

Chisamus, cicimus, sismusilis
Period: Medieval.
A variable fur "probably of the Pontic mouse". Named after the classical creature, possibly a weasel, mentioned by Pliny.

Chrome leather
Period: Late 19th century onwards.
The use of a chromium compound for tanning leather was developed in America and patented in 1884. It was quicker than vegetable tanning, and could make the leather tough and waterproof or soft and flexible. Such leather was used for bags, boots, gloves and shoes.

Ciclatoun
See Cheklaton.

Ciré
Period: 20th century onwards.
French term for a waxed finish and, although not really descriptive of fabric, the term was often used to describe satins with this surface treatment which created a lustrous, almost polished, finish.

Ciselé velvet
Period: 1876.
A fabric with satin ground having a raised pattern in velvet.

Civet
Period: 17th century.
The fur of the civet-cat. Also a musky substance extracted from the animal and used in perfume-making.

Clementine
Period: 1834.
A rich, thick silk **gauze** used for bonnet-linings, etc.

Cloth of gold, cloth of silver
Period: Medieval.
A very rich fabric of silk or wool interwoven with a high percentage of flat threads or strips of gold or silver.

Clotidienne
Period: 1833.
A ribbon-striped satin.

Coburg
Period: 1840s.
A wool and cotton twilled **stuff** resembling French **merino**.

Cobweb lawn
Period: ca. 1600.
Very fine, transparent linen.

Cogware
Period: 14th century.
A coarse, common cloth resembling **frieze**; made in the North of England.

Concertina cloth
Period: 1892.
A corded cloth with silk lines running through it.

Coney
Period: Medieval.
The fur of the mature rabbit.

Constitution
Period: 1800.
"A bold ribbed velvet cord", for riding breeches.

Corah silk
Period: 19th century.
A light, white washing silk from India.

Corded shag
Period: 1807.
A **shag** with a marked cord, resembling **corduroy**.

Corded silk
Period: 19th century.
A heavy silk with raised ribs or cords on the surface.

Cordelière
Period: 1846.
A silk and wool fabric.

Cordovan
Period: Medieval.
Fine Spanish leather.

Corduasoy
Period: 18th century.
"A thick silk woven over a coarse thread" according to Fairholt, but possibly confused with **corduroy**.

Corduroy
Period: 18th century onwards.
A thick corded stuff of cotton, with a pile like velvet.

Corduroy velveteen
Period: 1879.
A corded **velveteen**, used for dresses.

Cordwain
Period: Medieval.
Cordovan or Spanish leather.

Corfam
Period: 1960s.
Tradename of a synthetic shoe "leather" developed by the American firm of Du Pont in the 1960s; an improvement on previous synthetics, as it was supple and porous.

Corinna
Period: 1837.
A richly flowered silk fabric resembling embroidery.

Corkscrew
Period: 1870s.
A worsted cloth "having the appearance of a rib running across at a very low angle" (*Tailor & Cutter*).

Cornelly
Period: 1938.
Embroidery of a lacy design made by the Cornelly machine upon a cloth which is removed leaving just the embroidered design.

Corvella
Courtauld's tradename for a blend of **courtelle** and cotton.

Cotelé
Period: 1865.
A thick, ribbed silk.

Cotelette
Period: 1881.
A stocking-woven woollen which does not stretch.

Coteline
Period: 1892.
A striped, woollen **corduroy**.

Cotoline
Period: 1886.
A black mixture of faille and wool, resembling **Ottoman silk** but softer.

Cotswold
Period: 16th century.
Wool of a very high quality from Cotswold sheep in England; much used for making caps.

Cotton
Period: Medieval onwards.
The soft, downy fibres which cover the seeds of the cotton plant. In Europe originally used as padding or stuffing material and only later in its imported, woven form as a fabric.
See Calico.

Cotton cloth
Period: 15th–17th century.
Woollen cloth of which the nap has been "cottoned" or raised. "They rayse up the cotton of such Fustians." (1495, Act II, *of Henry VII*)

Cotton russet
Period: 16th century.
Russet cloth with a long nap.

Couchouc
Period: 19th century.

India rubber which began to be used for such articles of dress as garters and stays in the 1820s, in the woven version known as "elastic".

Courtauld's New Silk Crepe
Period: 1894.
"Almost as thin and soft as chiffon."

Courtelle
Period: 1950s.
Tradename for Courtauld's acrylic fibre which replaced viscose fibres in the 1950s.
See Corvella.

Coutil
Period: 1840s.
A French species of **jean**, but lighter in weight; a twilled cotton cloth.

Covert
Period: 19th century.
An all-wool cloth with worsted warp in two colours twisted together.

Crape, crepe, crêpe
Period: 17th century onwards.
A transparent, crimped silk gauze; originally black and as such used for mourning, for which purpose and colour the spelling "crape" remained in use; the later 19th century spelling "crepe" denoted a similar material, but of various colours and worn for general use.

Cravenette
Period: 1899.
Patented by Bradford Dyers Ltd. A process, applied to cloth, of rendering the fibres water-resistant; much used for covert coats.

Cremil, cremyle
Period: 14th century.
A cotton **lawn** used for kerchiefs.

Crêpe de Chine
Period: ca. 1860.
A very soft China crêpe of fine silk warp and tightly twisted worsted weft. Later, a finely crinkled, soft, silk crêpe.

Crêpe georgette
Period: 20th century.
Sheer, textured crêpe with a dull surface in cotton, rayon or silk.

Crepeline
Period: 1870s.
A cheap substitute for **crêpe de Chine**; made of mohair and worsted.

Crêpe mastic
Period: 1908.
"A glorified heavy crêpe de Chine".

Crêpe poplin
Period: 1871.
A silk and wool fabric, slightly repped, but crinkly like crêpe.

Crêpe royal
Period: 1889.
A transparent kind of **crêpe de Chine**.

Crêpe sultane
Period: 1910.
Crêpe with a lustrous surface.

Crêpe tizra
Period: 1928.
Wool **romaine**.

Crepon
Period: 1866.
A China crêpe with a silky lustre and a soft feel. By 1882 a wool or silk or mixed fabric with a silky surface resembling crêpe but thicker. In the 1890s a woollen textile creped to look puffed between stripes or squares of plain weave. Often with a slight admixture of silk in it.

Crêpotine
Period: 1904.
A summer fabric of soft wool and silk.

Crest cloth, cress cloth
Period: 15th and 16th centuries.
A species of linen often used for linings.

Cretonne
Period: 1867.
A twilled unglazed cotton fabric printed in colours.

Crewel
Period: 16th century.
Two-threaded worsted for embroidery and tapestry work (Bailey). Also used for garters, girdles and trimmings until ca. 1800. The term was reintroduced for crewel-work embroidery later in the century.

Crimplene
Period: Late 1950s.
A variant of polyester fibre introduced by ICI in the form of **Terylene** and, as Crimplene, used for clothing.

Crinoline
Period: 1829.
"A new material made of horsehair." Soon after it became a fabric of horsehair and cotton, used to make stiff under-petticoats. By 1856 the name was commonly applied to the "Artificial crinoline" or hoop, at first of whalebone and then of wire or watch-spring, containing a large number of circular hoops held together by fabric or tapes.

Crisp
Period: 14th and 15th centuries.
A **lawn**; the name then replaced by **Cyprus** or **pleasaunce**, but the original name was revived ca. 1600 for one of "the New Draperies".

Cristygrey
Period: Medieval.
A fur classed in 1393 as "Wildware". The fur being that taken from the animal's head or "crest".

Crocus
Period: 18th century.
Linen dyed yellow with saffron.

Croppes
Period: 15th century.
Fur made up of pieces cut from the rump part of an animal.

Cross lace
Period: 16th century.
A kind of braid lace.

Crushed velvet
Period: 20th century.
The velvet was pressed between rollers or otherwise processed to produce an irregular or antiqued surface.

Cubica
Period: 19th century.
A fine **shalloon**, made of **worsted**; for linings.

Culgee, culgar
Period: 17th and 18th centuries.
An East Indian silk fabric, richly coloured. "There are two sorts, the one is Satten, the other is Taffety. Much used for Handkerchiefs and for Gowns." (1696, *Merchants' Wharehouse Opened*)

Curled cloth
Period: 17th century.
A woollen cloth with a long napped surface.

Cuttanee, cottony
Period: 17th and 18th centuries.
A fine East Indian linen used for shirts, cravats, etc. Also of silk or with metal stripes.

Cut-work
See Broderie anglaise, White work; see also Cut-work in dictionary.

Cyclas
Period: Medieval.
See Ciclatoun.

Cypress
Period: 16th century.
A light, transparent material of silk and linen in plain or crepe weaves. Both white and black; the latter used for mourning.

Cyprus
See Crisp.

D

Dacron

Period: Mid-1950s.

Trade name of a synthetic polyester fibre manufactured by Du Pont in the USA.

Dagswain

Period: 15th and 16th centuries.

A very coarse cloth.

"Symple rayment doth serve us full well,

Wyth dagswaynes and rouges (rugs) we be content."

(1547, Boorde, *Introduction to Knowledge*)

Damasin, damasellours

Period: 17th and 18th centuries.

A silk brocaded with metal threads.

Damask

Period: Medieval onwards.

A figured, monochrome fabric of linen, silk or wool, of which the woven pattern appears reversed on the back by using contrasting faces of the weave.

Delaine

Period: 1830s.

A soft, all-wool fabric of plain weave, the warp of worsted; resembling but less "musliny" than **mousselaine de laine**. Some varieties were printed.

Denim

Period: 18th century onwards.

An imported **serge**; the name shortened from "serge de Nîmes". Later, the name of a coloured, twilled cotton fabric used for work clothes, most especially the blue trousers called **jeans**.

Denmark satin

Period: 19th century.

A variety of **lasting**, woven with a satin twill.

Derry

Period: 19th century.

"Brown derry as a strong wide-width linen is called" (1872, *Cassell's Household Guide,* Part 2).

Desoy, serge de soy

Period: 18th century.

A stout, twilled silk (Perkins); used for linings in the 19th century under the name of "silk serge".

Devoré

Period: Late 19th century onwards.

The term comes from the French *dévorer*, meaning to consume or devour. When a proprietary paste is applied to a fabric made from mixed fibres it can burn off the cellulose or viscose fibres, on cotton and linen for example, leaving the animal or polyester fibres, such as wool or silk, intact. On velvet the paste eats away at the viscose pile leaving a silk ground; on cotton and linen the result creates lace-like, open spaces.

Diagonal

Period: 1870s.

A **worsted** cloth with a multiple twill running diagonally in pronounced contrast. A fashionable cloth for coats.

Diamanté

Period: 19th century.

A net encrusted with glass imitation "diamonds".

Diamond lace

Period: 16th century.

A braid lace woven with a diamond pattern.

Diaper

Period: 15th century onwards.

A linen, or cotton and linen, fabric patterned simply by the directional alignment of the thread into diamonds or similar, with the light reflecting the design.

Dieppe serge

Period: 1872.

A **serge** with a coarse diagonal twill.

Dimity

Period: 17th century.

"A fine sort of fustian; a cotton stuff" (Bailey). In the 19th century the term was applied to a stout cotton fabric, plain or twilled, with a raised pattern on one side, sometimes printed.

Diphera

Period: 1842.

A fine, soft, kid leather; used for ladies' bonnets.

Djedda

Period: 1866.

A **poile de chevre** with silk spots.

Djersa kasha

Period: 1928.

A **jersey** fabric.

Doeskin

Period: 19th century.

A soft, fine, West of England cloth, the warp set very close so that the weave lines are invisible; the surface smooth and level. Designed to resemble soft doeskin leather. A fashionable cloth for trousers about the middle of the 19th century.

Dogskin

Period: 17th century onwards.

Used as a leather for gloves; sometimes refers to sheepskin.

Doily

Period: 17th century.

A woollen **stuff**, used for petticoats. Named after the originator "who kept a linnen-drapers shop in the Strand" (Sir Hans Sloane).

Domette

Period: 19th century.

A loosely woven kind of **flannel** with cotton warp and woollen weft.

Donegal tweed

Period: 1890.

"A kind of homespun tweed, brown in colour." Used for heavy overcoats. Made in plain or in two-and-two twill.

Dorcas

Period: 18th century.

An Indian cotton fabric.

Dorea

Period: 17th and 18th centuries.

An Indian **muslin** with very broad stripes.

Dorneck, dornick

Period: 16th century.

A cloth made in Norfolk, but copying Flemish fabrics of silk or worsted; in Scotland, a type of linen.

Dorretteen

Period: 1792.

A silk and wool twist in thin, invisible stripes; made in Norwich.

Dorsetteen

Period: 18th century.

A fabric of worsted warp and silk weft.

Double-faced

Period: 19th century onwards.

A fabric which is finished on both faces, thus allowing it to be made into a garment which can be worn inside out without further adjustment.

See Reversible clothing.

Dowlas

Period: 16th–19th century.

A coarse linen used chiefly for shirts, smocks, etc., worn by those less well placed financially.

Dozens

Period: 16th–18th century.

A kind of **kersey** or coarse woollen cloth. "Northern Whites commonly called Dosins" (1523). Also made in the West of England and known as "Western Dozens".

Drab

Period: 18th and 19th centuries.

A thick, strong cloth, usually twilled, of a dull brown or grey colour.

Draft

See Amen.

Dralon

Period: ca. 1955–1958.

A proprietary name for an acrylic fibre used in the production of textiles, and also the name of the resulting fabric. Much used for soft furnishings, it was experimented with in the 1960s to create mixed dralon and **nylon** dress fabrics.

Drap de Berry

Period: 17th and 18th centuries.

A woollen cloth woven at Berry in France.

Drap de France

Period: 1871.

A double-twilled **cashmere**.

Drap de Persse

Period: 1907.

A satin-faced, wool-backed cloth.

Drap de soie

Period: 19th century.

Synonymous with **poplin**.

Drap de velours

Period: 1861.

A thick, soft, velvety cloth.

Drap de Venise

Period: 1866.

A ribbed **poplin**.

Drap fourreau

Period: 1867.

A thick, smooth cloth with a plush surface on the inner side.

Drawboys

Period: 18th century.

A name given to **figured** fabrics which at first required the use of boys to regulate the treadles of the looms; superseded by the Jacquard loom. "Fine figured Drawboys for Women's coats with Fringe" (1750, *Boston Gazette*).

Drawn-work

Period: 16th century.

Drawn-thread work produced in a fabric by drawing out some of the weft threads and stitching the remaining warp and weft threads to produce a pattern.

Dreadnought

Period: 19th century.

A coarse, thick, woollen cloth with a shaggy nap; used for overcoats by countrymen.

Drill

Period: 18th century onwards.

Stout twilled linen, used for summer suits. "Dressed in ... a white drill Frock" (1757, *Norwich Mercury*).

Droguet

Period: 1860.

A kind of cloth of mixed yarns with brocaded figures in various colours upon it. A cheap imitation of brocaded silks.

Drugget

Period: 18th century.

A plain or corded woollen stuff "very thin and narrow, usually all wool, and sometimes half wool and half silk; having sometimes a twill but more usually without" (1741, Chambers).

Ducape

Period: 18th and 19th centuries.

A plain-wove, stout silk fabric. "Of softer texture than gros de Naples" (Beck). Often brocaded or glacé in the 19th century.

Duck

Period: 19th century.

Coarse white linen made from double warp and weft; much used for trousers in hot climates.

Duffel, duffle

Period: Late 17th century.

"A coarse woollen" (Defoe), originally from Brabant.

In the 19th century "a stout milled flannel, often friezed" (1835, Booth).

Later, a cloth with a thick, shaggy nap, used for overcoats; hence the nautical "duffle coat".

Dungaree

Period: 17th and 18th centuries.

A coarse Indian **calico**.

Dunster

Period: 14th–16th century.

A woollen **broadcloth** made in Somerset.

Durance

Period: 16th–18th century.

A durable woollen cloth; a **worsted** made at Norwich.

Durant

Period: 18th and 19th centuries.

"A glazed woollen stuff called by some "Everlasting"." (1828, *Webster's Dictionary*)

Duretto, durotta, duretty

Period: 17th century.

A sturdy fabric of mohair and woollen thread or silk. "6 yds durotta to line waistcoats 8/- (1723)".

Duroy

Period: 18th century.

A coarse, woollen, West of England cloth akin to **tammy**. "Wearing a grey Duroy coat and wastcoat" (1722, *London Gazette*).

Also a term for a glazed cotton in damask weave (1791, Norwich).

Dutty

Period: 17th century.

A fine cloth or possibly a calico.

Duvetyn, velours

Period: 20th century.

A soft, velvety material of wool or silk, or a mixture, with a fine, downy nap.

E

Eccelide

Period: 1837.

A cashmere and silk fabric, chiné and striped.

Ecru silk

Period: 20th century.

Silk from which only a small amount of natural gum was removed.

Ederella

Period: 1916.

A fabric that "has a panne-like surface".

Egyptian cloth

Period: 1866.

A soft fabric of silk with some wool.

Elastic

Period: 19th century.

The first patent for applying caoutchouc (india rubber) to thread to form "elastic" material was taken out by Hancock in 1820. The term "elastic", however, had been applied in the 18th century to stretchable fabrics cut on the cross. In 1884 the name was also applied to a new cloth "resembling a melton but as soft as a vicuna" (*Tailor & Cutter*).

Elatch, elatcha

Period: 17th century.

An Indian striped silk.

Elephant cloth

Period: 1869.

A cloth made of twisted flax-cord and having a basket-like mesh.

Ellementes

Period: 17th century.

A worsted cloth.

Elminetta

Period: 18th century.

A thin, cotton fabric.

Elysian

Period: 19th century.

A woollen, overcoating cloth with a nap finish in diagonal lines or ripples.

Embroidery

Period: Medieval onwards.

The enriching of cloth or fabric by stitching needlework patterns in silk or metal threads upon its surface.

Enamelled

Period: 18th century.

A term denoting a stiffening of a textile with gum.

Eolienne

Period: 20th century.

Similar to poplin but lighter in weight; usually of silk and wool.

Epangeline

Period: 1868.

An all-wool, rep-like cloth. In the 1890s the term was used for a woollen **sateen** with a slight cord.

Epinglé cloth
Period: 20th century.
A fabric with a fine rib effect running crosswise.

Éponge
Period: 1912.
A soft, loose fabric of cotton, wool or silk, similar to **ratine**; the warp usually firmly twisted with nubbly or looped filling yarns.

Ermine
Period: Medieval onwards.
The white winter fur of the stoat. Powdering of ermine (the spots made from the animal's tail to distinguish royal from ordinary ermine) began in the second half of the 14th century.

Erminetta
Period: 18th century.
A thin, linen or cotton fabric.

Esmeralda
Period: 1831.
A white crêpe or gauze embroidered in black and gold.

Estamine
Period: 17th and 18th centuries.
A loosely woven, woollen fabric. In the later 19th century it was a somewhat thick **serge**, firm in texture, "All-wool figured estamens" (1890s).

Estrich, estridge
Period: 16th century.
A felted material made from the down of ostrich feathers; used for hats as a substitute for **beaver**.

Etruscan cloth
Period: 1873.
A cloth with a rough surface like **terry towelling**.

Everlasting, lasting
Period: 18th century to ca. 1840.
A stout worsted fabric with double warps and single weft. "A cloth with a shining surface" (1829).

Exhibition checks
Period: 1851.
Cloth with a large-check pattern, used for trousers in the year of the Great Exhibition.

F

Fabric
Period: 19th century onwards.
A manufactured or woven textile used to make clothing; often used interchangeably with "material", though the latter is often used only for cloth, that is woollen products not silk or synthetic ones. "The increasing popularity of silks as opposed to what are known as "material" dresses" (1884, *Daily News*, 27 October).

Faced cloth
Any cloth which has a different weave or finish on the front from that on the back.

Faconné
French term describing fabrics incorporating small motifs in the weave; similar to **figured fabrics**.

Faille
Period: 1863.
"An unwatered moiré silk", softer and brighter than **grosgrain**.

Faillette
Period: 1898.
A soft, woollen fabric, ribbed, with a gloss like silk.

Falding
Period: Medieval.
A coarse cloth resembling **frieze**.

Farrenden, farrender, farendine
Period: 17th century.
A cloth of silk and wool.

Fearnought, fearnothing, dreadnought
Period: 18th century.
A stout cloth almost impenetrable to wind and rain. A thick cloth with a long pile. "A fear nothen Jacket and Wescot" (1741, Essex Records).

Feathers
Period: 15th century onwards.
Especially feathers of the ostrich; worn by men as decorative additions to headwear until the late 18th century, and by women from the 16th century onwards. In the 19th century, especially, feathers of every species of native and imported birds were used for headwear, muffs, mantles, etc.

Felt
Period: Medieval onwards.
A solid composition of the fibres of wool and the hairs of fur; united without weaving but by matting together by heat, moisture and pressure. A material much used for making hats.

Felted knitting
Period: 16th century.
A process whereby a knitted article, usually a cap, purposely knitted too large, is soaked, rubbed and pummelled to produce felting and shrinkage to the desired size.

Ferret
Period: 17th century.
A narrow ribbon of silk or cotton; a kind of tape.

Fibre
The basic entity that is the thread-like filaments of

natural or manufactured structures which are twisted into yarns and used to create a fabric.

Figured stuffs, figured fabrics
Period: 18th century.
"Designs of flowers, figures, branches, etc., impressed by means of hot irons" (1741, Chambers). In the 19th century the designs in coloured threads were woven into the fabric.

Figurero
Period: 17th century.
A woollen fabric.

Figuretto
Period: 17th century.
A costly flowered stuff; thought to have been woven with metallic threads.

Figury
Period: 15th century.
A satin and velvet woven with patterns.

Filled muslin
Period: Mid-19th century.
A fine **muslin** with "lappet spots" produced by zigzagging extra warp ends over the top of associated warp threads.

Fillozella, fillozetta, philiselie
Period: 17th century.
A double **camlet**. "A kinde of coarse silke" (1598).

Fingroms
Period: 18th century.
A coarse kind of **serge** principally made at Stirling in Scotland, according to Daniel Defoe.

Fish-net
Period: Late 19th century onwards.
Open-weave fabric or mesh, not dissimilar to fishing nets, used mainly for stockings and tights.

Fitchews, fitchet, filches
Period: Medieval.
The fur of the polecat or fitch, the under fur being yellow-buff, the upper fur a rich, glossy brown, close to black.

Flamingo
Period: 1928.
"A silk with wool to give it the fashionable crêpy effect".

Flanders serge
Period: 17th century.
An English-made **worsted** fabric.

Flannel
Period: Medieval onwards.
Originally a Welsh-made woollen cloth, though called in the 16th century "Welsh cottons". Made of woollen yarn, slightly twisted, with an open texture; of plain or twill weave.

Flannelette
Period: 1876.
Originally an American cloth, one side twilled, the other with a plush-like surface, and made mostly of wool; later, almost entirely of cotton, to imitate flannel.

Fleece
Period: Medieval onwards.
The woolly covering of a sheep or other long-haired animal, used to make garments. In the later 20th century the American firm, Malden Mills, patented Polarfleece in 1979 for making into non-technical garments, such as lightweight sports clothing. The same firm patented Polartec for use in technically demanding conditions.

Florameda
Period: 17th century.
A "flowered or figured stuff" (Beck).

Florence
Period: 15th century.
A woollen cloth originally imported from Italy.

Period: ca. 1840s.
The name denoted a corded **barege** or **grenadine**. It could also describe a thin kind of **taffeta** used for linings.

Florentina
Period: 18th and 19th centuries.
A variety of **prunella**; a material woven from combed wool.

Florentine
Period: 16th century.
A silk or satin textile imported from Florence.

Period: 19th century.
"A silk stuff chiefly used for men's waistcoats; striped, figured, plain, or twilled. Two other stuffs are known under this name, one composed of worsted (previously Florence); the other of cotton resembling **jean** and generally striped; used for trousers" (Beck). The latter was referred to in 1817 as "the newly invented National Florentine".

Florinelle
Period: Late 18th century.
A glazed **brocade**, striped and flowered; made at Norwich.

Flurt silk
Period: Medieval.
Figured silk.

Flushings
Period: 19th century.
A heavy woollen fabric similar to **duffel**.

Foines, foynes
Period: Medieval.
The fur of the beech marten, a member of the polecat family.

Forest cloth
Period: 16th–18th century.
A woollen cloth of good quality, originally from the Forest of Dean in England.

Forest white
Period: 16th and 17th centuries.
A white **homespun** made at Penistone, Yorkshire.

When dyed red or blue it was known as a **pennystone**.

Foulard

Period: 1820s.

Originally from India; later from France. A soft, light, washing silk, twilled.

Foulard poile de chèvre

Period: 1870.

A foulard-like fabric of goat's hair "with the brilliance of Jap silk".

Foule

Period: 1882.

"A material resembling casimir with a silky look." Soft and velvety. A twilled woollen.

Fox fur

Period: Medieval.

Fur of the native British fox was used from the early Middle Ages. The fur of the Russian black fox was used from ca. 1600. Later preferences included red and silver fox.

French jet

Period: 1893.

A dress trimming composed of jet facets applied to metal discs. This was a glass imitation of real jet, much used for beads, etc.

Frieze

Period: Medieval.

A napped woollen cloth, originally Irish. "A coarse kind of cloth manufactured in Wales" (1662, *Fuller's "Worthies"*).

Frisé

Period: Late 19th century.

Generally, a raised design or surface effect. In 1885 a brocade with the pattern standing up like terry velvet was fashionable, and a few years later "a raised frisé stripe in black silky wool" was mentioned (1892, *The Daily News*, 24 October).

Frizado

Period: 16th and 17th centuries.

A heavy worsted cloth similar to **baise**.

Frou-frou

Period: 1870.

A satin-like washing cloth.

Fulgurante

Period: 1920.

"A mixture of silk, satin and crêpe".

Fun fur

Period: 1960s onwards.

Fabrics imitating fur, using a range of synthetic fibres including acrylic and polyester and found in many colours and patterns. Dyed farmed rabbit pelts were also used.

Fur

Animal coats which are neither hair nor wool, but softer and thicker.

Throughout history the warmth offered by fur garments, linings and accessories have made the furs of particular animals much sought after; rabbit or **coney** was low in status terms, but ermine and sable were highly desirable. See individual entries, e.g. chinchilla, fox, mink, etc.

Fustian

Period: Medieval.

A coarse twilled fabric with linen warp and cotton weft (Beck). The surface resembling velvet; hence the term "mock velvet". The name appears to have been also applied in the 14th century to a woollen or worsted cloth made at Norwich.

Fustian anapes

Period: 17th century.

A fustian from Naples; a kind of **velveteen**. "Mock velvet or fustian anapes" (Cotgrave).

Fycheux

Period: 15th century.

Fur of the foumart, "otherwise called the Polecat or Fichet".

G

Gabardine

Period: 1879.

A patented cloth waterproofed before weaving. A fine worsted or worsted/cotton mixture twill, tightly woven and water repellent, more comfortable than rubberized cloths used for raincoats, etc. All-cotton gabardines were also made. The fabric was invented by Thomas Burberry.

Galatea

Period: 19th century.

A strong, firm, striped cotton fabric, woven in imitation of linen, with a marked twill.

Galloon

Period: 17th onwards.

A woollen or thread kind of **ferret** used as an edging of garments. In 1848. "Galloons are now of pure silk."

Gambroon

Period: 1817.

A twilled cloth of worsted and cotton warp and a cotton weft, in plain weave; also of mohair. Used for waistcoats, breeches and trousers.

Garlicks

Period: 17th century.

A linen from Gorlitz, in Prussian Silesia.

Gauze

Period: 13th century onwards.

A very thin silk textile, semi-transparent. By the 18th century it was made of linen as well as silk. In the 19th century it was also made of cotton.

Gauze illusion

Period: 1831.

A fine, close gauze of silk, resembling **tulle**.

Gauze sylphide

Period: 1832.

A fabric of alternate stripes of gauze and satin ribbon, the latter brocaded with bouquets of flowers.

Gazeline barege

Period: 1877.

A semi-transparent fabric of pure llama wool, resembling a **barege**.

Gaze perlee

Period: 1833.

Semi-transparent **gauze** with small, silk squares figured on it.

Genappe cloth

Period: 1863.

A fabric of wool and cotton, generally striped in two shades of the same colour.

Genet, jennet

Period: Medieval.

The fur of a species of civet cat, grey or black.

Genoa plush

Period: 1887.

A plush with a very short, thick pile resembling velvet. A cotton **velveteen**.

Genoa velvet

Period: 18th and 19th centuries.

An all-silk, brocaded velvet. "A term now applied when the ground is satin and the arabesque figures are velvet." (1876)

Gentish

Period: 16th and 18th centuries.

A fabric originating at Ghent in Flanders; at various times cloth or linen might be listed.

Geolaine

Period: 1928.

Woollen **georgette**.

Georgette

Period: 1914.

A filmy, silk crêpe, less dense than **crêpe de Chine**; later imitated in cotton, rayon and so forth.

German serge

Period: 18th century.

A **serge** made of worsted warp and woollen weft.

Gimp

Period: 17th century onwards.

A coarse lace formed by twisting threads round a foundation of wire or twine. Made in various qualities of silk, wool or cotton and used as a trimming.

See Glossary of Laces.

Gingerline

Period: 17th century.

A cloth, formerly a reddish-violet colour.

Gingham

Period: 17th century.

An imported cotton fabric from India made from dyed yarn and copied in Manchester and Glasgow in the 18th century. In the 19th century the name was given to a stout chequered cloth, originally of linen, later of cotton.

Glacé silk

Period: ca. 1840.

A plain **taffeta** with a peculiar lustrous surface.

Glazed holland

Period: 18th century.

A Dutch **chintz**.

Goaly

Period: 1874.

A kind of ecru silk, the fabric like fine canvas.

Godelming

Period: 14th century.

Calfskin leather prepared at Godalming, Surrey.

Gore-tex

Period: Late 20th century.

A registered trademark of W. L. Gore & Associates Inc. This fabric, introduced in 1989, used a Gore patent for membrane technology, which produced a fabric that could breathe but resisted wet and windy conditions.

Gossamer

Period: 19th century.

A rich silk **gauze** used for veils.

Gourgourans

Period: 1835.

"A dress material of a light-coloured ground with white satin stripes."

Granite

Period: 1820s.

A stuff made of **chenille** and used for head-dresses. In 1865 the term was applied to a chiné woollen fabric in two shades of one colour.

Grazet

Period: 18th century.

A cheap woollen **stuff** of a grey colour.

Grenadine

Period: 19th century.

A light silk or silk and wool gauze, resembling **barege** but with a more open mesh. Many varieties were made, both plain and figured; an all-wool grenadine was made, and some cotton was used.

Grey

Period: Medieval.

Thought to be the fur of the grey squirrel imported from Germany.

Gris

Period: Medieval.

A grey fur, possibly squirrel.

Grogram

Period: 17th and 18th centuries.

"A taffeta, thicker and coarser than ordinary" (Bailey). Originally of silk and mohair and then known as "Turkey grogram". The material was apparently stiffened with gum.

Gros, grosgrain

Period: 19th century onwards.

A stout silk fabric of rich quality, showing a cord, less perceptible than in poplin, running from selvedge to selvedge.

Gros de Londres

Period: 1883.

Similar to **Ottoman silk** but with a much finer cord comprising "two small grains between two large".

Gros de Naples

Period: 18th century.

Resembled **taffeta**, but stouter. "Lutestring now termed gros de Naples."

Period: 19th century.

A corded silk somewhat resembling Irish poplin.

Gros de Rome

Period: 1871.

A crinkled silk, between a **crêpe de Chine** and a foulard.

Gros des Indes

Period: 1827.

A heavy silk with narrow transverse stripes.

Gros de Suez

Period: 1867.

A silk fabric with "three small grains between two larger".

Gros de Tours

Period: 1833.

A rich, corded silk resembling terry velvet; almost identical with **rep imperial**.

Gros d'hiver

Period: 19th century.

A silk between a **tabby** and a **paduasoy**.

Gros tussore

Period: 1910.

Silk slightly knopped on a **rep** ground.

Guipure lace

See Glossary of Laces.

Gulik Holland

Period: 18th century.

A very fine, white **linen**, used for shirts.

Gutta-percha

Period: After 1842.

Sap taken from trees in south-east Asia, which acted as a natural latex, like **India rubber**, and was used in waterproofing clothing.

H

Habit cloth

Period: 19th century.

A smooth, close form of **broadcloth**, without a twill.

Habutai

Period: Early 19th century.

A fine, soft Japanese silk.

See Jap silk.

Hairbines

Period: Late 18th century.

A **worsted** in plain weave with a rough surface, resembling **mohair**. Made at Norwich.

Hambrow

Period: 16th and 17th centuries.

A fine linen from Hamborough in Germany.

Handewarpes

Period: 16th century.

A white or coloured cloth made in East Anglia.

Harden

Period: Early 15th–19th century.

A common linen made from tow or the coarsest quality of hemp or flax (Beck).

Hare

Period: Medieval.

The fur of the legs of hares; the white winter fur of the Irish hare was most esteemed.

Harlem stripes

Period: 18th century.

A **linen** from Holland.

Harrateen, harriteen

Period: 18th century.

An inexpensive woollen **stuff** made from combing wool; often used for bed hangings.

Harrington

Period: ca. 1835.

A stout cloth, "both sides smooth and napped", often with tufted surface. Used for winter overcoats.

Harris tweed

Period: After ca. 1850.

A rough, homespun, tweed cloth, of a loose weave; hand-made in the islands of Lewis and Harris in the Outer Hebrides. In the 20th century adapted for the fashionable markets in Europe and North America in several weights and colour combinations; the Orb logo on a label guarantees that the cloth is genuinely hand-woven Harris Tweed.

Harvards

Period: 1890s.

A cotton, striped shirting in two-and-two twill or in plain weave.

Hemp

Period: 17th century.

An annual herbaceous plant found in Asia and cultivated for its tough and resilient fibres which are used for ropes and for stout cloth similar to unbleached linen.

Henrietta cloth

Period: 1890s.

A cloth resembling fine cashmere, but with silk warp or weft.

Hercules braid

Period: ca. 1850.

A narrow braid in black or white, having a heavy, ribbed weave.

Herring-bone

Period: 19th century onwards.

A fabric woven with the direction of the twill alternated to produce a zig-zag effect which resembles the backbone of a herring.

Hessians

Period: 18th century.

A coarse cloth of **hemp** or **jute**.

Holland

Period: 15th to 18th century.

A fine **linen** first imported from Holland; later the name applied to any fine linen. "That manufactured in Frizeland and called frize holland is the strongest and best coloured." (1741, *Chambers's Encyclopædia*)

"There are two sorts of yarn or thread in Dutch or Flemish linen ... the warp is made of Flanders yarn; the shute of Silesia. The Scotch hollands are made of the same yarn both in warp and shute, either from home flax or the best foreign." (1742, *The Champion*)

Hollmes

Period: 17th century.

A sort of **fustian**.

Hollow lace

Period: 16th century.

A braid lace used for edging.

Homespun

Period: 16th century onwards.

Originally a local cloth, literally spun at home, later a coarse, loosely woven wool cloth, similar to local wares. In the 20th century, **tweeds** produced in Ireland or the Western Highlands.

Hoonan

Period: 1904.

The fine-grained variety of **tussore**.

Hopsack

Period: 1860s onwards.

A woollen in plain weave, the threads in weft and warp interlaced with two or more threads instead of one. The cloth patterned to produce the effect of a series of small squares. Became a fashionable dress material in the 1890s. Also applied more usually to a fabric with a rough surface finish.

Hopsack serge

Period: 1891.

A coarsely woven, woollen serge-canvas.

Hounscot say

Period: 15th century.

An English worsted cloth.

Housewife's cloth

Period: From 15th century.

"A middle sort of linnen cloth between fine and coarse, for family uses" (1727–1741, *Chambers's Encyclopædia*).

Hummums

Period: 18th century.

A plain-weave cotton cloth from East India.

I

Ikat

Period: Second half of the 20th century.

A resist dye technique whereby the yarn for both warp and weft is dyed before weaving in a tie-and-dye method. A traditional Indonesian skill which found favour in western dress in the 20th century.

Imperial, cloth imperial

Period: Medieval.

A silk fabric with figures in colours and gold thread. Originally made at Byzantium, the Eastern Roman Empire.

Imperial gauze

Period: 19th century.

"An open gauze having a white warp with a coloured weft."

Imperial velvet

Period: 1870.

A fabric in alternate stripes of **corded silk** and velvet, the latter double the width of the former.

Inderlins

Period: 18th century.

A coarse hempen cloth from Hamburg.

Indian

Period: 18th century.

Either drawn muslin lace ("Indian work") or **muslin**.

Indian dimity

Period: 18th century.

"Now called twilled calico" (Mrs Papendiek Journals, pub. 1887).

Ingrain

Period: Medieval.

Wool dyed before weaving, especially scarlets, crimsons and purples.

Inkle

Period: 16th–18th century.

A kind of linen tape, sometimes white but usually coloured, used as a cheap binding by less well off.

Interlock

Period: Early 20th century onwards.

A fabric in which the stitches are woven together to create a closely structured, knitted fabric, usually of cotton, used for men's underwear.

Ionetis

Period: Medieval.

The **genet**, the fur of which resembles that of the marten.

Ipsiboe

Period: 1821.

A yellow crêpe; named after the eponymous novel by Vicomte d"Arlincourt.

Irish cloth

Period: 13th–15th century.

Cloth made of wool, such as **frieze** or **linen**.

Italian cloth

Period: After 1850.

A cloth of botany weft and cotton warp, having a glossy face; used for coat linings.

Jacconet

Period: Early 19th century.

A thin, cotton fabric, between a **muslin** and **cambric**; similar to **nainsook**.

J

Jacquard fabric

Period: 19th century onwards.

Named after Joseph Marie Jacquard of Lyons, who invented an attachment which revolutionized the weaving of **figured fabrics** on the loom; there are many jacquard fabrics, from **brocade** to **muslin**.

Janus cord

Period: 1867.

A black **rep** of wool and cotton, the fine cord showing equally on both sides. Much used for mourning.

Japanese pongee

Period: 1870.

A silk of the same texture as crêpe, but with a smooth surface.

Japanese silk

Period: 1867.

A silk textile, hard and springy, resembling **alpaca**.

Japan muslin

Period: 18th century.

Muslin worked in a loom to produce an indistinct or "japanned" figure.

Japan stuff

Period: 17th and 18th centuries.

Thought to be **calico**. "Short under-petticoats, pure, fine, Some of Japan stuff, some of Chine" (1661, J. Evelyn, *Tyrannus or the Mode*).

Jap silk

Period: 20th century.

A plain-weave, flat-faced, lightweight silk, originally from Japan, "Printed Jap silks are lovely". (1902, *Today*, 14 May)

See Habutai.

Jardinière

Period: 1841.

A striped and gauffred **crêpe** strewn with small flowers.

Jean

Period: 16th century onwards.

A twilled cotton cloth or **fustian**. In the 19th century, a twilled **sateen**.

Jeans fustian

Period: 17th century.

A jean containing wool.

Jersey

Period: 16th century onwards.

The name originated from a worsted made of wool from the island of Jersey in the 16th century. In the 18th century the name applied to "the finest of the wool separated from the rest by combing" (Bailey). By 1879 the name was applied to a fine, elastic, plain-knitted fabric. Such fabrics, jersey, Milanese and tricot, were originally of wool or worsted but later were made from cotton, rayon or silk.

Jute

Period: 18th century onwards.

Fibre from the bark of the *Corchorus* plant, used to produce a tough rope or cloth, originally from Bengal but later variants were produced elsewhere.

K

Karakul

See Astrakhan.

Karamini

Period: 1878.

A light, woollen fabric with a slight fleecy surface.

Kasha

Period: 1926.

Name registered by Rodier of Paris. A worsted cloth, two-and-two twill, piece-dyed and given a soft finish and woolly handle; or a soft, silky flannel fabric of wool and threads of goat's hair in twill weave.

Kendal

Period: 14th century onwards.

A coarse woollen cloth, usually green, originally made at Kendal, in Cumberland.

Kenting

Period: 18th century.

A kind of fine linen from Holland; imported into Ireland in the mid-18th century and later made there.

Kersey, carsie

Period: Medieval to early 19th century.

A coarse woollen cloth with many varieties in quality and pattern. The name may record the Suffolk village where it possibly originated. It was much used for making stockings before the introduction of knitting. It was one of the traditional "narrow cloths" of Yorkshire, in the 18th century, and also made in Devonshire in the 17th and 18th centuries.

Kerseymere

Period: 18th and 19th centuries.

"A fine twilled woollen cloth of a peculiar texture, one third of the warp being always above and two thirds below each shoot of the weft" was a 19th-century description. However, its nature in the 18th century is uncertain. It seems to have been introduced as a rival to the patented **cassimir**, and was possibly very similar; the name first appears in an advertisement in the *Bath and Wilts Chronicle,* January 30, 1772, as "Kerzymear". Whether it was made of English or Spanish wool is uncertain, but after 1820 the Saxony merino wool was replacing the Spanish and at the same time the names "kerseymere" and "cassimir" were being used interchangeably in fashion journals. By 1845 writers on textiles, such as Perkins, regarded them as merely a matter of spelling, an example followed by Beck in 1885, and by later writers. The confusion in the earlier records is increased by the habit, in inventories and tailors' bills, of abbreviating names of materials, e.g. "Saxon drab kersey" (1822) may have been short for "kerseymere".

Kevlar

Period: Early 1970s onwards.

A proprietary name for a man-made fibre of great stiffness and tensile strength; used mainly as a reinforcing agent in composite fabrics. Within a synthetic fabric this fibre offers protection against fire, water and blows to the body.

Kid leather

Period: 17th century onwards.

The skin of young goats or lambs used for the preparation of fine, flexible leather for gloves and shoes.

Kilmarnock

Period: 18th century.

A Scottish woollen **serge** made in that town.

Kincob

Period: 18th century.

An Indian fabric generally embroidered with gold or silver; called a brocade in the mid-19th century.

Kluteen

Period: 1815.

A striped, French, figured silk, used for ladies' spencers and pelisses.

Knickerbocker

Period: 1867.

A thick, coarse, woollen stuff, self-coloured or speckled. The date coincides with the introduction of the garment of that name and presumably the material was designed for this use.

Knitting

Period: Medieval onwards.

A continuous web made by interlocking a series of loops in a single thread, using long metal needles. James Norbury, the distinguished practitioner informed the Cunningtons that, "You are perfectly safe in saying that "knit caps" were made in England during the 14th, 15th and 16th centuries. "Felted" caps were knitted first before being felted. ... As early as 1320 in an Oxford Inventory (Thorold Rogers, *History of Agricultural and Prices in England)* are listed two pairs of "Caligne de Wyrsted" – knitted gaiters."

Under Edward IV "certain Acts were passed to protect the British knitters from their Continental rivals ... Sleeves, caps, and some form of loose waistcoat were knitted in England at this time." Machine-knitting by a stocking frame was invented in 1589 by the Rev. William Lee (*see* **Stockinet**, **Stocking-kerseymere**). Both hand- and machine-knitted garments, especially caps, were found during excavations in the last quarter of the 20th century, many in a well-preserved state.

Knitted clothing produced by hand or on a machine became increasingly popular from the late 19th century onwards. in the 20th century it was a popular domestic pastime.

Knotting

Period: 17th and 18th centuries.

A fancy thread-work made by the knitting of knots in the thread; similar to **tatting**. Used for bordering garments, and at the end of the 18th century stockings were occasionally made of knotting.

L

Lace

Period: Medieval onwards.

A term denoting a variety of accessories to clothing. These are: a cord, usually of closely woven thread or silk and commonly with aglets at the ends, used for drawing together two edges, e.g. shoe-lace, stay-lace; secondly, a narrow braid woven on the loom; thirdly, braid lace as an edging to a garment from the second quarter of the 15th century onwards, often of metal thread; and lastly, an openwork fabric of linen, cotton, silk, woollen or metal threads, from the 16th century onwards. After 1660 a distinction was made between **bobbin lace** or **bone lace**, made on a pillow by threads attached to bobbins, and needlework, known as **point lace**.

See Glossary of Laces for various types, both hand- and machine-made.

Laid work

Period: 16th century.

A form of decoration corresponding to **appliqué**.

Laine foulard

Period: 1861.

A silk and wool washing silk fabric.

Lake

Period: Medieval.

"A kind of fine linen or perhaps lawn" (Strutt).

Lambskin

Period: 14th century onwards.

Black and white skins used for lining and facing garments.

Lambswool

Period: 20th century onwards.

The yarn spun from the fleece of young sheep, popular for knitted cardigans and jumpers.

Lamé

Period: 1920s onwards.

Term taken from the French for "metal strip" and given to fabrics woven with metallic threads; popular for women's evening wear.

Lampas, lawmpas, lampors

Period: 14th century.

A **figured fabric** of any type of weave, plain, satin or twill with weft floats, often coloured, bound with a warp thread and partial, as with brocade, or across the whole width of the fabric. The fibres can be silk, cotton and silk, or just cotton.

Lanital

Period: ca. 1936.

A man-made fibre based upon a constituent of milk. "The manufacture of artificial wool from milk has been successfully started in Italy, and the product known as lanital has been shown to possess properties suitable for the textile industry." (1937, *Nature*, 23 December).

Lapland beaver

Period: 1859.

A textile with "a twill on the face and has the appearance of plush; made in a variety of colours". Used for capes and outdoor garments.

Lastex

Period: Early 20th century.

The US Rubber Company's name for elastic yarn made of rubber combined with cotton, rayon or silk; used in foundation garments and underwear.

Lasting

See Everlasting.

Lawn

Period: 14th century onwards.

A very fine, semi-transparent linen cloth, but also mentioned in Sumptuary Laws of 1363 as a coarse country cloth, with ploughmen, shepherds, carters, etc., forbidden to wear any sort of cloth but "blanket and russet lawn". In the 17th century "lawns commonly called French lawns" were a very fine quality of **cambric**. The name was derived from the French town of Laon where the fabric was said to have been first made (Skeat). It was identical with cloth of Rheims, and similar to cambric, made in Cambrai – neighbouring cities famous for the quality of their linens.

Leather

Period: Medieval onwards.

Hide or animal skin prepared for use in clothing and accessories.

Lemister, lemster

Period: 16th century.

A fine woollen used for knitting caps; the Herefordshire wool being much used for this purpose.

See Bewdley caps, Monmouth caps.

Leno

Period: Late 18th and early 19th centuries.

A gauze-like linen fabric.

Leopard
Period: 15th century.
Leopard's fur; especially popular in the 16th century.

Lerion
Period: 12th century.
Possibly the fur of the grey dormouse.

Lettice
Period: Medieval.
A white fur resembling miniver; probably the fur of the snow weasel.

Levantine
Period: 1815.
A twilled **sarcenet**. In the 1840s it was a rich faced, stout twilled silk fabric similar to the **surah** of the 1870s.

Levantine folicé
Period: 1837.
A soft, rich silk with arabesque patterns.

Liberty Art silks
Period: 1870s onwards.
Originally East Indian tussore silks printed in Europe; becoming in the 1880s a generic name for artistically designed silks, usually of Indian weave, sold under that registered trademark.

Limousine
Period: 1874.
A thick, rough woollen, coarser than **cheviot** and having a hairy surface.

Lincloth
Period: 13th century.
Linen cloth.

Lincoln green
Period: 14th century.
A green cloth used especially by huntsmen, verderers, etc.

Linen
Period: Medieval onwards.
A woven fabric made of flax; made in England from Roman times or before. Many varieties and qualities.

Linsey-woolsey
Period: 16th century.
A cloth of linen and wool, said to have originally been made at Linsey, Suffolk. The warp of thread, the weft of worsted.

Lisle
Period: Mid-19th century onwards.
Hand-spun, two-ply cotton yarn, twisted to compact the fibres; often with a mercerized finish. The name reflects its original centre – Lille in France. Used mainly for stockings.

Lisse
Period: 19th century.
An uncrimped silk gauze. Described in 1894 as "the new name for improved uncrushable chiffon."

Livery lace
Period: 18th century onwards.

A worsted braid woven with a design peculiar to the household where it was to be worn.

Lizard, luzard
Period: 16th and 17th centuries.
The fur of the lynx.

Llama
Period: 1889.
"An elastic make of cloth of the vicuna class." Made from the hair of the South American animal of that name.

Llama cloth
Period: 19th century.
Cloths with a llama-wool face, and finished with a long nap. Used for overcoats.

Lockeram, lockram
Period: 15th–17th century.
A coarse **linen**, used for shirts and smocks, worn by the poorer classes.

Looking-glass silk
Period: 1892.
"A glacé with a suspicion of moiré on its shining surface."

Loretto
Period: 18th century.
A fine silk fabric used for waistcoats.

Louisine
Period: 1880s.
A very thin kind of **surah** silk.

Love
Period: 18th and 19th centuries.
A thin silk with narrow satin stripes in it; used for ribbons.

Lucern
Period: 16th century.
The fur of the **lynx**.

Luisine
Period: 1834.
A heavy **rep** silk.

Lumbardine
Period: 16th century.
Fine gauze identical with **pleasaunce**.

Lurex
Period: 1940s onwards.
Trademark name of the American Dow Badische Company for its metallic fibre yarn. Either woven or knitted with cotton, nylon, rayon, silk or wool fibres, lurex was and is made into garments, especially evening-wear.

Lustre
Period: 19th century.
A thin kind of **poplin**, of silk and worsted. In the 1890s the term was applied to a variety of **mohair** with a shiny surface.

Lutestring, lustring
Period: Late 16th–19th century.
Originally a fine, somewhat lustrous **taffeta**. In the 19th century, a very fine corded silk with a glossy face.

Lutherine
Period: 18th century.
Listed under "Mixed goods" and probably an early form of **lustre**.

Luvisca
Period: 1915.
A soft, sheeny, artificial silk made by Courtaulds.

Lycra
Period: 1958 onwards.

A man-made fibre introduced by Du Pont; its elasticity, abrasion resistance and stretch made it a significant component in underwear and also from the 1970s onwards in tights, exercise wear and swimsuits.

Lynx
Period: Medieval onwards.
A greyish-tawny fur with black markings, long and silky and used as a lining and trimming for garments.
See Lucern.

M

Macabre
Period: 1832.
A light, silk and wool fabric figured in small designs and edged with a gothic border.

Macramé
Period: 20th century.
A type of decorative knotting, originally from Arabia and used on furnishings before its entry into decoration on clothing and accessories in the 1960s.

Madonna
Period: 19th century.
A fancy **alpaca**; a plain weave with satin stripes.

Madras
Period: 1825.
A muslin with transparent ground having a pattern in thick, soft thread embroidered upon it. Madras muslin or Madras net muslin was one of several washable fabrics thought suitable for embroidered clothing. From the late 19th century the term also applied to a lightweight cotton fabric with non-run-resistant stripes or checks woven through the white ground, used for clothing.

Malines
Period: 1885.
A fancy canvas, closely woven, having the appearance of being interwoven.

Manchester cottons
Period: 16th century.
"Its woollen cloths which they call Manchester cottons..." (1590, Camden). The genuine cotton fabrics of that city date from ca. 1640.

Period: 18th century.
Term for a fabric with stripes of cotton and wool.

Manchester velvet
Period: 18th century.
Cotton velvet.

Mantling
Period: 18th century.
Rough, blue-and-white-checked cotton cloth for aprons.

Mantua silk
Period: 17th century.
"Those glorious Italian silks which our countrymen find more difficulty in imitating than any other" (1758, *A New Geographical and Historical Grammar*).

Marabout, marabou
Period: 19th century.
Feathers of a species of African stork. Also, by 1877, a term descriptive of a woollen soft to the touch but looking rough and mossy on the surface.

Maramuffe
Period: 17th century.
A cheap kind of cloth; also known as **pyramid**. Made of woollen yarn with a plain weave. Also a type of muff.

Marble
Period: 13th–18th century.
A cloth woven or dyed in colours to resemble marble markings. A similar fabric was made in silk.

Marbrinus
Period: 14th century.
Worsted cloths woven with pale-coloured warp and coloured wefts to imitate a marble appearance.

Marceline
Period: 1833.
"A brilliant but slight kind of sarcenet."

Marcella
Period: 18th to early 20th century.
A cotton quilting or coarse **piqué** with a **diaper** pattern in relief. Used for waistcoats.

Marguerite
Period: 18th century.
A dress fabric woven of silk, wool and linen.

Mariposa
Period: 1872.
A washing **sateen** with stripes alternately plain and dotted.

Marocain
Period: 20th century.
A plain-weave fabric woven from crêpe yarns with a "pebbly" finish. Also a ribbed crêpe fabric of silk, silk

and wool, or just wool.

Marquisette

Period: 1906.

"Between ninon and crêpe de Chine".

See Grenadine.

Martiniques

Period: Late 18th century.

A woollen fabric made at Norwich.

Martrons, marters

Period: Medieval.

The fur of the pine marten; a rich dark brown.

Matelassé

Period: 1839.

A firm, substantial silk woven to resemble **quilting**.

Mecca

Period: 1877.

Gauze of the thinnest texture with dashes of silk in the wool.

Mecklenburgh

Period: 18th century.

Wool **damask** with stripes in coloured floral designs. Made at Norwich.

Medley

Period: 16th–19th century.

A cloth made with wools of different colours for the warp and weft.

Melrose

Period: 18th century.

A fabric of silk warp and wool weft.

Melton

Period: 19th century onwards.

A heavily milled woollen cloth with a short dense nap; closely woven. Resembling **beaver** cloth.

Melusine

Period: 1948.

Long-haired felt, used for hats.

Memphis

Period: 1836.

A semi-transparent fabric of very fine cashmere wool.

Mercerization

Period: 1850 onwards.

A technique developed by John Mercer, a successful Lancashire calico dyer; this process treats cotton with caustic soda and gives a silky finish and strengthens the fabric.

Merino

Period: 1826.

A thin, twilled, woollen cloth originally made of wool from Spanish merino sheep. A worsted **plainback**, very soft to the touch. "French merino" indicated the better qualities, though made in England. Inferior qualities containing cotton appeared under many fancy names.

Merino crêpe

Period: 19th century.

A mixture of silk and worsted, having a shot effect.

Messellawny

Period: 17th century.

"A 17th century stuff" (Beck). Possibly a cotton or muslin.

Mexican cloth

Period: 1865.

Cloth of strong raw silk, washable.

Microfibre

Period: Late 20th century onwards.

Exceptionally fine manufactured fibres, eight times finer than wool and twice as fine as silk, which when used in fabrics offers qualities such as lightness, softness, gentle draping. Four such fibres are used for fabrics, acrylic microfibre, nylon microfibre, polyester microfibre and rayon microfibre.

Mignonette

Period: 18th century.

A light, fine pillow lace, fashionable for head-dresses after ca. 1750.

See Glossary of Laces.

Mikado

Period: 1875.

A silk alpaca imitating **Jap silk**; made by Lister of Bradford.

Milanese taffeta

Period: 1880.

A semi-transparent silk fabric woven on the cross.

Milk-and-water

Period: 16th century.

A cloth probably so named from its blue/white colour; possibly a woollen cloth.

Minikin

Period: 17th century.

A form of **baise**; a plain-weave worsted made in Norwich.

Miniver

Period: Medieval.

The winter fur of the red squirrel which was greyish-white. Two versions were used; the first with the grey retained, "miniver gros", and the other with only the white fur retained, "miniver pure".

Mink

Period: 15th century.

The black fur of the *Putorius lutreola,* the European stoat-like creature whose fur resembled sable but was shorter and glossier. This was gradually replaced in the late 19th and 20th centuries by its larger, North American cousin. It was found wild, or increasingly farmed from around 1940, and provided a dense, glossy fur. Originally dark in colour, ranched mink was both bred to provide various hues or dyed using the paler furs.

Mirror velvet

Period: 1890s.

A watered **velvet** having the appearance of reflections in its surface.

Mistake
Period: 1806.
A shaded silk used for ribbons.

Mockado
Period: 16th to end of 18th century.
An imitation of velvet, usually of wool.

Mock velvet
Period: 17th century.
Naples **fustian**; a twilled cotton fabric.

Modal
Period: 20th century.
An alternative to **viscose** but also using a cellulose base for a synthetic fibre which was seen as a good competitor to cotton. Its properties, such as absorbency, draping and taking dyes well, recommend it for knitting or weaving by itself or with other fibres.

Mohair
Period: 17th century onwards.
A closely woven stuff of the hair of the Angora goat; two varieties of the material, one plain, the other watered. In the 18th century described as "Of silk, both warp and woof, having its grain wove very close" (1738, Chambers). In the 19th century it was woven with silk, wool or cotton warps and resembled alpaca. In the 20th century imitations were produced using synthetic fibres or mixtures, and its appearance was often teased and fluffy rather than smooth.

Mohair lustre
Period: 1890s onwards.
Black fabric resembling alpaca, with mohair weft and cotton warp. This was produced in three qualities: closely woven "brilliantine", which has the most lustrous surface; "Sicilian", the heaviest quality; and "lustre", the lightest of all.

Moiré antique
Period: 19th century.
A heavy, stout, watered **grosgrain**, the watering being in irregular waves.

Moiré gauloise
Period: 1904.
A soft and subtle type of moiré antique.

Moirette
Period: 1896.
A worsted fabric, similar to **moreen** but lighter in weight, with a watered surface and slightly stiffened. Used for "rustling foundations" and petticoats.

Moiré velours
Period: 1897.
A silk and wool, watered velvet with a large, irregular design.

Moleskin
Period: 19th century.
A coarse **fustian**, strong and twilled; resembles barragon. Used for trousers by working-men.

Period: 20th century.
A firm, woven, cotton fabric with a velvety finish.

Molleton
Period: 1865.
A thick, smooth **flannel** in plain weave or two-and-two twill; used for dressing-gowns. Later often of cotton.

Momie cloth
Period: 1880s.
Cloth of cotton or silk warp and woollen weft, resembling a fine **crepe**; usually black and used for mourning.

Monkey
Period: Early 20th century.
A fur using the skin and long, silky, black hair of the Ethiopian monkey.

Monkey skin
Period: 1858.
A fashionable material for ladies' muffs.

Monks' cloth
Period: 15th century.
A worsted cloth.

Montpensier cloth
Period: 1871.
A smooth, soft cloth twilled on the wrong side.

Moravian work
Period: Early 19th century.
A revival of the 16th-century cutwork with button-holing at the edges; a forerunner of **broderie anglaise**.

Moreen, moireen
Period: 18th century onwards.
An all-worsted, plain-weave fabric with fine warp and thick weft, with a "watered" surface.

Morelly
Period: 17th century.
A kind of **tabby**. "A morelly coate striped yellow and black" (1681, *Verney Memoirs*).

Morisco work
Period: 16th century.
Couched embroidery in gold or silver in arabesque patterns. "A pair of sleeves of Morisco work" (1547, Inventory of the Wardrobe of Henry VIII).

Morocco leather
Period: 17th century onwards.
Goatskin leather tanned with sumac and generally red.

Moscow beaver
Period: 1868.
A shaggy, napped **beaver** cloth, for overcoats.

Moss cloth
Period: 1878.
A soft, rich fabric of silk and wool with a mossy texture.

Moss crêpe
Period: 20th century.
A fabric with an irregular, mossy surface.

Motley
Period: 14th century onwards.
A worsted of mixed coloured wool; originally a fine cloth,

later rather coarse. "A cloth which they [the Danish courtiers] call Kentish cloth, we call Motley" (1617, Fynes Moryson).

Moufflon serge
Period: 1918.
"A kind of brushed woollen textile".

Moultan muslin
Period: 1840s.
Muslin with a woven pattern "worked with a lappet wheel, made exclusively at Glasgow".

Mountain moss
Period: 1859.
"Resembles fur beaver but is lighter and softer." Used in mixed and plain colours; e.g. for loose capes.

Mousselaine de laine
Period: 1833.
A fine, light, woollen cloth of muslin-like texture; often "figured in gay patterns like a calico print". Of cotton warp and worsted weft, if of English make; of all wool if French.

Mousselaine de laine chiné
Period: 1841.
As **mousselaine de laine**, with **chiné** patterns.

Mousselaine de soie
Period: 19th century.
A very fine, soft, silk fabric with an open mesh; an early form of **chiffon**.

Mousselaine Thibet
Period: 1832.
A silk and wool fabric, semi-transparent, with a watered surface.

Mousselaine velours
Period: 1832.
Mousselaine de laine figured with cut velvet stripes.

Mozambique
Period: 1865.
A silk broché, wool **grenadine**.

Mull muslin
Period: 19th century.
Soft, thin muslin, not silky; finer than **nainsook**.

Mungo
Period: 19th century.

A cloth made from disintegrated woollen rags, especially those hard-twisted and felted.
See Shoddy.

Muscord
Period: 17th century.
A woollen cloth.

Muscovite
Period: 1884.
"A handsome thick corded silk."

Muscovite velvet
Period: 1883.
Velvet **brocade** on a ribbed silk ground.

Muser
Period: 16th century.
A **spangle** hanging by a thread from the surface of a garment instead of being stitched down.

Muslin
Period: 17th century onwards.
A fine cotton fabric having a downy nap on its surface. "The flimsy muslins from India" began to be imported into England ca. 1670, displacing the flaxen **linens** and **cambrics** in the fashionable world. Manufactured in England and Scotland ca. 1780. The varieties used in the 19th century may be divided into seven categories. First, **book muslin**, similar to Swiss but coarser; second, **Indian**, which was soft, thin, opaque, with a slight "greasy" feel; third, **leno** with a very open weave, but stiff. The fourth type was **Madras** with its transparent ground with a pattern in thread darned upon it; fifth was **mull muslin**; the sixth variety was **organdie**, a soft, opaque muslin with a raised spot worked in it; the last type was "Swiss muslin", with a hard finish but nearly transparent.

Musterdevillers, musterdevelin, must deviles
Period: 14th and 15th centuries.
A mixed grey woollen cloth woven at Montivilliers in Normandy.

Myllion
Period: 16th century.
A fustian from Milan. "A piece of millyan fustian..." (1588, Essex County Sessions Rolls).

N

Nacré velvet
The French term *nacré* means "pearly", and this style of velvet has a base colour which is different to that of the pile, giving a changeable effect.

Nainsook
Period: 18th century.
A somewhat heavy Indian muslin.

Nak, naquet
Period: Medieval.
A cloth of gold brocade imported from the Near East.

Nankeen, nankin
Period: 18th century.
A cotton cloth of a yellowish-brown colour, originally from Nankin.

Nappa leather
Period: ca. 1895 onwards.
A very soft leather, usually based on goat or sheep hides and alum tanned; originally used for gloves, it is now used for many other items of clothing.

Naps
Period: 18th century.
A term denoting cloths subjected to "friezing" or twisting the nap into knots.

Natte
Period: 1874.
A firm, substantial silk woven to resemble cane-plaiting.

Nattine
Period: 1916.
A thin, fine cloth with a canvas effect.

Neat's leather
Period: Medieval.
Leather made from the hide of "neat" cattle, i.e. oxen; used for footwear.

Needlework
Period: Medieval onwards.
The craft or art of sewing with a needle to make clothing, embroider, or create soft furnishings. The invention of the **sewing machine** in the mid-19th century did not end the need to finish garments by hand.

Neigeuse
Period: 1877.
A soft, twilled woollen with a surface speckled or "clotted", and rough-faced.

Net
Period: 16th century onwards.
A fabric of fine mesh, used for veils, etc.

Nettlecloth
Period: 17th century.
Linen made from nettle fibres in place of **hemp**; synonymous with **Scots cloth**. "Three linings for partlets, of nettle-cloth wrought with red silk" (1553, Hatfield Papers).

Network
Period: 16th and 17th centuries.
Lace consisting of a ground of net of square meshes on which is worked the pattern, sometimes cut out of linen and appliqué, but more usually darned with stitches like tapestry. "A sute of blacke net worke" (1574, Lord Middleton MSS). "A suit of network" appears to have been a set of matching bands, ruffs, ruffles, etc., sufficient to enhance a man's suit of clothes or a woman's dress.

New Drapery
Period: 16th century.
Refugee weavers, Walloons in 1561 and Netherlanders in 1568, settled in Colchester, Norwich, Maidstone, etc. and introduced **stuffs** to which they gave new names; known as "the New Drapery", to include "Sarges, Perpetuanoes, Bayes", etc. The "Old Draperies" were textiles such as **broadcloth** and the **kerseys**. It appears that some of the so-called "New Draperies" were old ones under new names, and that " a buffyn, a catalowne, and the pearl of beauty, are all one cloth; a peropus and paragon all one; a saye and pyramides all one; the same cloths bearing other names in times past" (Complaint by the Worsted Weavers of Norwich, reign of James VI & I).

Ninon
Period: 20th century.
A lightweight, plain-weave fabric, originally silk but later rayon and nylon.

None-so-pretty's
Period: ca. 1770.
A linen tape on which were woven figures in colours.

Norwich crepe
Period: 19th century.
A textile with silk warp and worsted weft, of two shades of a colour; it had the advantage of being reversible and, unlike **bombazine**, had no twill.

Norwich fustian
Period: 16th century.
A worsted cloth woven at Norwich in imitation of **fustian anapes**; the name legalized in 1554.

Norwich grograine
Period: 16th century.
A fine worsted cloth made at Norwich.

Norwich satin
Period: 16th century.
A worsted cloth made at Norwich; the name by which **russel satin** and **satin reverse** were known.

Novato
Period: 17th century.
A fabric of wool or silk. "A paire of ash couller novato hose" (1614, Lismore Papers).

Nun's cloth
Period: 1881.
"A fine thin untwilled woollen fabric formerly called mousselaine de laine; it is a kind of bunting."

Nun's thread, sister's thread
Period: 16th century.
A fine, white thread made in the convents of Italy and Flanders and used for netting and lace.

Nun's veiling
Period: 1879.
A kind of thin, woollen **barege**; synonymous with **voile**. Later, used as a synonym for **nun's cloth**.

Nylon
Period: ca. 1930 onwards.
Term for a range of synthetic fibres using polyamide structures; discovered around 1930 by Du Pont, the American company, and used for hosiery and clothing. A versatile synthetic, as it can be woven in many different weights and knitted to eliminate the feeling of stickiness associated with early nylon fabrics.

O

Oiled leather
Period: 18th century.
Leather dressed with fish oil, to imitate **chamois** leather; used for labourers' breeches.

Oldham
Period: Medieval.
A coarse worsted cloth made in Norfolk, the name probably a corruption of Aldham.

Ollyet
Period: 17th century.
A woollen cloth made at Norwich; similar to **bombazine**.

Ondine
Period: 1871.
A very soft and brilliant silk and wool mixture. By 1893, a corded silk **crepon**.

Ondule
Period: 1865.
Cloth having a wavy appearance in the warp.

Opossum
Period: Early 20th century.
Thick fur in shades of brown, grey and black, taken from a marsupial found in Australia, New Zealand and the USA; popular as a coat lining and trimming.

Orgagis
Period: 18th century.
A coarse Indian cotton cloth.

Organdie, organdy
Period: 19th century onwards.
Crisp-finished fine cotton gauze.
See Muslin.

Organza
Period: Early 19th century onwards.
A light, stiff, translucent silk fabric; in the 20th century often a synthetic fabric.

Oriental satin
Period: 1869.
A soft and thick, all-wool or silk and wool fabric, woven in two colours, one brilliant, the other dark.

Orleans cloth
Period: 1837.
Resembles an untwilled **Coburg**, the warp of thin cotton, and the weft of worsted.

Orlon
Period: 1940s onwards.
Tradename of a Du Pont acrylic fibre which was first made during World War II; often used in knitwear fabrics as a substitute for wool.

Orphrey
Period: Medieval.
Gold embroidery; later, a border of narrow strips of any kind of embroidery.

Osbro
Period: 17th century.
Worsted **fustian**, often mixed with silk.

Osnaburg, Ozenbrig
Period: 16th century.
A German **linen**.

Otter fur
Period: Medieval.
The fur of that animal used as a trimming on clothing.

Ottoman plush
Period: 1882.
A silk fabric having a broad, corded ground with plush figures of close, thick pile.

Ottoman rep
Period: 1882.
A lustrous satin **rep** woven on both sides with flat cording.

Ottoman satin
Period: 1832.
A rich, shaded satin brocaded with flowers.

Ottoman silk
Period: 1882.
"A term loosely applied to every kind of silk with a horizontal thick cord and two or three cords in between."

Ottoman velvet
Period: 1869.
A velvet with coloured patterns brocaded over it. By 1879, a richly repped, uncut velvet.

Ounce
Period: 16th century.
Originally the fur of the **lynx**, but later applied to that of other small feline animals.

Outnal thread, Wotenall thread
Period: 16th century.
Possibly "the Flemish brown flaxen thread", defined as such in the early 19th century.

Oxford
Period: Early 19th century.
A corded cotton and wool fabric.

Oxford shirting
Period: 19th century.
A cotton cloth, plain weave, with narrow coloured stripes.

P

Packing white
Period: 1483.
A woollen cloth mentioned in an English Act of Parliament of that year.

Padou
Period: 18th century.
A silk ribbon, imported from Padua.

Padua serge
Period: 18th century.
A cloth for poor women's gowns. In 1863, a silk **serge** used for linings.

Paduasoy, poodesoy, pattisway
Period: 17th and 18th centuries.
Anglicized from *pou de soie*, a 17th- century French term describing a strong, corded or grosgrain silk, often figured. Later revived as *poult de soie*.

Paillette silk
Period: 1904.
A lustrous silk; the least rich of the satins.

Paisley
Period: 19th century onwards.
Name of a Scottish town which became synonymous with the production of fine woollen cloth woven with a distinctive design of a cone (*buta* in Indian), much used for shawls in the 19th century. The design was printed on a range of fabrics in the post-1970 period.

Palmyrene
Period: 1827.
A textile between a **poplin** and a **barege**; embroidered in silks.

Palmyrienne
Period: 1831.
A shot wool-and-silk textile, resembling **mousselaine de soie**.

Pampilion
Period: 15th–16th century.
Black **budge** fur from Navarre. In the 16th century also a species of felt.

Panne
Period: 1899.
A soft, silk fabric between velvet and satin; a term sometimes applied to satin-faced velvet or silks with high lustre.
See Panne velvet.

Panne velvet
Period: Late 18th century onwards.
A soft, lustrous fabric woven from silk or rayon with a pile flattened in one direction to enhance the shiny surface.

Paragon
Period: 17th century.
A kind of double **camlet** similar to **peropus**. "The

Paragon, Peropus, and Philiselles may be affirmed to be double Chamlet, the difference being only the one was double in the warp and the other in the woof" (ca. 1605, "Allegations on behalf of the Worsted Weavers").
In the 18th century it was a **stuff** made from combing wool.

Paramatta
Period: 19th century.
A fabric at first made with a silk warp and worsted weft, resembling **Coburg**. Later, it was made with a cotton warp. Used chiefly for mourning.

Parapes
Period: 17th century.
A fabric which resembled **paragon**.

Parchmentier
Period: 19th century.
A thin, stiff, wool cloth made at Norwich.

Paris cloth, toile de Paris
Period: Medieval.
A fine white linen.
Period: 17th century.
A woollen cloth.

Parisian cloth
Period: 19th century.
An English fabric of cotton warp and worsted weft.

Parisienne
Period: 19th century.
A French cloth of merino wool with small brocaded designs; also, in 1842, an English worsted; a figured **Orleans cloth**.

Passementerie
Period: 16th–17th century.
Ornamental braids and other trimmings of gold and silver, silk or cotton threads.

Period: 19th century.
Colourful braids and fringes decorated with beads, silk and metallic threads.

Patchwork
Period: 18th century onwards.
Small pieces of fabric of various colours and patterns sewn together to form a larger item. Also printed fabric in this style, in the later 20th century.

Patent leather
Period: Late 18th century onwards.
Very glossy leather made from hide coated with layers of lacquer or varnish. Usually black, until the 20th century when other colours and synthetic substitutes were introduced.

Patent thread, Urling's patent
Period: 1817.
Cotton thread gassed to scorch off the finer fibres; from

which **Urling's lace** was formed.

Pearl of beauty
Period: 17th century.
A fancy name for "the New Drapery", but "a buffyn, a catalowne, and a pearl of beauty are all one cloth; may be affirmed single chamblettes, differing only in breadth" (1604). A striped worsted "by colours in the warp and tufted in the stripes".

Peau de soie
Period: 1880s.
A dull, heavy silk interwoven with a double satin weave with a **sateen** finish.

Peeling, peelon
Period: 18th century.
A kind of thin **satin**.

Pekin
Period: 1830s.
A silk fabric similar to **taffeta**, having fine stripes running through it; hence " Pekin stripes". By 1879 this term also applied to any fabric with alternate dull and lustrous stripes.

Pekine lainage
Period: 1912.
A thin oatmeal cloth with a knopped surface.

Pekin Labrador
Period: 1837.
A Pekin silk figured with wreaths.

Pekin point
Period: 1840.
A very rich white silk painted with flowers or bouquets with foliage, with a light mixture of gold in the pattern.

Pekin Victoria
Period: 1842.
A silk fabric with a satiné ground, shot in white and cherry or blue, with patterns in white.

Pelluce
Period: 16th century.
The early form of the word **plush**.

Pellure
Period: Medieval.
A generic name for furs.

Pelurin
Period: Medieval.
Purfled or edged with fur.

Penniston, pennystone
Period: 16th–18th century.
A coarse **frieze** made originally at Penistone, Yorkshire.
See Forest white

Percale
Period: Early 19th century.
A fine **calico**, slightly glazed and often having a small printed design. By 1863 described as "a fine glazed linen."

Percaline
Period: 1848.

A cotton fabric between a **gingham** and a **muslin**, striped or quadrilled, and printed in colours.

Pereale taffeta
Period: 1859.
A cambric **sarcenet**.

Perkale
Period: 1818.
French cambric muslin.

Perlaine
Period: 1921.
Soft woollen fabric resembling a thick face cloth.

Perlon
Period: 1941 onwards.
A proprietary name for a German **nylon** fibre. In 1960 an advertisement described a woman's girdle of "lightweight Perlon elastic".

Peropus
Period: 17th century.
A double **camlet**, often watered.
See Paragon.

Perpetuana, perpets
Period: Late 16th century.
One of the "New Draperies", a glossy-surfaced woollen fabric, the warp of combing wool, the woof of carding wool. "The sober perpetuana-suited Puritans" (1606, Dekker, *The Seven Deadly Sins*).

Perse
Period: 13th and 14th centuries.
A cloth, possibly **serge**, of a dark bluish colour.

Persian
Period: 17th–19th century.
A thin, soft silk, usually plain; much used for linings of coats, gowns, etc.

Persian lamb
See Karakul.

Persian thibet
Period: 1832.
A woollen cloth with embroidered designs similar to those on shawls.

Perspex
Period: 1935.
The tradename of a tough, transparent, acrylic plastic, lighter and less easy to splinter than glass; popular with jewellery designers.

Petersham cloth
Period: Mid-19th century onwards.
"A heavy woollen cloth having a round nap surface" (1904, *Tailor & Cutter*).

Petersham ribbon, petershams
Period: ca. 1840.
Thick double ribbon; watered, plain, figured or striped.

Philip and Cheney, Philip and China
Period: 17th and 18th centuries.
A woollen cloth akin to **camlet**, but it was capable

of being watered: "15 yeardes of water'd Philip and Cheney" (1627).

Philoselle
Period: 17th century.
A variety of **camlet**.
See Paragon.

Pile
Period: 16th century onwards.
The raised nap or surface on a heavy fabric such as **plush** or **velvet**, either left as a series of loops or cut.

Pillow
Period: 18th century.
A kind of plain **fustian**.

Pilot cloth
Period: 19th century.
A thick twilled cloth with a nap on one side; of indigo-blue colour. Used for greatcoats.

Pintado
Period: 17th century.
An East Indian cotton fabric printed in colours.

Piqué
Period: 19th century onwards.
Usually a cotton fabric, woven with a raised rib, often in a diamond pattern, also in straight horizontal or vertical ribs. "Waffle piqué" has a honeycomb pattern.

Plainback
Period: ca. 1813.
At first an imitation of cotton **jean** in **worsted**; later, single-twilled merinos were developed from it.

Plastic
Period: 20th century onwards.
Artificial resin-like substances used to create buckles, buttons, jewellery, etc. from the 1930s onwards. PVC was a plasticized fabric used for outerwear from the 1960s.

Pleasaunce
Period: 16th century.
"A fine species of gauze striped with gold" (Strutt). Used for head-coverings.
See Crisp.

Plodan
Period: 16th century.
A coarse, woollen, checked material. Worn by women for cloaks.

Plommett, plummet
Period: 16th and 17th centuries.
A woollen or mixed cloth made at Norwich. Possibly a form of **plunket**.

Ploughman's gauze
Period: 1801.
A fine **gauze** with satin spots; used for ladies' evening dresses.

Plunket, plonkete
Period: Medieval.
A woollen cloth, usually of a blue colour.

Plush
Period: 16th century.
A long-napped velvet of cotton or wool or silk; usually of wool and hair (e.g. goat's) mixed. In the 19th century it was a shaggy, hairy kind of cotton velvet with a long, soft nap resembling fur.

Poile de chevre
Period: 1861.
A plain-weave fabric with a goat's hair weft and silk warp; having a shiny, satin-like face.

Polayn
Period: Medieval.
Fur of the black squirrel, possibly from Poland.

Poldavis
Period: Late 16th century.
A coarse **linen**.

Polony wool
Period: Late 17th century.
Used in making imitation beaver hats.

Polyester
Period: 1940s onwards.
Discovered in 1941 and after 1946 used for furnishing fabrics. Once Du Pont of the USA launched **dacron** in 1963 polyester fibres came to be used for clothing fabrics. It is second only to cotton in worldwide use, due to its strength, resilience and ability to dry quickly.

Pompadour
Period: 18th century.
A rich silk **taffeta** with satin stripes and floral sprigs in colours. "Mr. Clarke was dressed in pompadour with gold buttons." (1762, Smollett, *Launcelot Greaves*)

Pompadour chiné
Period: 1840.
A woollen twilled cloth with a small chiné pattern and striped horizontally in minute, thread-like stripes.

Pompadour duchesse
Period: 1850.
A satin with broad stripes divided by other stripes sprinkled with tiny flowers.

Pompadour shantung
Period: 1880.
A thick washing silk like **foulard**, covered with Pompadour designs on a brilliant ground.

Pompadour silk
Period: 1832.
A silk fabric with black ground and a highly raised pattern in detached sprigs, in lemon, rose and green.

Pongee
Period: 1870s.
A **tussore** silk of an ecru colour.

Poodle cloth
Period: Late 19th century onwards.
A fabric, often of a mixture of mohair and wool, with a looped surface.

Popel, pople
Period: 15th century.
Squirrel fur, from the back of the animal.

Popes minsters
Period: 17th century.
Possibly linen imported from Munster.

Poplin
Period: 1685 onwards.
A kind of **rep** with silk warp and wool or worsted weft, having a fine cord on the surface. There are three classes: the single, the double, and the terry, the last being richly corded and, unlike terry velvet, the same on both sides. Poplin may be plain, watered or brocaded. Irish poplin, of worsted and silk, was made in that country from the 18th century, In the 20th century the term is applied to the structure rather than content of the fabric, and cotton poplins are well known.

Poplin broché
Period: 1841.
A poplin with **broché** patterning.

Poplinette
Period: 1859.
"Sometimes known as Norwich lustre and occasionally as Japanese silk." Made with a glazed thread and silk.

Poplin lactee
Period: 1837.
A poplin shot with white.

Poplin lama
Period: 1864.
Similar to **mousselaine de laine**, but softer and thicker.

Porraye
Period: Medieval.
A green, imported cloth. The name was used in the 16th century to denote the colour green.

Poult de soie
Period: 19th century.
A pure corded silk of a rich quality. By 1863, "a mixture of silk and alpaca with a shiny surface".
See Paduasoy.

President
Period: 1870s.
A heavy **union** cloth of two layers (see **double-faced**); the face with cotton warp and wool weft.

Princess stuff
Period: 17th and 18th centuries.
A dress fabric made of goat's-hair warp and silk weft.

Prince's stuff
Period: 18th century.
A black woollen cloth closely woven in plain weave, used for clerical and legal gowns and also for mourning.

Princetta
Period: 1800–1840.
A **worsted** of silk warp and worsted weft.

Printed fabrics
Period: 16th century onwards.
An early reference is: "1535–6. Wardrobe Warrant. For making of a shamewe of blacke printed satten". Printing of textiles began in London in 1676, at first for the printing of **calico**, using wood blocks. Printed materials for women's dresses were very fashionable in the 1830s and at various times in the 20th century.

Prunella, prunello
Period: 17th and 18th centuries.
A coarse form of black **shalloon**, used especially for academic, legal and clerical gowns.

Puke
Period: 15th and 16th centuries.
An imported woollen cloth, usually nearly black in colour, dyed before weaving.

Pullicat
Period: 16th–18th century.
From Pulicat near Madras. A cotton fabric used at the close of the 18th century for making coloured handkerchiefs.

Puntenado
Period: 17th century.
Italian needlepoint lace.
See Glossary of Laces.

Pured
Period: Medieval.
A term for the white fur of the underside of an animal.

Purl, purle
Period: 14th century onwards.
"A kind of edging for Bone Lace" (Bailey). "A narrow braid" (Planché).

Purled velvet, pirled velvet
Period: 16th century.
Velvet enriched with patterns worked in uncut loops of gold thread.

Purnellow
Period: 18th century.
A **worsted** cloth.

PVC
Period: 20th century onwards.
Polyvinyl chloride was discovered in 1844 and was used for domestic floor coverings, furnishing fabrics, etc. PVC fabric, with its easily-cleaned and waterproof surface, became popular for coats in the 1960s.

Pyramid
Period: 17th century.
A wide, coarse and thin form of **say**.

Q

Quiana
Period: 1960s onwards.
Light and wrinkle-free nylon fibre introduced by Du Pont and either knitted or woven into fabrics.

Quilting
Period: 18th and 19th centuries.
A ready-made padding, usually of satin interlined with cotton; used for petticoats and linings of gentlemen's coats.
See Quilting in main dictionary.

Quintin
Period: 17th century.
"A sort of French linnen cloth that comes from St. Quentin in Picardy" (1687, Miege).

R

Rabbit
Period: Medieval onwards.
A popular and inexpensive fur taken from the small rodent found in many countries. In recent times the fur has been dyed or patterned to resemble more expensive furs.
See Coney.

Raccoon
Period: 19th century onwards.
Fur taken from the American mammal; varying in colour from pale grey to brown-black; it was especially popular from 1920 to 1940.

Radium poplin
Period: 1916.
A fabric of silk and wool, resembling silk poplin.

Radzimir
Period: 1849.
A black, all-silk fabric used for mourning.

Raffia
Period: 19th century onwards.
The young leaves of the raffia palm produced a fibre used as an embroidery yarn, for knitting or woven into a coarse cloth. Plastic raffia was produced in the 20th century, when real and ersatz raffia bags and hats were popular at various times.

Ragmas, ragmersh
Period: 14th–16th century.
An oriental fabric figured in gold.

Raploch white
Period: 16th century.
A coarse, undyed, woollen **homespun**.

Ras du More
Period: 18th century.
A heavy, black silk resembling **armozeen**; used for mourning.

Rash
Period: 16th century.
A smooth fabric, either of silk and then called "silk rash", or of worsted and called "cloth rash"; later known as **shalloon**.

Rateen
Period: 17th century.
A thick, twilled cloth, usually friezed.

Period: 18th century.
The generic name of a class of coarse woollens.

Ratine
Period: 1910.
Loosely woven cotton or wool sponge cloth, with a rough, uneven surface with a "knopped" or tufted weave.

Ratinet
Period: 18th century.
A thin form of **rateen**.

Ray
Period: 14th century.
A word indicating that a fabric is striped, but the name appears also to have been applied to a fabric that was not coloured.

Raynes
Period: Medieval.
A fine quality of linen made at Rennes in France.

Rayon
Period: Early 20th century onwards.
Originally called artificial "art" silk, this was made from cellulose fibre and was used for stockings and then clothing after 1912. It was re-named in 1924 and its production increased as its use became widespread.

Red work
See Black work.

Regatta shirting
Period: ca. 1840.
A cotton fabric with narrow, coloured stripes.

Regence
Period: 1889.

A rich, silk textile with a ribbed, satin face.

Renforcée
Period: End of 17th century.
A strong, silk fabric akin to **alamode**, introduced by French refugee weavers after 1685.

Rep, repp
Period: 19th century onwards.
A cloth with heavily marked transverse ribs. There were many varieties – of wool, silk, or silk and wool, such as **poplin**. In the 20th century cotton rep was popular.

Rep bluet
Period: 19th century.
A dark-blue silk rep figured with black satin cornflowers.

Rep imperial
Period: 1835.
A rich silk imitating **terry velvet**.

Rep sarcenet
Period: 19th century.
A fabric between **gros de Naples** and a fine-cut French velvet.

Resilda fabrics
Period: 1908.
Uncrushable and unspottable **alpaca**.

Rhadames
Period: 1883.
A soft satin with a diagonal grain.

Rhinestone
Period: Late 19th century onwards.
Glass or paste imitation diamonds, often used as decoration on clothing and footwear, especially since the 1930s.

Ripple pony cloth
Period: 1914.
Resembled a finely ribbed **mirror velvet** with a bright finish.

Roanes
Period: 15th century onwards.
A fine woollen cloth, usually tawny in colour, made at Rouen. By the 17th century, a linen cloth from Rouen.

Romaine
Period: 1928.
A French lining fabric of warp satin weave; also "a light woollen with a dull surface and flat square weave".

Rosadimoi
Period: 1820.
A corruption of the name "Ras de St Maur" and later called **radzimir**.

Rosetta
Period: ca. 1700–1750.

A striped or checked fabric, probably silk.

Rosille de soie
Period: 1840.
A dull silk with pattern in **network** strewn with flowers in monochrome.

Roskyn, ruskin
Period: Medieval.
The summer fur of the squirrel; a red chestnut colour.

Rug
Period: 16th–18th century.
A coarse kind of **frieze** worn by the poorer classes.

Rum-swizzle
Period: 1850.
An Irish **frieze** made of undyed wool.

Russaline
Period: 18th century.
A woollen cloth made at Norwich.

Russel cord
Period: 1880s.
Originally an all-worsted cloth, but soon with cotton warps. Resembled a coarse, corded **alpaca**; used for linings.

Russells
Period: 16th century, revived in 18th century.
Worsted with a lustrous surface like satin; made at Norwich. Synonymous with **russel satin**.

Russel satin
Period: 16th century.
A Norwich fabric of worsted with a lustrous, satin-like finish.
See Norwich satin.

Russet
Period: 15th and 16th centuries.
A coarse cloth or homespun (Bailey). Sometimes brown but sometimes grey. Worn by the poorer classes.

Russian crêpe
Period: 1881.
A species of mat cloth, closely interwoven.

Russian duck
Period: 19th century.
A fine, bleached linen canvas; used for summer wear.

Russian velvet
Period: 1892.
A light woollen of even grain and checked, the stripes being small, round, raised twists of a different colour from the foundation.

Russienne
Period: Early 19th century.
A silk fabric.

S

Sabelline
Period: 17th century.
The skin of the zibelline marten.

Sable
Period: Medieval.
The fur of an animal resembling the weasel and of a rich, dark, glossy brown; some were black, hence the use of the word as a synonym for black.

Sackcloth
Period: 16th and 17th centuries.
A hempen material coarser than canvas; of various colours and worn for outer garments, chiefly by the lower classes.

Saddle twist
Period: 1865.
A trousering "with a narrow thread of a rib".

Sagathy
Period: 18th century.
A slight woollen stuff, a kind of **serge**; sometimes mixed with a little silk.

Sailcloth
Period: Late 19th century onwards.
Strong, densely woven, cotton canvas, though some **jute** and linen was also used. Lightweight sailcloth was used for clothing from the 1940s onwards.

Saint Omer
Period: 17th century.
An English worsted cloth.

Salisbury flannel
Period: 18th century.
"The principal manufactures of this city are flannels, druggets, and the cloths called Salisbury Whites" (1768).

Samite
Period: Medieval.
A costly silk fabric, frequently interwoven with threads of gold or silver.

Sammeron
Period: 16th century.
A fine quality of linen. "A cloth between flaxen and hempen, finer than the one and coarser than the other" (Halliwell).

Santoy
Period: 1904.
A silk and wool fabric with a rich sheen.

Sarata shirting
Period: ca. 1870.
A linen shirting material.

Sarcenet, sarsenet
Period: Medieval.
A thin, soft silk with a slight sheen on the surface; of plain and twill weave, variously coloured; sometimes "shot". Later much used for linings.

Sarciatus, sarzil
Period: Medieval.
A coarse woollen cloth, worn by the lowest classes (Strutt).

Sardinian
Period: 1870.
A heavy, twilled, woollen napped cloth, the nap slightly tufted. Used for overcoats.

Satarra cloth
Period: 1893.
"Like a hop-sack in texture but the surface finished to look like a fancy worsted."

Sateen
Period: 1838.
A cotton fabric with a shiny, satin-like face.

Satin
Period: Medieval onwards.
A silk twilled fabric woven with the warp or weft yarns passing over several of the other direction yarns before interlacing, resulting in a smooth finish. A smooth, glossy surface is enhanced by the application of heat; the back of the fabric remains dull. The brilliancy of the surface is augmented by dressing.

Satin Antoinette
Period: 1834.
Satin with white ground and satin-shaded **rays**, and small, detached bouquets of flowers.

Satin blonde
Period: 1833.
Satin flowered in white on coloured ground, resembling blonde lace on satin.

Satin cashmere
Period: 1893.
An uncrushable, all-wool fabric with soft, silky surface.

Satin de Chine
Period: 1850.
A satin of silk and worsted.

Satin de laine, satin cloth
Period: 1836.
A woollen cloth with a smooth surface, used for men's pantaloons.

Satin doubleface
Period: 1928.
A satin which is shiny on one face but moiré on the other.

Satin du Barry
Period: 1832.

A satin with alternate stripes of black and figuring.

Satin duchesse

Period: 1870.

A thick, plain satin, very durable.

Satine playé

Period: 1873.

A striped cotton and wool mixture, the face very satiny and the stripes twilled.

Satinesco

Period: 17th century.

An inferior kind of satin. One of the many "New Draperies" originating from Norwich.

Satin Esmeralda

Period: 1837.

A rich satin of various colours, with applications of velvet of a darker shade.

Satinet

Period: 17th–19th century.

A thin, slight satin, usually striped; "used by the ladies for summer Nightgowns". In 1816 also a silk and wool fabric with a satin stripe.

Satin fontange

Period: 1841.

A satin with broad stripes alternately white and coloured.

Satin foulard

Period: 1848.

A silk fabric satined either in stripes or spots.

Satin jean

Period: 1870.

A finely twilled cotton fabric with a satin gloss.

Satin Lisette

Period: 1916.

Fabric with a spun silk face and wool back.

Satin merino

Period: 1846.

A fabric of which the right side is finer and silkier than cashmere; the wrong side resembles plush.

Satin merveilleux, merv

Period: 1881.

A soft, twilled satin resembling thick, rich **surah**, but with a brighter face and duller back.

Satin Montespan

Period: 1833.

A rich silk of a dull white ground, striped in large squares.

Satin pompadour

Period: 1835.

A satin with white ground embroidered in coloured flowers.

Satin reverse

Period: 16th century.

A synonym of **Norwich satin**.

Satin turc

Period: 1868.

A soft and very brilliant woollen cloth.

Satin velouté

Period: 1837.

A satin "as rich as velvet and as supple as muslin".

Satin Victoria

A woollen material resembling silk, with narrow stripes.

Sattinet

Period: End of 18th century.

Worsted in satin weave; made in Norwich.

Saxony

Period: End of 18th century onwards.

The name given to a cloth made from the merino wool of Saxony. By ca. 1820, the name in the UK for a type of cloth of merino or botany quality, a group to which soft **tweeds** and fine **whipcords** belong. The cloth was noted for being smooth, soft and dense.

Say

Period: Medieval.

"A thin woollen serge" (Bailey). "A soft light twilled fabric of wool and silk" (Linthicum). The latter with a silk warp and wool weft.

Sayette

Period: Late 16th century.

One of "the New Draperies", a fabric of wool and silk.

Scarlet

Period: Medieval.

Originally a fine woollen fabric; later, a colour.

Scotia silk

Period: 1809.

A fabric of cotton and silk resembling **broché**.

Scots cloth

Period: 17th century.

Linen woven of nettle fibres.

See Nettlecloth.

Seal

Period: Late 18th century onwards.

Fur from this aquatic mammal began to be used for hats in the late 18th century and by the late 19th century the fur, dyed brown or black, was used for sealskin coats; it is a dense, luxurious fur.

Seal plush

Period: 19th century.

A type of **plush** with a dull surface.

Seersucker

Period: 18th century onwards.

An Indian cotton fabric. "Canterbury Muslins and Seersuckers 13/- to 28/- per gown" (1791, *Salisbury Journal*). Washable imitations made in other countries offered plain or striped crinkled fabrics of cotton, rayon or silk, with puckered warp stripes. It was popular for summer clothing worn by adults and children.

Selisie lawn

Period: 18th century.

A **cambric** imported from Silesia.

Selvytine
Period: 1906.
"Smooth and soft like velvet, waterproof and uncrushable".

Sempiternum
Period: 17th and 18th centuries.
A twilled woollen stuff resembling **serge**; named for its durability.

Sempringham
Period: 14th century.
A Lincolnshire cloth.

Sequin
Period: 19th century onwards.
From the Italian *zecchino*, a small Venetian coin, this decorative metallic disc was used on clothing and accessories; in the 20th century sequins were made of plastic.
See Spangle.

Serche
Period: ca. 1600.
Possibly a kind of **mohair** or **serge**.

Serge
Period: Medieval onwards.
A loosely woven, twilled **worsted**, much used from the 17th century. Many varieties were imported with their names of origin distorted, e.g. Serge of Chalon (1649) became **shalloon**, and Serge de Nimes became **denim**. The warp was usually worsted, the weft was wool.

Serge dusoy
Period: 18th century.
"A stout twilled silk, the twill curiously fine" (Perkins).

Sergenim
Period: 18th century.
Serge de Nimes.
See Denim.

Serge royale
Period: 1871.
A fabric of flax and wool, with a bright, silky appearance.

Shag
Period: 16th–18th century.
A shaggy cloth, generally of **worsted**. "A thick-piled cloth with a nap of worsted or silk" (Linthicum). Often used for linings.

Shagreen
Period: 18th and 19th centuries.
A silk fabric with a grained ground.

Shalloon
Period: 16th–19th century.
"A slight woollen stuff" (Swift), originally made at Chalon; first known as **rash**. Later, much used for linings of men's clothes. A loosely woven woollen stuff, twilled on both sides.

Shammy, shamoy
Period: 17th century onwards.
Chamois leather.

Shanks
Period: 15th and 16th centuries.
Black fur from the legs of kids, goats and lambs. For lining and bordering garments.

Shantung
Period: 1870s.
A thin, soft textile of undyed China silk. By 1904 it also described a coarse-grained variety of **tussore** silk. Later there were imitations of cotton and man-made fibres alongside silk, all dyed in a wide range of colours.

Sharkskin
Period: 20th century onwards.
A fabric made from rayon, silk or wool, in a twill weave which produces a smooth surface with a lustrous sheen.

Sheep's grey
Period: 17th century.
A **homespun** cloth of undyed, black and white wool.

Sheep's russet
Period: 16th century.
Probably identical with **fearnought**. "Sheep's russet cloth called friars' cloth or shepherd's clothing" (1598, John Florio, *A Worlde of Wordes*).

Shepherd's cloth
Period: 18th century.
Identical with **fearnought**.

Shoddy
Period: 19th century.
A remade cloth similar to **mungo**, but composed of rags of worsted and other loosely textured woollen cloths.

Shot silk
Period: Mid-19th century onwards.
A fabric woven with different coloured warp and weft yarns to create a changeable effect.

Sicilienne
Period: 1870.
A fine quality of **poplin**, the warp of silk, the weft of cashmere wool.

Silesia
Period: 18th and 19th centuries.
Thin, coarse linen with glazed surface. In the 18th century used for neckcloths and cravats, and in the 19th century much used for linings; usually of a brownish colour.

Silistrienne
Period: 1868.
A wool and silk fabric of a firm texture.

Silk
Period: Medieval onwards.
This product of the silkworm has always been imported into the UK, either in its raw state or as a silk fabric. Fabrics from the Near East, France, Italy, Spain, India and China reflect trade routes across the centuries. The actual manufacture of woven silk fabrics in this country was introduced by Flemish refugees in the 16th century

and much increased by every influx of foreign weavers, especially after 1685.

Silk damascene
Period: 1876.
A silk and wool fabric with fine stripes of wool and satin alternating.

Silk delaine
Period: 1830s.
A fabric of silk and worsted.

Silk serge
Period: 19th century.
A thin, twilled silk fabric, much used for coat linings.

Silverets
Period: 18th century.
A cloth used for mourning garments.

Sindon
Period: 15th century onwards.
A fine linen fabric.

Sipers
A fine lawn; also a synonym for **cypress**.

Sirge debaragon
Period: 17th century.
A light variety of **serge**.

Sirsaka
Period: 1835.
"A silk striped lengthwise in narrow light-coloured stripes and traversed horizontally by dark ones."

Siskin
Period: 14th century.
A Flemish cloth of a green colour.

Sister's thread
See Nun's cloth.

Skiver
Period: 18th century.
A thin kind of dressed leather.

Sleasy holland
Period: 18th century.
A name given to "all thin, slight, ill-wrought hollands" (1741, Chambers).

Sleaved silk
Period: 16th century.
Raw floss silk.

Slesia lawn
Period: 17th century.
A fine linen resembling cambric.

Slipper satin
Period: 20th century.
A hard-wearing, closely woven fabric with dull back and semi-glossy surface.

Soisette
Period: 19th century.
A fine, **muslin**-type, cotton fabric; plain weave with a soft finish.

Soosey
Period: 18th century.
A mixed striped fabric of silk and cotton, from India.

Soyeux linsey
Period: 1869.
A light and brilliant woollen **poplin**.

Spandex
Period: 1958 onwards.
Synthetic fibre introduced by Du Pont and used for hosiery, lingerie and swimwear because of its elasticity and lightweight qualities.

Spangle
Period: 15th–19th century.
Small, decorative pieces of glittering material, usually metallic; originally lozenge-shaped, later circular, sewn on garments.

Spanish crape
Period: 18th century.
An all-worsted cloth made at Norwich.

Spanish medley
Period: 17th and 18th centuries.
A Dorset **broadcloth** made of Spanish merino wool mixed with English.

Sparta velvet
Period: 17th century.
Another name for **fustian anapes**.

Spiral Witney
Period: 1861.
"A soft material with short curls on the face, somewhat between a napped Beaver and a Frieze."

Spun silk
Period: Late 19th century.
A yarn made by spinning short fibres, often from waste; sometimes known as "schappe silk".

Stamfortis
Period: Early Medieval.
A strong and costly cloth.

Stammel, stamin
Period: Medieval.
The earlier name of "stamin" denoted a fine worsted cloth, generally red. In the 16th century, under the name of "stammel", it described a good quality of **worsted** or **linsey-woolsey**, generally red.

Stockinet, stockingette
Period: 18th century onwards.
A closely woven woollen textile having a mesh resembling knitted material. Used for tight-fitting pantaloons in the early 19th century. Later made of silk, cotton and synthetics and offering a plain, smooth finish.

Stocking-kerseymere
Period: 1836.
"Has the face and firmness of a Saxony cloth and the elasticity of stocking." Used for evening-dress trousers.

Stone-washed
Period: 20th century.
A technique whereby a fabric is artificially aged or distressed. Usually associated with **denim**, the original

process involved real stones to abrade the surface and reduce colour, but this process was overtaken by a chemical one which was easier to control.

Strait

Period: 15th and 16th centuries.

Term denoting any "strait" or narrow cloth as opposed to **broadcloths**; their dimensions were fixed by statute in 1464.

Stranlyng

Period: Medieval.

The autumn fur of the squirrel.

Strasburg cloth

Period: 1881.

A cotton fabric resembling **corduroy** but without the plush face.

Striped plush

Period: 1865.

Plush with narrow stripes alternatively dull and shining.

Stuff

Period: Medieval onwards.

A term for worsteds made "of long or combing wool" (Caulfield and Stewart). "Distinguished from other woollen cloths by the absence of any nap or pile." The distinction was understood early in the 17th century.

Suede

Period: 19th century onwards.

Usually calfskin specially treated to produce a silky, slightly napped finish, this type of leather originated in Sweden (*Suède* in French). Used for clothing and accessories, such as gloves.

Sultane

Period: 1866.

A fabric of silk and mohair resembling fine **alpaca**, in alternate stripes of clear or satin or chiné.

Superfine

Period: 18th century.

A superior quality of **broadcloth** made of Spanish merino wool.

Period: 19th century.

A West of England broadcloth of merino yarn, fairly heavy, heavily felted, raised and cropped, with a soft, firm handle and lustrous face. It was much used for men's clothing until ca. 1880.

Surah

Period: 1873.

A soft and brilliant Indian silk twilled on both sides, more substantial than **foulard**.

Sussapine

Period: 16th century.

A costly silk textile.

Suzette

Period: 20th century.

A heavyweight **chiffon** with twisted yarns.

Swansdown

Period: 18th century onwards.

Originally the fine down feathers of the swan, used chiefly for muffs and pelerines. In the 19th century a mixed fabric, originally of wool and silk and later of wool and cotton.

Swanskin

Period: 18th and 19th centuries.

A thick, twilled **flannel** with a downy surface; used by working men for trouser-linings.

Swarry-Doo

Period: 1893.

"A very bright twilled silk" (*Tailor & Cutter*) used for facings of frock coats.

Sylvestrine

Period: 1831.

A fabric imitating silk, manufactured from wood; the first known attempt to make artificial silk.

See Rayon.

T

Tabaret

Period: 18th century.

"Worsted Tabaritts, the newest fashion; in imitation of a rich Brocaded Silk" (1749, *Boston Gazette*). Similar to **tabbinet**; a glazed, brocaded, woollen fabric.

Tabbinet

Period: Late 18th and 19th centuries.

A watered **poplin**.

Tabby

Period: 17th to early 20th century.

A thick **taffeta**, glossy and watered.

Taffeta

Period: 14th century onwards.

Originally a plain, glossy, silk fabric; later, a thin, glossy silk with a wavy lustre. There were many varieties; "changeable taffeta" in the 16th century was shot taffeta; "glacé silk" was a taffeta with a very glossy face. 20th-century versions can be made from synthetic fibres.

Taffeta coutil

Period: 1847.

A mixed fabric of silk and cotton in blue or lilac stripes on a white ground.

Taffetaline

Period: 1876.

A mohair fabric.

Tamatiye

Period: 1863.

A light woollen material resembling **grenadine** but thicker; the warp twisted once between each shoot of the weft, i.e. the gauze weave.

Tambour

Period: 18th and 19th centuries.

A form of embroidery worked on a drum-shaped frame.

Tamett

Period: 17th century.

A Norwich cloth.

Tamine

Period: 16th century.

A fine silk-and-wool fabric. In the 17th century it was a fine worsted with a glazed finish.

Tamise

Period: 1876.

A soft woollen fabric with a little silk in it.

Tammy

Period: 17th–19th century.

A worsted; apparently identical with **tamine**.

Tape

Period: Medieval onwards.

A narrow, flat, woven braid of flax or, later, of cotton.

Tarlatan

Period: 1830s.

Thin, gauze-like muslin, much stiffened.

Tartarian cachmere

Period: 1823.

"For ladies' dresses, soft and light; never creases; in all colours."

Tartaryn

Period: Medieval.

A rich silk fabric possibly imported from China.

Tattersal

Period: 1891.

A cloth in vivid checks resembling a horse-cloth.

Taunton

Period: 16th century.

A **broadcloth** made in Taunton.

Tavistock, Western dozens

Period: 16th century.

A species of **kersey** made in Tavistock.

Tawny

Period: 17th century.

A woollen cloth, usually yellowish brown in colour.

Terrendam

Period: 18th and 19th centuries.

An Indian cotton fabric.

Terry towelling, terry cloth

Period: Late 19th century onwards.

An absorbent cotton or linen fabric, often with a looped, uncut surface and used for beach robes, dressing-gowns, etc.

Terry velvet

Period: 19th century.

At first, an uncut velvet; later, a silk fabric having a fine, corded surface, with no resemblance to velvet.

Terylene

Period: 20th century onwards.

The tradename for the polyester fibre discovered by UK chemists in 1941 and eventually sold to American manufacturers by ICI. It was used for clothing alongside the earlier **nylon**.

The Union

Period: 1815.

A silk and cotton shot fabric.

Thibet cloth

Period: 1874.

A soft, thick, flannel-like cloth with long goat's-hair surface. The name also given, early in the century, to imitation cashmere first made in Yorkshire and in 1824 at Paisley.

Thickset

Period: 18th century.

A coarse **fustian** worn by the non-elite.

Thread

Period: Medieval onwards.

A thin cord for stitching, made of twisted flax, cotton, silk or wool; there were many named varieties, including Coleyn from Cologne in the 15th century; Bruges between the 15th and 17th centuries; Coventry, in the 16th century, a vivid blue, used chiefly for embroidery; "nun's thread", "sister's thread" and "ounce thread" in the 16th century were terms for a fine, white thread chiefly used in lace-making; many more can be identified.

Thunder and lightning

Period: 18th century.

A **serge** made of worsted warp and woollen weft; also known as "German serge".

Ticking

Period: 15th century onwards.

A linen fabric for mattress covers.

Ticklenburgs

Period: 17th and 18th centuries.

A coarse linen cloth from Tecklenburg in Germany.

Tie-dye

Period: 20th century onwards.

A traditional technique, much earlier than its use in the west, of twisting and knotting fabric and then using a dye. When opened, the original ground colour forms intricate patterns with the dyed areas.

Tie-silk

Period: 20th century.

A firm silk, similar to a **foulard**, originally used for men's ties but also for other items; "Charming and practical Tie-silk shirtwaisters" (1961, *Guardian*, 30 May).

Tiffany

Period: 17th century.

A transparent silk **gauze**.

Tigrine

Period: 1834.

A mixture of silk and cashmere resembling twilled satin; very soft and supple.

Tinsel, tylsent, tilson

Period: 16th century.

A rich silk fabric which could be plain or patterned interwoven with a weft with gold or silver threads or strips. Later a tinselled cloth could be of silk or wool interwoven with gold or silver. The term was also applied to a sparkling net, and to cheaper imitations using copper threads which were popular for theatrical costume.

Tiretaine

Period: 13th century.

A fine woollen cloth, generally scarlet, much used for women's dresses.

Tissue

Period: Medieval.

The most costly form of cloth of gold or silver, woven with raised loops of metal thread in various heights and thicknesses above a **brocatelle**, **lampas** or **velvet** ground. "Eight yerde of sea greene tyssue for double slevis for ridinge gownes" (1612–13, Part of the trousseau of Princess Elizabeth Stuart).

Period: 18th century onwards.

The term was gradually applied to sparkling but lightweight fabrics.

Tissue matalassé

Period: 1839.

A cloth of which the surface was "in small squares resembling quilting". Used for gentlemen's overcoats.

Tobin, tobine

Period: 17th century.

A striped woollen cloth made at Norwich; also of silk. "A silke tobine jerkyn" (1611, Will of Jeremy Wayman).

Period: 18th century.

A twilled silk resembling **Florentine**.

Period: 19th century.

A heavy twilled silk.

Tobralco

Period: 1912.

Washable Egyptian cotton fabric with a silky surface.

Toile de soie

Period: 1898.

A thick, silk-and-cotton shot, two-colour fabric with a thick rib.

Toilinet, toilonette

Period: End of the 18th century.

A fine woollen cloth, plain, striped or checked; somewhat like merino.

Period: First half of the 19th century.

"The warp of cotton and silk, the weft of woollen." Much used for waistcoats.

Treillis

Period: 18th century.

"Otherwise called Buckram."

Tricot

Period: 19th century.

The French term for knitting, applied to a knitted or occasionally woven fabric with fine vertical lines on the surface and cross lines on the reverse. It was used in England in 1838 as "a new material for pantaloons" resembling **stockinet**. Experiments with man-made fibres revolutionized its production and use in the 20th century.

See Jersey.

Tricot de Berlin

Period: 1808.

A very light form of knitted fabric, said to have resembled cotton gauze; used for ladies' walking dresses. "Shawls of silk net called Tricot de Berlin" (1835).

Tripe

Period: 15th–17th century.

Imitation velvet made of wool or thread. Also called **mock velvet**, **fustian anapes**, **velure**.

Tripoline

Period: 1874.

A twilled **satin turc**.

Tryko

Period: 1916.

A woollen fabric with a soft, suede-like surface

Tufted canvas

Period: 17th century.

"Stript or tufted canvas with thread", the "striping" or "tufting" done with linen thread or with silk.

Tufted dimity

Period: 18th century.

A fustian with a tufted surface; used for under-petticoats.

Tuft mockado

Period: 16th and 17th centuries.

A **mockado**, of wool or silk, in which the pattern, instead of being figured, consisted of a geometrical arrangement of tufts.

Tufttaffeta

Period: 16th and 17th centuries.

A **taffeta** with a pile left on it.

Tukes

Period: 16th century.

A kind of **buckram**.

Tulle

Period: 18th century onwards.

A fine silk bobbin net. First made by machinery in 1768 at Nottingham. Later imitated with synthetic nets.

Tulle arachne

Period: 1831.

A very clear **tulle** embroidered in light patterns with a mixture of gold and silk threads.

Tuly

Period: 16th century.

The name of a silk or thread fabric (Beck).

Turco poplinnes

Period: 1867.

A woollen fabric with a soft, silky sheen.

Turin gauze

Period: 19th century.

A **gauze** woven of raw silk.

Turin velvet

Period: 1860.

A silk and wool fabric imitating terry velvet.

Turkish velvet

Period: 1845.

Silk velvet ribbed across the stuff; "a group of ribs separated from another group by a plain satin bar".

Tussore

Period: 1869.

Half wool, half cotton fabric, looking like **poplin**. Later in the 19th century the name invariably indicated tussore silk.

Tussore silk

Period: 17th century onwards.

A "wild" silk of brownish, irregular appearance, originally imported from India and China. Much used for dress materials at the end of the 19th century.

Tweed

Period: 1825 onwards.

A woollen cloth originating in Scotland, the texture open and elastic. "The word "tweel" on an invoice being misread as "tweed" in 1825 led to the adoption of the latter as the trade name." (1875, *The Tailor & Cutter*)

The cloth is woven from dyed yarns in a variety of grades, from coarse and rough to fine and smooth. Varieties included **homespuns** made locally in the Western Highlands and Ireland, **Harris tweed**, **Donegal tweed** and West of England tweed. The name was indiscriminately applied to lightweight woollen cloths, but regained its original meaning in the later 20th century.

Twill

Period: Medieval onwards.

A fabric distinguished by the parallel diagonal ridges created by passing the weft threads over one and under two or more warp threads. Also a cotton fabric of this name.

Twist

Period: 16th century.

Thread composed of two or more filaments of cotton, hemp, silk or similar wound round one another.

Tylesent

Period: 16th century.

Synonymous with **tinsel** as a fabric glittering with metallic fibres.

U

Umritzur

Period: 1880.

A rough-faced fabric of camel's hair, soft and light, in art colours; introduced by Liberty and Co.

Union

Period: 19th century onwards.

A stout fabric of cotton and linen, much dressed and stiffened.

V

Vair

Period: Medieval.

The fur of a type of squirrel with a grey back and white belly. The whole fur or "gros vair" meant the back and belly fur; the "mean vair" (hence miniver) meant the belly fur alone.

Valence

Period: 14th century.

A thin cloth, possibly a kind of **say**.

Valencia

Period: ca. 1830 to 1840.

A fabric with a cotton warp and weft of worsted; much

used for waistcoats (Perkins). By 1850 the name was given to a kind of **habit cloth**.

Valentine

Period: 1833.

A slight, shaded, silk fabric.

Vandales, vandelas

Period: 17th century.

Coarse linens imported from France and the Netherlands.

Velcro

Period: 1960 onwards.

A proprietary name for strip fasteners to hold fabrics,

leather, etc. together. Velcro is produced in two inter-locking strips which can be cut to length; one strip is covered with tiny nylon loops, the other with tiny nylon hooks which can be pressed together and pulled apart.

Veletine
Period: 1812.
A small-figured silk fabric.

Velluto
Period: 1883.
A cloth imitating **Genoa velvet**.

Velour
Period: 19th century.
Wool or wool mixture cloth, soft and smooth with a closely-cut pile or nap resembling **velvet**.

Velours broché
Period: 19th century.
Velvet having a satin **broché** pattern on it.

Velours de laine
Period: 1894.
A fabric with velvet stripes or checks on a woollen ground.

Velours du dauphin
Period: 1777.
Velvet with small stripes of different colours; made at Spitalfields in London.

Velours du nord
Period: 1881.
A fabric with a black satin ground shot with a colour, and covered with velvet flowers stamped in relief.

Velours épinglé
Period: 19th century.
A **terry velvet**.

Velure
Period: 17th century.
Imitation velvet. "My velure (breeches) ... that you thought had been velvet" (1604, *The London Prodigal*).

Velveret
Period: 18th century.
A variety of **fustian** with a velvet-like face.

Velvet
Period: Medieval onwards.
An imported silk fabric, from Spain, Italy or France, with a short dense pile, which could be cut or uncut, above a satin ground which might incorporate gold or silver threads. With the introduction of synthetic fibres in the 20th century velvet was no longer made from silk.

Velveteen
Period: Late 18th century onwards.
An imitation of silk velvet, the pile being silk on a cotton back or all cotton.

Velvet imperatrice
Period: 1860.
A kind of dark **terry velvet**.

Venetian
Period: 18th century.

A closely woven twilled cloth.
Period: 19th century.
A fine worsted fabric with a lustre finish.

Verano cloth
Period: 1880.
A kind of ribbed **cretonne**.

Verdours
Period: 16th century.
Thought to have been green **baise**.

Verglas
Period: 1894.
A **moiré** with a peculiar form of watering, resembling reflections on water.

Vermilion
Period: 17th century.
A cotton cloth dyed scarlet; sometimes called **barmillion**.

Vervise
Period: Medieval.
A blue cloth similar to **plunket**.

Vesses
Period: Late 15th century.
A worsted cloth, made in Suffolk.

Victoria cloth
Period: 1865.
A substantial cloth "replacing meltons or undressed cloths", for men's overcoats.

Victoria crape
Period: 19th century.
A **crape** made entirely of cotton.

Victoria serge
Period: 1893.
A fabric which resembled silk **serge**; used as a lining for lounge jackets.

Victoria silk
Period: 1893.
A silk and wool fabric for petticoats "guaranteed to rustle".

Vicugna, vicuna
Period: 1877.
A very soft cloth of llama wool, generally plain. Later, of worsted warp and woollen weft. "A fine material known as Vicuna though different houses call it by different names such as "Saxony Melton", "Meltonia", etc." (1888, *Tailor & Cutter*)

Vigogne
Period: 19th century.
An all-wool cloth, twilled and in neutral colours.

Vigonia cloth
Period: 1809.
Cloth of Spanish wool, "soft and warm resembling the texture of the Indian shawl". Used for women's dresses.

Virly
Period: Late 13th and early 14th centuries.
A green cloth made at Vire in Normandy.

Viscose

Period: 20th century onwards.

The most readily available type of **rayon**, it is produced in greater quantities than cuprammonium rayon. "Candy pink and white cotton and viscose shirtwaister" (1972, *Vogue*, June edition).

Viyella

Period: 1894 onwards.

Proprietary brand of 50% wool, 50% cotton mixture, originally manufactured by William Hollins & Co. Ltd., Nottingham.

Voile

Period: 1885 onwards.

A very thin, woollen fabric very similar to, or identical with, **nun's veiling**. Later made of cotton or rayon.

W

Waborne lace

Period: 16th century.

A braid lace made at Waborne, Norfolk.

Wadmol

Period: Medieval.

A coarse woollen cloth, used chiefly by the non-elite for their doublets, jerkins, etc.

Warp

The threads held lengthways in a loom and usually held tauter than the **weft** threads which are passed through to create a piece of cloth.

Wash-leather

Period: 15th century onwards.

Very soft, pliable leather, buff colour; made by splitting sheepskin.

Watchet

Period: Medieval.

A kind of blue cloth.

Watered stuffs

Stuffs impressed with close wavy lines and generally known as **tabbies** in the 18th century and **moirés** from the 19th century onwards.

Waterproof

Period: 19th century.

The use of india-rubber solution applied to a textile was patented by Charles Macintosh of Glasgow in 1823. "The cloth called *waterproof* is generally lined with calico or figured cotton; these materials are well imbued and stiffened with gum and firmly sewn together. The smell of the gum is not the only unpleasant quality in this kind of cloth for on approaching the fire the lining shrinks." (1829, *The Gentleman's Magazine of Fashion*)

Weaving

Period: From the earliest period.

The interlacing of yarns to form a fabric on a loom, either by hand or driven by machinery. There are three basic weaves – plain, **satin** and **twill** – and all others are variants of these. Plain weave is the simplest form, with warp and weft threads being linked in a one-over, one-under movement, like darning.

Weft, woof

The threads which pass across the **warp** in weaving in plain, satin, twill or combination weaves.

Whalebone

Period: Medieval onwards.

A cartilaginous material from the upper jaw of the whale; a flexible material used especially for the ribs of women's stays until the 20th century.

Whipcord cloth

Period: 1863.

A large-diagonal ribbed cloth, heavy and stiff. Used for riding breeches.

Whites

Period: Medieval.

A generic term for undyed cloth, particularly in the Middle Ages.

Wildbore

Period: 18th century.

A stout **tammy**, closely woven.

Wildware

Period: Medieval.

Imported furs of various animals.

Wilton

Period: Medieval.

Linen from Wilton, Wiltshire.

Period: 18th century.

A type of woollen cloth.

Winceyette

Period: 20th century.

A fabric, usually of cotton, with a soft, raised nap; made into nightclothes for adults and children.

Winsey

Period: 19th century.

A cotton and wool mixture resembling **linsey-woolsey**.

Witney blanket

Period: 1844.

A heavy cloth produced at Witney, Oxfordshire, and used for men's overcoats.

Wool

Period: Medieval onwards.

The hair of the sheep, the quality varying according to the breed of the animal and the locality where it was bred. English wool was the staple medieval industry. Wool was imported into the UK from Spain from the late 16th century, from Saxony in the second half of 18th century, and from Australia from ca. 1840. Wool can be divided into two principal groups according to the length of the hairs, producing the long-stapled textiles, **worsteds**, and the short-stapled, woollens. Blends of the two sorts or blends with other materials, such as silk, cotton, goat's-hair, mohair, etc., have produced innumerable textiles having distinctive names.

Wool barege
Period: 1850s.
A **barege** made of fine wool; used for shawls.

Worcesters
Period: 15th and 16th centuries.
A cloth, usually white, made in Worcestershire.

Worsted
Period: Medieval onwards.
At first known, in the 13th century, as "cloth of Worthstede"; a cloth made of long-stapled wool combed straight and smooth before spinning.

X and Y

Yeddo crêpe
Period: 1880.
A cotton fabric as thick as linen but soft; printed with Chinese designs.

Yeddo poplin
Period: 1865.

A fabric made of pure llama wool, resembling French merino.

Yokohama crêpe
Period: 1880.
A cotton textile printed in stripes with Japanese floral designs.

Z

Zephirina
Period: 1841.
"A new material for coats; a mixture of various colours."

Zephyr
Period: 1880s.
A light, fine **gingham**, thin and silky, often with coloured warp and finer weft.

Zephyr shirting
Period: 1880s.

A very fine **flannel** with silk warp; for hot climates.

Zephyr silk barege
Period: 1840s.
A barege of silk and wool with a gauze weave.

Zibeline, zibelline
Period: 1856.
A fabric between a **barege** and a **paramatta**; apparently a mixture of wool and cotton.

Glossary of Laces

Alençon, point d'
Period: 18th and 19th centuries.
Fine needle lace with delicate twisted and looped mesh, with floral patterns outlined by buttonhole stitches worked over a hair.

Antwerp
Period: 17th century.
Densely worked bobbin lace, most typically patterned with a vase of flowers (*'potlen kant'*). Diminished into a coarse, cheap lace.

Argentan, point d'
Period: 18th and 19th centuries.
Related to Alençon lace but heavier and with a hexagonal mesh oversewn in buttonhole stitch.

Binche
Period: 18th century.
Delicate, soft bobbin lace distinguished by its *'point de neige'* (cobwebby) ground and tiny, indistinct, floral patterns.

Black lace
Period: 17th century.
Probably **Mechlin** or **Brussels** lace; this and "black and white" lace were fashionable after the Restoration of Charles II in 1660.

Blonde
Period: ca. 1730–1850.
Cream-coloured, silk bobbin lace of Chantilly type but with more densely worked patterned areas. A very heavy variety was made in Spain, in black as well as white silk.

Bobbin lace
A generic term for all lace made by the twisting and plaiting together of threads wound on bobbins. In the 16th century a lace composed of a coarse thread, made using bobbins rather than needles.

Bone lace
Period: 16th and early 17th centuries.
Another name for **bobbin lace**; the name derived from the small bones originally used for bobbins. From the late 16th century onwards this lace was made on a pillow with bone bobbins.

Brabant lace
Period: 18th century.
Bobbin lace similar to Brussels lace but worked on a larger, coarser scale.

Brussels laces
A variety of laces. In the 18th century primarily a fine bobbin lace with a hexagonal mesh (drochel) and floral patterns outlined by a raised "woven" edging.
Also fine, flat needle and mixed laces. In the 19th century *Point de Gaze,* a delicate needle lace with raised petals and a fine looped mesh; also a popular heavier *Duchesse* bobbin lace of the guipure type.
See Point d'Angleterre.

Buckinghamshire lace
Period: 18th and 19th centuries.
Bobbin lace of the Lille type with a twisted net ground, small patterns with a gimp outline. Called "Bucks Point". Similar laces were made in Bedfordshire and Northamptonshire, all in England.

Burano
Period: 18th and early 19th centuries.
Needle lace, originally of the 18th-century Venetian type; flat and elaborately patterned. In the late 19th century various needle laces were produced by the Burano Lace School.

Campane lace
Period: 17th century.
"A kind of narrow lace, picked or scalloped" (1694, *Ladies' Dictionary*). The scallops in the shape of little bells. From *campane*, meaning a bell.

Carrickmacross
Period: After 1850.
Not a true lace but cut-muslin work; either applied to a machine net ground or left as a guipure.

Catgut lace
Period: 17th and 18th centuries.
Tradename for a kind of lace, possibly of horsehair; certainly not of catgut. "5¾ (yards) of fine broad cattgutt border at 20/-" (1693, Bill for lace, for Queen Mary).

Chantilly
Period: Late 18th and 19th centuries.
Silk bobbin lace of great delicacy made in Chantilly, Bayeux, and surrounding districts. Fine ground, with the patterned areas outlined by a glossy cordonnet.

Chemical lace
See Machine lace.

Chenille lace
Period: 18th century.
A French lace, the ground silk honeycomb in geometrical designs, filled with thick stitches and outlined with white chenille.

Cheveux de frize
Period: 18th century.
A narrow lace with a vandyke edge, used as a trimming. Often spoken of as "frize".

Colberteen
Period: 17th and 18th centuries.
"A kind of open lace with a square grounding" (Randle Holme, 1688). "A lace resembling network" (1694, *Ladies' Dictionary*).

Cordonnet

A sharp outline to patterned areas provided either by a thick thread, called gimp in English laces, or by a raised, woven strip in Brussels lace, or bundles of threads in 19th-century Belgian lace, or a hair in Alençon lace.

In needle lace the thread, threads or hair are oversewn in buttonhole stitch.

Crown lace

Period: 16th century.

A lace, "the pattern worked on a succession of crowns with acorns and roses".

Cut-and-slash lace

Period: 17th century.

Cut-work lace; "... apron laced with cut and slash lace" (1677, *London Gazette*).

Dentelle

The French word for lace; a term often used in the 19th century, in books and magazines.

Dresden lace

Period: 18th century.

Mainly used for the very fine **white work** that was decorated with such elaborate pulled-fabric work that it resembled Brussels bobbin lace. Some bobbin lace was also made at Dresden.

English point lace

Period: ca. 1670.

A name applied to **Brussels lace** smuggled into England; so called to avoid tax.

Filet lace, lacis

Period: 16th and 17th centuries.

A fashionable darned net; normally hand-made fisherman's net, but sometimes a woven net was used. In the 18th and 19th centuries it was seen as a peasant art rather than fashionable.

Flemish lace, Flanders lace

Period: Late 16th and 17th centuries.

During the 17th century this developed from densely-patterned, solid bobbin laces into soft, delicate laces from which emerged the distinctive laces of Brussels, Mechlin, Binche, etc. "Madam," tis right Mechlin ... smuggled ... The State prohibits Flanders Lace" (1709. T. Baker, *Fine Lady's Airs*).

Also, in the second half of the 17th century this denoted a boldly patterned, fairly large-scale tape lace comparable with that of Milan.

Gassed lace

Period: Early 19th century.

The thread first was passed through a gas flame to scorch off superfluous fibres. "British Gassed Lace commonly known by the name of Urling's Lace" (1823).

Genoese

Period: 16th and 17th centuries.

Fairly heavy bobbin lace, usually scalloped and distinguished by the frequent use of "wheat-ear" motifs and circles.

Gimp

Period: 16th–18th century.

An open bobbin lace, the threads of which are made by twisting yarns round wire or strips of parchment, etc., giving a stiff texture. The term was also applied to the thick thread outlining the pattern in many bobbin laces.

Guipure

Period: 17th century onwards.

Originally another name for **gimp**. It came to mean laces, often with a tape foundation, made without a ground mesh: the parts either touching or linked by occasional bars. In the 19th century the term was used loosely for many laces with large patterns.

Hamilton lace

Period: 18th century.

A coarse lace of diamond pattern made at Hamilton, Scotland from 1752; named after the Duchess of Hamilton.

Herringbone lace

Period: 16th century.

Lace having a chevron pattern.

Hollie point

Period: 18th century.

English needle lace. Small-scale, solidly-worked and with a voided pattern. Used particularly to trim baby clothes.

Honiton

Period: 18th century onwards.

Bobbin lace similar to that of Brussels but coarser and with more simple floral patterns, particularly roses. With a mesh ground in the 18th century, but applied to machine net, or made as a **guipure**, in the 19th century.

Huguenot lace

Period: Early 19th century.

An imitation lace with a muslin net ground on which floral cut-out designs were sewn.

Hungerland lace

Period: 17th century.

A lace made at Halle in the Hungarian style. "Your Hungerland bands and Spanish quellio ruffs" (ca. 1630, Massinger, *The City Madam*).

Lille

Period: 18th and 19th centuries.

Simple bobbin lace used mainly for trimmings. Delicate, twisted net ground decorated with *point d'esprit*. Small floral patterns outlined with gimp.

Limerick

Period: 19th century.

Not a true lace but embroidered machine net. Either worked with a hooked tambour needle or needle-run.

Loom lace

Period: 16th century onwards.

Lace woven on a loom, imitating bobbin or point lace. "For loome lace to make Mistris Margarett a payre of ruffez" (1554–5, Willoughby Accounts, Lord Middleton's MSS).

Machine lace

Period: 19th century onwards.

The earliest machine-made net was produced on knitting frames during the 1760s, but a more important development was Heathcote's invention of the "Bobbinnet" machine in 1808. Machine-made patterned nets followed and, from the 1840s, increasingly elaborate machine laces were produced. The Swiss invention of "chemical" or "burnt-out" lace in 1883 enabled the manufacture, by embroidery machine, of exact copies of elaborate needle laces.

Madras lace

Period: 1880s.

Bobbin lace similar in style to Maltese lace, the result of a lace-making school being established in Madras.

Maltese

Period: 19th century.

Heavy, silk bobbin lace with wheat-ear motifs and/or Maltese crosses. Particularly popular in England after being shown at the 1851 Exhibition.

Marly-lace

Period: 18th and 19th centuries.

A lace of a hexagonal mesh net powdered with small, round rosettes. Originally of cotton; later of thread and of silk.

Maskel lace

Period: 15th century.

A spotted lace net.

Mechlin

Period: Late 17th to mid-19th century.

Bobbin lace with a hexagonal ground mesh, distinguished by its softness and by the silky gimp thread used to outline the pattern. A summer lace.

Metal laces

Period: 16th–18th century.

Bobbin laces, usually decorated with spangles in the 16th and 17th centuries.

Milanese

Period: 17th and early 18th century.

Bobbin lace with a tape-like foundation. Bold, scrolling patterns, normally floral; sometimes with elaborate fillings.

Mixed lace

Lace made with both needle and bobbin techniques.

Naples lace

Period: 16th and 17th centuries.

A black silk lace made at Naples.

Needle lace, needle point

Generic term for all laces made by the needle, not with bobbins.

Needlework lace

Period: Late 16th century to ca. 1660.

The name given at that time to **point lace**.

Orris lace

Period: 17th and 18th centuries.

A lace woven with designs in gold or silver threads.

Parchment lace

Period: 16th and 17th centuries.

A pillow lace, usually of gold or silver but occasionally of coloured silks.

See Gimp.

Patent lace

Period: ca. 1800–ca. 1820.

A term commonly denoting machine-made lace.

Peak lace

Period: 16th and 17th centuries.

Lace with the outer edge margined by a series of angular indentations.

Point d'Angleterre

Period: 17th and 18th centuries.

High-quality bobbin and also needle laces made in Brussels. In the 19th century the term was also applied to machine net with applied bobbin-lace patterns, again from Brussels. The name was first used for laces smuggled into England from Brussels in the 1670s, when a ban was put on their importation. It remained widely in use after this was lifted. *'Onze aunes d'Angleterre de Flandre'* (1738, Duc de Penthieve Accounts).

Point de France

Period: 1665 to early 18th century.

Originally a copy of Venetian needle lace, but with a distinctive French character by the 1670s. Elaborate, formal designs, sometimes incorporating figures. Developed into **Alençon** and **Argentan**.

Point de Venise

Period: From 1660 onwards.

"I never saw anything prettier than this high-work on your point d"Espagne. ... "Tis not so rich as point de Venise." (1676, Etherege, *Man of Mode*)

Point Jean

Period: From 1660 onwards.

A bobbin lace found in England after this date.

Point lace, point

Period: Late 16th century onwards.

A thread lace made wholly with the needle on a parchment pattern. The term "needle-point" is modern. Known as "point lace" from 1660; previously as **needlework lace** to distinguish it from **bone lace**, **cut-work** and **drawn-work**. NB Point lace is the generic term which should only refer to **needle lace**, as distinct from **bobbin lace**, but was widely misused to mean any fine lace, e.g. **point d'Angleterre**.

Point of Spain

Period: From 1660 onwards.

Spanish point lace.

Pomet lace

Period: 16th century.

A silk lace.

Punto in aria

Period: 16th and 17th centuries.

An early form of needle lace following **reticella**; made without the linen ground but with free-flowing patterns.

Reticella

Period: 16th and 17th centuries.

The earliest form of **needle lace**. Built-up with button-hole stitches on a rectangular grid of threads formed by cutting and "drawing" a piece of linen and creating geometric patterns.

Saint Martin's lace

Period: 16th and 17th centuries.

A cheap, copper braid lace made in the parish of St Martin's, in the City of London.

Seaming lace

Period: 17th century.

A moderately wide net lace of **cut-work**, **bone lace** or **needlework**, without edges; used instead of a seam to unite the breadths of linen in a shirt or smock.

Sedan lace

Period: 17th century.

Cutwork lace made at Sedan in France.

Spider work

Period: 19th century.

A cheap, machine-made lace.

Statute lace

Period: 1571.

Lace woven according to the statute enacted in that year; probably a native-made lace to be worn by those who were forbidden to wear foreign-made lace.

Tape lace

Period: All periods.

Either a needle or bobbin lace, occasionally of woven tapes. A term descriptive of any lace in which the designs are built up of tape-like forms.

Tawdry

Period: 16th and 17th centuries.

A silk lace, originally called St Audry's lace.

Torchon lace

Period: 19th century.

Bobbin lace with simple patterns and little net ground, made by peasants and by amateurs for general use.

Trolly lace

Period: 17th and 18th centuries.

A coarse Flanders bobbin lace; the pattern outlined with thicker thread or with a flat, narrow border composed of several thicker threads.

Urling's lace

See Gassed lace.

Valenciennes

Period: 18th century.

A delicate, soft bobbin lace, like **binche** but with distinct floral patterns and a mesh ground.

Period: 19th century.

Distinguished by its square, or round, plaited mesh and very white, clear patterns.

Venetian lace

Period: 16th and 17th centuries.

Needle lace developing from **reticella**, through **punto in aria**, into very elaborate, raised laces with scrolling, flower-decorated patterns. According to scale, these were called: "gros point"; "rose point"; "point de neige". Also worked without the raised elaborations as "point plat". One variety with a pattern of small, branching stems was known as "coraline".

Period: 18th century.

A flat, densely patterned needle-lace of high quality.

White work

Period: 16th century onwards.

Initially a synonym for **cut-work**. However, this white-on-white form of embroidery traditionally used other techniques, such as drawn thread and pulled work and shadow work to create effects similar to those of needle lace, though white work is now usually considered **embroidery**.

See Broderie anglaise.

Yak lace

Period: 19th century.

A coarse and rather heavy lace made of the hair of the yak; fashionable for shawls, etc., ca. 1870–1880.

Youghal point, yougal point

Period: After 1850.

Irish needle lace, flat and rather open, with naturalistic floral patterns.

Glossary: Obsolete Colour Names

Abraham, Abram
Period: 16th century.
Brown.

Bowdy
Period: 17th century.
Scarlet from the dye house established at Bow, East London, for dyeing scarlet by a new method.

Brassel
Period: 16th century.
A red colour obtained from the wood of an East Indian tree.

Bristol
Period: 16th century.
Red.

Carnation
Period: 16th century.
A colour "resembling raw flesh".

Cottony
See Cuttanee.

Crepe, crêpe
See Crape.

Crocus
Period: 17th century.
A yellow dye obtained from saffron.

Falwe
Period: Medieval.
Yellow.

Gingerline
Period: 16th century.
Reddish-violet.

Goose-turd
Period: 16th century.
Yellowish-green.

Hair
Period: 16th century.
Bright tan.

Incarnate
Period: 16th century.
Red.

Inde
Period: Medieval.
Azure blue.

Isabelle
Period: 16th century.
Yellow or light buff.

Lustie-gallant
Period: 16th century.
Light red.

Maidenhair
Period: 16th century.
Bright tan.

Marble
Period: 16th century.
Parti-coloured.

Medley
Period: 16th century.
A mixture of colours.

Milk-and-water
Period: 16th century.
Bluish-white.

Murrey
Period: 16th century.
Purplish-red.

Orange tawny
Period: 16th century.
Orange-brown.

Pear
Period: 16th century.
Russet red.

Perse
Period: Medieval.
Bluish-grey.

Plunket
Period: 16th century.
Light blue or sky blue.

Popinjay
Period: 16th century.
Green or blue.

Puke
Period: 16th century.
A dirty brown.

Rats colour
Period: 16th century.
Dull grey.

Roy
Period: 16th century.
A bright tawny.

Russet
Period: Medieval.
A dark brown.

Sad
Period: 16th century.
A dark tint of any colour.

Sanguin
Period: 16th century.
Blood red.

Sheeps colour
> *Period:* 16th century.
> A neutral colour.

Stammel
> *Period:* 16th century.
> Red.

Tawny
> *Period:* Medieval.
> A dusky brown-orange.

Toley
> *Period:* Medieval.
> Scarlet.

Vermel
> *Period:* Medieval.
> Vermilion.

Watchet
> *Period:* Medieval.
> Pale blue inclining towards green.

Bibliography

Adburgham, Alison. *Shopping in Style*. London, 1979.

Alexander, Hélène. *Fans*. London, 1984.

Anon. *Yesterday's Shopping: Gamages General Catalogue 1914*. Ware, Hertfordshire, 1994.

Ashelford, Jane. *The Art of Dress, Clothes and Society 1500–1914*.

Ashelford, Jane. *The Visual History of Costume: The Sixteenth Century*. London, 1983

Blum, Stella (ed.). *Ackermann's Costume Plates: Women's Fashions in England, 1818–1828*. New York, 1978.

Blum, Stella (ed.). *Victorian Fashions & Costumes from Harper's Bazar: 1867–1898*. New York, 1974.

Brand, Jan and Teunissen, José (eds.). *Fashion Accessories*. Arnhem, 2007.

Buck, Anne. *Dress in Eighteenth-century England*. London, 1979.

Buck, Anne. *Victorian Costume and Costume Accessories*, 2nd edn. Bedford, 1984.

Burman, Barbara and Denbo, Seth. *Pockets of History*. Museum of Costume, Bath, 2007.

Byrde, Penelope and Wilson, Verity (eds.). *Costume. The Journal of the Costume Society*, vol. 43, Leeds, 2009.

Byrde, Penelope. *The Visual History of Costume: The Twentieth Century*. London, 1989.

Calasibetta, Charlotte Mankey and Tortora, Phyllis. *The Fairchild Dictionary of Fashion*. New York, 2003.

Carroll, David. *The Dictionary of Foreign Terms in the English Language*. New York, 1973.

Clabburn, Pamela. *The Norwich Shawl*. London, 1995.

Clark, Fiona. *Hats*. London, 1982.

Coleridge, Lady Georgina (intro.) *The Lady's Realm: A Selection from November 1904 to April 1905*. London, 1972.

Cumming, Valerie. *Gloves*. London, 1982.

Cumming, Valerie. *The Visual History of Costume Accessories*. London, 1998.

Cumming, Valerie. *Understanding Fashion History*. London, 2004.

Cunnington, C. W. & P. E. and Beard, Charles. *A Dictionary of English Costume*. London, 1972 and 1976 edns.

Cunnington, C. Willett and Cunnington, Phillis. *Handbook of English Costume in the Eighteenth Century*, 3rd edn. London, 1972.

Cunnington, C. Willett and Cunnington, Phillis. *Handbook of English Costume in the Nineteenth Century*, 3rd edn. London, 1970.

Cunnington, C. Willett and Cunnington, Phillis. *Handbook of English Costume in the Seventeenth Century*, 3rd edn. London, 1972.

Cunnington, C. Willett and Cunnington, Phillis. *Handbook of English Costume in the Sixteenth Century*, 3rd edn. 1970.

Cunnington, C. Willett and Cunnington, Phillis. *Handbook of English Mediaeval Costume*, 2nd edn. London, 1973.

Cunnington, C. Willett. *English Women's Clothing in the Nineteenth Century*. London, 1937.

Cunnington, C. Willett. *English Women's Clothing in the Present Century*. London, 1952.

De Marly, Diana. *Costume on the Stage 1600–1940*. London, 1982.

Essinger, James. *Spell Bound: The Improbable Story of English Spelling*. London, 2006.

Farrell, Jeremy. *Socks & Stockings*. London, 1992.

Farrell, Jeremy. *Umbrellas & Parasols*. London, 1985.

Foster, Vanda. *Bags and Purses*. London, 1982.

Foster, Vanda. *The Visual History of Costume: The Nineteenth Century*. London, 1984.

Fukai, Akiko et al. *Fashion: The Collection of the Kyoto Costume Institute*. Cologne, 2002.

Harrison, E.P. *Scottish Estate Tweeds*. Elgin, 1995.

Hashagen, Joanna and Levey, Santina. *Fine & Fashionable: Lace from the Blackborne Collection*. The Bowes Museum, County Durham, 2006.

Haye, Amy de la. *Fashion Source Book*. London, 1988.

Hayward, Maria. *Dress at the Court of Henry VIII*. Leeds, 2007.

Herald, Jacqueline. *Renaissance Dress in Italy 1400–1500*. London, 1981.

Holding, T. H. *Coats*, 4th edn. London, 1902.

Ironside, Janey. *A Fashion Alphabet*. London, 1968.

Kennan, Brigid. *The Women We Wanted to Look Like*. New York, 1978.

Levitt, Sarah. *Victorians Unbuttoned: Registered Designs for Clothing, their Makers and Weavers 1839–1900*. London, 1986.

Lynam, Ruth (ed.). *Paris Fashion: The Great Designers and their Creations*. London, 1972.

Mansfield, Alan & Cunnington, Phillis E. *Handbook of English Costume in the 20th Century 1900–1950*. London, 1973.

McDowell, Colin. *McDowell's Directory of Twentieth Century Fashion*. London, 1984.

Mendes, Valerie & de la Haye, Amy. *20th Century Fashion*. London, 1999.

Mulvagh, Jane. *Vogue History of 20th Century Fashion*. London, 1988.

Mulvagh, Jane. *Costume Jewelry in Vogue*. London, 1988.

Newman, Alex & Shariff, Zakee. *Fashion A to Z.* London, 2009.

Newton, Stella Mary. *Health, Art & Reason: Dress Reformers of the 19th Century.* London, 1974.

O'Hara Callan, Georgina. *The Thames and Hudson Dictionary of Fashion and Fashion Designers.* London, 1998.

Oxford English Dictionary. Oxford, 2009, paper and online edns.

Ribeiro, Aileen & Cumming, Valerie. *The Visual History of Costume.* London, 1989.

Ribeiro, Aileen. *Dress in Eighteenth Century Europe 1715–1789.* London, 1984.

Ribeiro, Aileen. *Fashion and Fiction.* London, 2005.

Ribeiro, Aileen. *The Gallery of Fashion.* London, 2000.

Rieff Anawalt, Patricia. *The Worldwide History of Dress.* London, 2007.

Saunders, Ann (ed.). *Costume. The Journal of the Costume Society,* vols 1–9, London, 1967–1975; vols 10–39, London, 1976–2005; vols 40–42, Leeds, 2006–2008.

Scott, Margaret. *Late Gothic Europe.* London, 1980.

Scott, Margaret. *The Visual History of Costume: The Fourteenth and Fifteenth Centuries.* London, 1986

Swann, June. *Shoes.* London, 1982.

Thornton, Peter. *Baroque and Rococo Silks.* London, 1965.

Vergani, Guido (ed.). *Fashion Dictionary.* New York, 2006.

Wardle, Patricia. *Victorian Lace.* London, 1968.

Worsley, Harriet. *Decades of Fashion.* Köln, 2000.

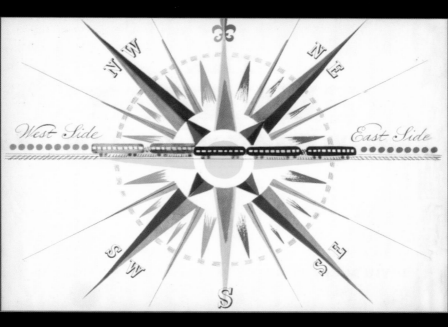

YOU
ARE
HERE

*Personal Geographies and
Other Maps of the Imagination*

Katharine Harmon

PRINCETON ARCHITECTURAL PRESS

NEW YORK

Published by
Princeton Architectural Press
37 East Seventh Street
New York, New York 10003

For a free catalog of books, call 1.800.722.6657.
Visit our web site at www.papress.com.

PROJECT EDITING: Jennifer N. Thompson
TEXT EDITING: Clare Jacobson, Nicola Bednarek
DESIGN: Jane Jeszeck, Jigsaw
RESEARCH: Abby Fifer, Janet Fryberger
PERMISSIONS: Melissa Flamson, FreelancePermissions.com
EDITORIAL CONSULTATION: Dean Holmes

Special thanks to: Nettie Aljian, Janet Behning, Megan Carey, Penny (Yuen Pik) Chu,
Russell Fernandez, Jan Haux, Mark Lamster, Nancy Eklund Later, Linda Lee, Nancy
Levinson, Katharine Myers, Jane Sheinman, Scott Tennent, Joe Weston, and Deb
Wood of Princeton Architectural Press —Kevin C. Lippert, publisher

Library of Congress Cataloging-in-Publication Data
Harmon, Katharine A., 1960-
  You are here : personal geographies and other maps of the imagination/
Katharine Harmon.
     p. cm.
  ISBN 1-56898-430-8 (pbk. : alk. paper)
  1. Cartography. 2. Thematic maps. I. Title.
  GA105.3.H346 2003
  912--dc22
                              2003015044

Author's acknowledgments appear on page 190–191.

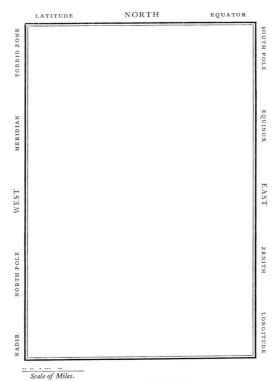

OCEAN-CHART.

He had brought a large map
      representing the sea,
Without the least vestige of land:
And the crew were much pleased
      when they found it to be
A map they could all understand.

           — Lewis Carroll,
           The Hunting of the Snark

For John Held, Jr.,
and all of the inspired mapmakers
before and since.

EXCERPTS

PAGES 4–5: Lewis Carroll, *The Hunting of the Snark: An Agony, in Eight Fits* (London: Macmillan & Co., 1876).

PAGE 13: Leonardo da Vinci, *The Notebooks of Leonardo da Vinci*

PAGES 15–19: Stephen S. Hall's essay "I, Mercator" is adapted from a longer original, which appeared in the spring 1994 issue of *Orion* magazine.

PAGES 54-55, 105, 124-125: Part or all of the captions for maps by Ernest Dudley Chase were written by Joseph Garver for a 2003 exhibition of Chase's work at Harvard College Library.

PAGE 56: German poem translated by Anke Betz.

PAGE 65: "The Map-Maker on His Art" by Howard Nemerov appears by permission of Margaret Nemerov. From *The Collected Poems of Howard Nemerov* by Howard Nemerov (Chicago: The University of Chicago Press, 1977).

PAGES 66–69: Roger Sheffer's essay "The Mental Geography of Appalacian Trail Hikers" is adapted from a longer original, which appeared in the fall 1999 issue of *You Are Here: The Journal of Creative Geography.*

PAGE 130: Katie Davis's essay "Memory Map" originally aired on NPR's "All Things Considered" as part of the ongoing Neighborhood Stories series.

PAGES 148-149: From *Treasure Island* by Robert Louis Stevenson (New York: Scribners, 1909).

PAGE 192: From *The BFG* by Roald Dahl. Copyright © 1982 by Roald Dahl. Reprinted by permission of Farrar, Straus and Giroux, LLC and David Higham Associates.

ILLUSTRATIONS

FRONT COVER: Lordy Rodriguez, *Farm Strip,* 2002. Ink on paper, 36 x 28 inches. Courtesy of Clementine Gallery, New York

INSIDE COVERS: *Map of the Various Paths of Life,* published by Benjamin Johnson, Philadelphia, 1805 (originally published as a jigsaw puzzle in 1794). Courtesy of Map Collection, Yale University Library.

PAGE 1: Dorothea Dana, illustration for *The Runaway Train* by Muriel Fuller (Philadelphia: David McKay Company, 1946).

PAGE 2: Istvan Banyai, *You Are Here: SPS Signal Reception,* 2003. Courtesy of the artist.

PAGE 12: *The Arterial System,* an illustration from the *Encyclopédie,* the first published compendium of human knowledge, created in France from 1745 to 1765.

PAGE 64: Boris Artzybasheff, illustration from advertisement for *Time* magazine (detail). © 1941 Time Inc.

BACK COVER: From left to right, top to bottom, details from pages 33, 44, 100–101, 25, 96–97, 72, 51, 144–145, 56, 43, 22, 108–109, 156, and 91.

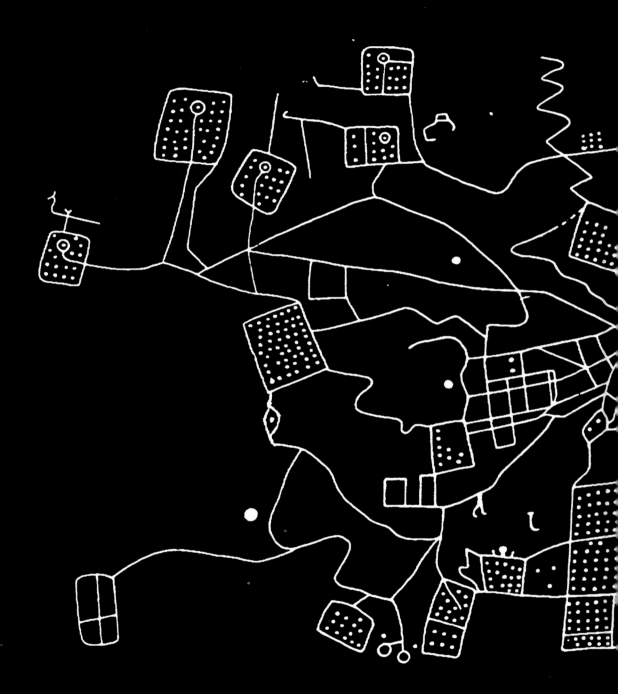

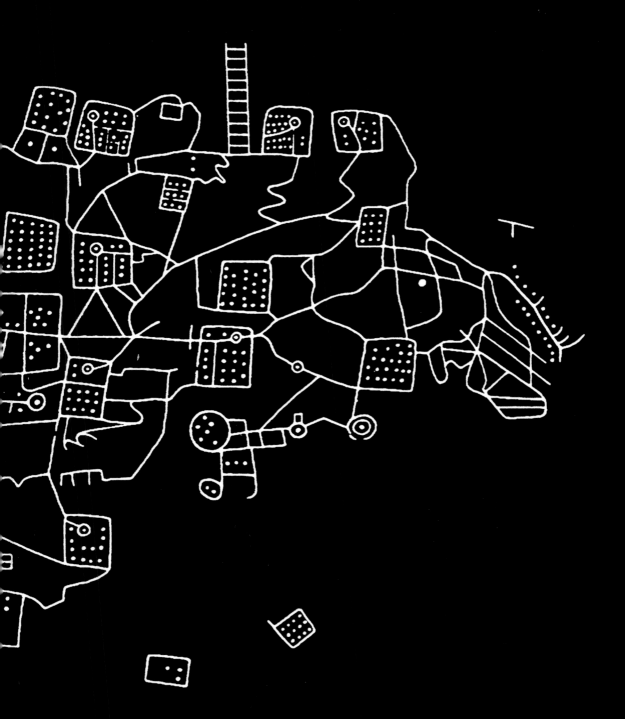

Introduction

I SENSE THAT HUMANS have an urge to map—and that this mapping instinct, like our opposable thumbs, is part of what makes us human. Consider the map on the preceding two pages, from an area called Valcamonica in the center of northern Italy, between Milan and Venice. In this part of Lombardy, glaciers retreated and left smooth swaths of rock, on which, over a period of eight thousand years, prehistoric people carved one of the world's greatest collections of petroglyphs. This image dates to the Iron Age and is thought to be among the oldest-known maps extant, perhaps showing a farming settlement at the bottom of the valley it faces. Four thousand or so years ago someone sat on the rock and made this map, and it captivates me.

As a youngster, in the bedroom I shared with my sister, I came to know intimately the ceiling of the room where I was supposed to be napping. I stared upward for hours, making out forms of imagined countries in the water-stained plaster. Why was I seeing international borders even before I knew the meaning of the concept? It was a natural way to pass the time and kept my restless imagination engaged far beyond that bedroom while my body got the rest my mother thought it needed.

Maps intrigue us, perhaps none more than those that ignore mapping conventions. These are maps that find their essence in some other goal than just taking us from point A to point B. They are a vehicle for the imagination, fuelled up and ready to go. We look at these maps, and our minds know just what to do: take

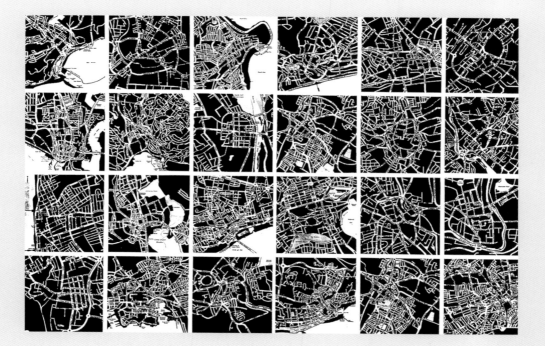

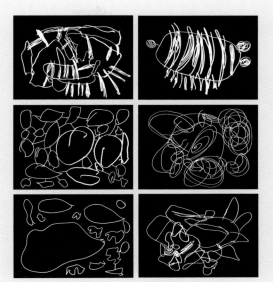

the information and extrapolate from it a place where they can leap, play, gambol—without that distant province of our being, the body, dragging them down.

Of course, part of what fascinates us when looking at a map is inhabiting the mind of its maker, considering that particular terrain of imagination overlaid with those unique contour lines of experience. If I had mapped that landscape, we ask ourselves, what would I have chosen to show, and how would I have shown it? The coded visual language of maps is one we all know, but in making maps of our worlds we each have our own dialect.

I map, therefore I am: this could be the motto for the contributors to this book. *You Are Here* is my own personal proof of the mapping instinct: an idiosyncratic collection of maps that transcend the norm, either because of the mapmaker's personal viewpoint, or sense of humor, or ingenuity, or all of the above. These are maps of the imagination, as all maps are, only more so.

Try making a map like these, and you might realize that the mapping instinct is of the "use it or lose it" variety. My three-year-old daughter, on the other hand, can generate map after map, such as the ones shown at right, each with an elaborate verbal narrative in place of a key. She has learned about maps in preschool but not to the extent that she thinks there is any "right" way to draw them. Three-year-olds are born cartographers, eager to claim their own territories and impose order on surroundings that are widening and becoming more complex by the day.

I hope I can help keep her mapping facility alive. I look forward to the day I will hand her a copy of *The Collected Works of John Held, Jr.*, a book I discovered one rainy summer day on my grandparents' bookshelf. I recognized immediately that this was an exuberant mapmaker, and the products of his mapping urge were a form of creative cartography I wanted to find more of. Here, many years later, is a book filled with it—from works by artists like Guillermo Kuitca and Joyce Kozloff, who have used maps as part of a marvelous artistic output, to the witty creations of illustrators like Ernest Dudley Chase, Jo Mora, and Istvan Banyai, to the poem-maps of Edwin Morgan and Howard Horowitz, to maps used by novelists over the past two hundred years to enhance their fiction. This collection of maps represents, for me, an exhilarating form of graphic expression, and I hope it will inspire other creative cartographers for years to come.

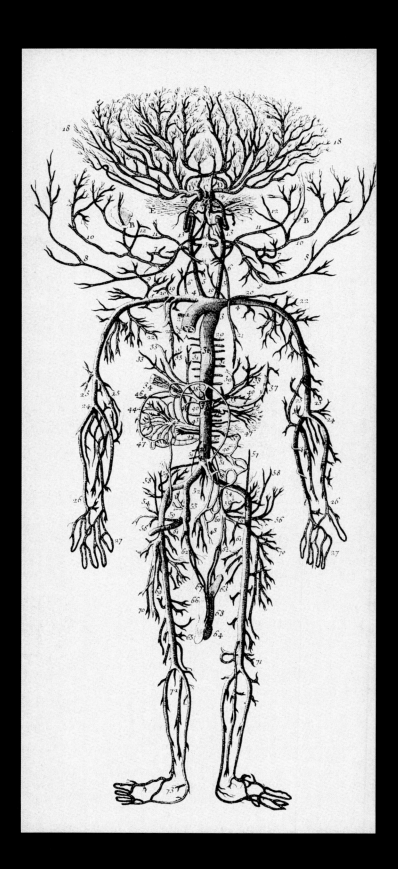

Personal Geography

Man is called by the ancients a world in miniature and certainly this name is well applied, for just as man is composed of earth, water, air and fire, so is the body of the earth. If man has in him bones which are the support and armor of the flesh, the world has rocks which are the support of the earth; if man has in himself the sea of blood, in which the lungs rise and fall in breathing, so the body of the earth has its oceanic sea which also rises and falls every six hours for the world to breathe. If from the said sea of blood spring veins which go on ramifying throughout the human body, similarly the oceanic sea fills the body of the earth with infinite veins of water.

—Leonardo da Vinci

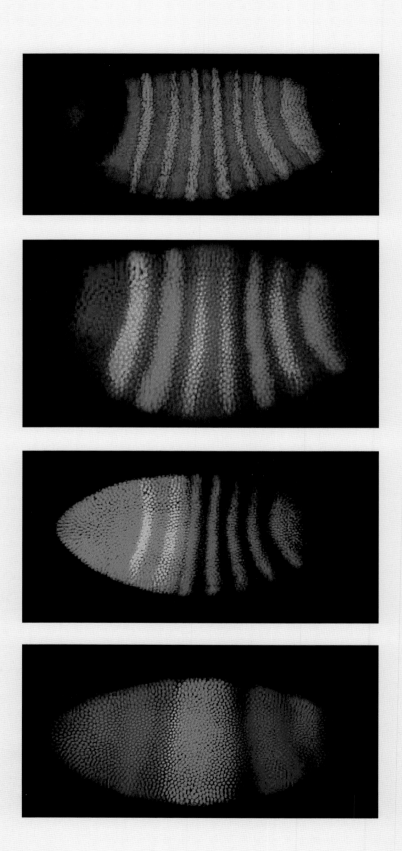

I, Mercator

STEPHEN S. HALL

A NUMBER OF YEARS AGO, two men of dubious moral compass (being the counselors of the wilderness school to which many parents, mine included, sent their sullen offspring for "toughening") abandoned about a dozen of us soft lads in the middle of Nowhere, Minnesota. We found ourselves alarmingly alone in a lovely but none-too-friendly landscape dominated by lakes and bogs and a big hazy sky. Our mission was to read a map and slog through miles of brack and bramble, to find our way back.

That was my first taste of orienteering—crashing through a landscape without paths, provisioned only with vague bearings and a distant destination. "Orienteering" is such an odd but impressive word that it has always stuck with me, and in fact moves me to propose a related concept to describe a process somewhat like orienteering but more personal, more historical, more associative, more metaphorical, perhaps more spiritual: "orientating," or crashing through the larger landscapes of memory and experience and knowledge, trying to get a fix on where we are in a multitude of landscapes that together compose the grander scheme of things. Orientating begins with geography, but it reflects a need of the conscious, self-aware organism for a kind of transcendent orientation that asks not just where am I, but where do I fit in this landscape? Where have I been? Where shall I go, and what values will I pack for the trip? What culture of knowledge allows me to know what I know, which is often another way of knowing where I am? And what pattern, what grid of wisdom, can I impose on my accumulated, idiosyncratic geographies? The coordinates marking this territory are unique to each individual and lend themselves to a very private kind of cartography.

I like to say that I never travel without a map, but then none of us do. We all travel with many maps, neatly folded and tucked away in the glove compartment of memory—some of them communal and universal, like our autonomic familiarity with seasonal constellations and the shape of continents, and some as particular as the local roads we have each traipsed. As we navigate on the trip that Dante called "our life's way," we are all creating our private maps. Like Mercator, we are not discovering entirely new worlds; rather, we are laying a new set of lines down on a known but changing world, arranging and rearranging metaphysical rhumbs that we associate with successful navigation. To each, her or his private meridians. To each, a unique projection. I, Mercator, and you, too.

To orientate is to hop back and forth between landscape and time, geography and emotion, knowledge and behavior. As I write this, I am sitting on the back porch of a house in the valley of Pantherkill Stream in upstate New York, looking out at a wild and thickly wooded landscape that created an association in my mind: a memory of something that happened in Minnesota. And that led to another memory, of something that occurred on an island off the coast of Sicily, and then to another memory, same island but different year, and then back to the Pantherkill, to the summer rental house, and to the beloved mate rustling in a different corner of it. It all happens in the span of a few moments. Never out of earshot of the Pantherkill, which tumbles in a rush off to my left, I have roamed across state lines and oceans and continents, backwards in time, each thought colored according to a personal legend corresponding to the elevation and depressions of my private humors: pride, wonder, sadness, remorse.

Like memory, geography is associative. In this process I call orientating we all carry a personal atlas in our brains (which obliges this psychic gazetteering because it happens to be the most sophisticated, supple map-making device ever created). We flip through it with synaptic rapidity; we crash just so through a wilderness of neurons primed and aligned by experience, traveling a decade in an instant, traversing hemispheres in the span of a few axons, snagging now and then on the nettles of a sad recollection, exhilarated by the sheer expanse of territory covered, surprised at how our brains can organize so much information along emotional latitudes, their very architecture a kind of microscopic merging of all the cartography we have acquired and stored. We are damned by the arrogance with which we ignore the immensity of the territories we presume to tame with our absurdly precise instruments of measure, and redeemed by a cunning, even courageous naïveté that persuades us to believe that they are approachable, knowable, chartable.

All maps are thematic, personal maps even more so; like everyone else, I lay down my lines and sail the wobbly grid. I, Mercator; you, Mercator, too.

※

Maps are not intrinsically sentimental documents. But I am always surprised at how, in a phase transition every bit as magical and elemental as that from vapor to water, I can shift in one glance from information-retrieval to inspiration, followed shortly thereafter by aspiration. Reading Shelby Foote's history of the Civil War recently, I was struck by a passage describing Robert E. Lee, who, poring over a map of the Virginia countryside, conceived of perhaps his greatest military maneuver, the flanking attack that crushed much superior Union forces at Chancellorsville in 1863. Lee, according to Foote's account, "kept peering at a map spread on his knees; he peered so intently, indeed, that he seemed to be trying to make it give him information which it did not contain."

And yet it did. At one point, the Confederate general asked Stonewall Jackson, "How do we get at those people?" and then, apparently in answer to his own question (Foote continues), "Lee traced a fingertip

westward along the map from their present location, as if to sketch in an ideal route past the front of the enemy position." There turned out to be a road where Lee's finger traveled; the rebel troops took it, and the rout was soon on. The story beautifully conveys that covenant between map-reader and map, the reader with his almost petulant demand for more information, the wishful fingertip grazing that abstract representation of Virginia countryside, and that phase transition between vision and volition, tipped off by Foote's phrase "an ideal route," in which resides all that creativity can bring to one's imagined passage through the physical world (passages, one hopes, less bloody than this one). What the map fails to supply, the human mind (or human yearning) sometimes has the power to conjure. It seems somehow easier to conjure up possibility out of a map than out of the sheer ether; perhaps we imagine the coordinates of latitude and longitude as a safety net.

When it comes to orientating, the mood of the map-reader colors the map itself. The ability to conjure, the willingness to fill in the blanks, the urgency with which one needs to know—all contribute to what the map becomes in the hands of the inspired imaginer: an instrument of destiny. It can involve public, national destinies, as in Lee's military maneuver, or simply a more intimate and personal campaign, a document of familial geography and history, a goad to take the transforming journey on which you meet the person or see the landscape or have the experience that changes if not a life, then at least its trajectory. It is hard to look at a map without sensing, in our bones, private hopes and secret fears about change. In my Mercator daydreams, I see: An erasure, perhaps, of the laid-down lines of the past. A willingness to draw new meridians. A reconfiguring of the private globe. A silent earthquake.

※

In the last thirty years, mapping has come a long way. Scientists have mapped the most forlorn bits of acreage on this Earth in a multitude of ways. Paleoclimatologists can tell us what kind of trees grew there nine thousand years ago, how much it rained, how fiercely the winds blew; seismic tomographers can tell us if the planet's geologically fluid mantle, hundreds of miles beneath the surface, is warm or cold, moving up or down. Geologists have mapped the shifting tides of the Earth's magnetic field as it has washed this way and that over the region. Molecular biologists can chop up the genetic lineage of any plant or animal in the zone like so much parsley and trace its evolution back hundreds of millions of years, while population biologists can chart the waxing and waning numbers of individual species, including some creatures that died out millennia ago.

Out of one territory, one map, can bloom a thousand geographies, and all the technologies that have allowed those new maps have come to fruition in a relatively short time. One is tempted to remark about how rapidly our world has changed, but what has really changed, even more rapidly, are our ways of seeing this world. With our telescopes and our microscopes, our remote-sensing satellites and our fluorescing molecular probes, we have expanded notions of the chartable world, creating a holistic, multidimensional cartography. There are maps to anywhere: chromosomes, galaxies, the brain, the cell, the spaces between atoms, cracks in the double helix, the edge of time. If maps invite travel, these new maps inspire journeys of an altogether different, more associative sort. At the same time, they still connect to our traditional geographies and are potential destinations of the orientating process; they lend themselves to a form of bushwhacking that is more interior, philosophic, imaginative.

In the past few years, I have had the privilege of visiting a great many scientific laboratories where the most ingenious and far-reaching mapping is occurring. Maps are no longer just the province of geographers; many new and previously inaccessible physical domains are being mapped, while many "known" territories are being reexplored and mapped all over again in novel ways. Another message, both surprising and exhilarating, is that no matter how distant or abstract the landscape, each has resonance for our more terrestrial, down-to-earth peregrinations. These disparate landscapes have nothing in common except the imaginer; it is as if I blaze paths between

dimensions that exist nowhere but in my head. In my private atlas, there is not just a birthplace, childhood homes, Rome, and a beautiful morning along the Pantherkill, but the egg and the chromosome, the ocean floor and the atmosphere, galaxies and the map of time, all the way back to the singularity that is said to have marked the beginning of our universe, a single point. To walk all these territories, I have only imagination, but that is not, I would argue, a poor man's instrument of measure.

Consider the landscape of the fertilized egg. A map showing the microscopic convulsions of a fertilized fruit-fly egg as it throbs into embryonic activity serves no practical or useful purpose, except wonder. I have looked at these maps dozens of times (they are called "fate maps" and have enjoyed a renaissance in the last decade, thanks to molecular biology); they reveal the exquisite beauty of cellular organization. In order to build itself into an organism, the egg must first in effect become a map— it must create north and south poles,  where head and tail will develop, equatorial zones for the internal compartments where organs will later appear. This early geographical delineation is accomplished by genes, which turn on in certain regions of the egg at certain times, like clockwork, and it is in fact the sequential appearance of these genes that have been mapped. Even though their colors come courtesy of a computer, not nature, each fate map has a trembling and penultimate architecture about it, the look of biological domains about to dissolve and borders about to break down and reform, as in a color field painted by Mark Rothko (art imitating, perhaps, the beginning of life). It is not simply that the science is beautiful and fills us with wonder; that foundation of geographical order is essential to the subsequent unfurling of individual difference. We all, human and fruit fly alike, start out with the same floorplan, yet how diverse and unique are the mansions we erect upon our little plots of cytoplasm.

Genetic maps have never struck me as beautiful in the same way as geographical maps, but they encourage me to imagine DNA as a landscape, one at first so monotonous and unvarying that it makes Flatland look like the Grand Canyon. And yet when x-ray crystallographers, with their electron density maps and three-dimensional structures, provide a closer look at the physical lay of the land (at a scale measured in ten

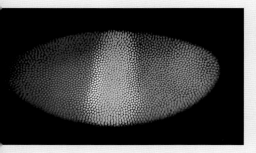

billionths of a meter, where a wavelength of light would fall upon and smother the molecule like a tarpaulin), that drearily monotonous thread of DNA reveals itself to be a bumpy, grooved, protruding, and twisting landscape of infinitesimally subtle outcrops and ravines. Each apparently has a biological purpose, most recognizable by proteins, the overall geography imaginable not only as a solid, palpable territory, but also as a stormy climate in which clouds of evanescent electro-atomic attractions and repulsions known as van der Waals forces tug and shove at atoms, and amid which storms delicate hydrogen bonds hold the rungs of the double helix together.

I wonder what it would be like to watch a hydrogen bond uncouple, as many must do when we dole out a half of the helix to our sex cells and package them in egg or sperm, a billion messages stuffed in a billion bottles so that one might reach that far shore known as fertilization. I wonder why so many of the messages we receive at our bumbling human scale, at the level of day-to-day wisdom, stress the virtues of strength, power, and resolve, when the message from that part of nature most essential to our proliferation as individual, as species, and as family is altogether different.

The message from DNA is one about suppleness more than strength, flexibility more than firmness, the virtue of coming apart as well as holding fast. The "importance of weak interactions" is how James Watson describes it in *Molecular Biology of the Gene*. We cannot choose our metaphors if we do not truly know the territory.

Or consider our recent attempts to chart the universe. Until some new knowledge comes to light, I suppose the Big Bang and all its implications will do; I admire the sheer cathedral of intellect built to apprehend something as large as the universe and create something perhaps even larger, an explanation for it, out of the meager light that swims back from the birth of time and, by chance, happens to land on our telescopes. But oceans of theorizing have been based on a cupful of data—only fifty thousand or so galaxies have been mapped out of resplendent millions, and ninety percent of the matter in the universe (purported to be dark) remains as yet undiscovered. To look at the galactic maps of the universe, with their unexpected clumps and voids, and formulate a tentative explanation is to realize that sometimes, often, we have to proceed with a theory (or a decision, or a commitment, as to a mate) knowing that all the information is not in hand, could not in a thousand lifetimes be at hand. In life as in cosmology, making do with incomplete information is as much an art as a science, and the style with which we fashion decisions may be as important as whether they turn out to be right or wrong.

If there is a thread running through all these ruminations, it stretches all the way back to one of my earliest memories. Someone recently asked me how I became interested in maps, and I suddenly saw myself as a young child sitting on the floor of a sun porch in the first home I remember, assembling a thick wooden puzzle of the United States, putting each state in its proper place. Before ever becoming conscious of its lesson, I am sure the exercise imbued me with a sense of external order, with the idea that things belong in their proper place. It was a fiction, of course, but an important fiction. Everything from the x-ray universe to yesterday's newspaper brings to our attention unexpected cataclysms, operatic bursts of disorder, intimations of a world bewildering precisely because of its randomness, its disturbing excesses and mysteries. The lesson I draw from the childhood puzzle is not that the world beyond the sun porch is orderly, or should be orderly. Rather, like the fertilized egg, which requires a core of order to realize its potential, we need some secure oasis of order, even if only a memory (or a fiction), as a home port for our various explorations, our attempts to make sense of the unknown. This is the place we call "home," which appears on page one of every private atlas. Home can literally be home, an abode, or our notion of family, or even a comfortable spot apart from our dwelling place, like work; whatever it is, home is where the lines are straight, the order clear, where even disorder seems predictable and the displacements tolerably temporary. And perhaps that is why when disorder invades the home—when illness, death, divorce, or any of a dozen domestic estrangements upsets the order—our metaphors for the ensuing emotional distress are so often geographical: we are lost, disoriented, have lost our bearings, we are at sea.

The surpassing virtue of Mercator's 1569 projection, of course, was that it facilitated ocean-going navigation, which in turn enabled and expedited further exploration. Just so, by rearranging the lines we privately knit, we enable and expedite our own exploratory thoughts; and while the world is changing much faster than it did for Mercator, at the same time it provides many more possibilities for connection, understanding, evolution. As we nose around these new-found territories, we may begin to create an ever more complex and useful geography of survival: atop our maps of land, sea, planet, chromosome, and cosmos, we superimpose maps of pain, of revelation, of joy, of disappointment. To each emotion, there is a pin on the map, the pattern of each accumulating and filling in until they have the appearance of growth rings.

Maps ultimately testify to our belief in the value of exploration, whether the compass is pointed inward or out. To do so is to appreciate the value of the mind as a dynamic vessel of exploration; it does not travel according to the limits of the compass rose, but moves by association. And when the mind comes to rest, when it ceases its orientating leaps and shunts and associations, we find ourselves back where we started, where Here intersects Now.

It might be a few yards up from Pantherkill Stream or it might be standing on the side of a road in northern Minnesota, waiting for a truck. For we did emerge from the wilderness those many years ago, with the help of a map. When I think of that map now, the one that showed us the fire road that would lead us out of those Minnesota woods, it is as if I am floating above the landscape; I see our journey as a capillary of expediency and hope running through an immense landscape that for the most part we did not see and could not possibly have understood. Looking down, I am reminded that the most important thing a map shows, if we pause to look at it long enough, if we travel upon it widely enough, if we think about it hard enough, is all the things we still do not know.

Stephen S. Hall has worked as an editor and contributing writer for The New York Times Magazine *and is the author of* Invisible Frontiers *(1987),* Mapping the Next Millennium *(1992),* A Commotion in the Blood *(1997), and, most recently,* Merchants of Immortality *(2003).*

Images on pages 14, 18: Gene expression patterns in Drosophila (fruit fly) embryos, from the laboratory of Dr. John Reinitz, Department of Applied Mathematics and Statistics, Stony Brook University/SUNY, Stony Brook, New York. © 1997 and 1998 by David Kosman and John Reinitz

Image on page 17: A blastoderm-stage *Drosophila* embryo stained for nuclear Hunchback protein (in red, restricted to the anterior half of the embryo) and cytoplasmic Extradenticle protein (in green, present throughout the embryo). Courtesy of Dr. Richard S. Mann, Department of Biochemistry and Molecular Biophysics, Columbia University.

TAB. XXIV.

Untitled relief halftone, 1939
From *Der Mensch, Desund und Krank*, volume 2, by Fritz Kahn (Zurich-Leipzig: Albert Mueller, 1939)

A body map illustrates the healthful effects of sunlight on internal systems.

LEFT:
Paolo Mascagni, Tab. XXIV
From *Vasorum Lymphaticorum Corporis Humani Historia et Ichnographia,* 1787
Courtesy of the Health Sciences Library, University of Washington

When Mascagni (1755–1815), a professor of anatomy at the University of Siena, Italy, began studying the human lymph system, only half of the lymphatic vessels were known; he is credited with discovering the other half. Mascagni injected mercury as a contrast medium into cadavers' vessels to make them more visible, and carefully dissected around them to chart their courses.

Otto Soglow, *Main Route of Expedition through the Alimentary Canal,* 1930
From *Through the Alimentary Canal with Gun and Camera* by George S. Chappell
(New York: Frederick A. Stokes Co., 1930)

Chappell, a humorist of the 1920s and 1930s, wrote a parody of the popular adventure narrative featuring four intrepid explorers venturing forth into unknown interior territories. Soglow, the book's illustrator (1900–1975), was a popular cartoonist best known for his work in *The New Yorker* and a syndicated feature, "The Little King."

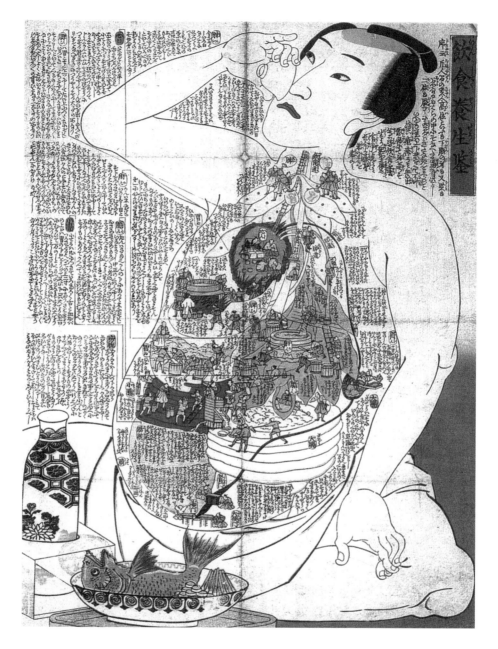

Kunisada Utagawa, *Rules of Dietary Life,* ca. 1850
Woodcut print, 20 x 15 inches
Courtesy of the Naito Museum of Pharmaceutical Science and Industry, Kawashima Gifu, Japan

An example of Ukiyo-e, a movement in Japanese
painting depicting scenes and objects from everyday life. It shows the functions of the respective
internal organs and instructs the reader about
proper nutrition.

Paula Scher, *The Truth Behind the Overused Publicity Photo (Circa 1985)*, 1992
Acrylic on canvas, 9¾ inches diameter
Courtesy of the artist

RIGHT:
Arthur Merton, *A Symbolic Head*, 1879
From *Descriptive Mentality from the Head, Face and Hand* by Holmes Merton
(Philadelphia: D. McKay, 1899)

Like other phrenologists of his time, Merton believed that "psychologic physiognomy is the only art by which all the powers of the Intellect, Affection, and the Will can be thoroughly and accurately measured." He recommended this "natural, practical, and prophetic art" as an important tool in everyday life, in particular for businessmen in assessing the strengths and weaknesses of clients and employees; for husbands and wives wishing to avoid marital discord; and

for parents seeking to understand the subtle natures of their offspring ("Much time and money is often wasted where a study of their children's faces would have revealed the natural trend of power and desire"). Professor Merton ended his book with an address in Staten Island where, by appointment, readers could obtain personal interviews with the author for between five and twenty dollars.

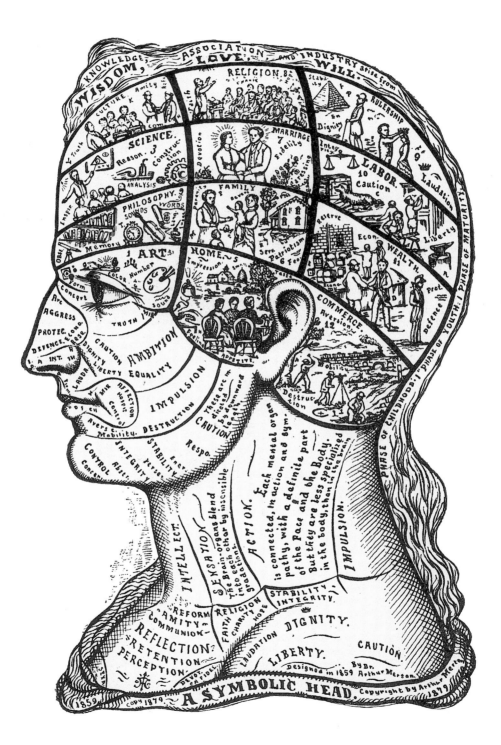

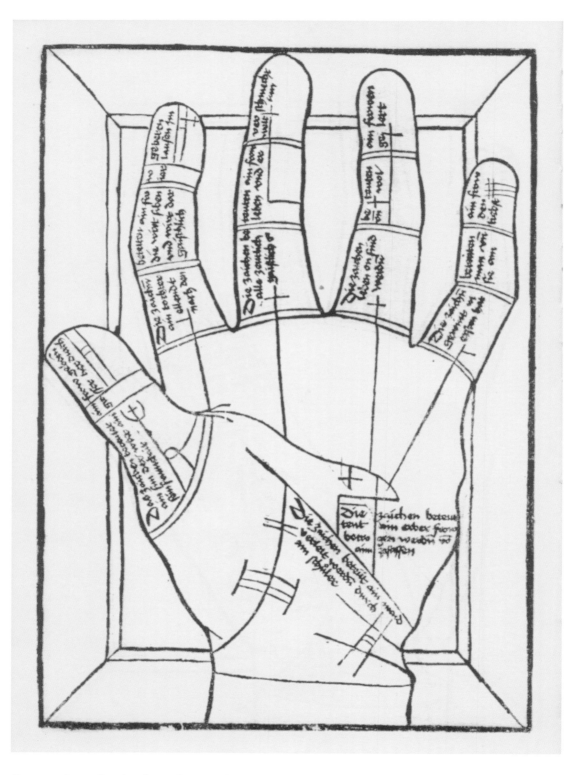

German palm reading chart from *Die Kunst Chiromantia*
by Johann Hartlieb, c. 1480

Aidan, *Hand Map*, 2000

Aidan, a seven-year-old from County Tyrone, Northern Ireland, took part in a drawing project to explore the personal landscape of the hand. The exercise was led by Julie Forester, an artist in residence with Multimedia Maps, a three-year project that placed artists in schools in the border counties of Ireland to investigate the uses of mapping for generating creativity and change.

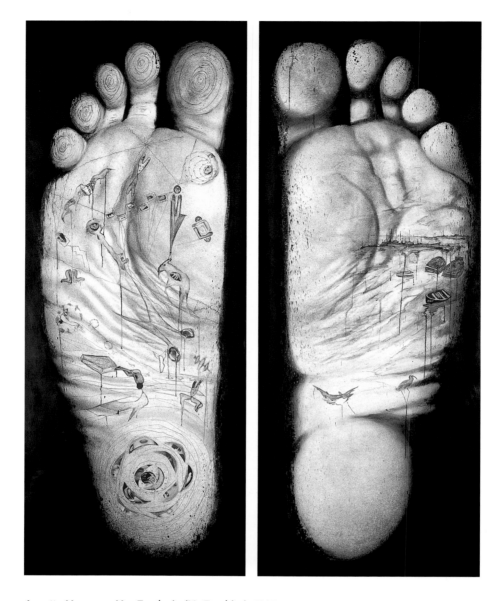

Annette Messager, *Mes Tropheés (My Trophies)*, 1987
Acrylic, charcoal, and pastel on two gelatin silver prints, 81⅛ x 67 inches (overall)
Collection of Los Angeles County Museum of Art. Purchased with funds provided by the Ralph M. Parsons Fund, Clyde A. Beswick, Mr. and Mrs. Barry Smooke, Linda and Jerry Janger, Ronnie and Vidal Sassoon, Sharleen Cooper Cohen, David and Susan Gersh, and Bonnie Wilke. Photograph © 2003 Museum Associates/LACMA

In this and many other related works, Messager explored a theme inspired by Madeleine de Scudéry's seventeenth-century *Carte du Pays de Tendre*, an illustrated "map of tenderness" featuring a woman's emotions and parts of her anatomy. Messager embellished her personal topography to create the many images in the series *Mes Tropheés*.

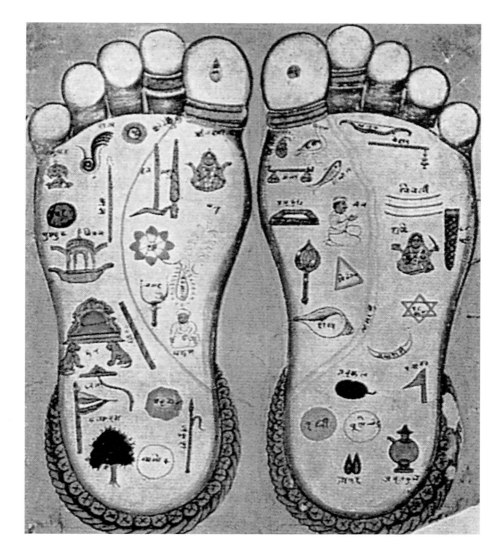

Vishnu's Footprints as Constellations of His Earthly Symbols, Rajasthan, 18th century
Artist unknown
From *The Redstone Diary of True Places* (London: Redstone Press, 1997)

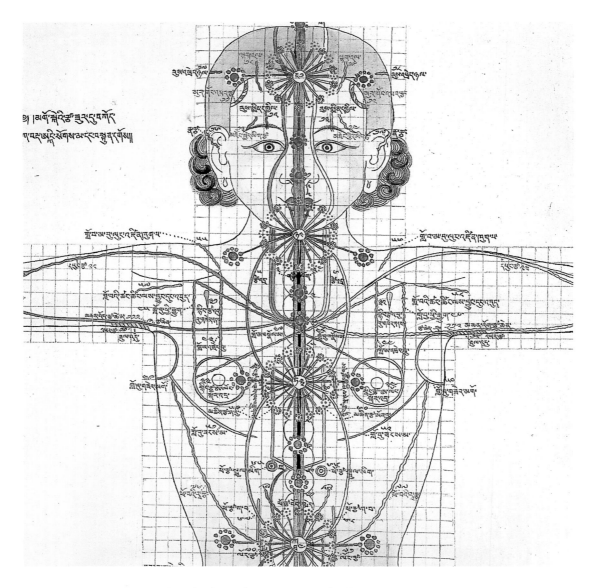

Sangye Gyamtso, *Interconnecting Blood Vessels: Anterior View* (detail), c. 1680s
From *Tibetan Medical Paintings: Illustrations to the Blue Beryl Treatise of Sangye Gyamtso* (London, 1992).
Reprinted by permission of Serindia Publications, Inc.

Sangye Gyamtso (1653–1705), a Tibetan regent and erudite scholar, was the author of *Blue Beryl*, an ambitious commentary on the *Four Tantras,* the cornerstone of Tibetan medicine. This anatomical chart is from one of the more than seventy *thangkas* (hand-painted scrolls) that illustrate the commentary. The chart depicts three of the four major "channels" of Tibetan Buddhist medicine, with information on which blood vessels are acceptable for bloodletting. The author also created an authoritative text on astrology, the *White Beryl*.

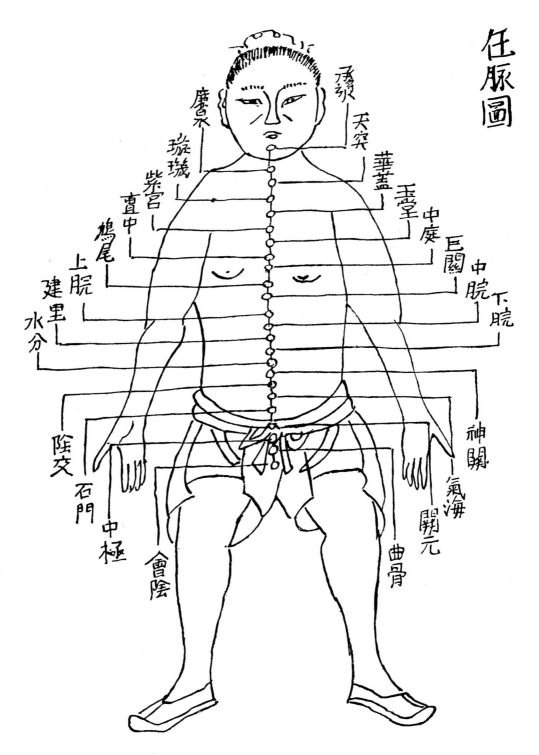

Acupuncture diagram, artist and date unknown
From *L'Acuponcture Chinoise* by George Soulié de Morant
(Paris: Mercure de France, 1939)

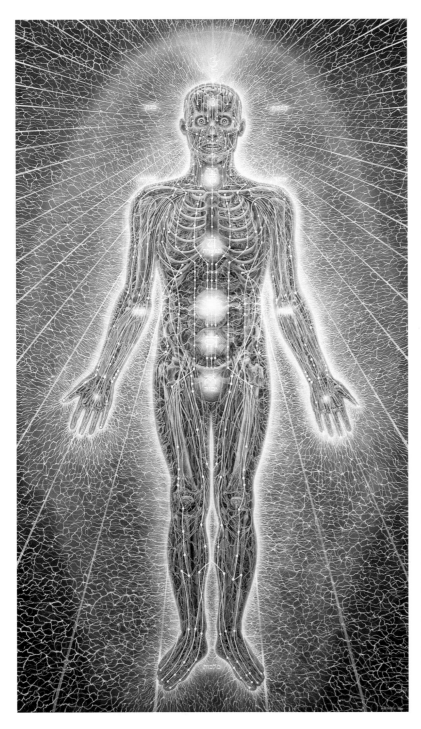

Alex Grey, *Psychic Energy System,* 1980
Acrylic on linen, 84 x 48 inches
From www.sacredmirrors.org.
Reprinted by permission of the
Alex Grey Studio

From *The Sacred Mirrors*, a series of twenty-one images that examine in fine detail the human physical and metaphysical anatomy. Each depicts a life-size figure facing forward, enabling the viewer to stand before the "mirror" image and have a sense of seeing into oneself. The series is intended as a means of visualizing and focusing healing energy to particular parts of the body. *Psychic Energy System* weaves the psycho-spiritual energies into an x-ray view of the physical body. Grey used descriptions from clairvoyants and aura readers of the colors and shapes of the astral and etheric auras surrounding the body, the seven central chakras, and the golden white light of the acupuncture meridians and points. The entire body is immersed in a lattice-work of energy called the *prana*, or vital ether, one of the pervasive life-supplying sources recognized in both Eastern and Western occult spiritual traditions.

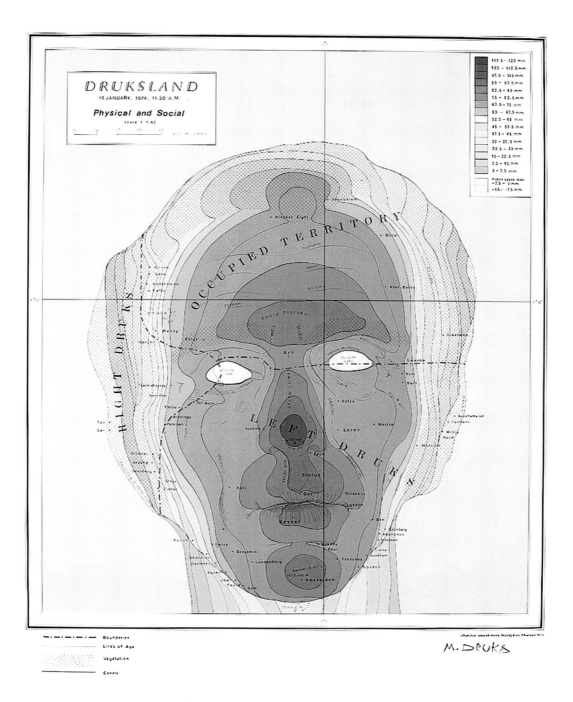

Michael Druks, *Druksland Physical and
Social 15 January 1974, 11:30 am,* 1974
From a folio collection, *Flexible Geography: My Private Atlas*
Lithograph, 18 x 15 inches
Courtesy England & Co. Gallery, London

An Israeli-born artist, Druks has explored the notion of borders, boundaries, and their social and political ramifications. The 1970s *Flexible Geography* project was an experiment in applying the international and visual language of mapping for individual purposes.

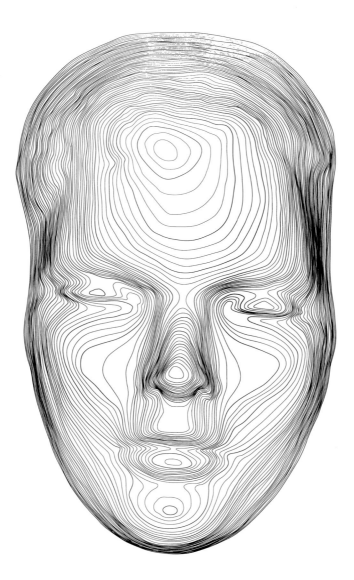

Gerald Fremlin, *Topography of a Face,* c. 1960s
Courtesy of the artist

RIGHT:

Dr. Robin Williams, *Contour Map of Identical Female Twins Face to Face,* date unknown
© SPL/Photo Researchers Inc.

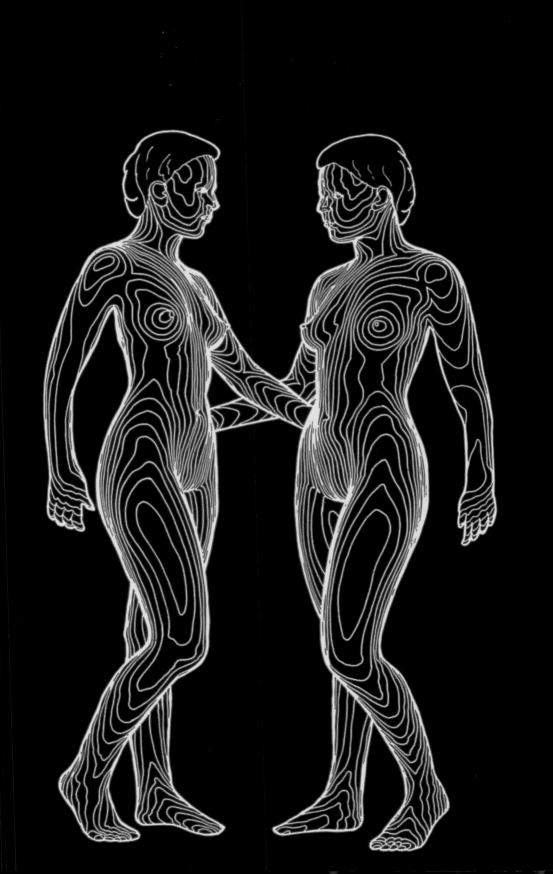

Body Map of My Life

①

Location: Top of right ear
Cause: Odd lump of tissue, referred to by second-grade classmates as the "Rice Krispie"
Diagnosis: Cartilaginous growth
Treatment: Removed by physician father's colleague
Follow-up: Small scar persists.

②

Location: Lower lip
Cause: Sudden burst of confidence during sole ice-skating attempt
Diagnosis: Face-first tumble results in front teeth puncturing lip.
Treatment: Father, saying stitches are unnecessary, applies antibiotic ointment and bandaging.
Follow-up: During dinner that night, sister asks if I can feel the Campbell's chicken noodle soup trickling through the hole. Today, tiny cross-shaped mark is barely visible.

③

Location: Top of left hand
Cause: Shattered glass from car wreck, sustained when a mother of two runs a red light and smashes into a pick-up truck, which smashes into me. At moment of impact, "My Sharona" by The Knack was on the radio, leaving a kind of psychological scar.
Diagnosis: Slice in hand; a bit shaken up
Treatment: Series of bandages
Follow-up: Replaced totaled VW Rabbit with another VW Rabbit. The psychological scar pulses whenever I hear "My Sharona."

④

Location: Left forearm midway between wrist and elbow

Cause: Angry Oscar fish (*Astronotus ocellatus*). Acquired while reaching into aquarium of rock-guitarist boyfriend who was living in bachelor pad during mid-eighties Atlanta party scene.
Diagnosis: Gashed arm
Treatment: Series of bandages
Follow-up: Subtle scar remains. Oscar fish later committed piscine suicide by jumping out of tank onto floor of bachelor pad, where it died a slow, suffocating death. Boyfriend moved to New Orleans and got married.

⑤

Location: Equal parts head and heart
Cause: First crush in college (clean-cut preppy) suddenly stops calling and appears at parties with a shiny, diminutive Southern belle.
Diagnosis: Bruised ego
Treatment: Learned to play quarters with (not so clean-cut) members of Beta Phi Zeta fraternity.
Follow-up: Later learned that freshman flame became a dentist in Pittsburgh. No regrets.

⑥

Location: Left palm and short-term memory bank
Cause: As the Halloween party my sister and I are hosting kicks into gear, I hilariously demonstrate my *Psycho* knife technique on the deli roast chicken. Unfortunately, I am holding the bird in my hand, and the tender poultry body and flimsy foam holder are no match for the Henckel twelve-inch blade. Realizing that I have stabbed myself, I put the fowl on the counter and proceed to pass out on the kitchen floor.
Diagnosis: Margaritas + party-induced bravado = lapse in judgment.
Treatment: I regain consciousness and look up into the faces of Ernie from *Sesame Street*, the Oak Ridge Boys, and a bloody, pecked Tippie Hedren from *The*

36 YOU ARE HERE

Birds. Realize I am not hallucinating, but in fact surrounded by concerned, costumed friends, who take charge.
Follow-up: The Henckel blade is duller.

⑦

Location: Front and side of left knee
Cause: Warm-up drills in preparation for first North Carolina women's team appearance at Ultimate Frisbee National Championships, West Palm Beach, Florida
Diagnosis: Tournament clinic worker recommends leg massage. Later diagnosed by orthopedist as torn anterior cruciate ligament (ACL).
Treatment: Knee reconstruction. First (and only) exposure to mmmmorphine.
Follow-up: Active participant in spectator sports

⑧

Location: Part of brain marking the nexus of anger and disbelief
Cause: While on the way to do laundry, spot then-boyfriend (now referred to as "psycho chef") coming out of his comely coworker's apartment early on a Sunday morning. Claims he was merely dropping off Percocet to help relieve her of menstrual cramps.
Diagnosis: Need for heavy reality dose. OK, so he cooks amazing gourmet meals, but, really, the guy's an asshole.
Treatment: Wordless, late-night phone calls from chef reinforce diagnosis (above).
Follow-up: Chef begins to lose his hair and is later seen in advanced stage of balding. Incident also results in two rather amusing short stories.

⑨

Location: Right shoulder
Cause: Too much sun growing up in South Florida
Diagnosis: Undetermined growth, possible precancerous lesion
Treatment: Dermatologist removes growth and photographs entire body for CD archiving, which allows baseline comparison on quarterly basis.
Follow-up: Lots of sunscreen

⑩

Location: Lower abdomen
Cause: Surgery
Diagnosis: Breech baby
Treatment: Cesarean section
Follow-up: A pink, screaming, healthy little girl

⑪

Location: Top of left ear
Cause: Overstimulated preschool daughter whacks mother with plastic pail in Disney World swimming pool
Diagnosis: Broken cartilage
Treatment: New hairstyle
Follow-up: No more Disney World ever again

⑫

Location: Gums
Cause: Age, not enough flossing
Diagnosis: Early stages of gingivitis
Treatment: A bit more flossing
Follow-up: Actively dodging recommended procedure of gum tissue replacement surgery

⑬

Location: Right breast
Cause: Biopsy for possible cancerous growth
Diagnosis: Benign lump
Treatment: None needed
Follow-up: Schedule repeat mammograms every six months

⑭

Location: Worry center in depths of psyche
Cause: Marriage, motherhood, middle age
Diagnosis: Increased responsibility, less spontaneity
Treatment: New blonde hairpiece, spur-of-the-moment bike rides, and a toe ring
Follow-up: To be continued.

Bridget Booher is a freelance writer living in Hillsborough, North Carolina.

Chukchi drawing, Siberia, 19th century
From *Dreams: Visions of the Night* by David Coxhead and Susan Hiller
(New York: Thames & Hudson, 1989)

The Chukchi are an indigenous Siberian people, the largest native nation on the Asian side of the North Pacific. This map lays out paths to dreamed destinations. The roads lead to middle earth, the heavens, and the underworld, and to dawn, evening, and night; all pass through the pole star at the center of the world. The map uses notations that are collectively understood to guide others in their dreams and prevent them from becoming lost.

Biá, untitled drawing, c. 1970s
From Beyond the Milky Way: Hallucinatory Imagery of the Tukano Indians
by G. Reichel-Dolmatoff (Los Angeles: UCLA Latin American Center Publications, 1978), plate 3, page 55.
© 1978 by The Regents of the University of California. Reproduced with permission

After ingesting a potion prepared from local narcotic plants, men of the Turkano Indians of the Amazon, guided by shamans, experience ritualistic visions. While living among the Turkano, anthropologist Gerardo Reichel-Dolmatoff (1912–1994) asked participants to convey what they had experienced, resulting in vision maps such as this one. Biá's drawing charts the first stage of the journey, in which the visual effects are highly colorful and rich in geometric patterns. Here the central image involves fertility, with a vagina (at the crossroads) being approached by drops of semen (the red and blue dots).

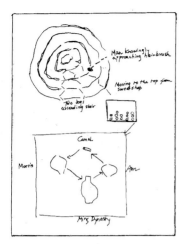

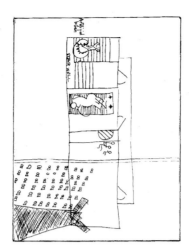

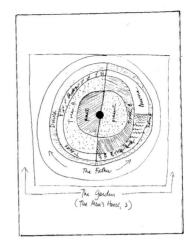

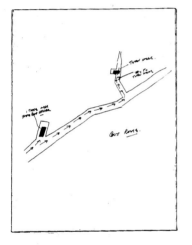

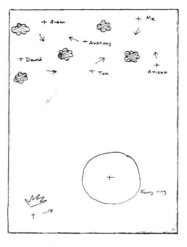

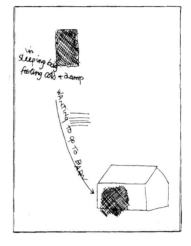

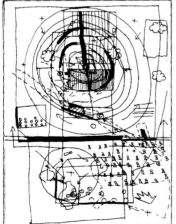

**Susan Hiller, *Composite Group Dream Map,
Night of 23/24 August,* from *Dream Mapping,* 1974**
Courtesy of the artist

In 1974, conceptual artist Susan Hiller invited ten participants to sleep outdoors for three nights in the countryside
of Hampshire where there is a proliferation of fairy rings.
These are circles of *marasmius oreades* mushrooms, and,
according to myth, after sleeping inside one, you are
granted entry to fairy land. Together the participants in
Hiller's "group investigation" collaborated on a notation
system for recording their dreams, and each morning they
mapped the events and structures they encountered while
dreaming. Hiller then superimposed the maps on one
another to create a collective dream map. The purpose
was not to determine if they had visited fairy land, but to
enable the participants to experience revelations in the
process of mapping ephemeral locations.

Adolf Wölfli, *General View of the Island Neveranger,* 1911
and *The West Coast of Europe, or the Atlantic Ocean,* 1911
Colored pencil on newsprint
Courtesy of the Adolf Wölfli Foundation, Bern

Adolf Wölfli (1864–1930) was diagnosed with schizophrenia at the age of thirty-one and committed to a mental asylum near Bern, where he lived until his death thirty-five years later. While confined he produced an astounding œuvre of drawings, collages, sheet music, prose, and poetry. These illustrations are included in *From the Cradle to the Grave,* a series of nine hand-bound books (2,970 total pages, with 752 illustrations) that recount Wölfli's imaginary life story from ages two through eight. The protagonist travels around the globe, imposing his own sense of order on it. Wölfli based his descriptions and depictions of faraway places on the familiar topography of Bern and the Swiss countryside, and also on a school atlas he owned, but clearly they are fantastical visions very much his own.

Falls of Eternal Despair, 1895
Artist unknown. Lithograph, 32 x 26 inches
Courtesy of Eleanor Dickinson. Photo: Meagen Geer

"The River flows through the 'Land of Sin,' better known by some as the 'Land of Selfishness,' and by others as the 'Land of Unbelief.' This Land abounds with sterile deserts and deadly swamps, and is infested by ravenous wild beasts and venomous serpents. Pitfalls and quicksands are numerous. . . . The River of Death, with its Tributaries, flows through this Land, poisoning the inhabitants, and bearing them over the *Falls of Eternal Despair* to their awful doom." So begins the text of a lengthy sermon published in 1901 by Martin Wells Knapp with this illustration as a preaching diagram. Each of the ten tributaries of the River of Death merits its own chapter full of atmospheric detail; note that Satan has created swampy regions such as "Dancing School" and "Sunday Papers" to lure souls into the treacherous waters. Artist Eleanor Dickinson uses this artifact in exhibitions exploring the revivalist culture of the Appalachian region.

Missionary Map, late 19th century
Artist unknown
Metallic paint and pencil on muslin, 50 x 69 inches
Smithsonian American Art Museum, Washington, D.C./Art Resource, New York

Howard Finster, *All Roads One Road Headed the Same Way,* 1978
Enamel on wood
Courtesy of photographer Victor Faccinto

Baptist preacher and renowned folk artist Howard Finster
(1916–2001) devoted his life to art and his art to God. Where
Wells's map (page 44) makes Heaven seem a distant and
lofty destination, Finster generously offers many routes
to a paradise that is detailed in its delights.

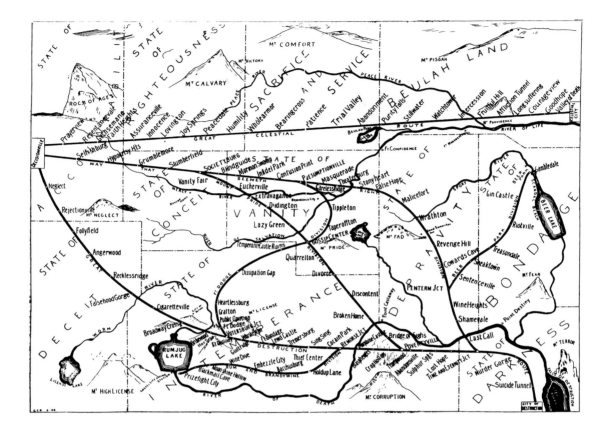

G. E. Bula, *Gospel Temperance Railroad Map,* 1908
From *An Atlas of Fantasy* by J. B. Post
(Baltimore: Mirage Press, Ltd., 1973)

Maps that guide the wanderer through life were abundant in
the nineteenth century, each with a compelling agenda. In
this map, refraining from drink ensured that a life's traveler
would avoid being marooned on Blockhead Island in the
middle of Rum Lake, or sent up Turn-stomach River to Bad
Wine Lake.

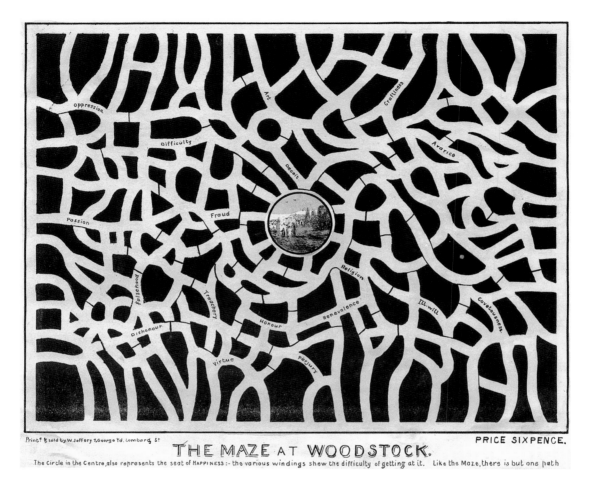

The Maze at Woodstock, c. 1840

Artist unknown

© 2003 Hordern-Dalgety Collection, www.puzzlemuseum.com

The text on this map reads: "Printed and sold by W. Jeffery. London. Price Six Pence. The circle in the centre also represents the seat of Happiness: The various windings shew (*sic*) the difficulty of getting at it. Like the maze, there is but one path."

The Road to Success
Artist and date unknown
Courtesy of Cooper Edens

Boarding a train at the Right System Railroad Station means
that bad habits, bad memory, or bad temper will not deter
the traveler from reaching the terminus of success.

The Highest or Greatest Degrees of Virtue, Grace, and Glory.

GLORY The Saints Rest

Mansions of Blessedness or HEAVEN Eternal Life Immortality

Foretastes of Heaven The Valley of the River Jordan Shadow of Death Believing Prospects of Glory

Victory over the World, the Flesh, and the Devil Faithfulness to Death River of Doubt

Hopes full of Immortality Resignation

PERSEVERANCE

Steadfastness in the Faith Tranquility Union to God

Mountns of Spiritual-mindedness Longing for Rest Reconciliation with God Delight in God Views of Covenant Love

Vale of Retirement Trust in the Promises Witnessings of the Spirit Mount of Contemplation

Divine breathings

Converse with Heaven Serenity Peace in believing

Groves of Religious Pleasures Ejaculation Hills Love of God Joy in the Holy Ghost Benevolence

Fields of Meditation Walking with God Hope Delight in Duties Contentment Charity

Divine supports Confidence in God Experience Communion with God Brotherly kindness

Trials Mortified Affections Streams of Comfort Patience Godliness Temperance

FAITH Uprightness Spiritual Affections Knowledge Virtue

Spiritual Wisdom Integrity Justification Adoption Adversity

Good Works Self knowledge Zeal Godly Sincerity Holy Jealousy

Grace in the Heart Self Examination Weak Faith

Holy Fear River of Self denial Affliction Probation Anxiety

Grief Holy Desire True Piety Devotion Serious reflection

REPENTANCE Praise Religion Peaceable Fruits of Righteousness

Fields of Regeneration Meekness Sanctification Fields of Circumspection

Penitence and Reformation Conversion Humility Watchfulness and

Prayer Hatred of Sin

Self Abhorrence Sorrow for Sin

Conviction

Private Duties Discretion Pious Prudence Sobriety Moderation Urbanity Friendship

Common Honesty Probity Relative Duties Good nature

Plains of Freewill and Morality Affability Generosity

Outward Profession Honour Loyalty Justice Social Duties

Boundaries of Conscience

City of Realm or Natural Man Conscience overcome Self will Self love

Gaiety Folly Conscience silenced Bad Company Swearing Bad Inclinations

Theft Fraud Lying & Sinful Compliances Disobedience of Parents

Little Sins falsely so called Injustice Sabbath Breaking Commissions of Sin Backsliding Evil Communications

Thoughtlessness Extravagance Omissions of Duty Worldly mindedness Corrupt Dispositions

INDIFFERENCE Love of the World Debauchery Gaming Evil Habits Irregular Appetites

Unconcern Licentiousness Carnality Corrupt Affections Stupidity

Vanity Fleshly Indulgence Entire Neglect of Duty

River of Unbelief False Pleasures

Luxury Self deceit Wilful Blindness Streams of False Joys

OBDURACY Contempt of Religion Deism Free thinking

Plains of Revelling and Immorality Voluptuousness Stubbornness Vain Glory Streams of Vice

Passion Impiety Blasphemy Arrogance Pride Hills

Malice Anger Carnal Security Hatred of God his Ways, Ordinances & People Envy

Revenge Atheism Fretfulness Discontent

Dissimulation Libertinism Love of Sin

Plains of Sensuality and Hardheartedness

Self delusion Open Rebellion Total Apostacy Continuance in Sin

Mountains of Sin and Iniquity Mountns of Presumption of unrepented Guilt

IMPENITENCE Satan's Triumph Despair Inevitable Ruin

Borders of Hell Gulf of Death Borders of Hell

THE BOTTOMLESS PIT OF DESTRUCTION; or **HELL**

The Greatest Degrees of Vice and Misery.

To know Reader, which Road you are travelling, & what Counties Towns &c. you have past, or are going thro'; seriously examine how matters stand between God and your own Soul; what are your Thoughts, Words, and Actions? what Life do you live? what Company do you keep? what Pleasures do you pursue? and, which are you (professedly) in the Way to, Heaven or Hell?

Say happy Christian, for you only know,   Vice its own Punishment will ever prove.
What real Pleasures from Religion flow;   **MAN KNOW THYSELF.**   Religion leads to blissful Realms above.

Search the Scriptures.

T. Conder Sculp.

Published according to Act of Parliament by J. Buckland & W. Otridge.
18th Jany 1775.

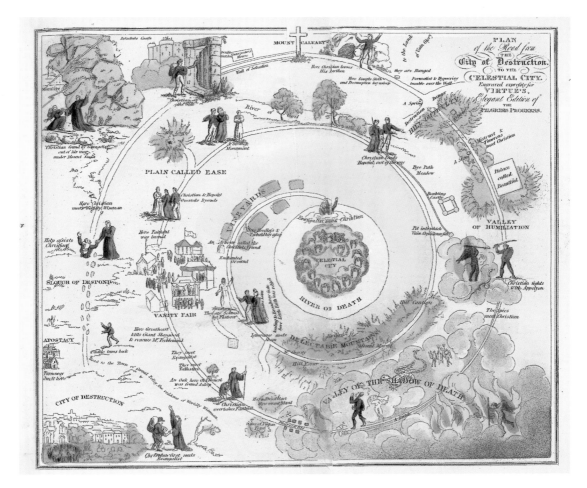

LEFT:
New Map of the Journey of Life:
The Roads to Happiness and Misery
Artist unknown
From *Walking Amusements for Chearful Christians*
by George Wright (London, 1775)
13 x 7¾ inches
Courtesy of Map Collection, Yale University Library

The guide to this map states: "The degrees of vice are
marked but little at first, and end in exceeding large ones,
to shew (*sic*) that no one is wicked all at once, but go on
from little to great lengths of wickedness, 'till they assuredly
terminate in the highest degrees of vice and misery,
according to that common observation, *Nemo repente fuit
turpissimus* [No man becomes a villain all at once]."

*Plan of the Road from the City of Destruction
to the Celestial City*
Artist unknown
From *The Pilgrim's Progress* by John Bunyan
(London: George Virtue, 1850)

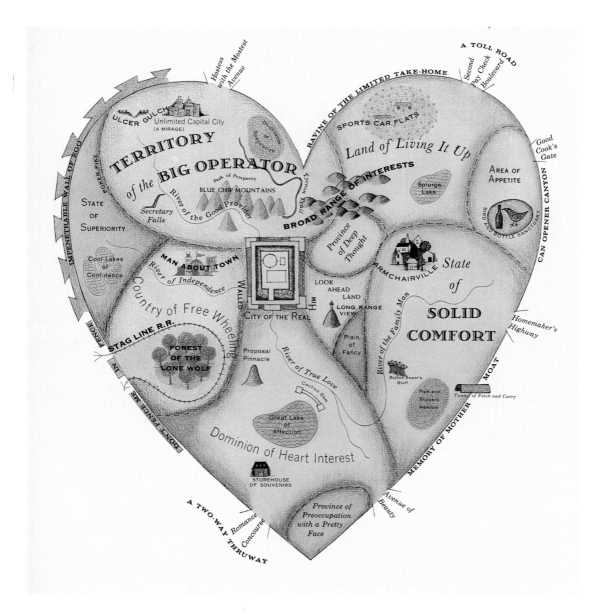

Geographical Guide to a Man's Heart with Obstacles and Entrances Clearly Marked,
and *Geographical Guide to a Woman's Heart Emphasizing Points of Interest to the Romantic Traveler* (RIGHT)
From *McCall's* Magazine, January 1960

Inspired by a pair of Victorian lithographs, whose original
artist-author is unknown. These versions were created by
artist Jo Lowrey and the editors of *McCall's*.

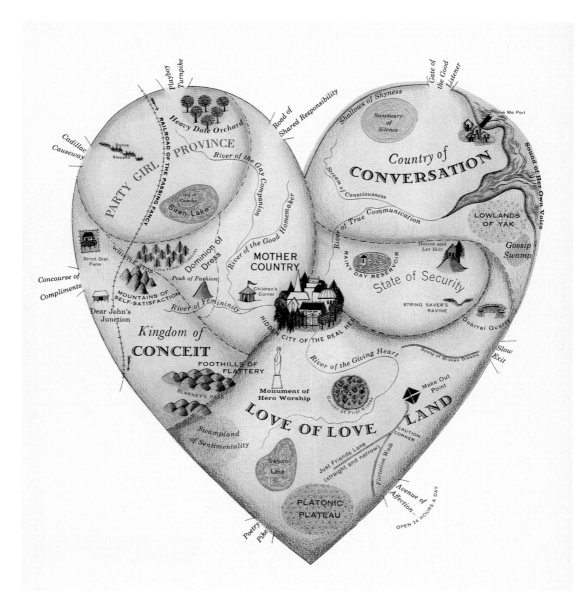

Playboy Turnpike · Heavy Date Orchard · Road of Shared Responsibility · Gate of the Good Listener · Shallows of Shyness · Sanctuary of Silence · Phone Me Port · Cadillac Causeway · Dance Steppes · PARTY GIRL PROVINCE · River of the Gay Companion · Country of CONVERSATION · Sound of Her Own Voice · Isle of Caprice · Siren Lake · Stream of Consciousness · LOWLANDS OF YAK · Strict Diet Farm · Dominion of Dress · River of the Good Homemaker · River of True Communication · Gossip Swamp · Concourse of Compliments · Little Forest · Peak of Fashion · MOUNTAINS OF SELF-SATISFACTION · MOTHER COUNTRY · House and Lot Hill · RAINY DAY RESERVOIR · State of Security · Dear John's Junction · River of Femininity · Children's Corner · STRING SAVER'S RAVINE · Kingdom of CONCEIT · HIDDEN CITY OF THE REAL HEART · Quarrel Quarry · FOOTHILLS OF FLATTERY · River of the Giving Heart · Byway of Broken Dreams · Slow Exit · BLARNEY'S PASS · Monument of Hero Worship · Garden of First Kisses · Make Out Point · Swampland of Sentimentality · LOVE OF LOVE LAND · CAUTION CORNER · Swoon Lake · Just Friends Lane (straight and narrow) · Flirtation Walk · PLATONIC PLATEAU · Poetry Pike · Avenue of Affection – OPEN 24 HOURS A DAY

FOLLOWING PAGES:
Ernest Dudley Chase, *A Pictorial Map of Loveland*, 1943
Courtesy of Frederic Holland. Photo: Harvard College Library

Chase (1876–1966) was a graphic artist from Massachusetts who combined his artistic facility with business savvy. He created and published more than fifty pictorial maps during the last thirty years of his life, both as the owner of his own publishing company and as an employee of another. A man of abundant energy, he traveled extensively and recorded his experiences in thousands of detailed drawings, which he later used as models for the intricate renderings of monuments, industries, people, and landscapes that cover every inch of his maps.

Here, in Loveland, it's always Valentine's Day; Cupid's arrows always strike their marks, and lovers perennially live in a state of besotted devotion. And, of course, everything is heart-shaped—leaves, icicles, smoke rings, even pyramids. Distance is measured in "scales of smiles."

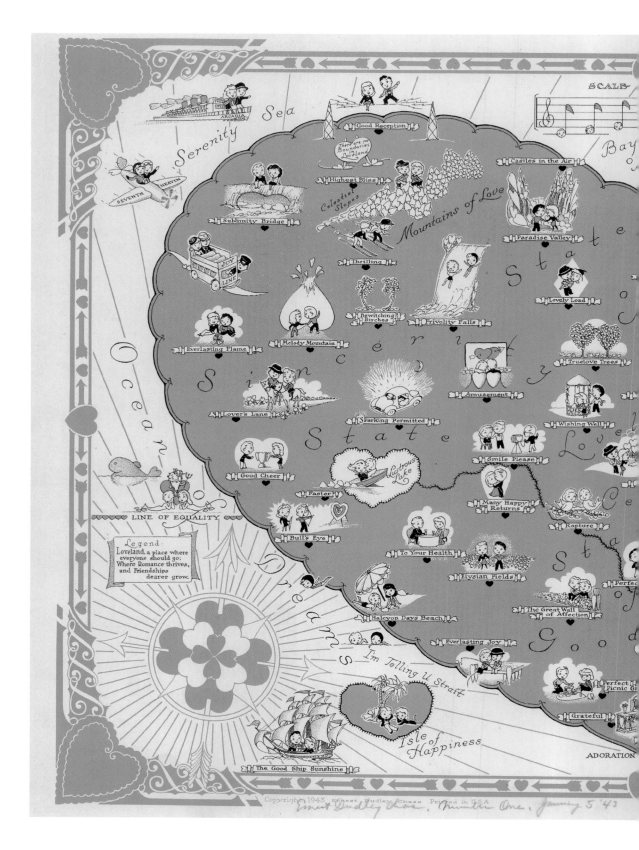

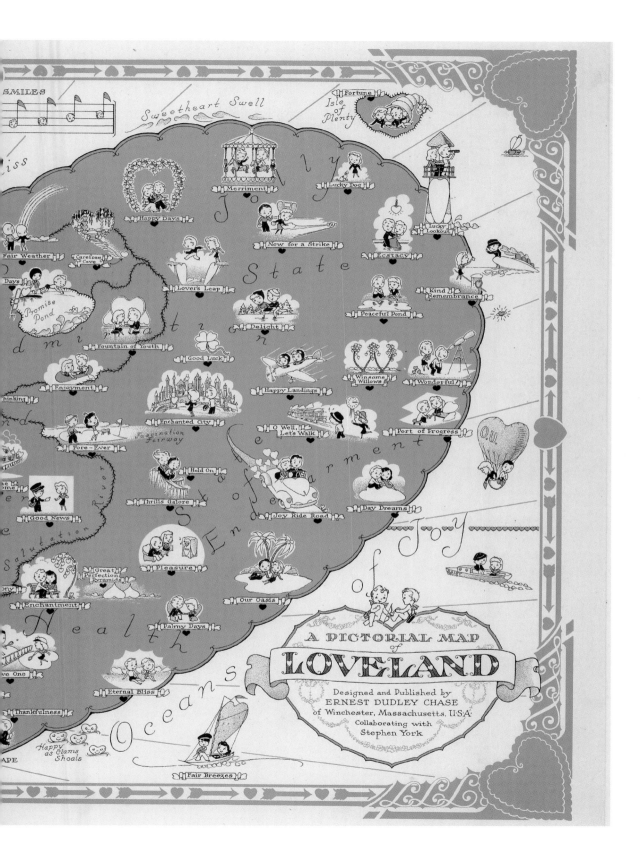

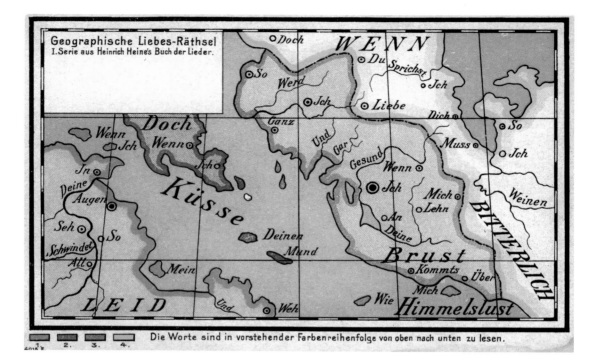

Geographische Liebes-Räthsel
I. Serie aus Heinrich Heine's Buch der Lieder.

Die Worte sind in vorstehender Farbenreihenfolge von oben nach unten zu lesen.

Geographische Liebes-Räthsel, ca. 1905
Artist unknown
© 2003 Hordern-Dalgety Collection, www.puzzlemuseum.com

The creator of this pictorial map incorporated the words of a
poem by Heinrich Heine:
When I look into your eyes
All my sorrow and agony disappears
But when I kiss your lips
I recover completely
When I lean onto your chest
It comes over me like heavenly delight
But when you say I love you
I have to weep so bitterly

RIGHT:
Louise van Swaaij and Jean Klare, *Passion*
From *The Atlas of Experience* (New York: Bloomsbury USA,
2000). Courtesy of Meteor Press

From the Bay of Wisdom to the Sea of Plenty and up the
Stream of Ideas, *The Atlas of Experience* covers the water-
front and explores all the inland territories of life's moods,
emotions, and other states of being. On the map of Chaos,
a mountain range is labeled the Heights of Exasperation; a
city named Entrée is located on the map of Haute Cuisine.

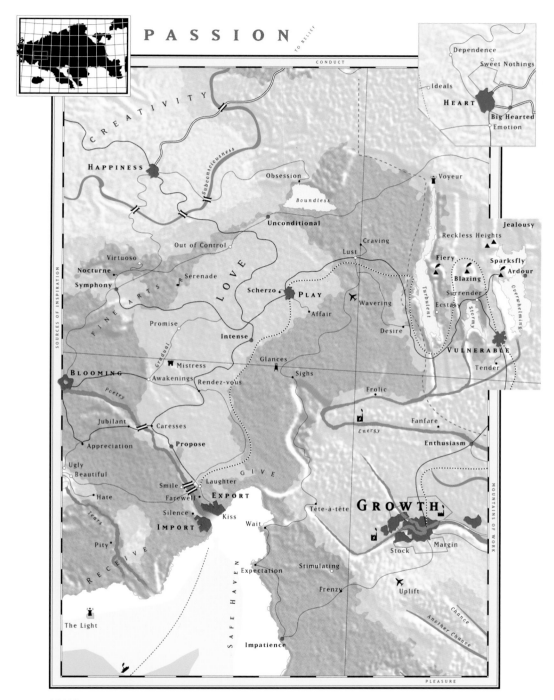

PASSION

TO BELIEF

CONDUCT

CREATIVITY

HAPPINESS

Subconsciousness

Obsession

Boundless

Voyeur

Unconditional

Craving

Out of Control

Reckless Heights

Jealousy

Virtuoso

Lust

Fiery

Sparksfly

Nocturne

LOVE

Blazing

Ardour

Symphony

Serenade

Scherzo

PLAY

Wavering

Surrender

FINE ARTS

Affair

Ecstasy

Stormy

Promise

Desire

Intense

Turbulent

Overwhelming

Gradual

Glances

VULNERABLE

Mistress

Sighs

Tender

Awakenings

Rendez-vous

Frolic

BLOOMING

Poetry

Energy

Fanfare

Jubilant

Caresses

Enthusiasm

Appreciation

Propose

Ugly

GIVE

Beautiful

MOUNTAINS OF WORK

Smile

Laughter

GROWTH

Hate

Farewell

EXPORT

Tête-à-tête

Silence

Kiss

IMPORT

Wait

Stock

Margin

Pity

RECEIVE

Expectation

Stimulating

The Light

SAFE HAVEN

Frenzy

Uplift

Chance

Impatience

Another Chance

SOURCES OF INSPIRATION

PLEASURE

SCALE

10   20   30   40   50

COPYRIGHT © 2002 METEOR PRESS BV/HOOFDZAKEN, THE NETHERLANDS. BASED ON AN IDEA BY JEAN KLARE AND LOUISE VAN SWAAIJ

WORLDOFEXPERIENCE® IS AN INTERNATIONAL REGISTERED TRADEMARK. ALL RIGHTS RESERVED. WWW.WORLDOFEXPERIENCE.COM

HEART

Dependence

Sweet Nothings

Ideals

Big Hearted

Emotion

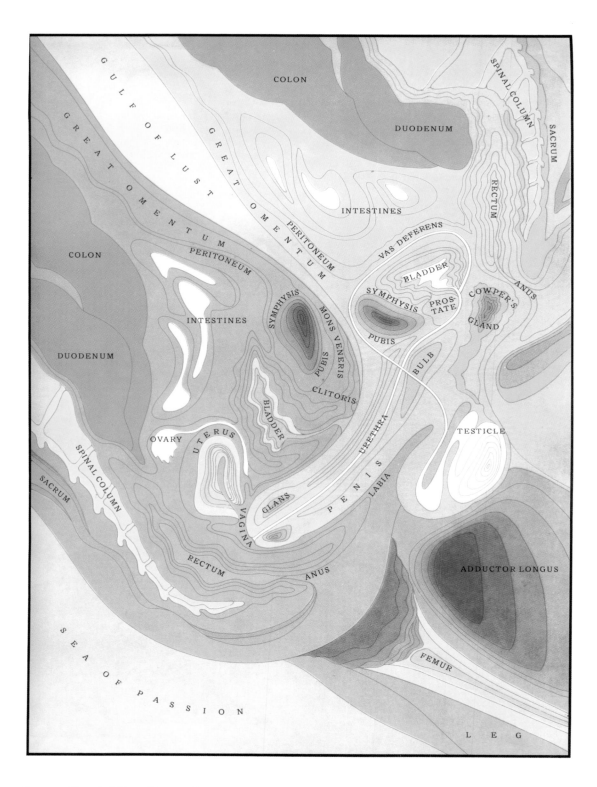

Seymour Chwast, *A Map of Lovemaking,* 1980
Reprinted with permission of Seymour Chwast, The Pushpin Group

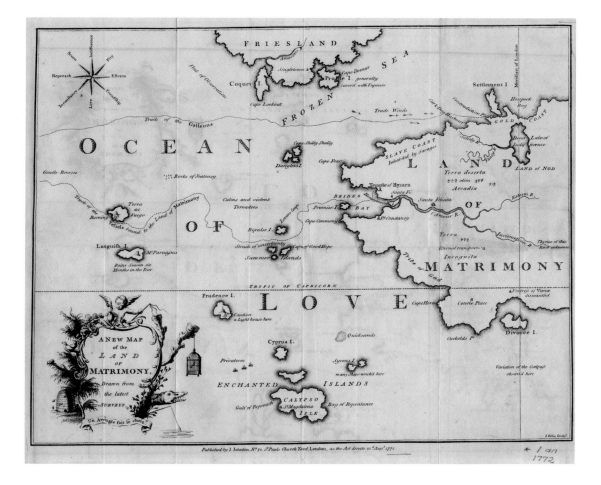

New Map of the Land of Matrimony, 1772
Artist unknown
10½ x 13 inches
Courtesy of Map Collection, Yale University Library

Joyce Kozloff, *Bodies of Water: Songlines,* 1997–98
Acrylic and collage on canvas, 72 x 72 inches
Courtesy of DC Moore Gallery, New York

Kozloff has spent over ten years exploring issues of conquest
and control in multi-layered mapping pieces, from globes to
mosaics to complete environments, and often incorporating
text. Her work questions the dominance of imperialistic
powers including various forms of cultural occupation.

Guillermo Kuitca, *House Plan with Blood Flows,* 1991
Acrylic on canvas, 37 x 27½ inches
Collection of Nan and Gene Corman, Beverly Hills, California
Courtesy of Sperone Westwater, New York

The artist is fascinated by cartographical forms, from
maps of vast swaths of territory to compressed urban
grids to compact floor plans. In many paintings he has
reproduced the layout of a small apartment. Here the
space is a living, pulsating organism, both nurturing
and ominous.

Sara Fanelli, *Map of My Day*, 1995
Mixed media, 10 x 23 inches
From *My Map Book* (New York: HarperCollins, 1995)

Italian artist and illustrator Sara Fanelli charts
various facets of a child's world and inspires kids
to create maps of their own, in *My Map Book*.

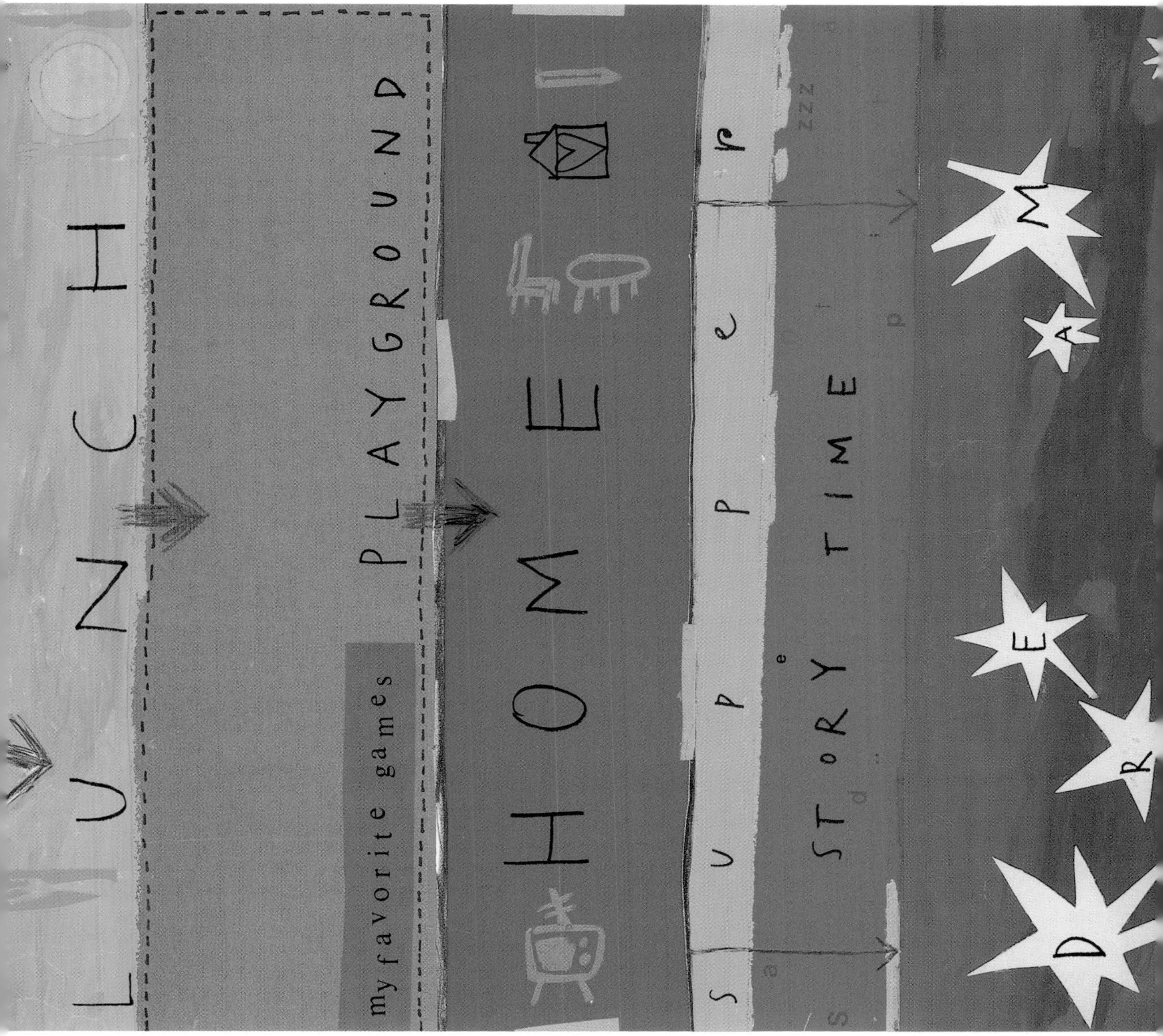

LUNCH ➤

PLAYGROUND ➤

my favorite games

HOME

SUPPER

STORY TIME

zzz

DREAMLAND

At Home in the World

THE MAP-MAKER ON HIS ART

After the bronzed, heroic traveler
Returns to the television interview
And cocktails at the Ritz, I in my turn
Set forth across the clean, uncharted paper.
Smiling a little at his encounters with
Savages, bugs, and snakes, for the most part
Skipping his night thoughts, philosophic notes,
Rainy reflexions, I translate his trip
Into my native tongue of bearings, shapes,
Directions, distances. My fluent pen
Wanders and cranks as his great river does,
Over the page, making the lonely voyage
Common and human.
     This my modest art
Brings wilderness well down into the range
Of any budget; under the haunted mountain
Where he lay in delirium, deserted
By his safari, they will build hotels
In a year or two. I make no claim that this
Much matters (they will name a hotel for him
And none for me), but lest the comparison
Make me appear a trifle colorless,
I write the running river a rich blue
And—let imagination rage!—wild green
The jungles with their tawny meadows and swamps
Where, till the day I die, I will not go.

        —*Howard Nemerov*

The Mental Geography of Appalachian Trail Hikers

ROGER SHEFFER

THE APPALACHIAN TRAIL runs more than two thousand miles from start to finish, all of it mapped at a scale of an inch to the mile or better, with contour lines and vertical profiles detailing every up and down. A complete set of official maps exists for every section. Carrying all those maps from Georgia to Maine would add at least another pound to the hiker's pack weight and increase not only the physical burden of hiking, but also the mental burden, to which, it seems, the body is often more sensitive. And so the long-distance hikers along the AT often rely on other maps—not for detailed directions, but for a sense of what they are doing, of where they are along this almost incomprehensible continuum.

Mapless, the weary hikers sign in for the night at the next shelter, and there, in the register notebook, they find unconventional representations of the trailscape—some useful, some entertaining. The caretaker of the shelter has drawn a map to the nearest water source, detailed down to the last fencepost, with apologies in case the spring has run dry. A knowledgeable "local" has scribbled a relocation for the next ten miles, a necessary bypass not mentioned in the guidebook. An anonymous artist has provided an illustrated map of "the trail between here and Route 309," making it easier to take, perhaps, by turning various features of the landscape into familiar household objects: Bake Oven Knob becomes a four-burner stove with its oven door open, Bayer's Rocks are three big aspirin tablets set side by side, and, of course, the Knife Edge is a knife edge. A thin green line, marked "AT," threads its way through these illustrated landmarks from south to north.

The thru-hikers have all signed in with comments and itineraries and customized "signatures" or "logos" incorporating their trail identities and, often, a part of the abstract map that has stamped itself on the collective hiking mind. Richard J. Bailey (trail name, "The Old Fhart"), a frequent distance hiker on the Appalachian Trail, has created an address-label-size sticker that he places in the register of every shelter he visits on his way north from Georgia to Maine. Bailey's logo is an extreme reduction of the vertical profiles of all fourteen states thrown together, marking only the most important peaks, like Springer Mountain and Katahdin, with a vertical exaggeration factor of 413.6, resulting in a profile that looks something like the spiky record of a volatile stock market or an erratic EKG. The address portion of the sticker blocks out the more forgettable ups and downs of relatively flat Maryland, Pennsylvania, and New Jersey.

Other hikers draw their profile maps freehand. In their designs, they may respond to the idea of the entire hike or merely the experiences of one day. They may offer descriptions of what they have just experienced (as "Van Go" does in his almost-vertical descent into the Pennsylvania town of Port Clinton) or as a premonition of what is to come (as "Pixie" shows in her profile map from Dick's Dome shelter in northern Virginia, looking north towards Harpers Ferry). The seventeen identical hills of "Pixie's Profile Map" are, no

How about that killer decent into Port Clinton?

Van-Go

You must get here

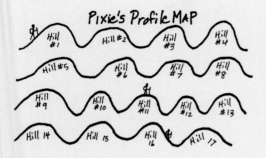

Pixie's Profile MAP

Hill #1, Hill #2, Hill #3, Hill #4, Hill #5, Hill #6, Hill #7, Hill #8, Hill #9, Hill #10, Hill #11, Hill #12, Hill #13, Hill 14, Hill 15, Hill 16, Hill 17

doubt, out of scale with respect to the four antlike hikers who clamber up and down them; for, in these mental maps of the trail, it is never possible to show the true size of the mountain, physically or psychologically, in relation to the person who labors upon its slopes, wearing busted boots and ragged clothes, hauling a forty-pound pack.

A profile from a Pennsylvania shelter is both clever and sadly deluded. "Bull Moose" has drawn a moose

PA.-KATAHDIN PROFILE
GA.-PA. PROFILE
"BULL MOOSE"
GA→HAGGIS BATHROOM 96
Celibacy Tour

logo with antlers to display two vertical profiles. The antler on the left, representing Georgia to Pennsylvania, is quite jagged; the one on the right, Pennsylvania to Mt. Katahdin, is much less so, as if this hiker believes things will get easier. They won't. New England is certainly as difficult as the South, perhaps more difficult, as it features less ridge hiking and more base-to-summit ascents. That some thru-hikers combine GA and ME into one word when they sign the register may say something about the space between those two locations. In the minds of certain AT hikers, the two-thousand-mile space is already gone, because they have willed it to be, and they prefer to consider it a GAME.

A "dialogue" among several hikers in the Windsor Furnace shelter in Pennsylvania demonstrates typical trail humor:

7-8-85: I came here to find myself. Instead, I found Windsor Furnace turquoise. —*Red Man*

7-8-85: Go Slow Go Far—maybe we're waiting for ourselves at the Pinnacle [Pennsylvania landmark]? We been looking for over a 1,000 miles. Hey Drifters! Have you found yourselves? So, where are you? Wherever you are, there you are. GA-ME! (There I am!) —*Jenny and Katy from CA*

7-9-85: Have I found myself? After the last five days, I'm not only wondering where I am, but who I am. I'm here, but where is here? I want to get to there, but I was told I can't get there from here. I suppose it doesn't matter, because how can I be in two places at once, when I'm actually nowhere at all. So there. —*Drifting Jimmy*

7-9-85: We're on our way to everywhere. . . . Today I'm Pokey, but I've been Yogi, Kaz. . . . Slowly up that ridge, over those rocks. Know thyself.

The hikers are all caught in the "long green tunnel," an endless trail without many open views or signs of real progress, a trail that often follows a convoluted track so as to avoid the towns and cities that would have given these people a better sense of where they were. The rocks have destroyed the hikers' boots and their backs. They have passed through the Duncannon Monster, one of the worst stretches of rocks on the entire trail, which in the imagination of one hiker takes the form of a grotesque rock-head, larger than any mountain. And when they reach the famous Pinnacle, there is no reward. The overlook is socked in with fog.

THE ALMIGHTY BOOT EATER

GA   NC/TN   VA   WVA   MD   PA
DUNCANNON

For decades hikers have engaged in similar map-making. A page from the 1924 Carter Notch Hut register in the White Mountains of New Hampshire is like a work of primitive art: ten absurdly steep mountains shown in sequence, with stick-figure hikers struggling up and tumbling down the slopes. The Peabody River, between Mt. Washington and Mt. Jefferson, has its own "peaks," stylized waves to indicate the struggle of crossing them. One hiker appears to be standing on his head between two crests of water, as if he tumbled and landed there. The steepness of the mountains is a running joke. In one example of register art from the 1940s, the discordance between guidebook language, "ascends steeply," and the true experience of hiking is graphically represented.

The complete hike from Georgia to Maine (the usual direction) can be indirect, involving gaps, reversals, backing, and filling. A northbound hiker may go off the trail at some intermediate point, get picked up by friends and dropped off at the northern terminus, and then begin to hike south, to cover the sections missed. This is called flip-flopping, which is the way I interpret Jimmy 1 Note's diagram—that he will skip a few states and make them up later. His plan to "reappear" a couple of weeks later in Hanover, New Hampshire, is part of that dream image thru-hikers sometimes develop, a sense of magical abilities that may help to transcend the landscape. One hiker in the Smokies (another "Pixie") claims to have discovered a shortcut: "Did you know that part of the trail from Little Laurel Shelter to here is really a wormhole that connects you to the trail in Georgia? It really is! I swear." Suggesting something out of science fiction, Pixie's "wormhole" seems an apt metaphor for spells of trail amnesia. The AT feels so long that the only imaginable way to get to the end is by magically skipping parts of it.

The most complex itinerary diagram I've ever seen is not a map, really, but a travelog (past, present, and future) imposed upon a chain of states, all fourteen listed in order, with various truths and fantasies attached to each. The hiker loses his girlfriend in Virginia, visits a prostitute in New York, where he is arrested—as if the trail would take him directly through New York City, when in fact it passes some fifty miles north of there. In Connecticut, he "resorts to flip-flops." This does not mean hiking the trail out of sequence, but rather adopting flip-flops as his footgear after having ruined his third pair of boots—none of which had happened yet, at the time when "Bruce on the Loose" actually composed this itinerary in Pennsylvania.

All along the AT, there are geographical thresholds important to weary thru-hikers. Passing through Harpers Ferry, headquarters for the Appalachian Trail Conference, and crossing the Potomac and joining the C&O Canal Towpath for an hour or two, becomes a significant moment for these hikers. Other important mileposts are the Delaware Water Gap, Bear Mountain

Bridge in New York, and the state of Vermont. At the Vermont state line register, just across the border from Massachusetts, a hiker notes, "We are officially out of rattlesnake habitat (according to "Wingfoot") and officially in Maple Syrup and Ben & Jerry habitat. (Hmmm, rattlesnakes and maple syrup…. Mixin' the 2 sounds like a marketable idea)."

Because the actual length of the trail is hard to measure, due to frequent reroutes, it has been impossible to establish a reliable halfway point. Two hikers who stayed at Rausch Gap Shelter, Pennsylvania, during the summer of 1984—separated by a month—disputed the subject in the shelter register:

6/11/84: Finally—the last of the halfway points! First there was Harpers Ferry—spiritual halfway point of the AT. Then PenMar and the Mason Dixon line—cross from the South into the North. Then Pine Grove Furnace and the half-gallon club. Then Whisky Spring Road—supposed halfway point according to the 1984 Data Book. Then Center Point Knob. Then the Cumberland Valley roadwalk and US 11—my own personally calculated halfway point. Then Duncannon—"Halfway Point of the Appalachian Trail." And now the Halfway Hilton—now I can honestly say I'm halfway from Springer to Katahdin…. —Chris

7/9/84: Enough of this halfway bullshit. First it was Harpers Ferry, then PenMar, then some cedar tree in East Bumfuck, now it's supposedly here. We're already past the halfway mark and shouldn't have to be subject to these continual psychological teasings insisting that we're only halfway. We've returned from the locker room, redevised our new strategy, and listened to some inspirational words from Coach Boston. On to Katahdin and best of luck to all thru hikers in the second half of their journey. —The Sleeping Cinema

As pictured in the shelter register, Pooh and Piglet arrive at Windsor Furnace, Pennsylvania, "the Halfway House." Piglet says, "I heard someone say there's only

1,000 miles left to Mt. Kindergarten [Katahdin]." And Pooh replies, "That still sounds like a lot to me, Piglet, probably even more than twenty!" For twenty is about as much as the mind—or at least the body—can comprehend, especially in rock-strewn Pennsylvania.

The hike spins into a stall. It's raining. The rocks are slippery. There's nothing to do but wait it out in the shelter. But the roof leaks and the next shelter is twelve miles north, too far to reach before dark. The register comes down out of its wooden box with the ballpoint pen or pencil, and the hiker draws a map of what matters: the pattern of holes in the shelter roof. Of what use is this map? It is the picture of what matters now, what will benefit the next party of hikers. Here's the front of the shelter; here's the back. One inch equals two feet. The diameters of the leak-holes are only slightly exaggerated. The Big Five, displayed on a grid, are like stars in a constellation. The hiker connects the dots, then slides his sleeping bag to the far corner of the shelter, closes his eyes, and dreams of the last ascent, to the top of Katahdin—or, perhaps, a comforting mental map of that climb.

Roger Sheffer teaches creative writing at Minnesota State University, Mankato, and is the author of three collections of short fiction. His essays on the outdoors have regularly appeared in Adirondack Life *and* Appalachia.

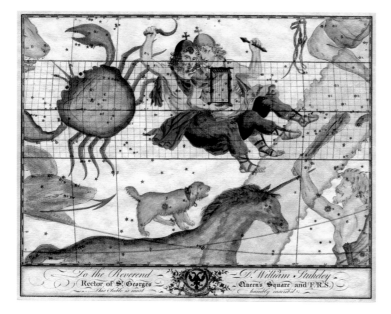

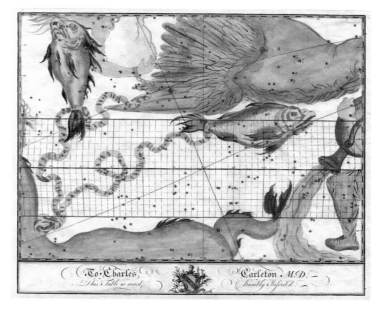

John Bevis, *Pisces* and *Gemini,* 1740s
Hand-colored copperplate engravings, 14 x 18 inches each
From *Atlas Céleste (Celestial Atlas),* c. 1786
Courtesy of George Glazer Gallery, www.georgeglazer.com

A pair of British celestial prints showing constellations based on figures in classical mythology, as identified by Ptolemy. Bevis, a British physician and amateur astronomer, created maps of heavenly beauty; but the charts were also important scientific works, featuring the latest celestial discoveries of the famous astronomers of the day, along with Bevis's own astronomical observations.

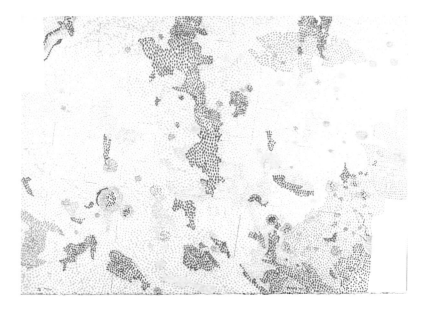

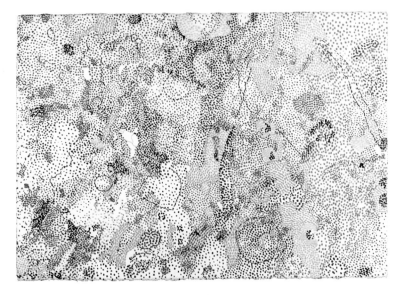

Nancy Graves, *Maestlin G Region of the Moon* (TOP) **and** *Fra Maura Region of the Moon*
Both 22½ x 30 inches
From *Lithographs Based on Geologic Maps of Lunar Orbiter and Apollo Landing Sites* (a series of ten), 1972
Courtesy of Carl Solway Gallery

In the early 1970s, when images of the Moon were deeply impressed on American minds, artist Nancy Graves (1940–1995) immersed herself in lunar maps prepared by NASA in advance of the Apollo space missions. In producing artistic versions of these maps, Graves layered abstraction upon abstraction: of precise scientific data (itself conceptually abstract for most people) and of maps (themselves abstractions of three-dimensional space). Graves left off any interpretive key, giving the viewer no clues to form, scale, or meaning of the content. We are left to explore these maps of the Moon in our own fashion and, Graves hopes, to understand the underlying information more deeply as a result.

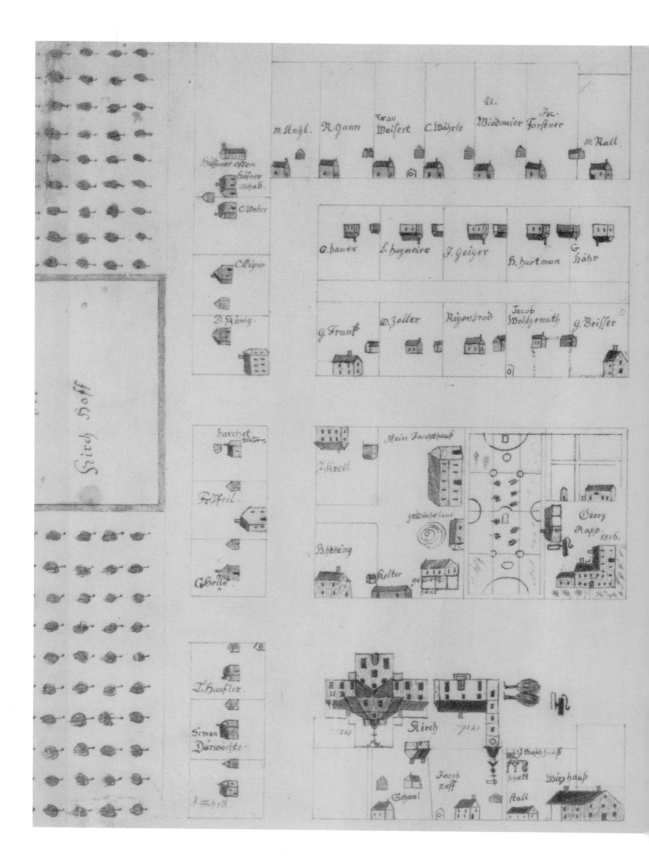

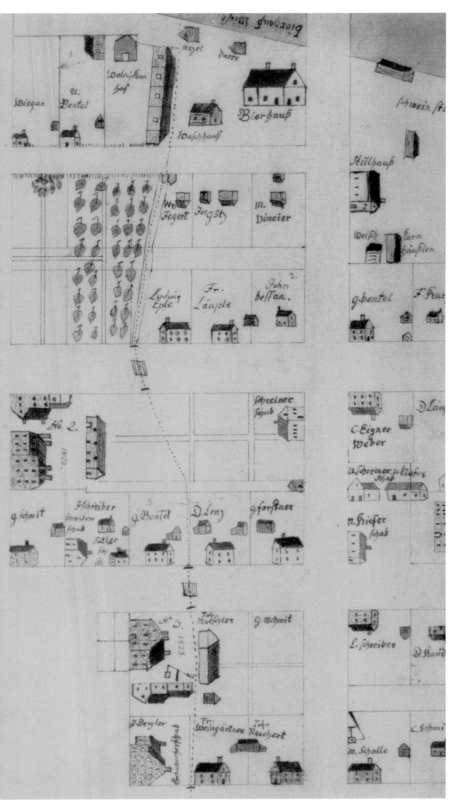

Wallrath Weingartner, *Map of New Harmony, Indiana,* 1832
Courtesy of the Pennsylvania State Archives, Harrisburg (MG-185 Harmony Society Papers)

In the Shaker religious communities of the nineteenth century, artists created highly detailed drawings of their settlements. Weingartner's representation of New Harmony reflects the neatness and sense of order that characterized the Shaker culture. As is typical of Shaker cartographers, he drew buildings as elevations oriented to the facing road, so that no matter which way you turn the map, some portion of the structures and notations are upside down.

Claes Oldenburg, *Soft Manhattan #1: Postal Codes,* 1966
Stenciled canvas stuffed with kapok, 80 x 30 inches
Courtesy Albright-Knox Art Gallery, Buffalo, New York

The artist's soft sculptures played an important role in developing the Pop Art movement of the 1960s and 70s. Oldenburg recreated an assortment of modern consumer objects in cloth, vinyl, and other pliant materials, including this "map" sculpture of Manhattan and another, similar one, of the New York subway system.

The island's tip
was sliced by a ship
canal that tamed the
Spuyten Duyvil shoals,
but severed Marble Hill
from Inwood. Medieval
tapestry unicorns grace
the Cloisters; a flag-
pole and stockade mark
old Fort Tryon. Lofty
crags overlook the
broad Hudson River
as bedrock & history
anchor the Heights to
the George Washington Bridge. Walk east
toward the Bronx across High Bridge;
gaze to the south
from Sugar Hill,
where trumpeters
and tap dancers
stepped up into
the sun. Ages ago
Iapetus (an older
Atlantic Ocean)
closed; the kiss
with Africa heated
a melting pot. Lava
was injected in veins
of rock and coagulated
to form Palisade cliffs.
The legacy of Algonquian
life is hidden in our place
names and our meals. The new-
comers (first the Dutch, then
English, African, Irish, German,
Italian, Jewish, Chinese, Greek,
Ukrainian, Armenian, Puerto Rican,
Pakistani, Cuban, Dominican, Haitian,
Filipino, and all) have shed blood in a
thousand places, but millions live. Legends
of Gotham: Father Knickerbocker, Boss Tweed,
Emma Lazarus, Fiorello, the roar of the El,
the blizzard of '47, Giants at the Polo Grounds.
Offshore, barges ply swirling brown water near
North River sewage pipes, as striped bass and
shad swim up "the river that flows both ways" : a
tidal reach of the sea all the way up to Albany.
Brownstone, bodega, ball court & bus stop: on warm
nights in Harlem, noisy streets and quiet rooftops.
Kids splash around a hydrant as lovers embrace on a
Riverside Park bench and rush-hour traffic is stalled on the Triborough Bridge.
Some uptown options: gospel choir on Sunday, sooty
Grant's Tomb, hiphop the Apollo, ribs at Sylvia's,
law at Columbia, mangos in El Barrio, peace garden
in the Cathedral, rowboat on the Meer, pub-crawl the
West Side; listen to poetry at the 92nd St. Y, nosh at
Zabar's, spiral up the Guggenheim, tour Gracie Mansion.
Songbirds alight in leafy woods as a turtle lays eggs
near a pond in Central Park. Grand museums flank the
green with dinosaur bones and Egyptian tombs. When it
snows, we ramble out to Sheep Meadow & the Great Lawn;
in sunshine, to Strawberry Fields, the Lake, & the Zoo.
Buy hot dogs from pushcarts near Madison boutiques, or
hear grand opera at the Met. Step down to the world of
subways. (Take the A train, ride the Lexington line,
or change at 59th Street for the IRT. Catch the F out to Queens.)
Gneiss but full of schist, the bedrock sparkles with
mica. It bears the weight of midtown: skyscrapers
at Columbus Circle, Fifth Avenue, and Park Avenue.
Attend concerts at Carnegie, ice skating shows at
Rockefeller Center, Mass at St. Patrick's Cathedral.
Our eyes are drawn up to a blue slice of sky as
vertical walls enclose us. 100 gridlocked taxis honk
at police blockades as Fidel speaks at the U.N.
Revelers jam Times Square on New Year's Eve, to
jostle and sing as the ball drops. Buses come in
(the Lincoln Tunnel) to Port Authority, trains to Grand Central. The
lion-flanked public library was once a reservoir;
we love the Art Deco classic Chrysler spire. From
Hell's Kitchen walk to Broadway, buy tickets for
"Showboat" or "Cats"—hey, the Knicks won at the
buzzer in the Garden! See Macy's float parade, then
gape from atop the Empire State, where mighty Kong
took a fall. Diamond jewelers join fur-clad window
shoppers as herds of jaywalkers cross against the
light in the Garment District. Graffiti-scrawled
boards near the Flatiron Building enclose pits
of unconsolidated sediment Consolidated Edison
must dig. Workers repair Gramercy Park cables,
reroute Chelsea steam pipes, plug a burst main
flooding streets by Union Square. (Tap water
flows down from the Catskills in deep tunnels;
garbage is hauled to a landfill at Fresh Kills.)
The riverfront was filled for barnacle-crusted
piers, and Minetta Brook wetlands became lots
in Greenwich Village. A sweatshop horror: 146
locked-in women lost their lives in the Triangle
Shirtwaist fire. Watch skateboard demons cavort
among panhandlers as old men play chess near the
arch in Washington Square. N.Y.U. students, art
film fans, coffee drinkers, & East Village poets
crowd smoky joints on Saturday night; some cross
(the Holland Tunnel) back out to New Jersey. Cheap gallery space
is a memory in SoHo; cast-iron lofts rent high,
as do TriBeCa warehouses. A bag lady seeks warmth
huddled over a sidewalk grate on the Bowery, where
Stuyvesant's farm once spread in old New Amsterdam.
The original steal (this island, traded for $24 in
beads) lies plastered in myth and concrete, obscured
like the African Burial Grounds. A Lower East Side
delicatessen sells good chicken soup; enjoy zuppa di
pesca at the Festival of San Gennaro, or bird's nest
soup in Chinatown. Marchers to City Hall cross the Brooklyn Bridge
to demonstrate, as tourists at South Street Seaport
eat lunch with a view. The Fulton Fish Market is
mobbed before dawn. Precambrian stocks bond the
upper crust with solid foundations below the
Trade Towers, Trinity Church and Wall Street.
Ferryboats to Staten Island, Ellis
Island, the Statue of Liberty,
and Governor's Island
depart from wind-
swept docks
at Battery
Park.

Howard Horowitz, *Manhattan*, 1997
Originally appeared in *The New York Times*,
August 30th, 1997
Courtesy of the author

It took the author one-and-a-half years to write and design this poem about Manhattan, in the form of a map as crowded as the place it represents. Horowitz, a professor of environmental studies at Ramapo College, crams in descriptions of physical geography, cultural attractions, buildings, institutions, individuals, and his own memories. His affection for the place is readily apparent as he leads the reader from "lofty crags overlook[ing] the broad Hudson River" at the island's northern tip, to "a blue slice of sky as vertical walls enclose us" in midtown, to downtown neighborhoods where one can "enjoy zuppa di pesca at the Festival of San Gennaro, or bird's nest soup in Chinatown."

```
                    chaffinch
              chaffinchchaffinch
        chaffinchchaffinchchaffinch
        chaffinchchaffinchchaffinch
              chaffinchchaffinch
                    chaffinch
              chaffie     chye     chaffiechaffie
              chaffie     chye     chaffiechaffie
                          chye     chaffie
                    chaffiechaffiechaffie
                    chaffiechaffiechaffie
                          chaffiechaffie
                          chaffiechaffie
                          chaffiechaffie
                          chaffiechaffie


                    shilly shelly
              shelfyshilfyshellyshilly
                    shelfyshillyshilly
                    shilfyshellyshelly
              shilfyshelfyshelly
                          shellyfaw
                    shielyshellyfaw
              shilfy
              shilfyshelfy  shielyshiely
        shilfyshelfyshelfy        shielychaffie
              chaffiechaffie          chaffiechaffie
              chaffiechaffie
        shilfyshilfyshilfyshelfyshelfy
        chaffieshilfyshilfyshelfyshelfyshelfyshelfy
        chaffieshilfyshilfyshelfyshelfyshelfyshelfyshelfy
        shilfyshilfyshilfyshelfy          shelfyshelfy
        shilfy        shilfy
                    shilfy
              shilfyshelfy


              brichtie
```

Edwin Morgan,
Chaffinch Map of Scotland, 1965
From *Collected Poems* (Manchester,
England: Carcanet Press
Limited, 1990)
Reprinted with permission

In this visual poem/map, the
Scottish poet Edwin Morgan
shows the geographic range of various
Scottish names for a bird, *Fringilla
coelebs,* commonly known as the
chaffinch. Recent studies have
shown that the chaffinch's song
varies according to region,
similar to human dialects.

RIGHT:
Nina Katchadourian,
Austria, 1997
Dissected paper road map,
approx. 7 x 5 inches
Collection of the artist. Courtesy Debs
& Co., New York, and Catharine Clark
Gallery, San Francisco

Brooklyn-based artist Nina
Katchadourian is fascinated by the
connection between the geographical and the anatomical. This piece,
one of a series of works made from
dissected maps, is shaped to reflect
Austria's nickname as "the heart of
Europe." The original map was
large, approximately 40 x 50
inches; the result is a dense yet
fragile bundle of highways and
byways, the vessels of a country.

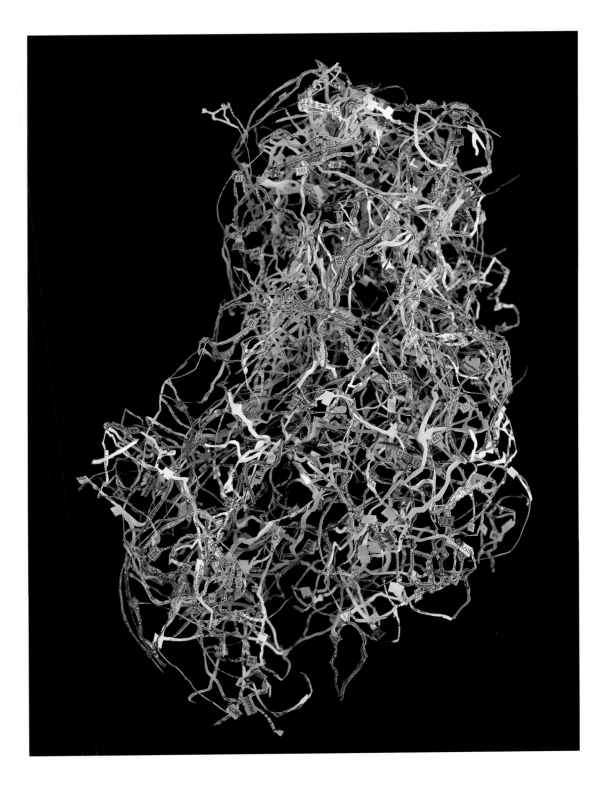

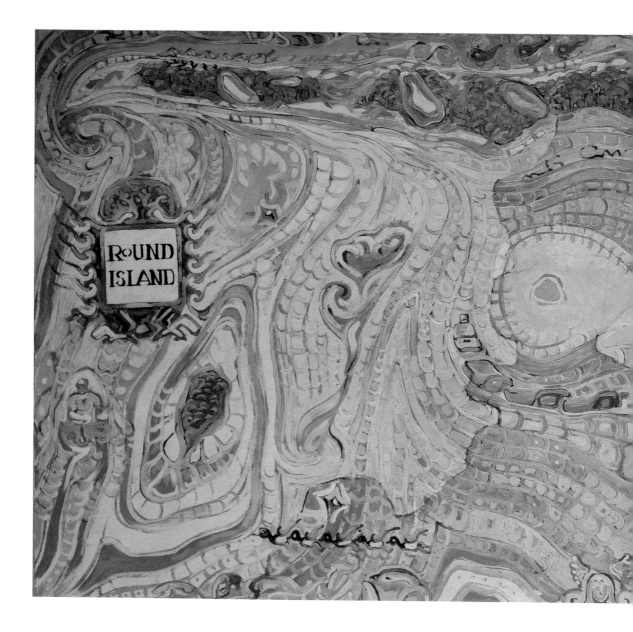

Walter Anderson, *Map of Horn Island*, c. 1960
Oil on plywood panel, 4 x 8 feet
© Shearwater Pottery, Ltd., agent and attorney-in-fact for the family of Peter Anderson: James Anderson,
Patricia Anderson Findeisen, Peter Michael Anderson, and Annette Anderson Ashley

Artist Walter Anderson (1903–1965) painted the water, marshes, and woods of the Mississippi Gulf Coast. He spent much of the last fifteen years of his life alone on Horn Island, a barrier island ten miles from his home in Ocean Springs. In a small sailboat he loaded trash cans filled with paper, paints, brushes, food, and bedding, and crossed the open sea to his place of creative isolation. The crossing, often perilous, was a rite of passage for him. This map of Horn Island is a uniquely artistic sea chart of the waters he knew so intimately. The painter in his boat is on the far left side.

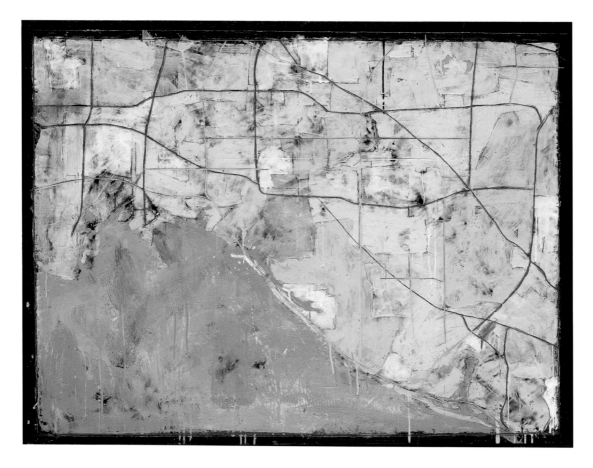

Kevin Wilson, *Coastline 1*, 2000
Encaustic on panel, 36 x 45 inches
Courtesy of Solomon Fine Art, Seattle

Wilson enjoys painting simple, everyday objects or images
imbued with a certain mystique. His map paintings are based
on atlases and AAA trip documents, featuring locations (such
as the California coast, here) that have personal significance
to him.

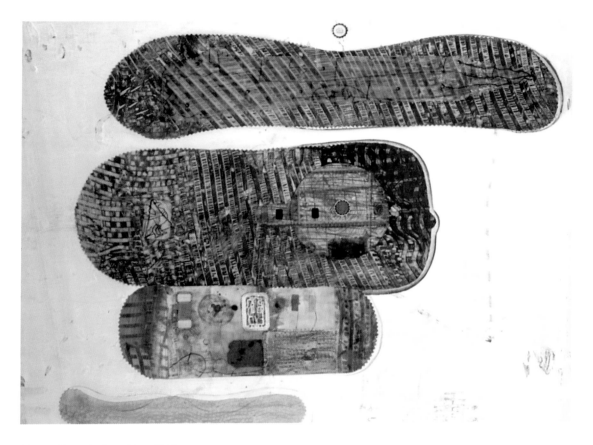

Sharon Horvath, *Step, Trap,* 1998
Oil and mixed media on linen, 20 x 20 inches
Private collection. Courtesy of Tibor de Nagy Gallery, New York

For years American artist Sharon Horvath has incorporated
topographical imagery in her art. In 1997 she spent a year in
Rome and used medieval Roman maps as the inspiration
for a related series of paintings.

Map of Srinigar, 19th century
Artist unknown
Embroidered in fine wool on cloth, 90 x 77 inches
Courtesy of V&A Images, The Victoria and Albert Museum, London

A shawl presents a map of the city of Srinigar, located at the
foot of the Himalayas in Kashmir, India. In fine detail it depicts
canals, bridges, lakes, gardens, and even inhabitants of the city.

Harry Allen, *Map* (rug with detail of map of Salzburg, Austria), 2001
6 x 9 feet
Courtesy of Dune, New York

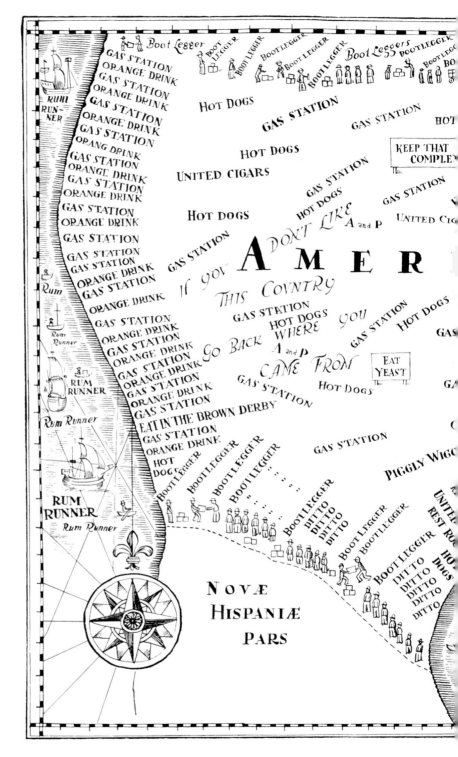

John Held, Jr.,
Map of Americana, 1928
Pen and ink, 12⅞ x 18⅛ inches
Reproduced with permission of
Illustration House and the estate
of Margaret Held

Celebrated illustrator John Held,
Jr. (1889–1958) was best known
for his magazine-cover depictions
of Joe College and the flappers of
the Roaring Twenties. He was
also a serious artist and sculptor,
but used illustration to display his
marvelous sense of whimsy—as
in a succession of maps that
simultaneously poked fun at various topics and cartography itself.
Held wrote on one of his maps,
"The scale is nobody's business,"
and "One of the charms of a map
like this is that nothing is any
where near correct. What are you
going to do about it?"

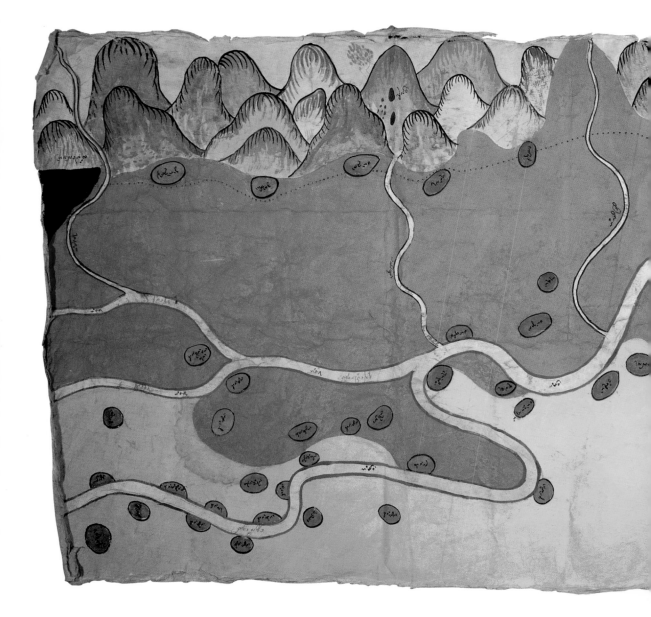

Shan map relating to a border dispute between (British) Burma and China along the Nam Mao River
Artist and date unknown
By permission of the Syndics of Cambridge University Library

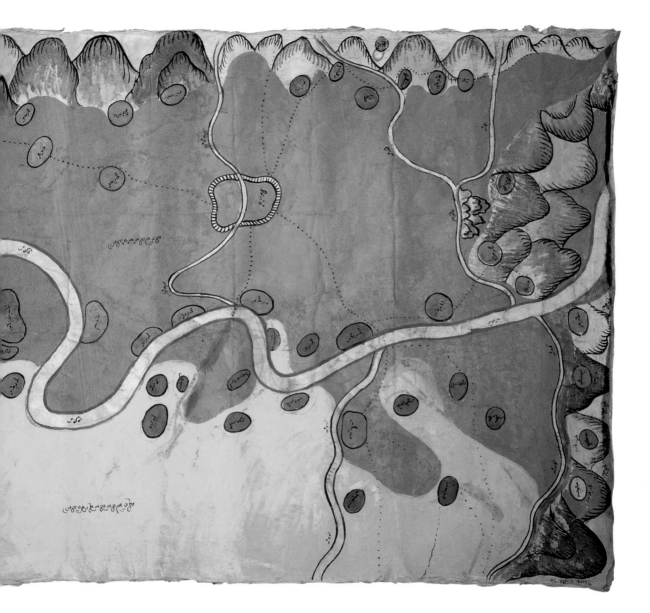

COOLING MY FEET IN A RIVER

Richard Long, selected pages from *A Walk Across England: A Walk of 382 Miles in 11 Days from the West Coast to the East Coast of England*
(New York: Thames & Hudson, 1997)
By permission of the artist

Richard Long (b. 1940) investigates the interaction between a single man and a solitary landscape. In a series of "walks" begun in 1967— examples include *Walking a Line in Peru 1972; Alpine Stones, A Thirteen Day Mountain Walk, Switzerland 2000*; and *A 15 Day Walk in the Three Sisters Wilderness, Oregon 2002*—Long "explores relationships between time, distance, geography, and measurement," and records the results in various combinations of photographs, maps, and text. His walks have been called conceptual drawings on the Earth, though Long thinks of them as sculptures. In a sense, he takes mapping to its origins: feet connected to the Earth.

PEEING IN THE MIDDLE OF THE ROAD

A BIRD DROPPING

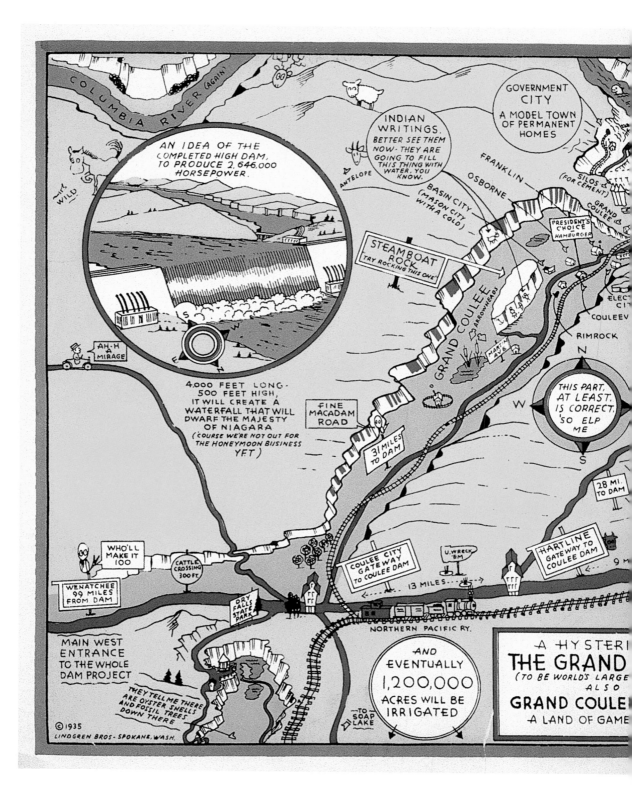

The map contains the following labels:

MASON CITY ALL ELECTRIC. NO CHIMNEY TOWN. (WHICH CAUSES CONSTERNATION AMONG STORKS)

UNTOLD WEALTH IN UNDEVELOPED MINERAL RESOURCES!

MESS HALL THE BEST CHICKEN DINNER BY A DAM SITE

COULEE CENTER

COULEE HEIGHTS

TAKE-OFF

SERVICE

COFFERDAMS

NOW WE WON'T HAVE A PIT TO HISS IN

THIS WILL BE A GREAT PLACE FOR DOCKS.

COLUMBIA RIVER

SANPOIL RIVER

KELLAR

SALMON FISHING

FREE FERRY

YOU CAN SEE THE CASCADE MOUNTAINS FROM HERE

26 MILES TO DAM

GOOD GRAVEL ROAD

KELLER NESPELEM OMAK ETC.

21 MI TO DAM

WILBUR GATEWAY TO COULEE DAM

U.S. 10

12 MILES

JACKRABBIT (PRESSED)

ALMIRA GATEWAY TO COULEE DAM.

SPOKANE 92 MILES FROM DAM

MAIN EAST ENTRANCE TO THE WHOLE DAM PROJECT

L MAP OF OULEE DAM ONCRETE (EXAMPLE) E DRY FALLS SCENIC SPLENDOR

CHOICE BLENDING HARD WHEAT RAISED HERE

HATCHED & SCRATCHED By Jolly Lindgren 1935

WA.—EASTERN

"Jolly" Lindgren,
A Hysterical Map of the Grand Coulee Dam, 1935
Published by Lindgren Bros.,
Spokane, Washington
Courtesy of MSCUA, University of
Washington Libraries, UW 22220z

FOLLOWING PAGES:
Kathy Prendergast, *Lost,* 1999
Computer-generated image on paper,
34 x 47 inches
© Kathy Prendergast. Courtesy of
Kerlin Gallery, Dublin

This map of the United States by an Irish artist shows state borders and topographical information about mountain ranges, rivers, and lakes, but the only places identified with a name are those that include the word "lost." The names might refer to the geographic confusion of the explorers who named them, or perhaps Prendergast is pointing to prospects that never materialized in a land of opportunity. Or maybe she is making a larger statement about the history and development of the country as a whole. The title brings to mind its antonym; for so many people, the country's development is about places found, but for its native populations, it was the opposite.

Lost

Alighiero e Boetti, *Mappa del mondo,* 1984 and *Mappa del mondo,* 1988
Embroidery on cloth, 46¼ x 70⅞ inches (blue) and 45 x 84 inches (green)
Courtesy of Sperone Westwater, New York

While in Afghanistan in 1970, Italian artist Alighiero e Boetti (1940–1994) contracted with weavers to create a series of embroidered tapestries, maps of the world in various colors using the flag of each country to define its shape. He continued to design the maps over the course of many years, and the borders of each describe Boetti's location at the time the piece was created. These "souvenirs," stitched by women artisans he had befriended, were perhaps a response to the global consolidation they graphically portray. "To my mind, the work of the embroidered maps represents supreme beauty," Boetti once said. "For these works, I made nothing, selected nothing, in the sense that the world is the way it is and I have not drawn it; the flags are those that exist anyway . . . Once the basic idea is there, the concept, then everything else is chosen."

Jaune Quick-to-See Smith, *Indian Country Today,* 1996
Acrylic and collage on canvas, 60 x 100 inches
Courtesy of the artist

Quick-to-See Smith, a member of the Confederated Salish
and Kootenai Nation and an Indian rights advocate, explores
in her art issues of race, politics, the environment, and bicul-
turalism. This painting uses what she calls the "coyote sneak-
up" to draw attention to Native American issues. The base is
a collage of newspaper clippings on topics pertaining to
Native Americans' lives—for example, a report on the status
of education on Indian reservations, or an advertisement for
a company called Savage Tans. The artist overlays this with
the iconographic contours of the United States to draw in
the viewer, coyote-like. State borders and place names
washed in red paint point to the complete makeover of a
land formerly roamed and named by other inhabitants.

FOLLOWING PAGES:
Paula Scher, *The World,* 1998
Acrylic on canvas, 8 x 5 feet
Courtesy of the artist

In her 2002 book, *Make It Bigger,* graphic designer Paula
Scher explains that she began painting "small opinionated
maps in the early nineties. Over time they grew larger and
more obsessive. In the late nineties and now the map
paintings serve as an antidote to laborious corporate design
projects frustrated by indecisive committees."

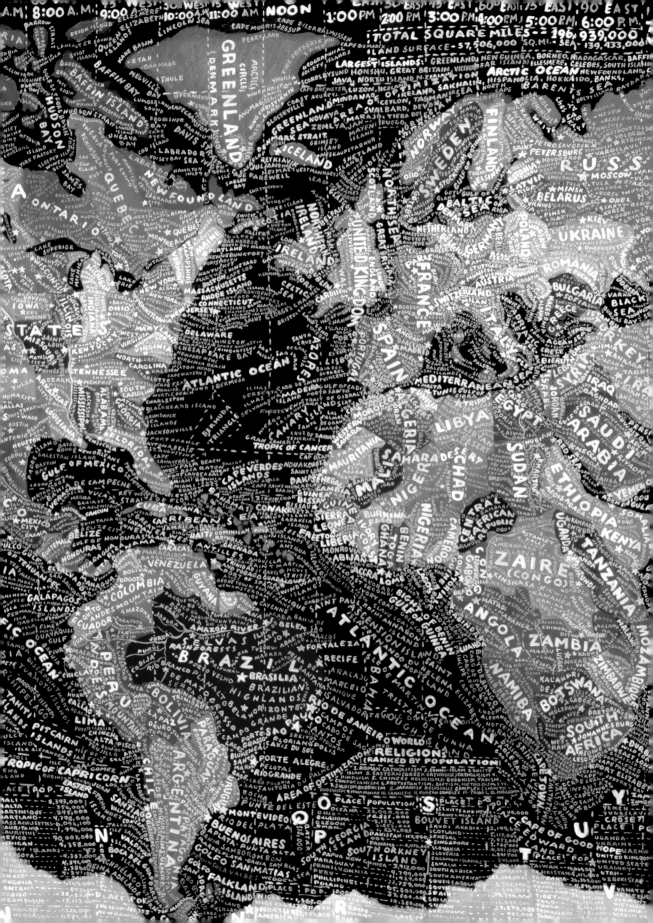

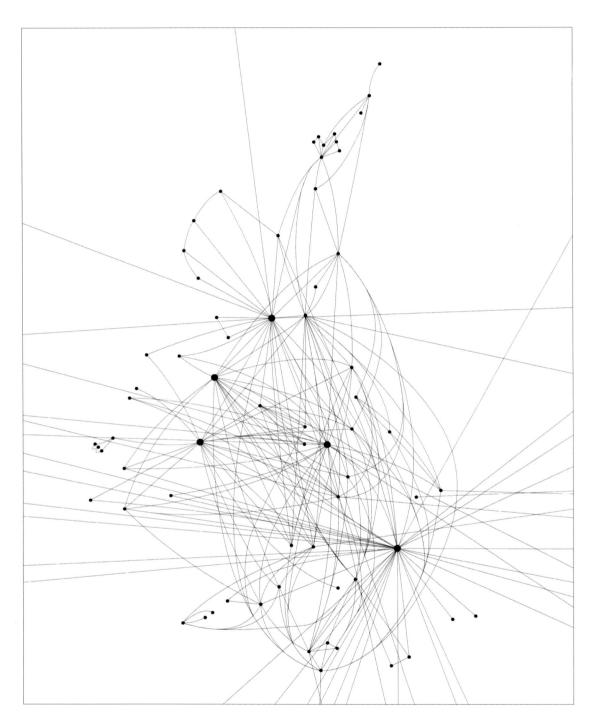

Langlands & Bell, *Air Routes of Britain (Day)* and *Air Routes of Britain (Night)*, 2002
Screen print, 27¼ x 21½ inches
Published by Alan Cristea Gallery. © 2002 Langlands & Bell. Reprinted by permission

In this diptych, British artists Ben Langlands and Nikki Bell
portray "a mile-high state of permanent flux frozen in time."

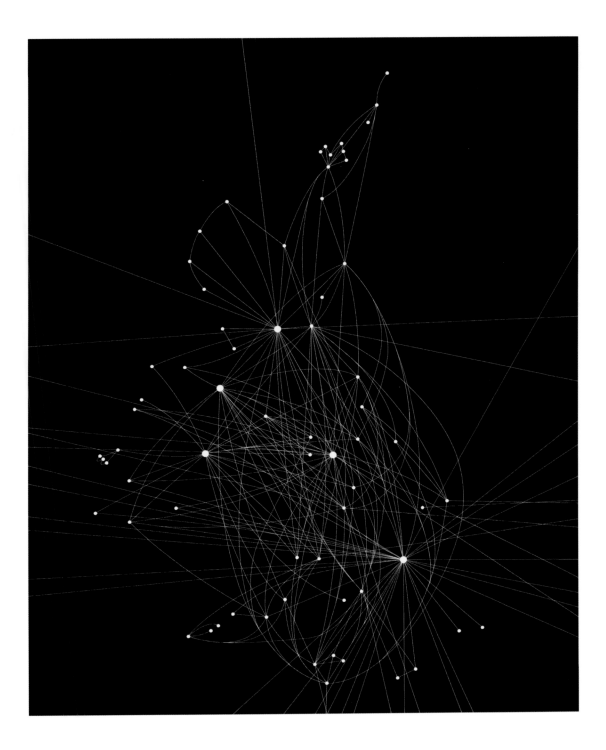

Jo Mora, *Grand Canyon,* **1931**
(Monterey, California: Jo Mora
Publications, 1931)
Color photo process print on glossy paper,
14 x 18 inches (image)
Courtesy of Diane Ross

Born in Uruguay, Jacinto "Jo" Mora
(1876–1947) was fascinated by his
adopted home in the western U.S. and
spent much of his adult life studying its
history and culture. He was a sculptor,
painter, and photographer as well as an
illustrator, and approached mapmaking
as a way to convey information in an
artistic manner. Fewer than a dozen of his
pictorial maps were published, but those
of the Grand Canyon, Yosemite,
Yellowstone, Los Angeles, and San Diego
are masterpieces of the form and prized
by collectors. He dedicates this map to
"those unfortunate souls who through
ignorance, apathy, or misfortune, have
never seen the abysmal silent climax this
carte humorously depicts."

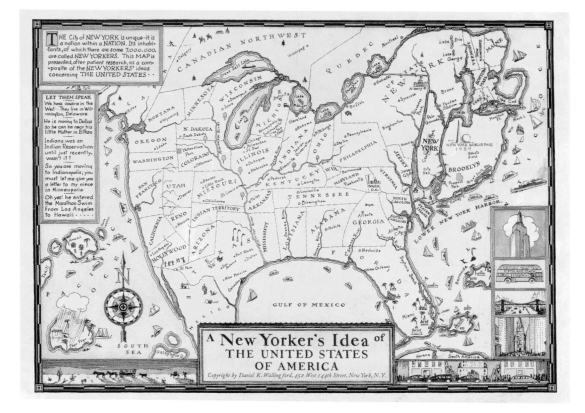

Daniel K. Wallingford, *A New Yorker's Idea of the United States of America*, c. 1939
Color-process print on glossy paper, 11 x 16 inches
Courtesy of George Glazer Gallery, www.georgeglazer.com

Wallingford's map precedes Saul Steinberg's 1975 version, *View of the World from 9th Avenue,* by thirty-five years. Produced for the 1939 New York World's Fair, it pokes fun at New Yorkers' worldly provincialism with incorrect or fictitious place names in the American hinterlands; for example, Minneapolis and Indianapolis are humorously shown together in Michigan as "The Twin Cities."

RIGHT:
Ernest Dudley Chase, *The United States as Viewed by California (Very Unofficial),* 1940
22 x 16 inches
By permission of Fred Holland
Courtesy of Harvard College Library

Most likely inspired by Wallingford's map, Chase's version pokes fun at those who tout California as a land of eternal sunshine and boundless delights. The cartouche itself is a cornucopia spilling fruit and flowers. The rest of the country (except for New England, which is "kissed by the sun part of the time") is shrouded under a pall of clouds.

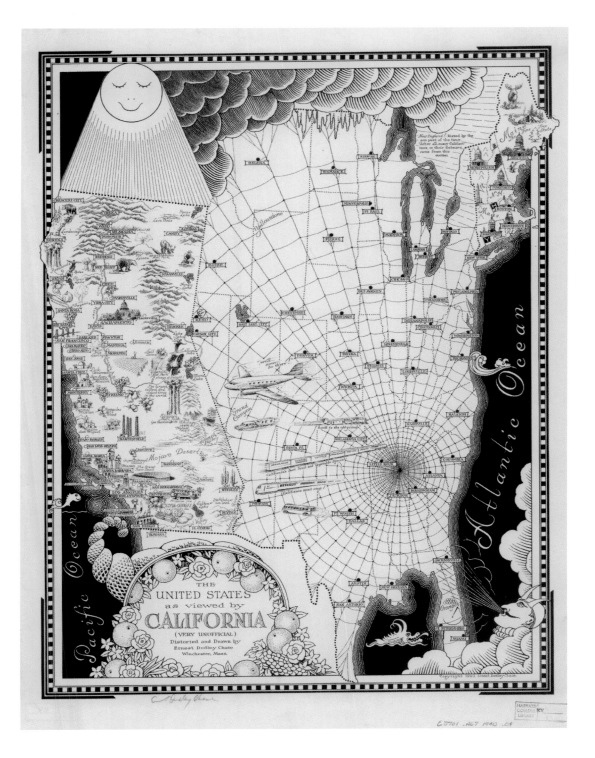

THE
UNITED STATES
as viewed by
CALIFORNIA
(VERY UNOFFICIAL)
Distorted and Drawn by
Ernest Dudley Chase
Winchester, Mass.

Two Maps of Boylan Heights

DENIS WOOD

THE IDEA WAS TO SEE what we could learn about neighborhoods by mapping them. Because we didn't know much about neighborhoods, we didn't know what to look for, so we mapped everything in Boylan Heights, a neighborhood in Raleigh, North Carolina. We mapped the streets and what was under the streets—the sewers, water mains, and gas lines. We wanted to map the tree roots, mirroring underground the branches spread out overhead. We did map the trees.

We mapped the power lines and the telephone lines and the cables for televisions. We mapped the street lights. Later we mapped the light cast by the street lights and all the other lights, prowling the neighborhood after dark with a light meter. Up above the lights we saw the stars, and we mapped the stars you could see from the neighborhood.

We mapped the traffic and the colors of the leaves in the fall and the fences. We mapped the graffiti made in wet cement and the street signs and the dollar value of the real estate, the colors of the houses and the number of stories and the number of steps from the sidewalk to the front porches, and where the wind chimes were and the clotheslines. We mapped everything we could figure out how to map.

One Halloween—it was 1982—we mapped the pumpkins. While everyone else was trick-or-treating, I walked through the neighborhood with a camera and took pictures of all the jack-o'-lanterns. We made high-contrast contact prints of the photographs and pasted them on a street map, so there's a jack-o'-lantern at every address where there was a pumpkin on a porch. In most cases the photograph is of the jack-o'-lantern that was at the address, but in some cases my photographs didn't turn out (in these cases we duplicated an image from another porch), and in other cases there

was more than one pumpkin (in these cases one does duty for the rest). Then we blacked out everything but the faces of the jack-o'-lanterns: Halloween in Boylan Heights! The pattern will not be clear without the streets to imply the extent of the neighborhood, but the readers of the neighborhood atlas in which this map was intended as a plate would, by the time they looked at it, be so familiar with the layout of the neighborhood as to pick up the pattern immediately: most of the pumpkins are on the porches of the big houses at the top of the hill.

It made us think of another map we had made. By that Halloween the Boylan Heights neighborhood association had been publishing its monthly newsletter for eight years. We had recorded on a map the addresses of every one of the 923 mentions in those ninety-six newsletters. The addresses most frequently referenced were those of the big houses at the top of the hill.

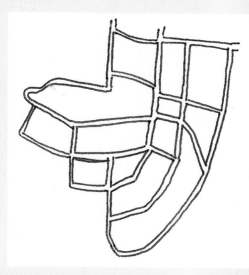

Boylan Heights baseline map

Boylan Heights pumpkin map, 1982

*indicates a porch
with more than one pumpkin*

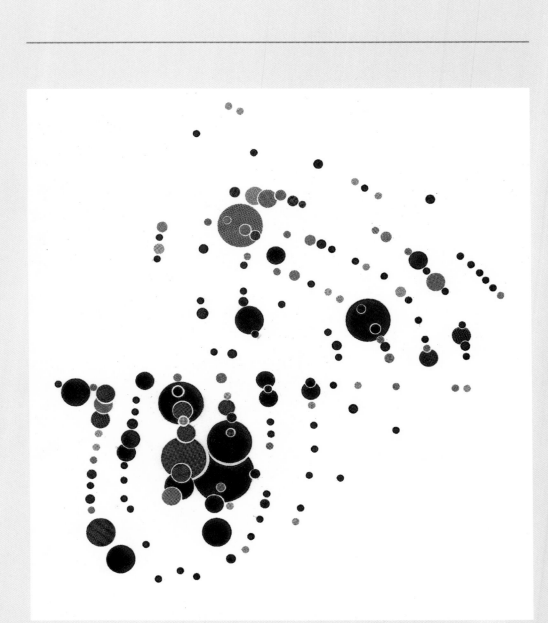

Boylan Heights newsletter map, 1982

The size of the circle indicates the number of times a household was mentioned in the community newsletter, with the biggest circle indicating sixty or more mentions, and the smallest fewer than four. The shading differentiates between family business and neighborhood business. The darkest circles indicate fewer than twenty percent of references were personal in nature; the lighter the circle, the more likely the newsletter references had to do with a householder's return from a visit to a sick relative, or with friends or relatives coming to visit. (An example of personal news: "Mrs. Harry Caldwell of 1030 W. South St., has a Sister, Mrs. Ruby Tunnell, who has been quite ill in Wilson Memorial Hospital." An example of community news: "Our special thanks to Mr. and Mrs. Clyde Edwards, who invited us to their beautiful backyard at 417 South Boylan Avenue for the June meeting [of the neighborhood association.]") The distinction shows not only that most of the addresses that appeared in the newsletter are at the top of the hill, but that those located elsewhere are likely to be of the "sick relative" character.

What was interesting was that the people who lived at these addresses changed. The people could come and go, but the addresses kept on being referred to. What this suggested was that people who were going to be movers and shakers in the neighborhood were attracted to certain kinds of houses, bigger ones, toward the top of the hill; and those who weren't going to be movers and shakers were attracted to others, smaller ones, down toward the streams and the railroad tracks that surrounded the neighborhood.

People living in the big houses at the top of the hill were mentioned all the time. The address referenced most frequently is currently occupied by Raleigh's mayor, Charles Meeker. But it was referenced at the same rate when it was occupied by Ben Floyd, who lived there in 1974, the year the newsletter was founded. That year Ben was president of the neighborhood association. The family that moved in when Ben moved out played a lesser but similar role in the newsletter. After that, Charles moved in. He played a strong leadership role in the neighborhood and, before becoming mayor, was a city councilman.

During the eight years these different people lived there, their address was referenced sixty-six times; the house across the street to its side was referenced forty-seven times; the one directly across the street from it was referenced thirty times; and the one five doors down from that house was referenced thirty times. Those four houses account for a fifth of all the references made to any address during the newsletter's first eight years. Only two other addresses in the neighborhood are referenced at least thirty times—and a full third of the addresses were never referenced at all. As far as the newsletter was concerned, these people didn't exist. Their addresses could be anywhere, but they predominated among the small houses lower down the hill.

People who get mentioned in the newsletter carve jack-o'-lanterns and put them on their porches on Halloween. Both of these are measures of class. They are also measures of a certain respect for tradition, especially the traditions of a certain kind of neighborhood, which Boylan Heights has always imagined itself

to be. All this would have warmed the cockles of the hearts of Kelsey and Guild, the Boston landscape architects who laid out the neighborhood in 1907. Because they meant for upper-class folk to live at the top of the hill, they laid these lots out large. Down slope they were smaller. At the bottom of the hill the lots were tiny, long, and narrow. Their plan worked.

Nowadays the whole neighborhood has been substantially gentrified, and while the 1982 patterns we found persist, there are more jack-o'-lanterns everywhere. After the kids have trick-or-treated, folks carry their pumpkins to the Boylan Avenue Bridge, where they line them up for a group portrait taken by Michael Zirkle, one of the neighborhood's professional photographers. These portraits hang in many homes.

Want to bet on where the homes are?

Denis Wood initiated the mapping of Boylan Heights, North Carolina, in 1974 as an assignment for students at the School of Design at North Carolina State University. It grew into a long-term project, documented in the as-yet unpublished book, Dancing and Singing: A Narrative Atlas of Boylan Heights. *Wood writes frequently about mapping for a variety of publications and is the author of* The Power of Maps.

Clarence Peter Helck, *The American Road: 21,000,000 Passenger Cars,* 1931
From *Fortune* Magazine, December 1931

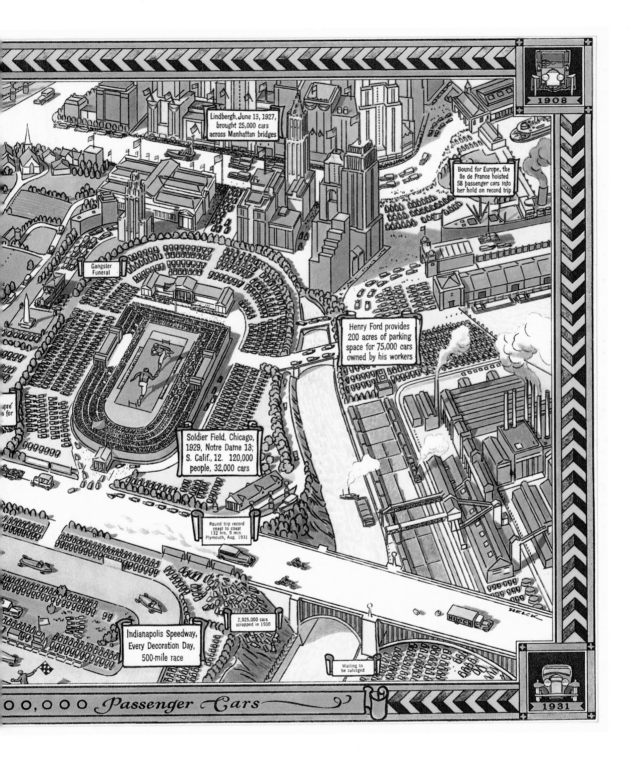

Lindbergh, June 13, 1927, brought 25,000 cars across Manhattan bridges

Bound for Europe, the Ile de France hoisted 58 passenger cars into her hold on record trip

1908

Gangster Funeral

Henry Ford provides 200 acres of parking space for 75,000 cars owned by his workers

Soldier Field, Chicago, 1929, Notre Dame 13; S. Calif., 12. 120,000 people, 32,000 cars

Round trip record coast to coast 132 hrs, 9 min. Plymouth, Aug. 1931

2,925,000 cars scrapped in 1930

Indianapolis Speedway, Every Decoration Day, 500-mile race

Waiting to be salvaged

HOOCH

HELCK

1931

00,000 *Passenger Cars*

From this map you'll learn that in 1931 the round-trip record for driving coast to coast was 132 hours, 9 minutes, in a Plymouth. Perhaps it would have been faster without the barrels rolling out of the back of the "Hooch" truck ahead.

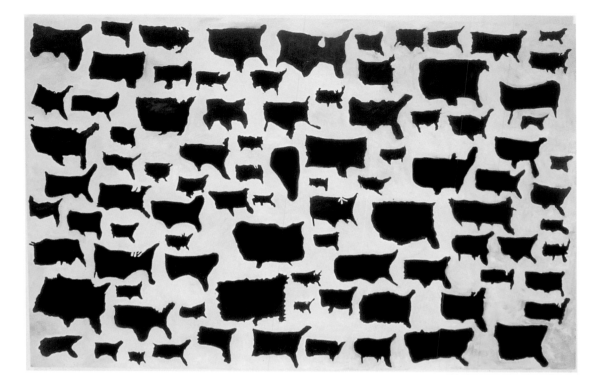

Kim Dingle, *United Shapes of America (Maps Drawn by Las Vegas Teenagers)*, 1991
Oil on wood, 48 x 72 inches
Courtesy of Sperone Westwater, New York

What happens when you ask American students to draw the outline of their country, a profile they have seen countless times and studied over the course of years in school? Dingle asked, and then painted the resulting shapes as a compilation of the ways that visual recall can distort the most basic and familiar of maps—perhaps commenting not so much on the state of U.S. geography education as on our enduring need for maps.

C. F. Korten, *Michigan*, 1947
Gouache on paperboard, 25¼ x 19⁹⁄₁₆ inches (sheet)
From *The United States Series* commissioned by the Container Corporation of America
Smithsonian American Art Museum, Washington, D.C./Art Resource, New York

Oyvind Fahlstrom, *World Map,* 1972
Acrylic on vinyl, 36 x 72 inches
Private collection, New York
Courtesy of Sharon Avery-Fahlstrom

Born of a Swedish mother and a Norwegian father in Sao Paulo, Brazil, Oyvind Fahlstrom (1928–1976) was destined to become a citizen of the world. Separated from his parents by World War II, he lived in Stockholm for many years before moving to Paris, Rome, and, ultimately, New York. He was hugely energetic, producing writings and artworks in an astonishing variety and combination of forms, rife with political and social content. This rich mix is on display in *World Map*, where a deliciously redrawn international landscape, dense with barbed commentary, partakes of the comic book and the jigsaw puzzle.

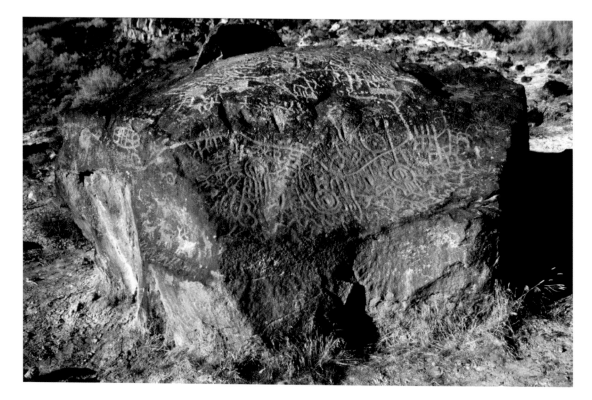

Map Rock, artist and date unknown
Size of rock: approximately 7 x 6 x 5 feet
Photo: Barry Rose, 1991
Courtesy of Bureau of Land Management, Lower Snake River
District, Idaho

Though not officially proven, this petroglyph in an archaeological park southeast of Boise, Idaho has long been thought
to be a map of the upper Snake River and its surroundings,
possibly a depiction of Shoshone territory, or a representation of the spiritual relationships between the human inhabitants, the animals they hunted, and the land. The basalt
boulder is located at a prominent spot, easy for anyone traveling down the river valley to spot.

RIGHT:
Peralta Stone Maps
Artist and date unknown
Photo: Greg Davis. Courtesy of the Superstition Mountain
Historical Society

Treasure maps and tall tales go hand in hand, and the
Superstition Mountains of Arizona have given rise to both.
There are many versions of the story about Jacob Waltz, the
German prospector who in the 1860s supposedly discovered a super-rich vein of gold southeast of Phoenix; he died
not long thereafter, and prospectors have been risking life
and limb to find the famous Lost Dutchman Mine ever since.
Then there is the story of "Jack," a man vacationing with his
family in Arizona—in 1949, or in 1956—who pulled off the
highway and got out of his car to take a look at the
Superstition Mountains. He climbed a small hill to get a better view and stumbled over a treasure map carved in stone.
He returned a year later and dug up two more stone maps,
the "heart map" and the "trail map" that, when placed side
by side, lead the way to boundless riches. Be the first to
decipher the maps, and you'll live happily ever after.

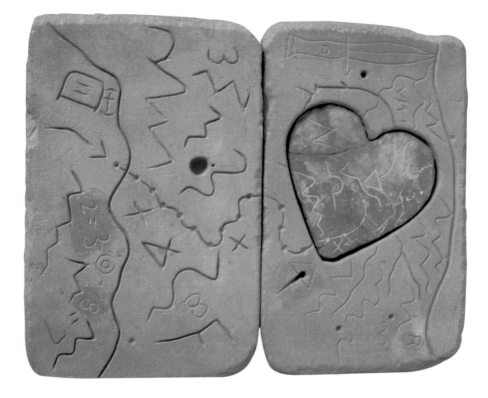

Kisaburo Ohara, *A Humorous Diplomatic Atlas of Europe and Asia* (detail), 1904
From *The Playful Eye* by Julian Rothenstein and Mel Gooding (San Francisco: Chronicle Books, 2000)

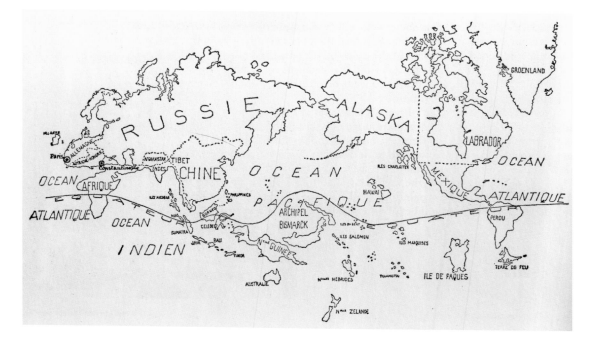

Surrealist Map of the World, 1929
Artist unknown
From a special issue of *Variétés*, a Brussels-based magazine,
entitled "Le Surréalisme en 1929"

The Surrealists amused themselves by creating a map that
puts imperialist powers in their place. For example: other
than Alaska, the United States are invisible; mainland Britain
is dwarfed by Ireland; Easter Island looms over a tiny
Australia; and only two cities are marked, Paris and
Constantinople, with the rest of France and Turkey missing.
More than anything, this is a map of the Surrealists' cultural
ideals. A 1925 Surrealist declaration stated, "Even more than
patriotism—which is a quite commonplace sort of hysteria,
though emptier and shorter-lived than most—we are dis-
gusted by the idea of belonging to a country at all, which is
the most bestial and least philosophic of the concepts to
which we are subjected.... Wherever Western civilization is
dominant, all human contact has disappeared, except
contact from which money can be made—payment in
hard cash."

T/4 John G. Drury, 214th Ordnance Battalion,
Mem-O-Map of Europe, 1946
10½ x 13¾ inches
Published by Mem-O-Map Company

With this souvenir map, and another one like it for those stationed in Oahu, military personnel who served in World War II could chart their adventures, including bivouac sites and participation in troop movements.

William Wegman, *Vacationland,* 2003
Oil and found postcards on three wooden panels, 84 x 144 x 2 inches
Courtesy of Sperone Westwater, New York

Wegman's postcard collages feature vintage postcards from distinct periods and places, evoking nostalgia for summer cross-country road trips. Each card is fragmented with a graphic division (often yellow) that connects the cards as they fall into a grid. Rather than an idealized landscape, the finished whole is a scrapbook-map of imaginary travel.

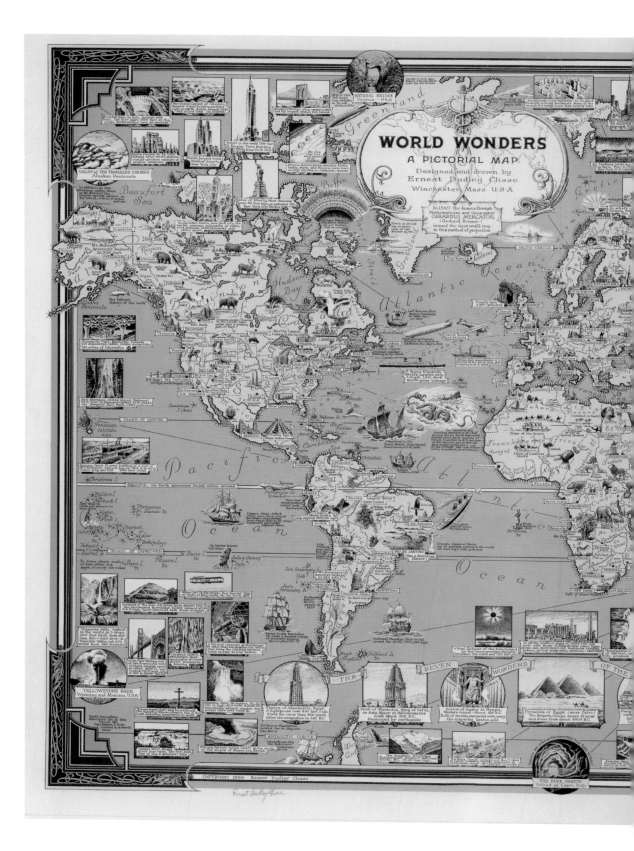

Ernest Dudley Chase,
World Wonders:
A Pictorial Map, 1939
By permission of Fred Holland
Photo: Harvard College Library

An encyclopedic compendium of superlatives, this map depicts a broad range of cultural and natural wonders—from the Hanging Gardens of Babylon to the Waldorf Astoria, from the Great Buddha of Bamian to the Brooklyn Bridge, from the Dionne quintuplets to the Aurora Borealis. Chase records these phenomena on the Mercator projection.

SCOTLAND.

A gallant piper, struggling through the bogs,
His wind bag broken, wearing his clay clogs;

Yet, strong of heart, a fitting emblem makes
For Scotland—land of heroes and of cakes.

Vincent Brooks, Day & Son, Lith. London, W.C.

Aleph, *Scotland* and *Ireland*, 1869
9½ x 8 inches (image), 10½ x 9 inches (sheet)
From *Geographical Fun: Being Humourous Outlines of Various Countries*
(London: Hodder and Stoughton, 1869). Courtesy of Map Collection, Yale University Library

IRELAND.

And what shall typify the Emerald Isle?
A Peasant, happy in her baby's smile?

No fortune her's,—though rich in native grace,—
Herrings, potatoes, and a joyous face.

The *Geographical Fun* atlas consists of twelve maps of European countries created by William Harvey, writing under the pseudonym "Aleph." England takes the form of Queen Victoria; Italy is a revolutionary figure; Denmark is an ice skater, and Russia—of course—is a bear. In the introduction the author stated his intention: "It is believed that illustrations of Geography may be rendered educational, and prove of service to young Scholars who commonly think Globes and Maps but wearisome aids to knowledge. If these geographical puzzles excite the mirth of children, the amusement of the moment may lead to the profitable curiosity of youthful students and imbue the mind with a healthful taste for foreign lands."

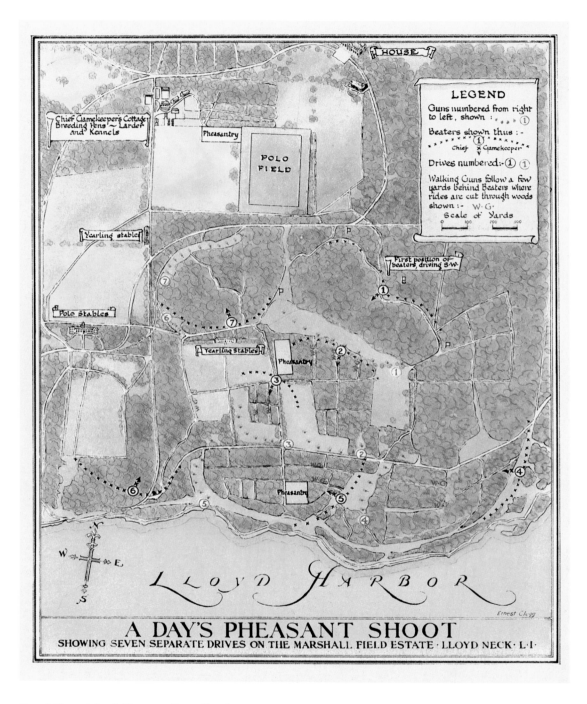

Ernest Clegg, *A Day's Pheasant Shoot Showing Seven Separate Drives on the Marshall Field Estate,*
Lloyd Neck, Long Island, 1931
From *Fortune* magazine, October 1931

"The day's shoot illustrated by the map is one of four available on this acreage," reads the accompanying text. "The whole plan affords a two-day shoot every two weeks from late November through February, with 4,000 to 7,000 birds raised in the breeding pens according to weather and luck with plagues."

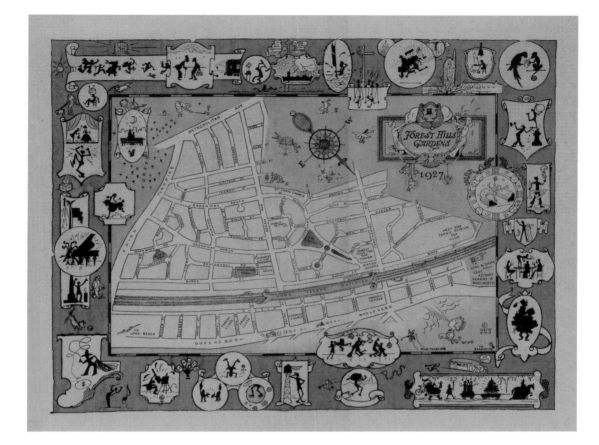

Forest Hills Gardens, 1927
Artist unknown
Photo-process print with hand coloring, 16 x 20 inches
Courtesy of George Glazer Gallery, www.georgeglazer.com

A nostalgic print from an era when the borough of Queens
was a weekend leisure destination for New Yorkers. The
West Side Tennis Stadium and Club in Forest Hills first
hosted the U.S. men's doubles tournament in 1915. By
1927, the year this map was published, both the men's
and women's singles tournaments were played in Forest
Hills. In 1978 the U.S. Open was moved to nearby
Flushing Meadows.

FOLLOWING PAGES:
Dr. Woody Sullivan, *Earth at Night,* 2002
© 2002 W. T. Sullivan, III

Humankind reveals its nighttime activities in this mosaic
of images recorded by the Defense Meteorological Satellite
Program. Most of the images are from the 1990s and
have been selected and processed to best illustrate various
phenomena; purple: city lighting, orange: seasonal agricultural
fires, yellow: natural gas flares in oil fields, gray: lights bedeck-
ing squid and saury fleets, aqua: aurora borealis.

Memory Map

BY KATIE DAVIS

I WAS REPORTING in Nicaragua a few years after the revolution and needed to find the office of the censor. A Sandinista official pointed north. "Go a few blocks and take a left where the big tree used to be before the earthquake," she said.

"Where the tree used to be?"

Well, I got lost and missed my interview. I complained to friends, "That official steered me the wrong way on purpose." They told me, "That's just how directions are given in Nicaragua, all over Latin America." Eventually, I began to use the story as an example of how different it is down south.

Until one day, a few years back, I caught myself using memory as a map. A new neighbor asked where to make a key. "There's a key maker," I said, "right next door to where Gartenhaus Furs used to be." Used to be.

My neighbor stared blankly. I clarified. "Oh, it's a check cashing place now." But in my mind, it will forever be the elegant limestone building that had fur for garbage. A dumpster full of fur. When I was eleven, I'd climb up and pull out scraps to make mink stoles for my Barbie dolls.

I noticed more and more that memory was my map. When people wanted a recommendation for my favorite Ethiopian restaurant on 18th Street, I'd say, "the one where the post office used to be." Then I'd describe the way the brass post office boxes would shine through the twelve-foot windows. "Yes, but is the food good?," they'd ask.

I met a new neighbor on the street where I grew up. I said, "Oh, you're the one who lives in Mrs. Retz's house." He gave me a look and said, "Well, we live there now and have for more than a year."

How to explain that I meant no slight? That for me it will always be Mrs. Retz's house. She was a gardener who could coax clouds of roses from her miniature front yard.

At home when speaking with my mom, we have whole conversations with twenty-year-old signposts.

Mom says, "The tenants in 1773 are fighting eviction."

"You mean Frank Sanchez's building?"

"Right," she clarifies, "two doors up from the Nelson's." Never mind that these two families haven't lived on the block for years.

I stopped trying to explain to people and now I censor myself. Not everyone wants to know this kind of history about their street: that the eighteen narrow apartments squeezed into one lot were once a single, sprawling house with a wraparound porch. And that no one cared if you cut through the yard to the ice cream store where Giuseppe cranked the cream by hand.

So, yes, I walk my street among the departed and disappeared—Mrs. Retz tying up her rose bushes, Giuseppe cutting peaches for the ice cream. Some days, what's missing is more vivid than what is.

I realize now what the Nicaraguan woman was saying when she told me to turn where the tree used to be. She was saying that she'd seen a lot of change—an earthquake, a revolution. And that the tree that used to be there, it was missed.

Katie Davis is a writer in Washington D.C.
This essay is from her ongoing public radio series,
Neighborhood Stories.

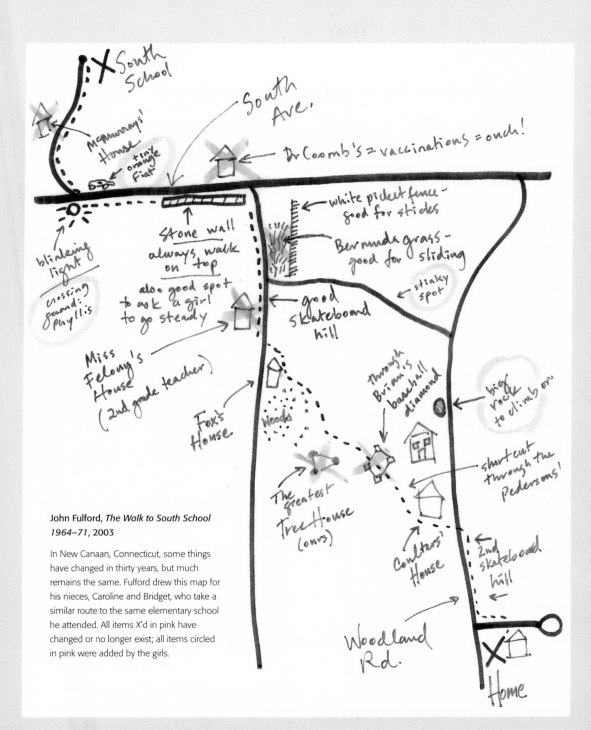

John Fulford, *The Walk to South School* 1964–71, 2003

In New Canaan, Connecticut, some things have changed in thirty years, but much remains the same. Fulford drew this map for his nieces, Caroline and Bridget, who take a similar route to the same elementary school he attended. All items X'd in pink have changed or no longer exist; all items circled in pink were added by the girls.

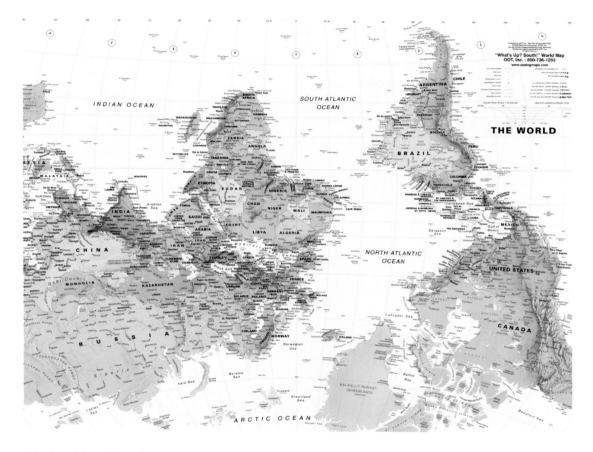

What's Up? South! (detail), 2002
Courtesy of ODT, Inc., Amherst, Massachusetts
© 2002 www.odt.org

The publisher of this alternative view of the world reminds
us: "It takes many points of view to see the truth."

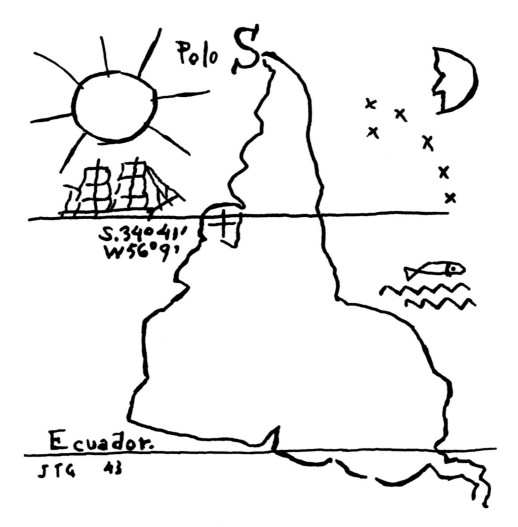

Joaquín Torres-García, *Upside-down Map*, 1934
From *La escuela del sur (The School of the South)*

The Uruguayan modernist artist Joaquín Torres-García (1874–1949) drew a map that became the guiding symbol for a movement. The School of the South was a group of Latin American artists wishing to promote the unique qualities of Latin American art and claim a prominent place in an art world dominated by Europe and the U.S. He wrote, "There should be no North for us, except in opposition to our South. That is why we now turn the map upside down, and now we know what our true position is, and it is not the way the rest of the world would like to have it. From now on, the elongated tip of South America will point insistently at the South, our North. Our compass as well; it will incline irremediably and forever toward the South, toward our pole. When ships sail from here traveling north, they will be traveling down, not up as before. Because the North is now below."

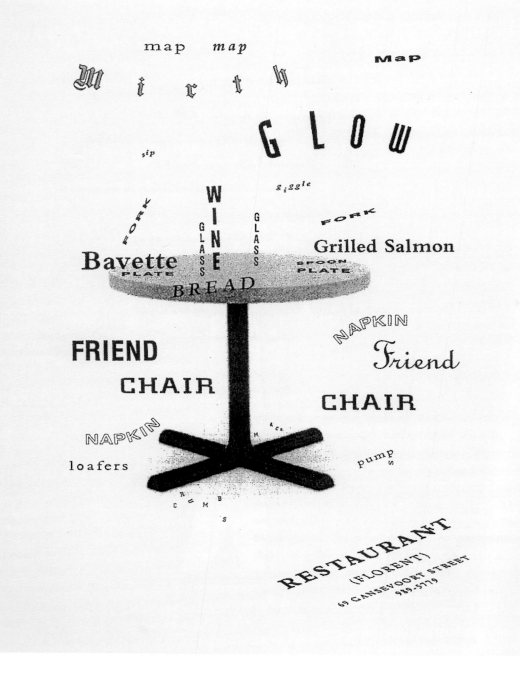

Tibor Kalman, *Untitled,* c. 1980s
M + Co., for Restaurant Florent, New York City
M + Co. Collection, Cooper-Hewitt, National Design Museum, Smithsonian Institution.
Reprinted by permission

Kalman (1949–1999), a graphic designer and principal of
M + Co. in New York City, created this word map with table
as a promotional post card.

Remy Hetreau, *Vins de Roussillon–Midi–Provence,* c. 1930s
Color poster on paper, 27 x 33 inches
Printed by Editions Publi-Mab, Paris
Courtesy of George Glazer Gallery, www.georgeglazer.com

One of a series of posters, *Les Vignobles de France,* created to promote the country's
wine-making regions.

Barosi, Untitled drawing, c. 1932
From *The Futurist Cookbook* by Filippo Tommaso Marinetti
(London: Trefoil Publications Ltd., 1989)

Marinetti, leading theorist of the Futurist movement founded in 1909, asserted that
"men think dream and act according to what they eat and drink." He proposed a program for the total renewal of food and cooking, and published his manifesto-as-cook-
book in 1932. It included a recipe for a cocktail called "Fire in the Mouth," which can be
assembled using the map shown here, noting that the cherries should be rolled in
cayenne pepper before being placed in the bottom of the glass, and the honey layer
should be one centimeter thick so as to form an impermeable division in the middle of
the drink. The cocktail's creator, Futurist engineer Barosi (first name unknown), also
concocted a dish called "Dolceforte" (Sweetstrong) consisting of bread covered with
anchovies, bananas, butter, and mustard.

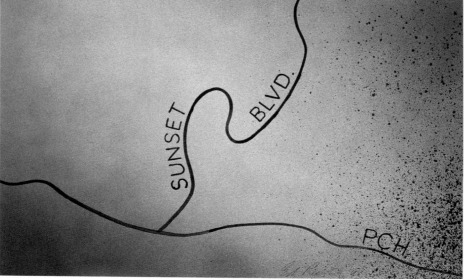

Ed Ruscha, *Pico and Sepulveda*, 1999
Acrylic on linen, 24 x 30 inches

Sunset/P.C.H, 1998
Acrylic on paper, 14 x 22 inches
Photos: Paul Ruscha

Road language, maps, and the city of Los Angeles: these are three of the themes Ruscha has mined throughout his artistic career. In his relatively recent series of images of intersections, the three converge.

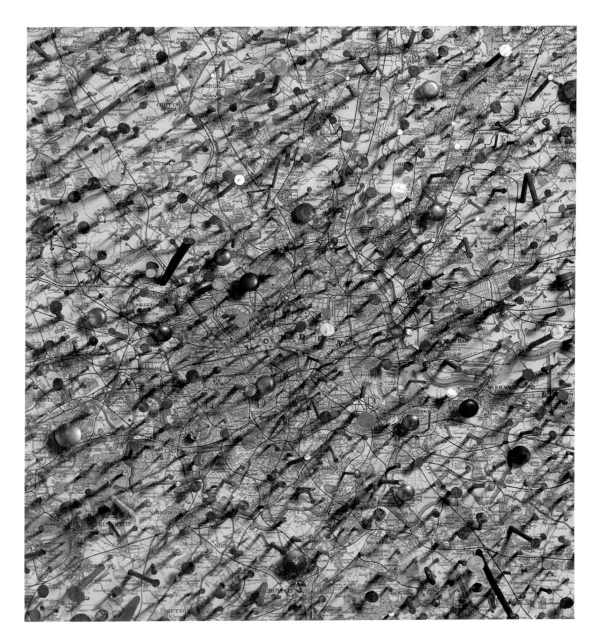

Chris Kenny, *Fetish Map of London I* (detail), 2000
Mixed media box construction, 21 x 26½ x 3¼ inches
Collection of Museum of London
Photo courtesy of England & Co. Gallery, London

"Maps are already fetishes of a type," the artist has written. "They draw up associations of home and abroad, the known and the unknown, belonging and longing. In my *Fetish Map of London* I combine their sophisticated code with a more primal symbolism of nailing, jewelling, and pinpointing."

Life in Los Angeles

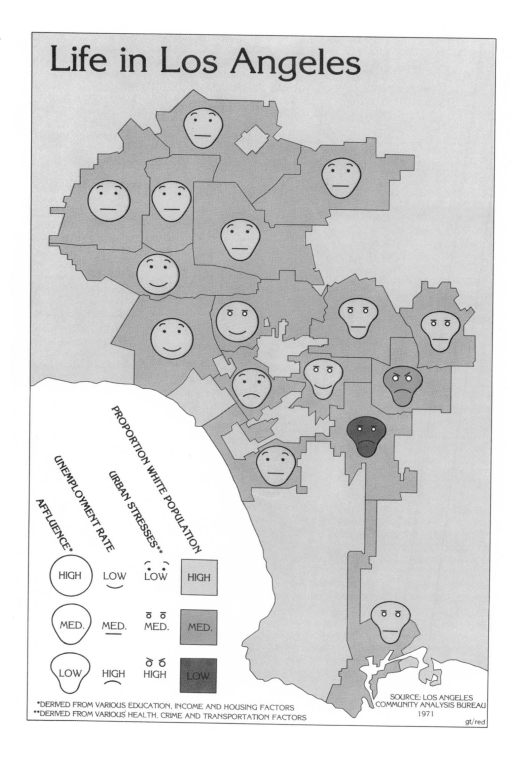

PROPORTION WHITE POPULATION

URBAN STRESSES**

UNEMPLOYMENT RATE

AFFLUENCE*

AFFLUENCE*	UNEMPLOYMENT RATE	URBAN STRESSES**	PROPORTION WHITE POPULATION
HIGH	LOW	LOW	HIGH
MED.	MED.	MED.	MED.
LOW	HIGH	HIGH	LOW

*DERIVED FROM VARIOUS EDUCATION, INCOME AND HOUSING FACTORS
**DERIVED FROM VARIOUS HEALTH, CRIME AND TRANSPORTATION FACTORS

SOURCE: LOS ANGELES
COMMUNITY ANALYSIS BUREAU
1971

gt/red

Istvan Banyai, *Ecological L.A.,* 1990
Created for inclusion in Spade & Archer's
50 Maps of L.A. by J. C. Suarés
(New York: H. M. Gousha, 1990)
Courtesy of the artist

Banyai, a New York–based illustrator, created
a base map on which Spade & Archer noted
sixteen Los Angeles locations representing a
sampling of best and worst environmental
achievements—from storm drains spewing
pathogens and industrial waste into the Pacific
to film producer David Zucker's electric car.

LEFT:
Eugene Turner, *Life in Los Angeles,* 1971

Turner, a geography professor at California
State University, made this map/chart as an
experiment in presenting multiple variables in a
way that people can readily grasp. To do so he
uses Chernoff Faces, developed by Herman
Chernoff on the theory that people are sensitive to subtle differences in facial expressions,
and thus able to comprehend complex data
when it is assigned one of eleven facial charac-
teristics (e.g., eyebrow slope, mouth curvature,
pupil size). In Turner's map, each of the variables is an aggregation of multiple sources of
data; for example, stress levels are gauged in
response to a number of lifestyle factors. The
map achieves its end: one knows its point
before reading the data headings.

Guillermo Kuitca, *Untitled (San Francisco)*, 1995
Oil and acrylic on canvas, 76 x 79 inches
Collection of John and Francis Bowes, San Francisco
Courtesy of Sperone Westwater, New York

Giullermo Kuitca, *Untitled,* 1989
Oil on vinyl-covered mattress (3 parts),
86⅝ x 55⅛ inches each, 86⅝ x 165⅛ inches overall
Collection of Herbert Cummings Charitable Trust
Courtesy of Sperone Westwater, New York

In Kuitca's artistic considerations of the human condition, the
Argentinean-born artist examines the spaces people occupy,
"the silent theaters of human interaction." What is private
becomes public, and vice versa—as with a city mapped in
bones, or mattresses marked with road maps to untold
destinations.

Ellsworth Kelly, *Fields on a Map (Meschers, Gironde)*, 1950
Collage in four parts, 25⅞ x 72 inches

The influential abstract artist Ellsworth Kelly is known for
large, often monochromatic paintings of geometric shapes.
These bear little similarity to his complex drawings of the late
1940s and early 50s, yet in these early works he began to
develop the reduced geometric forms for which he is so well
known. During this period he lived in France and was inspired
by the topographical grids of cultivated fields he saw there.
Another story claims that he found a map in a Paris bookstall,
transcribed its routes, and used them to create a grid form
that became *Fields on a Map*.

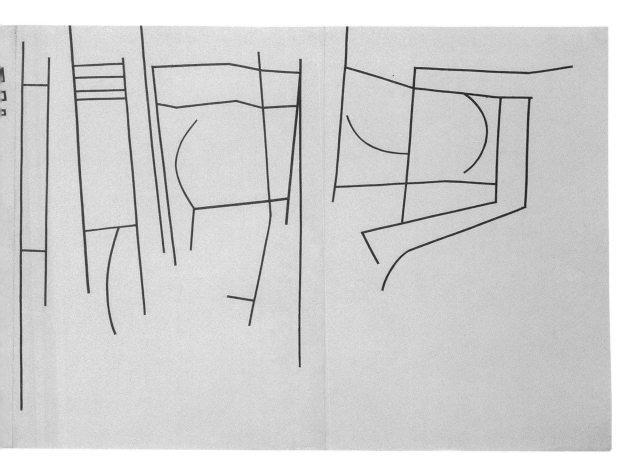

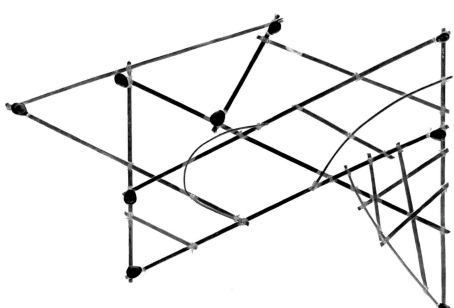

Marshall Islands navigation chart, c. 1960
Catalogue No. 398230, Department of Anthropology, Smithsonian Institution, Washington. D.C.

The stick charts of the Marshall Islanders, made of palm ribs tied with coconut fiber and shells or pieces of coral to indicate islands, are tools for studying ocean patterns in the surrounding South Pacific. The charts show the relationship between wave masses, or swells, and land masses.

Allied Advertising artists,
Whimsical Map of Hollywood,
1937
Photo-process poster on paper,
13 x 17 inches
Courtesy of George Glazer Gallery,
www.georgeglazer.com

One of the earliest souvenir maps of Tinseltown. From the reverse side: "Hollywood! Where stars are born, dreams are realized, and hearts are broken; where fortunes are made and fortunes are lost; Hollywood, fickle mistress of the cinema world, beckons you to its enchanted city."

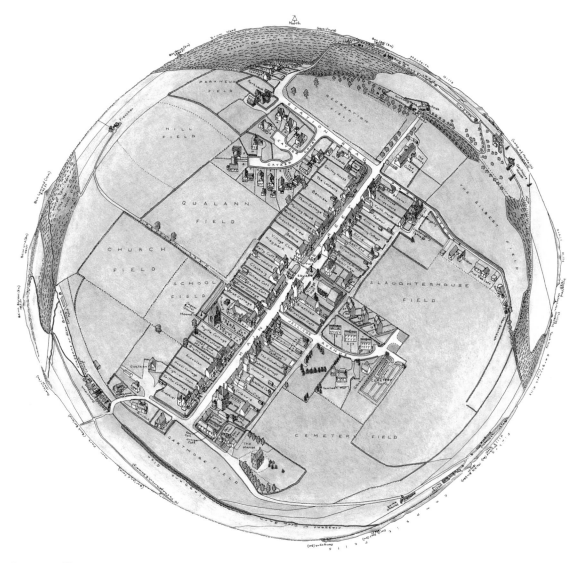

Gartmore Village Map Group, *Gartmore Village Map* (detail), 1994
25 x 23½ inches
Gartmore Heritage Society. Reproduced by permission

Common Ground is an organization founded in London in 1983 to promote the cultural heritage of areas in Britain and celebrate their local distinctiveness and histories. The map of Gartmore was created as part of the Parish Maps project, initiated by Common Ground, whose message is, in short: "Know your place—make a map of it!" The project encourages the creation of local maps by the people, for the people. Their booklet states, "By making parish maps and putting on them the places and features that you love and displaying them in a prominent position in the neighborhood, there is a better chance that these things will not only be recognized and enjoyed by others, but respected and protected as well." Over two thousand parish maps have been created since the project's inception.

Ten members of the community of Gartmore, Scotland, formed a committee and circulated a questionnaire to gather as much relevant information as possible for use in preparing their village map. The group chose a circular format to reflect the village's hilltop location and give a sense of the surrounding panoramic views. Thus the fisheye-lens projection gives some idea of what a person in the village sees on the horizon. By the end of 2001 the group had sold over 1,400 maps and donated the proceeds to Children's Hospice Association Scotland.

Various artists, *Common Ground Apple Map* (detail), 1993
Common Ground. Reproduced by permission

This poster/map, also from Common Ground, celebrates
orchards, diversity, and local distinctiveness by showing the
many varieties of apple grown across Britain.

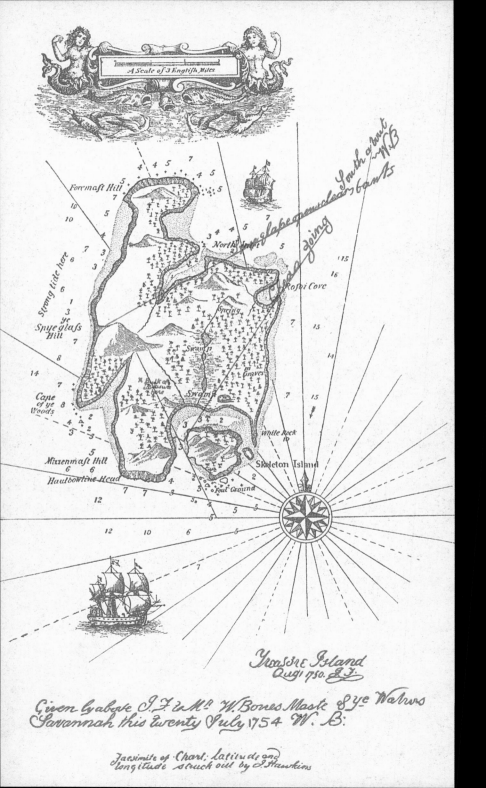

A Scale of 3 English Miles

Foremast Hill

Strong tide here

ye
Spye glass
Hill

Cape
of ye
Woods

Mizzenmast Hill

Haulbowline Head

North Inlet

Spring

Swamp

Bulk of
Tresure

Swamp

Skeleton Island

White Rock

Foot Ground

Graves

Rossi Cove

Cape opens clear of banks

South about N.B.

tide going

TREASURE ISLAND
Augt 1750. J.F.

Given by above J.F. & Mr W. Bones Maste of ye Walrus
Savannah this Twenty July 1754 W. B:

Facsimile of Chart: latitude and
longitude struck out by J. Hawkins

Realms of Fantasy

I made the map of the island; it was elaborately and (I thought) beautifully coloured; the shape of it took my fancy beyond expression; it contained harbours that pleased me like sonnets; and with the unconsciousness of the predestined, I ticketed my performance *Treasure Island*. I am told there are people who do not care for maps, and I find it hard to believe. The names, the shapes of the woodlands, the courses of the roads and rivers, the prehistoric footsteps of man still distinctly traceable up hill and down dale, the mills and the ruins, the ponds and the ferries, per–haps the *Standing Stone* or the *Druidic Circle* on the heath; here is an inexhaustible fund of interest for any man with eyes to see, or tuppenceworth of imagination to understand with. No child but must remember lay–ing his head in the grass, staring into the infinitesimal forest, and seeing it grow populous with fairy armies. Somewhat in this way, as I pored upon my map of *Treasure Island*, the future characters of the book began to appear there visibly among imaginary woods; and their brown faces and bright weapons peeped out upon me from unexpected quarters, as they passed to and fro, fighting and hunting treasure, on these few square inches of a flat projection.

—*Robert Louis Stevenson,*
Treasure Island

The Lure of Maps in Arthur Ransome

HUGH BROGAN

SUSCEPTIBILITY TO the beauty and suggestiveness of maps may not be a universal human trait—what is?—but the works of many storytellers show that it is at least very common. The early editions of Arthur Ransome's *Swallows and Amazons* (first published in 1930) carry a Stephen Spurrier endpaper map that had much to do with attracting its first readers. In it (all green and blue and black) a Lancashire lake is transformed into a wild surmise at the end of the known world, surrounded by forests and great mountains. Native settlements dot its shore, an octopus can be seen lurking in a lagoon, a stately galleon runs before the breath of the South Wind, a whale spouts among the islands, and a splendid pair of pirates serve as supporters for the coat-of-arms of the Swallows and the bare-breasted Amazons. At one end of the lake is the Antarctic, at the other the Arctic—marked "unexplored." Spurrier's map is not only a thing of beauty and wonder in itself, it also expresses the underlying theme of the book, indeed of all Arthur Ransome's writing for children: the transmuting power of the young imagination. It is worse than lamentable that in later editions it was replaced by a pedestrian, ill-drawn substitute.

Ransome was a powerfully original writer for children, but he worked in a well-established tradition that almost dictated that he provide maps for his books. The tradition seems to have started with *Treasure Island* (1883), to which there is constant reference in *Swallows*; Robert Louis Stevenson's example was soon followed by Rider Haggard in *King Solomon's Mines* (1886). In the twentieth century a flood followed: Erskine Childers's *The Riddle of the Sands* (1903), L. Frank Baum's *Wizard of Oz* books, A. A. Milne's *Winnie-the-Pooh* (1926), J. R. R. Tolkien's *The Hobbit* (1937), and many, many others. Maps were drawn for new editions of Rudyard Kipling's *The Jungle Book* and Richard Jefferies's *Bevis* (1932). The tradition ran on after Ransome, by way of Tolkien's *The Lord of the Rings,* C. S. Lewis's *Chronicles of Narnia,* and Ursula Le Guin's *Earthsea* cycle. Perhaps it still persists.

The device of a map to excite and assist readers' fancy seems obvious enough nowadays, but it is a comparatively recent invention. *Robinson Crusoe* (another reference point for the Swallows) was sent into the world without a map. It was not until the late nineteenth century that techniques of reproduction grew sufficiently cheap and various to make the great Victorian age of illustration possible, and maps are, after all, only a form of illustration. Nevertheless, it is probably not a coincidence that the magic of maps was first exploited when the British Empire was at its height. For several centuries the history of the world was dominated by the Europeans, as explorers, traders, and conquerors, and among those nations the British were eventually preeminent. *Treasure Island* looks back joyously to one moment in the rise of the empire (the map is carefully dated by its first owner, Captain Flint, to "August, 1750")—the age of pirates on the Spanish Main; and Rider Haggard, in *King Solomon's*

was influenced by Jefferies, but looks as if Shepard may have studied Spurrier's map for *Swallows and Amazons*. All these maps are deliberate re-imaginings of actual geography, yet in the end it is of limited interest that Jefferies, A. A. Milne, and Arthur Ransome made use of identifiable locations. It is the process that counts. This is even truer of the maps in Tolkien, Lewis, and Le Guin: they were drawn to give concreteness

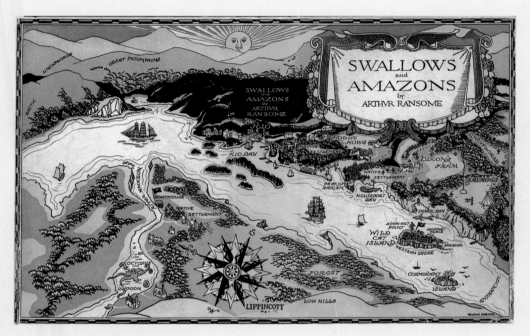

Mines, exploited the legend of Africa as the Dark Continent, which, even as he wrote, was being explored and annexed by the European powers, Britain as usual in the lead. In my childhood, long ago, I was taught to take pride in the fact that so much of the world's map was colored red, to show British imperial sovereignty; how much more exciting it must have been when the red tide was spreading further and further in every decade!

If the idea of the fictional map was born of history, its exploitation became as diverse as the authors and artists who took it up. E. H. Shepard's map of the Bevis country is palpably related to his map of the Pooh books, and in some details (the River Nile, the Forest, Fir Tree Gulf) not only reminds us how much Ransome

to wholly imagined worlds. Statements are made in the texts that can be verified by the maps; details in the maps can be confirmed or explained in the texts. The map is a powerful tool of what Tolkien calls "sub-creation": the invention of a secondary world.

Arthur Ransome was well aware of these considerations: they can all be derived from his theory of illustration, which was that pictures in a tale should be useful, not merely ornamental. They should tell the story, as fully and precisely as possible (which is why he was always dissatisfied with the illustrations supplied for his work by professional artists, and eventually drew everything himself, in spite of his very limited skills as a draftsman). He went further than any other children's writer known to me by putting mapmaking at the very center of his fictions. When for the first time the Swallow and her crew sail off to Wild Cat Island, the children combine in their play the games of being mariners and of being explorers. Captain John carries with him an everyday map of the lake, but says, "We'll give everything our own names, of course." At the end of the book the Swallows' "chart" is still incomplete ("There are lots of names you haven't got," says Captain Nancy), but that is a welcome spur to further exploration.

John had entered the explorers' new names on his chart ("Shark Bay," "Amazon River," "Rio"), but the mapping aspect of the stories did not at once become a major theme. Ransome always made sure that every volume had its own map, however, for even in the "lake" stories (*Swallowdale, Winter Holiday, Pigeon Post, The Picts and the Martyrs*) the scene is never exactly repeated; new territories are explored every time, so new maps are needed. The first big innovation comes with *Peter Duck*, a tale of piracy invented, recounted, and illustrated (we are told) by the Swallows and Amazons themselves. The influence of *Treasure Island* hangs heavily on the story (but not, in my judgment, to its detriment), never more so than in the map of Crab Island, where Peter Duck's treasure is buried, and which is clearly inspired by Captain Flint's map. The overall likeness is superficial (Ransome was too good a writer to plagiarize), but perhaps it gave him pleasure to capture the superficiality, so true is it to life. Confronted with the need to depict a Crab Island, children would inevitably turn to *Treasure Island* for ideas: Ransome made sure that his did so.

In the hands of the Swallows and Amazons the great, brutal, imperial adventure has shrunk to a harmless game (as, earlier, the wars of the eighteenth century produced the game "French and English," or the conquest of the Wild West set all children to playing at cowboys and Indians), but it may have come to embarrass Ransome slightly. The Swallows, venturing across their unknown sea for the first time, dealt with the steamers and pleasure-craft criss-crossing the lake by ignoring them or, at most, deeming them mere "native" boats, just as the farms ashore are dismissed

as "native" settlements. The Swallows are ready to have dealings with the natives if they must (they get their morning milk from Dixon's Farm), but they do not altogether trust them. This part of the fantasy gradually fades out. In *Winter Holiday,* the lake being frozen, the children become competitors in a race to the North Pole. In *Pigeon Post* they are prospectors for gold.

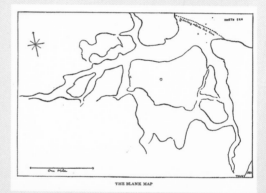

THE BLANK MAP

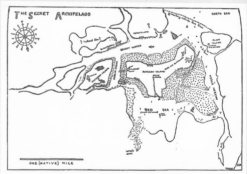

THE MAP: WITH BLACKBERRY COAST AND PEEWITLAND

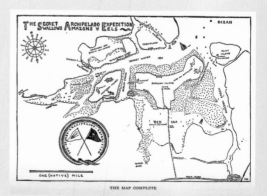

THE MAP COMPLETE

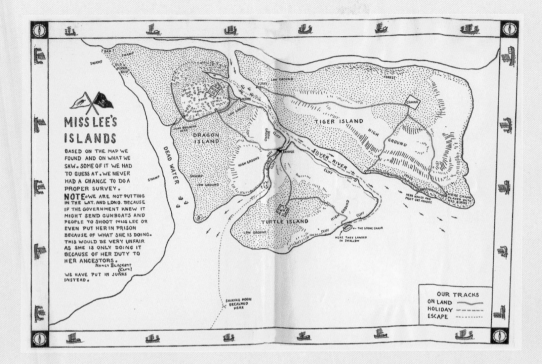

MISS LEE'S
ISLANDS

BASED ON THE MAP WE
FOUND AND ON WHAT WE
SAW. SOME OF IT WE HAD
TO GUESS AT. WE NEVER
HAD A CHANCE TO DO A
PROPER SURVEY.
NOTE.WE ARE NOT PUTTING
IN THE LAT. AND LONG. BECAUSE
IF THE GOVERNMENT KNEW IT
MIGHT SEND GUNBOATS AND
PEOPLE TO SHOOT MISS LEE OR
EVEN PUT HER IN PRISON
BECAUSE OF WHAT SHE IS DOING.
THIS WOULD BE VERY UNFAIR
AS SHE IS ONLY DOING IT
BECAUSE OF HER DUTY TO
HER ANCESTORS.
         NANCY BLACKETT
              (CAPT.)
WE HAVE PUT IN JUNKS
INSTEAD.

OUR TRACKS
ON LAND ————
HOLIDAY – – – –
ESCAPE ········

In *Coot Club* the protagonists form a bird protection society; in the other book about the Norfolk Broads, *The Big Six,* they are detectives. In all these stories, maps play a key part in the plot, in addition to assisting the reader. The most exciting are probably the charts of the North Sea in *We Didn't Mean to Go to Sea,* in which we can follow John's desperate course as he negotiates fog, night, shoals, tides, and arrogant steamers in his attempt to find sea-room and save the Goblin from wreck.

But maps are central to the narratives of *Secret Water, Missee Lee,* and *Great Northern?.* In the first the exploring game is revived: the Swallows' mission is to produce an accurate map of the Walton Backwaters in Essex, as if they were members of the Ordinance Survey. In the other two books, the plots turn to the extreme importance of concealing geographical information: the whereabouts of pirate islands and a rare bird's nest. In both instances the maps provide information and withhold it at the same time. They tantalize. They hint. They say just enough to engage a

child's imagination and curiosity. This may be taken as the mapmaker's attempt simultaneously to convey, as before, the allure of mapping while preserving the sense of mystery at the edge of the world. Together these somewhat contradictory impulses embodied, in Ransome's view, the vision of childhood, the vision so completely realized in his books.

Hugh Brogan is research professor of history at the University of Essex and the author of The Life of Arthur Ransome *(1984).*

PAGE 150: The cover of the first edition of *Swallows and Amazons* (London: Jonathan Cape, 1930), illustrated by Stephen Spurrier. PAGE 151: The cover of the American edition of *Swallows and Amazons* (New York: J. B. Lippincott, 1958), illustrated by Helene Carter. PAGE 152: A selection of maps from *Secret Water* (London: Jonathan Cape, 1939), illustrated by Arthur Ransome. PAGE 153: Endsheet map from *Missee Lee* (London: Jonathan Cape, 1941), illustrated by Arthur Ransome. Images reprinted by permission of the Random House Group. Ltd.

Richard Becker, *Voodoo Isle*
From *Bloodthirsty Pirate Tales* #6
(Mountain View, California:
Black Swan Press, 1997)

Lordy Rodriguez, *Island in the Center,* 2002
Ink on paper, 46 x 32 inches
Courtesy of Clementine Gallery, New York City

This piece is part of a series of abstract map images without words, entitled "Dislocations"; it is one of two ongoing bodies of map-related artwork Rodriguez is building. The other, "States," is a multi-year project to rearrange the United States, including adding five new ones.

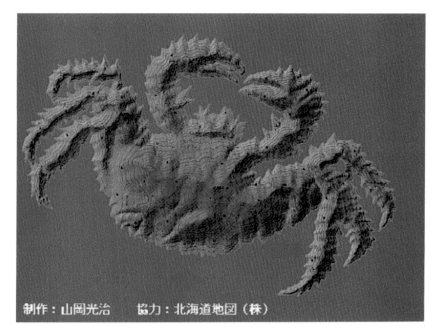

制作：山岡光治　協力：北海道地図（株）

制作：山岡光治　協力：北海道地図（株）

Imaginary Animal Islands, 1999
Designed by Mitsuharu Yamaoka (Planning Department GSI); drawn by Takeshi Hattori, Toshiyuki Okeya and Hiroki Sasahara
(Hokkaido Regional Survey Department GSI); digital shading by Hokkaido Chizu Co Ltd.
Geographical Survey Institute, www.gsi.go.jp

A group of cartographers with the Hokkaido Regional Survey Department, Japan, created a series of six imaginary islands, each in the form of an animal native to Hokkaido. Realizing that their collective passion for mapmaking began in childhood, they decided—just for fun—to return to some of their early imaginative musings. "When we were young, we gazed at maps all day long and tried to imagine the landscapes and cultures they represented," the collaborators write on their website. "We found that the sparks of interest ignited so long ago still burn within."

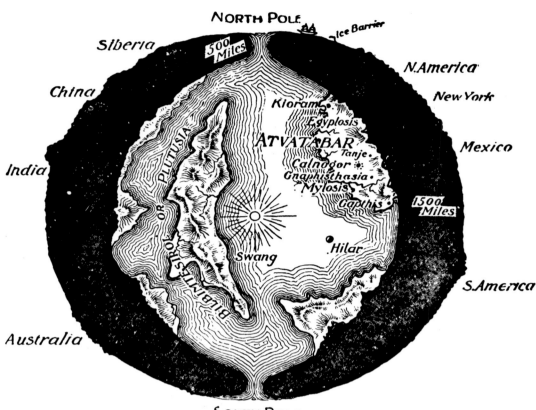

The Interior World
Artist and date unknown
From *Goddess of Atvatabar: Being the History of the Interior World and Conquest of Atvatabar*
by William R. Bradshaw (New York: J. F. Douthitt, 1892)

This map comes from one of a slew of speculative novels inspired by the "hollow Earth" theory (most notably Jules Verne's *Journey to the Center of the Earth,* 1864). In the seventeenth century British astronomer Edmond Halley (of Halley's Comet fame) first advanced the theory, which was expanded in the nineteenth century by John Cleves Symmes, an eccentric American who believed that at each of the Earth's poles was an opening (popularly called a "Symmes Hole") where the oceans flowed in and out. The interior of the Earth, he claimed, was inhabited. He traveled around the country sharing his theory and raising money to send an expedition to the hole at the North Pole. Symmes went so far as to petition Congress for money to finance the voyage, and the proposal received twenty-five votes.

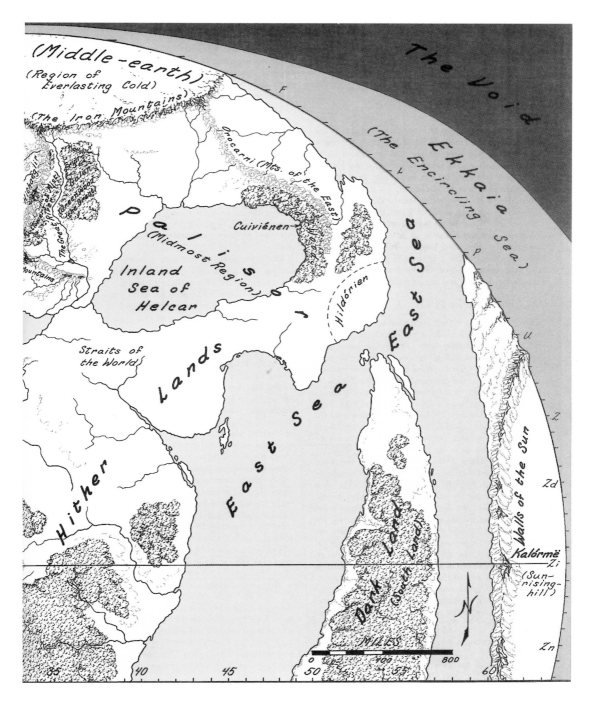

The map contains the following labels:

(Middle-earth)
(Region of Everlasting Cold)
(The Iron Mountains)
Orocarni (Mts. of the East)
The Void
Ekkaia (The Encircling Sea)
Cuiviénen
Palisor (Midmost Region)
Inland Sea of Helcar
Hildórien
East Sea
Straits of the World
Lands
Hither
Walls of the Sun
Dark Land (South Land)
Kalórmë (Sun-rising-hill)
N
MILES
0   50   400   800
35   40   45   50   60

Karen Wynn Fonstad, *First Age of Arda* (detail)
From *The Atlas of Middle-Earth,* Revised Edition
(Boston: Houghton Mifflin, 1991)
© 1991 by Karen Wynn Fonstad
Reprinted by permission of Houghton Mifflin Company
All rights reserved

This atlas of the realms described in J. R. R. Tolkien's books is just one of several guides to fantasy worlds by Fonstad, including *The Atlas of Pern* (based on the *Dragonriders of Pern* series by Anne McCaffrey), *Atlas of the Land* (*The Chronicles of Thomas Covenant the Unbeliever,* by Stephen R. Donaldson), and *Atlas of the Dragonlance World* (*Dragonlance* series by Margaret Weis).

Joyce Kozloff, *Calvino's Cities on the Amazon,* 1995
Collage, watercolor and acrylic on paper, mounted on fabric with audiotape
60 x 112 inches
Courtesy DC Moore Gallery, New York City

In *Invisible Cities,* a novel by Italo Calvino, Marco Polo describes fifty-six imaginary cities in the empire of Kublai Khan. Kozloff created *Cities on the Amazon* as a tribute to the book, and in exhibitions the artwork appears with a soundtrack of a voice reading key passages. "After many readings," Kozloff said in an interview, "I realized that the cities, all named for women, are metaphors for male fantasies (among other things). I isolated something that moved me from each story. Going down the Amazon is another adventure fantasy, and so I collapsed the two preoccupations into one work."

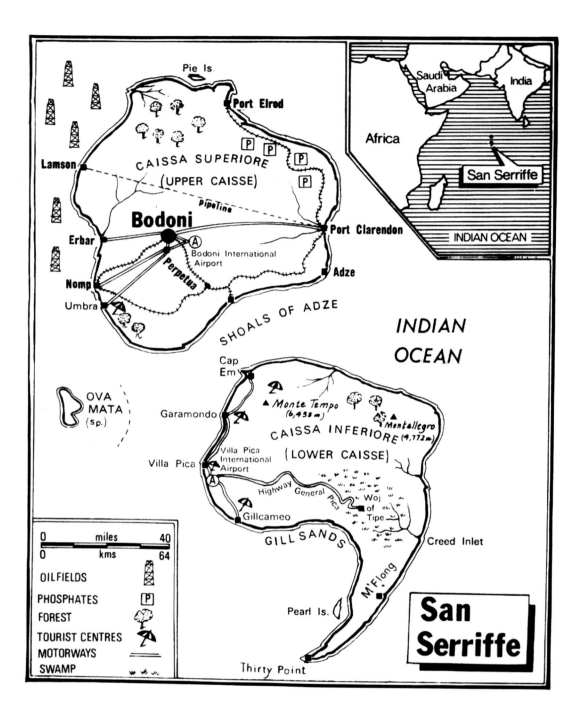

San Seriffe: An April Fool's Joke Map, 1 April 1978
Artist unknown
© The Guardian, London

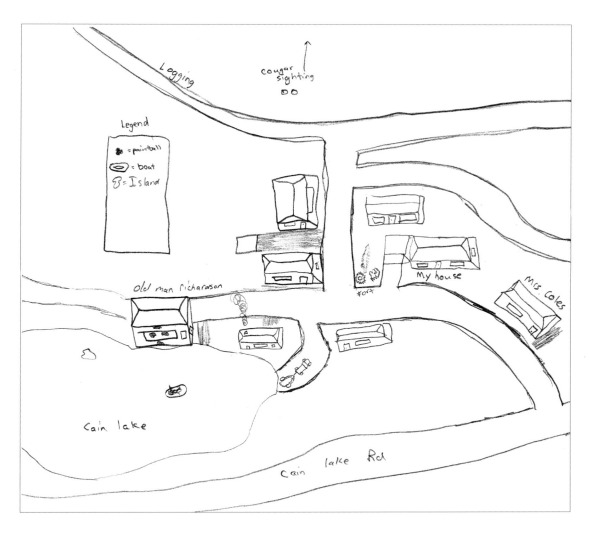

Michael Jensen, *Untitled* **(revenge map), 2003**

Whenever Michael takes his inflatable boat out onto the lake, Old Man Richardson gets out his BB gun ... or so Michael claims. The twelve-year-old artist has made a fantasy map of a paintball payback.

FOLLOWING PAGES:

Julie Mehretu, *Looking Back to a Bright New Future,* **2003**
Ink and acrylic on canvas, 95 x 119 inches
Courtesy of The Project, New York

Born in Ethiopia in 1970, artist Julie Mehretu grew up in Michigan. She has studied in Senegal and the U.S. and has exhibited in Harlem, Houston, and Ghent, Belgium. Not surprisingly, her paintings have an international flavor and frequently can be seen, in her words, as "story maps of no location." In *Looking Back to a Bright New Future*, abstract forms coalesce into a map of the world, apparently exploding outward in a colorful Big Bang.

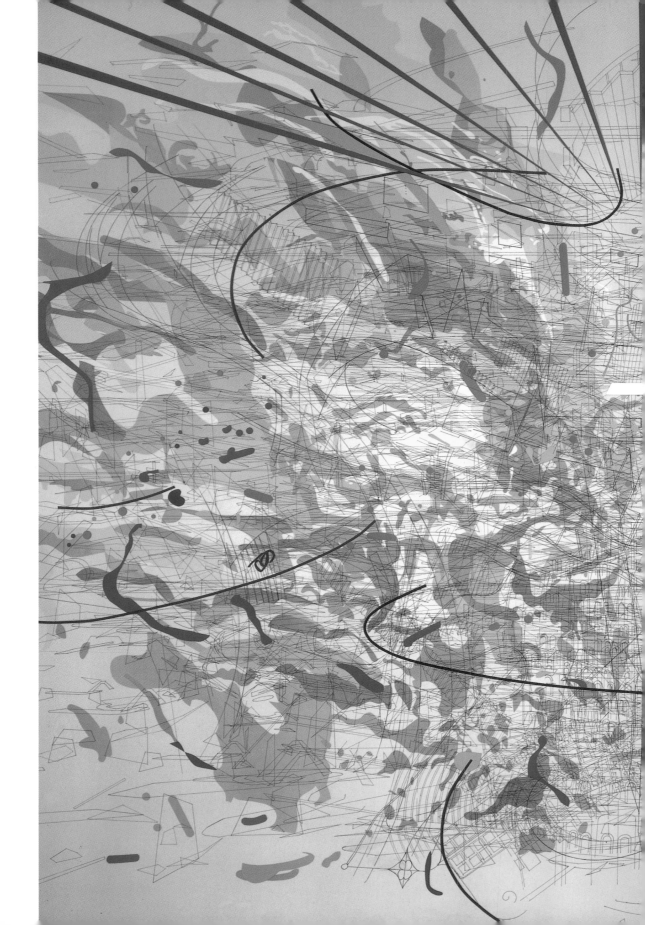

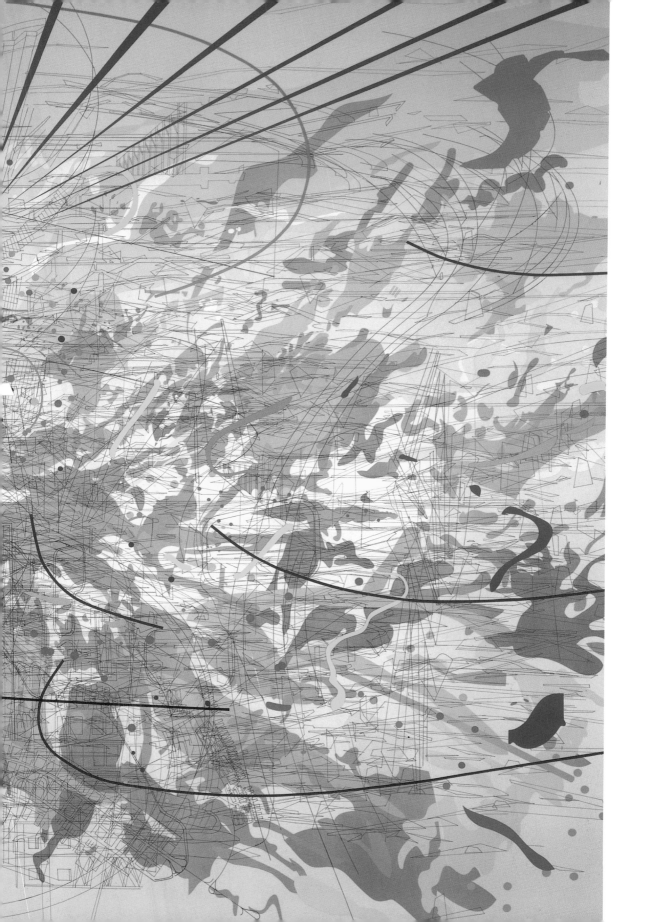

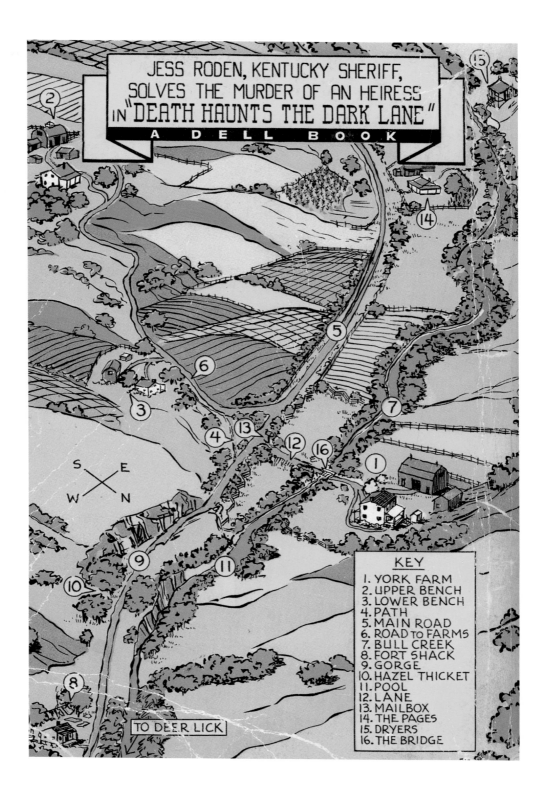

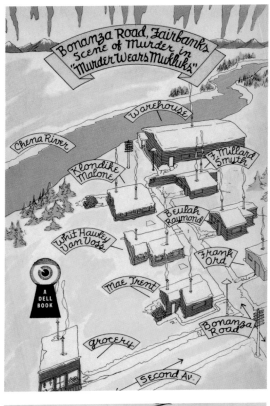

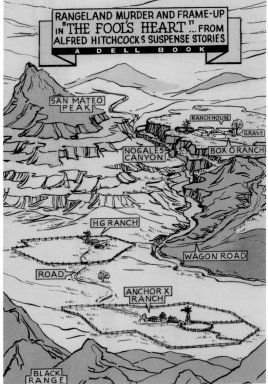

Back cover art:
Death Haunts the Dark Lane by A. B. Cunningham
(New York: Dell Books, 1948)
Murder Wears Mukluks by Eunice Mays Boyd
(New York: Dell Books, 1955)
The Strawstack Murders by Dorothy Cameron Disney
(New York: Dell Books, 1939)
Suspense Stories selected by Alfred Hitchcock
(New York: Dell Books, 1949)

Through the 1940s Dell Books built a highly successful line of paperback novels by incorporating maps on the books' back covers. The "mapbacks" were works of genre fiction—in mystery, romance, Western, and science fiction categories—and featured a map or diagram that depicted a central location from each plot line. Between 1941 and 1952, various illustrators created 552 original maps for the books. Mapbacks sold for twenty-five cents apiece; today they are collector's items.

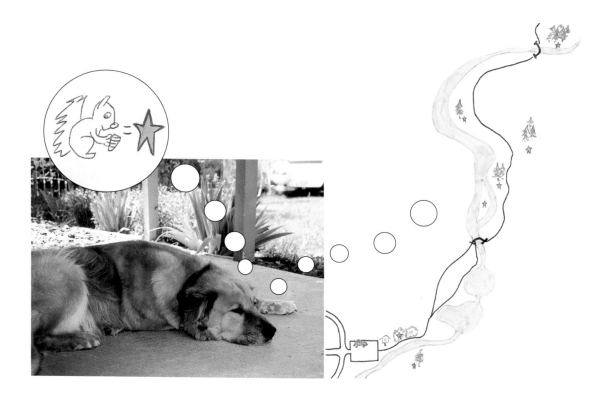

John Held, Jr., *A Dog's Idea of the Ideal Country Estate,* 1920s
From *The Works of John Held, Jr.* (Ives Washburn, 1931)
Image reproduced with permission of Illustration House and the estate of Margaret Held

TOP LEFT:
All Roads Lead to the Doghouse, from a placemat from Bob Murray's Doghouse restaurant, Seattle
Artist and date unknown. Courtesy of MSCUA, University of Washington Libraries, UW 22218z

BOTTOM LEFT:
Neera Tetreault, *Cyrus's Squirrel Map of Spring Creek, Noting All the Choicest Hang-Outs of Those Elusive Critters, the Chasing of Which Gives Such Meaning to Life,* 2003

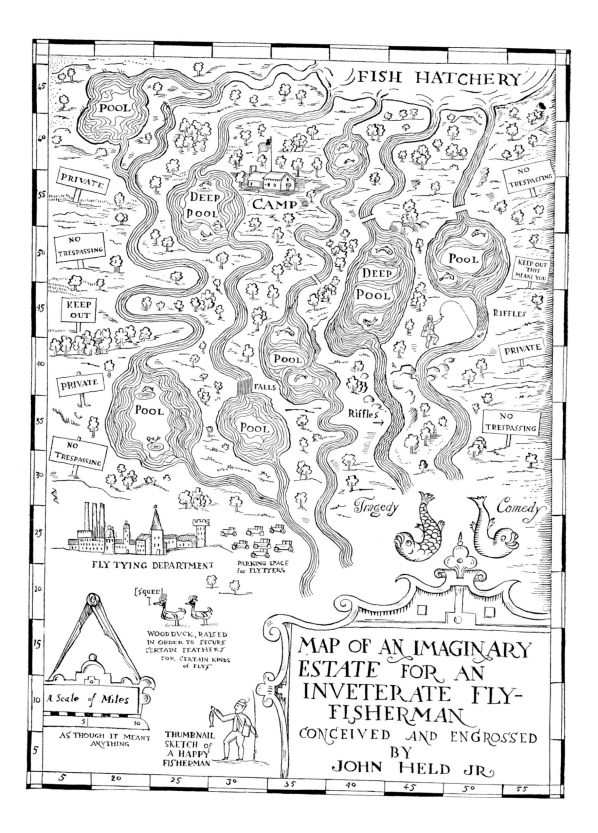

LEFT:

John Held, Jr., *Map of an Imaginary Estate for an Inveterate Fly-Fisherman*, 1920s
Image reproduced with permission of Illustration House and the estate of Margaret Held

Sugaroku, a children's board game of the journey to paradise, Japan
Artist and date unknown
Courtesy of Redstone Press

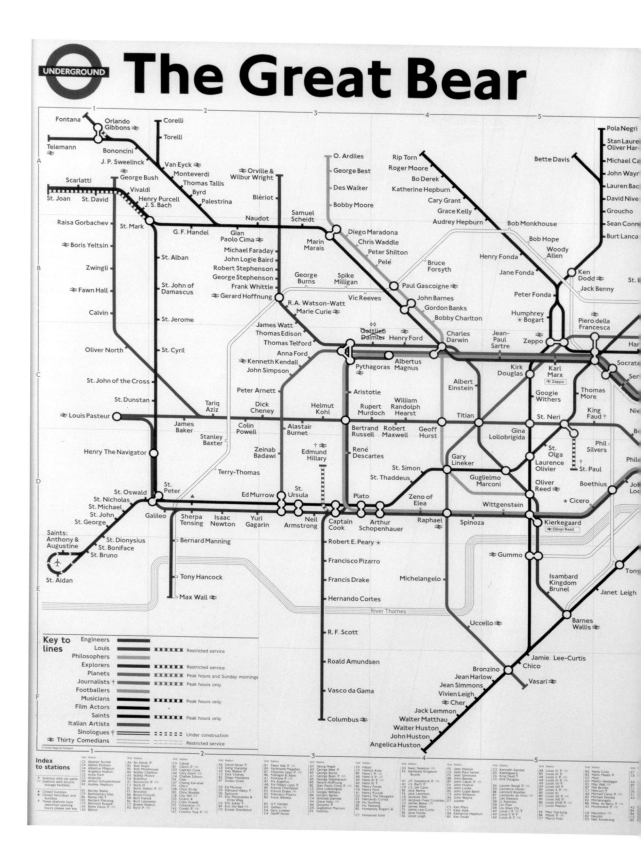

Simon Patterson, *The Great Bear,* 1992
Four-color lithographic print in anodized
aluminum frame, 43 x 53 x 2 inches
Courtesy of Lisson Gallery

In his art, Patterson transmutes familiar information classification systems—maps, slide
rules, air traffic route plans, and star charts,
for example—by imposing new information
on them. The map of London's Underground
(so effective in its 1930s graphic design that
it has become iconic) becomes something
else; tube riders can joy-ride among figures
of history and popular culture travel, traveling
from a philosopher to a newscaster and
passing a comedian, a newscaster, or a saint
on the way. Are the names placed at random,
or is there some method here? The reader
uses accepted mapping "rules" to try and
figure it out.

Rojan (Fedor Rojankowski), *Untitled*
Lithographic illustration from *Plouf*
(Paris: Flammarion, 1935)

RIGHT:
Rojan, *Terrain de Chasse,*
Lithographic illustration from *Froux le Lièvre* (Paris:
Flammarion, 1935)
By permission of the publisher

Rojankovsky (1891–1970), a Latvian artist known early in
his career as "Rojan," was an adept and adaptive illustrator—
of children's books and also of erotic fiction—in Paris in the
1920s and 30s; later, he settled in the U.S. Here, in two
examples from the Père Castor series of children's books,
he displays the bold style and colors of the fauvists.

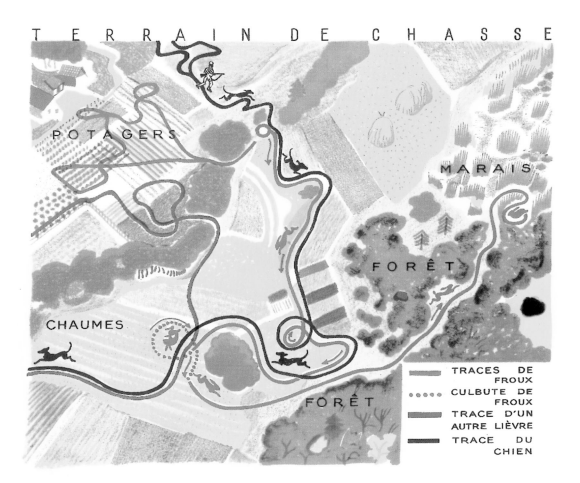

TERRAIN DE CHASSE

POTAGERS

MARAIS

FORÊT

CHAUMES

FORÊT

TRACES DE FROUX
CULBUTE DE FROUX
TRACE D'UN AUTRE LIÈVRE
TRACE DU CHIEN

FOLLOWING PAGES:
Mark Bennett, *Town of Mayberry,* **199.**
Lithograph, 24¼ x 36¼ inches
Courtesy of Mark Moore Gallery, Santa Monica

Mark Bennett is a Beverly Hills postal worker with a Wilshire
Boulevard route. He grew up in Chattanooga, where his family spent leisure time touring suburban model home sites. At
home with his brother, Bennett drew houses and watched
countless hours of television to escape from an unhappy
childhood. As an adult, he began meticulously mapping the
settings for the sit-coms he had watched for years, and over
a twenty-year period he produced a series of forty plans,
mostly blueprints of houses. Bennett has said that the
process of mapping them made the places and the people
who lived there seem within reach—though both maps and
sit-coms call attention to their limited dimensions.

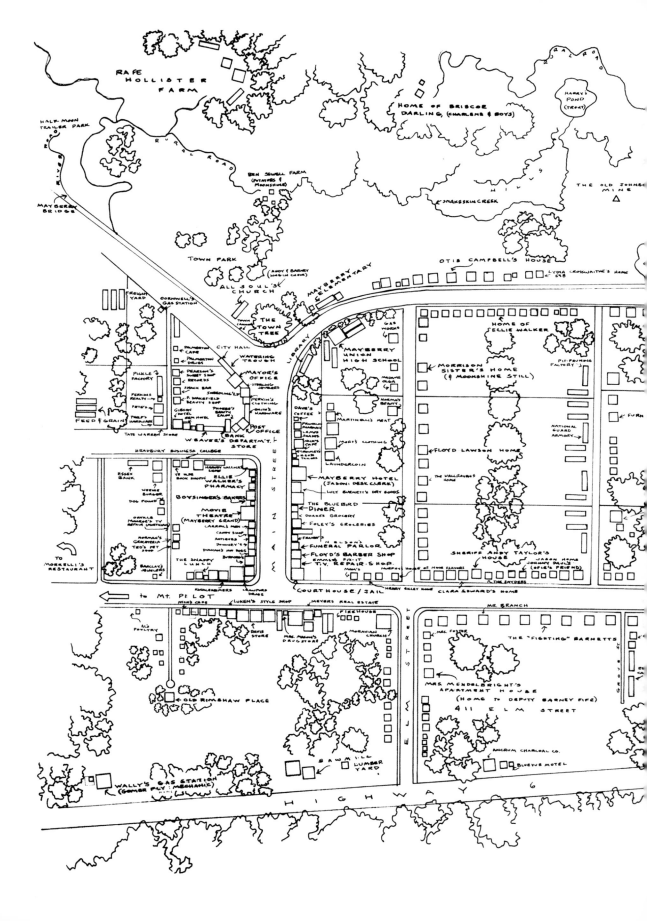

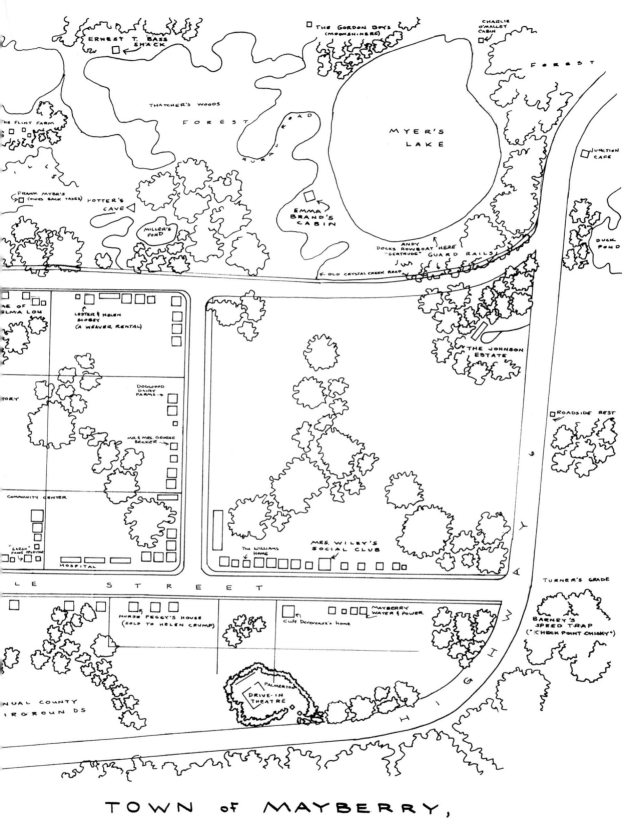

TOWN of MAYBERRY,
NORTH CAROLINA, U.S.A.

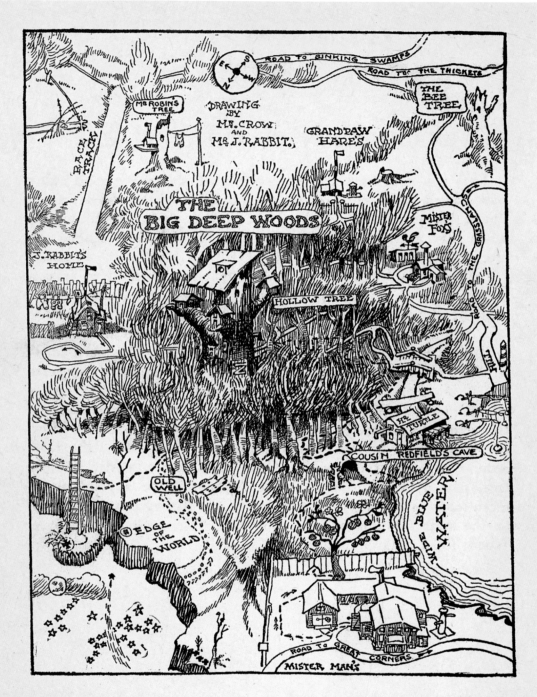

A NEW MAP OF THE HOLLOW TREE AND DEEP WOODS COUNTRY

A New Map of the Hollow Tree and Deep Woods Country
Artist unknown. From *Hollow Tree Nights and Days* by Albert
Bigelow Paine (New York: Harper & Bros. Publishers, 1915)

This map appears to have been inspired by E.H. Shepherd's
illustration of the Hundred-Acre Wood for *Winnie-the-Pooh*,
but in fact preceded it by eleven years.

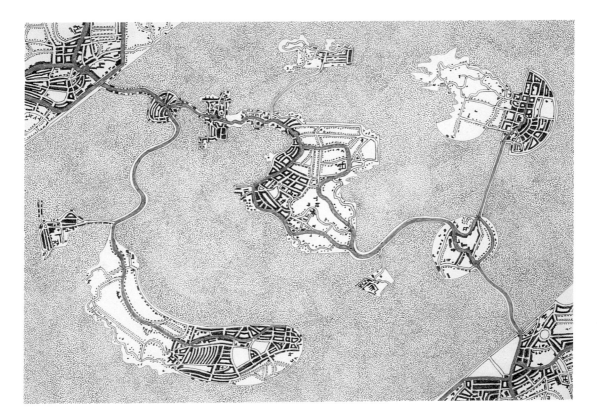

Michael the Cartographer, *Untitled*, **early 1980s**
Felt-tip pen on paper, 8 x 12 inches
Courtesy of the Musgrave-Kinley Outsider Collection

The late Victor Musgrave, a writer, filmmaker, and London gallery owner, was a champion of outsider artists and coorganized the groundbreaking 1979 Outsiders exhibition in London. Around the same period, Musgrave met a man called Michael and admired his cartographic drawings. The man would not part with them, but later sent two to Musgrave, who was unable to locate the artist thereafter. "We still hope he might turn up one day," says Monika Kinley, the Outsider Collection's current curator and caretaker.

FOLLOWING PAGES:
Quentin Blake, *Untitled*
From *Our Village* by John Yeoman
(New York: Atheneum, 1988)
Illustration © 1988 Quentin Blake
Reproduced by permission of Walker Books Ltd.

The map provides the front endsheets and sets the scene for rhymes about the memorable residents of a village, including the baker, Mr. Crumb; the absent-minded Dotty Lou, who is cared for by her cows; and Samuel Flowerbutts: "He's the smallest man I know, but whatever is in his garden seems to grow and grow and grow."

The
Blacksmith's

The School

Dr P
Hou

The Bakery

The
Village
Green

Mr
Pennin
Sh

Tabitha Tripp
lives here

Mr To
shop

Mr Flowerbutts' Garden

Podg

Mr Arkwright's
House
d Bicycle
hed

To the Swimming Pond ↑

Farmer
Parsnip's Farm

→

This is where
Lily Binns and
Elsie Crumb
live

Farmer Trott
Farm

The Scarecrow ────────→

on's

ral Store

The
Skating
Pond ────→

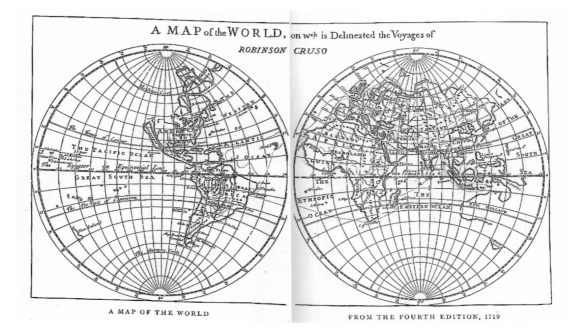

A Map of the World, on Which Is Delineated the Voyages of Robinson Crusoe
Artist unknown. From *The Life and Strange Surprising Adventures of Robinson Crusoe* by Daniel Defoe
(Boston: The Athenæum Press, 1916)

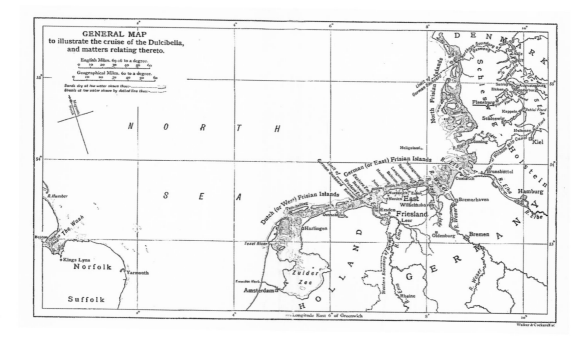

General Map to Illustrate the Cruise of the Dulcibella, and Matters Relating Thereto
Artist unknown. From *The Riddle of the Sands: A Record of Secret Service Recently Achieved by Erskine Childers*
(London: Smith, Elder & Co., 1904)

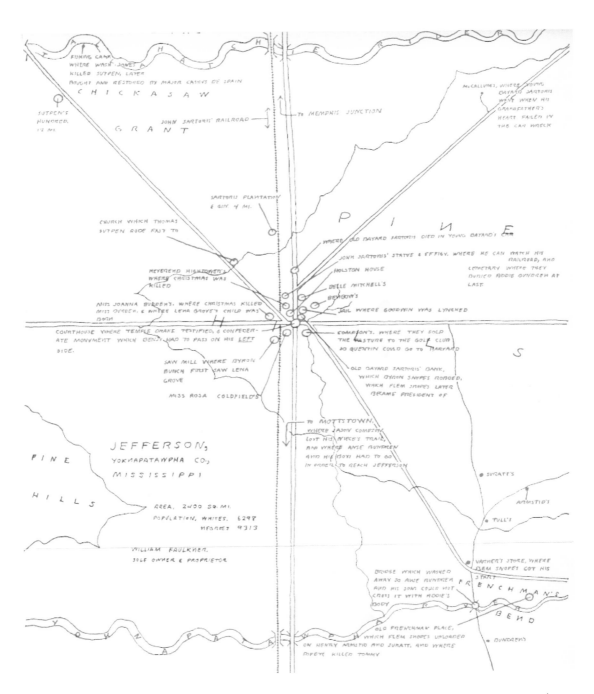

William Faulkner, *Map of Yoknapatawpha County*
From *Absalom, Absalom!* by William Faulkner
(New York: Random House, 1936)
© 1936 by William Faulkner and renewed 1964 by Estelle
Faulkner and Jill Faulkner Summers. Used by permission of
Random House, Inc. and Curtis Brown Group Ltd.

The Nobel Prize winner set several of his greatest novels—
including *The Sound and the Fury* (1929), *As I Lay Dying*
(1930), and *Light in August* (1932)—in this fictional county,
which in its geographic layout resembles Mississippi's
Lafayette County. The purpose of this map is more historical
than geographic, citing events that befall Faulkner's characters in *Absalom, Absalom!* and the earlier Yoknapatawpha
works. The effect is to make his fictional world seem almost
real, and to accent its grim, murderous nature.

Edward Gorey, *The Western Sea*
From *The Jumblies* by Edward Lear (New York: Young Scott Books, 1968)
Reprinted by permission of Donadio & Olson, Inc.
© 1968 by Edward Gorey

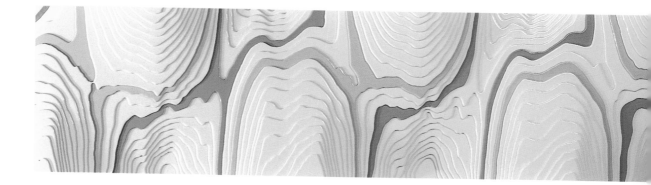

The Hills of the Chankly Bore

THE WESTERN SEA

BELOW:
Leo Saul Berk, *Hogbacks Back to Back,* 2002
MDF and tinted lacquer, 13 x 97 x 4 inches (diptych)
Collection of Ben and Aileen Krohn
Courtesy of Howard House, Seattle

Berk's three-dimensional topographical maps are actually
something else. The artist selects sheets of plywood for their
grain patterns and assembles shapes outlined in the wood.
Each grain line becomes a new level, a visual representation
of a tree's growth. The resulting sculptures are about form
and shape, but their clean surfaces evoke clear-cut hillsides
from whence the wood—in theory if not reality—has come.

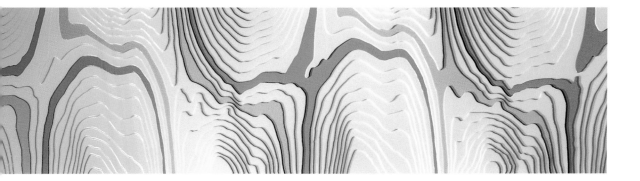

Wim Delvoye, *Atlas #2*, 2003
C-print on aluminum (edition of 6), 39⅜ x 49¼ inches
Sperone Westwater, New York

Delvoye published a catalog of paintings entitled *Atlas*,
which laid out an entire world of his imagining. More
recently the artist has created an enormous digital file
depicting a new version of that world, of which a detail
appears above.

Hal Aber, *Bermuda Triangle,* 1975
Mixed media, 22 x 28 inches
Courtesy of the artist

A subscription-based social studies publication, "Headline Focus Wall Maps" was published by Scholastic, Inc. and sent to junior and senior high school classes every two weeks. Most maps in the series focused on geography and socio-political topics (e.g., oil resources, unrest in northern Ireland, endangered species). Aber, the designer and art director of the series, gave this map a more light-hearted treatment.

Julia Ricketts, *Notations on a River,* 2001
Oil on canvas, 26 x 38 inches
Courtesy of Solomon
Fine Art, Seattle

Seattle painter Julia Ricketts often adopts an aerial viewpoint to explore the visual intersections of natural and man-made forms. The mapping elements laid onto the landscape allude to the human tendency to quantify and divide land, and frame a scene both scenic and utilitarian.

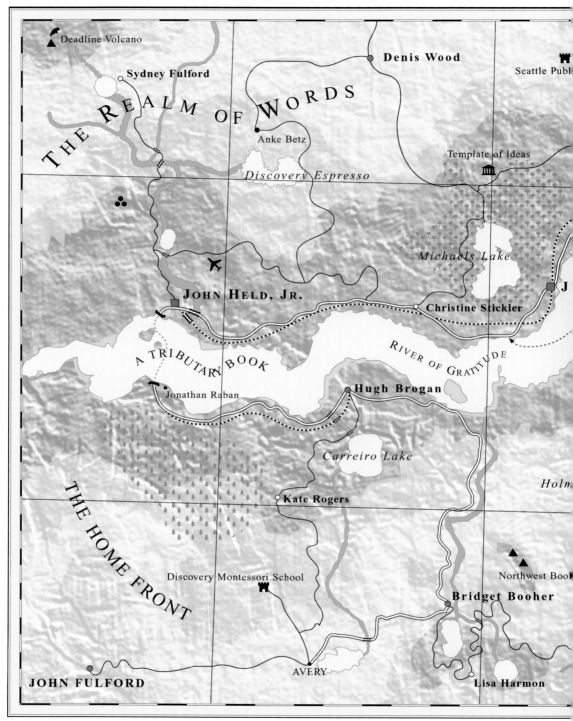

The River of Gratitude, 2003
A customized map created online at www.worldofexperience.com
© Meteor Press

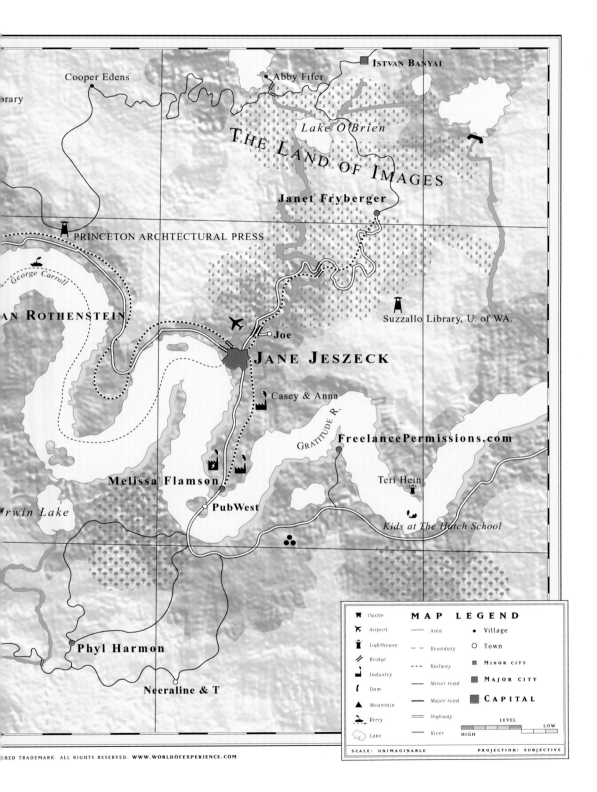

Cooper Edens

Istvan Banyai

Abby Fifer

Lake O'Brien

THE LAND OF IMAGES

Janet Fryberger

PRINCETON ARCHITECTURAL PRESS

George Carroll

AN ROTHENSTEIN

Suzzallo Library, U. of WA.

Joe

JANE JESZECK

Casey & Anna

GRATITUDE R.

FreelancePermissions.com

Melissa Flamson

Teri Hein

Irwin Lake

PubWest

Kids at The Hutch School

Phyl Harmon

Neeraline & T

MAP LEGEND

Castle		Village
Airport	Area	Town
Lighthouse	Boundary	MINOR CITY
Bridge	Railway	MAJOR CITY
Industry	Minor road	CAPITAL
Dam	Major road	
Mountain	Highway	LEVEL
Ferry	River	
Lake		HIGH LOW

SCALE: UNIMAGINABLE   PROJECTION: SUBJECTIVE

In the leading machine the Head of the Air Force was sitting beside the pilot. He had a world atlas on his knees and he kept staring first at the atlas, then at the ground below, trying to figure out where they were going. Frantically he turned the pages of the atlas.

"Where the devil are we going?" he cried.

"I haven't the foggiest idea," the pilot answered. "The Queen's orders were to follow the giant and that's exactly what I'm doing."

The pilot was a young Air Force officer with a bushy moustache. He was very proud of his moustache. He was also quite fearless and he loved adventure. He thought this was a super adventure. "It's fun going to new places," he said.

"New places!" shouted the Head of the Air Force. "What the blazes d'you mean new places?"

"This place we're flying over now isn't in the atlas, is it?" the pilot said, grinning.

"You're darn right it isn't in the atlas!" cried the Head of the Air Force. "We've flown clear off the last page!"

"I expect that old giant knows where he's going," the young pilot said.

"He's leading us to disaster!" cried the Head of the Air Force. He was shaking with fear. In the seat behind him sat the Head of the Army who was even more terrified.

"You don't mean to tell me we've gone right out of the atlas?" he cried, leaning forward to look.

"That's exactly what I am telling you!" cried the Air Force man. "Look for yourself. Here's the very last map in the whole flaming atlas! We went off that over an hour ago!" He turned the page. As in all atlases, there were two completely blank pages at the very end. "So now we must be somewhere here," he said, putting a finger on one of the blank pages.

"Where's here?" cried the Head of the Army.

The young pilot was still grinning broadly. He said to them, "That's why they always put two blank pages at the back of the atlas. They're for new countries. You're meant to fill them in yourself."

—*Roald Dahl,*
The BFG